MW00327431

The Ultimate
Instant Pot
Cookbook for Beginners

1000
Foolproof, Quick & Easy Home-made Instant Pot Recipes with Cooking Tips
for Beginners and Advanced Users
(Pressure Cooker Cookbook)

By Charles H. Lewis

Copyright © 2021 – By Charles H. Lewis

All Rights Reserved.

The content contained within this book may not be reproduced, duplicated or transmitted without direct written permission from the author or the publisher.

Under no circumstances will any blame or legal responsibility be held against the publisher, or author, for any damages, reparation, or monetary loss due to the information contained within this book, either directly or indirectly.

Legal Notice:

This book is copyright protected. It is only for personal use. You cannot amend, distribute, sell, use, quote or paraphrase any part of the content within this book, without the consent of the author or publisher.

Disclaimer Notice:

Please note the information contained within this document is for educational and entertainment purposes only. All effort has been executed to present accurate, up to date, reliable, complete information. No warranties of any kind are declared or implied. Readers acknowledge that the author is not engaged in the rendering of legal, financial, medical or professional advice. The content within this book has been derived from various sources. Please consult a licensed professional before attempting any techniques outlined in this book.

By reading this document, the reader agrees that under no circumstances is the author responsible for any losses, direct or indirect, that are incurred as a result of the use of the information contained within this document, including, but not limited to, errors, omissions, or inaccuracies.

Table of Content

Chapter 5 Poultry 50

Chapter 6 Beef 66

Chapter 7 Pork 81

Chapter 8 Lamb 92

Chapter 9 Pasta and Rice 98

Chapter 10 Grains and Beans 110

Chapter 11 Soups, Stews, and Chilis 125

Chapter 12 Appetizers and Snacks 141

Chapter 13 Side Dishes 152

Chapter 14 Sauce and Broth 164

Introduction

The success of Instant Pot seems to be everywhere in the world. In recent years, an army of these programmable pressure cookers has appeared on kitchen counters around the world. Instant Pots seems to have attracted the hearts of countless home cooks overnight.

The uniqueness and advantages of Instant Pot attracted me when Instant Pot coming to the market. I bought my first Instant Pot two years ago. After receiving the Instant Pot, I could not wait to open the box and use it for cooking. At first, I cooked many different dishes according to the bonus recipes manual. It didn't take long for me to cook all the recipes. So, I started searching for relevant Instant Pot recipes from the Internet, and recorded those delicious and easy-to-use dishes one by one in my own blank recipe book. At the same time, I was not satisfied with the first Instant Pot I bought. Later I bought two Instant Pot of different models and sizes to facilitate the use of different occasions. Two years have passed, and I have accumulated a large number of delicious and simple Instant Pot recipes, including simple breakfast, chicken soup, porridge, delicious slow-cooked beef brisket, desserts and more.

With the popularity of Instant Pot, the demand for Instant Pot recipes from home cooks is also increasing. Therefore, I would like to share some of my experience and over 1000 accumulated recipes in the past two years with readers. I hope that this book becomes a new classic in your kitchen and encourages you to plug in your Instant Pot and get cooking right away. If you're new to Instant Pot cooking, welcome! I will tell you the everything about Instant Pot to you in the Chapter 1.

Chapter 1 Understanding the Instant Pot

Whether you have already bought it or you are thinking about buying an instant pot, know that this revolutionary appliance will be the star of your kitchen and your new best friend. Why? Because it replaces 7 different kitchen gadgets. **That being said, you can use your one and not-expensive Instant Pot for 7 different cooking methods:**

1. A Pressure Cooker
2. A Sauté Pan
3. A Slow Cooker
4. A Steamer
5. A Rice Cooker
6. A Yogurt Maker
7. A Warming Pot

Why Choose the Instant Pot?

If you're still in two minds about the advantages of owning a multicooker, here are some further reasons why an Instant Pot is one of the top kitchen appliances out there.

- **Easy and Effortless**

There's no need to check on the food, as it's continuously cooked. You don't have to constantly stir or keep an eye on the temperature to make sure nothing burns. The only effort you have to go through is prepping the vegetables and meat and putting it all in the pot! In a few minutes, you'll have a warm meal to share with your family.

- **Safe and Secure**

You can relax knowing that there's no possibility that your Instant Pot will blow up. This modern-day cooker has built-in safety features and sensors that the old-school pressure cookers don't have.

- **Straightforward to Clean**

One would think that an appliance with the ability to cook a whole meal will require some aftercare hassles and complicated cleaning instructions. Not at all! There's only one inner pot and a few smaller elements to wash, and they're all dishwasher safe. Gone are the days of having to wash three pots, casseroles, and utensils galore.

- **No Nutrients Go to Waste**

It's an unfortunate fact that the longer you cook food, the more nutrients go to waste. But, seeing that the cooking time is so much shorter when you use a multicooker, your food will still be loaded with vitamins and minerals.

- **Gets Rid of Germs**

Your kitchen may be spotless, but there's no way of knowing if the food you're bringing from outside is bacteria-free. Luckily, since the Instant Pot not only cooks food at a low temperature but also under pressure, bacteria and germs will die during the process.

- **No Shortage of Recipes**

Not only will you find recipes in this book, but you can also do a quick internet search and be flooded with Instant Pot recipe blogs. You'll find anything from making a delicious beef stew, to how to make yogurt, and even wine!

It's exciting, right? Now that you know what makes the Instant Pot special, it is time to look at factors you should keep in mind when selecting your multicooker.

What to Do When You Get Your Cooker?

You will see the following when you open the box your cooker came in (apart from the actual Instant Pot, of course):

- Manual
- Quick reference guide
- Condensation collector
- Steamer rack
- Soup scoop
- Rice measuring cup
- Rice paddle
- Recipe book

The manual and quick reference guide will give you all the information required to set up your cooker. Read through it properly. While some multicookers will come already assembled, others do not, and you will have to install the inner pot, sealing ring, and the lid.

Before you do, wash all the elements with warm water and dry with a cloth. Wipe–do not submerge–the Instant Pot with a warm wet cloth and then dry. When all elements are completely dry, you can insert the inner pot. Next, put in the sealing ring and make sure it is fixed securely. Make sure all other components of the lid are in place by referring to the manual.

Once done, you're ready to test your pot!

Water Test

Although it is not absolutely necessary to do this step, I recommend you do it, nonetheless. It will give you peace of mind that the Instant Pot is in complete working order.

After assembling your multicooker and reading through the manual and quick reference guide to see what all the buttons do and icons mean, it is time to go through a water test.

1. Plug the cooker into the wall socket and switch it on.

2. Place the inner pot inside the cooker and add three cups of water.

3. Make sure the sealing ring is inserted securely.

4. Seal the Instant Pot with the lid. You will hear the pot beep three times to indicate that the lid is sealed.

5. Select 'Sealing' on the steam release handle.

6. Press the Pressure Cook/Steam button and set the timer to two minutes. Then press 'Start.'

7. If a lot of steam is escaping out of the sides, switch the machine off, and check the silicone ring is in place correctly. Try again.

8. Once the pot comes to pressure, a countdown will begin. The water should be boiling after two minutes. If that is the case, your water test was successful, and your Instant Pot doesn't have any defects.

How Does It Work?

I know it can be overwhelming when you first get your Instant Pot. Don't worry, after reading this section you'll be ready to dish up your first culinary masterpiece!

So, first things first: How does it actually work?

The cooker is made up out of three components called the inner pot, the cooker base, and the lid.

The **inner pot** is the container that goes inside the actual cooker. You will put all your ingredients in this part of the cooker. As the liquid inside the inner pot heats, it creates steam that cannot escape. This, in turn, creates pressure.

The **cooker base** is where all the electric and safety mechanisms are housed. The microprocessor, pressure and temperature sensors, heating element, and display and control panel all form part of this element.

The **lid** is a critical part of your multicooker; if it doesn't seal completely, the pot will not come to pressure. The lid itself contains numerous small parts, including the steam release, sealing ring, float valve and silicone cap, and anti-block shield. All of these work together to seal and regulate pressure.

The **steam release** can be set to either venting or sealed, and also acts as a safety feature where if the pressure increases to an unsafe level, the excess steam will push the valve up to release pressure.

The sealing ring is made from durable silicone rubber and creates an airtight seal.

The **float valve and silicone cap** fully seal the cooker. The float valve also acts as a latch lock, which prevents the lid from turning when force is applied.

The **anti-block shield** prevents blockage of the steam release pipe and ensures a steady release of steam when depressurizing.

Okay, now that you know what each of the components does, let's have a look at the buttons and icons.

The Buttons

The exact buttons will depend on the model and make you have, so you will have to use the user manual as guidance when you're unsure. But I will cover the general buttons for your convenience.

Sauté

You can use this multicooker to sauté food as you would using a skillet. The Instant Pot will warm to the temperature you selected (low, normal/medium, high) and let you know with a beep that you can start sautéing.

The time limit for this specific setting is 30-minutes, but you will usually only need 10 to 15 minutes. If you do require more time, just press the 'Sauté' button again, and you'll have 30 more minutes.

Be sure to add a little oil to ensure food doesn't get stuck to the bottom of the pan.

Manual or Pressure Cook

Your machine will either have a 'Manual' or 'Pressure cook' button. This is what you'll press if you want your pot to come to pressure.

Setting the Cooking Time

You have to let your pot know for how long it must cook. Just hit the plus or minus button to set the amount of time required per the recipe you're following. It will take a few seconds for 'On' to display, and your pot will start to build pressure. On some models, the timer is set by turning a knob and hitting 'Start.' Usually, on these models, the timer countdown will only begin once the cooker has come to pressure, and the cooking process has started.

When the time is up, you will see L0:00 or 00:00 appear on the screen. The timer will then start counting up to indicate how long it has been since the cooking process concluded. This is essential information when a recipe calls for a timed natural release (more on that later).

Keep Warm/Cancel

Your cooker may have these buttons separately or as one. For the "Keep Warm" function, most Instant Pots will automatically revert to this setting when the cooking time has ended.

If you want to cancel a function or switch to another, press the 'Cancel' button. This is also the button you will use to turn off your Instant Pot after use. Just hold in the 'Cancel' button for a few seconds until 'Off' is displayed on the screen.

Delay Start

A delayed start is convenient if you want cooking to start later on. I use this function almost every day. You can prep the ingredients, add them to the pot, and then set the timer so that the food is ready when your guests arrive. Just think, no more running between the kitchen while entertaining friends or family—the multicooker does everything for you.

Just keep in mind that not all food is safe to stay out of the refrigerator for too long before cooking. Chicken is a good example of meat you won't be able to place in the pot in the morning to start cooking four to six hours later.

Pressure/Steam Release

The lid is an important aspect when it comes to the pressure/steam release of your Instant Pot. Although the lids of various models differ slightly, they all have two positions: venting and sealing.

You will position the pressure release on 'Sealing' when you want to pressure cook anything. When the cooking process is done, you will move the position to 'Venting' to allow steam to escape and depressurizing to take place.

There, however, are three different types of pressure release methods. If you're following a specific recipe, this information will be included. The method you end up using also depends on the type of food in the pot.

Quick pressure release (QPR) is when you let all the steam escape at once. Foods like fish, veggies, or anything else that doesn't require a lot of cooking time will make use of QPR.

Natural pressure release (NPR) is when you don't move the pressure release to venting at all but instead let the pot depressurize as it cools. This can take anywhere from a few minutes up to 10 hours. The "Keep Warm" function automatically kicks in once cooking has stopped, the pot will stay on for 10 hours during which it will slowly depressurize.

Timed NPR is where you wait a certain amount of time before venting the steam. The recipe you're using will usually indicate how long you should wait.

The Icons

If you buy a basic multicooker, it will come with a red or blue LED. The more expensive models have digital screens, and you will see different icons appear at certain times during the process.

Flame under a pot

The pot is busy warming up. The icon will also go on and off as the pot regulates its heat while cooking.

'P' in a pot

The "Pressure Cook" function is selected.

Thermometer

"Keep Warm" mode has been activated.

Speaker with an 'X' next to it

All sounds have been muted. If your pot still makes sound and you would like to turn it off, do the following:

On the Duo, Duo Plus, Duo Nova, SV, or Viva models, press the minus button until the machine displays 'Off.' Alternatively, to turn it on, you will have to press the plus button until 'On' is shown.

If you own an Ultra or Duo Evo Plus, while 'Off' is displayed on the screen, press and hold the knob for a few seconds. You can then turn the knob to select 'On' or 'Off,' and press the knob again to set the sound setting in place.

The Best Cooker for You

There are various makes and models on the market, and this makes it hard to know which one will fulfill your needs. Ask yourself the questions below, and you'll be able to get the right multicooker for you.

How big is your family?

If you're only cooking for two, then there's no need to buy an 8-quart cooker. Here are the breakdowns of the different sizes.

- **3-quart = one or two people**
- **6-quart = three to six people**
- **8-quart = six to nine people**

8 Safety Cooking Tips

Furthermore, there are some safety tips you need to keep in mind:

- Check that the inner pot and heating plate are both clean and dry.

- Check the lid for any stuck food particles. Pay extra attention to the float valve, exhaust valve, and anti-block shield.

- Check the sealing ring is secure.

- Check the steam release valve is set to 'Sealing.'

- Make sure not to overfill the Instant Pot. At no time should the contents in the pot surpass the three-quarter mark. If you're cooking starchy foods, the halfway mark is ideal.

- Be careful when you release the steam.

- Unplug the multicooker when not in use.

- No part of the pot that contains electrical components should be submerged in water.

Pressure Release

It may seem complicated to pressure cook your meals, but the Instant Pot is the most hassle-free appliance among its fellow pressure cookers. **There are two ways in which you can release the pressure:**

- » **Quick Pressure Release (QPR)** – If you choose this method, you will let the pressure out of the pot quickly and all at once. You can use this with seafood, veggies, or even meat. Just make sure that your pot isn't full because it will result in spillage.

- » **Naturally Pressure Release (NPR)** – When the food you are cooking is larger in volute, is foamy, or has a high liquid content, a natural pressure release is required in order to prevent leaking.

- » **Timed Natural Pressure Release** - I often wait 10 or 15 minutes after the end of a cooking program, then move the Pressure Release to Venting to release a less geyser-like amount of steam from the pot.

Cooking Time Chart

Now is the time when you'll realize just how much time an Instant Pot will save you in the kitchen!

Food	Cooking Time	Food	Cooking Time
Vegetables		**Meat, Fish, & Eggs**	
Asparagus	1-2 min	Beef stew	20 min (per 1lb)
Broccoli	1-2 min	Beef large	20-25 min (per 1lb)
Brussel sprouts	2-3 min	Beef ribs	20-25 min (per 1lb)
Cabbage (whole)	2-3 min	Chicken whole	8 min (per 1lb)
Beans	1-2 min	Chicken breasts	6-8 min (per 1lb)
Butternut squash	4-6 min	Chicken bone stock	40-45 min (per 1lb)
Carrots	6-8 min	Lamb leg	15 min (per 1lb)
Corn on the cob	3-5 min	Pork roast	15 min (per 1lb)
Potatoes (Large)	12-15 min	Pork baby back ribs	15-20 min (per 1lb)
Potatoes (Small)	8-10 min	Fish whole	4-5 min
Potatoes (Cubes)	3-5 min	Fish fillet	2-3 min
Sweet potatoes (Whole)	12-15 min	Lobster	2-3 min
Sweet potatoes (Cubes)	2-4 min	Shrimp	1-3 min
Cauliflower (florets)	2-3 min	Seafood stock	7-8 min
Mixed vegetables	3-4 min	Eggs	5 min
Rice & Grains		**Beans & Lentils (Dry)**	
Barley	20-22 min	Black Beans	20-25 min
Oatmeal	2-3 min	Kidney Beans (Red)	20-25 min
Oats	3-5 min	Kidney Beans (White)	25-30 min
Quinoa	1 min	Lima Beans	12-14 min
Porridge	5-7 min	Lentils (Green)	8-10 min
Rice (Brown)	20-22 min	Lentils (Yellow)	1-2 min
Rice (Jasmine)	4 min	Chickpeas	30-40 min
Rice (Basmati)	2-3 min	Navy Beans	20-24 min
Rice (White)	4 min	Pinto Beans	25-30 min
Rice (Wild)	20-25 min	Soy Beans	35-45 min

Chapter 2 Breakfast and Brunch

Cherry and Almond Oatmeal

Prep time: 10 minutes | Cook time: 5 minutes | Serves 6

4 cups vanilla almond milk, plus additional as needed
1 cup steel-cut oats
⅓ cup packed brown sugar
1 cup dried cherries
½ teaspoon ground cinnamon
½ teaspoon salt

1. Combine all ingredients in the Instant Pot.
2. Secure the lid. Select the Manual mode and set the cooking time for 5 minutes at High Pressure.
3. Once cooking is complete, do a natural pressure release for 10 minutes, then release any remaining pressure. Carefully open the lid.
4. Allow the oatmeal to sit for 10 minutes. Serve with additional almond milk, if desired.

Almond Pancakes

Prep time: 10 minutes | Cook time: 15 minutes per batch | Serves 6

4 eggs, beaten
2 cups almond flour
½ cup butter, melted
2 tablespoons granulated erythritol
1 tablespoon avocado oil
1 teaspoon baking powder
1 teaspoon vanilla extract
Pinch of salt
¾ cup water, divided

1. In a blender, combine all the ingredients, except for the ½ cup of the water. Pulse until fully combined and smooth. Let the batter rest for 5 minutes before cooking.
2. Fill each cup with 2 tablespoons of the batter, about two-thirds of the way full. Cover the cups with aluminum foil.
3. Pour the remaining ½ cup of the water and insert the trivet in the Instant Pot. Place the cups on the trivet.
4. Set the lid in place. Select the Manual mode and set the cooking time for 15 minutes on High Pressure. When the timer goes off, do a quick pressure release. Carefully open the lid.
5. Repeat with the remaining batter, until all the batter is used. Add more water to the pot before cooking each batch, if needed.
6. Serve warm.

Apple Risotto

Prep time: 10 minutes | Cook time: 12 minutes | Serves 4 to 6

2 tablespoons butter
1½ cups Arborio rice
2 apples, cored and sliced
3 cups plant-based milk
1 cup apple juice
⅓ cup brown sugar
1½ teaspoons cinnamon powder
Salt to taste
½ cup dried cherries

1. Set your Instant Pot to Sauté and melt the butter.
2. Add rice, stir and cook for 5 minutes.
3. Add the remaining ingredients, except the cherries, to the Instant Pot. Stir well.
4. Lock the lid. Select the Manual mode and set the cooking time for 6 minutes at High Pressure.
5. When the timer beeps, perform a natural pressure release for 6 minutes, then release any remaining pressure. Carefully remove the lid.
6. Stir in the cherries and close the lid. Let sit for 5 minutes. Serve warm.

Egg Cups with Broccoli

Prep time: 10 minutes | Cook time: 6 minutes | Serves 4

7 large eggs, divided
1½ cups half-and-half
3 tablespoons shredded Swiss cheese
1 teaspoon minced fresh basil
2 teaspoons minced fresh parsley
¼ teaspoon salt
⅛ teaspoon cayenne pepper
Cooking spray
1½ cups frozen broccoli florets, thawed
1 cup water

1. Spritz four ramekins with cooking spray and set aside.
2. Beat together three eggs with the half-and-half, cheese, basil, parsley, salt, and cayenne pepper in a large bowl until well incorporated.
3. Pour the egg mixture evenly into the greased ramekins. Divide the broccoli florets among the ramekins and top each with one remaining egg.
4. Add the water and trivet to the Instant Pot, then place the ramekins on top of the trivet. Cover them loosely with foil.
5. Lock the lid. Select the Steam mode and set the cooking time for 6 minutes at High Pressure.
6. Once cooking is complete, do a quick pressure release. Carefully open the lid.
7. Allow to cool for 5 minutes before removing and serving.

Banana and Amaranth Bread with Walnuts

Prep time: 5 minutes | Cook time: 4 minutes | Serves 4

1 cup amaranth
2 cups sliced bananas
2 ½ cups vanilla-flavored rice milk
2 tablespoons brown sugar
½ teaspoon nutmeg
½ teaspoon cinnamon
¼ teaspoon salt
½ cup chopped walnuts

1. Combine all the ingredients, except for the walnuts, in the Instant Pot.
2. Secure the lid. Select the Manual mode and set the cooking time for 4 minutes at High Pressure.
3. Once cooking is complete, do a natural pressure release for 10 minutes, then release any remaining pressure. Carefully open the lid.
4. Stir in the walnuts before serving.

Bacon Wrapped Avocado

Prep time: 5 minutes | Cook time: 10 minutes | Serves 4

1 avocado, peeled, pitted and halved
½ teaspoon chili flakes
½ teaspoon ground cinnamon
1 teaspoon coconut cream
4 bacon slices

1. Sprinkle the avocado with the chili flakes and ground cinnamon.
2. Fill the avocado with the coconut cream and wrap in the bacon slices. Secure the avocado bomb with toothpicks, if needed.
3. Select the Sauté mode on the Instant Pot. Place the wrapped avocado bomb in the pot. Cook for 10 minutes on both sides, or until the bacon is crispy.
4. Transfer to a platter. Slice and serve.

Applesauce Oatmeal

Prep time: 10 minutes | Cook time: 5 minutes | Serves 8

6 cups water
1½ cups steel-cut oats
1½ cups unsweetened applesauce
¼ cup maple syrup, plus more for topping
½ teaspoon ground nutmeg
1½ teaspoons ground cinnamon
⅛ teaspoon salt
1 large apple, chopped

1. Except for the apple, combine all the ingredients in the Instant Pot.
2. Lock the lid. Select the Manual mode and set the cooking time for 5 minutes at High Pressure.
3. Once cooking is complete, do a natural pressure release for 10 minutes, then release any remaining pressure. Carefully open the lid.
4. Add the chopped apple and stir well. Allow the oatmeal to sit for 10 minutes. Ladle into bowls and top with a drizzle of maple syrup, if desired. Serve warm.

Quinoa and Banana Breakfast Bowl

Prep time: 5 mins, Cook Time: 12 mins, Servings: 2

½ cup peeled and sliced banana
¾ cup quinoa, soaked in water for at least 1 hour
1 (8 oz.) can almond milk
2 tbsps. honey
1 tsp. vanilla extract
Pinch of salt
¾ cup water

1. Combine all the ingredients in the Instant Pot. Stir to mix well.
2. Lock the lid. Set to Rice mode, then set the timer for 12 minutes at Low Pressure.
3. Once the timer goes off, perform a quick pressure release. Carefully open the lid.
4. Serve immediately.

Eggs In Purgatory

Prep time: 15 minutes | Cook time: 24 minutes | Serves 4

2 (14½-ounce / 411-g) cans fire-roasted diced tomatoes, undrained
½ cup water
1 medium onion, chopped
2 garlic cloves, minced
2 tablespoons canola oil
2 teaspoons smoked paprika
½ teaspoon crushed red pepper flakes
½ teaspoon sugar
¼ cup tomato paste
4 large eggs
¼ cup shredded Monterey Jack cheese
2 tablespoons minced fresh parsley
1 (18-ounce / 510-g) tube polenta, sliced and warmed (optional)

1. Place the tomatoes, water, onion, garlic, oil, paprika, red pepper flakes, and sugar into the Instant Pot and stir to combine.
2. Secure the lid. Select the Manual mode and set the cooking time for 4 minutes at High Pressure.
3. Once cooking is complete, do a quick pressure release. Carefully open the lid.
4. Set the Instant Pot to Sauté and stir in the tomato paste. Let it simmer for about 10 minutes, stirring occasionally, or until the mixture is slightly thickened.
5. With the back of a spoon, make 4 wells in the sauce and crack an egg into each. Scatter with the shredded cheese.
6. Cover (do not lock the lid) and allow to simmer for 8 to 10 minutes, or until the egg whites are completely set.
7. Sprinkle the parsley on top and serve with the polenta slices, if desired.

Egg Stuffed Bell Peppers

Prep time: 5 minutes | Cook time: 14 minutes | Serves 2

2 eggs, beaten
1 tablespoon coconut cream
¼ teaspoon dried oregano
¼ teaspoon salt
1 large bell pepper, cut into halves and deseeded
1 cup water

1. In a bowl, stir together the eggs, coconut cream, oregano and salt.
2. Pour the egg mixture in the pepper halves.
3. Pour the water and insert the trivet in the Instant Pot. Put the stuffed pepper halves on the trivet.
4. Set the lid in place. Select the Manual mode and set the cooking time for 14 minutes on High Pressure. When the timer goes off, do a quick pressure release. Carefully open the lid.
5. Serve warm.

Orange and Blackberry Egg Cake

Prep time: 12 mins, Cook Time: 8 mins, Servings: 3

Zest from ½ an orange
½ cup fresh blackberries
1 tbsp. coconut oil
3 tbsps. coconut flour
5 eggs, whisked
1 cup water
Pinch salt

1. Place a steamer basket in the Instant Pot and pour in a cup of water.
2. In a mixing bowl, combine the eggs, coconut oil, and coconut flour until well combined. Season with a pinch of salt.
3. Add the blackberries and orange zest.
4. Pour into muffin cups.
5. Place the muffin cups in the steamer basket.
6. Lock the lid. Press the Steam button and set the cooking time for 8 minutes at High Pressure.
7. Once cooking is complete, do a quick pressure release. Carefully open the lid.
8. Allow to cool for 5 minutes before serving.

Almond and Blueberry Oatmeal

Prep time: 5 minutes | Cook time: 25 minutes | Serves 4

1½ cups old-fashioned rolled oats
⅓ cup coconut sugar
1 tablespoon flax meal
1 teaspoon baking powder
1 teaspoon ground cinnamon
1 cup almond milk
1 teaspoon freshly grated
orange zest
1 teaspoon pure vanilla extract
¼ cup applesauce
¾ cup fresh blueberries
1 cup water
⅓ cup slivered almonds, toasted

1. Stir together the oats, coconut sugar, flax meal, baking powder, and cinnamon in a medium bowl until combined.
2. Add the almond milk, orange zest, vanilla, and applesauce. Fold in the blueberries and stir to incorporate. Spoon the oat mixture into 4 ramekins. Cover each ramekin tightly with foil.
3. Pour the water into the Instant Pot and insert a trivet. Place the ramekins on the trivet.
4. Lock the lid. Select the Manual mode and set the cooking time for 25 minutes at High Pressure.
5. When the timer beeps, perform a quick pressure release. Carefully remove the lid. Using potholders, remove the ramekins and remove the foil.
6. Serve topped with the toasted almonds.

Bread Coconut Pudding

Prep time: 12 mins, Cook Time: 15 mins, Servings: 8

½ cup maple syrup
1 bread loaf, cubed
½ cup butter

2 cups coconut milk
4 eggs
2 cups water

1. In a blender, blend the coconut milk with eggs, butter and maple syrup until smooth.
2. Transfer the mixture to a pudding pan and add the bread cubes. Cover the pan with tin foil.
3. Add 2 cups water and trivet to your Instant Pot. Place the pudding pan on the trivet.
4. Lock the lid. Select the Manual mode and cook for15 minutes at High Pressure.
5. Once cooking is complete, do a quick pressure release. Carefully open the lid.
6. Allow to cool for 5 minutes before serving.

Chicken and Cheddar Casserole

Prep time: 10 minutes | Cook time: 20 minutes | Serves 6

1 cup ground chicken
1 teaspoon olive oil
1 teaspoon chili flakes
1 teaspoon salt

1 cup shredded Cheddar cheese
½ cup coconut cream

1. Press the Sauté button on the Instant Pot and heat the oil. Add the ground chicken, chili flakes and salt to the pot and sauté for 10 minutes. Stir in the remaining ingredients.
2. Set the lid in place. Select the Manual mode and set the cooking time for 10 minutes on High Pressure. When the timer goes off, do a quick pressure release. Carefully open the lid.
3. Let the dish cool for 10 minutes before serving.

Scrambled Tofu with Burrito

Prep time: 5 minutes | Cook time: 7 minutes | Serves 2

2 cups water
2 small Yukon Gold potatoes, cut into 1-in (2.5 cm) chunks
2 tablespoons extra-virgin olive oil
10 ounces (283 g) firm organic tofu, drained and crumbled
½ teaspoon ground turmeric
2 tablespoons nutritional yeast
½ teaspoon sea salt

Pinch of freshly ground black pepper
¼ cup unsweetened plant-based milk
2 flour tortillas, warmed
½ avocado, sliced
1 cup fresh baby spinach or arugula
¼ cup salsa

1. Pour the water into the Instant Pot and insert a steamer basket. Put the potato chunks in the steamer basket.
2. Secure the lid. Select the Manual mode and set the cooking time for 2 minutes at High Pressure.
3. When the timer beeps, perform a quick pressure release. Carefully remove the lid and steamer basket. Pour the water out of the Instant Pot and wipe it dry.
4. Press the Sauté button on the Instant Pot and heat the olive oil until very hot. Add the potatoes and sauté for about 3 minutes, flipping occasionally, until crisp on the outside. Remove the potatoes from the pot and set aside on a plate.
5. Add the crumbled tofu, turmeric, nutritional yeast, salt, and pepper to the pot, and sauté for 1 to 2 minutes. For a softer scramble, you can add the milk and simmer until warm and the milk has evaporated and absorbed.
6. Assemble the burritos: Place the potatoes and tofu scramble onto the tortillas. Top with equal portions of avocado, baby spinach, and salsa. Roll into burritos and serve immediately.

Coconut, Plum, and Apple Cobbler

Prep time: 12 mins, Cook Time: 15 mins, Servings: 2

2 tbsps. honey
¼ cup shredded coconut
1 plum, pitted and chopped

3 tbsps. coconut oil, divided
1 apple, cored and chopped

1. In the Instant Pot, combine the plum with apple, half of the coconut oil, and honey, and blend well.
2. Lock the lid. Select the Manual mode and cook for 10 minutes at High Pressure.
3. Once cooking is complete, do a quick pressure release. Carefully open the lid.
4. Transfer the mixture to bowls and clean your Instant Pot.
5. Set your Instant Pot to Sauté and heat the remaining coconut oil. Add the coconut, stir, and toast for 5 minutes.
6. Sprinkle the coconut over fruit mixture and serve.

Quinoa with Chickpea and Cucumber Salad

Prep time: 15 minutes | Cook time: 1 minute | Serves 4

2 cups quinoa, rinsed well
2 cups vegetable or chicken broth
Salad:
1 (15-ounce / 425-g) can chickpeas, drained and rinsed
1 cucumber, diced
1 cup chopped flat-leaf parsley
¼ cup extra-virgin olive oil

1 red onion, diced
1 red bell pepper, diced
3 cloves garlic, minced
Juice of 2 lemons
2 tablespoons red wine vinegar
Salt and pepper, to taste
1 to 2 cups crumbled feta cheese (optional)

1. Place the quinoa and broth into the Instant Pot and stir to incorporate.
2. Lock the lid. Select the Manual mode and set the cooking time for 1 minute at High Pressure.
3. Once cooking is complete, do a natural pressure release for 10 minutes, then release any remaining pressure. Carefully open the lid.
4. Fluff the quinoa with a fork and allow to cool for 5 to 10 minutes.
5. Remove the quinoa from the pot to a large bowl and toss together with all the salad ingredients until combined. Serve immediately.

Potato and Cheddar Casserole

Prep time: 20 minutes | Cook time: 35 minutes | Serves 6

6 large eggs
½ cup 2% milk
½ teaspoon salt
¼ teaspoon pepper
4 cups frozen shredded hash brown potatoes, thawed

2 cups shredded Cheddar cheese
1 cup cubed fully cooked ham
½ medium onion, chopped
1 cup water

1. In a medium bowl, beat together the eggs with the milk, salt, and pepper until combined. In another bowl, thoroughly combine the potatoes, cheese, ham, and onion, then transfer to a greased baking dish. Pour the egg mixture over top. Cover the dish with foil.
2. Pour the water into the Instant Pot and insert a trivet. Place the baking dish on top of the trivet.
3. Secure the lid. Select the Manual mode and set the cooking time for 35 minutes at High Pressure.
4. Once cooking is complete, do a natural pressure release for 10 minutes, then release any remaining pressure. Carefully open the lid.
5. Allow the casserole cool for 5 to 10 minutes before serving.

Rice Pudding

Prep time: 12 mins, Cook Time: 12 mins, Servings: 6

1 cup coconut cream
¼ cup maple syrup
1¼ cups water
1 cup basmati rice
2 cups almond milk

1. In the Instant Pot, mix together the milk with water, rice, cream and maple syrup.
2. Lock the lid. Select the Manual mode and cook for 12 minutes at Low Pressure.
3. Once cooking is complete, do a natural pressure release for 5 minutes, then release any remaining pressure. Carefully open the lid.
4. Stir the pudding again and divide into bowls to serve.

Egg and Broccoli Casserole

Prep time: 5 mins, Cook Time: 15 mins, Servings: 6

6 eggs, beaten
⅓ cup all-purpose flour
3 cups cottage cheese
¼ cup butter, melted
Salt and pepper, to taste
2 tbsps. chopped onions
3 cups broccoli florets

1. Combine the eggs, flour, cheese, butter, salt, and pepper in a large bowl. Stir to mix well.
2. Put the onions and broccoli in the Instant Pot. Pour the egg mixture over. Stir to combine well.
3. Lock the lid. Set to Manual mode, then set the timer to 15 minutes at High pressure.
4. Once the timer goes off, perform a natural pressure release for 10 minutes, then release any remaining pressure. Carefully open the lid.
5. Transfer them on a plate and serve immediately.

Hawaiian Sweet Potato Hash

Prep time: 20 minutes | Cook time: 20 minutes | Serves 6

4 bacon strips, chopped
1 tablespoon canola or coconut oil
2 large sweet potatoes, peeled and cut into ½-inch pieces
1 cup water
2 cups cubed fresh pineapple
½ teaspoon salt
¼ teaspoon paprika
¼ teaspoon chili powder
¼ teaspoon pepper
⅛ teaspoon ground cinnamon

1. Press the Sauté button on the Instant Pot and add the bacon. Cook for about 7 minutes, stirring occasionally, or until crisp.
2. Remove the bacon with a slotted spoon and drain on paper towels. Set aside.
3. In the Instant Pot, heat the oil until it shimmers.
4. Working in batches, add the sweet potatoes to the pot and brown each side for 3 to 4 minutes. Transfer the sweet potatoes to a large bowl and set aside.
5. Pour the water into the pot and cook for 1 minute, stirring to loosen browned bits from pan.
6. Place a steamer basket in the Instant Pot. Add the pineapple, salt, paprika, chili powder, pepper, and cinnamon to the large bowl of sweet potatoes and toss well, then transfer the mixture to the steamer basket.
7. Secure the lid. Select the Steam mode and set the cooking time for 2 minutes at High Pressure.
8. Once cooking is complete, do a quick pressure release. Carefully open the lid.
9. Top with the bacon and serve on a plate.

Pineapple and Carrot Oatmeal

Prep time: 10 minutes | Cook time: 10 minutes | Serves 8

4½ cups water
2 cups shredded carrots
1 cup steel-cut oats
1 (20-ounce / 567-g) can crushed pineapple, undrained
1 cup raisins
2 teaspoons ground cinnamon
1 teaspoon pumpkin pie spice
Cooking spray
Brown sugar (optional)

1. Spritz the bottom of the Instant Pot with cooking spray. Place the water, carrots, oats, raisins, pineapple, cinnamon, and pumpkin pie spice into the Instant Pot and stir to combine.
2. Secure the lid. Select the Manual mode and set the cooking time for 10 minutes at High Pressure.
3. Once cooking is complete, do a natural pressure release for 10 minutes, then release any remaining pressure. Carefully open the lid.
4. Let the oatmeal stand for 5 to 10 minutes. Sprinkle with the brown sugar, if desired. Serve warm.

Broccoli and Cheese Egg Bites

Prep time: 10 minutes | Cook time: 10 minutes | Serves 7

5 eggs, beaten
3 tablespoons heavy cream
⅛ teaspoon salt
⅛ teaspoon black pepper
1 ounce (28 g) finely chopped
broccoli
1 ounce (28 g) shredded Cheddar cheese
½ cup water

1. In a blender, combine the eggs, heavy cream, salt and pepper and pulse until smooth.
2. Divide the chopped broccoli among the egg cups equally. Pour the egg mixture on top of the broccoli, filling the cups about three-fourths of the way full. Sprinkle the Cheddar cheese on top of each cup.
3. Cover the egg cups tightly with aluminum foil.
4. Pour the water and insert the trivet in the Instant Pot. Put the egg cups on the trivet.
5. Lock the lid. Select the Manual mode and set the cooking time for 10 minutes on High Pressure. Once the timer goes off, perform a natural pressure release for 5 minutes, then release any remaining pressure. Carefully open the lid.
6. Serve immediately.

Arugula Frittata

Prep time: 5 minutes | Cook time: 5 minutes | Serves 2

3 eggs, beaten
¼ cup loosely packed arugula
¼ red onion, chopped
¼ cup feta cheese crumbles
¼ teaspoon garlic powder
Kosher salt, to taste
Freshly ground black pepper, to taste
1 cup water

1. Stir together the eggs, arugula, onion, feta cheese crumbles, garlic powder, salt, and pepper in a medium bowl. Pour the egg mixture into a greased round cake pan and cover with foil.
2. Add the water and trivet to the Instant Pot, then place the cake pan on top of the trivet.
3. Lock the lid. Select the Manual mode and set the cooking time for 5 minutes at High Pressure.
4. Once cooking is complete, do a natural pressure release for 10 minutes, then release any remaining pressure. Carefully open the lid.
5. Let the frittata rest for 5 minutes in the pan before cutting and serving.

Bacon and Cheese Quiche

Prep time: 5 mins, Cook Time: 10 mins, Servings: 6

2 tbsps. olive oil
6 eggs, lightly beaten
1 cup milk
Salt and pepper, to taste

2 cups Monterey Jack cheese, grated
1 cup bacon, cooked and crumbled

1. Grease the Instant Pot with olive oil.
2. Combine the eggs, milk, salt, and pepper in a large bowl. Stir to mix well.
3. Put the cheese and bacon in the pot, then pour the egg mixture over. Stir to mix well.
4. Lock the lid. Set to Manual mode, then set the timer for 10 minutes at High Pressure.
5. Once the timer goes off, perform a natural pressure release for 5 minutes. Carefully open the lid.
6. Transfer the quiche on a plate and serve.

Bacon Egg Muffins

Prep time: 12 mins, Cook Time: 8 mins, Servings: 4

4 cooked bacon slices, crumbled
4 tbsps. shredded Cheddar cheese

¼ tsp. salt
1 green onion, chopped
4 eggs, beaten
1½ cups water

1. In a bowl, mix the eggs with cheese, bacon, onion and salt, and whisk well. Pour the egg mixture evenly into four muffin cups.
2. Add 1½ cups water and steamer basket to the Instant Pot. Place the muffin cups in the basket.
3. Lock the lid. Select the Manual mode and set the cooking time for 8 minutes at High Pressure.
4. Once cooking is complete, do a quick pressure release. Carefully open the lid.
5. Divide the muffins between plates and serve warm.

Orange and Strawberry Compote

Prep time: 10 mins, Cook Time: 15 mins, Servings: 4

2 lbs. fresh strawberries, rinsed, trimmed, and cut in half
2 oz. fresh orange juice
1 vanilla bean, chopped

½ tsp. ground ginger
¼ cup sugar
Toast, for serving

1. Put all the ingredients into the Instant Pot. Stir to mix well.
2. Lock the lid. Set to the Manual Mode, then set the timer for 15 minutes at High Pressure.
3. When the timer goes off, perform a natural pressure release for 10 minutes. Carefully open the lid.
4. Allow to cool and thicken before serving with the toast.

Spinach and Ham Frittata

Prep time: 3 mins, Cook Time: 10 mins, Servings: 8

1 cup diced ham
2 cups chopped spinach
8 eggs, beaten

½ cup coconut milk
1 onion, chopped
1 tsp. salt

1. Put all the ingredients into the Instant Pot. Stir to mix well.
2. Lock the lid. Set to Manual mode, then set the timer for 10 minutes at High Pressure.
3. Once the timer goes off, perform a natural pressure release for 5 minutes. Carefully open the lid.
4. Transfer the frittata on a plate and serve immediately.

Asparagus and Gruyère Cheese Frittata

Prep time: 10 minutes | Cook time: 22 minutes | Serves 6

6 eggs
6 tablespoons heavy cream
½ teaspoon salt
½ teaspoon black pepper
1 tablespoon butter
2½ ounces (71 g) asparagus, chopped

1 clove garlic, minced
1¼ cup shredded Gruyère cheese, divided
Cooking spray
3 ounces (85 g) halved cherry tomatoes
½ cup water

1. In a large bowl, stir together the eggs, cream, salt, and pepper.
2. Set the Instant Pot on the Sauté mode and melt the butter. Add the asparagus and garlic to the pot and sauté for 2 minutes, or until the garlic is fragrant. The asparagus should still be crisp.
3. Transfer the asparagus and garlic to the bowl with the egg mixture. Stir in 1 cup of the cheese. Clean the pot.
4. Spritz a baking pan with cooking spray. Spread the tomatoes in a single layer in the pan. Pour the egg mixture on top of the tomatoes and sprinkle with the remaining ¼ cup of the cheese. Cover the pan tightly with aluminum foil.
5. Pour the water in the Instant Pot and insert the trivet. Place the pan on the trivet.
6. Set the lid in place. Select the Manual mode and set the cooking time for 20 minutes on High Pressure. When the timer goes off, perform a quick pressure release. Carefully open the lid.
7. Remove the pan from the pot and remove the foil. Blot off any excess moisture with a paper towel. Let the frittata cool for 5 to 10 minutes before transferring onto a plate.

Apple Pumpkin Butter

Prep time: 12 mins, Cook Time: 10 mins, Servings: 6

30 oz. pumpkin purée
4 apples, cored, peeled, and cubed

12 oz. apple cider
1 cup sugar
1 tbsp. pumpkin pie spice

1. In the Instant Pot, stir together the pumpkin purée with apples, apple cider, sugar, and pumpkin pie spice.
2. Lock the lid. Select the Manual mode and cook for 10 minutes at High Pressure.
3. Once cooking is complete, do a quick pressure release. Carefully open the lid.
4. Remove from the pot and serve in bowls.

Apple Butter

Prep time: 15 minutes | Cook time: 3 minutes | Makes 5 cups

4 pounds (1.8 kg) large apples, cored and quartered
¾ to 1 cup sugar
¼ cup water
3 teaspoons ground cinnamon

¼ teaspoon ground cloves
¼ teaspoon ground allspice
¼ teaspoon ground nutmeg
¼ cup creamy peanut butter

1. Combine all the ingredients except the butter in the Instant Pot.
2. Secure the lid. Select the Manual mode and set the cooking time for 3 minutes at High Pressure.
3. Once cooking is complete, do a natural pressure release for 5 minutes, then release any remaining pressure. Carefully open the lid.
4. Blend the mixture with an immersion blender. Add the peanut butter and whisk until smooth.
5. Let the mixture cool to room temperature. Serve immediately.

French Eggs

Prep time: 12 mins, Cook Time: 8 mins, Servings: 4

¼ tsp. salt
4 bacon slices
1 tbsp. olive oil

4 tbsps. chopped chives
4 eggs
1½ cups water

1.Grease 4 ramekins with a drizzle of oil and crack an egg into each ramekin.
2.Add a bacon slice on top and season with salt. Sprinkle the chives on top.
3.Add 1½ cups water and steamer basket to your Instant Pot. Transfer the ramekins to the basket.
4.Lock the lid. Select the Manual mode and set the cooking time for 8 minutes at High Pressure.
5.Once cooking is complete, do a quick pressure release. Carefully open the lid.
6.Serve your baked eggs immediately.

Raisin and Apple Oatmeal

Prep time: 10 minutes | Cook time: 5 minutes | Serves 6

3 cups vanilla almond milk
¾ cup steel-cut oats
3 tablespoons brown sugar
¾ cup raisins
4½ teaspoons butter

½ teaspoon salt
¾ teaspoon ground cinnamon
1 large apple, peeled and chopped
¼ cup chopped pecans

1.Combine all the ingredients except the apple and pecans in the Instant Pot.
2.Secure the lid. Select the Manual mode and set the cooking time for 5 minutes at High Pressure.
3.Once cooking is complete, do a natural pressure release for 10 minutes, then release any remaining pressure. Carefully open the lid.
4.Scatter with the chopped apple and stir well. Allow the oatmeal to sit for 1o minutes. Ladle into bowls and sprinkle the pecans on top. Serve immediately.

Cheese and Spinach Strata

Prep time: 5 minutes | Cook time: 40 minutes | Serves 4

1 cup filtered water
6 eggs
1 cup chopped spinach
1 cup shredded full-fat
Cheddar cheese
¼ small onion, thinly sliced
½ tablespoon salted grass-fed
butter, softened
½ teaspoon Dijon mustard

½ teaspoon kosher salt
½ teaspoon freshly ground
black pepper
½ teaspoon cayenne pepper
½ teaspoon paprika
½ teaspoon dried sage
½ teaspoon dried cilantro
½ teaspoon dried parsley

1.Pour the water into the the Instant Pot, then place the trivet.
2.Whisk together the eggs, spinach, cheese, onion, butter, mustard, salt, black pepper, cayenne pepper, paprika, sage, cilantro, and parsley in a large bowl until well incorporated. Pour the egg mixture into a greased baking dish. Cover the dish loosely with aluminum foil. Put the dish on top of the trivet.
3.Secure the lid. Select the Manual mode and set the cooking time for 40 minutes at High Pressure.
4.Once cooking is complete, do a natural pressure release for 10 minutes, then release any remaining pressure. Carefully open the lid.
5.Let the strata rest for 5 minutes and serve warm.

Coffee Cake

Prep time: 10 minutes | Cook time: 45 minutes | Serves 8

Cake:
2 cups almond flour
1 cup granulated erythritol
1 teaspoon baking powder
Pinch of salt
2 eggs
½ cup sour cream
4 tablespoons butter, melted

2 teaspoons vanilla extract
2 tablespoons Swerve
1½ teaspoons ground
cinnamon
Cooking spray
½ cup water

Icing:
2 ounces (56 g) cream cheese, softened
1 cup powdered erythritol
1 tablespoon heavy cream
½ teaspoon vanilla extract

1.In the bowl of a stand mixer, combine the almond flour, granulated erythritol, baking powder and salt. Mix until no lumps remain. Add the eggs, sour cream, butter and vanilla to the mixer bowl and mix until well combined.
2.In a separate bowl, mix together the Swerve and cinnamon.
3.Spritz the baking pan with cooking spray. Pour in the cake batter and use a knife to make sure it is level around the pan. Sprinkle the cinnamon mixture on top. Cover the pan tightly with aluminum foil.
4.Pour the water and insert the trivet in the Instant Pot. Put the pan on the trivet.
5.Set the lid in place. Select the Manual mode and set the cooking time for 45 minutes on High Pressure. When the timer goes off, do a quick pressure release. Carefully open the lid.
6.Remove the cake from the pot and remove the foil. Blot off any moisture on top of the cake with a paper towel, if necessary. Let rest in the pan for 5 minutes.
7.Meanwhile, make the icing: In a small bowl, use a mixer to whip the cream cheese until it is light and fluffy. Slowly fold in the powdered erythritol and mix until well combined. Add the heavy cream and vanilla extract and mix until thoroughly combined.
8.When the cake is cooled, transfer it to a platter and drizzle the icing all over.

Leek and Asparagus Frittata

Prep time: 10 minutes | Cook time: 10 minutes | Serves 4

6 eggs
¼ teaspoon fine sea salt
Freshly ground black pepper,
to taste
8 ounces (227 g) asparagus
spears, woody stems removed
and cut into 1-inch pieces
1 cup thinly sliced leeks

¼ cup grated Parmesan
cheese
1 cup water
Chopped green onions, for
garnish (optional)
Fresh flat-leaf parsley, for
garnish (optional)

1.Whisk together the eggs, salt, and black pepper in a large mixing bowl until frothy.
2.Add the asparagus pieces, leeks, and cheese and stir to combine. Pour the mixture into a greased round cake pan.
3.Add the water and trivet to the Instant Pot, then place the pan on top of the trivet.
4.Lock the lid. Select the Manual mode and set the cooking time for 10 minutes at High Pressure.
5.Once cooking is complete, do a natural pressure release for 10 minutes, then release any remaining pressure. Carefully open the lid.
6.Allow the frittata to cool for 5 minutes. Garnish with the green onions and parsley, if desired. Cut the frittata into wedges and serve warm.

Buckwheat and Strawberry Pudding

Prep time: 5 minutes | Cook time: 7 minutes | Serves 4

1 cup buckwheat groats
3 cups coconut milk
1 cup chopped fresh strawberries
½ cup unsweetened shredded coconut

1 teaspoon cinnamon
½ teaspoon almond extract
½ teaspoon pure vanilla extract
½ cup sliced almonds
½ cup cold coconut cream

1. Stir together all the ingredients, except for the almonds and coconut cream, in the Instant Pot.
2. Secure the lid. Select the Manual mode and set the cooking time for 7 minutes at High Pressure.
3. Once cooking is complete, do a natural pressure release for 20 minutes, then release any remaining pressure. Carefully open the lid.
4. Spoon the buckwheat pudding into serving dishes. Garnish with coconut cream and almonds before serving.

Raisin and Cranberry Compote

Prep time: 5 minutes | Cook time: 3 minutes | Makes 2½ cups

1 (12-ounce / 340-g) package fresh or 3 cups frozen cranberries
¼ cup thawed orange juice concentrate
⅔ cup packed brown sugar

2 tablespoons raspberry vinegar
½ cup golden raisins
½ cup chopped dried apricots
½ cup chopped walnuts, toasted

1. Combine the cranberries, orange juice concentrate, brown sugar, and vinegar in the Instant Pot.
2. Secure the lid. Select the Manual mode and set the cooking time for 3 minutes at High Pressure.
3. Once cooking is complete, do a natural pressure release for 5 minutes, then release any remaining pressure. Carefully open the lid.
4. Stir in the raisins, apricots, and walnuts and serve warm.

Tex Mex Tofu Scramble

Prep time: 5 minutes | Cook time: 10 minutes | Serves 4

1 tablespoon olive oil
3 cloves garlic, minced
1 cup chopped red bell pepper
¼ cup canned green chilies, chopped
1 teaspoon ground cumin
1 teaspoon paprika
1 teaspoon chili powder
½ teaspoon salt

½ teaspoon black pepper
1 package extra firm tofu, cubed
1 cup fresh corn kernels
1 cup diced tomatoes
¼ cup vegetable broth or water
1 avocado, sliced
¼ cup chopped fresh cilantro (optional)

1. Set your Instant Pot to Sauté and heat the olive oil.
2. Add the garlic, red bell pepper, green chilies, cumin, paprika, chili powder, salt, and black pepper, stirring well, and sauté for 5 minutes.
3. Stir in the remaining ingredients, except for the avocado and cilantro.
4. Lock the lid. Select the Manual mode and set the cooking time for 4 minutes at High Pressure.
5. When the timer beeps, perform a quick pressure release. Carefully remove the lid and stir.
6. Serve garnished with avocado slices and fresh cilantro (if desired).

Quinoa and Tomato Cream Bowl

Prep time: 12 mins, Cook Time: 12 mins, Servings: 6

1 tbsp. grated ginger
1 (28 oz) can tomatoes, chopped

¼ cup quinoa
14 oz. coconut milk
1 small yellow onion, chopped

1. In the Instant Pot, mix the onion with quinoa, tomatoes, milk and ginger, and stir well.
2. Lock the lid. Select the Manual mode and cook for 12 minutes at High Pressure.
3. Once cooking is complete, do a natural pressure release for 5 minutes, then release any remaining pressure. Carefully open the lid.
4. Stir the mixture one more time and divide into bowls to serve.

Peanut Butter Granola Bars

Prep time: 5 minutes | Cook time: 20 minutes | Serves 10

1 cup quick-cooking oats
½ cup all-natural peanut butter
⅓ cup pure maple syrup
1 tablespoon extra-virgin olive oil

¼ teaspoon fine sea salt
⅓ cup dried cranberries or raisins
½ cup raw pumpkin seeds
1 cup water

1. Line a 7-inch round pan with parchment paper.
2. Combine the oats, peanut butter, maple syrup, olive oil, and salt in a large bowl and stir well. Fold in the dried cranberries and pumpkin seeds, then scrape the batter into the prepared pan. Use a spatula to press the batter evenly into the bottom of the pan.
3. Pour the water into the Instant Pot and insert a trivet. Place the pan on the trivet. Cover the pan with another piece of parchment to protect the granola bars from condensation.
4. Secure the lid. Select the Manual mode and set the cooking time for 20 minutes at High Pressure.
5. Once cooking is complete, do a natural pressure release for 10 minutes, then release any remaining pressure. Carefully open the lid.
6. Remove the trivet and let the granola cool completely in the pan. Cut the cooled granola into 10 pieces and serve.

Steel-Cut Oatmeal

Prep time: 5 minutes | Cook time: 14 minutes | Serves 2

½ cup steel-cut oats
1½ cups water
¼ cup maple syrup, plus additional as needed
2 tablespoons packed brown

sugar
¼ teaspoon ground cinnamon
Pinch kosher salt, plus additional as needed
1 tablespoon unsalted butter

1. Press the Sauté button on the Instant Pot. Add the steel-cut oats and toast for about 2 minutes, stirring occasionally.
2. Add the water, ¼ cup of maple syrup, brown sugar, cinnamon, and pinch salt to the Instant Pot and stir well.
3. Lock the lid. Select the Manual mode and set the cooking time for 12 minutes at High Pressure.
4. Once cooking is complete, do a natural pressure release for 10 minutes, then release any remaining pressure. Carefully open the lid.
5. Stir the oatmeal and taste, adding additional maple syrup or salt as needed.
6. Let the oatmeal sit for 10 minutes. When ready, add the butter and stir well. Ladle into bowls and serve immediately.

Egg Benedict

Prep time: 5 minutes | Cook time: 1 minute | Serves 3

1 teaspoon butter	pepper
3 eggs	1 cup water
¼ teaspoon salt	3 turkey bacon slices, fried
½ teaspoon ground black	

1. Grease the eggs molds with the butter and crack the eggs inside. Sprinkle with salt and ground black pepper.
2. Pour the water and insert the trivet in the Instant Pot. Put the eggs molds on the trivet.
3. Set the lid in place. Select the Manual mode and set the cooking time for 1 minute on High Pressure. When the timer goes off, do a quick pressure release. Carefully open the lid.
4. Transfer the eggs onto the plate. Top the eggs with the fried bacon slices.

Hard-Boiled Eggs

Prep time: 5 minutes | Cook time: 5 minutes | Serves 6

½ cup water	6 eggs

1. Place the trivet in the Instant Pot and pour in the water.
2. Crack each egg into a silicone cup. Carefully place the cups on top of the trivet.
3. Set the lid in place. Select the Manual mode and set the cooking time for 5 minutes on High Pressure. When the timer goes off, perform a quick pressure release. Carefully open the lid.
4. Carefully remove the cups from the pot. Use a spoon to pop the eggs out of the cups. Serve immediately.

Lettuce Wrapped Chicken Sandwich

Prep time: 10 minutes | Cook time: 15 minutes | Serves 4

1 tablespoon butter	½ teaspoon ground nutmeg
3 ounces (85 g) scallions, chopped	1 tablespoon coconut flour
	1 teaspoon salt
2 cups ground chicken	1 cup lettuce

1. Press the Sauté button on the Instant Pot and melt the butter. Add the chopped scallions, ground chicken and ground nutmeg to the pot and sauté for 4 minutes. Add the coconut flour and salt and continue to sauté for 10 minutes.
2. Fill the lettuce with the ground chicken and transfer it on the plate. Serve immediately.

Bacon and Egg Risotto

Prep time: 12 mins, Cook Time: 12 mins, Servings: 2

1½ cups chicken stock	cheese
2 poached eggs	3 chopped bacon slices
2 tbsps. grated Parmesan	¾ cup Arborio rice

1. Set your Instant Pot to Sauté and add the bacon and cook for 5 minutes until crispy, stirring occasionally.
2. Carefully stir in the rice and let cook for an additional 1 minute.
3. Add the chicken stock and stir well.
4. Lock the lid. Select the Manual mode and set the cooking time for 6 minutes at Low Pressure.
5. Once cooking is complete, do a quick pressure release. Carefully open the lid.
6. Add the Parmesan cheese and keep stirring until melted. Divide the risotto between two plates. Add the eggs on the side and serve immediately.

Eggs En Cocotte

Prep time: 10 mins, Cook Time: 20 mins, Servings: 4

1 cup water	4 eggs
1 tbsp. butter	1 tbsp. chives
4 tbsps. heavy whipping cream	Salt and pepper, to taste

1. Arrange a steamer rack in the Instant Pot, then pour in the water.
2. Grease four ramekins with butter.
3. Divide the heavy whipping cream in the ramekins, then break each egg in each ramekin.
4. Sprinkle them with chives, salt, and pepper.
5. Arrange the ramekins on the steamer rack.
6. Lock the lid. Set to the Manual mode, then set the timer for 20 minutes at High Pressure.
7. Once the timer goes off, perform a natural pressure release for 10 minutes, then release any remaining pressure. Carefully open the lid.
8. Transfer them on a plate and serve immediately.

Pumpkin Oatmeal

Prep time: 5 minutes | Cook time: 10 minutes | Serves 6

3 cups water	spice
1½ cups 2% milk	1 teaspoon ground cinnamon
1¼ cups steel-cut oats	¾ teaspoon salt
3 tablespoons brown sugar	1 (15-ounce / 425-g) can solid-pack pumpkin
1½ teaspoons pumpkin pie	

1. Place all the ingredients except the pumpkin into the Instant Pot and stir to incorporate.
2. Secure the lid. Select the Manual mode and set the cooking time for 10 minutes at High Pressure.
3. Once cooking is complete, do a natural pressure release for 10 minutes, then release any remaining pressure. Carefully open the lid.
4. Add the pumpkin and stir well. Allow the oatmeal to sit for 5 to 10 minutes to thicken. Serve immediately.

Rhubarb Compote

Prep time: 10 minutes | Cook time: 3 minutes | Serves 6

Compote:

2 cups finely chopped fresh rhubarb	¼ cup sugar
	⅓ cup water

For Serving:

3 cups reduced-fat plain Greek yogurt	2 tablespoons honey
	¾ cup sliced almonds, toasted

1. Combine the rhubarb, sugar, and water in the Instant Pot.
2. Secure the lid. Select the Manual mode and set the cooking time for 3 minutes at High Pressure.
3. Once cooking is complete, do a natural pressure release for 10 minutes, then release any remaining pressure. Carefully open the lid.
4. Transfer the mixture to a bowl and let rest for a few minutes until cooled slightly. Place in the refrigerator until chilled.
5. When ready, whisk the yogurt and honey in a small bowl until well combined. Spoon into serving dishes and top each dish evenly with the compote. Scatter with the almonds and serve immediately.

Sweet Potato and Kale Egg Bites

Prep time: 7 minutes | Cook time: 20 minutes | Makes 7 egg bites

1 (14-ounce / 397-g) package firm tofu, lightly pressed
¼ cup coconut milk
¼ cup nutritional yeast
1 tablespoon cornstarch
½ to 1 teaspoon sea salt
½ teaspoon onion powder
½ teaspoon garlic powder
½ teaspoon ground turmeric
½ cup shredded sweet potato
Handful kale leaves, chopped small
1 cup plus 1 tablespoon water, divided
Freshly ground black pepper, to taste
Nonstick cooking spray

1. Lightly spray a silicone egg bites mold with nonstick cooking spray. Set aside.
2. Combine the tofu, milk, yeast, cornstarch, sea salt, onion powder, garlic powder, and turmeric in a food processor. Pulse until smooth.
3. Press the Sauté button to heat your Instant Pot until hot.
4. Add the sweet potato, kale, and 1 tablespoon of water. Sauté for 1 to 2 minutes. Stir the veggies into the tofu mixture and spoon the mixture into the prepared mold. Cover it tightly with aluminum foil and place on a trivet.
5. Pour the remaining 1 cup of water into the Instant Pot and insert the trivet.
6. Lock the lid. Select the Manual mode and set the cooking time for 18 minutes at High Pressure.
7. When the timer beeps, perform a natural pressure release for 10 minutes, then release any remaining pressure. Carefully remove the lid.
8. Remove the silicone mold from the Instant Pot and pull off the foil. Allow to cool for 5 minutes on the trivet. The bites will continue to firm as they cool.
9. Season to taste with pepper and serve warm.

Coconut Muesli Stuffed Apples

Prep time: 10 minutes | Cook time: 3 minutes | Serves 2

⅓ cup water
2 large unpeeled organic apples, cored and tops removed
Filling:
½ cup coconut muesli
2 tablespoons butter, cubed
½ teaspoon ground cinnamon
2 teaspoons packed brown sugar

1. Pour the water into the Instant Pot and set aside.
2. Mix together all the ingredients for the filling in a bowl, mashing gently with a fork until incorporated.
3. Stuff each apple evenly with the muesli mixture, then arrange them in the Instant Pot.
4. Lock the lid. Select the Manual mode and set the cooking time for 3 minutes at Low Pressure, depending on how large the apples are.
5. Once cooking is complete, do a natural pressure release for 10 minutes, then release any remaining pressure. Carefully open the lid.
6. Let the apples cool for 5 minutes and serve.

Spiced Fruit Medley

Prep time: 5 minutes | Cook time: 1 minute | Serves 6

1 pound (454 g) frozen pineapple chunks
1 pound (454 g) sliced frozen peaches
1 cup frozen and pitted dark sweet cherries
2 ripe pears, sliced
¼ cup pure maple syrup
1 teaspoon curry powder, plus more as needed

1. Combine all the ingredients in the Instant Pot.
2. Secure the lid. Select the Manual mode and set the cooking time for 1 minute at High Pressure.
3. Once cooking is complete, do a quick pressure release. Carefully open the lid.
4. Stir the mixture well, adding more curry powder if you like it spicy. Serve warm.

Vanilla Pancake

Prep time: 5 minutes | Cook time: 50 minutes | Serves 6

3 eggs, beaten
½ cup coconut flour
¼ cup heavy cream
¼ cup almond flour
3 tablespoons Swerve
1 teaspoon vanilla extract
1 teaspoon baking powder
Cooking spray

1. In a bowl, stir together the eggs, coconut flour, heavy cream, almond flour, Swerve and vanilla extract. Whisk in the baking powder until smooth.
2. Spritz the bottom and sides of Instant Pot with cooking spray. Place the batter in the pot.
3. Set the lid in place. Select the Manual mode and set the cooking time for 50 minutes on Low Pressure. Once the timer goes off, perform a natural pressure release for 5 minutes, then release any remaining pressure. Carefully open the lid.
4. Let the pancake rest in the pot for 5 minutes before serving.

Tropical Fruit Chutney

Prep time: 5 minutes | Cook time: 20 minutes | Serves 6

2 mangoes, chopped
1 medium-sized pear, peeled and chopped
1 papaya, chopped
1 cup apple cider vinegar
½ cup brown sugar
¼ cup golden raisins
2 tablespoons fresh grated ginger
2 teaspoons lemon zest
½ teaspoon coriander
½ teaspoon cinnamon
¼ teaspoon cardamom

1. Stir together all the ingredients in the Instant Pot.
2. Secure the lid. Select the Manual mode and set the cooking time for 6 minutes at High Pressure.
3. Once cooking is complete, do a natural pressure release for 20 minutes, then release any remaining pressure. Carefully open the lid.
4. Press the Sauté button on the Instant Pot. Cook the chutney, stirring, for approximately 12 to 15 minutes, or until thickened. Serve warm.

Baked Eggs with Parmesan

Prep time: 5 minutes | Cook time: 10 minutes | Serves 1

1 tablespoon butter, cut into small pieces
2 tablespoons keto-friendly low-carb Marinara sauce
3 eggs
2 tablespoons grated Parmesan cheese
¼ teaspoon Italian seasoning
1 cup water

1. Place the butter pieces on the bottom of the oven-safe bowl. Spread the marinara sauce over the butter. Crack the eggs on top of the marinara sauce and top with the cheese and Italian seasoning.
2. Cover the bowl with aluminum foil. Pour the water and insert the trivet in the Instant Pot. Put the bowl on the trivet.
3. Set the lid in place. Select the Manual mode and set the cooking time for 10 minutes on Low Pressure. When the timer goes off, do a quick pressure release. Carefully open the lid.
4. Let the eggs cool for 5 minutes before serving.

Buttery Herbed Sirloin Steak

Prep time: 5 minutes | Cook time: 1 minute | Serves 2

½ cup water
1 pound (454 g) boneless beef sirloin steak
½ teaspoon salt
½ teaspoon black pepper
1 clove garlic, minced
2 tablespoons butter, softened
¼ teaspoon dried rosemary
¼ teaspoon dried parsley
Pinch of dried thyme

1. Pour the water into the Instant Pot and put the trivet in the pot.
2. Rub the steak all over with salt and black pepper. Place the steak on the trivet.
3. In a small bowl, stir together the remaining ingredients. Spread half of the butter mixture over the steak.
4. Set the lid in place. Select the Manual mode and set the cooking time for 1 minute on Low Pressure. When the timer goes off, perform a quick pressure release. Carefully open the lid.
5. Remove the steak from the pot. Top with the remaining half of the butter mixture. Serve hot.

Cabbage and Zucchini Hash Browns

Prep time: 5 minutes | Cook time: 8 minutes | Serves 3

1 cup shredded white cabbage
3 eggs, beaten
½ teaspoon ground nutmeg
½ teaspoon salt
½ teaspoon onion powder
½ zucchini, grated
1 tablespoon coconut oil

1. In a bowl, stir together all the ingredients, except for the coconut oil. Form the cabbage mixture into medium hash browns.
2. Press the Sauté button on the Instant Pot and heat the coconut oil.
3. Place the hash browns in the hot coconut oil. Cook for 4 minutes on each side, or until lightly browned.
4. Transfer the hash browns to a plate and serve warm.

Buckwheat Breakfast Bowls

Prep time: 5 minutes | Cook time: 1 minute | Serves 6

2 cups buckwheat groats, soaked for at least 20 minutes and up to overnight
3 cups water
¼ cup pure maple syrup
1 teaspoon vanilla extract
1 teaspoon ground cinnamon
¼ teaspoon fine sea salt
Almond milk, for serving
Chopped or sliced fresh fruit, for serving

1. Drain and rinse the buckwheat. In the Instant Pot, combine the buckwheat with the water, maple syrup, cinnamon, vanilla, and salt.
2. Lock the lid. Select the Manual mode and set the cooking time for 1 minute at High Pressure.
3. When the timer beeps, perform a natural pressure release for 10 minutes, then release any remaining pressure. Carefully remove the lid and stir the cooked grains.
4. Serve the buckwheat warm with almond milk and fresh fruit.

Mini Bell Pepper and Cheddar Frittata

Prep time: 12 mins, Cook Time: 5 mins, Servings: 6

1 chopped red bell pepper
1 tbsp. almond milk
¼ tsp. salt
2 tbsps. grated Cheddar
cheese
5 whisked eggs
1½ cups water

1. In a bowl, combine the salt, eggs, cheese, almond milk, and red bell pepper, and whisk well. Pour the egg mixture into 6 baking molds.
2. Add 1½ cups water and steamer basket to your Instant Pot. Transfer the baking molds to the basket.
3. Lock the lid. Select the Manual mode and cook for 5minutes at High Pressure.
4. Once cooking is complete, do a quick pressure release. Carefully open the lid. Serve hot.

Raisin, Apple, and Pecan Oatmeal

Prep time: 10 minutes | Cook time: 5 minutes | Serves 4

¾ cup steel-cut oats
¾ cup raisins
3 cups vanilla almond milk
3 tablespoons brown sugar
4½ teaspoons butter
¾ teaspoon ground cinnamon
½ teaspoon salt
1 large apple, peeled and chopped
¼ cup chopped pecans

1. Combine all the ingredients, except for the apple and pecans, in the Instant Pot.
2. Lock the lid. Select the Manual mode and set the cooking time for 5 minutes at High Pressure.
3. When the timer beeps, perform a natural pressure release for 10 minutes, then release any remaining pressure. Carefully remove the lid.
4. Stir in the apple and let sit for 10 minutes. Spoon the oatmeal into bowls and sprinkle the pecans on top before serving.

Walnut and Pear Oatmeal

Prep time: 5 minutes | Cook time: 7 minutes | Serves 2

1 cup old-fashioned oats
1¼ cups water
1 medium pear, peeled, cored, and cubed
¼ cup freshly squeezed orange juice
¼ cup chopped walnuts
¼ cup dried cherries
¼ teaspoon ground ginger
¼ teaspoon ground cinnamon
Pinch of salt

1. In the Instant Pot, combine the oats, water, pear, orange juice, walnuts, cherries, ginger, cinnamon, and salt.
2. Secure the lid. Select the Manual mode and set the cooking time for 7 minutes at High Pressure.
3. Once cooking is complete, do a natural pressure release for 10 minutes, then release any remaining pressure. Carefully open the lid.
4. Stir the oatmeal and spoon into two bowls. Serve warm.

Pork Quill Egg Cups

Prep time: 15 minutes | Cook time: 15 minutes | Serves 4

10 ounces (283 g) ground pork
1 jalapeño pepper, chopped
1 tablespoon butter, softened
1 teaspoon dried dill
½ teaspoon salt
1 cup water
4 quill eggs

1. In a bowl, stir together all the ingredients, except for the quill eggs and water. Transfer the meat mixture to the silicone muffin molds and press the surface gently.
2. Pour the water and insert the trivet in the Instant Pot. Put the meat cups on the trivet.
3. Crack the eggs over the meat mixture.
4. Set the lid in place. Select the Manual mode and set the cooking time for 15 minutes on High Pressure. When the timer goes off, do a quick pressure release. Carefully open the lid.
5. Serve warm.

Carrot and Pineapple Oatmeal

Prep time: 10 minutes | Cook time: 10 minutes | Serves 8

4½ cups water
2 cups shredded carrots
1 cup steel-cut oats
1 (20-ounce/ 567-g) can crushed pineapple, undrained
1 cup raisins
1 teaspoon pumpkin pie spice
2 teaspoons ground cinnamon
Brown sugar (optional)
Cooking spray

1. Spray the bottom of the Instant Pot with cooking spray.
2. Combine the remaining ingredients except the brown sugar in the Instant Pot.
3. Secure the lid. Select the Manual mode and set the cooking time for 10 minutes at High Pressure.
4. Once cooking is complete, do a natural pressure release for 10 minutes, then release any remaining pressure. Carefully open the lid.
5. Serve sprinkled with the brown sugar, if desired.

Stone Fruit Compote

Prep time: 5 minutes | Cook time: 3 minutes | Makes about 2 cups

4 cups sliced stone fruit (plums, apricots, or peaches)
⅛ cup water
1 tablespoon pure maple syrup, plus additional as needed
1 tablespoon fresh lemon juice
½ teaspoon vanilla bean paste or extract
Pinch of ground cinnamon

1. Stir together all the ingredients in the Instant Pot.
2. Lock the lid. Select the Manual mode and set the cooking time for 1 minute at High Pressure.
3. When the timer beeps, perform a natural pressure release for 10 minutes, then release any remaining pressure. Carefully remove the lid.
4. Allow to simmer on Sauté for 2 minutes, stirring, or until thickened.
5. Taste and add additional maple syrup, as needed. Serve warm.

Special White Pancake

Prep time: 12 mins, Cook Time: 30 mins, Servings: 4

2½ tsps. baking powder
2 eggs, beaten
2 tbsps. sugar
1½ cups milk
2 cups white flour

1. In a bowl, mix the flour with eggs, milk, sugar, and baking powder. Stir to incorporate.
2. Spread out the mixture onto the bottom of the Instant Pot.
3. Lock the lid. Select the Manual mode and cook for 30 minutes at High Pressure.
4. Once cooking is complete, do a quick pressure release. Carefully open the lid.
5. Let the pancake cool for a few minutes before slicing to serve.

Veggie Quiche

Prep time: 12 mins, Cook Time: 20 mins, Servings: 6

½ cup milk
1 red bell pepper, chopped
2 green onions, chopped
Salt, to taste
8 whisked eggs
1 cup water

1. In a bowl, combine the whisked eggs with milk, bell pepper, onions and salt, and stir well. Pour the egg mixture into a pan.
2. In your Instant Pot, add the water and trivet. Place the pan on the trivet and cover with tin foil.
3. Lock the lid. Select the Manual mode and cook for 20 minutes at High Pressure.
4. Once cooking is complete, do a quick pressure release. Carefully open the lid.
5. Slice the quiche and divide between plates to serve.

Bacon and Spinach Quiche
Prep time: 5 minutes | Cook time: 35 minutes | Serves 3

1 cup filtered water
5 eggs, lightly beaten
½ cup spinach, chopped
½ cup full-fat coconut milk
½ cup shredded full-fat
Cheddar cheese
2 slices no-sugar-added bacon,

cooked and finely chopped
½ teaspoon dried parsley
½ teaspoon dried basil
½ teaspoon freshly ground
black pepper
¼ teaspoon kosher salt

1.Pour the water into the the Instant Pot, then place the trivet.
2.Stir together the remaining ingredients in a baking dish. Cover the dish loosely with aluminum foil. Place the dish on top of the trivet.
3.Secure the lid. Select the Manual mode and set the cooking time for 35 minutes at High Pressure.
4.Once cooking is complete, do a natural pressure release for 10 minutes, then release any remaining pressure. Carefully open the lid.
5.Serve warm.

Strawberry and Pumpkin Spice Quinoa Bowl
Prep time: 12 mins, Cook Time: 2 minute, Servings: 4

2¼ cups water
2 tbsps. honey
2 cups chopped strawberries

¼ tsp. pumpkin pie spice
1 ½ cups quinoa

1.In the Instant Pot, mix the quinoa with honey, water, spice, and strawberries. Stir to combine.
2.Lock the lid. Select the Manual mode and set the cooking time for 2 minutes at High Pressure.
3.Once cooking is complete, do a natural pressure release for 10 minutes, then release any remaining pressure. Carefully open the lid.
4.Let the quinoa rest for 10 minutes. Give a good stir and serve immediately.

Vanilla Applesauce
Prep time: 10 minutes | Cook time: 3 minutes | Makes 5 cups

7 medium apples (about 3
pounds / 1.4 kg), peeled and
cored
½ cup water

½ cup sugar
1 tablespoon lemon juice
¼ teaspoon vanilla extract

1.Slice each apple into 8 wedges on your cutting board, then slice each wedge crosswise in half.
2.Add the apples to the Instant Pot along with the remaining ingredients. Stir well.
3.Secure the lid. Select the Manual mode and set the cooking time for 3 minutes at High Pressure.
4.Once cooking is complete, do a natural pressure release for 10 minutes, then release any remaining pressure. Carefully open the lid.
5.Blend the mixture with an immersion blender until your desired consistency is achieved.
6.Serve warm.

Western Omelet
Prep time: 12 mins, Cook Time: 30 mins, Servings: 4

½ cup half-and-half
4 chopped spring onions
6 whisked eggs

¼ tsp. salt
8 oz. bacon, chopped
1½ cups water

1.Place the steamer basket in the Instant Pot and pour in 1½ cups water.
2.In a bowl, combine the eggs with half-and-half, bacon, spring onions and salt, and whisk well. Pour the egg mixture into a soufflé dish and transfer to the steamer basket.
3.Lock the lid. Select the Steam mode and cook for 30 minutes at High Pressure.
4.Once cooking is complete, do a quick pressure release. Carefully open the lid.
5.Allow to cool for 5 minutes before serving.

Chapter 3 Vegetables

Spicy Zucchini

Prep time: 5 minutes | Cook time: 4 minutes | Serves 4

1½ tablespoons olive oil
2 garlic cloves, minced
1½ pounds (680 g) zucchinis, sliced
½ cup vegetable broth

1 teaspoon dried basil
½ teaspoon smoked paprika
½ teaspoon dried rosemary
Salt and pepper, to taste

1. Set the Instant Pot to the Sauté mode and heat the olive oil. Add the garlic to the pot and sauté for 1 minute, or until fragrant. Stir in the remaining ingredients.
2. Lock the lid. Select the Manual mode and set the cooking time for 3 minutes on Low Pressure. When the timer goes off, perform a quick pressure release. Carefully open the lid.
3. Serve immediately.

Asparagus with Copoundy Cheese

Prep time: 5 minutes | Cook time: 1 minute | Serves 4

1½ pounds (680 g) fresh asparagus
1 cup water
2 tablespoons olive oil
4 garlic cloves, minced

Sea salt, to taste
¼ teaspoon ground black pepper
½ cup shredded Copoundy cheese

1. Pour the water into the Instant Pot and put the steamer basket in the pot.
2. Place the asparagus in the steamer basket. Drizzle the asparagus with the olive oil and sprinkle with the garlic on top. Season with salt and black pepper.
3. Close and secure the lid. Select the Manual mode and set the cooking time for 1 minute at High Pressure. Once cooking is complete, do a quick pressure release. Carefully open the lid.
4. Transfer the asparagus to a platter and served topped with the shredded cheese.

Beet Thoran Keralite Sadhya

Prep time: 10 minutes | Cook time: 20 minutes | Serves 4

1 cup water
½ pound (227 g) small beets
2 tablespoons olive oil
½ chili pepper, chopped
1 garlic clove, minced

½ cup shallots, chopped
5 curry leaves
⅓ teaspoon turmeric powder
Sea salt and ground black pepper, to taste

1. Pour the water in the Instant Pot and fit in a steamer basket. Place the beets in the steamer basket.
2. Secure the lid. Choose the Steam mode and set the cooking time for 15 minutes at High pressure.
3. Once cooking is complete, perform a quick pressure release. Carefully open the lid. Allow the beets to cool for a few minutes.
4. Once the beets are cool enough to touch, transfer them to a cutting board, then peel and chop them into small pieces.
5. Press the Sauté button and heat the olive oil until shimmering.
6. Add and sauté the chili pepper, garlic, shallots, and curry leaves for about 4 minutes or until softened.
7. Sprinkle with the turmeric, salt, and black pepper. Fold in the cooked beets. Serve warm.

Braised Red Wine Collards

Prep time: 5 minutes | Cook time: 2 minutes | Serves 4

1 pound (454 g) Collards, torn into pieces
¾ cup water
¼ cup dry red wine
1½ tablespoons sesame oil

1 teaspoon ginger-garlic paste
½ teaspoon fennel seeds
½ teaspoon mustard seeds
Sea salt and ground black pepper, to taste

1. Add all the ingredients to the Instant Pot and stir to combine.
2. Lock the lid. Select the Manual mode and set the cooking time for 2 minutes on High Pressure. When the timer goes off, perform a quick pressure release. Carefully open the lid.
3. Ladle into individual bowls and serve warm.

Bok Choy with Soy Sauce

Prep time: 5 minutes | Cook time: 6 minutes | Serves 4

1 teaspoon sesame oil
1 clove garlic, pressed
1 pound (454 g) Bok choy

½ cup water
1 tablespoon rice wine vinegar
2 tablespoons soy sauce

1. Press the Sauté button and heat the sesame oil in the Instant Pot.
2. Add the garlic and sauté for 1 minute or until fragrant. Add the Bok choy and pour in the water.
3. Secure the lid. Choose the Manual mode and set the cooking time for 5 minutes at High pressure.
4. Meanwhile, in a small bowl, whisk the rice vinegar and soy sauce.
5. Once cooking is complete, do a quick pressure release. Carefully open the lid.
6. Drizzle the sauce over the Bok choy and serve immediately.

Cauliflower Tots

Prep time: 30 minutes | Cook time: 10 minutes | Serves 4

1 cup water
1 large cauliflower
1 egg, beaten
1 cup almond meal
1 cup grated Parmesan cheese

1 cup grated Gruyere cheese
2 garlic cloves, minced
Salt, to taste
3 tablespoons olive oil

1. Pour the water in the Instant Pot, then fit in a trivet and place the cauliflower on top.
2. Seal the lid. Select the Manual mode and set the time for 3 minutes at High Pressure.
3. Once cooking is complete, do a quick pressure release. Carefully open the lid.
4. Transfer the cauliflower to a food processor and pulse to rice the cauliflower.
5. Pour the cauliflower rice into a bowl. Mix in the egg, almond meal, cheeses, garlic, and salt.
6. Make the tots: Form the mixture into 2-inch oblong balls. Place on a baking sheet and chill in the refrigerator for 20 minutes.
7. Set the Instant Pot on Sauté mode. Heat the olive oil until shimmering.
8. Remove tots from refrigerator and fry in the oil for 6 minutes on all sides until golden brown. Flip the tots in the oil during the frying. Work in batches to avoid overcrowding.
9. Place the tots on a paper towel-lined plate to pat dry and serve.

Broccoli with Roasted Almonds

Prep time: 10 minutes | Cook time: 4 minutes | Serves 4 to 6

6 cups broccoli florets
1 cup water
1½ tablespoons olive oil
8 garlic cloves, thinly sliced
2 shallots, thinly sliced
½ teaspoon crushed red pepper flakes
Grated zest and juice of 1

medium lemon
½ teaspoon kosher salt
Freshly ground black pepper, to taste
¼ cup chopped roasted almonds
¼ cup finely slivered fresh basil

1. Pour the water into the Instant Pot. Place the broccoli florets in a steamer basket and lower into the pot.
2. Close and secure the lid. Select the Steam setting and set the cooking time for 2 minutes at Low Pressure. Once the timer goes off, use a quick pressure release. Carefully open the lid.
3. Transfer the broccoli to a large bowl filled with cold water and ice. Once cooled, drain the broccoli and pat dry.
4. Select the Sauté mode on the Instant Pot and heat the olive oil. Add the garlic to the pot and sauté for 30 seconds, tossing constantly. Add the shallots and pepper flakes to the pot and sauté for 1 minute.
5. Stir in the cooked broccoli, lemon juice, salt and black pepper. Toss the ingredients together and cook for 1 minute.
6. Transfer the broccoli to a serving platter and sprinkle with the chopped almonds, lemon zest and basil. Serve immediately.

Baby Eggplants with Coconut

Prep time: 20 minutes | Cook time: 10 minutes | Serves 4

¼ cup dried coconut powder
1 tablespoon coriander powder
1 teaspoon cumin powder
½ teaspoon red chili powder
½ teaspoon garam masala
¼ teaspoon turmeric powder
1 teaspoon salt, divided
12 baby eggplants (1 pound / 454 g in total), each eggplant

is 2 inches, rinsed and patted dry
1 tablespoon olive oil
½ teaspoon mustard seeds
1 medium red onion, chopped
1 teaspoon ginger garlic paste
2 medium tomatoes, chopped
¾ cup water, divided
Cilantro, for garnish

1. In a bowl, mix the coconut powder, coriander powder, cumin powder, red chili powder, garam masala, turmeric powder and ½ teaspoon salt.
2. Make crosswise and lengthwise slits through the flesh of each eggplant, but without cutting all the way through. Carefully open the eggplants up and divide half of the coconut mixture in each baby eggplant. Reserve remaining half of the coconut stuffing for the curry. Set the stuffed eggplants and reserved stuffing mixture aside.
3. Press the Sauté button on the Instant Pot. Add the oil and the mustard seeds and let them heat until they pop.
4. Add the onion and cook for 2 minutes until soft and translucent.
5. Add the ginger garlic paste and cook for 1 minute, then add the tomatoes and ¼ cup of water. Cook the tomatoes for 2 minutes until they turn soft, and then add the reserved coconut stuffing. Cook for 1 minute and then add ½ cup of water and ½ teaspoon of salt and mix well.
6. Put the stuffed eggplants on top of the masala and close the lid.
7. Press the Manual button. Set cooking time for 4 minutes on High Pressure.
8. When timer beeps, do a quick pressure release.
9. Open the pot, garnish with cilantro and serve.

Walnut and Beet Burgers

Prep time: 10 minutes | Cook time: 45 minutes | Serves 4

5 medium beets, quartered
1½ cups water
1½ cups chopped walnuts
4 teaspoons cornstarch, combined with ¼ cup warm water
½ cup chopped yellow onions
⅛ cup all-purpose flour

1 cup shredded Cheddar cheese
2 tablespoons soy sauce
2 tablespoons olive oil
Salt and ground black pepper, to taste
4 burger buns

1. Add the beets and water to the Instant Pot. Lock the lid, then press the Manual button, and set the timer to 15 minutes at High Pressure.
2. When the timer beeps, let pressure release naturally for 5 minutes, then release any remaining pressure. Unlock lid.
3. Drain the beets and add to a large bowl. Add the remaining ingredients, except for the buns, and mash the mixture with a potato masher. Form the beet mixture into 4 patties.
4. Preheat the oven to 350ºF (180ºC). Spray a baking pan with cooking spray.
5. Place the patties on the prepared baking pan and bake for 25 to 30 minutes.
6. Allow the patties to cool, then assemble the patties with buns and serve.

Mushroom and Cauliflower Risotto

Prep time: 7 mins, Cook time: 10 mins, Servings: 3

1 cup freshly squeezed coconut milk
1 tbsp. coconut oil
1 cauliflower head, cut into florets

1 onion, chopped
1 lb. shiitake mushrooms, sliced
Salt and pepper, to taste

1. Press the Sauté button and heat the coconut oil.
2. Sauté the onions for 3 minutes or until fragrant. Add the cauliflower and shiitake mushrooms.
3. Sprinkle salt and pepper for seasoning.
4. Add the coconut milk in three batches.
5. Allow to simmer for 10 minutes.
6. Garnish with chopped parsley if desired.

Baked Cabbage with Pepper

Prep time: 15 minutes | Cook time: 25 minutes | Serves 2

1 tablespoon olive oil, divided
½ pound (227 g) green cabbage, shredded
1 garlic clove, sliced
1 onion, thinly sliced
1 Serrano pepper, chopped
1 sweet pepper, thinly sliced
Sea salt and ground black

pepper, to taste
1 teaspoon paprika
1 cup cream of mushroom soup
4 ounces (113 g) Colby cheese, shredded
1 cup water

1. Grease a baking dish with ½ tablespoon of olive oil. Add the cabbage, garlic, onion, and peppers. Stir to combine.
2. Drizzle with remaining oil and season with salt, black pepper, and paprika. Pour in the mushroom soup. Top with the shredded cheese and cover with aluminum foil.
3. Pour the water in the Instant Pot and fit in a trivet. Lower the dish onto the trivet.
4. Secure the lid. Choose the Manual mode and set the cooking time for 25 minutes at High pressure.
5. Once cooking is complete, perform a quick pressure release. Carefully open the lid. Serve warm.

Brussels Sprouts with Peanuts

Prep time: 10 minutes | Cook time: 8 minutes | Serves 4

3 tablespoons sesame oil
1½ pounds (680 g) Brussels sprouts, halved
2 tablespoons fish sauce

1 cup chicken stock
½ cup chopped roasted peanuts

1. Set the Instant Pot to Sauté and heat the sesame oil until shimmering.
2. Add and fry Brussels sprouts for 5 minutes or until golden. Mix in the fish sauce and chicken stock.
3. Seal the lid. Select the Manual mode and set the time for 3 minutes.
4. Once cooking is complete, do a quick pressure release, then unlock the lid.
5. Mix in the peanuts. Serve immediately.

Olive and Cauliflower Salad

Prep time: 10 minutes | Cook time: 2 minutes | Serves 4

1 cup water
½ pound (227 g) cauliflower, cut into florets
1 bell pepper, thinly sliced
½ red onion, thinly sliced
¼ cup fresh flat-leaf parsley,
Dressing:
1 teaspoon hot mustard
2 tablespoons fresh lime juice
3 tablespoons extra-virgin olive

coarsely chopped
¼ cup green olives, pitted and coarsely chopped
2 ounces (57 g) Mozzarella cheese, crumbled

oil
Sea salt and ground black pepper, to taste

1. Pour the water in the Instant Pot and fit in a steamer basket. Place the cauliflower in the steamer basket.
2. Secure the lid. Choose the Steam mode and set the cooking time for 2 minutes at High pressure.
3. Once cooking is complete, perform a quick pressure release. Carefully open the lid.
4. Toss the cooked cauliflower with pepper, onion, parsley, and olives in a large bowl.
5. In a small bowl, combine the ingredients for the dressing.
6. Dress the salad and serve garnished with the crumbled Mozzarella cheese.

Pecan and Cherry Stuffed Pumpkin

Prep time: 20 minutes | Cook time: 20 minutes | Serves 4

1 (2-pound / 907-g) pumpkin, halved lengthwise, stems trimmed
2 tablespoons olive oil
1 cup water
½ cup dried cherries
1 teaspoon dried parsley

5 toasted bread slices, cubed
1 teaspoon onion powder
1½ cups vegetable broth
Salt and black pepper, to taste
½ cup chopped pecans, for topping

1. Brush the pumpkin with olive oil. Pour the water in the Instant Pot and fit in a trivet. Place the pumpkin, skin-side down, on the trivet.
2. Seal the lid. Select the Manual mode and set the cooking time for 15 minutes at High Pressure.
3. Once cooking is complete, do a quick pressure release. Carefully open the lid.
4. Remove the pumpkin and water. Press the Sauté button, add the remaining ingredients. Stir for 5 minutes or until the liquid is reduced by half.
5. Divide the mixture between pumpkin halves and top with pecans.

Broccoli with Mushrooms

Prep time: 15 mins, Cook Time: 8 mins, Servings: 4

2 tbsps. coconut oil
1 cup sliced mushrooms
2 cups broccoli florets

1 tbsp. soy sauce
1 cup vegetable broth
Salt and pepper, to taste

1. Set the Instant Pot to Sauté mode and add the coconut oil to melt.
2. Add the mushrooms and sauté for 4 to 5 minutes.
3. Add broccoli and soy sauce and sauté for 1 more minute.
4. Pour the broth over. Sprinkle with salt and pepper.
5. Lock the lid. Set the Instant Pot to Manual mode, then set the timer for 2 minutes at High Pressure.
6. Once cooking is complete, do a quick pressure release. Carefully open the lid.
7. Serve the veggies drizzled with the cooking liquid.
8. Serve immediately!

Raisin and Broccoli Seed Salad

Prep time: 10 minutes | Cook time: 1 minutes | Serves 2 to 4

1 cup water
½ pound (227 g) broccoli, cut into florets
2 tablespoons raisins
2 scallion stalks, chopped
Sea salt and ground black pepper, to taste
2 tablespoons sesame seeds,

toasted
2 tablespoons sunflower seeds, to toasted
1 tablespoon balsamic vinegar
⅓ cup mayonnaise
1 tablespoon fresh lemon juice
⅓ cup sour cream

1. Pour the water in the Instant Pot and fit in a steamer basket. Place the broccoli in the steamer basket.
2. Secure the lid. Choose the Manual mode and set the cooking time for 1 minute at High pressure.
3. Once cooking is complete, perform a quick pressure release. Carefully open the lid. Allow to cool for a few minutes.
4. Transfer the broccoli florets to a serving bowl. Toss in the raisins, scallions, salt, black pepper, and seeds.
5. Stir in the balsamic vinegar, mayo, lemon juice, and sour cream. Serve immediately.

Cabbage with Cream Sauce

Prep time: 10 minutes | Cook time: 13 minutes | Serves 4

1 tablespoon unsalted butter
½ cup diced pancetta
¼ cup diced yellow onion
1 cup chicken broth
1 pound (454 g) green cabbage, finely chopped
1 bay leaf

⅓ cup heavy cream
1 tablespoon dried parsley
1 teaspoon fine grind sea salt
¼ teaspoon ground nutmeg
¼ teaspoon ground black pepper

1. Press the Sauté button on the Instant Pot and melt the butter. Add the pancetta and onion to the pot and sauté for about 4 minutes, or until the onion is tender and begins to brown.
2. Pour in the chicken broth. Using a wooden spoon, stir and loosen any browned bits from the bottom of the pot. Stir in the cabbage and bay leaf.
3. Lock the lid. Select the Manual mode and set the cooking time for 4 minutes on High Pressure. When the timer goes off, perform a quick pressure release. Carefully open the lid.
4. Select Sauté mode and bring the ingredients to a boil. Stir in the remaining ingredients and simmer for 5 additional minutes.
5. Remove and discard the bay leaf. Spoon into serving bowls. Serve warm.

Spinach and Broccoli Avocado Mash

Prep time: 15 minutes | Cook time: 3 minutes | Serves 4

1 medium broccoli, cut into florets
2 cups spinach
1 cup vegetable broth
2 avocados, halved, pitted, and peeled

2 tablespoons chopped parsley
2 tablespoons butter
Salt and black pepper, to taste
3 tablespoons Greek yogurt
2 tablespoons toasted pine nuts, for topping

1. Add the broccoli, spinach, and broth to the Instant Pot. Stir to mix well.
2. Seal the lid. Select the Manual mode and set the cooking time for 3 minutes on High Pressure.
3. Once cooking is complete, do a quick pressure release. Carefully open the lid. Stir in the avocado, parsley, butter, salt, pepper, and Greek yogurt.
4. Pour the mixture in a food processor and pulse until smooth. Spoon into serving bowls and top with pine nuts. Serve immediately.

Butternut Squash and Mushrooms

Prep time: 10 minutes | Cook time: 40 minutes | Serves 4

1 tablespoon olive oil
2 cups butternut squash, peeled and diced
1 red bell pepper, diced
½ cup onion, chopped
3 garlic cloves, minced
8 ounces (227 g) white mushrooms, sliced
1½ cups Arborio rice

3½ cup vegetable soup
¼ teaspoon oregano
2 teaspoons ground coriander
1 teaspoon salt
1 teaspoon ground black pepper
½ cup dry white wine
1½ tablespoons nutritional yeast

1. Put the oil to the Instant Pot and select the Sauté function.
2. Add the butternut squash, bell pepper, onion, and garlic to the oil and sauté for 5 minutes.
3. Stir in the mushrooms, rice, soup, oregano, coriander, salt, pepper, and wine.
4. Secure the lid and select the Bean / Chili function and set the cooking time for 30 minutes at High Pressure.
5. When the timer beeps, do a natural pressure release for 10 minutes, then release any remaining pressure. Open the lid.
6. Mix in the nutritional yeast, then cook for another 5 minutes on Sauté setting. Serve warm.

Parmesan Asparagus

Prep time: 10 minutes | Cook time: 8 minutes | Serves 4

1 cup water
1 pound (454 g) asparagus, chopped
2 garlic cloves, minced
2 tablespoons butter, softened

Salt and black pepper, to taste
1 tablespoon olive oil
½ lemon, juiced
2 tablespoons grated Parmesan cheese

1. In the Instant pot, pour the water and fit in a trivet. Cut out a foil sheet, place the asparagus on top with garlic and butter. Season with salt and black pepper. Wrap the foil and place on the trivet.
2. Seal the lid. Select the Manual mode and set to 8 minutes on High Pressure.
3. Once cooking is complete, do a quick pressure release. Carefully open the lid.
4. Remove the foil, then transfer the asparagus onto a platter. Drizzle with lemon juice, and top with Parmesan cheese to serve.

Khoreshe Karafs

Prep time: 20 minutes | Cook time: 11 minutes | Serves 2

1 tablespoon unsalted butter
½ onion, chopped
1 garlic clove, minced
½ pound (227 g) celery stalks, diced
1 Persian lime, prick a few holes
1 tablespoon fresh cilantro,

roughly chopped
1 tablespoon fresh mint, finely chopped
½ teaspoon mustard seeds
2 cups vegetable broth
½ teaspoon cayenne pepper
Sea salt and ground black pepper, to taste

1. Press the Sauté button of the Instant Pot. Add and melt the butter.
2. Add and sauté the onions and garlic for about 3 minutes or until tender and fragrant.
3. Stir in the remaining ingredients, except for the basmati rice.
4. Secure the lid. Choose the Manual mode and set the cooking time for 18 minutes at High pressure.
5. Once cooking is complete, use a natural pressure release for 15 minutes, then release any remaining pressure. Carefully open the lid.
6. Serve hot.

Mushrooms with Green Beans

Prep time: 15 minutes | Cook time: 5 minutes | Serves 8

2 cups finely chopped mushrooms
1 cup chopped onion
3 cloves garlic, minced
1 teaspoon kosher salt
½ teaspoon black pepper
¼ cup water
1 pound (454 g) trimmed fresh

green beans
2 tablespoons diced cream cheese, at room temperature
¼ cup half-and-half
Sliced toasted almonds (optional)
Fried onions (optional)

1. In the Instant Pot, combine the mushrooms, onion, garlic, salt, pepper, and water. Put the green beans on top. Set the cream cheese on top of the beans.
2. Lock the lid. Select Manual mode and set the timer for 3 minutes on High Pressure.
3. When timer beeps, use a quick pressure release. Open the lid.
4. Select Sauté mode. Stir in the half-and-half. Cook, stirring frequently, until the sauce has thickened, about 2 minutes.
5. Transfer them to a serving bowl. Top with almonds and fried onions, and serve.

Caramelized Onions

Prep time: 6 mins, Cook time: 35 mins, Servings: 2

1 tbsp. freshly squeezed lemon juice
3 tbsps. coconut oil

Salt and pepper, to taste
3 white onions, sliced
1 cup water

1. Press the Sauté button on the Instant Pot and heat the coconut oil.
2. Sauté the onions for 5 minutes and add the remaining ingredients.
3. Add the water and stir.
4. Lock the lid. Set the Instant Pot to Manual mode, then set the timer for 20 minutes at High Pressure.
5. Once cooking is complete, do a quick pressure release. Carefully open the lid.
6. Press the Sauté button and continue cooking for another 10 minutes.
7. Serve warm.

Broccoli Stuffed Potatoes

Prep time: 10 minutes | Cook time: 20 minutes | Serves 4

1 cup water
1 head broccoli, cut into florets
4 small russet potatoes
¾ cup half-and-half

1 tablespoon butter
2 cups Gruyere cheese, grated
1 teaspoon cornstarch
¼ cup chopped fresh chives

1. Pour the water in the Instant Pot and fit in a steamer basket.
2. Add the broccoli. Seal the lid. Select the Manual mode and set the cooking time for 1 minute at High Pressure.
3. Once cooking is complete, do a quick pressure release, then unlock the lid and transfer the broccoli to a bowl.
4. In the steamer basket, place the potatoes. Seal the lid again. Select the Manual mode and set the cooking time for 15 minutes on High Pressure.
5. Once cooking is complete, do a quick pressure release. Unlock the lid and let the potatoes cool.
6. Take out the steamer basket and discard the water. Press the Sauté button and warm half-and-half and butter until the butter melts.
7. In a bowl, mix the cheese with cornstarch and pour the mixture into the pot. Stir until the cheese melts. Transfer the mixture in a large bowl.
8. Toss the broccoli with the mixture to combine well. Cut a slit into each potato and stuff with the broccoli mixture. Scatter with chives to serve.

Celeriac and Cauliflower Mix

Prep time: 10 minutes | Cook time: 2 minutes | Serves 4

1 cup water
1 head cauliflower, cut into florets
1 carrot, sliced

½ cup celeriac, sliced
2 tablespoons butter
Salt and black pepper, to taste

1. Pour the water into the Instant Pot and fit in a steamer basket. Place the cauliflower, carrots, and celeriac in the basket.
2. Seal the lid. Select the Steam mode, then set the cooking time for 2 minutes at High Pressure.
3. Once cooking time is complete, perform a quick pressure release. Unlock the lid and transfer the veggies to a bowl.
4. Stir in the butter and sprinkle with salt and pepper before serving.

Cheesy Chanterelle Mushrooms

Prep time: 10 minutes | Cook time: 5 minutes | Serves 4

1 tablespoon olive oil
2 cloves garlic, minced
1 (1-inch) ginger root, grated
16 ounces (454 g) Chanterelle mushrooms, brushed clean and sliced
½ cup unsweetened tomato purée
½ cup water

2 tablespoons dry white wine
1 teaspoon dried basil
½ teaspoon dried thyme
½ teaspoon dried dill weed
⅓ teaspoon freshly ground black pepper
Kosher salt, to taste
1 cup shredded Cheddar cheese

1. Press the Sauté button on the Instant Pot and heat the olive oil. Add the garlic and grated ginger to the pot and sauté for 1 minute, or until fragrant. Stir in the remaining ingredients, except for the cheese.
2. Lock the lid. Select the Manual mode and set the cooking time for 5 minutes on Low Pressure. When the timer goes off, perform a quick pressure release. Carefully open the lid..
3. Serve topped with the shredded cheese.

Cauliflower Mash

Prep time: 12 mins, Cook time: 10 mins, Servings: 4

1 cup water
1 cauliflower head, cut into florets
¼ tsp. salt

¼ tsp. ground black pepper
¼ tsp. garlic powder
1 handful chopped chives

1. Set a trivet in the Instant Pot and pour in the water.
2. Place the cauliflower.
3. Lock the lid. Set the Instant Pot to Steam mode, then set the timer for 10 minutes at High Pressure.
4. Once cooking is complete, do a quick pressure release. Carefully open the lid.
5. Using a food processor, pulse the cauliflower.
6. Add the garlic powder, salt, and pepper.
7. Garnish with chives, then serve.

Spinach and Cauliflower Medley

Prep time: 10 minutes | Cook time: 3 minutes | Serves 4

1 pound (454 g) cauliflower, cut into florets
1 yellow onion, peeled and chopped
1 red bell pepper, deseeded and chopped
1 celery stalk, chopped
2 garlic cloves, crushed

2 tablespoons olive oil
1 tablespoon grated lemon zest
1 teaspoon Hungarian paprika
Sea salt and ground black pepper, to taste
2 cups spinach, torn into pieces

1. Add all the ingredients, except for the spinach, to the Instant Pot.
2. Close and secure the lid. Select the Manual setting and set the cooking time for 3 minutes at High Pressure. Once the timer goes off, use a quick pressure release. Carefully open the lid.
3. Stir in the spinach and lock the lid. Let it sit in the residual heat for 5 minutes, or until wilted.
4. Serve warm.

Jamaican Potato and Pumpkin Curry

Prep time: 15 minutes | Cook time: 6 minutes | Serves 6

2 tablespoons vegetable oil
3 cloves garlic, minced
1 tablespoon minced fresh ginger
1 cup chopped onion
1 tablespoon plus 1½ teaspoons Jamaican curry powder
1 stemmed, deseeded, and sliced Scotch bonnet pepper
3 sprigs fresh thyme

1 teaspoon kosher salt
½ teaspoon ground allspice
4 cups (1-inch cubes) peeled pumpkin
1½ cups (1-inch cubes) peeled potatoes
2 cups stemmed, deseeded, and diced red, yellow bell peppers
1 cup water

1. Select Sauté on the Instant Pot. Heat the vegetable oil.
2. Add the garlic and ginger. Sauté for a minute or until fragrant.
3. Add the onion and sauté for 2 minutes or until translucent.
4. Fold in the curry powder, Scotch bonnet pepper, thyme, salt, and allspice. Stir to coat well. Add the pumpkin, potatoes, bell peppers, and water.
5. Lock the lid. Select Manual mode and set the timer for 3 minutes at High Pressure.
6. When timer beeps, perform a natural pressure release for 10 minutes, then release any remaining pressure. Open the lid.
7. Serve immediately.

Spinach with Almonds and Olives

Prep time: 15 minutes | Cook time: 2 to 3 minutes | Serves 4

1 tablespoon olive oil
3 cloves garlic, smashed
Bunch scallions, chopped
2 pounds (907 g) spinach, washed
1 cup vegetable broth
1 tablespoon champagne vinegar
½ teaspoon dried dill weed
¼ teaspoon cayenne pepper
Seasoned salt and ground

black pepper, to taste
½ cup almonds, soaked overnight and drained
2 tablespoons green olives, pitted and halved
2 tablespoons water
1 tablespoon extra-virgin olive oil
2 teaspoons lemon juice
1 teaspoon garlic powder
1 teaspoon onion powder

1. Press the Sauté button on the Instant Pot and heat the olive oil. Add the garlic and scallions to the pot and sauté for 1 to 2 minutes, or until fragrant.
2. Stir in the spinach, vegetable broth, vinegar, dill, cayenne pepper, salt and black pepper.
3. Lock the lid. Select the Manual mode and set the cooking time for 1 minute on High Pressure. When the timer goes off, perform a quick pressure release. Carefully open the lid.
4. Stir in the remaining ingredients.
5. Transfer to serving plates and serve immediately.

Green Beans with Toasted Peanuts

Prep time: 10 minutes | Cook time: 1 minutes | Serves 4

1 cup water
1 pound (454 g) green beans, trimmed
1 lemon, juiced

2 tablespoons olive oil
Salt and black pepper, to taste
2 tablespoons toasted peanuts

1. Pour the water in the Instant Pot, then fit in a steamer basket and arrange the green beans on top.
2. Seal the lid. Select the Manual mode and set the time for 1 minute on High Pressure.
3. Once cooking is complete, do a quick pressure release. Unlock the lid.
4. Transfer the green beans onto a plate and mix in lemon juice, olive oil, salt, pepper, and toasted peanuts. Serve immediately.

Tomatillo and Jackfruit Tinga

Prep time: 15 minutes | Cook time: 21 minutes | Serves 4

1 tablespoon olive oil
1½ cups minced onion
6 cloves garlic, minced
2 tablespoons minced jalapeño
1 (20-ounce / 565-g) can jackfruit in brine, rinsed, shredded
1 (14.5-ounce / 411-g) can

diced tomatoes
1 cup diced tomatillos
1½ teaspoons dried thyme
1 teaspoon dried oregano
¼ cup water
½ teaspoon ground cumin
Salt, to taste

1. Select the Sauté setting of the Instant Pot and heat the oil until shimmering.
2. Add the onion and sauté for 5 minutes or until transparent. Then add the garlic and jalapeño and sauté for 1 minute more.
3. Add the jackfruit, tomatoes, tomatillos, thyme, oregano, water, and cumin to the pot and stir to combine.
4. Put the lid on. Select the Manual setting and set the timer for 15 minutes on High Pressure.
5. When timer beeps, allow the pressure to release naturally for 5 minutes, then release any remaining pressure. Open the lid.
6. Sprinkle with salt and serve.

Boiled Egg and Gold Potato Salad

Prep time: 20 minutes | Cook time: 12 minutes | Serves 4

1 cup water
1 pound (454 g) small Yukon Gold potatoes
2 boiled eggs, peeled and chopped
1 celery rib, diced
¼ cup pickle relish
½ yellow onion, sliced

1 garlic clove, minced
⅓ cup mayonnaise
½ teaspoon fresh rosemary, chopped
½ tablespoon yellow mustard
⅓ teaspoon cayenne pepper
Sea salt and ground black pepper, to taste

1. Pour the water in the Instant Pot and fit in a steamer basket. Place the potatoes in the steamer basket.
1. Secure the lid. Choose the Manual mode and set the cooking time for 12 minutes at High pressure.
2. Once cooking is complete, do a quick pressure release. Carefully remove the lid. Allow to cool for a few minutes until cool enough to handle.
3. Peel and slice the potatoes, then place them in a large bowl and toss with the remaining ingredients. Stir to combine.
4. Serve immediately.

Spaghetti Squash with Spinach

Prep time: 10 minutes | Cook time: 8 minutes | Serves 4

1 large spaghetti squash, cut into 8 pieces
1½ cups water
3 tablespoons olive oil
8 cloves garlic, thinly sliced
½ cup slivered almonds

1 teaspoon red pepper flakes
4 cups chopped fresh spinach
1 teaspoon kosher salt
1 cup shredded Parmesan cheese

1. Pour the water into the Instant Pot. Put a trivet in the pot. Set the squash on the trivet.
2. Lock the lid. Select Manual mode and set the timer for 7 minutes on High Pressure.
3. When timer beeps, perform a natural pressure release for 10 minutes, then release any remaining pressure.
4. Remove the squash, and cut it in half lengthwise. Use a fork to scrape the strands of one half into a large bowl. Measure out 4 cups. Reserve the other half for other use.
5. Set the squash shell aside to use as a serving vessel. Clean the pot.
6. Select Sauté mode. When the pot is hot, add the olive oil. Once the oil is hot, add the garlic, almonds, and pepper flakes. Cook, stirring constantly and being careful not to burn the garlic for 1 minute.
7. Add the spinach, salt, and spaghetti squash. Stir well to thoroughly combine ingredients until the spinach wilts.
8. Transfer the mixture to the reserved squash shell. Sprinkle with the Parmesan cheese before serving.

Steamed Tomato with Halloumi Cheese

Prep time: 5 minutes | Cook time: 3 minutes | Serves 4

8 tomatoes, sliced
1 cup water
½ cup crumbled Halloumi cheese
2 tablespoons extra-virgin olive

oil
2 tablespoons snipped fresh basil
2 garlic cloves, smashed

1. Pour the water into the Instant Pot and put the trivet in the pot. Place the tomatoes in the trivet.
2. Lock the lid. Select the Manual mode and set the cooking time for 3 minutes on High Pressure. When the timer goes off, perform a quick pressure release. Carefully open the lid.
3. Toss the tomatoes with the remaining ingredients and serve.

Chinese Pe-Tsai

Prep time: 5 minutes | Cook time: 8 minutes | Serves 4

2 tablespoons sesame oil
1 yellow onion, chopped
1 pound (454 g) pe-tsai cabbage, shredded
¼ cup rice wine vinegar

1 tablespoon coconut aminos
1 teaspoon finely minced garlic
½ teaspoon salt
¼ teaspoon Szechuan pepper

1.Set the Instant Pot on the Sauté mode and heat the sesame oil. Add the onion to the pot and sauté for 5 minutes, or until tender. Stir in the remaining ingredients.
2.Lock the lid. Select the Manual mode and set the cooking time for 3 minutes on High Pressure. When the timer goes off, perform a quick pressure release. Carefully open the lid.
3.Transfer the cabbage mixture to a bowl and serve immediately.

Coconut Cabbage

Prep time: 6 mins, Cook time: 20 mins, Servings: 4

2 cups freshly squeezed coconut milk
1 halved onion
1 thumb-size ginger, sliced

1 garlic bulb, crushed
1 cabbage head, shredded
Salt and pepper, to taste

1.In the Instant Pot, add all the ingredients. Stir to mix well.
2.Lock the lid. Set the Instant Pot to Manual mode, then set the timer for 20 minutes at High Pressure.
3.Once cooking is complete, do a quick pressure release. Carefully open the lid.
4.Serve warm.

Vegetable Burgers

Prep time: 20 minutes | Cook time: 55 minutes | Serves 2

2 tablespoons olive oil, divided
½ medium red bell pepper, deseeded and chopped
½ medium yellow onion, chopped
½ medium zucchini, chopped
½ cup chopped yellow squash
4 cloves garlic, minced
1 cup dried black beans

8 cups water
1 teaspoon salt
½ cup panko bread crumbs
½ jalapeño, deseeded and minced
Pinch freshly ground black pepper
2 burger buns

1.Press the Sauté button on the Instant Pot and heat 1 tablespoon of olive oil until shimmering.
2.Add the bell pepper and onion and sauté for 3 minutes or until the onion is translucent.
3.Add the zucchini, squash, and garlic and sauté for 3 minutes. Transfer the vegetables in the pot to a small bowl and set aside.
4.Add the beans, water, and salt to the pot. Lock the lid. Press the Bean button and set the cooking time for 30 minutes at High Pressure.
5.When the timer beeps, let pressure release naturally for 10 minutes. Release any remaining pressure, then unlock lid.
6.Press the Sauté button on the pot and simmer bean mixture for 10 minutes to thicken.
7.Transfer the mixture to a large bowl and mash with forks. When cool enough to handle, quickly mix in the vegetable mixture, panko, jalapeño, and pepper and blend thoroughly.
8.Form the mixture into 2 patties. Cook in a skillet over remaining 1 tablespoon of olive oil for 2 to 3 minutes on each side until browned.
9.Remove from heat and assemble each patty with a bun. Serve warm.

Couscous with Vegetables

Prep time: 30 mins, Cook time: 10 mins, Servings: 3

2 tsps. olive oil
1 onion, chopped
1 red bell pepper, chopped
1 cup grated carrot

2 cups couscous
2 cups water
Salt, to taste
½ tbsp. lemon juice

1.Grese the Instant Pot with olive oil. Add the onion.
2.Set to the Sauté mode and sauté the onion for 2 minutes.
3.Add the red bell pepper and carrot.
4.Cook for 3 minutes.
5.Add the couscous and water.
6.Season with salt.
7.Lock the lid. Set the Instant Pot to Manual mode, then set the timer for 2 minutes at High Pressure.
8.Once cooking is complete, do a natural pressure release. Carefully open the lid.
9.Fluff the couscous with a fork.
10.Drizzle with the lemon juice before serving.

Cauliflower and Tomato Curry

Prep time: 10 minutes | Cook time: 2 minutes | Serves 4 to 6

1 medium head cauliflower, cut into bite-size pieces
1 (14-ounce / 397-g) can sugar-free diced tomatoes, undrained
1 bell pepper, thinly sliced
1 (14-ounce / 397-g) can full-fat coconut milk
½ to 1 cup water

2 tablespoons red curry paste
1 teaspoon salt
1 teaspoon garlic powder
½ teaspoon onion powder
½ teaspoon ground ginger
¼ teaspoon chili powder
Freshly ground black pepper, to taste

1.Add all the ingredients, except for the black pepper, to the Instant Pot and stir to combine.
2.Lock the lid. Select the Manual setting and set the cooking time for 2 minutes at High Pressure. Once the timer goes off, use a quick pressure release. Carefully open the lid.
3.Sprinkle the black pepper and stir well. Serve immediately.

Italian Carrot and Potato Medley

Prep time: 15 minutes | Cook time: 11 minutes | Serves 4

2 tablespoons olive oil
1 cup potatoes, peeled and chopped
3 carrots, peeled and chopped
3 garlic cloves, minced

1 cup vegetable broth
1 teaspoon Italian seasoning
Salt and black pepper, to taste
1 tablespoon chopped parsley
1 tablespoon chopped oregano

1.Set the Instant Pot to the Sauté mode. Heat the olive oil until shimmering.
2.Add and sauté the potatoes and carrots for 5 minutes or until tender.
3.Add the garlic and cook for a minute or until fragrant. Pour in the vegetable broth, season with Italian seasoning, salt, and black pepper.
4.Seal the lid. Select the Manual mode and set the time for 5 minutes at High Pressure.
5.Once cooking is complete, do a quick pressure release, then unlock the lid.
6.Spoon the potatoes and carrots into a serving bowl and mix in the parsley and oregano. Serve warm.

Zucchinis with Eggplant

Prep time: 6 mins, Cook time: 8 mins, Servings: 6

3 zucchinis, sliced
1 eggplant, chopped
3 tbsps. olive oil
3 tomatoes, sliced

1 onion, diced
Salt and pepper, to taste
¼ cup water

1. Press the Sauté button on the Instant Pot and heat the olive oil.
2. Sauté the onions for 3 minutes or until translucent, then add the eggplants. Sauté for another 2 minutes.
3. Add the tomatoes and zucchini.
4. Sprinkle salt and pepper for seasoning.
5. Add the water.
6. Lock the lid. Set the Instant Pot to Manual mode, then set the timer for 6 minutes at High Pressure.
7. Once cooking is complete, do a quick pressure release. Carefully open the lid.
8. Serve warm.

Lettuce and Falafel Salad

Prep time: 10 minutes | Cook time: 6 to 8 minutes | Serves 4

1 cup shredded cauliflower
⅓ cup coconut flour
1 teaspoon grated lemon zest
1 egg, beaten
2 tablespoons coconut oil

2 cups chopped lettuce
1 cucumber, chopped
1 tablespoon olive oil
1 teaspoon lemon juice
½ teaspoon cayenne pepper

1. In a bowl, combine the cauliflower, coconut flour, grated lemon zest and egg. Form the mixture into small balls.
2. Set the Instant Pot to the Sauté mode and melt the coconut oil. Place the balls in the pot in a single layer. Cook for 3 to 4 minutes per side, or until they are golden brown.
3. In a separate bowl, stir together the remaining ingredients.
4. Place the cooked balls on top and serve.

Mushroom and Cabbage Dumplings

Prep time: 20 minutes | Cook time: 15 to 16 minutes | Makes 12 dumplings

1 tablespoon olive oil
1 cup minced shiitake mushrooms
1½ cups minced cabbage
½ cup shredded carrot

2 tablespoons soy sauce
1 tablespoon rice wine vinegar
1 teaspoon grated fresh ginger
12 round dumpling wrappers
1½ cups water

1. Select the Sauté setting of the Instant Pot. Heat the oil until shimmering.
2. Add the mushrooms and sauté for 3 or 4 minutes until the mushrooms release the juices.
3. Add the cabbage, carrot, soy sauce and rice wine vinegar and sauté for 5 minutes or until the mixture is dry. Mix in the ginger.
4. Line a steamer with parchment paper. Prepare a small bowl of water.
5. Put a wrapper on the clean work surface and rub the water around the edge of the wrapper. Add 1 tablespoon of the vegetable filling to the middle of the wrapper and fold in half. Press to make a dumpling. Then put the dumpling in the steamer. Repeat with remaining wrappers and fillings.
6. Arrange the trivet in the pot. Put the steamer on the trivet and pour the water in the pot.
7. Put the lid on. Select the Steam setting and set the timer for 7 minutes on High Pressure.
8. When timer beeps, use a natural pressure release for 5 minutes, then release any remaining pressure. Open the lid.
9. Serve hot.

Simple Spiced Russet Potatoes

Prep time: 15 minutes | Cook time: 12 minutes | Serves 3 to 4

2 large russet potatoes, cut in half and skin left on
1 tablespoon olive oil
1¼ teaspoon cumin seeds
2 teaspoons coriander seeds, roughly crushed
2 green chilies, sliced

1-inch piece ginger, chopped
½ teaspoon turmeric powder
⅛ teaspoon red chili powder
½ teaspoon salt
2 teaspoons lemon juice
Cilantro, to garnish

1. Add 1 cup of water to the Instant Pot. Put the trivet inside the pot, then put the potatoes, cut side up, on top of the trivet.
2. Secure the lid. Press the Manual button and set the timer for 10 minutes on High Pressure.
3. When timer beeps, let the pressure release naturally for 5 minutes, then release any remaining pressure. Open the lid.
4. Carefully remove the potatoes from the trivet. When they have cooled down a bit, peel the potatoes and dice them into small pieces.
5. Drain the water from the pot, wipe it dry and then put it back into the Instant Pot.
6. Press the Sauté button, add the oil and then the cumin seeds. Let the seeds sizzle for a few seconds, then add the coriander seeds and green chilies. Sauté for a few seconds and then add the ginger. Sauté for a minute until the ginger is golden.
7. Add the potatoes, turmeric powder, red chili powder and salt and mix, until all the potato pieces are well coated with the spices. Mix gently.
8. Add the lemon juice and toss to combine. Garnish with cilantro and serve.

Garlicky Baby Potatoes

Prep time: 30 mins, Cook Time: 11 mins, Servings: 4

1 tbsp. olive oil
3 garlic cloves
2 lbs. baby potatoes

1 sprig rosemary
1 cup vegetable stock
Salt and pepper, to taste

1. Hit the Sauté button in the Instant Pot.
2. Add the olive oil.
3. Add the garlic, baby potatoes and rosemary.
4. Brown the outside of the potatoes.
5. Pierce each potato with a fork.
6. Add the vegetable stock.
7. Lock the lid. Set the Instant Pot to Manual mode, then set the timer for 11 minutes at High Pressure.
8. Once cooking is complete, do a quick pressure release. Carefully open the lid.
9. Season with salt and pepper and serve.

Veggie Stew

Prep time: 6 mins, Cook time: 10 mins, Servings: 5

½ cup chopped tomatoes
1 stalk celery, minced
2 zucchinis, chopped

1 lb. mushrooms, sliced
1 onion, chopped
Salt and pepper, to taste

1. Place all ingredients in the Instant Pot.
2. Pour in enough water until half of the vegetables are submerged.
3. Lock the lid. Set the Instant Pot to Manual mode, then set the timer for 10 minutes at High Pressure.
4. Once cooking is complete, do a quick pressure release. Carefully open the lid.
5. Serve warm.

Ratatouille

Prep time: 20 mins, Cook Time: 10 mins, Servings: 4

2 cups water	2 eggplants, sliced
2 medium zucchini, sliced	1 tbsp. olive oil
3 tomatoes, sliced	Salt and pepper, to taste

1. Pour the water into the Instant Pot.
2. In a baking dish, arrange a layer of the zucchini.
3. Top with a layer of the tomatoes.
4. Place a layer of eggplant slices on top.
5. Continue layering until you use all the ingredients.
6. Drizzle with olive oil.
7. Place the baking dish on the trivet and lower it.
8. Lock the lid. Set the Instant Pot to Manual mode, then set the timer for 10 minutes at High Pressure.
9. Once cooking is complete, do a quick pressure release. Carefully open the lid.
10. Sprinkle with salt and pepper and serve warm!

Artichokes with Onion

Prep time: 6 mins, Cook time: 30 mins, Servings: 8

½ cup organic chicken broth	and cleaned
Salt and pepper, to taste	1 onion, chopped
4 large artichokes, trimmed	1 garlic clove, crushed

1. Place all ingredients in the Instant Pot.
2. Lock the lid. Set the Instant Pot to Manual mode, then set the timer for 30 minutes at High Pressure.
3. Once cooking is complete, do a quick pressure release. Carefully open the lid.
4. Serve the artichokes with lemon juice.

Spaghetti Squash Noodles

Prep time: 5 minutes | Cook time: 18 minutes | Serves 4

2 pounds (907 g) spaghetti squash	almonds
1 cup water	¼ cup flat-leaf parsley
3 garlic cloves	3 tablespoons grated
1 cup fresh basil leaves	Parmesan cheese
½ cup olive oil	½ teaspoon fine grind sea salt
⅓ cup unsalted toasted	½ teaspoon ground black pepper

1. Using a knife, pierce all sides of the squash to allow the steam to penetrate during cooking.
2. Pour the water into the Instant Pot and put the trivet in the pot. Place the squash on the trivet.
3. Lock the lid. Select the Manual mode and set the cooking time for 18 minutes at High Pressure. When the timer goes off, use a natural pressure release for 10 minutes, then release any remaining pressure. Carefully open the lid.
4. Remove the trivet and squash from the pot. Set aside to cool for 15 minutes, or until the squash is cool enough to handle.
5. Make the pesto sauce by placing the remaining ingredients in a food processor. Pulse until the ingredients are well combined and form a thick paste. Set aside.
6. Cut the cooled spaghetti squash in half lengthwise. Using a spoon, scoop out and discard the seeds.
7. Using a fork, scrape the flesh of the squash to create the noodles. Transfer the noodles to a large bowl.
8. Divide the squash noodles among 4 serving bowls. Top each serving with the pesto sauce. Serve hot.

Garlicky Baby Bok Choy

Prep time: 9 mins, Cook time: 4 mins, Servings: 6

1 tsp. peanut oil	4 garlic cloves, minced
1 lb. baby Bok choy, trimmed and washed	1 tsp. red pepper flakes
Salt and pepper, to taste	1 cup water

1. Press the Sauté button on the Instant Pot.
2. Heat the oil and sauté the garlic for 1 minute until fragrant.
3. Add the Bok choy and sprinkle salt and pepper for seasoning.
4. Pour in the water.
5. Lock the lid. Set the Instant Pot to Manual mode, then set the timer for 4 minutes at High Pressure.
6. Once cooking is complete, do a quick pressure release. Carefully open the lid.
7. Sprinkle with red pepper flakes, then serve.

Brussels Sprouts with Cranberries

Prep time: 10 minutes | Cook time: 3 minutes | Serves 6

1½ cups	½ cup orange marmalade
2 pounds (907 g) small Brussels sprouts, rinsed and trimmed	2 tablespoons butter, melted
	1 teaspoon kosher salt
1 cup dried cranberries	½ teaspoon cayenne pepper

1. Pour the water into the Instant Pot. Put a steamer basket in the pot. Put the Brussels sprouts and cranberries in the steamer basket.
2. Lock the lid. Select Manual mode and set the timer for 3 minutes on High Pressure.
3. When timer beeps, use a quick pressure release. Open the lid.
4. Transfer the Brussels sprouts and cranberries to a serving bowl. Add the orange marmalade, butter, salt, and cayenne. Toss to combine well. Serve hot.

Satarash with Eggs

Prep time: 10 minutes | Cook time: 5 minutes | Serves 4

2 tablespoons olive oil	1 teaspoon paprika
1 white onion, chopped	½ teaspoon dried oregano
2 cloves garlic	½ teaspoon turmeric
2 ripe tomatoes, puréed	Kosher salt and ground black pepper, to taste
1 green bell pepper, deseeded and sliced	1 cup water
1 red bell pepper, deseeded and sliced	4 large eggs, lightly whisked

1. Press the Sauté button on the Instant Pot and heat the olive oil. Add the onion and garlic to the pot and sauté for 2 minutes, or until fragrant. Stir in the remaining ingredients, except for the eggs.
2. Lock the lid. Select the Manual mode and set the cooking time for 3 minutes on High Pressure. When the timer goes off, perform a quick pressure release. Carefully open the lid.
3. Fold in the eggs and stir to combine. Lock the lid and let it sit in the residual heat for 5 minutes. Serve warm.

Daikon and Zucchini Fritters

Prep time: 10 minutes | Cook time: 8 minutes | Serves 4

2 large zucchinis, grated
1 daikon, diced
1 egg, beaten

1 teaspoon ground flax meal
1 teaspoon salt
1 tablespoon coconut oil

1. In the mixing bowl, combine all the ingredients, except for the coconut oil. Form the zucchini mixture into fritters.
2. Press the Sauté button on the Instant Pot and melt the coconut oil.
3. Place the zucchini fritters in the hot oil and cook for 4 minutes on each side, or until golden brown.
4. Transfer to a plate and serve.

Lemony Broccoli

Prep time: 5 minutes | Cook time: 4 minutes | Serves 4

2 cups broccoli florets
1 tablespoon ground paprika
1 tablespoon lemon juice
1 teaspoon grated lemon zest

1 teaspoon olive oil
½ teaspoon chili powder
1 cup water

1. Pour the water in the Instant Pot and insert the trivet.
2. In the Instant Pot pan, stir together the remaining ingredients.
3. Place the pan on the trivet.
4. Set the lid in place. Select the Manual mode and set the cooking time for 4 minutes on High Pressure. When the timer goes off, do a quick pressure release. Carefully open the lid.
5. Serve immediately.

Tofu and Mango Curry

Prep time: 15 minutes | Cook time: 9 minutes | Serves 2

8 ounces (227 g) extra-firm tofu, pressed to remove the moisture, cubed
¼ teaspoon smoked paprika
¼ teaspoon crushed red pepper
1¼ teaspoon salt, divided
⅛ teaspoon ground black pepper
2 tablespoons olive oil, divided

½ teaspoon mustard seeds
2 dried red chilies
½ medium white onion, diced
1½-inch piece ginger, grated
¾ cup gresh mango purée
½ cup coconut milk
1 teaspoon curry powder
½ cup water
Juice of ½ lemon
Cilantro, to garnish

1. Toss the tofu cubes with smoked paprika, crushed red pepper, ¼ teaspoon salt and ground black pepper.
2. Press the Sauté button on the Instant Pot. Add 1 tablespoon of oil to the pot, then add the spiced tofu cubes and cook for 4 minutes, or until lightly browned on all sides. Remove the tofu cubes to a bowl and set aside.
3. Add another tablespoon of oil to the pot, then add the mustard seeds. Let the mustard seeds pop and then add the dried red chilies. Sauté for a few seconds, then add the onion and ginger. Cook the onion and ginger for a minute until the onion turns a little soft.
4. Add the mango purée, coconut milk, and curry powder, then add 1 teaspoon of salt and let it all cook for a minute.
5. Add the water along with the sautéed tofu cubes and close the lid. Press the Manual button and set the timer for 3 minutes on High Pressure.
6. When timer beeps, do a quick pressure release. Open the lid.
7. Stir in the lemon juice, then transfer the curry to a serving bowl. Garnish with cilantro and serve.

Gobi Masala

Prep time: 5 minutes | Cook time: 4 to 5 minutes | Serves 4 to 6

1 tablespoon olive oil
1 teaspoon cumin seeds
1 white onion, diced
1 garlic clove, minced
1 head cauliflower, chopped

1 tablespoon ground coriander
1 teaspoon ground cumin
½ teaspoon garam masala
½ teaspoon salt
1 cup water

1. Set the Instant Pot to the Sauté mode and heat the olive oil. Add the cumin seeds to the pot and sauté for 30 seconds, stirring constantly. Add the onion and sauté for 2 to 3 minutes, stirring constantly. Add the garlic and sauté for 30 seconds, stirring frequently.
2. Stir in the remaining ingredients.
3. Lock the lid. Select the Manual mode and set the cooking time for 1 minute on High Pressure. When the timer goes off, perform a quick pressure release. Carefully open the lid.
4. Serve immediately.

Grape Leaves and Nut Rice Bowl

Prep time: 15 minutes | Cook time: 4 minutes | Serves 4

1 cup chopped onion
1 cup chopped tomato
1 cup basmati rice, rinsed and drained
1 cup pine nuts
8 ounces (227 g) brined grape leaves, drained and chopped
2 tablespoons olive oil

3 cloves garlic, minced
1 tablespoon dried parsley
1½ teaspoons ground allspice
1 teaspoon kosher salt
1 teaspoon black pepper
1 cup water
⅓ cup fresh lemon juice
¼ cup chopped fresh mint

1. In the Instant Pot, combine the onion, tomato, rice, pine nuts, grape leaves, olive oil, garlic, parsley, allspice, salt, pepper, and water. Stir to combine.
2. Lock the lid. Select Manual mode and set the timer for 4 minutes on High Pressure.
3. When timer beeps, perform a natural pressure release for 10 minutes, then release any remaining pressure. Open the lid.
4. Stir in the lemon juice and mint and serve.

Green Beans with Coconut

Prep time: 10 minutes | Cook time: 3 minutes | Serves 4

2 tablespoons vegetable oil
1 teaspoon mustard seeds
1 teaspoon cumin seeds
1 cup diced onion
1 teaspoon ground turmeric
1 teaspoon kosher salt
½ teaspoon cayenne pepper

1 (12-ounce / 340-g) package frozen green beans
¼ cup unsweetened shredded coconut
½ cup water
¼ cup chopped fresh cilantro

1. Select Sauté mode on the Instant Pot. When the pot is hot, add the oil. Once the oil is hot, add the mustard seeds and cumin seeds, and allow to sizzle for 15 to 20 seconds.
2. Stir in the onion. Add the turmeric, salt, and cayenne and stir to coat. Add the green beans, coconut, and water; stir to combine.
3. Lock the lid. Select Manual mode and set the timer for 2 minutes at High Pressure.
4. When timer beeps, use a quick pressure release. Open the lid.
5. Transfer to a serving dish and garnish with the cilantro. Serve warm.

Mushrooms with Garlic

Prep time: 12 mins, Cook Time: 10 mins, Servings: 1

½ cup water
4 oz. mushrooms, sliced
2 garlic cloves, minced
1 tbsp. olive oil
Salt and pepper, to taste

1. Pour water along with mushrooms in an Instant Pot.
2. Lock the lid. Set the Instant Pot to Manual mode, then set the timer for 5 minutes at High Pressure.
3. Once cooking is complete, do a quick pressure release. Carefully open the lid.
4. Drain the mushroom and then return back to the Instant Pot.
5. Now add olive oil to the pot and mix.
6. Press the Sauté function of the pot and let it cook for 3 minutes.
7. Sauté every 30 seconds.
8. Add the garlic and sauté for 2 minutes or until fragrant. Sprinkle with salt and pepper, then serve the dish.

Mini Tofu and Vegetable Frittatas

Prep time: 15 minutes | Cook time: 25 to 26 minutes | Serves 4

1 tablespoon olive oil
½ cup minced onion
½ cup minced mushrooms
⅓ cup minced bell pepper
⅓ cup grated carrot
⅓ cup minced kale, collards or spinach
1 (14-ounce / 397-g) package firm tofu, quickly pressed to

remove most of the liquid
2 tablespoons nutritional yeast
2 teaspoons Italian herb seasoning
1½ teaspoons salt
½ teaspoon ground turmeric
Salt and ground black pepper, to taste
1½ cups water

1. Select the Sauté setting of the Instant Pot. Heat the oil until shimmering, add the onion and sauté until translucent, 5 minutes.
2. Add the mushrooms and cook for 3 minutes or until they release juices, then add the bell pepper and carrot, and sauté for 2 or 3 minutes or until the mixture is dry. Stir in the kale and set aside to cool.
3. Add the tofu, nutritional yeast, Italian herb seasoning, salt, and turmeric to the blender. Blend until smooth.
4. Combine the cooled vegetables and tofu mixture in a bowl. Sprinkle with salt and pepper.
5. Grease 4 ramekins and divide the mixture among them. Cover with foil. Put the trivet in the Instant Pot and pour in the water. Arrange the ramekins on the trivet.
6. Put the lid on. Set to Manual mode and set cooking time for 15 minutes at High Pressure.
7. When timer beeps, allow a natural pressure release for 5 minutes, then release any remaining pressure. Open the lid.
8. Serve hot.

Sesame Zoodles with Scallions

Prep time: 10 minutes | Cook time: 3 minutes | Serves 6

2 large zucchinis, trimmed and spiralized
¼ cup chicken broth
1 tablespoon chopped scallions
1 tablespoon coconut aminos
1 teaspoon sesame oil
1 teaspoon sesame seeds
¼ teaspoon chili flakes

1. Set the Instant Pot on the Sauté mode. Add the zucchini spirals to the pot and pour in the chicken broth. Sauté for 3 minutes and transfer to the serving bowls.
2. Sprinkle with the scallions, coconut aminos, sesame oil, sesame seeds and chili flakes. Gently stir the zoodles.
3. Serve immediately.

Zucchini Sticks

Prep time: 5 minutes | Cook time: 8 minutes | Serves 2

2 zucchinis, trimmed and cut into sticks
2 teaspoons olive oil
½ teaspoon white pepper
½ teaspoon salt
1 cup water

1. Place the zucchini sticks in the Instant Pot pan and sprinkle with the olive oil, white pepper and salt.
2. Pour the water and put the trivet in the pot. Place the pan on the trivet.
3. Lock the lid. Select the Manual setting and set the cooking time for 8 minutes at High Pressure. Once the timer goes off, use a quick pressure release. Carefully open the lid.
4. Remove the zucchinis from the pot and serve.

Vinegary Broccoli with Cheese

Prep time: 5 minutes | Cook time: 5 minutes | Serves 4

1 pound (454 g) broccoli, cut into florets
1 cup water
2 garlic cloves, minced
1 cup crumbled Cottage cheese
2 tablespoons balsamic vinegar
1 teaspoon cumin seeds
1 teaspoon mustard seeds
Salt and pepper, to taste

1. Pour the water into the Instant Pot and put the steamer basket in the pot. Place the broccoli in the steamer basket.
2. Close and secure the lid. Select the Manual setting and set the cooking time for 5 minutes at High Pressure. Once the timer goes off, do a quick pressure release. Carefully open the lid.
3. Stir in the remaining ingredients.
4. Serve immediately.

Soya Granules and Green Pea Tacos

Prep time: 20 minutes | Cook time: 8 minutes | Serves 8

2 cups soya granules, soaked in water for at least 20 minutes, drained
½ cup frozen green peas, soaked in water for at least 5 minutes, drained
1 tablespoon olive oil
1 medium red onion, chopped
2 teaspoons ginger garlic paste
3 jalapeños, deseeded, sliced, plus more for garnish
1 tablespoon tomato paste
¾ teaspoon taco seasoning
½ teaspoon garam masala
½ teaspoon coriander powder
1 teaspoon salt
1 cup plus 2 tablespoons water
2 tablespoons cilantro, chopped, plus more for garnish
2 teaspoons lime juice
8 small corn tortillas
Sliced onions, for garnish
Salsa, for garnish
Diced avocados, for garnish

1. Press the Sauté button on the Instant Pot. Add the oil and then add the chopped onion. Cook the onion for 2 minutes until softened.
2. Add the ginger garlic paste and cook for another minute
3. Add the sliced jalapeños and cook for 30 seconds. Add the soya granules to the pot along with the green peas.
4. In a small bowl, mix the tomato paste with 2 tablespoons of water, then add it to the pot, along with the taco seasoning, garam masala, coriander powder and salt, and mix until well combined. Add the remaining water and close the lid.
5. Press the Manual button and set the timer for 4 minutes at High Pressure.
6. When timer beeps, let the pressure release naturally for 5 minutes, then release any remaining pressure.
7. Remove the lid, add the cilantro and lime juice and mix.
8. Warm the tortillas and fill with the prepared keema filling. Top with sliced onions, jalapeños, cilantro, salsa and diced avocados and serve.

Quinoa and Veggies

Prep time: 15 mins, Cook Time: 5 mins, Servings: 4

1½ cups water
1 cup rinsed and drained uncooked quinoa
¼ cup crumbled feta cheese

Greek seasoning and olive oil mixture
¼ cup sliced cucumber
¼ cup diced black olives

1. Pour the water into the Instant Pot.
2. Add the quinoa.
3. Lock the lid. Set the Instant Pot to Manual mode, then set the timer for 1 minute at High Pressure.
4. Once cooking is complete, do a natural pressure release. Carefully open the lid.
5. In a bowl, mix cucumber and black olives.
6. Top with the quinoa and feta cheese.
7. Drizzle with the dressing, then serve.

Honey Carrot Salad

Prep time: 10 minutes | Cook time: 3 minutes | Serves 2 to 4

1 cup water
1 pound (454 g) carrots, sliced to 2-inch chunks
1 scallion, finely sliced
½ tablespoon Dijon mustard
½ tablespoon lime juice

1 teaspoon honey
¼ teaspoon red pepper flakes
½ teaspoon Himalayan salt
¼ teaspoon ground white pepper
1 tablespoon olive oil

1. Pour the water in the Instant Pot and fit in a steamer basket. Place the carrots in the steamer basket.
2. Secure the lid. Choose the Steam mode and set the cooking time for 3 minutes at High pressure.
3. Once cooking is complete, perform a quick pressure release. Carefully open the lid.
4. Toss the carrots with the remaining ingredients in a serving bowl and serve chilled.

Potatoes and Cauliflower Masala

Prep time: 15 minutes | Cook time: 13 to 14 minutes | Serves 4

1 tablespoon vegetable oil
½ teaspoon cumin seeds
1 large red onion, finely chopped
1½ teaspoons ginger garlic paste
2 medium tomatoes, chopped
½ teaspoon dried mango powder
¼ teaspoon garam masala
¼ teaspoon red chili powder

1 teaspoon coriander powder
½ teaspoon turmeric powder
¾ teaspoon salt
6 tablespoons water, divided
2 medium potatoes, diced into 1-inch pieces
1 (1-pound / 454-g) medium head cauliflower, cut into medium to large florets
2 tablespoons cilantro, chopped, plus more for garnish

1. Press the Sauté button on the Instant Pot. Add the oil and the cumin seeds and let them sizzle for a few seconds.
2. Add the chopped onion and cook for 3 minutes until soft and translucent.
3. Add the ginger garlic paste and cook for another minute or until fragrant.
4. Add the tomatoes and cook for 2 minutes or until the tomatoes are soft.
5. Add the dried mango powder, garam masala, red chili powder, coriander powder, turmeric powder, and salt and mix to combine.
6. Cook the spices for 30 seconds, and then add 2 tablespoons of water and diced potatoes.
7. Toss to coat well. Cover the pot and let the potatoes cook for 3 to 4 minutes, stirring once halfway through.

8. Remove the lid, add 4 tablespoons of water and mix well to deglaze the pot.
9. Put the cauliflower florets on top. Sprinkle 2 tablespoons of cilantro on top of the cauliflower.
10. Close the pot. Press the Manual button and set the timer for 3 minutes on Low Pressure. When timer beeps, do a quick pressure release.
11. Open the pot and gently mix the cauliflower with the potatoes and the masala. Transfer them to a serving bowl, garnish with more cilantro and serve.

Lush Veg Medley

Prep time: 50 mins, Cook Time: 8 mins, Servings: 4

1 cup water
1 tbsp. raisins
1 zucchini, sliced
1 eggplant, cubed

3 tbsps. olive oil
10 halved cherry tomatoes
2 potatoes, cubed
2 tbsps. raisins

1. In the Instant Pot, add the water. Add the potatoes and zucchini.
2. Lock the lid. Set the Instant Pot to Manual mode, then set the timer for 8 minutes on High Pressure.
3. Once cooking is complete, do a quick pressure release. Carefully open the lid.
4. Drain water and add olive oil.
5. Mix in the tomatoes and eggplant. Let cook for 2 minutes.
6. Top with the raisins before serving.

Tofu with Sweet Potatoes and Kale

Prep time: 45 mins, Cook time: 6 mins, Servings: 4

1 tbsp. tamari sauce
⅔ cup vegetable broth
1 sweet potato, cubed

2 cups chopped kale
8 oz. cubed tofu
Salt and pepper, to taste

1. Add tofu in the Instant Pot.
2. Drizzle with half of the tamari and the broth.
3. Cook for about 3 minutes on Sauté function.
4. Add the rest of the ingredients.
5. Lock the lid. Set the Instant Pot to Manual mode, then set the timer for about 3 minutes at High Pressure.
6. Once cooking is complete, do a quick pressure release. Carefully open the lid.
7. Serve immediately!

Zucchini and Bell Pepper Stir Fry

Prep time: 6 mins, Cook time: 5 mins, Servings: 6

2 large zucchinis, sliced
1 tbsp. coconut oil
4 garlic cloves, minced
2 red sweet bell peppers,

julienned
1 onion, chopped
Salt and pepper, to taste
¼ cup water

1. Press the Sauté button on the Instant Pot.
2. Heat the coconut oil and sauté the onion and garlic for 2 minutes or until fragrant.
3. Add the zucchini and red bell peppers.
4. Sprinkle salt and pepper for seasoning.
5. Pour in the water.
6. Lock the lid. Set the Instant Pot to Manual mode, then set the timer for 5 minutes at High Pressure.
7. Once cooking is complete, do a quick pressure release. Carefully open the lid.
8. Serve warm.

Sautéed Brussels Sprouts And Pecans

Prep time: 4 mins, Cook time: 6 mins, Servings: 4

¼ cup chopped pecans
2 garlic cloves, minced
Salt and pepper, to taste

2 tbsps. water
2 cups baby Brussels sprouts
1 tbsp. coconut oil

1. Press the Sauté button on the Instant Pot and heat the oil.
2. Sauté the garlic for 1 minute or until fragrant.
3. Add the Brussels sprouts. Sprinkle salt and pepper for seasoning.
4. Add the water.
5. Lock the lid. Set the Instant Pot to Manual mode, then set the timer for 3 minutes at High Pressure.
6. Once cooking is complete, do a quick pressure release. Carefully open the lid.
7. Add the pecans and set to the Sauté mode and sauté for 3 minutes or until the pecans are roasted.
8. Serve immediately.

Vegetarian Mac and Cheese

Prep time: 30 mins, Cook time: 4 mins, Servings: 10

4 cups water
1 tsp. garlic powder
16 oz. elbow macaroni pasta
Salt and pepper, to taste
2 cups frozen mixed

vegetables
1 cup shredded Cheddar
1 cup milk
Fresh parsley, for garnish

1. To the Instant Pot, add the water, garlic powder and pasta. Sprinkle with salt and pepper.
2. Lock the lid. Set the Instant Pot to Manual mode, then set the timer for 4 minutes at High Pressure.
3. Once cooking is complete, do a quick pressure release. Carefully open the lid.
4. Add the vegetables, Cheddar and milk, then cover the pot and press Sauté.
5. Simmer until the vegetables have softened.
6. Garnish with fresh parsley and serve.

Stuffed Sweet Potatoes

Prep time: 42 mins, Cook Time: 17 mins, Servings: 2

1 cup cooked couscous
2 sweet potatoes
1 tbsp. olive oil
1 tsp. paprika

Salt and pepper, to taste
1 cup cooked chickpeas
2 spring onions, chopped

1. Use a fork to pierce sweet potatoes.
2. To the Instant Pot, add enough water to cover.
3. Add the steamer rack inside and set the potatoes on top.
4. Lock the lid. Set the Instant Pot to Manual mode, then set the timer for 8 minutes on High Pressure.
5. Once cooking is complete, do a natural pressure release for 5 minutes. Carefully open the lid.
6. Set the sweet potato aside on a plate. Drain the pot.
7. While the Instant Pot is on Sauté mode, heat the olive oil. Set in chickpeas and paprika with salt and pepper.
8. Half the potatoes and mash the inside.
9. Add the chickpeas and couscous.
10. Top with the chopped spring onion and serve.

Sesame Bok Choy

Prep time: 6 mins, Cook Time: 4 mins, Servings: 4

1 tsp. soy sauce
½ tsp. sesame oil
1½ cups water

1 medium Bok choy
2 tsps. sesame seeds

1. Pour the water into the Instant Pot.
2. Place the Bok choy inside the steamer basket.
3. Lower the basket
4. Lock the lid. Set the Instant Pot to Manual mode, then set the timer for 4 minutes at High Pressure.
5. Once cooking is complete, do a quick pressure release. Carefully open the lid.
6. In a serving bowl, set in the Bok choy. Toss with the remaining ingredients to coat.
7. Serve immediately!

Simple Cauliflower Gnocchi

Prep time: 5 minutes | Cook time: 2 minutes | Serves 4

2 cups cauliflower, boiled
½ cup almond flour
1 tablespoon sesame oil

1 teaspoon salt
1 cup water

1. In a bowl, mash the cauliflower until puréed. Mix it up with the almond flour, sesame oil and salt.
2. Make the log from the cauliflower dough and cut it into small pieces.
3. Pour the water in the Instant Pot and add the gnocchi.
4. Lock the lid. Select the Manual mode and set the cooking time for 2 minutes on High Pressure. Once the timer goes off, perform a natural pressure release for 5 minutes, then release any remaining pressure. Carefully open the lid.
5. Remove the cooked gnocchi from the water and serve.

Sumptuous Vegetable and Tofu Curry

Prep time: 5 minutes | Cook time: 6 minutes | Serves 4

2 cups diced peeled butternut squash
2 cups chopped bok choy
1 cup button or cremini mushrooms, trimmed and quartered
1 cup stemmed, deseeded,

and roughly chopped yellow bell pepper
1 block Japanese curry paste, diced
2 cups water
1 (14-ounce / 397-g) package firm tofu, diced

1. In the Instant Pot, combine the butternut squash, bok choy, mushrooms, bell pepper, curry paste, and water. Stir to mix well.
2. Lock the lid. Select Manual mode and set the timer for 4 minutes at High Pressure.
3. When timer beeps, perform a natural pressure release for 10 minutes, then release any remaining pressure.
4. Open the lid. Stir in the tofu. Set the pot to Sauté mode and sauté for 2 minutes or until the tofu is lightly browned.
5. Serve immediately.

Zoodles with Mediterranean Sauce

Prep time: 10 minutes | Cook time: 5 minutes | Serves 2

1 tablespoon olive oil
2 tomatoes, chopped
½ cup water
½ cup roughly chopped fresh parsley
3 tablespoons ground almonds
1 tablespoon fresh rosemary, chopped
1 tablespoon apple cider vinegar
1 teaspoon garlic, smashed
2 zucchinis, spiralized and cooked
½ avocado, pitted and sliced
Salt and ground black pepper, to taste

1. Add the olive oil, tomatoes, water, parsley, ground almonds, rosemary, apple cider vinegar and garlic to the Instant Pot.
2. Lock the lid. Select the Manual mode and set the cooking time for 5 minutes on High Pressure. When the timer beeps, perform a natural pressure release for 10 minutes, then release any remaining pressure. Carefully open the lid.
3. Divide the cooked zucchini spirals between two serving plates. Spoon the sauce over each serving. Top with the avocado slices and season with salt and black pepper.
4. Serve immediately.

Spaghetti Squash Noodles with Tomatoes

Prep time: 15 minutes | Cook time: 14 to 16 minutes | Serves 4

1 medium spaghetti squash
1 cup water
2 tablespoons olive oil
1 small yellow onion, diced
6 garlic cloves, minced
2 teaspoons crushed red pepper flakes
2 teaspoons dried oregano
1 cup sliced cherry tomatoes
1 teaspoon kosher salt
½ teaspoon freshly ground black pepper
1 (14.5-ounce / 411-g) can sugar-free crushed tomatoes
¼ cup capers
1 tablespoon caper brine
½ cup sliced olives

1. With a sharp knife, halve the spaghetti squash crosswise. Using a spoon, scoop out the seeds and sticky gunk in the middle of each half.
2. Pour the water into the Instant Pot and place the trivet in the pot with the handles facing up. Arrange the squash halves, cut side facing up, on the trivet.
3. Lock the lid. Select the Manual mode and set the cooking time for 7 minutes on High Pressure. When the timer goes off, use a quick pressure release. Carefully open the lid.
4. Remove the trivet and pour out the water that has collected in the squash cavities. Using the tines of a fork, separate the cooked strands into spaghetti-like pieces and set aside in a bowl.
5. Pour the water out of the pot. Select the Sauté mode and heat the oil.
6. Add the onion to the pot and sauté for 3 minutes. Add the garlic, pepper flakes and oregano to the pot and sauté for 1 minute.
7. Stir in the cherry tomatoes, salt and black pepper and cook for 2 minutes, or until the tomatoes are tender.
8. Pour in the crushed tomatoes, capers, caper brine and olives and bring the mixture to a boil. Continue to cook for 2 to 3 minutes to allow the flavors to meld.
9. Stir in the spaghetti squash noodles and cook for 1 to 2 minutes to warm everything through.
10. Transfer the dish to a serving platter and serve.

Steamed Paprika Broccoli

Prep time: 6 mins, Cook time: 6 mins, Servings: 2

¼ tsp. ground black pepper
1 tbsp. freshly squeezed lemon juice
¼ tsp. salt
1 head broccoli, cut into florets
1 tbsp. paprika
1 cup water

1. Place a trivet or the steamer rack in the Instant Pot and pour in the water.
2. Place the broccoli florets on the trivet and sprinkle salt, pepper, paprika, and lemon juice.
3. Lock the lid. Set the Instant Pot to Steam mode, then set the timer for 6 minutes at High Pressure.
4. Once cooking is complete, do a quick pressure release. Carefully open the lid.
5. Serve immediately.

Tofu and Greens with Fenugreek Sauce

Prep time: 25 minutes | Cook time: 15 to 18 minutes | Serves 3

1 yellow onion, quartered
15 cashews
3 cloves garlic
1-inch piece ginger
1 green chili
4 green cardamoms
1½ cups water, divided
1½ tablespoons olive oil
1 bay leaf
1 teaspoon coriander powder
¼ teaspoon garam masala
¼ teaspoon turmeric powder
¼ teaspoon red chili powder
1 teaspoon salt
1½ cups fenugreek leaves, stems removed, chopped
6 ounces (170 g) extra-firm tofu, cubed
1 teaspoon fenugreek leaves, crushed
¼ cup heavy cream
½ teaspoon sugar
1 cup broccoli florets
10 thin asparagus stalks, hard end removed and then cut into 1-inch pieces

1. Put the onion and cashews into the steamer basket. Pour 1 cup of water in the Instant Pot and then put the steamer basket inside it.
2. Close the lid and then press the Steam button. Set cooking time for 2 minutes on High Pressure.
3. When timer beeps, do a quick pressure release. Open the lid.
4. Transfer the steamed onion and cashews to a blender and add the garlic, ginger, green chili, green cardamoms and ½ cup of water and purée to a smooth paste.
5. Press the Sauté button on the Instant Pot. Add the oil and then add the bay leaf along with the prepared onion paste. Cook the onion paste for 4 to 5 minutes, until there's no smell of raw onion, and then stir in the coriander powder, garam masala, turmeric powder, red chili powder and salt. Cook for 1 minute, then add the chopped fenugreek leaves and cook for another 1 to 2 minutes.
6. Add 1 cup of water and the tofu, mix well and then close the lid. Press the Manual button and set the timer for 3 minutes on High Pressure.
7. When timer beeps, do a quick pressure release.
8. Open the lid and press the Sauté button. Add the fenugreek leaves, heavy cream, sugar, broccoli florets and asparagus.
9. Cover the pot and let it simmer for 4 to 5 minutes. Serve warm.

Lemony Peas with Bell Pepper

Prep time: 5 minutes | Cook time: 1 minutes | Serves 4

2 cups frozen peas
1 cup stemmed, deseeded, and diced red bell pepper
1 cup thinly sliced onion
1 tablespoon butter, melted
2 tablespoons water

1 teaspoon kosher salt
½ teaspoon black pepper
2 tablespoons chopped fresh mint
Zest of 1 lemon
1 tablespoon fresh lemon juice

1. In the Instant Pot, combine the peas, bell pepper, onion, butter, water, salt, and pepper. Stir to mix well.
2. Lock the lid. Select Manual mode and set the timer for 1 minute on High Pressure.
3. When timer beeps, use a quick pressure release. Open the lid.
4. Stir in the mint along with the lemon zest and juice and serve.

Ritzy Green Pea and Cauliflower Curry

Prep time: 20 minutes | Cook time: 8 minutes | Serves 4

3 large tomatoes
4 large cloves garlic
1-inch piece ginger
1 green chili
12 raw cashews
1½ tablespoons olive oil
1 bay leaf
3 green cardamoms
6 peppercorns
3 cloves
1 large red onion, chopped
1½ teaspoons coriander powder

1 teaspoon garam masala
½ teaspoon red chili powder
½ teaspoon turmeric powder
1 teaspoon salt
¼ cup plain yogurt, at room temperature
½ cup plus 2 tablespoons coconut milk
¼ cup water
1 large head cauliflower, cut into florets
½ cup frozen green peas
Cilantro, for garnish

1. Using a blender, purée the tomatoes, garlic, ginger, green chili and cashews to a smooth paste. Set aside.
2. Press the Sauté button on the Instant Pot. Add the oil and then add the bay leaf, green cardamoms, peppercorns and cloves. Sauté for a few seconds until the spices are fragrant and then add the onion. Cook the onion until soft, around 2 minutes.
3. Add the puréed tomato mixture. Cook for 2 minutes and then add the coriander powder, garam masala, red chili powder, turmeric powder and salt. Stir to combine the spices and cook them for 30 seconds.
4. Add the yogurt, whisking continuously until well combined.
5. Add the coconut milk and the water and mix to combine.
6. Add the cauliflower florets and peas and toss to combine them with the masala.
7. Close the lid and press the Manual button. Set the timer for 3 minutes on Low Pressure.
8. When timer beeps, do a quick pressure release.
9. Open the pot, give them a stir. Garnish with cilantro and serve.

Vegetarian Smothered Cajun Greens

Prep time: 6 mins, Cook time: 3 mins, Servings: 4

2 tsps. crushed garlic
Salt and pepper, to taste
1 onion, chopped

6 cups raw greens
1 tbsp. coconut oil
1 cup water

1. Press the Sauté button on the Instant Pot and heat the coconut oil.
2. Sauté the onion and garlic for 2 minutes or until fragrant.
3. Add the greens and Sprinkle salt and pepper for seasoning.
4. Add the water.
5. Lock the lid. Set the Instant Pot to Manual mode, then set the timer for 3 minutes at High Pressure.
6. Once cooking is complete, do a quick pressure release. Carefully open the lid.
7. Sprinkle with red chili flakes, then serve.

Minty Paneer Cubes with Cashews

Prep time: 20 minutes | Cook time: 10 to 11 minutes | Serves 4

1½ cups cilantro, roughly chopped
¾ cup mint leaves
1 small red onion
2 green chilies
15 cashews
1-inch piece ginger
2 cloves garlic
¼ teaspoon ground black pepper
1¼ cups water, divided
1 tablespoon olive oil or unsalted butter
1 bay leaf

¾ teaspoon cumin seeds
½ cup yogurt, whisked with ¼ teaspoon cornstarch
½ teaspoon cumin powder
½ teaspoon coriander powder
¼ teaspoon crushed red pepper, optional
½ teaspoon salt
2 teaspoons heavy cream
Garam masala, to sprinkle
½ teaspoon sugar
1 cup paneer, cut into cubes
Sliced onions, for serving

1. In a blender, grind together the cilantro, mint leaves, onion, green chilies, cashews, ginger, garlic, black pepper and ¼ cup of water to form a smooth paste. Set it aside.
2. Press the Sauté button on the Instant Pot. Add the oil, bay leaf and cumin seeds and let the cumin seeds sizzle for a few seconds.
3. Then add the prepared cilantro mint paste to the pot and cook for 2 to 3 minutes, or until the raw smell of the onion in the paste goes away.
4. Whisk the yogurt with the cornstarch and then fold into the pot. Cook for 2 minutes.
5. Add cumin powder, coriander powder, crushed red pepper and ¾ cup of water and cook for a few seconds.
6. Close the lid, and then press the Soup button and set the cooking time for 3 minutes on High Pressure.
7. When timer beeps, do a quick pressure release.
8. Open the pot, stir the curry and press the Sauté button. Add ¼ cup of water along with the salt, heavy cream, garam masala and sugar. Mix well and then add the paneer cubes.
9. Let the curry simmer for 2 minutes. Serve with sliced onions on the side.

Kashmiri Tofu

Prep time: 20 minutes | Cook time: 20 minutes | Serves 4

8 small dried red chilies
5 cloves
3 tablespoons coriander seeds
5 green cardamoms
2 tablespoons unsalted butter
½ tablespoon olive oil
½ tablespoon grated garlic
½ tablespoon grated ginger
2 small red onions, cubed
4 large tomatoes
½ teaspoon kashmiri red chili powder
¾ cup water, divided

1 small green bell pepper, diced, divided
1 small red bell pepper, diced, divided
1 pound (454 g) extra-firm tofu, cubed
1½ teaspoons fenugreek leaves, crushed
3 tablespoons heavy cream
1 teaspoon sugar
2 tablespoons cilantro, chopped

1. In a pan over medium heat, roast the red chilies, cloves, coriander seeds, and green cardamoms for 6 minutes or until fragrant.
2. Turn off the heat. Transfer them to a spice grinder and grind to a fine powder. Set aside.
3. Press the Sauté button on the Instant Pot. Add the butter and oil to the pot and then add the garlic and ginger and sauté for a few seconds.
4. Add the onion and sauté for 2 minutes until softened. Add the tomatoes and sauté for 3 minutes.
5. Add the kashmiri red chili powder, salt, and the prepared spice mix. Mix until well combined and then add ½ cup of water and half of the bell peppers.
6. Close the pot, and then press the Manual button. Set cooking time for 4 minutes on High Pressure.
7. When timer beeps, do a quick pressure release.
8. Open the pot and press the Sauté button. Add the remaining water and then stir in the cubed tofu and the remaining half of the bell peppers.
9. Fold in the fenugreek leaves, heavy cream, sugar, and cilantro and simmer for 4 minutes.
10. Serve hot.

Zucchini and Tomato Melange

Prep time: 13 mins, Cook time: 10 mins, Servings: 4

5 garlic cloves, minced
3 medium zucchinis, chopped
1 lb. puréed tomatoes
1 onion, chopped

1 tbsp. coconut oil
Salt and pepper, to taste
1 cup water

1. Place the tomatoes in a food processor and blend until smooth.
2. Press the Sauté button on the Instant Pot and heat the oil.
3. Sauté the garlic and onions for 2 minutes or until fragrant.
4. Add the zucchini and tomato purée.
5. Sprinkle salt and pepper for seasoning.
6. Add the water to add more moisture.
7. Lock the lid. Set the Instant Pot to Manual mode, then set the timer for 10 minutes at High Pressure.
8. Once cooking is complete, do a quick pressure release. Carefully open the lid.
9. Serve warm.

Lemony Asparagus with Gremolata

Prep time: 15 minutes | Cook time: 2 minutes | Serves 2 to 4

Gremolata:
1 cup finely chopped fresh Italian flat-leaf parsley leaves
3 garlic cloves, peeled and

grated
Zest of 2 small lemons

Asparagus:
1½ pounds (680 g) asparagus, trimmed

1 cup water

Lemony Vinaigrette:
1½ tablespoons fresh lemon juice
1 teaspoon Swerve
1 teaspoon Dijon mustard

2 tablespoons extra-virgin olive oil
Kosher salt and freshly ground black pepper, to taste

Garnish:
3 tablespoons slivered almonds

1. In a small bowl, stir together all the ingredients for the gremolata.
2. Pour the water into the Instant Pot. Arrange the asparagus in a steamer basket. Lower the steamer basket into the pot.
3. Lock the lid. Select the Steam mode and set the cooking time for 2 minutes on Low Pressure.
4. Meanwhile, prepare the lemony vinaigrette: In a bowl, combine the lemon juice, swerve and mustard and whisk to combine. Slowly drizzle in the olive oil and continue to whisk. Season generously with salt and pepper.
5. When the timer goes off, perform a quick pressure release. Carefully open the lid. Remove the steamer basket from the Instant Pot.
6. Transfer the asparagus to a serving platter. Drizzle with the vinaigrette and sprinkle with the gremolata. Serve the asparagus topped with the slivered almonds.

Steamed Asparagus

Prep time: 5mins, Cook time: 5 mins, Servings: 1

7 asparagus spears, washed and trimmed
¼ tsp. pepper
1 tbsp. extra virgin olive oil

Juice from freshly squeezed ¼ lemon
¼ tsp. salt
1 cup water

1. Place a trivet or the steamer rack in the Instant Pot and pour in the water.
2. In a mixing bowl, combine the asparagus spears, salt, pepper, and lemon juice.
3. Place on top of the trivet.
4. Lock the lid. Set the Instant Pot to Steam mode, then set the timer for 5 minutes at High Pressure.
5. Once cooking is complete, do a quick pressure release. Carefully open the lid.
6. Drizzle the asparagus with olive oil.

Mixed Veggies

Prep Time: 10 Mins |Total Time: 22 Mins |Serves: 3

1 tablespoon olive oil	1 garlic clove, minced
8 oz. mushrooms, sliced	1 tablespoon tomato paste
1 zucchini, sliced	1 teaspoon oregano
1 bell pepper, diced	1 teaspoon basil
1 Japanese eggplant, peeled and sliced	3 tablespoons water
	¼ teaspoon red pepper flakes
1 medium potato, peeled and diced	½ cup Parmigiano-Reggiano cheese, grated
1 small onion, thinly sliced	Salt and pepper, to taste

1.Put the olive oil, onions, garlic and potatoes in the Instant Pot and select "Sauté".
2.Sauté for 3 minutes and add rest of the ingredients except cheese.
3.Set the Instant Pot to "Manual" at high pressure for 10 minutes.
4.Release the pressure naturally and add Parmigiano-Reggiano cheese.

Delicious Succotash

Prep Time: 7 Mins |Total Time: 20 Mins |Serves: 6

1 cup bell peppers	2 cups lima beans
2 cups complete corn kernels	2 cups tomatoes
2 cups water	2 teaspoons salt
3 tablespoons butter	

1.Put the butter and bell peppers in the Instant Pot and select "Sauté".
2.Sauté for 3 minutes and add rest of the ingredients.
3.Set the Instant Pot to "Manual" at high pressure for 10 minutes.
4.Release the pressure naturally and serve hot.

Vegetable Medley

Prep Time: 5 Mins |Total Time: 14 Mins |Serves: 3

1 small sweet potato, peeled and diced	1 tablespoon olive oil
2 carrots, peeled and diced	1 sprig rosemary
3 pink potatoes, quartered	½ cup water
1½ cups butternut squash	Salt and pepper, to taste

1.Put the olive oil and rosemary sprig in the Instant Pot and select "Sauté".
2.Sauté for 2 minutes and add rest of the ingredients.
3.Set the Instant Pot to "Manual" at high pressure for 7 minutes.
4.Release the pressure naturally and serve hot.

Simple Broccoli

Prep Time: 5 Mins |Total Time: 10 Mins |Serves: 3

1 pound broccoli florets	Salt and freshly ground black pepper, to taste
1 cup water	
2 tablespoons butter, melted	

1.Place the steamer trivet in the bottom of Instant Pot and add water.
2.Put the broccoli florets on the trivet.
3.Set the Instant Pot to "Manual" at high pressure for 5 minutes.
4.Release the pressure quickly and remove the trivet.
5.Drizzle with butter and season with salt and black pepper.

Couscous Stuffed Peppers

Prep Time: 10 Mins |Total Time: 46 Mins |Serves: 4

1 cup couscous	2 teaspoons dried oregano
4 tablespoons pine nuts, roasted	1 teaspoon salt
	½ teaspoon black pepper
4 large red bell peppers	¼ cup feta cheese, crumbled
2 cups water	

1.Put the water and couscous in the Instant Pot.
2.Set the Instant Pot to "Manual" at high pressure for 3 minutes.
3.Release the pressure naturally and add rest of the ingredients.
4.Sauté for 3 minutes and fill this stuffing evenly in the bell peppers.
5.Bake in a pre-heated oven at 375oF for 30 minutes.

Spicy Cauliflower

Prep Time: 10 Mins |Total Time: 15 Mins |Serves: 3

1 pound cauliflower	1 teaspoon red pepper flakes, crushed
½ cup vegetable broth	
1 tablespoon fresh lemon juice	Salt, to taste
1 tablespoon olive oil	

1.Season the cauliflower with salt and red pepper flakes.
2.Put the olive oil and cauliflowers in the Instant Pot and select "Sauté".
3.Sauté for 4 minutes and add vegetable broth.
4.Set the Instant Pot to "Manual" at high pressure for 6 minutes.
5.Release the pressure naturally and stir in the lemon juice.

Nutty Brussels Sprouts

Prep Time: 5 Mins |Total Time: 9 Mins |Serves: 3

1 pound brussels sprouts, trimmed and halved	½ cup almonds, chopped
	1 teaspoon salt
½ tablespoon butter, melted	

1.Place the steamer trivet in the bottom of Instant Pot and add water.
2.Put the brussels sprouts on the trivet.
3.Set the Instant Pot to "Manual" at high pressure for 4 minutes.
4.Release the pressure quickly and remove the trivet.
5.Drizzle with butter and top with almonds.

Refreshing Green Beans

Prep Time: 5 Mins |Total Time: 11 Mins |Serves: 6

2 pounds fresh green beans	3 cups water
2 garlic cloves, minced	Salt and freshly ground black pepper, to taste
4 tablespoons butter	

1.Put the fresh green beans and all other ingredients in the Instant Pot.
2.Set the Instant Pot to "Manual" at high pressure for 6 minutes.
3.Release the pressure quickly and serve hot.

Chapter 4 Fish and Seafood

Almond-Crusted Tilapia
Prep time: 5 minutes | Cook time: 5 minutes | Serves 4

1 cup water
2 tablespoons Dijon mustard
1 teaspoon olive oil
¼ teaspoon lemon pepper
4 tilapia fillets
⅔ cup sliced almonds

1. Pour the water into the Instant Pot and add a trivet.
2. Whisk together the Dijon mustard, olive oil, and lemon pepper in a small bowl. Brush both sides of the tilapia fillets with the mixture.
3. Spread the almonds on a plate. Roll the fillets in the almonds until well coated. Place the fillets on top of the trivet.
4. Secure the lid. Select the Manual mode and set the cooking time for 5 minutes at High Pressure.
5. Once cooking is complete, do a quick pressure release. Carefully open the lid.
6. Divide the fillets among the plates and serve.

Chili Salmon
Prep time: 3 mins, Cook time: 7 mins, Servings: 4

¼ cup soy sauce
4 salmon fillets
5 tbsps. organic sugar-free chili sauce
Salt and pepper, to taste
¼ cup water
3 tbsps. chopped green onions

1. In the Instant Pot, add all the ingredients except for the green onions.
2. Lock the lid. Select the Manual mode and cook for 7 minutes at Low Pressure.
3. Once cooking is complete, do a quick pressure release. Carefully open the lid.
4. Garnish with green onions and serve.

Monkfish Stew
Prep time: 5 minutes | Cook time: 6 minutes | Serves 6

Juice of 1 lemon
1 tablespoon fresh basil
1 tablespoon fresh parsley
1 tablespoon olive oil
1 teaspoon garlic, minced
1½ pounds (680 g) monkfish
1 tablespoon butter
1 bell pepper, chopped
1 onion, sliced
½ teaspoon cayenne pepper
½ teaspoon mixed
peppercorns
¼ teaspoon turmeric powder
¼ teaspoon ground cumin
Sea salt and ground black pepper, to taste
2 cups fish stock
½ cup water
¼ cup dry white wine
2 bay leaves
1 ripe tomato, crushed

1. Stir together the lemon juice, basil, parsley, olive oil, and garlic in a ceramic dish. Add the monkfish and marinate for 30 minutes.
2. Set your Instant Pot to Sauté. Add and melt the butter. Once hot, cook the bell pepper and onion until fragrant.
3. Stir in the remaining ingredients.
4. Lock the lid. Select the Manual mode and set the cooking time for 6 minutes at High Pressure.
5. When the timer beeps, perform a quick pressure release. Carefully remove the lid.
6. Discard the bay leaves and divide your stew into serving bowls.
7. Serve hot.

Salmon and Avocado Burgers
Prep time: 5 minutes | Cook time: 5 minutes | Serves 4

2 tablespoons coconut oil
1 pound (454 g) salmon fillets
⅓ cup finely ground pork rinds
2 tablespoons finely diced onion
2 tablespoons mayonnaise
½ teaspoon salt
¼ teaspoon chili powder
¼ teaspoon garlic powder
1 egg
1 avocado, pitted
Juice of ½ lime

1. Set your Instant Pot to Sauté. Add and heat the coconut oil.
2. Remove skin from the salmon filets. Finely mince the salmon and add to a large bowl.
3. Stir in the remaining ingredients except the avocado and lime and form 4 patties.
4. Place the burgers into the pot and sear for about 3 to 4 minutes per side, or until the center feels firm and reads at least 145ºF (63ºC) on a meat thermometer.
5. Scoop flesh out of the avocado. In a small bowl, mash the avocado with a fork and squeeze the lime juice over the top.
6. Divide the mash into four sections and place on top of salmon burgers. Serve warm.

Coconut Cod Curry
Prep time: 4 mins, Cook time: 8 mins, Servings: 4

2 tsps. curry powder
2 tsps. grated ginger
4 cod fillets
1½ cups coconut milk
1 cilantro sprig, chopped
Salt and pepper, to taste

1. In the Instant Pot, set in all ingredients excluding the cilantro. Give a good stir to combine.
2. Lock the lid. Select the Steam mode and cook for 8 minutes at Low Pressure.
3. Once cooking is complete, do a quick pressure release. Carefully open the lid.
4. Garnish with chopped cilantro before serving.

Cod Fillets with Cherry Tomatoes
Prep time: 2 minutes | Cook time: 15 minutes | Serves 4

2 tablespoons butter
¼ cup diced onion
1 clove garlic, minced
1 cup cherry tomatoes, halved
¼ cup chicken broth
¼ teaspoon dried thyme
¼ teaspoon salt
⅛ teaspoon pepper
4 (4-ounce / 113-g) cod fillets
1 cup water
¼ cup fresh chopped Italian parsley

1. Set your Instant Pot to Sauté. Add and melt the butter. Once hot, add the onions and cook until softened. Add the garlic and cook for another 30 seconds.
2. Add the tomatoes, chicken broth, thyme, salt, and pepper. Continue to cook for 5 to 7 minutes, or until the tomatoes start to soften.
3. Pour the sauce into a glass bowl. Add the fish fillets. Cover with foil.
4. Pour the water into the Instant Pot and insert a trivet. Place the bowl on top.
5. Lock the lid. Select the Manual mode and set the cooking time for 3 minutes at Low Pressure.
6. Once cooking is complete, do a quick pressure release. Carefully open the lid.
7. Sprinkle with the fresh parsley and serve.

Cod Fillets with Dill

Prep time: 5 minutes | Cook time: 5 minutes | Serves 2

1 cup water	to taste
2 cod fillets	2 sprigs fresh dill
¼ teaspoon garlic powder	4 slices lemon
Salt and ground black pepper,	2 tablespoons butter

1. Add the water to the Instant Pot and put the trivet in the bottom of the pot.
2. Arrange the cod fillets on the trivet. Sprinkle with the garlic powder, salt, and pepper.
3. Layer 1 sprig of dill, 2 lemon slices, and 1 tablespoon of butter on each fillet.
4. Secure the lid. Select the Manual mode and set the cooking time for 5 minutes on High Pressure.
5. Once the timer beeps, use quick pressure release. Carefully remove the lid.
6. Serve.

Fish and Veggie Bake

Prep time: 10 minutes | Cook time: 5 minutes | Serves 4

1½ cups water	florets
Cooking spray	1 pound (454 g) tilapia fillets,
2 ripe tomatoes, sliced	sliced
2 cloves garlic, minced	Sea salt, to taste
1 teaspoon dried oregano	1 tablespoon olive oil
1 teaspoon dried basil	1 cup crumbled feta cheese
½ teaspoon dried rosemary	⅓ cup Kalamata olives, pitted
1 red onion, sliced	and halved
1 head cauliflower, cut into	

1. Pour the water into your Instant Pot and insert a trivet.
2. Spritz a casserole dish with cooking spray. Add the tomato slices to the dish. Scatter the top with the garlic, oregano, basil, and rosemary.
3. Mix in the onion and cauliflower. Arrange the fish fillets on top. Sprinkle with the salt and drizzle with the olive oil.
4. Place the feta cheese and Kalamata olives on top. Lower the dish onto the trivet.
5. Lock the lid. Select the Manual mode and set the cooking time for 5 minutes at High Pressure.
6. When the timer beeps, perform a quick pressure release. Carefully remove the lid.
7. Allow to cool for 5 minutes before serving.

Cod with Orange Sauce

Prep time: 10 minutes | Cook time: 7 minutes | Serves 4

4 cod fillets, boneless	Salt and ground black pepper,
1 cup white wine	to taste
Juice from 1 orange	4 spring onions, chopped
A small grated ginger piece	

1. Combine the wine, orange juice, and ginger in your Instant Pot and stir well.
2. Insert a steamer basket. Arrange the cod fillets on the basket. Sprinkle with the salt and pepper.
3. Secure the lid. Press the Manual button on your Instant Pot and set the cooking time for 7 minutes on High Pressure.
4. Once the timer beeps, do a quick pressure release. Carefully remove the lid.
5. Drizzle the sauce all over the fish and sprinkle with the green onions.
6. Transfer to a serving plate and serve immediately.

Lemon-Chili Sockeye Salmon

Prep time: 5 minutes | Cook time: 5 minutes | Serves 4

4 wild sockeye salmon fillets	Salt and ground black pepper,
¼ cup lemon juice	to taste
2 tablespoons assorted chili	1 cup water
pepper seasoning	

1. Drizzle the salmon fillets with lemon juice. Season with the chili pepper seasoning, salt, and pepper.
2. Pour the water into the Instant Pot and add a steamer basket. Put the salmon fillets in the steamer basket.
3. Secure the lid. Select the Manual mode and set the cooking time for 5 minutes at High Pressure.
4. Once cooking is complete, do a quick pressure release. Carefully open the lid.
5. Remove from the Instant Pot and serve.

Fish and Tomato Soup

Prep time: 10 minutes | Cook time: 8 minutes | Serves 4

2 teaspoons olive oil	fillets
1 yellow onion, chopped	1 cup shrimp
1 bell pepper, sliced	1 tablespoon sweet Hungarian
1 celery, diced	paprika
2 garlic cloves, minced	1 teaspoon hot Hungarian
3 cups fish stock	paprika
2 ripe tomatoes, crushed	½ teaspoon caraway seeds
¾ pound (340 g) haddock	

1. Set the Instant Pot to Sauté. Add and heat the oil. Once hot, add the onions and sauté until soft and fragrant.
2. Add the pepper, celery, and garlic and continue to sauté until soft.
3. Stir in the remaining ingredients.
4. Lock the lid. Select the Manual mode and set the cooking time for 5 minutes at High Pressure.
5. When the timer beeps, perform a quick pressure release. Carefully remove the lid.
6. Divide into serving bowls and serve hot.

Garam Masala Cod

Prep time: 10 minutes | Cook time: 10 minutes | Serves 4

2 tablespoons sesame oil	1 tablespoon chopped fresh dill
½ teaspoon cumin seeds	leaves
½ cup chopped leeks	1 tablespoon chopped fresh
1 teaspoon ginger-garlic paste	curry leaves
1 pound (454 g) cod fillets,	1 tablespoon chopped fresh
boneless and sliced	parsley leaves
2 ripe tomatoes, chopped	Coarse sea salt, to taste
1½ tablespoons fresh lemon	½ teaspoon smoked cayenne
juice	pepper
½ teaspoon garam masala	¼ teaspoon ground black
½ teaspoon turmeric powder	pepper, or more to taste

1. Set the Instant Pot to Sauté. Add and heat the sesame oil until hot. Sauté the cumin seeds for 30 seconds.
2. Add the leeks and cook for another 2 minutes until translucent. Add the ginger-garlic paste and cook for an additional 40 seconds.
3. Stir in the remaining ingredients.
4. Lock the lid. Select the Manual mode and set the cooking time for 6 minutes at Low Pressure.
5. When the timer beeps, perform a quick pressure release. Carefully remove the lid.
6. Serve immediately.

Easy Cod Meal

Prep time: 6 mins, Cook Time: 5 mins, Servings: 2

1 cup water
2 tbsps. ghee

1 fresh large fillet cod
Salt and pepper, to taste

1. Cut fillet into 3 pieces. Coat with the ghee and season with salt and pepper.
2. Pour the water into the pot and place steamer basket/trivet inside.
3. Arrange the fish pieces over the basket/trivet.
4. Lock the lid. Select the Manual mode and cook for 5 minutes at Low Pressure.
5. Once cooking is complete, do a quick pressure release. Carefully open the lid.
6. Serve warm.

Tuna with Eggs

Prep time: 5 minutes | Cook time: 15 minutes | Serves 4

2 cans tuna, drained
2 eggs, beaten
1 can cream of celery soup
2 carrots, peeled and chopped
1 cup frozen peas
½ cup water

¾ cup milk
¼ cup diced onions
2 tablespoons butter
Salt and ground black pepper, to taste

1. Combine all the ingredients in the Instant Pot and stir to mix well.
2. Secure the lid. Select the Manual mode and set the cooking time for 15 minutes at High Pressure.
3. Once cooking is complete, do a quick pressure release. Carefully open the lid.
4. Divide the mix into bowls and serve.

Crispy Salmon Fillets

Prep time: 5 minutes | Cook time: 5 minutes | Serves 2

1 tablespoon avocado oil
2 (3-ounce / 85-g) salmon fillets
1 teaspoon paprika
½ teaspoon salt

¼ teaspoon dried thyme
¼ teaspoon onion powder
¼ teaspoon pepper
⅛ teaspoon cayenne pepper

1. Drizzle the avocado oil over salmon fillets. Combine the remaining ingredients in a small bowl and rub all over fillets.
2. Press the Sauté button on the Instant Pot. Add the salmon fillets and sear for 2 to 5 minutes until the salmon easily flakes with a fork.
3. Serve warm.

Broccoli and Halibut Casserole

Prep time: 6 mins, Cook Time: 6 mins, Servings: 6

1 tbsp. Dijon mustard
1¼ cup full-fat coconut cream
2 tbsps. olive oil

1½ lbs. halibut fillets, sliced
1 cup broccoli florets
Salt and pepper, to taste

1. In the Instant Pot, add all the ingredients. Give a good stir.
2. Lock the lid. Select the Manual mode and set the cooking time for 8 minutes at Low Pressure.
3. Once cooking is complete, do a quick pressure release. Carefully open the lid.
4. Let the fish and broccoli cool for 5 minutes before serving.

Salmon with Dijon Mustard

Prep time: 5 minutes | Cook time: 5 minutes | Serves 2

1 cup water
2 fish fillets or steaks, such as salmon, cod, or halibut (1-inch thick)

Salt and ground black pepper, to taste
2 teaspoons Dijon mustard

1. Add the water to the Instant Pot and insert a trivet.
2. Season the fish with salt and pepper to taste. Put the fillets, skin-side down, on the trivet and top with the Dijon mustard.
3. Secure the lid. Select the Manual mode and set the cooking time for 5 minutes at High Pressure.
4. Once cooking is complete, do a quick pressure release. Carefully open the lid.
5. Divide the fish between two plates and serve.

Salmon Packets

Prep time: 8 minutes | Cook time: 6 minutes | Serves 4

1½ cups cold water
4 (5-ounce / 142-g) salmon fillets
½ teaspoon fine sea salt
¼ teaspoon ground black

pepper
1 lime, thinly sliced
4 teaspoons extra-virgin olive oil, divided
Fresh thyme leaves

1. Pour the cold water into the Instant Pot and insert a steamer basket.
2. Sprinkle the fish on all sides with the salt and pepper.
3. Take four sheets of parchment paper and place 3 lime slices on each sheet. Top the lime slices with a piece of fish.
4. Drizzle with 1 teaspoon of olive oil and place a few thyme leaves on top. Cover each fillet with the parchment by folding in the edges and folding down the top like an envelope to close tightly.
5. Stack the packets in the steamer basket, seam-side down.
6. Secure the lid. Select the Manual mode and set the cooking time for 6 minutes at Low Pressure.
7. When the timer beeps, perform a natural pressure release for 10 minutes, then release any remaining pressure. Carefully remove the lid.
8. Remove the fish packets from the pot.
9. Serve the fish garnished with the fresh thyme.

Veggie and Haddock Foil Packets

Prep time: 5 minutes | Cook time: 10 minutes | Serves 4

1½ cups water
1 lemon, sliced
2 bell peppers, sliced
1 brown onion, sliced into rings
4 sprigs parsley
2 sprigs thyme
2 sprigs rosemary

4 haddock fillets
Sea salt, to taste
⅓ teaspoon ground black pepper, or more to taste
2 tablespoons extra-virgin olive oil

1. Pour the water and lemon into your Instant Pot and insert a steamer basket.
2. Assemble the packets with large sheets of heavy-duty foil.
3. Place the peppers, onion rings, parsley, thyme, and rosemary in the center of each foil. Place the fish fillets on top of the veggies.
4. Sprinkle with the salt and black pepper and drizzle the olive oil over the fillets. Place the packets in the steamer basket.
5. Lock the lid. Select the Manual mode and set the cooking time for 10 minutes at Low Pressure.
6. When the timer beeps, perform a quick pressure release. Carefully remove the lid.
7. Serve warm.

Steamed Salmon

Prep time: 5 minutes | Cook time: 10 minutes | Serves 2

1 cup water
2 salmon fillets

Salt and ground black pepper,
to taste

1. Pour the water into the Instant Pot and add a trivet.
2. Season the salmon fillets with salt and black pepper to taste. Put the salmon fillets on the trivet.
3. Secure the lid. Select the Steam mode and set the cooking time for 10 minutes at High Pressure.
4. Once cooking is complete, do a natural pressure release for 10 minutes, then release any remaining pressure. Carefully open the lid.
5. Serve hot.

Salmon with Broccoli

Prep time: 5 minutes | Cook time: 5 minutes | Serves 2

1 cup water
8 ounces (227 g) salmon fillets
8 ounces (227 g) broccoli, cut

into florets
Salt and ground black pepper,
to taste

1. Pour the water into the Instant Pot and insert a trivet.
2. Season the salmon and broccoli florets with salt and pepper. Put them on the trivet.
3. Secure the lid. Select the Steam mode and set the cooking time for 5 minutes at High Pressure.
4. Once cooking is complete, do a natural pressure release for 10 minutes, then release any remaining pressure. Carefully open the lid.
5. Serve hot.

Fish Fillets with Asparagus

Prep time: 5 minutes | Cook time: 3 minutes | Serves 4

2 lemons
2 cups cold water
2 tablespoons extra-virgin olive oil
4 (4-ounce / 113-g) white fish fillets, such as cod or haddock
1 teaspoon fine sea salt

1 teaspoon ground black pepper
1 bundle asparagus, ends trimmed
2 tablespoons lemon juice
Fresh dill, for garnish

1. Grate the zest off the lemons until you have about 1 tablespoon and set the zest aside. Slice the lemons into ⅛-inch slices.
2. Pour the water into the Instant Pot. Add 1 tablespoon of the olive oil to each of two stackable steamer pans.
3. Sprinkle the fish on all sides with the lemon zest, salt, and pepper.
4. Arrange two fillets in each steamer pan and top each with the lemon slices and then the asparagus. Sprinkle the asparagus with the salt and drizzle the lemon juice over the top.
5. Stack the steamer pans in the Instant Pot. Cover the top steamer pan with its lid.
6. Lock the lid. Select the Manual mode and set the cooking time for 3 minutes at High Pressure.
7. Once cooking is complete, do a natural pressure release for 7 minutes, then release any remaining pressure. Carefully open the lid.
8. Lift the steamer pans out of the Instant Pot.
9. Transfer the fish and asparagus to a serving plate. Garnish with the lemon slices and dill.
10. Serve immediately.

Pesto Fish Packets with Parmesan

Prep time: 8 minutes | Cook time: 6 minutes | Serves 4

1½ cups cold water.
4 (4-ounce / 113-g) white fish fillets, such as cod or haddock
1 teaspoon fine sea salt
½ teaspoon ground black pepper

1 (4-ounce / 113-g) jar pesto
½ cup shredded Parmesan cheese (about 2 ounces / 57 g)
Halved cherry tomatoes, for garnish

1. Pour the water into your Instant Pot and insert a steamer basket.
2. Sprinkle the fish on all sides with the salt and pepper. Take four sheets of parchment paper and place a fillet in the center of each sheet.
3. Dollop 2 tablespoons of the pesto on top of each fillet and sprinkle with 2 tablespoons of the Parmesan cheese.
4. Wrap the fish in the parchment by folding in the edges and folding down the top like an envelope to close tightly.
5. Stack the packets in the steamer basket, seam-side down.
6. Lock the lid. Select the Manual mode and set the cooking time for 6 minutes at Low Pressure.
7. Once cooking is complete, do a natural pressure release for 10 minutes, then release any remaining pressure. Carefully open the lid.
8. Remove the fish packets from the pot. Transfer to a serving plate and garnish with the cherry tomatoes.
9. Serve immediately.

Flounder Fillets with Capers

Prep time: 3 mins, Cook time: 10 mins, Servings: 4

1 cup water
1 tbsp. chopped fresh dill
4 lemon wedges

2 tbsps. chopped capers
4 flounder fillets
Salt and pepper, to taste

1. In the Instant Pot, set in a steamer basket and pour the water into the pot.
2. Sprinkle salt and pepper to the flounder fillets. Sprinkle with dill and chopped capers on top. Add lemon wedges on top for garnish.
3. Place the fillets on the trivet.
4. Lock the lid. Select the Steam mode and cook for 10 minutes at Low Pressure.
5. Once cooking is complete, do a quick pressure release. Carefully open the lid.
6. Serve warm.

Lemon and Garlic Cod

Prep time: 10 minutes | Cook time: 5 minutes | Serves 4

1 pound (454 g) cod fillets
4 cloves garlic, smashed
1 medium lemon, cut into wedges

½ teaspoon salt
¼ teaspoon black pepper
1 tablespoon olive oil
1 cup water

1. Place the cod, garlic, and lemon in the center of aluminum foil. Sprinkle with the salt and pepper. Drizzle the oil over the top. Fold the foil up on all sides and crimp the edges tightly.
2. Place the trivet in the bottom of your Instant Pot. Pour in the water. Carefully lower the foil packet into the pot.
3. Secure the lid. Select the Manual mode and cook for 5 minutes on Low Pressure.
4. Once the timer goes off, do a quick release pressure. Carefully open the lid.
5. Lift the foil packet out of your Instant Pot. Carefully open the foil packet.
6. Squeeze fresh lemon juice over the cod and serve.

Halibut En Papillote
Prep time: 12 mins, Cook time: 10 mins, Servings: 4

1 cup water
1 cup chopped tomatoes
1 thinly sliced shallot

4 halibut fillets
½ tbsp. grated ginger
Salt and pepper, to taste

1.In the Instant Pot, set in a steamer basket and pour the water into the pot.
2.Get a large parchment paper and place the fillet in the middle. Season with salt and pepper. Add the grated ginger, tomatoes, and shallots. Fold the parchment paper to create a pouch and crimp the edges.
3.Place the parchment paper containing the fish.
4.Lock the lid. Select the Steam mode and cook for 10 minutes at Low Pressure.
5.Once cooking is complete, do a quick pressure release. Carefully open the lid.
6.Serve warm.

Halibut Stew with Bacon
Prep time: 10 minutes | Cook time: 10 minutes | Serves 4

4 slices bacon, chopped
1 celery, chopped
½ cup chopped shallots
1 teaspoon garlic, smashed
1 pound (454 g) halibut
2 cups fish stock
1 tablespoon coconut oil,

softened
¼ teaspoon ground allspice
Sea salt and crushed black peppercorns, to taste
1 cup Cottage cheese, at room temperature
1 cup heavy cream

1.Set the Instant Pot to Sauté. Cook the bacon until crispy.
2.Add the celery, shallots, and garlic and sauté for another 2 minutes, or until the vegetables are just tender.
3.Mix in the halibut, stock, coconut oil, allspice, salt, and black peppercorns. Stir well.
4.Lock the lid. Select the Manual mode and set the cooking time for 7 minutes at Low Pressure.
5.When the timer beeps, perform a natural pressure release for 10 minutes, then release any remaining pressure. Carefully remove the lid.
6.Stir in the cheese and heavy cream. Select the Sauté mode again and let it simmer for a few minutes until heated through.
7.Serve immediately.

Salmon with Honey Sauce
Prep time: 10 minutes | Cook time: o minutes | Serves 4

Salmon:
1 cup water
1 pound (454 g) salmon fillets
Sauce:
½ cup honey
4 cloves garlic, minced
4 tablespoons soy sauce

½ teaspoon salt
¼ teaspoon black pepper

2 tablespoons rice vinegar
1 teaspoon sesame seeds

1.Pour the water into the Instant Pot and insert a trivet.
2.Season the salmon fillets with salt and pepper to taste, then place on the trivet.
3.Secure the lid. Select the Manual mode and set the cooking time for 0 minutes at High Pressure.
4.Once cooking is complete, do a natural pressure release for 10 minutes, then release any remaining pressure. Carefully open the lid.
5.Meanwhile, whisk together all the ingredients for the sauce in a small bowl until well mixed.
6.Transfer the fillets to a plate and pour the sauce over them. Serve hot.

Pesto Halibut
Prep time: 12 mins, Cook time: 8 mins, Servings: 4

2 tbsps. extra virgin olive oil
1 tbsp. freshly squeezed lemon juice
1 cup basil leaves

2 garlic cloves, minced
4 halibut fillets
¼ cup water
Salt and pepper, to taste

1.Place the halibut fish in the Instant Pot. Set aside.
2.In a food processor, pulse the basil, olive oil, garlic, and lemon juice until coarse. Sprinkle salt and pepper for seasoning.
3.Spread pesto sauce over halibut fillets. Add the water.
4.Lock the lid. Select the Manual mode and cook for 8 minutes at Low Pressure.
5.Once cooking is complete, do a quick pressure release. Carefully open the lid.
6.Serve warm.

Curried Salmon
Prep time: 6 mins, Cook Time: 8 mins, Servings: 4

2 cups coconut milk
2 tbsps. coconut oil
1 onion, chopped

1 lb. raw salmon, diced
1½ tbsps. minced garlic

1.Press the Sauté button on the Instant Pot and heat the oil.
2.Sauté the garlic and onions until fragrant, about 2 minutes.
3.Add the diced salmon and stir for 1 minute.
4.Pour in the coconut milk.
5.Lock the lid. Select the Manual mode and cook for 4 minutes at Low Pressure.
6.Once cooking is complete, do a quick pressure release. Carefully open the lid.
7.Let the salmon cool for 5 minutes before serving.

Steamed Cod and Veggies
Prep time: 5 minutes | Cook time: 2 to 4 minutes | Serves 2

½ cup water
Kosher salt and freshly ground black pepper, to taste
2 tablespoons freshly squeezed lemon juice, divided
2 tablespoons melted butter
1 garlic clove, minced
1 zucchini or yellow summer

squash, cut into thick slices
1 cup cherry tomatoes
1 cup whole Brussels sprouts
2 (6-ounce / 170-g) cod fillets
2 thyme sprigs or ½ teaspoon dried thyme
Hot cooked rice, for serving

1.Pour the water into your Instant Pot and insert a steamer basket.
2.Sprinkle the fish with the salt and pepper. Mix together 1 tablespoon of the lemon juice, the butter, and garlic in a small bowl. Set aside.
3.Add the zucchini, tomatoes, and Brussels sprouts to the basket. Sprinkle with the salt and pepper and drizzle the remaining 1 tablespoon of lemon juice over the top.
4.Place the fish fillets on top of the veggies. Brush with the mixture and then turn the fish and repeat on the other side. Drizzle any remaining mixture all over the veggies. Place the thyme sprigs on top.
5.Lock the lid. Select the Steam mode and set the cooking time for 2 to 4 minutes on High Pressure, depending on the thickness of the fish.
6.Once cooking is complete, use a quick pressure release. Carefully open the lid.
7.Serve the cod and veggies over the cooked rice.

Lemon Pepper Salmon

Prep time: 15 mins, Cook time: 5 mins, Servings: 4

1 cup water	2 tbsps. olive oil
1 tsp. ground dill	Salt, to taste
1 tsp. ground tarragon	4 lemon slices
1 tsp. ground basil	1 carrot, sliced
4 salmon fillets	1 zucchini, sliced

1. In the Instant Pot, add the water, dill, tarragon, and basil.
2. Place the steamer basket inside.
3. Set in the salmon. Drizzle with a tablespoon of olive oil, pepper and salt. Top with lemon slices.
4. Lock the lid. Select the Steam mode and cook for 3 minutes at Low Pressure.
5. Once cooking is complete, do a quick pressure release. Carefully open the lid.
6. Transfer the fish to a plate and discard the lemon slices.
7. Drizzle the Instant Pot with remaining olive oil. Add the carrot and zucchini to the Instant Pot. Set to Sauté mode, then sauté for 2minutes or until the vegetables are tender.
8. Serve the salmon with the veggies.
9. Garnish with fresh lemon wedges.

Herbed Cod Steaks

Prep time: 5 minutes | Cook time: 4 minutes | Serves 4

1½ cups water	peppercorns, crushed
2 tablespoons garlic-infused oil	2 sprigs thyme
4 cod steaks, 1½-inch thick	1 sprig rosemary
Sea salt, to taste	1 yellow onion, sliced
½ teaspoon mixed	

1. Pour the water into your Instant Pot and insert a trivet.
2. Rub the garlic-infused oil into the cod steaks and season with the salt and crushed peppercorns.
3. Lower the cod steaks onto the trivet, skin-side down. Top with the thyme, rosemary, and onion.
4. Lock the lid. Select the Manual mode and set the cooking time for 4 minutes at High Pressure.
5. When the timer beeps, perform a quick pressure release. Carefully remove the lid.
6. Serve immediately.

Lemony Salmon with Avocados

Prep time: 10 minutes | Cook time: 7 minutes | Serves 2

2 (3-ounce / 85-g) salmon fillets	⅓ cup mayonnaise
½ teaspoon salt	Juice of ½ lemon
¼ teaspoon pepper	2 avocados
1 cup water	½ teaspoon chopped fresh dill

1. Season the salmon fillets on all sides with the salt and pepper. Add the water to the Instant Pot and insert a trivet.
2. Arrange the salmon fillets on the trivet, skin-side down.
3. Secure the lid. Select the Steam mode and set the cooking time for 7 minutes at Low Pressure.
4. Once cooking is complete, do a quick pressure release. Carefully open the lid. Set aside to cool.
5. Mix together the mayonnaise and lemon juice in a large bowl. Cut the avocados in half. Remove the pits and dice the avocados. Add the avocados to the large bowl and gently fold into the mixture.
6. Flake the salmon into bite-sized pieces with a fork and gently fold into the mixture.
7. Serve garnished with the fresh dill.

Italian Salmon with Lemon Juice

Prep time: 6 mins, Cook Time: 8 mins, Servings: 5

1½ lbs. salmon fillets	3 tbsps. freshly squeezed
2 tbsps. butter	lemon juice
3 tbsps. olive oil	Salt and pepper, to taste
1 tbsp. Italian herb seasoning mix	⅓ cup water

1. Place all ingredients in the Instant Pot and stir well.
2. Lock the lid. Select the Manual mode and set the cooking time for 8 minutes at Low Pressure. Flip the fish halfway through the cooking time.
3. Once cooking is complete, do a quick pressure release. Carefully open the lid.
4. Divide the salmon among plates and serve.

Tilapia with Pineapple Salsa

Prep time: 10 minutes | Cook time: 2 minutes | Serves 4

1 pound (454 g) tilapia fillets	½ cup pineapple salsa
¼ teaspoon salt	1 cup water
⅛ teaspoon black pepper	

1. Put the tilapia fillets in the center of a 1½ piece of aluminum foil. Sprinkle the salt and pepper to season.
2. Fold the sides of the aluminum foil up to resemble a bowl and pour in the pineapple salsa. Fold foil over top of tilapia fillets and crimp the edges.
3. Pour the water into the Instant Pot and insert a trivet, then put the foil packet on top of the trivet.
4. Secure the lid. Select the Manual mode and set the cooking time for 2 minutes at High Pressure.
5. Once cooking is complete, do a quick pressure release. Carefully open the lid.
6. Remove the foil packet and carefully open it. Serve the tilapia fillets hot with the salsa as garnish.

Snapper with Spicy Tomato Sauce

Prep time: 5 minutes | Cook time: 5 minutes | Serves 6

2 teaspoons coconut oil, melted	¾ cup vegetable broth
1 teaspoon celery seeds	1 (14-ounce / 113-g) can fire-roasted diced tomatoes
½ teaspoon fresh grated ginger	1 bell pepper, sliced
½ teaspoon cumin seeds	1 jalapeño pepper, minced
1 yellow onion, chopped	Sea salt and ground black pepper, to taste
2 cloves garlic, minced	
1½ pounds (680 g) snapper fillets	¼ teaspoon chili flakes
	½ teaspoon turmeric powder

1. Set the Instant Pot to Sauté. Add and heat the sesame oil until hot. Sauté the celery seeds, fresh ginger, and cumin seeds.
2. Add the onion and continue to sauté until softened and fragrant.
3. Mix in the minced garlic and continue to cook for 30 seconds. Add the remaining ingredients and stir well.
4. Lock the lid. Select the Manual mode and set the cooking time for 3 minutes at Low Pressure.
5. When the timer beeps, perform a quick pressure release. Carefully remove the lid.
6. Serve warm

Mahi-Mahi Fillets with Peppers
Prep time: 10 minutes | Cook time: 3 minutes | Serves 3

2 sprigs fresh rosemary
2 sprigs dill, tarragon
1 sprig fresh thyme
1 cup water
1 lemon, sliced
3 mahi-mahi fillets
2 tablespoons coconut oil,
melted
Sea salt and ground black pepper, to taste
1 serrano pepper, seeded and sliced
1 green bell pepper, sliced
1 red bell pepper, sliced

1. Add the herbs, water, and lemon slices to the Instant Pot and insert a steamer basket.
2. Arrange the mahi-mahi fillets in the steamer basket.
3. Drizzle the melted coconut oil over the top and season with the salt and black pepper.
4. Lock the lid. Select the Manual mode and set the cooking time for 3 minutes at Low Pressure.
5. When the timer beeps, perform a natural pressure release for 10 minutes, then release any remaining pressure. Carefully remove the lid.
6. Place the peppers on top. Select the Sauté mode and let it simmer for another 1 minute.
7. Serve immediately.

Tilapia Fillets with Arugula
Prep time: 5 minutes | Cook time: 4 minutes | Serves 4

1 lemon, juiced
1 cup water
1 pound (454 g) tilapia fillets
½ teaspoon cayenne pepper, or more to taste
2 teaspoons butter, melted
Sea salt and ground black pepper, to taste
½ teaspoon dried basil
2 cups arugula

1. Pour the fresh lemon juice and water into your Instant Pot and insert a steamer basket.
2. Brush the fish fillets with the melted butter.
3. Sprinkle with the cayenne pepper, salt, and black pepper. Place the tilapia fillets in the basket. Sprinkle the dried basil on top.
4. Lock the lid. Select the Manual mode and set the cooking time for 4 minutes at Low Pressure.
5. When the timer beeps, perform a quick pressure release. Carefully remove the lid.
6. Serve with the fresh arugula.

Lime Tilapia Fillets
Prep time: 10 minutes | Cook time: 2 minutes | Serves 4

1 cup water
4 tablespoons lime juice
3 tablespoons chili powder
½ teaspoon salt
1 pound (454 g) tilapia fillets

1. Pour the water into Instant Pot and insert a trivet.
2. Whisk together the lime juice, chili powder, and salt in a small bowl until combined. Brush both sides of the tilapia fillets generously with the sauce. Put the tilapia fillets on top of the trivet.
3. Secure the lid. Select the Manual mode and set the cooking time for 2 minutes at High Pressure.
4. Once cooking is complete, do a quick pressure release. Carefully open the lid.
5. Remove the tilapia fillets from the Instant Pot to a plate and serve.

Salmon with Mayo
Prep time: 5 minutes | Cook time: 15 minutes | Serves 4 to 6

½ cup mayonnaise
4 cloves garlic, minced
1 tablespoon lemon juice
1 teaspoon dried basil leaves
2 pounds (907 g) salmon fillets
Salt and ground pepper, to taste
2 tablespoons olive oil
Chopped green onion, for garnish

1. Stir together the mayo, garlic, lemon juice, and basil in a bowl. Set aside.
2. Season the salmon fillets with salt and pepper to taste.
3. Press the Sauté button on the Instant Pot and heat the olive oil.
4. Add the seasoned fillets and brown each side for 5 minutes. Add the mayo mixture to the Instant Pot and coat the fillets. Continue cooking for another 5 minutes, flipping occasionally.
5. Remove from the Instant Pot to a plate and serve garnished with the green onions.

Panko Tilapia
Prep time: 15 minutes | Cook time: 18 minutes | Serves 4

1 pound (454 g) tilapia fillets
1 teaspoon salt
½ teaspoon black pepper
1 cup whole milk
3 large eggs, lightly beaten
½ cup panko bread crumbs
6 tablespoons olive oil, divided

1. Season the tilapia with salt and black pepper. Set aside.
2. Place the milk in a shallow bowl, the beaten eggs in a separate shallow bowl, and the panko in a dish.
3. Press the Sauté button on the Instant Pot and heat 2 tablespoons of olive oil.
4. Dredge the tilapia fillets in the milk, then dip in the eggs, shaking off any excess, and finally coat with the panko.
5. Working in batches, place the coated fillets in the hot oil. Cook each side for 3 minutes until evenly browned. Transfer the fillets to a paper towel-lined plate. Repeat with the remaining 4 tablespoons of olive oil and fillets.
6. Cool for 5 minutes and serve.

Perch Fillets with Red Curry
Prep time: 5 minutes | Cook time: 6 minutes | Serves 4

1 cup water
2 sprigs rosemary
1 large-sized lemon, sliced
1 pound (454 g) perch fillets
1 teaspoon cayenne pepper
Sea salt and ground black pepper, to taste
1 tablespoon red curry paste
1 tablespoons butter

1. Add the water, rosemary, and lemon slices to the Instant Pot and insert a trivet.
2. Season the perch fillets with the cayenne pepper, salt, and black pepper. Spread the red curry paste and butter over the fillets.
3. Arrange the fish fillets on the trivet.
4. Lock the lid. Select the Manual mode and set the cooking time for 6 minutes at Low Pressure.
5. When the timer beeps, perform a quick pressure release. Carefully remove the lid.
6. Serve with your favorite keto sides.

Dill-Lemon Salmon

Prep time: 3 minutes | Cook time: 5 minutes | Serves 2

2 (3-ounce / 85-g) salmon
fillets, 1-inch thick
1 teaspoon chopped fresh dill
½ teaspoon salt

¼ teaspoon pepper
1 cup water
2 tablespoons lemon juice
½ lemon, sliced

1. Season salmon with dill, salt, and pepper.
2. Pour the water into the Instant Pot and insert the trivet. Place the salmon on the trivet, skin-side down. Squeeze lemon juice over fillets and scatter the lemon slices on top.
3. Lock the lid. Select the Steam mode and set the cooking time for 5 minutes at High Pressure.
4. Once cooking is complete, do a quick pressure release. Carefully open the lid.
5. Serve warm.

Pesto Salmon with Almonds

Prep time: 5 minutes | Cook time: 12 minutes | Serves 4

1 tablespoon butter
¼ cup sliced almonds
4 (3-ounce / 85-g) salmon
fillets

½ cup pesto
¼ teaspoon pepper
½ teaspoon salt
1 cup water

1. Press the Sauté button on the Instant Pot and add the butter and almonds.
2. Sauté for 3 to 5 minutes until they start to soften. Remove and set aside.
3. Brush salmon fillets with pesto and season with salt and pepper.
4. Pour the water into Instant Pot and insert the trivet. Place the salmon fillets on the trivet.
5. Secure the lid. Select the Steam mode and set the cooking time for 7 minutes at High Pressure.
6. Once cooking is complete, do a quick pressure release. Carefully open the lid.
7. Serve the salmon with the almonds sprinkled on top.

Quick Salmon

Prep time: 12 mins, Cook Time: 5 mins, Servings: 4

1 cup water
¼ cup lemon juice
1 tbsp. butter

¼ tsp. salt
4 boneless salmon fillets
1 bunch dill, chopped

1. Place the water in the Instant Pot, add lemon juice, add steamer basket, add salmon inside, season with some salt, sprinkle dill and drizzle melted butter.
2. Lock the lid. Select the Manual mode and cook for 5 minutes at Low Pressure.
3. Once cooking is complete, do a quick pressure release. Carefully open the lid.
4. Divide salmon between plates and serve with a side dish.

Red Curry Halibut

Prep time: 3 mins, Cook time: 10 mins, Servings: 4

2 tbsps. chopped cilantro
4 skinless halibut fillets
3 green curry leaves
1 cup chopped tomatoes

1 tbsp. freshly squeezed lime
juice
Salt and pepper, to taste

1. Place all ingredients in the Instant Pot. Give a good stir to combine the ingredients.
2. Lock the lid. Select the Manual mode and cook for 10 minutes at Low Pressure.
3. Do a quick pressure release.

Salmon Cakes

Prep time: 15 minutes | Cook time: 9 minutes | Serves 4

½ pound (227 g) cooked
salmon, shredded
2 medium green onions, sliced
2 large eggs, lightly beaten
1 cup bread crumbs
½ cup chopped flat leaf parsley
¼ cup soy sauce

1 tablespoon Worcestershire
sauce
1 teaspoon salt
½ tablespoon garlic powder
½ teaspoon cayenne pepper
¼ teaspoon celery seed
4 tablespoons olive oil, divided

1. Stir together all the ingredients except the olive oil in a large mixing bowl until combined.
2. Set your Instant Pot to Sauté and heat 2 tablespoons of olive oil.
3. Scoop out golf ball-sized clumps of the salmon mixture and roll them into balls, then flatten to form cakes.
4. Working in batches, arrange the salmon cakes in an even layer in the Instant Pot.
5. Cook each side for 2 minutes until golden brown. Transfer to a paper towel-lined plate. Repeat with the remaining 2 tablespoons of olive oil and salmon cakes.
6. Serve immediately.

Salmon with Bok Choy

Prep time: 5 minutes | Cook time: 8 minutes | Serves 4

1½ cups water
2 tablespoons unsalted butter
4 (1-inch thick) salmon fillets
½ teaspoon cayenne pepper
Sea salt and freshly ground
pepper, to taste

2 cups Bok choy, sliced
1 cup chicken broth
3 cloves garlic, minced
1 teaspoon grated lemon zest
½ teaspoon dried dill weed

1. Pour the water into your Instant Pot and insert a trivet.
2. Brush the salmon with the melted butter and season with the cayenne pepper, salt, and black pepper on all sides.
3. Lock the lid. Select the Manual mode and set the cooking time for 3 minutes at Low Pressure.
4. When the timer beeps, perform a quick pressure release. Carefully remove the lid.
5. Add the remaining ingredients.
6. Lock the lid. Select the Manual mode and set the cooking time for 5 minutes at High Pressure.
7. When the timer beeps, perform a quick pressure release. Carefully remove the lid.
8. Serve the poached salmon with the veggies on the side.

Thai Fish Curry

Prep time: 6 mins, Cook Time: 6 mins, Servings: 6

1½ lbs. salmon fillets
2 cups fresh coconut milk
¼ cup chopped cilantro

⅓ cup olive oil
2 tbsps. curry powder
Salt and pepper, to taste

1. In the Instant Pot, add all the ingredients. Give a good stir.
2. Lock the lid. Select the Manual mode and set the cooking time for 6 minutes at Low Pressure.
3. Once cooking is complete, do a quick pressure release. Carefully open the lid. Set warm.

Salmon Tandoori

Prep time: 2 hours, Cook Time: 6 mins, Servings: 4

1½ lbs. salmon fillets
3 tbsps. coconut oil

Salt and pepper, to taste
1 tbsp. tandoori spice mix

1. In a bowl, add all the ingredients. Toss well until the fish is fully coated. Allow the fish to marinate for 2 hours in the fridge.
2. Place the marinated salmon in the Instant Pot.
3. Lock the lid. Select the Manual mode and cook for 6 minutes at Low Pressure. Flip the fish halfway through the cooking time.
4. Once cooking is complete, do a quick pressure release. Carefully open the lid.
5. Remove from the pot and serve on a plate.

Salmon with Garlicky Yogurt

Prep time: 2 minutes | Cook time: 4 minutes | Serves 4

1 cup water
2 tablespoons olive oil
4 salmon steaks
Coarse sea salt and ground
black pepper, to taste
Garlicky Yogurt:

1 (8-ounce / 227-g) container
full-fat Greek yogurt
2 cloves garlic, minced
2 tablespoons mayonnaise
⅓ teaspoon Dijon mustard

1. Pour the water into the Instant Pot and insert a trivet.
2. Rub the olive oil into the fish and sprinkle with the salt and black pepper on all sides. Put the fish on the trivet.
3. Lock the lid. Select the Manual mode and set the cooking time for 4 minutes at High Pressure.
4. When the timer beeps, perform a quick pressure release. Carefully remove the lid.
5. Meanwhile, stir together all the ingredients for the garlicky yogurt in a bowl.
6. Serve the salmon steaks alongside the garlicky yogurt.

Salmon with Basil Pesto

Prep time: 6 mins, Cook Time: 6 mins, Servings: 6

3 garlic cloves, minced
1½ lbs. salmon fillets
2 cups basil leaves
2 tbsps. freshly squeezed

lemon juice
½ cup olive oil
Salt and pepper, to taste

1. Make the pesto sauce: Put the basil leaves, olive oil, lemon juice, and garlic in a food processor, and pulse until smooth.
2. Season with salt and pepper.
3. Place the salmon fillets in the Instant Pot and add the pesto sauce.
4. Lock the lid. Select the Manual mode and set the cooking time for 6 minutes at Low Pressure.
5. Once cooking is complete, do a quick pressure release. Carefully open the lid.
6. Divide the salmon among six plates and serve.

Salmon with Dill

Prep time: 12 mins, Cook Time: 10 mins, Servings: 2

2 tbsps. dill
⅓ cup olive oil
1 tbsp. fresh lemon juice
2 tbsps. butter

2 salmon fillets
1 cup water
Salt and pepper, to taste

1. Add the water and steam rack to the Instant Pot.
2. Put the remaining ingredients in a heatproof dish and stir well.
3. Place the dish on the steam rack.
4. Lock the lid. Select the Steam mode and cook for 10 minutes at Low Pressure.
5. Once cooking is complete, do a quick pressure release. Carefully open the lid.
6. Divide the salmon fillets among two serving plates and serve.

Chili-Rubbed Tilapia

Prep time: 6 mins, Cook time: 10 mins, Servings: 4

1 cup water
½ tsp. garlic powder
1 lb. skinless tilapia fillet

2 tbsps. extra virgin olive oil
Salt and pepper, to taste
2 tbsps. chili powder

1. Set a trivet in the Instant Pot and pour the water into the pot.
2. Season the tilapia fillets with salt, pepper, chili powder, and garlic powder. Drizzle with olive oil on top.
3. Place in the steamer basket.
4. Lock the lid. Select the Steam mode and cook for 10 minutes at Low Pressure.
5. Once cooking is complete, do a quick pressure release. Carefully open the lid.
6. Serve warm.

Greek Snapper

Prep time: 6 mins, Cook time: 10 mins, Servings: 4

1 cup water
12 snapper fillets
3 tbsps. olive oil

2 tbsps. Greek yogurt
1 garlic clove, minced
Salt and pepper, to taste

1. Set a trivet in the Instant Pot and pour the water into the pot.
2. In a mixing bowl, combine the olive oil, garlic, and Greek yogurt. Sprinkle salt and pepper for seasoning.
3. Apply Greek yogurt mixture to the fish fillets. Place the fillets on the trivet.
4. Lock the lid. Select the Steam mode and cook for 10 minutes at Low Pressure.
5. Once cooking is complete, do a quick pressure release. Carefully open the lid.
6. Serve warm.

Tuna Fillets with Lemon Butter

Prep time: 5 minutes | Cook time: 3 minutes | Serves 4

1 cup water
⅓ cup lemon juice
2 sprigs fresh thyme
2 sprigs fresh parsley
2 sprigs fresh rosemary
1 pound (454 g) tuna fillets

4 cloves garlic, pressed
Sea salt, to taste
¼ teaspoon black pepper, or
more to taste
2 tablespoons butter, melted
1 lemon, sliced

1. Pour the water into your Instant Pot. Add the lemon juice, thyme, parsley, and rosemary and insert a steamer basket.
2. Put the tuna fillets in the basket. Top with the garlic and season with the salt and black pepper.
3. Drizzle the melted butter over the fish fillets and place the lemon slices on top.
4. Lock the lid. Select the Manual mode and set the cooking time for 3 minutes at Low Pressure.
5. When the timer beeps, perform a quick pressure release. Carefully remove the lid.
6. Serve immediately.

Herbed Red Snapper

Prep time: 3 mins, Cook time: 12 mins, Servings: 4

1 cup water
4 red snapper fillets
1½ tsps. chopped fresh herbs
¼ tsp. paprika

3 tbsps. freshly squeezed lemon juice
Salt and pepper, to taste

1. Set a trivet in the Instant Pot and pour the water into the pot.
2. Mix all ingredients in a heat-proof dish that will fit in the Instant Pot. Combine to coat the fish with all ingredients.
3. Place the heat-proof dish on the trivet.
4. Lock the lid. Select the Manual mode and cook for 12 minutes at Low Pressure.
5. Once cooking is complete, do a quick pressure release. Carefully open the lid.
6. Serve warm.

Teriyaki Salmon

Prep time: 5 minutes | Cook time: 0 minutes | Serves 4

1 pound (454 g) salmon fillets
½ cup packed light brown sugar
½ cup rice vinegar

½ cup soy sauce
1 tablespoon cornstarch
1 teaspoon minced ginger
¼ teaspoon garlic powder

1. Place the salmon fillets into the Instant Pot.
2. Whisk together the remaining ingredients in a small bowl until well combined. Pour the mixture over the salmon fillets, turning to coat.
3. Secure the lid. Select the Manual mode and set the cooking time for 0 minutes at High Pressure.
4. Once cooking is complete, do a natural pressure release for 10 minutes, then release any remaining pressure. Carefully open the lid.
5. Serve hot.

Simple Broccoli Mackerel

Prep Time: 5 Mins | Total Time: 10 Mins | Serves: 4

4 Mackerel Fillets
10 ounces Broccoli Florets

1 tsp Garlic Powder
1 ½ cup Water

1. Sprinkle the mackerel with garlic powder and arrange them inside the steamer basket.
2. Place the broccoli florets on top.
3. Pour the water into the IP.
4. Lower the steamer basket into the pot.
5. Close the lid and choose MANUAL.
6. Cook on HIGH for 2 minutes.
7. Do a quick pressure release.
8. Serve and enjoy!

Instant Pot Citrus Tilapia

Prep Time: 10 Mins | Total Time: 2H 10 Mins | Serves: 4

4 tilapia filets
1 10-ounce can mandarin oranges

2 tbsp. minced garlic
2 tbsp. coconut oil
Sea salt and pepper

1. Arrange fish side by side onto a large piece of aluminum foil and sprinkle with garlic and coconut oil evenly.
2. Top the fish with oranges and season with salt and pepper; fold the foil to wrap the content well.
3. Place in an instant pot and lock lid; cook on high for 15 minutes.

Hot Lemony Instant Pot Tilapia with Asparagus

Prep Time: 15 Mins | Total Time: 2H 15 Mins | Serves: 6

6 tilapia filets
1 bundle of asparagus
12 tbsp. lemon juice

Lemon pepper seasoning
3 tbsp. melted coconut oil

1. Divide asparagus into equal amounts per each fillet.
2. Place each fillet in the center of a foil and sprinkle with about 1 tsp. of lemon pepper seasoning; drizzle with about 2 tbsp. of lemon juice and about ½ tbsp. melted coconut oil.
3. Top each filet with the asparagus and fold the foil to form a packet.
4. Repeat with the remaining ingredients and then place the packets into an instant pot.
5. Lock lid and cook on high for 15 minutes.

Salmon on Veggie Noodles

Prep Time: 5 Mins | Total Time: 15 Mins | Serves: 4

4 Salmon Fillets
1 Zucchini, Spiralized
1 large Carrot, Spiralized
2 Potatoes, Spiralized

1 cup of Water
1 Thyme Sprig
2 tsp Olive Oil
Pinch of Pepper

1. Pour the water into the Instant Pot and place the thyme inside.
2. In the steamer basket, arrange the veggies.
3. Place the salmon on top.
4. Drizzle with olive oil and sprinkle with pepper.
5. Lower the basket into the pot and close the lid.
6. Close the lid and hit STEAM.
7. Cook for 5 minutes.
8. Do a quick pressure release.
9. Serve and enjoy!

Lemon Salmon

Prep Time:5 Mins | Cook Time:6Mins | Servings: 4

1 pound skin-on salmon fillets
1 Tablespoon ghee, melted
Pinch of salt, white pepper
½ medium fresh lemon, thinly sliced

Sprigs of fresh dill, fresh parsley, fresh tarragon, fresh basil
1 cup of water

1. Add 1 cup water, herbs, and a steamer rack to Instant Pot.
2. Season salmon with salt, white pepper. Drizzle with melted ghee.
3. Place fillets on steamer rack. Top with lemon slices.
4. Close, seal the lid. Press "Steam" button. Cook on HIGH 3 minutes.
5. When done, manually release pressure. Remove the lid.
6. Transfer to platter. Garnish with fresh herbs. Serve.

Instant Pot Coconut Curry Shrimp

Prep Time: 5 Mins | Total Time: 20 Mins | Serves: 4

1 pound shelled shrimp
15 ounces water
4 cups coconut milk

½ cup Thai red curry sauce
¼ cup cilantro
2½ tsp. garlic-lemon seasoning

1. In your instant pot, combine water, coconut milk, red curry paste, cilantro, and lemon garlic seasoning;
2. Stir to mix well and lock lid; cook on high for 10 minutes and then release the pressure quickly.
3. Add shrimp and continue cooking for another 5 minutes and then release pressure naturally.
4. Serve garnished with cilantro.

Thyme-Sesame Crusted Halibut

Prep time: 6 mins, Cook time: 8 mins, Servings: 4

1 cup water
1 tsp. dried thyme leaves
1 tbsp. toasted sesame seeds
8 oz. halibut, sliced

Salt and pepper, to taste
1 tbsp. freshly squeezed lemon juice

1. Set a trivet in the Instant Pot and pour the water into the pot.
2. Season the halibut with lemon juice, salt, and pepper. Sprinkle with dried thyme leaves and sesame seeds.
3. Place the fish on the trivet.
4. Lock the lid. Select the Steam mode and cook for 8 minutes at Low Pressure.
5. Once cooking is complete, do a quick pressure release. Carefully open the lid.
6. Serve warm.

Tilapia Fish Cakes

Prep time: 15 minutes | Cook time: 15 minutes | Serves 4

½ pound (227 g) cooked tilapia fillets, shredded
1½ cups bread crumbs
2 large eggs, lightly beaten
1 cup peeled and shredded russet potato
2 teaspoons lemon juice

2 tablespoons full-fat sour cream
1 teaspoon salt
¼ teaspoon black pepper
½ teaspoon chili powder
⅛ teaspoon cayenne pepper
4 tablespoons olive oil, divided

1. Mix together all the ingredients except the olive oil in a large bowl and stir until well incorporated.
2. Scoop out golf ball-sized clumps of the tilapia mixture and roll them into balls, then flatten to form cakes.
3. Set your Instant Pot to Sauté and heat 2 tablespoons of olive oil.
4. Put the tilapia cakes in the Instant Pot in an even layer. You'll need to work in batches to avoid overcrowding.
5. Sear for 2 minutes per side until golden brown. Transfer to a paper towel-lined plate. Repeat with the remaining 2 tablespoons of olive oil and tilapia cakes.
6. Serve immediately.

Tuna Noodle Casserole

Prep time: 5 minutes | Cook time: 4 minutes | Serves 4

3 cups water
28 ounces (794 g) cream of mushroom soup
14 ounces (397 g) canned tuna, drained
20 ounces (567 g) egg noodles

1 cup frozen peas
Salt and ground black pepper, to taste
4 ounces (113 g) grated Cheddar cheese
¼ cup bread crumbs (optional)

1. Combine the water and mushroom soup in the Instant Pot.
2. Stir in the tuna, egg noodles, and peas. Season with salt and pepper.
3. Secure the lid. Select the Manual mode and set the cooking time for 4 minutes at High Pressure.
4. When the timer beeps, perform a quick pressure release. Carefully remove the lid.
5. Scatter the grated cheese and bread crumbs (if desired) on top. Lock the lid and allow to sit for 5 minutes.
6. Serve warm.

Tuna Salad with Lettuce

Prep time: 12 mins, Cook Time: 10 mins, Servings: 4

2 tbsps. olive oil
½ lb. tuna, sliced
1 tbsp. fresh lemon juice
2 eggs

1 head lettuce
Salt and pepper, to taste
1 cup water

1. In a large bowl, season the tuna with lemon juice, salt and pepper. Transfer the tuna to a baking dish.
2. Add the eggs, water, and steamer rack to the Instant Pot. Place the baking dish on the steamer rack.
3. Lock the lid. Select the Steam mode and set the cooking time for 10 minutes at Low Pressure.
4. Once cooking is complete, do a quick pressure release. Carefully open the lid.
5. Allow the eggs and tuna to cool. Peel the eggs and slice into wedges. Set aside.
6. Assemble the salad by shredding the lettuce in a salad bowl. Toss in the cooled tuna and eggs.
7. Sprinkle with olive oil, then serve.

Wild Alaskan Cod with Cherry Tomatoes

Prep time: 5 minutes | Cook time: 8 minutes | Serves 2

1 large fillet wild Alaskan Cod
1 cup cherry tomatoes, chopped

Salt and ground black pepper, to taste
2 tablespoons butter

1. Add the tomatoes to your Instant Pot. Top with the cod fillet. Sprinkle with the salt and pepper.
2. Secure the lid. Press the Manual button on your Instant Pot and set the cooking time for 8 minutes on High Pressure.
3. Once the timer goes off, perform a quick pressure release. Carefully remove the lid.
4. Add the butter to the cod fillet. Secure the lid and let stand for 1 minute.
5. Transfer to a serving plate and serve.

Salmon with Lemon Mustard

Prep time: 8 mins, Cook time: 10 mins, Servings: 4

1 cup water
1 garlic clove, minced
4 skinless salmon fillets
2 tbsps. Dijon mustard

Salt and pepper, to taste
2 tbsps. freshly squeezed lemon juice

1. Set a trivet in the Instant Pot and pour the water into the pot.
2. In a bowl, mix lemon juice, mustard, and garlic. Sprinkle salt and pepper for seasoning.
3. Top the salmon fillets with the mustard mixture. Place the fish fillets on the trivet.
4. Lock the lid. Select the Steam mode and cook for 10 minutes at Low Pressure.
5. Once cooking is complete, do a quick pressure release. Carefully open the lid.
6. Serve warm.

Chapter 5 Poultry

Honey-Garlic Chicken

Prep time: 5 minutes | Cook time: 15 minutes | Serves 6

1½ pounds (680 g) chicken breasts, cut into cubes
3 cloves of garlic, minced
6 tablespoons honey
2 tablespoons online powder
1½ tablespoons soy sauce

½ tablespoon sriracha sauce
1 cup water
1 tablespoon cornstarch + 2 tablespoons water
1 tablespoon sesame oil
Green onions, chopped

1. Add all the ingredients except the cornstarch slurry, sesame oil, and green onions to the Instant Pot and stir to combine.
2. Secure the lid. Select the Poultry mode and cook for 15 minutes on High Pressure.
3. Once the timer goes off, use a quick pressure release. Carefully open the lid.
4. Select the Sauté mode. Fold in the cornstarch slurry. Stir well.
5. Let simmer until the sauce is thickened.
6. Mix in the sesame oil and green onions and stir to combine.
7. Serve immediately.

Tomato Chicken Soup

Prep time: 6 mins, Cook time: 20 mins, Servings: 4

¼ cup fresh basil leaves
8 chopped plum tomatoes
4 skinless chicken breasts,

halved
Salt and pepper, to taste
5 cups water

1. Place all ingredients into the Instant Pot. Give a good stir to mix everything.
2. Lock the lid. Select the Manual mode and set the timer to 20 minutes at High Pressure.
3. Once cooking is complete, do a natural pressure release for 10 minutes, then release any remaining pressure. Carefully open the lid.
4. Let the soup cool for 10 minutes and serve warm.

BBQ Chicken, Sausage, and Veggies

Prep time: 10 minutes | Cook time: 25 minutes | Serves 8

4 chicken drumsticks, skin removed
4 bone-in chicken thighs, skin removed
1 large sweet red pepper, cut into 1-inch pieces

1 medium onion, chopped
1 cup chicken broth
1 (12-ounce / 340-g) package smoked sausage links, cut into 1-inch pieces
1 cup barbecue sauce

1. Place the chicken pieces, sausage, pepper, onion, and broth in the Instant Pot and drizzle with the barbecue sauce.
2. Secure the lid. Select the Manual mode and set the cooking time for 12 minutes on High Pressure.
3. Once the timer goes off, use a quick pressure release. Carefully open the lid.
4. Remove the chicken, sausage and veggies from the Instant Pot and keep warm.
5. Set the Instant Pot to Sauté and bring the liquid to a boil. Let simmer for 12 to 15 minutes, or until the sauce is thickened, stirring frequently.
6. Serve the chicken, sausage and veggies with the sauce.

Baked Mushroom Chicken

Prep time: 5 minutes | Cook time: 15 minutes | Serves 4

1 tablespoon butter
2 cloves garlic, smashed
½ cup chopped yellow onion
1 pound (454 g) chicken breasts, cubed
10 ounces (283 g) button mushrooms, thinly sliced
1 cup chicken broth
½ teaspoon shallot powder

½ teaspoon turmeric powder
½ teaspoon dried basil
½ teaspoon dried sage
½ teaspoon cayenne pepper
⅓ teaspoon ground black pepper
Kosher salt, to taste
½ cup heavy cream
1 cup shredded Colby cheese

1. Set your Instant Pot to Sauté and melt the butter.
2. Add the garlic, onion, chicken, and mushrooms and sauté for about 4 minutes, or until the vegetables are softened.
3. Add the remaining ingredients except the heavy cream and cheese to the Instant Pot and stir to incorporate.
4. Lock the lid. Select the Meat/Stew mode and set the cooking time for 6 minutes at High Pressure.
5. When the timer beeps, perform a natural pressure release for 10 minutes, then release any remaining pressure. Carefully remove the lid.
6. Stir in the heavy cream until heated through. Pour the mixture into a baking dish and scatter the cheese on top.
7. Bake in the preheated oven at 400ºF (205ºC) until the cheese bubbles.
8. Allow to cool for 5 minutes and serve.

Chicken with Yogurt Salsa

Prep time: 15 mins, Cook Time: 15 mins, Servings: 4

1 medium jar salsa
½ cup water

1 cup plain Greek yogurt
4 chicken breasts

1. Add all the ingredients to the Instant Pot. Using a spatula, gently stir to combine well.
2. Lock the lid. Select the Poultry mode and set the cooking time for 15 minutes at High Pressure.
3. Once cooking is complete, do a natural pressure release for 8 minutes, then release any remaining pressure. Carefully open the lid.
4. Transfer the cooked mixture to a salad bowl and serve warm.

Barbecue Chicken Wings

Prep time: 5 minutes | Cook time: 12 minutes | Serves 4

1 pound (454 g) chicken wings
1 teaspoon salt
½ teaspoon pepper
¼ teaspoon garlic powder

1 cup sugar-free barbecue sauce, divided
1 cup water

1. Toss the chicken wings with the salt, pepper, garlic powder, and half of barbecue sauce in a large bowl until well coated.
2. Pour the water into the Instant Pot and insert the trivet. Place the wings on the trivet.
3. Secure the lid. Select the Manual mode and set the cooking time for 12 minutes at High Pressure.
4. Once cooking is complete, do a quick pressure release. Carefully open the lid.
5. Transfer the wings to a serving bowl and toss with the remaining sauce. Serve immediately.

Salsa Chicken Legs

Prep time: 5 minutes | Cook time: 16 minutes | Serves 5

5 chicken legs, skinless and boneless
½ teaspoon sea salt
Salsa Sauce:

1 cup puréed tomatoes	2 tablespoons minced fresh
1 cup onion, chopped	cilantro
1 jalapeño, chopped	3 teaspoons lime juice
2 bell peppers, deveined and	1 teaspoon granulated garlic
chopped	

1. Press the Sauté button to heat your Instant Pot.
2. Add the chicken legs and sear each side for 2 to 3 minutes until evenly browned. Season with sea salt.
3. Thoroughly combine all the ingredients for the salsa sauce in a mixing bowl. Spoon the salsa mixture evenly over the browned chicken legs.
4. Lock the lid. Select the Manual mode and set the cooking time for 10 minutes at High Pressure.
5. When the timer beeps, perform a natural pressure release for 10 minutes, then release any remaining pressure. Carefully remove the lid. Serve warm.

Sesame Chicken

Prep time: 6 mins, Cook time: 25 mins, Servings: 12

1½ cup soy sauce	5 lbs. chicken breasts or thighs
1 bay leaf	2 tbsps. toasted sesame seeds
2 packets dried star anise	2 cups water
flowers	

1. Place the chicken breasts, soy sauce, star anise flowers, and bay leaf into the Instant Pot.
2. Lock the lid. Select the Manual mode and set the cooking time for 25 minutes at High Pressure.
3. Once cooking is complete, do a natural pressure release for 15 minutes, then release any remaining pressure. Carefully open the lid.
4. Allow the chicken breasts cool for 5 minutes and serve.

Shredded Chicken

Prep time: 5 minutes | Cook time: 14 minutes | Serves 4

½ teaspoon salt	2 (6-ounce / 170-g) boneless,
½ teaspoon pepper	skinless chicken breasts
½ teaspoon dried oregano	1 tablespoon coconut oil
½ teaspoon dried basil	1 cup water
½ teaspoon garlic powder	

1. In a small bowl, combine the salt, pepper, oregano, basil, and garlic powder. Rub this mix over both sides of the chicken.
2. Set your Instant Pot to Sauté and heat the coconut oil until sizzling.
3. Add the chicken and sear for 3 to 4 minutes until golden on both sides.
4. Remove the chicken and set aside.
5. Pour the water into the Instant Pot and use a wooden spoon or rubber spatula to make sure no seasoning is stuck to bottom of pot.
6. Add the trivet to the Instant Pot and place the chicken on top.
7. Secure the lid. Select the Manual mode and set the cooking time for 10 minutes at High Pressure.
8. Once cooking is complete, do a natural pressure release for 5 minutes, then release any remaining pressure. Carefully open the lid.
9. Remove the chicken and shred, then serve.

Smoky Chicken

Prep time: 5mins, Cook time: 15 mins, Servings: 6

2 tbsps. smoked paprika	1 tbsp. olive oil
2 lbs. chicken breasts	½ cup water
Salt and pepper, to taste	

1. Press the Sauté button on the Instant Pot and heat the olive oil.
2. Stir in the chicken breasts and smoked paprika and cook for 3 minutes until lightly golden.
3. Season with salt and pepper and add ½ cup water.
4. Lock the lid. Select the Manual mode and cook for 12 minutes at High Pressure.
5. Once cooking is complete, do a natural pressure release for 8 minutes, then release any remaining pressure. Carefully open the lid.
6. Garnish with cilantro or scallions, if desired.

Spiced Chicken Drumsticks

Prep time: 6 mins, Cook time: 15 mins, Servings: 10 to 12

¼ tsp. dried thyme	½ tsp. onion powder
1½ tbsps. paprika	12 chicken drumsticks
Salt and pepper, to taste	2 cups water

1. On a clean work surface, rub the chicken drumsticks generously with the spices. Season with salt and pepper.
2. Transfer the chicken to the Instant Pot and add the water.
3. Lock the lid. Select the Poultry mode and cook for 15 minutes at High Pressure.
4. Once cooking is complete, do a natural pressure release for 8 minutes, then release any remaining pressure. Carefully open the lid.
5. Remove from the pot to a plate and serve.

Spicy Chicken with Smoked Sausage

Prep time: 35 minutes | Cook time: 15 minutes | Serves 11

1 (6-ounce / 170-g) can tomato paste	1½ teaspoons dried oregano
1 (14½-ounce / 411-g) can diced tomatoes, undrained	½ teaspoon hot pepper sauce
1 (14½-ounce / 411-g) can beef broth or chicken broth	1¼ teaspoons salt
2 medium green peppers, chopped	½ teaspoon cayenne pepper
1 medium onion, chopped	1 pound (454 g) smoked sausage, halved and cut into ¼-inch slices
5 garlic cloves, minced	1 pound (454 g) boneless, skinless chicken breasts, cut into 1-inch cubes
3 celery ribs, chopped	½ pound (227 g) uncooked shrimp, peeled and deveined
3 teaspoons dried parsley flakes	Hot cooked rice, for serving
2 teaspoons dried basil	

1. Mix together the tomato paste, tomatoes, and broth in your Instant Pot. Stir in the green peppers, onion, garlic, celery, and seasonings. Fold in the sausage and chicken.
2. Secure the lid. Press the Manual button and set the cooking time for 8 minutes on High Pressure.
3. Once the timer goes off, do a quick pressure release. Carefully open the lid.
4. Set the Instant Pot to sauté. Add the shrimp and stir well. Cook for another 5 minutes, or until the shrimp turn pink, stirring occasionally.
5. Serve over the cooked rice.

Moringa Chicken Soup

Prep time: 3 minutes | Cook time: 18 minutes | Serves 8

1½ pounds (680 g) chicken breasts
5 cups water
1 cup chopped tomatoes
2 cloves garlic, minced

1 onion, chopped
1 thumb-size ginger
Salt and pepper, to taste
2 cups moringa leaves or kale leaves

1. Combine all the ingredients except the moringa leaves in the Instant Pot.
2. Secure the lid. Select the Poultry mode and set the cooking time for 15 minutes at High Pressure.
3. Once cooking is complete, do a natural pressure release for 10 minutes, then release any remaining pressure. Carefully open the lid.
4. Set your Instant Pot to Sauté and stir in the moringa leaves. Allow to simmer for 3 minutes until softened.
5. Divide into bowls and serve warm.

Orange Chicken Breasts

Prep time: 5 minutes | Cook time: 18 minutes | Serves 4

4 chicken breasts
¾ cup orange marmalade
¾ cup barbecue sauce
¼ cup water
2 tablespoons soy sauce

1 tablespoon cornstarch, mixed with 2 tablespoons water
2 tablespoons green onions, chopped

1. Combine all the ingredients except the cornstarch mixture and green onions in the Instant Pot.
2. Secure the lid. Select the Poultry mode and set the cooking time for 15 minutes at High Pressure.
3. Once cooking is complete, do a quick pressure release. Carefully open the lid.
4. Set your Instant Pot to Sauté and stir in the cornstarch mixture. Simmer for a few minutes until the sauce is thickened.
5. Add the green onions and stir well. Serve immediately.

Paprika Chicken with Cucumber Salad

Prep time: 10 minutes | Cook time: 20 minutes | Serves 4

1 tablespoon olive oil
1 yellow onion, chopped
2 chicken breasts, skinless, boneless and halved
Salad:
2 cucumbers, sliced
1 tomato, cubed
1 avocado, peeled, pitted, and

1 cup chicken stock
1 tablespoon sweet paprika
½ teaspoon cinnamon powder

cubed
1 tablespoon chopped cilantro

1. Press the Sauté button on the Instant Pot and heat the olive oil until it shimmers.
2. Add the onion and chicken breasts and sauté for 5 minutes, stirring occasionally, or until the onion is translucent. Stir in the chicken stock, paprika, and cinnamon powder.
3. Secure the lid. Select the Manual mode and set the cooking time for 15 minutes at High Pressure.
4. Meanwhile, toss all the ingredients for the salad in a bowl. Set aside.
5. Once cooking is complete, do a natural pressure release for 10 minutes, then release any remaining pressure. Carefully open the lid.
6. Divide the chicken breasts between four plates and serve with the salad on the side.

Paprika Chicken with Tomatoes

Prep time: 10 mins, Cook Time: 20 mins, Servings:4

1 tbsp. avocado oil
1½ lbs. chicken breast, skinless, boneless, and cubed
1 cup tomatoes, cubed
1 cup chicken stock

1 tbsp. smoked paprika
1 tsp. cayenne pepper
A pinch of salt and black pepper

1. Set your Instant Pot to Sauté and heat the oil. Cook the cubed chicken in the hot oil for 2 to 3 minutes until lightly browned.
2. Add the remaining ingredients to the pot and stir well.
3. Lock the lid. Select the Poultry mode and set the cooking time for 18 minutes at High Pressure.
4. Once cooking is complete, do a natural pressure release for 10 minutes, then release any remaining pressure. Carefully open the lid.
5. Serve the chicken and tomatoes in bowls while warm.

Parmesan Drumsticks

Prep time: 5 minutes | Cook time: 25 minutes | Serves 4

2 pounds (907 g) chicken drumsticks (about 8 pieces)
1 teaspoon salt
1 teaspoon dried parsley
½ teaspoon garlic powder
½ teaspoon dried oregano
¼ teaspoon pepper
1 cup water

1 stick butter
2 ounces (57 g) cream cheese, softened
½ cup grated Parmesan cheese
½ cup chicken broth
¼ cup heavy cream
⅛ teaspoon pepper

1. Sprinkle the salt, parsley, garlic powder, oregano, and pepper evenly over the chicken drumsticks.
2. Pour the water into the Instant Pot and insert the trivet. Arrange the drumsticks on the trivet.
3. Secure the lid. Select the Manual mode and set the cooking time for 15 minutes at High Pressure.
4. Once cooking is complete, do a quick pressure release. Carefully open the lid.
5. Transfer the drumsticks to a foil-lined baking sheet and broil each side for 3 to 5 minutes, or until the skin begins to crisp.
6. Meanwhile, pour the water out of the Instant Pot. Set your Instant Pot to Sauté and melt the butter.
7. Add the remaining ingredients to the Instant Pot and whisk to combine. Pour the sauce over the drumsticks and serve warm.

Prosciutto-Wrapped Chicken

Prep time: 5 minutes | Cook time: 15 minutes | Serves 5

1½ cups water
5 chicken breast halves, butterflied
2 garlic cloves, halved
1 teaspoon marjoram

Sea salt, to taste
½ teaspoon red pepper flakes
¼ teaspoon ground black pepper, or more to taste
10 strips prosciutto

1. Pour the water into the Instant Pot and insert the trivet.
2. Rub the chicken breast halves with garlic. Sprinkle with marjoram, salt, red pepper flakes, and black pepper. Wrap each chicken breast into 2 prosciutto strips and secure with toothpicks. Put the chicken on the trivet.
3. Lock the lid. Select the Poultry mode and set the cooking time for 15 minutes at High Pressure.
4. When the timer beeps, perform a natural pressure release for 10 minutes, then release any remaining pressure. Carefully remove the lid.
5. Remove the toothpicks and serve warm.

BLT Chicken Salad

Prep time: 15 minutes | Cook time: 17 minutes | Serves 4

4 slices bacon
2 (6-ounce / 170-g) chicken breasts
1 teaspoon salt
½ teaspoon garlic powder
¼ teaspoon dried parsley
Sauce:
⅓ cup mayonnaise
1 ounce (28 g) chopped pecans

¼ teaspoon pepper
¼ teaspoon dried thyme
1 cup water
2 cups chopped romaine lettuce

½ cup diced Roma tomatoes
½ avocado, diced
1 tablespoon lemon juice

1. Press the Sauté button to heat your Instant Pot.
2. Add the bacon and cook for about 7 minutes, flipping occasionally, until crisp. Remove and place on a paper towel to drain. When cool enough to handle, crumble the bacon and set aside.
3. Sprinkle the chicken with salt, garlic powder, parsley, pepper, and thyme.
4. Pour the water into the Instant Pot. Use a wooden spoon to ensure nothing is stuck to the bottom of the pot. Add the trivet to the pot and place the chicken on top of the trivet.
5. Secure the lid. Select the Manual mode and set the cooking time for 10 minutes at High Pressure.
6. Meanwhile, whisk together all the ingredients for the sauce in a large salad bowl.
7. Once cooking is complete, do a quick pressure release. Carefully open the lid.
8. Remove the chicken and let sit for 10 minutes. Cut the chicken into cubes and transfer to the salad bowl, along with the cooked bacon. Gently stir until the chicken is thoroughly coated. Mix in the lettuce right before serving.

Chicken Alfredo with Bacon

Prep time: 10 minutes | Cook time: 27 minutes | Serves 4

2 (6-ounce / 170-g) boneless, skinless chicken breasts, butterflied
½ teaspoon garlic powder
¼ teaspoon dried parsley
¼ teaspoon dried thyme
¼ teaspoon salt
⅛ teaspoon pepper

2 tablespoons coconut oil
1 cup water
1 stick butter
2 cloves garlic, finely minced
¼ cup heavy cream
½ cup grated Parmesan cheese
¼ cup cooked crumbled bacon

1. Sprinkle the chicken breasts with the garlic powder, parsley, thyme, salt, and pepper.
2. Set your Instant Pot to Sauté and melt the coconut oil.
3. Add the chicken and sear for 3 to 5 minutes until golden brown on both sides.
4. Remove the chicken with tongs and set aside.
5. Pour the water into the Instant Pot and insert the trivet. Place the chicken on the trivet.
6. Secure the lid. Select the Manual mode and set the cooking time for 20 minutes at High Pressure.
7. Once cooking is complete, do a quick pressure release. Carefully open the lid.
8. Remove the chicken from the pot to a platter and set aside.
9. Pour the water out of the Instant Pot, reserving ½ cup; set aside.
10. Set your Instant Pot to Sauté again and melt the butter.
11. Add the garlic, heavy cream, cheese, and reserved water to the Instant Pot. Cook for 3 to 4 minutes until the sauce starts to thicken, stirring frequently.
12. Stir in the crumbled bacon and pour the mixture over the chicken. Serve immediately.

Broccoli Chicken with Black Beans

Prep time: 10 mins, Cook Time: 25 mins, Servings: 4

1 tbsp. olive oil
2 chicken breasts, skinless and boneless
1 cup broccoli florets
1½ cups chicken stock

2 tbsps. tomato sauce
1 cup black beans, soaked overnight and drained
A pinch of salt and black pepper

1. Set your Instant Pot to Sauté and heat the olive oil. Add the chicken breasts and sauté for 5 minutes until lightly browned.
2. Add the remaining ingredients to the pot and stir well.
3. Lock the lid. Select the Poultry mode and cook for 20 minutes at High Pressure.
4. Once cooking is complete, do a natural pressure release for 10 minutes, then release any remaining pressure. Carefully open the lid.
5. Remove from the pot and serve on plates.

Parmesan Chicken with Broccoli

Prep time: 8 mins, Cook Time: 5 mins, Servings: 2 to 3

⅓ cup grated Parmesan cheese
1 cup chicken broth
2 cups broccoli florets

½ cup heavy cream
3 cups cooked and shredded chicken
Salt and pepper, to taste

1. In the Instant pot, add the broth, broccoli, chicken, salt, and pepper. Using a spatula, stir the ingredients.
2. Lock the lid. Select the Steam mode and cook for 3 minutes at High Pressure.
3. Once cooking is complete, do a quick pressure release. Carefully open the lid.
4. Set your Instant Pot to Sauté and stir in the cream.
5. Cook for 2 minutes. Transfer to a large plate and serve.

Chicken Lo Mein

Prep time: 10 minutes | Cook time: 10 minutes | Serves 4

1 tablespoon toasted sesame oil
1 garlic clove, minced
1½ pounds (680 g) boneless, skinless chicken breast, cut into bite-size pieces
8 ounces (227 g) dried linguine, broken in half
1 cup broccoli florets
1 carrot, peeled and thinly sliced

1 cup snow peas
Sauce:
1½ cups low-sodium chicken broth
1 tablespoon fish sauce
1 tablespoon soy sauce
1 tablespoon Shaoxing rice wine
1 tablespoon brown sugar
1 teaspoon grated fresh ginger

1. Press the Sauté button on the Instant Pot and heat the sesame oil until shimmering.
2. Add the garlic and chicken and sauté for about 5 minutes, stirring occasionally, or until the garlic is lightly browned.
3. Fan the noodles across the bottom of the Instant Pot. Top with the broccoli florets, carrot, finished by snow peas.
4. Whisk together all the ingredients for the sauce in a medium bowl until the sugar is dissolved. Pour the sauce over the top of the vegetables.
5. Secure the lid. Select the Manual mode and set the cooking time for 5 minutes at High Pressure.
6. Once cooking is complete, do a quick pressure release. Carefully open the lid.
7. Stir the noodles, breaking up any clumps, or until the liquid has absorbed. Serve warm.

Browned Chicken with Veggies

Prep time: 10 minutes | Cook time: 25 minutes | Serves 4

2 tablespoons olive oil
1 yellow onion, chopped
2 chicken breasts, skinless, boneless and cubed
1 cup cubed mixed bell peppers
1 cup cubed tomato
1 cup chicken stock
1 teaspoon Creole seasoning
A pinch of cayenne pepper

1. Set your Instant Pot to Sauté and heat the olive oil until hot.
2. Add the onion and chicken cubes and brown for 5 minutes. Stir in the remaining ingredients.
3. Secure the lid. Select the poultry mode and set the cooking time for 20 minutes at High Pressure.
4. Once cooking is complete, do a natural pressure release for 10 minutes, then release any remaining pressure. Carefully open the lid.
5. Serve warm.

Bruschetta Chicken

Prep time: 5 minutes | Cook time: 20 minutes | Serves 2

2 boneless, skinless chicken breasts
½ cup filtered water
1 (14-ounce / 397-g) can sugar-free or low-sugar crushed tomatoes
¼ teaspoon dried basil
½ cup shredded full-fat Cheddar cheese
¼ cup heavy whipping cream

1. Combine all the ingredients except the cheese and whipping cream in the Instant Pot.
2. Secure the lid. Select the Manual mode and set the cooking time for 20 minutes at High Pressure.
3. Once cooking is complete, do a quick pressure release. Carefully open the lid.
4. Stir in the cheese and whipping cream until the cheese melts, and serve.

Chicken with Cheese Mushroom Sauce

Prep time: 8 minutes | Cook time: 14 minutes | Serves 4

2 tablespoons unsalted butter or coconut oil
2 cloves garlic, minced
¼ cup diced onions
2 cups sliced button or cremini mushrooms
4 boneless, skinless chicken breast halves
½ cup chicken broth
¼ cup heavy cream
1 teaspoon fine sea salt
1 teaspoon dried tarragon leaves
½ teaspoon dried thyme leaves
½ teaspoon ground black pepper
2 bay leaves
½ cup grated Parmesan cheese
Fresh thyme leaves, for garnish

1. Set your Instant Pot to Sauté and melt the butter.
2. Add the garlic, onions, and mushrooms and sauté for 4 minutes, stirring often, or until the onions are softened.
3. Add the remaining ingredients except the Parmesan cheese and thyme leaves to the Instant Pot and stir to combine.
4. Lock the lid. Select the Manual mode and set the cooking time for 10 minutes at High Pressure.
5. When the timer beeps, perform a natural pressure release for 10 minutes, then release any remaining pressure. Carefully remove the lid.
6. Discard the bay leaves and transfer the chicken to a serving platter.
7. Add the Parmesan cheese to the Instant Pot with the sauce and stir until the cheese melts.
8. Pour the mushroom sauce from the pot over the chicken. Serve garnished with the fresh thyme leaves.

Chicken with Pesto

Prep time: 5 minutes | Cook time: 25 minutes | Serves 2

2 (6-ounce / 170-g) boneless, skinless chicken breasts, butterflied
½ teaspoon salt
¼ teaspoon pepper
¼ teaspoon dried parsley
¼ teaspoon garlic powder
2 tablespoons coconut oil
1 cup water
¼ cup whole-milk ricotta cheese
¼ cup pesto
¼ cup shredded whole-milk Mozzarella cheese
Chopped parsley, for garnish (optional)

1. Sprinkle the chicken breasts with salt, pepper, parsley, and garlic powder.
2. Set your Instant Pot to Sauté and melt the coconut oil.
3. Add the chicken and brown for 3 to 5 minutes. Remove the chicken from the pot to a 7-cup glass bowl.
4. Pour the water into the Instant Pot and use a wooden spoon or rubber spatula to make sure no seasoning is stuck to bottom of pot.
5. Scatter the ricotta cheese on top of the chicken. Pour the pesto over chicken, and sprinkle the Mozzarella cheese over chicken. Cover with aluminum foil. Add the trivet to the Instant Pot and place the bowl on the trivet.
6. Secure the lid. Select the Manual mode and set the cooking time for 20 minutes at High Pressure.
7. Once cooking is complete, do a natural pressure release for 10 minutes, then release any remaining pressure. Carefully open the lid.
8. Serve the chicken garnished with the chopped parsley, if desired.

Garlic Chicken

Prep time: 10 minutes | Cook time: 20 minutes | Serves 4

2 chicken breasts, skinless, boneless and halved
1 cup tomato sauce
¼ cup sweet chili sauce
¼ cup chicken stock
4 garlic cloves, minced
1 tablespoon chopped basil

1. Combine all the ingredients in the Instant Pot.
2. Secure the lid. Select the Poultry mode and set the cooking time for 20 minutes at High Pressure.
3. Once cooking is complete, do a natural pressure release for 10 minutes, then release any remaining pressure. Carefully open the lid.
4. Divide the chicken breasts among four plates and serve.

Chicken with Jalapeño

Prep time: 15 mins, Cook Time: 12 mins, Servings: 3

1 lb. boneless chicken breast
3 jalapeños, sliced
8 oz. Cheddar cheese
¾ cup sour cream
8 oz. cream cheese
Salt and pepper, to taste
½ cup water

1. Add ½ cup water, cream cheese, jalapeños, chicken breast, salt, and pepper to the pot. Stir to combine well.
2. Lock the lid. Select the Manual mode and set the cooking time for 12 minutes at High Pressure.
3. Once cooking is complete, do a natural pressure release for 8 minutes, then release any remaining pressure. Carefully open the lid.
4. Mix in the sour cream and Cheddar cheese, and serve warm!

Ginger Chicken Congee

Prep time: 12 mins, Cook Time: 25 mins, Servings: 4

2 cups rice
8 medium chicken breasts
4 cups water

4-inch minced ginger piece
1 chicken stock cube
Salt and pepper, to taste

1.Add the rice, water, chicken breasts, chicken stock, and ginger to the Instant Pot. Season with salt and pepper.
2.Lock the lid. Select the Poultry mode and set the cooking time for 25 minutes at High Pressure.
3.Once cooking is complete, do a natural pressure release for 10 minutes, then release any remaining pressure. Carefully open the lid. Serve warm.

Chicken Pasta Puttanesca

Prep time: 10 minutes | Cook time: 9 minutes | Serves 4

2 (6- to 7-ounce / 170- to 198-g) boneless, skinless chicken breasts
Salt and freshly ground black pepper, to taste
2 tablespoons olive oil
12 ounces (340 g) dry penne pasta
1 (14.5-ounce / 411-g) can diced tomatoes with Italian

herbs, with juices
2½ cups store-bought chicken or vegetable broth, or homemade
4 oil-packed rolled anchovies with capers, plus 1 tablespoon oil from the jar
½ cup oil-cured black or Kalamata olives
Pinch of red pepper flakes

1.Using paper towels, pat the chicken dry. Sprinkle with the salt and pepper.
2.Press the Sauté button on your Instant Pot. Add and heat the oil.
3.Add the chicken and cook for 3 minutes, or until the chicken is nicely browned on one side.
4.Stir in the penne, tomatoes, broth, anchovies and oil, olives, red pepper flakes, and pepper. Place the chicken on top.
5.Secure the lid. Select the Manual mode and set the cooking time for 6 minutes on Low Pressure.
6.When the timer beeps, do a quick pressure release. Carefully open the lid.
7.Remove the chicken from the Instant Pot to a cutting board and cut into bite-size pieces. Transfer the chicken back to the pot and stir until well mixed.
8.Lock the lid and let sit for 5 minutes, or until the liquid is thickened.
9.Serve immediately.

Chicken with Cilantro

Prep time: 5 minutes | Cook time: 25 minutes | Serves 4

2 chicken breasts, skinless, boneless and halved
1 cup tomato sauce
1 cup plain Greek yogurt
¾ cup coconut cream

¼ cup chopped cilantro
2 teaspoons garam masala
2 teaspoons ground cumin
A pinch of salt and black pepper

1.Thoroughly combine all the ingredients in the Instant Pot.
2.Lock the lid. Select the Poultry mode and set the cooking time for 25 minutes at High Pressure.
3.Once cooking is complete, do a natural pressure release for 5 minutes, then release any remaining pressure. Carefully open the lid.
4.Transfer the chicken breasts to a plate and serve.

Chicken Fajita Bowls

Prep time: 5 minutes | Cook time: 10 minutes | Serves 2

1 pound (454 g) boneless, skinless chicken breasts, cut into 1-inch pieces
2 cups chicken broth
1 cup salsa
1 teaspoon paprika
1 teaspoon fine sea salt, or

more to taste
1 teaspoon chili powder
½ teaspoon ground cumin
½ teaspoon ground black pepper
1 lime, halved

1.Combine all the ingredients except the lime in the Instant Pot.
2.Lock the lid. Select the Manual mode and set the cooking time for 10 minutes at High Pressure.
3.When the timer beeps, perform a quick pressure release. Carefully remove the lid.
4.Shred the chicken with two forks and return to the Instant Pot. Squeeze the lime juice into the chicken mixture. Taste and add more salt, if needed. Give the mixture a good stir.
5.Ladle the chicken mixture into bowls and serve.

Buffalo Wings

Prep time: 5 minutes | Cook time: 12 minutes | Serves 4

2 pounds (907 g) chicken wings, patted dry
1 teaspoon seasoned salt
¼ teaspoon pepper
½ teaspoon garlic powder

¼ cup buffalo sauce
¾ cup chicken broth
⅓ cup blue cheese crumbles
¼ cup cooked bacon crumbles
2 stalks green onion, sliced

1.Season the chicken wings with salt, pepper, and garlic powder.
2.Pour the buffalo sauce and broth into the Instant Pot. Stir in the chicken wings.
3.Lock the lid. Select the Manual mode and set the cooking time for 12 minutes at High Pressure.
4.Once cooking is complete, do a quick pressure release. Carefully open the lid. Gently stir to coat wings with the sauce.
5.If you prefer crispier wings, you can broil them for 3 to 5 minutes until the skin is crispy.
6.Remove the chicken wings from the pot to a plate. Brush them with the leftover sauce and serve topped with the blue cheese, bacon, and green onions.

Chicken with Black Bean

Prep time: 10 minutes | Cook time: 8 minutes | Serves 8

1½ pounds (680 g) boneless, skinless chicken breasts
1 medium green pepper, chopped
1 medium sweet red pepper, chopped

2 (16-ounce /454-g) jars black bean and corn salsa
1 (12-ounce / 340-g) package tortilla chips
2 cups shredded Mexican cheese blend

1.Add the chicken, peppers, and salsa to your Instant Pot.
2.Secure the lid. Press the Manual button on the Instant Pot and set the cooking time for 8 minutes on High Pressure.
3.Once cooking is complete, use a natural pressure release for 7 minutes and then release any remaining pressure. Carefully open the lid.
4.Remove the chicken from the pot to a plate and shred with two forks.
5.Transfer the chicken back to the Instant Pot and stir to combine.
6.Serve the chicken over chips with a slotted spoon. Scatter the cheese on top.

Butter-Parmesan Wings

Prep time: 5 minutes | Cook time: 12 minutes | Serves 4

2 pounds (907 g) chicken wings, patted dry
1 teaspoon seasoned salt
½ teaspoon garlic powder
½ teaspoon pepper

1 cup water
3 tablespoons butter
1 teaspoon lemon pepper
¼ cup grated Parmesan cheese

1. Season the chicken wings with the salt, garlic powder, and pepper.
2. Pour the water into the Instant Pot and insert the trivet. Arrange the wings on the trivet.
3. Secure the lid. Select the Manual mode and set the cooking time for 10 minutes at High Pressure.
4. Once cooking is complete, do a quick pressure release. Carefully open the lid.
5. Remove the chicken wings and set aside on a plate.
6. For crispy wings, you can place them on a foil-lined baking sheet and broil for 3 to 5 minutes, or until the skin is crispy.
7. Pour the water out of the Instant Pot. Set your Instant Pot to Sauté and melt the butter.
8. Stir in the lemon pepper and return the wings to the pot, tossing to coat. Scatter with the cheese and serve warm.

Cashew Chicken

Prep time: 3 minutes | Cook time: 15 minutes | Serves 6

2 pounds (907 g) chicken thighs, bones, and skin removed
¼ cup soy sauce
¼ teaspoon black pepper
2 tablespoons ketchup
2 tablespoons rice vinegar
1 clove of garlic, minced

1 tablespoon brown sugar
1 teaspoon grated ginger
1 tablespoon cornstarch + 2 tablespoons water
⅓ cup cashew nuts, toasted
2 tablespoons sesame seeds, toasted
¼ cup green onions, chopped

1. Add all the ingredients except for the cashew nuts, sesame seeds, cornstarch slurry, and green onions to the Instant Pot and stir to combine.
2. Secure the lid. Select the Manual mode and cook for 15 minutes on High Pressure.
3. Once cooking is complete, use a quick pressure release. Carefully open the lid.
4. Select the Sauté mode and stir in the cornstarch slurry. Let simmer until the sauce is thickened.
5. Stir in the cashew nuts, sesame seeds, and green onions.
6. Transfer to a serving dish and serve immediately.

Chicken with Artichokes and Bacon

Prep time: 10 mins, Cook Time: 25 mins, Servings:4

2 chicken breasts, skinless, boneless, and halved
2 cups canned artichokes, drained, and chopped
1 cup bacon, cooked and

crumbled
1 cup water
2 tbsps. tomato paste
1 tbsp. chives, chopped
Salt, to taste

1. Mix all the ingredients in your Instant Pot until well combined.
2. Lock the lid. Select the Poultry mode and set the cooking time for 25 minutes at High Pressure.
3. Once cooking is complete, do a natural pressure release for 10 minutes, then release any remaining pressure. Carefully open the lid.
4. Remove from the pot to a large plate and serve.

Cashew Chicken with Sautéed Vegetables

Prep time: 15 mins, Cook time: 20 mins, Servings: 6

2 lbs. chicken breasts, thinly sliced
Salt and pepper, to taste
1 head broccoli florets

1 cup cubed red bell pepper
1 cup cashew nuts, toasted
½ cup water

1. Press the Sauté button on the Instant Pot. Stir in the chicken breasts and cook for 5 minutes. Sprinkle pepper and salt for seasoning. Pour in ½ cup water for additional moisture.
2. Press the Poultry button and set the cooking time for 10 minutes at High Pressure.
3. Once cooking is complete, do a quick pressure release. Carefully open the lid. Transfer the chicken breast to a large plate.
4. Press the Sauté button and stir in the broccoli and red bell pepper. Allow to simmer for 5 minutes. Scatter the toasted cashew nuts over the vegetables.
5. Serve the chicken breasts with sautéed vegetables on the side.

Double-Cheesy Drumsticks

Prep time: 3 minutes | Cook time: 23 minutes | Serves 5

1 tablespoon olive oil
5 chicken drumsticks
½ cup chicken stock
¼ cup unsweetened coconut milk
¼ cup dry white wine
2 garlic cloves, minced
1 teaspoon shallot powder
½ teaspoon marjoram

½ teaspoon thyme
6 ounces (170 g) ricotta cheese
4 ounces (113 g) Cheddar cheese
½ teaspoon cayenne pepper
¼ teaspoon ground black pepper
Sea salt, to taste

1. Set your Instant Pot to Sauté and heat the olive oil until sizzling.
2. Add the chicken drumsticks and brown each side for 3 minutes.
3. Stir in the chicken stock, milk, wine, garlic, shallot powder, marjoram, thyme.
4. Lock the lid. Select the Manual mode and set the cooking time for 15 minutes at High Pressure.
5. When the timer beeps, perform a natural pressure release for 10 minutes, then release any remaining pressure. Carefully remove the lid.
6. Shred the chicken with two forks and return to the Instant Pot.
7. Set your Instant Pot to Sauté again and add the remaining ingredients and stir well.
8. Cook for another 2 minutes, or until the cheese is melted. Taste and add more salt, if desired. Serve immediately.

Lemon Garlic Chicken

Prep time: 1 hour 20 mins, Cook time: 12 mins, Servings: 6

3 tbsps. olive oil, divided
2 tsps. dried parsley
6 chicken breasts

3 minced garlic cloves
1 tbsp. lemon juice
Salt and pepper, to taste

1. Mix together 2 tablespoons olive oil, chicken breasts, parsley, garlic cloves, and lemon juice in a large bowl. Place in the refrigerator to marinate for 1 hour.
2. Press the Sauté button on the Instant Pot and heat the remaining olive oil.
3. Cook the chicken breasts for 5 to 6 minutes per side until cooked through.
4. Allow to cool for 5 minutes before serving.

Bacon and Chicken Ranch Casserole
Prep time: 5 minutes | Cook time: 30 minutes | Serves 4

4 slices bacon
4 (6-ounce / 170-g) boneless, skinless chicken breasts, cut into 1-inch cubes
½ teaspoon salt
¼ teaspoon pepper
1 tablespoon coconut oil
½ cup chicken broth
½ cup ranch dressing
½ cup shredded Cheddar cheese
2 ounces (57 g) cream cheese

1. Press the Sauté button to heat your Instant Pot.
2. Add the bacon slices and cook for about 7 minutes until crisp, flipping occasionally.
3. Remove from the pot and place on a paper towel to drain. Set aside.
4. Season the chicken cubes with salt and pepper.
5. Set your Instant Pot to Sauté and melt the coconut oil.
6. Add the chicken cubes and brown for 3 to 4 minutes until golden brown.
7. Stir in the broth and ranch dressing.
8. Secure the lid. Select the Manual mode and set the cooking time for 20 minutes at High Pressure.
9. Once cooking is complete, do a quick pressure release. Carefully open the lid.
10. Stir in the Cheddar and cream cheese. Crumble the cooked bacon and scatter on top. Serve immediately.

Broccoli and Chicken Rice Bowl
Prep time: 5 minutes | Cook time: 10 minutes | Serves 4

Cooking spray
2 boneless, skinless chicken breasts, cut into 1-inch pieces
4 cups broccoli florets
4 cups low-sodium chicken broth
1 cup long-grain white rice
½ teaspoon fine sea salt
¼ teaspoon ground black pepper
1½ cups shredded Cheddar cheese

1. Spitz the inner pot of your Instant Pot with cooking spray. Add the chicken, broccoli, broth, rice, salt, and pepper.
2. Secure the lid. Press the Manual button and set the cooking time for 10 minutes on High Pressure.
3. Once cooking is complete, do a quick pressure release. Carefully open the lid.
4. Add the cheese and stir until melted.
5. Serve immediately.

Super Garlicky Chicken
Prep time: 5 minutes | Cook time: 20 minutes | Serves 6

1 tablespoon butter
1 tablespoon olive oil
2 chicken breasts, bone and skin not removed
4 chicken thighs, bone and skin not removed
Salt and pepper, to taste
40 cloves of garlic, peeled and sliced
2 sprigs of thyme
¼ cup chicken broth
¼ cup dry white wine
Parsley, for garnish

1. Set your Instant Pot to Sauté. Add the butter and oil.
2. Fold in the chicken pieces and stir well. Sprinkle with the salt and pepper.
3. Mix in the garlic cloves and sauté for an additional 5 minutes until fragrant.
4. Add the thyme, chicken broth, and white wine. Stir well.
5. Secure the lid. Select the Manual mode and set the cooking time for 15 minutes on High Pressure.
6. Once cooking is complete, use a quick pressure release. Carefully open the lid.
7. Transfer to a serving dish and serve garnished with parsley.

Lime-Chili Chicken
Prep time: 12 mins, Cook time: 6 mins, Servings:5

6 garlic cloves, minced
1 tbsp. chili powder
1 tsp. cumin
1 lb. skinless and boneless
chicken breasts
1 ½ limes, juiced
1 cup water

1. In the Instant Pot, add the chicken breasts, garlic, chili powder, cumin, lime juice, salt, pepper, and water.
2. Lock the lid. Select the Manual mode and cook for 6 minutes at High Pressure.
3. Once cooking is complete, do a natural pressure release for 5 minutes, then release any remaining pressure. Carefully open the lid.
4. Cool for 5 minutes and serve warm.

Mixed Greens and Chicken Salad
Prep time: 5 minutes | Cook time: 20 minutes | Serves 4

Chicken:
2 tablespoons avocado oil
1 pound (454 g) chicken breast, cubed
½ cup filtered water
½ teaspoon ground turmeric
½ teaspoon dried parsley
½ teaspoon dried basil
½ teaspoon kosher salt
½ teaspoon freshly ground black pepper
Salad:
1 avocado, mashed
1 cup chopped arugula
1 cup chopped Swiss chard
1 cup chopped kale
½ cup chopped spinach
2 tablespoons pine nuts, toasted

1. Combine all the chicken ingredients in the Instant Pot.
2. Secure the lid. Select the Manual mode and set the cooking time for 20 minutes at High Pressure.
3. Meanwhile, toss all the salad ingredients in a large salad bowl.
4. Once cooking is complete, do a quick pressure release. Carefully open the lid.
5. Remove the chicken to the salad bowl and serve.

Chicken Liver Pâté
Prep time: 5 minutes | Cook time: 15 minutes | Serves 8

2 tablespoons olive oil
1 pound (454 g) chicken livers
2 garlic cloves, crushed
½ cup chopped leeks
1 tablespoon poultry seasonings
1 teaspoon dried rosemary
½ teaspoon paprika
½ teaspoon dried marjoram
½ teaspoon red pepper flakes
½ teaspoon ground black pepper
¼ teaspoon dried dill weed
Salt, to taste
1 cup water
1 tablespoon stone ground mustard

1. Set your Instant Pot to Sauté and heat the olive oil.
2. Add the chicken livers and sauté for about 3 minutes until no longer pink.
3. Add the remaining ingredients except the mustard to the Instant Pot and stir to combine.
4. Lock the lid. Select the Manual mode and set the cooking time for 10 minutes at High Pressure.
5. When the timer beeps, perform a quick pressure release. Carefully remove the lid.
6. Transfer the cooked mixture to a food processor, along with the mustard. Pulse until the mixture is smooth. Serve immediately.

Pea and Chicken Casserole

Prep time: 10 minutes | Cook time: 30 minutes | Serves 4

2 pounds (907 g) chicken breast, skinless, boneless and cubed
1 cup veggie stock
1 cup peas
1 tablespoon Italian seasoning

1 tablespoon sweet paprika
A pinch of salt and black pepper
1 cup coconut cream
1 cup shredded Cheddar cheese

1. Stir together the chicken cubes, veggie stock, peas, Italian seasoning, paprika, salt, and pepper in the Instant Pot. Pour the coconut cream over top.
2. Secure the lid. Select the Poultry mode and set the cooking time for 20 minutes at High Pressure.
3. Once cooking is complete, do a quick pressure release. Remove the lid.
4. Scatter the shredded cheese all over. Put the lid back on and cook on High Pressure for an additional 10 minutes.
5. Once cooking is complete, do a quick pressure release. Carefully open the lid.
6. Serve warm.

Chicken Cacciatore

Prep time: 5 minutes | Cook time: 22 minutes | Serves 4 to 5

6 tablespoons coconut oil
5 chicken legs
1 bell pepper, diced
½ onion, chopped
1 (14-ounce / 397-g) can sugar-free or low-sugar diced tomatoes

½ teaspoon dried basil
½ teaspoon dried parsley
½ teaspoon kosher salt
½ teaspoon freshly ground black pepper
½ cup filtered water

1. Press the Sauté button on the Instant Pot and melt the coconut oil.
2. Add the chicken legs and sauté until the outside is browned.
3. Remove the chicken and set aside.
4. Add the bell pepper, onion, tomatoes, basil, parsley, salt, and pepper to the Instant Pot and cook for about 2 minutes.
5. Pour in the water and return the chicken to the pot.
6. Lock the lid. Select the Manual mode and set the cooking time for 18 minutes at High Pressure.
7. Once cooking is complete, do a quick pressure release. Carefully open the lid. Serve warm.

Chicken Curry

Prep time: 6 mins, Cook time: 15 mins, Servings: 6

2 cups freshly squeezed coconut milk
1½ lbs. boneless chicken breasts

2 cups chopped tomatoes
2 tbsps. curry powder
1 ginger
Salt and pepper, to taste

1. Press the Sauté button on the Instant Pot. Add the chicken breasts and cook for 3 minutes until lightly golden. Season with salt and pepper.
2. Stir in the curry powder and continue cooking for 2 minutes more. Add the remaining ingredients and whisk well.
3. Press the Poultry button and set the cooking time for 10 minutes.
4. Once cooking is complete, do a natural pressure release for 6 minutes, then release any remaining pressure. Carefully open the lid.
5. Cool for 5 minutes and serve on plates.

Chicken with Cheese Sauce

Prep time: 5 minutes | Cook time: 10 minutes | Serves 4

1 tablespoon olive oil
1 pound (454 g) chicken fillets
½ teaspoon dried basil
Cheese Sauce:
3 teaspoons butter, at room temperature
⅓ cup grated Gruyère cheese
⅓ cup Neufchâtel cheese, at room temperature

Salt and freshly ground black pepper, to taste
1 cup chicken broth

⅓ cup heavy cream
3 tablespoons unsweetened coconut milk
1 teaspoon shallot powder
½ teaspoon granulated garlic

1. Set your Instant Pot to Sauté and heat the olive oil until sizzling.
2. Add the chicken and sear each side for 3 minutes. Sprinkle with the basil, salt, and black pepper.
3. Pour the broth into the Instant Pot and stir well.
4. Lock the lid. Select the Manual mode and set the cooking time for 6 minutes at High Pressure.
5. When the timer beeps, perform a natural pressure release for 10 minutes, then release any remaining pressure. Carefully remove the lid.
6. Transfer the chicken to a platter and set aside.
7. Clean the Instant Pot. Press the Sauté button and melt the butter.
8. Add the cheeses, heavy cream, milk, shallot powder, and garlic, stirring until everything is heated through.
9. Pour the cheese sauce over the chicken and serve.

Crispy Wings

Prep time: 15 mins, Cook time: 15 mins, Servings: 8

1 tbsp. paprika
1 tsp. rosemary leaves
Salt and pepper, to taste

2 lbs. chicken wings
1 cup water

1. Put all the ingredients in the Instant Pot and stir well.
2. Lock the lid. Select the Manual mode and set the cooking time for 15 minutes at High Pressure.
3. Once cooking is complete, do a natural pressure release for 10 minutes, then release any remaining pressure. Carefully open the lid.
4. Transfer to a plate and serve.

Chili Chicken Zoodles

Prep time: 10 minutes | Cook time: 20 minutes | Serves 4

2 chicken breasts, skinless, boneless and halved
1½ cups chicken stock
3 celery stalks, chopped
1 tablespoon tomato sauce

1 teaspoon chili powder
A pinch of salt and black pepper
2 zucchinis, spiralized
1 tablespoon chopped cilantro

1. Mix together all the ingredients except the zucchini noodles and cilantro in the Instant Pot.
2. Secure the lid. Select the Manual mode and set the cooking time for 15 minutes at High Pressure.
3. Once cooking is complete, do a natural pressure release for 10 minutes, then release any remaining pressure. Carefully open the lid.
4. Set your Instant Pot to Sauté and add the zucchini noodles. Cook for about 5 minutes, stirring often, or until softened.
5. Sprinkle the cilantro on top for garnish before serving.

Chicken Tacos with Cheese Shells

Prep time: 5 minutes | Cook time: 25 minutes | Serves 6

Chicken:
4 (6-ounce / 170-g) boneless, skinless chicken breasts
1 cup chicken broth
1 teaspoon salt
¼ teaspoon pepper
1 tablespoon chili powder
2 teaspoons garlic powder
2 teaspoons cumin

Cheese Shells:
1½ cups shredded whole-milk Mozzarella cheese

1. Combine all ingredients for the chicken in the Instant Pot.
2. Secure the lid. Select the Manual mode and set the cooking time for 20 minutes at High Pressure.
3. Once cooking is complete, do a quick pressure release. Carefully open the lid.
4. Shred the chicken and serve in bowls or cheese shells.
5. Make the cheese shells: Heat a nonstick skillet over medium heat.
6. Sprinkle ¼ cup of Mozzarella cheese in the skillet and fry until golden. Flip and turn off the heat. Allow the cheese to get brown. Fill with chicken and fold. The cheese will harden as it cools. Repeat with the remaining cheese and filling.
7. Serve warm.

Chinese Steamed Chicken

Prep time: 6 mins, Coo time: 10 mins, Servings: 6

1 tsp. grated ginger
1½ lbs. chicken thighs
1 tbsp. five-spice powder
¼ cup soy sauce
3 tbsps. sesame oil
1 cup water
Salt and pepper, to taste

1. In the Instant Pot, stir in all the ingredients.
2. Lock the lid. Select the Poultry mode and set the cooking time for 10 minutes at High Pressure.
3. Once cooking is complete, do a natural pressure release for 7 minutes, then release any remaining pressure. Carefully open the lid.
4. Serve the chicken thighs while warm.

Chicken Verde with Green Chile

Prep time: 5 minutes | Cook time: 15 minutes | Serves 4

3 pounds (1.4 kg) bone-in, skin-on chicken drumsticks and/or thighs
1 (27-ounce / 765-g) can roasted poblano peppers, drained
1 (15-ounce / 425-g) jar salsa verde (green chile salsa)
1 (7-ounce / 198-g) jar chopped green chiles, drained
1 onion, chopped
1 tablespoon chopped jalapeño (optional)
1 tablespoon ground cumin
4 teaspoons minced garlic
1 teaspoon fine sea salt

1. Mix together all the ingredients in your Instant Pot and stir to combine.
2. Secure the lid. Press the Manual button and set the cooking time for 15 minutes on High Pressure.
3. Once the timer goes off, use a quick pressure release. Carefully open the lid.
4. Remove the chicken from the Instant Pot to a plate with tongs. Let cool for 5 minutes.
5. Remove the bones and skin and discard. Shred the chicken with two forks.
6. Transfer the chicken back to the sauce and stir to combine.
7. Serve immediately.

Creamy Chicken with Mushrooms

Prep time: 12 mins, Cook time: 13 mins, Servings: 6

4 garlic cloves, minced
1 onion, chopped
1 cup mushrooms, sliced
6 boneless chicken breasts,
halved
½ cup coconut milk
½ cup water

1. Press the Sauté button on the Instant Pot and stir in the chicken breasts.
2. Fold in the onions and garlic and sauté for at least 3 minutes until tender. Season with salt and pepper. Add the remaining ingredients to the Instant Pot and whisk well.
3. Lock the lid. Select the Poultry mode and cook for 8 minutes at High Pressure.
4. Once cooking is complete, do a natural pressure release for 5 minutes, then release any remaining pressure. Carefully open the lid.
5. Allow to cool for 5 minutes before serving.

Crispy Herbed Chicken

Prep time: 10 mins, Cook Time: 30 mins, Servings: 2 to 3

2 tbsps. butter, softened
½ head of garlic, crushed
1 thyme sprig, crushed
1 rosemary sprig, crushed
½ tbsp. paprika
Salt and ground black pepper, to taste
1½ lbs. whole chicken, patted dry
2 cups water

1. Mix together the butter, garlic, thyme, rosemary, paprika, salt, and pepper in a shallow dish, and stir to incorporate.
2. Slather the butter mixture all over the chicken until well coated. Add the water and chicken to the Instant Pot.
3. Lock the lid. Select the Manual mode and cook for 20 minutes at High Pressure.
4. Once cooking is complete, do a natural pressure release for 10 minutes, then release any remaining pressure. Carefully open the lid.
5. Remove the chicken from the pot and place it under the broiler for 10 minutes, or until the skin is just lightly crisped. Serve warm.

Curried Chicken Legs with Mustard

Prep time: 10 minutes | Cook time: 20 minutes | Serves 5

5 chicken legs, boneless, skin-on
2 garlic cloves, halved
Sea salt, to taste
½ teaspoon smoked paprika
¼ teaspoon ground black pepper
2 teaspoons olive oil
1 tablespoon yellow mustard
1 teaspoon curry paste
4 strips pancetta, chopped
1 shallot, peeled and chopped
1 cup vegetable broth

1. Rub the chicken legs with the garlic halves. Sprinkle with salt, paprika, and black pepper.
2. Set your Instant Pot to Sauté and heat the olive oil.
3. Add the chicken legs and brown for 4 to 5 minutes. Add a splash of chicken broth to deglaze the bottom of the pot.
4. Spread the chicken legs with mustard and curry paste.
5. Add the pancetta strips, shallot, and remaining vegetable broth to the Instant Pot.
6. Lock the lid. Select the Manual mode and set the cooking time for 14 minutes at High Pressure.
7. When the timer beeps, perform a natural pressure release for 10 minutes, then release any remaining pressure. Carefully remove the lid.
8. Serve warm.

Asian Chicken

Prep time: 12 mins, Cook time: 10 mins, Servings: 5

3 minced garlic cloves | breasts
¼ cup chicken broth | 3 tbsps. soy sauce
1½ lbs. boneless chicken | 1 tbsp. ginger slices

1. Place all ingredients in the Instant Pot. Give a good stir.
2. Lock the lid. Press the Poultry button and set the cooking time for 10 minutes.
3. Once cooking is complete, do a natural pressure release for 8 minutes, then release any remaining pressure. Carefully open the lid.
4. Garnish with chopped scallions and drizzle with sesame oil, if desired.

Kung Pao Chicken

Prep time: 5 minutes | Cook time: 17 minutes | Serves 5

2 tablespoons coconut oil | ½ teaspoon chili powder
1 pound (454 g) boneless, skinless chicken breasts, cubed | ½ teaspoon finely grated ginger
1 cup cashews, chopped | ½ teaspoon kosher salt
6 tablespoons hot sauce | ½ teaspoon freshly ground black pepper

1. Set the Instant Pot to Sauté and melt the coconut oil.
2. Add the remaining ingredients to the Instant Pot and mix well.
3. Secure the lid. Select the Manual mode and set the cooking time for 17 minutes at High Pressure.
4. Once cooking is complete, do a quick pressure release. Carefully open the lid.
5. Serve warm.

Chicken Legs with Mayo Sauce

Prep time: 5 minutes | Cook time: 20 minutes | Serves 4

4 chicken legs, bone-in, skinless | pepper flakes
2 garlic cloves, peeled and halved | ¼ teaspoon ground black pepper, or more to taste
½ teaspoon coarse sea salt | 1 tablespoon olive oil
½ teaspoon crushed red | ¼ cup chicken broth
Dipping Sauce:
¾ cup mayonnaise | 1 teaspoon fresh lemon juice
2 tablespoons stone ground mustard | ½ teaspoon Sriracha
For Garnish:
¼ cup roughly chopped fresh | cilantro

1. Rub the chicken legs with the garlic. Sprinkle with salt, red pepper flakes, and black pepper.
2. Set your Instant Pot to Sauté and heat the olive oil.
3. Add the chicken legs and brown for 4 to 5 minutes. Add a splash of chicken broth to deglaze the bottom of the pot.
4. Pour the remaining chicken broth into the Instant Pot and mix well.
5. Lock the lid. Select the Manual mode and set the cooking time for 14 minutes at High Pressure.
6. Meanwhile, whisk together all the sauce ingredients in a small bowl.
7. When the timer beeps, perform a natural pressure release for 10 minutes, then release any remaining pressure. Carefully remove the lid.
8. Sprinkle the cilantro on top for garnish and serve with the prepared dipping sauce.

Citrus Chicken Tacos

Prep time: 5 minutes | Cook time: 20 minutes | Serves 12

¼ cup olive oil | squeezed
12 chicken breasts, skin and bones removed | 2 tablespoons ground cumin
8 cloves of garlic, minced | 1 tablespoon dried oregano
⅔ cup orange juice, freshly squeezed | 1 tablespoon orange peel
⅔ cup lime juice, freshly | Salt and pepper, to taste
| ¼ cup cilantro, chopped

1. Set your Instant Pot to Sauté. Add and heat the oil.
2. Add the chicken breasts and garlic. Cook until the chicken pieces are lightly browned.
3. Add the orange juice, lime juice, cumin, oregano, orange peel, salt, and pepper. Stir well.
4. Secure the lid. Select the Poultry mode and cook for 15 minutes on High Pressure.
5. Once cooking is complete, do a quick pressure release. Carefully remove the lid.
6. Serve garnished with the cilantro.

Chicken Breasts with Cream Cheese

Prep time: 5 minutes | Cook time: 15 minutes | Serves 2

½ pound (227 g) boneless, skinless chicken breasts | friendly ranch dressing
2 ounces (57 g) cream cheese, softened | ½ cup shredded full-fat Cheddar cheese
½ cup grass-fed bone broth | 3 slices bacon, cooked and chopped into small pieces
¼ cup tablespoons keto-

1. Combine all the ingredients except the Cheddar cheese and bacon in the Instant Pot.
2. Secure the lid. Select the Manual mode and set the cooking time for 15 minutes at High Pressure.
3. Once cooking is complete, do a quick pressure release. Carefully open the lid.
4. Add the Cheddar cheese and bacon and stir well, then serve.

Chicken Wingettes with Cilantro Sauce

Prep time: 5 minutes | Cook time: 6 minutes | Serves 6

12 chicken wingettes | 1 teaspoon sea salt
10 fresh cayenne peppers, trimmed and chopped | 1 teaspoon onion powder
3 garlic cloves, minced | ½ teaspoon black pepper
1½ cups white vinegar | 2 tablespoons olive oil
Dipping Sauce:
½ cup sour cream | 2 cloves garlic, minced
½ cup mayonnaise | 1 teaspoon smoked paprika
½ cup cilantro, chopped

1. In a large bowl, toss the chicken wingettes, cayenne peppers, garlic, white vinegar, salt, onion powder, and black pepper. Cover and marinate for 1 hour in the refrigerator.
2. When ready, transfer the chicken wingettes to the Instant Pot, along with the marinade and olive oil.
3. Lock the lid. Select the Manual mode and set the cooking time for 6 minutes at High Pressure.
4. Meanwhile, thoroughly combine all the sauce ingredients in a mixing bowl.
5. When the timer beeps, perform a quick pressure release. Carefully remove the lid.
6. Serve the chicken warm alongside the dipping sauce.

Fennel Chicken
Prep time: 10 mins, Cook Time: 25 mins, Servings: 4

2 tbsps. olive oil
2 tbsps. grated ginger
2 chicken breasts, skinless, boneless and halved
1 cup chicken stock
2 fennel bulbs, sliced
1 tbsp. basil, chopped
A pinch of salt and black pepper

1. Set your Instant Pot to Sauté and heat the olive oil. Cook the ginger and chicken breasts for 5 minutes until evenly browned.
2. Add the remaining ingredients to the pot and mix well.
3. Lock the lid. Select the Poultry mode and cook for 20 minutes at High Pressure.
4. Once cooking is complete, do a natural pressure release for 10 minutes, then release any remaining pressure. Carefully open the lid.
5. Allow the chicken cool for 5 minutes before serving.

Filipino Chicken Adobo
Prep time: 3 mins, Cook Time: 30 mins, Servings:4

4 chicken legs
⅓ cup soy sauce
¼ cup white vinegar
¼ cup sugar
5 cloves garlic, crushed
2 bay leaves
1 onion, chopped
Salt and pepper, to taste

1. Add all the ingredients to your Instant Pot and stir to combine well.
2. Lock the lid. Select the Poultry mode and cook for 30 minutes at High Pressure.
3. Once cooking is complete, do a natural pressure release for 10 minutes, then release any remaining pressure. Carefully open the lid.
4. Divide the chicken legs among four plates and serve warm.

Indian Butter Chicken
Prep time: 10 minutes | Cook time: 15 minutes | Serves 4

3 tablespoons butter or ghee, at room temperature, divided
1 medium yellow onion, halved and sliced through the root end
1 (10-ounce / 284-g) can Ro-Tel tomatoes with green chilies, with juice
2 tablespoons mild Indian curry
paste
1½ pounds (680 g) boneless, skinless chicken thighs, fat trimmed, cut into 2- to 3-inch pieces
2 tablespoons all-purpose flour
Salt and freshly ground black pepper, to taste

1. Add 1 tablespoon of the butter in the Instant Pot and select the Sauté mode. Add the onion and sauté for 6 minutes until browned.
2. Stir in the tomatoes and scrape any browned bits from the pot. Add the curry paste and stir well. Fold in the chicken and stir to coat.
3. Secure the lid. Press the Manual button on the Instant Pot and cook for 8 minutes on High Pressure.
4. Once cooking is complete, use a quick pressure release.
5. Combine the remaining 2 tablespoons of butter and the flour in a small bowl and stir until smooth.
6. Select the Sauté mode. Add the flour mixture to the chicken in two additions, stirring between additions. Sauté for 1 minute, or until the sauce is thickened.
7. Sprinkle with the salt and pepper and serve.

Honey-Glazed Chicken with Sesame
Prep time: 5 minutes | Cook time: 25 minutes | Serves 6

1 tablespoon olive oil
2 cloves garlic, minced
½ cup diced onions
4 large boneless, skinless chicken breasts
Salt and pepper, to taste
½ cup soy sauce
½ cup honey
¼ cup ketchup
2 teaspoons sesame oil
¼ teaspoon red pepper flakes
2 green onions, chopped
1 tablespoon sesame seeds, toasted

1. Press the Sauté button on the Instant Pot and heat the olive oil.
2. Add the garlic and onions and sauté for about 3 minutes until fragrant.
3. Add the chicken breasts and sprinkle with the salt and pepper. Brown each side for 3 minutes.
4. Stir in the soy sauce, honey, ketchup, sesame oil, and red pepper flakes.
5. Secure the lid. Select the Poultry mode and set the cooking time for 20 minutes at High Pressure.
6. Once cooking is complete, do a natural pressure release for 10 minutes, then release any remaining pressure. Carefully open the lid.
7. Sprinkle the onions and sesame seeds on top for garnish before serving.

Huli Huli Chicken
Prep time: 5 minutes | Cook time: 10 minutes | Serves 8

1 cup crushed pineapple, drained
⅓ cup reduced-sodium soy sauce
¾ cup ketchup
3 tablespoons lime juice
3 tablespoons packed brown sugar
1 garlic clove, minced
8 boneless, skinless chicken thighs, about 2 pounds (907 g)
Hot cooked rice, for serving

1. Mix together the pineapple, soy sauce, ketchup, lime juice, sugar, and clove in a mixing bowl.
2. Add the chicken to your Instant Pot and place the mixture on top.
3. Secure the lid. Press the Manual button on the Instant Pot and set the cooking time for 10 minutes at High Pressure.
4. Once cooking is complete, use a natural pressure release for 5 minutes and then release any remaining pressure. Carefully open the lid.
5. Serve with the cooked rice.

Bruschetta Chicken
Prep time: 5 minutes | Cook time: 20 minutes | Serves 2

½ cup filtered water
2 boneless, skinless chicken breasts
1 (14-ounce / 397-g) can sugar-free or low-sugar
crushed tomatoes
¼ teaspoon dried basil
½ cup shredded full-fat Cheddar cheese
¼ cup heavy whipping cream

1. Add the filtered water, chicken breasts, tomatoes, and basil to your Instant Pot.
2. Lock the lid. Press the Manual button and set the cooking time for 20 minutes on High Pressure.
3. Once cooking is complete, use a quick pressure release. Carefully open the lid.
4. Fold in the cheese and cream and stir until the cheese is melted.
5. Serve immediately.

Chicken Piccata

Prep time: 5 minutes | Cook time: 25 minutes | Serves 4

4 (6-ounce / 170-g) boneless, skinless chicken breasts
½ teaspoon salt
½ teaspoon garlic powder
¼ teaspoon pepper
2 tablespoons coconut oil
1 cup water
2 cloves garlic, minced
4 tablespoons butter
Juice of 1 lemon
¼ teaspoon xanthan gum

1. Sprinkle the chicken with salt, garlic powder, and pepper.
2. Set your Instant Pot to Sauté and melt the coconut oil.
3. Add the chicken and sear each side for about 5 to 7 minutes until golden brown.
4. Remove the chicken and set aside on a plate.
5. Pour the water into the Instant Pot. Using a wooden spoon, scrape the bottom if necessary to remove any stuck-on seasoning or meat. Insert the trivet and place the chicken on the trivet.
6. Secure the lid. Select the Manual mode and set the cooking time for 10 minutes at High Pressure.
7. Once cooking is complete, do a natural pressure release for 10 minutes, then release any remaining pressure. Carefully open the lid.
8. Remove the chicken and set aside. Strain the broth from the Instant Pot into a large bowl and return to the pot.
9. Set your Instant Pot to Sauté again and add the remaining ingredients. Cook for at least 5 minutes, stirring frequently, or until the sauce is cooked to your desired thickness.
10. Pour the sauce over the chicken and serve warm.

Jamaican Curry Chicken Drumsticks

Prep time: 5 minutes | Cook time: 20 minutes | Serves 4

1½ pounds (680 g) chicken drumsticks
1 tablespoon Jamaican curry powder
1 teaspoon salt
1 cup chicken broth
½ medium onion, diced
½ teaspoon dried thyme

1. Sprinkle the salt and curry powder over the chicken drumsticks.
2. Place the chicken drumsticks into the Instant Pot, along with the remaining ingredients.
3. Secure the lid. Select the Manual mode and set the cooking time for 20 minutes at High Pressure.
4. Once cooking is complete, do a quick pressure release. Carefully open the lid. Serve warm.

Mexican Shredded Chicken

Prep time: 12 mins, Cook time: 18 mins, Servings: 4

½ tsp. paprika
3 lbs. chicken breasts
½ tsp. dried oregano
1 tbsp. chili powder
¼ tsp. cumin powder
Salt and pepper, to taste
2 cups water

1. Place all ingredients in the Instant Pot and whisk well.
2. Lock the lid. Select the Poultry mode and set the cooking time for 18 minutes at High Pressure.
3. Once cooking is complete, do a natural pressure release for 12 minutes, then release any remaining pressure. Carefully open the lid.
4. Remove the chicken breasts from the pot and shred them. Serve immediately.

Chicken and Cranberry Salad

Prep time: 10 minutes | Cook time: 6 to 10 minutes | Serves 2

1 pound (454 g) skinless, boneless chicken breasts
½ cup water
2 teaspoons kosher salt, plus more for seasoning
½ cup mayonnaise
1 celery stalk, diced
2 tablespoons diced red onion
½ cup chopped dried
cranberries
¼ cup chopped walnuts
1 tablespoon freshly squeezed lime juice
¼ shredded unpeeled organic green apple
Freshly ground black pepper, to taste

1. Add the chicken, water, and 2 teaspoons of salt to your Instant Pot.
2. Lock the lid. Press the Poultry button on the Instant Pot and cook for 6 minutes on High Pressure.
3. Once cooking is complete, use a natural pressure release for 5 minutes and then release any remaining pressure. Carefully open the lid.
4. Remove the chicken from the Instant Pot to a cutting board and let sit for 5 to 10 minutes.
5. Shred the meat, transfer to a bowl, and add ¼ cup of the cooking liquid.
6. Mix in the mayonnaise and stir until well coated. Add the celery, onion, cranberries, walnuts, lime juice, and apple. Sprinkle with the salt and pepper.
7. Serve immediately.

Chicken and Spinach Stew

Prep time: 13 mins, Cook time: 10 mins, Servings: 6

1 ginger, sliced
3 garlic cloves, minced
2 cups spinach leaves
1 cup chopped tomatoes
1 lb. chicken breasts
1 cup water
Salt and pepper, to taste

1. Press the Sauté button on the Instant Pot and add the chicken and garlic. Stir-fry for 3 minutes until the garlic becomes fragrant.
2. Add the ginger, tomatoes, spinach, and water. Season with salt and pepper.
3. Lock the lid. Select the Manual mode and set the cooking time for 6 minutes at High Pressure.
4. Once cooking is complete, do a natural pressure release for 5 minutes, then release any remaining pressure. Carefully open the lid.
5. Cool for a few minutes and serve warm.

Chicken and Eggplant Sauté

Prep time: 6 mins, Cook time: 10 mins, Servings: 6

3 eggplants, sliced
1 tbsp. coconut oil
1 tsp. red pepper flakes
1 lb. ground chicken
Salt and pepper, to taste

1. Press the Sauté button on the Instant Pot and heat the coconut oil.
2. Stir in the ground chicken and cook for 3 minutes until lightly golden.
3. Add the remaining ingredients and stir to combine.
4. Lock the lid. Select the Poultry mode and set the cooking time for 6 minutes at High Pressure.
5. Once cooking is complete, do a quick pressure release. Carefully open the lid.
6. Transfer to a large plate and serve warm.

Instant Pot Ranch Chicken

Prep time: 5 minutes | Cook time: 20 minutes | Serves 6

1 teaspoon salt
½ teaspoon garlic powder
¼ teaspoon pepper
¼ teaspoon dried oregano
3 (6-ounce / 170-g) skinless chicken breasts

1 stick butter
8 ounces (227 g) cream cheese
1 dry ranch packet
1 cup chicken broth

1. In a small bowl, combine the salt, garlic powder, pepper, and oregano. Rub this mixture over both sides of chicken breasts.
2. Place the chicken breasts into the Instant Pot, along with the butter, cream cheese, ranch seasoning, and chicken broth.
3. Secure the lid. Select the Manual mode and set the cooking time for 20 minutes at High Pressure.
4. Once cooking is complete, do a natural pressure release for 10 minutes, then release any remaining pressure. Carefully open the lid.
5. Remove the chicken and shred with two forks, then return to the Instant Pot. Use a rubber spatula to stir and serve on a plate.

Lemony Fennel Chicken

Prep time: 12 mins, Cook time: 12 mins, Servings: 8

3 tbsps. freshly squeezed lemon juice
1 tsp. cinnamon
¼ cup fennel bulb
4 garlic cloves, minced

2 lbs. boneless and skinless chicken thighs
Salt and pepper, to taste
½ cup water

1. Place lemon juice, cinnamon, fennel bulb, garlic, and chicken thighs in the Instant Pot. Sprinkle pepper and salt for seasoning. Add ½ cup of water for moisture.
2. Lock the lid. Select the Manual mode and cook for 12 minutes at High Pressure.
3. Once cooking is complete, do a natural pressure release for 8 minutes, then release any remaining pressure. Carefully open the lid.
4. Remove the chicken from the pot and shred it, then serve.

Whole Roasted Chicken with Lemon and Rosemary

Prep time: 2 hours, Cook time: 25 to 30 mins, Servings: 12

1 (5 to 6 pounds) whole chicken
6 minced garlic cloves
Salt and pepper, to taste

1 sliced lemon
1 rosemary sprig
1 cup water or chicken broth

1. On a clean work surface, rub the chicken with the minced garlic cloves, salt and pepper.
2. Stuff the lemon slices and rosemary sprig into the cavity of the chicken. Place the chicken into the Instant Pot and add the water or chicken broth.
3. Lock the lid. Select the Poultry mode and cook for 25 to 30 minutes at High Pressure.
4. Once cooking is complete, do a natural pressure release for 15 minutes, then release any remaining pressure. Carefully open the lid.
5. Remove the chicken from the pot and shred it. Serve immediately.

Chicken Enchilada Bowl

Prep time: 10 minutes | Cook time: 35 minutes | Serves 4

2 (6-ounce / 170-g) boneless, skinless chicken breasts
2 teaspoons chili powder
½ teaspoon garlic powder
½ teaspoon salt
¼ teaspoon pepper
2 tablespoons coconut oil
¾ cup red enchilada sauce
¼ cup chicken broth

1 (4-ounce / 113-g) can green chilies
¼ cup diced onion
2 cups cooked cauliflower rice
1 avocado, diced
½ cup sour cream
1 cup shredded Cheddar cheese

1. Sprinkle the chili powder, garlic powder, salt, and pepper on chicken breasts.
2. Set your Instant Pot to Sauté and melt the coconut oil. Add the chicken breasts and sear each side for about 5 minutes until golden brown.
3. Pour the enchilada sauce and broth over the chicken. Using a wooden spoon or rubber spatula, scrape the bottom of pot to make sure nothing is sticking. Stir in the chilies and onion.
4. Secure the lid. Select the Manual mode and set the cooking time for 25 minutes at High Pressure.
5. Once cooking is complete, do a quick pressure release. Carefully open the lid.
6. Remove the chicken and shred with two forks. Serve the chicken over the cauliflower rice and place the avocado, sour cream, and Cheddar cheese on top.

Lemony Chicken With Potatoes

Prep time: 5 minutes | Cook time: 21 minutes | Serves 4

2 pounds (907 g) chicken thighs
1 teaspoon fine sea salt
½ teaspoon ground black pepper
2 tablespoons olive oil
¼ cup freshly squeezed lemon juice

¾ cup low-sodium chicken broth
2 tablespoons Italian seasoning
2 to 3 tablespoons Dijon mustard
2 to 3 pounds (907 to 1361 g) red potatoes, quartered

1. Sprinkle the chicken with the salt and pepper.
2. Add the oil to your Instant Pot. Select the Sauté mode. Add the chicken and sauté for 3 minutes until browned on both sides.
3. Meanwhile, make the sauce by stirring together the lemon juice, chicken broth, Italian seasoning, and mustard in a medium mixing bowl.
4. Drizzle the sauce over the chicken. Fold in the potatoes.
5. Secure the lid. Press the Manual button on the Instant Pot and cook for 15 minutes on High Pressure.
6. Once cooking is complete, do a quick pressure release. Carefully remove the lid.
7. Transfer the chicken to a serving dish and serve immediately.

Mongolian Chicken

Prep time: 5 minutes | Cook time: 20 minutes | Serves 6

2 tablespoons olive oil
10 cloves garlic, minced
1 onion, minced
4 large boneless, skinless chicken breasts, cut into cubes
1 cup water
1 cup soy sauce

1 cup brown sugar
1 cup chopped carrots
1 tablespoon garlic powder
1 tablespoon grated ginger
1 teaspoons red pepper flakes
1 tablespoon cornstarch, mixed with 2 tablespoons water

1. Set your Instant Pot to Sauté and heat the olive oil.
2. Add the garlic and onion and sauté for about 3 minutes until fragrant.
3. Add the chicken cubes and brown each side for 3 minutes. Add the remaining ingredients except the cornstarch mixture to the Instant Pot and stir well.
4. Secure the lid. Select the Poultry mode and set the cooking time for 15 minutes at High Pressure.
5. Once cooking is complete, do a natural pressure release for 10 minutes, then release any remaining pressure. Carefully open the lid.
6. Set your Instant Pot to Sauté again and whisk in the cornstarch mixture until the sauce thickens.
7. Serve warm.

Spinach and Feta Stuffed Chicken

Prep time: 10 minutes | Cook time: 25 minutes | Serves 4

½ cup frozen spinach
⅓ cup crumbled feta cheese
1¼ teaspoons salt, divided
4 (6-ounce / 170-g) boneless, skinless chicken breasts, butterflied

¼ teaspoon pepper
¼ teaspoon dried oregano
¼ teaspoon dried parsley
¼ teaspoon garlic powder
2 tablespoons coconut oil
1 cup water

1. Combine the spinach, feta cheese, and ¼ teaspoon of salt in a medium bowl. Divide the mixture evenly and spoon onto the chicken breasts.
2. Close the chicken breasts and secure with toothpicks or butcher's string. Sprinkle the chicken with the remaining 1 teaspoon of salt, pepper, oregano, parsley, and garlic powder.
3. Set your Instant Pot to Sauté and heat the coconut oil.
4. Sear each chicken breast until golden brown, about 4 to 5 minutes per side.
5. Remove the chicken breasts and set aside.
6. Pour the water into the Instant Pot and scrape the bottom to remove any chicken or seasoning that is stuck on. Add the trivet to the Instant Pot and place the chicken on the trivet.
7. Secure the lid. Select the Manual mode and set the cooking time for 15 minutes at High Pressure.
8. Once cooking is complete, do a natural pressure release for 15 minutes, then release any remaining pressure. Carefully open the lid. Serve warm.

Thai Peanut Chicken

Prep time: 6 mins, Cook time: 12 mins, Servings: 6

2 tbsps. chopped scallions
Salt and pepper, to taste
1½ cups toasted peanuts, divided

2 garlic cloves, minced
1½ lbs. chicken breasts
1 cup water

1. Place 1 cup of toasted peanuts in a food processor and pulse until smooth. This will serve as your peanut butter.
2. On a flat work surface, chop the remaining toasted peanuts finely and set aside.
3. Press the Sauté button on the Instant Pot and add the chicken breasts and garlic. Keep on stirring for 3 minutes until the meat has turned lightly golden. Sprinkle pepper and salt for seasoning.
4. Pour in the prepared peanut butter and water. Give the mixture a good stir.
5. Lock the lid. Select the Poultry mode and set the cooking time for 8 minutes at High Pressure.
6. Once cooking is complete, do a natural pressure release for 5 minutes, then release any remaining pressure. Carefully open the lid.
7. Garnish with chopped peanuts and scallions before serving.

Thyme Chicken with Brussels Sprouts

Prep time: 10 mins, Cook Time: 25 mins, Servings: 4

1 tbsp. olive oil
2 chicken breasts, skinless, boneless and halved
2 cups Brussels sprouts, halved

1 cup chicken stock
2 thyme springs, chopped
A pinch of salt and black pepper

1. Set your Instant Pot to Sauté and heat the olive oil. Add the chicken breasts and brown for 5 minutes.
2. Add the remaining ingredients to the pot and whisk to combine.
3. Lock the lid. Select the Poultry mode and set the cooking time for 20 minutes at High Pressure.
4. Once cooking is complete, do a natural pressure release for 10 minutes, then release any remaining pressure. Carefully open the lid.
5. Divide the chicken and Brussels sprouts among four plates and serve.

Chicken with White Wine Mushroom Sauce

Prep time: 5 minutes | Cook time: 22 minutes | Serves 12

2 tablespoons vegetable oil
4 cloves garlic, minced
1 onion, chopped
6 chicken breasts, halved
1¼ pounds (567 g) cremini
mushrooms, sliced
1½ cups dry white wine
1 cup chicken broth
1 tablespoon lemon juice,
freshly squeezed
1 tablespoon thyme
2 bay leaves
Salt and pepper, to taste
2 tablespoons cornstarch,
mixed with 2 tablespoons
water

1. Set your Instant Pot to Sauté and heat the vegetable oil.
2. Add the garlic, onion, and chicken and brown for about 5 minutes.
3. Fold in the mushrooms, white wine, chicken broth, lemon juice, thyme, bay leaves, salt, and pepper and stir to incorporate.
4. Secure the lid. Select the Poultry mode and set the cooking time for 15 minutes at High Pressure.
5. Once cooking is complete, do a quick pressure release. Carefully open the lid.
6. Set your Instant Pot to Sauté again and stir in the cornstarch mixture. Let simmer for a few minutes until the sauce is thickened.
7. Allow to cool for 5 minutes before serving.

Chipotle Chicken Fajita

Prep time: 15 minutes | Cook time: 10 minutes | Serves 2

1 tablespoon oil
½ green bell pepper, sliced
¼ red onion, sliced
2 skinless, boneless chicken
breasts
½ cup water
2 canned chipotle chiles in
adobo sauce, deseeded and
minced
Kosher salt, to taste
3 tablespoons mayonnaise
¼ cup sour cream
½ tablespoon freshly squeezed
lime juice
Freshly ground black pepper,
to taste

1. Set your Instant Pot to Sauté and heat the oil until it shimmers.
2. Add the bell pepper and onion and sauté for 3 to 4 minutes until tender.
3. Remove from the Instant Pot to a small bowl and set aside to cool.
4. Add the chicken breasts, water, and a few teaspoons of adobo sauce to the pot and season with salt to taste.
5. Lock the lid. Select the Poultry mode and set the cooking time for 6 minutes at High Pressure.
6. Once cooking is complete, do a natural pressure release for 5 minutes, then release any remaining pressure. Carefully open the lid.
7. Remove the chicken from the pot to a cutting board and allow to cool for 10 minutes. Slice the chicken breasts into cubes and place in a medium bowl.
8. Add the cooked bell pepper and onion, mayo, sour cream, chipotle chiles, lime juice, salt, and pepper to the bowl of chicken and toss to coat. Serve immediately.

Crack Chicken with Bacon

Prep time: 5 minutes | Cook time: 15 minutes | Serves 2

½ cup grass-fed bone broth
½ pound (227 g) boneless,
skinless chicken breasts
2 ounces (57 g) cream cheese,
softened
¼ cup tablespoons keto-
friendly ranch dressing
3 slices bacon, cooked,
chopped into small pieces
½ cup shredded full-fat
Cheddar cheese

1. Add the bone broth, chicken, cream cheese, and ranch dressing to your Instant Pot and stir to combine.
2. Secure the lid. Press the Manual button and set the cooking time for 15 minutes on High Pressure.
3. When the timer goes off, do a quick pressure release. Carefully open the lid.
4. Add the bacon and cheese and stir until the cheese has melted.
5. Serve.

Chicken Cordon Bleu

Prep time: 12 minutes | Cook time: 15 minutes | Serves 6

4 boneless, skinless chicken
breast halves, butterflied
4 (1-ounce / 28-g) slices Swiss
cheese
Sauce:
1½ ounces (43 g) cream
cheese (3 tablespoons)
¼ cup chicken broth
1 tablespoon unsalted butter
8 (1-ounce / 28-g) slices ham
1 cup water
Chopped fresh flat-leaf parsley,
for garnish
¼ teaspoon ground black
pepper
¼ teaspoon fine sea salt

1. Lay the chicken breast halves on a clean work surface. Top each with a slice of Swiss cheese and 2 slices of ham. Roll the chicken around the ham and cheese, then secure with toothpicks. Set aside.
2. Whisk together all the ingredients for the sauce in a small saucepan over medium heat, stirring until the cream cheese melts and the sauce is smooth.
3. Place the chicken rolls, seam-side down, in a casserole dish. Pour half of the sauce over the chicken rolls. Set the remaining sauce aside.
4. Pour the water into the Instant Pot and insert the trivet. Place the dish on the trivet.
5. Lock the lid. Select the Manual mode and set the cooking time for 15 minutes at High Pressure.
6. When the timer beeps, perform a natural pressure release for 10 minutes, then release any remaining pressure. Carefully remove the lid.
7. Remove the chicken rolls from the Instant Pot to a plate. Pour the remaining sauce over them and serve garnished with the parsley.

Chapter 6 Beef

Apricot Preserved Flank Steak
Prep time: 10 minutes | Cook time: 45 minutes | Serves 4

¼ cup apricot preserves
⅛ cup apple cider vinegar
¼ cup ketchup
⅛ cup honey
¼ cup soy sauce
1 teaspoon ground mustard
⅛ teaspoon cayenne pepper
¼ teaspoon ground black

pepper
1 (2-pound / 907-g) flank steak
2 tablespoons avocado oil, divided
1 large sweet onion, peeled and sliced
1½ cups beef broth

1.In a small bowl, combine the preserves, vinegar, ketchup, honey, soy sauce, mustard, cayenne pepper, and pepper. Spread half of the mixture on all sides of the flank steak on a clean work surface. Set the remaining mixture aside.
2.Press the Sauté button on Instant Pot. Heat 1 tablespoon of avocado oil. Add and sear the meat on each side for about 5 minutes. Remove the meat and set aside.
3.Add remaining 1 tablespoon of avocado oil and onions. Sauté for 3 to 5 minutes or until translucent.
4.Pour in the beef broth. Set meat on the onions. Pour the remaining preserve mixture over. Lock the lid.
5.Press the Meat / Stew button and set the cooking time for 35 minutes at High Pressure.
6.When timer beeps, let pressure release naturally for 15 minutes, then release any remaining pressure. Unlock the lid.
7.Transfer the meat to a serving platter. Thinly slice and serve immediately.

Beef Ribs with Radishes
Prep time: 20 minutes | Cook time: 56 minutes | Serves 4

¼ teaspoon ground coriander
¼ teaspoon ground cumin
1 teaspoon kosher salt, plus more to taste
½ teaspoon smoked paprika
Pinch of ground allspice (optional)
4 (8-ounce / 227-g) bone-in

beef short ribs
2 tablespoons avocado oil
1 cup water
2 radishes, ends trimmed, leaves rinsed and roughly chopped
Freshly ground black pepper, to taste

1.In a small bowl, mix together the coriander, cumin, salt, paprika, and allspice. Rub the spice mixture all over the short ribs.
2.Set the Instant Pot to Sauté mode and add the oil to heat. Add the short ribs, bone side up. Brown for 4 minutes on each side.
3.Pour the water into the Instant Pot. Secure the lid. Press the Manual button and set cooking time for 45 minutes on High Pressure.
4.When timer beeps, allow the pressure to release naturally for 10 minutes, then release any remaining pressure. Open the lid.
5.Remove the short ribs to a serving plate.
6.Add the radishes to the sauce in the pot. Place a metal steaming basket directly on top of the radishes and place the radish leaves in the basket.
7.Secure the lid. Press the Manual button and set cooking time for 3 minutes on High Pressure.
8.When timer beeps, quick release the pressure. Open the lid. Transfer the leaves to a serving bowl. Sprinkle with with salt and pepper.
9.Remove the radishes and place on top of the leaves. Serve hot with the short ribs.

Beef and Bacon Fig Chutney
Prep time: 20 minutes | Cook time: 35 minutes | Serves 4

3 bacon slices, chopped
1 teaspoon olive oil
4 pounds (1.8 kg) beef short ribs
Salt and black pepper, to taste
1 pound (454 g) cherry tomatoes, halved

1 medium white onion, chopped
3 garlic cloves, minced
1 cup Marsala wine
¼ cup fig preserves
2 cups beef broth
3 tablespoons thyme leaves

1.Set the Instant Pot to Sauté mode and brown the bacon for 5 minutes until crispy. Place the bacon on a paper towel-lined plate and set aside.
2.Heat the olive oil, then season beef ribs with salt, and pepper. Sear the beef in the pot for 5 minutes on both sides or until brown. Transfer the beef next to bacon.
3.Add the cherry tomatoes, onion, and garlic to Instant Pot, then sauté for 5 minutes or until soft.
4.Stir in Marsala wine, fig preserves, beef broth, and thyme. Return beef and bacon to the pot.
5.Seal the lid, then select the Manual mode and set the time for 20 minutes at High Pressure.
6.Once cooking is complete, allow a natural release for 10 minutes, then release any remaining pressure. Unlock the lid.
7.Serve immediately.

Beef Empanadas
Prep time: 20 minutes | Cook time: 20 minutes | Serves 4

2 tablespoons olive oil, divided
¼ pound (113 g) ground beef
1 garlic clove, minced
½ white onion, chopped
6 green olives, pitted and chopped
¼ teaspoon cumin powder

¼ teaspoon paprika
¼ teaspoon cinnamon powder
2 small tomatoes, chopped
1 cup water
8 square wonton wrappers
1 egg, beaten

1.Select the Sauté mode of the Instant Pot and heat 1 tablespoon of olive oil.
2.Add and sauté the ground beef, garlic, and onion for 5 minutes or until fragrant and the beef is no longer pink.
3.Stir in olives, cumin, paprika, and cinnamon, and cook for 3 minutes.
4.Add the tomatoes and water, and cook for 1 minute.
5.Seal the lid, then select the Manual mode and set the time for 8 minutes on High Pressure.
6.When timer beeps, allow a natural release for 10 minutes, then release any remaining pressure. Carefully open the lid.
7.Spoon the beef mixture onto a plate and let cool for a few minutes. Lay the wonton wrappers on a flat surface.
8.Place 2 tablespoons of the beef mixture in the middle of each wrapper. Brush the edges of the wrapper with egg and fold in half to form a triangle. Pinch the edges together to seal.
9.Heat the remaining oil in the Instant Pot and fry the empanadas for a minute each. Work in batches to avoid overcrowding.
10.Remove to paper towels to soak up excess fat before serving.

Red and Green Cabbage with Beef
Prep time: 20 minutes | Cook time: 22 minutes | Serves 4

1 tablespoon olive oil
1 pound (454 g) ground beef
1 tablespoon grated ginger
3 garlic cloves, minced
Salt and black pepper, to taste
1 medium red cabbage, shredded
1 medium green cabbage, shredded
1 red bell pepper, chopped
1 cup water
2 tablespoons tamarind sauce
½ tablespoon honey
1 tablespoon hot sauce
1 tablespoon sesame oil
2 tablespoons walnuts
1 teaspoon toasted sesame seeds

1. Set the Instant Pot to Sauté mode and heat the olive oil.
2. Add the beef, then season with ginger, garlic, salt, black pepper. Cook for 5 minutes.
3. Add the red and green cabbage, bell pepper, and sauté for 5 minutes.
4. Pour in the water and seal the lid. Select the Manual mode and set the time to 10 minutes on High Pressure.
5. When timer beeps, allow a natural release for 10 minutes, then release any remaining pressure. Unlock the lid.
6. Meanwhile, in a bowl, combine the tamarind sauce, honey, hot sauce, and sesame oil. Stir in the pot, add walnuts, and cook for 1 to 2 minutes on Sauté mode.
7. Dish out and garnish with sesame seeds. Serve warm.

Beef, Bacon and Cauliflower Rice Casserole
Prep time: 15 minutes | Cook time: 26 minutes | Serves 5

2 cups fresh cauliflower florets
1 pound (454 g) ground beef
5 slices uncooked bacon, chopped
8 ounces (227 g) unsweetened tomato purée
1 cup shredded Cheddar cheese, divided
1 teaspoon garlic powder
½ teaspoon paprika
½ teaspoon sea salt
¼ teaspoon ground black pepper
¼ teaspoon celery seed
1 cup water
1 medium Roma tomato, sliced

1. Spray a round soufflé dish with coconut oil cooking spray. Set aside.
2. Add the cauliflower florets to a food processor and pulse until a riced. Set aside.
3. Select Sauté mode. Once the pot is hot, crumble the ground beef into the pot and add the bacon. Sauté for 6 minutes or until the ground beef is browned and the bacon is cooked through.
4. Transfer the beef, bacon, and rendered fat to a large bowl.
5. Add the cauliflower rice, tomato purée, ½ cup Cheddar cheese, garlic powder, paprika, sea salt, black pepper, and celery seed to the bowl with the beef and bacon. Mix well to combine.
6. Add the mixture to the prepared dish and use a spoon to press and smooth the mixture into an even layer.
7. Place the trivet in the Instant Pot and add the water to the bottom of the pot. Place the dish on top of the trivet.
8. Lock the lid. Select Manual mode and set cooking time for 20 minutes on High Pressure.
9. When cooking is complete, quick release the pressure.
10. Open the lid. Arrange the tomato slices in a single layer on top of the casserole and sprinkle the remaining cheese over top.
11. Secure the lid and let the residual heat melt the cheese for 5 minutes.
12. Open the lid, remove the dish from the pot.
13. Transfer the casserole to a serving plate and slice into 5 equal-sized wedges. Serve warm.

Beery Back Ribs
Prep time: 20 minutes | Cook time: 50 minutes | Serves 2 to 4

½ pound (227 g) back ribs
4 ounces (113 g) beers
½ cup BBQ sauce
½ red chili, sliced
½ onion, chopped
1 garlic clove, minced
1-inch piece fresh ginger,
minced
2 tablespoons tamari
1 tablespoon agave nectar
Sea salt and ground black pepper, to taste
1 teaspoon toasted sesame seeds

1. Place the back ribs, beers, BBQ sauce, red chili, onion, garlic, and ginger in the Instant Pot.
2. Secure the lid. Choose the Manual mode and set the cooking time for 40 minutes at High pressure.
3. Once cooking is complete, perform a natural pressure release for 10 minutes, then release any remaining pressure. Carefully open the lid.
4. Add the tamari sauce, agave, salt and pepper and place the beef ribs under the broiler.
5. Broil ribs for 10 minutes or until well browned. Serve with sesame seeds.

Bell Pepper and Beef
Prep time: 12 mins, Cook time: 30 mins, Servings: 4

1½ lbs. beef tenderloin
1 tsp. sea salt
4 green bell peppers, deseeded and stems removed
1 tbsp. extra virgin olive oil
1 red onion, peeled and diced
1 cup water

1. On a clean work surface, cut the beef into 1-inch thick slices, sprinkle with salt
2. Cut the bell peppers into ¼-inch slices.
3. Set Instant Pot to Sauté setting, then add extra virgin olive oil and heat until hot.
4. Add the beef and cook for 4 to 5 minutes or until browned.
5. Add peppers and onion, and sauté for 2 minutes. Pour in the water.
6. Lock the lid. Set the Instant Pot to the Manual setting and set the timer at 30 minutes at High Pressure.
7. When the timer beeps, press Cancel, then use a quick pressure release.
8. Carefully open the lid and allow to cool for a few minutes. Serve warm.

Big Papa's Roast
Prep time: 12 mins, Coo Time: 1 hour, Servings: 6

3 lbs. beef chuck roast
2 tsps. salt
6 peppercorns, crushed
2 tbsps. extra virgin olive oil
2 cups beef stock

1. On a clean work surface, rub the beef with salt and peppercorns.
2. Coat the Instant Pot with olive oil and set the Sauté setting. Heat the oil until shimmering.
3. Add and brown the beef roast for 4 to 5 minutes.
4. Pour in the beef stock.
5. Lock the lid. Set to Manual mode, set the cooking time for 60 minutes at High Pressure.
6. Once cooking is complete, use a natural pressure release for 10 minutes, then release any remaining pressure.
7. Carefully open the lid. Allow to cool for a few minutes. Transfer them on a large plate and serve immediately.

Broccoli with Beef

Prep time: 15 minutes | Cook time: 25 minutes | Serves 4

½ cup grass-fed bone broth
1 pound (454 g) chuck steak, sliced
1 jalapeño pepper, sliced
1 green onion, chopped
½ teaspoon ginger, grated
½ teaspoon garlic
2 tablespoons coconut oil

½ teaspoon crushed red pepper
½ teaspoon kosher salt
½ teaspoon freshly ground black pepper
½ teaspoon dried parsley
1 cup broccoli, chopped
1 teaspoon sesame seeds

1. Pour the bone broth into the Instant Pot, then add the steak, jalapeño, green onion, ginger, garlic, coconut oil, red pepper, salt, black pepper, and parsley.
2. Close the lid and select the Manual mode. Set the cooking time for 20 minutes on High Pressure.
3. When timer beeps, let the pressure naturally release for about 10 minutes, then release any remaining pressure. Carefully open the lid.
4. Transfer the steak mixture on a plate. Add the broccoli and set to the Sauté mode. Cook for 5 minutes or until tender. Remove the broccoli from the pot.
5. Top the beef with the sesame seeds, serve with the broccoli.

Beef and Cauliflower

Prep time: 12 mins, Cook Time: 30 mins, Servings: 4

1 tbsp. extra virgin olive oil
1½ lbs. ground beef
1 tsp salt
1 cup puréed tomato

6 cups cauliflower, cut into florets
1 cup water

1. Set the Instant Pot to Sauté setting, then add the olive oil and heat until shimmering.
2. Add the beef and sauté for 4 or 5 minutes or until browned.
3. Add the rest of the ingredients.
4. Lock the lid. Select the Manual setting and set the timer at 30 minutes on High Pressure.
5. When the timer beeps, press Cancel, then use a quick pressure release.
6. Carefully open the lid and allow to cool for a few minutes. Serve warm.

Corn Chili Beef

Prep time: 12 mins, Cook Time: 30 mins, Servings: 4

1 tbsp. olive oil
2 small onions, chopped
2 small chili peppers, diced
¼ cup canned corn

10 oz. lean ground beef
3 cups water
Salt and pepper, to taste

1. Press Sauté on the Instant Pot. Heat the olive oil in the pot.
2. Add the onions, chili peppers, corn, and beef. Sauté for 2 to 3 minutes or until the onions are translucent and the peppers are softened.
3. Add the water to the Instant Pot, and sprinkle with salt and pepper. Mix to combine well.
4. Lock the lid. Press Meat/Stew. Set the timer to 20 minutes at High Pressure.
5. Once cooking is complete, press Cancel, then use a quick pressure release.
6. Open the lid, transfer them on 4 plates and serve.

Vegetable and Beef Pot

Prep time: 15 minutes | Cook time: 21 minutes | Serves 4

2 tablespoons olive oil
1 pound (454 g) ground beef
¾ cup chopped baby Bella mushrooms
1 carrot, peeled and chopped
1 small onion, finely chopped
1 celery stick, chopped

1 garlic clove, minced
1 tablespoon Worcestershire Sauce
2 tablespoons tomato paste
1 teaspoon cinnamon powder
2 cups beef stock
2 sweet potatoes, chopped

1. Set the Instant Pot to the Sauté mode, then heat the olive oil.
2. Brown the beef in the pot for 5 minutes. Mix in mushrooms, carrot, onion, celery, and garlic. Sauté for 5 minutes or until softened.
3. Mix in Worcestershire sauce, tomato paste, and cinnamon. Cook for 1 minute.
4. Pour in the beef stock and add the potatoes. Seal the lid, then select the Manual mode and set the cooking time for 10 minutes.
5. Once cooking is complete, allow a natural release for 5 minutes, then release any remaining pressure and unlock the lid.
6. Serve warm.

Beef Stuffed Kale Rolls

Prep time: 15 minutes | Cook time: 30 minutes | Serves 4

8 ounces (227 g) ground beef
1 teaspoon chives
¼ teaspoon cayenne pepper
4 kale leaves

1 tablespoon cream cheese
¼ cup heavy cream
½ cup chicken broth

1. In the mixing bowl, combine the ground beef, chives, and cayenne pepper.
2. Then fill and roll the kale leaves with ground beef mixture.
3. Place the kale rolls in the Instant Pot.
4. Add cream cheese, heavy cream, and chicken broth. Close the lid.
5. Select Manual mode mode and set cooking time for 30 minutes on High Pressure
6. When timer beeps, make a quick pressure release. Open the lid.
7. Serve warm.

Beef Masala Curry

Prep time: 10 minutes | Cook time: 20 minutes | Serves 4

2 tomatoes, quartered
1 small onion, quartered
4 garlic cloves, chopped
½ cup fresh cilantro leaves
1 teaspoon garam masala
½ teaspoon ground coriander

1 teaspoon ground cumin
½ teaspoon cayenne
1 teaspoon salt
1 pound (454 g) beef chuck roast, cut into 1-inch cubes

1. In a blender, combine the tomatoes, onion, garlic, and cilantro.
2. Process until the vegetables are puréed. Add the garam masala, coriander, cumin, cayenne, and salt. Process for several more seconds.
3. To the Instant Pot, add the beef and pour the vegetable purée on top.
4. Lock the lid. Select Manual mode and set cooking time for 20 minutes on High Pressure.
5. When timer beeps, let the pressure release naturally for 10 minutes, then release any remaining pressure. Unlock the lid.
6. Stir and serve immediately.

Beef Lasagna

Prep time: 20 minutes | Cook time: 20 minutes | Serves 4

1 cup water
1 pound (454 g) ground beef
1 cup spinach, chopped
1 (14-ounce / 397-g) can fire roasted tomatoes
1 egg
¼ (4-ounce / 113-g) small onion, sliced
¾ cup Mozzarella cheese, shredded

½ cup Parmesan cheese, grated
1½ cups whole milk ricotta cheese
2 tablespoons coconut oil
½ teaspoon garlic
½ teaspoon dried basil
½ teaspoon fennel seeds
½ teaspoon dried parsley
½ teaspoon dried oregano

1. Pour the water into the Instant Pot, then insert the trivet.
2. In a large bowl, combine the remaining ingredients in the pot. Transfer the mixture into a baking pan.
3. Place the pan onto the trivet, and cover with aluminum foil.
4. Close the lid, then select the Manual mode. Set the cooking time for 20 minutes on High Pressure.
5. When timer beeps, naturally release the pressure for about 10 minutes, then release any remaining pressure. Carefully open the lid.
6. Let cool and serve.

Japanese Beef Shanks

Prep time: 15 minutes | Cook time: 30 minutes | Serves 4

1 pound (454 g) beef shank
½ teaspoon Five-spice powder
1 teaspoon instant dashi granules
½ teaspoon garlic, minced
1 tablespoon tamari or soy

sauce
¼ cup rice wine
1 clove star anise
½ dried red chili, sliced
1 tablespoon sesame oil
¾ cup water

1. Combine all ingredients to the Instant Pot.
2. Secure the lid. Choose the Manual mode and set the cooking time for 30 minutes at High pressure.
3. Once cooking is complete, use a natural pressure release for 10 minutes, then release any remaining pressure. Carefully open the lid.
4. Slice the beef shank and serve hot.

Spinach and Beef Tagliatelle

Prep time: 15 minutes | Cook time: 18 minutes | Serves 4

1 tablespoon olive oil
1 pound (454 g) ground beef
1 cup sliced cremini mushrooms
1 small yellow onion, chopped
2 garlic cloves, minced
8 ounces (227 g) tagliatelle

2 (26-ounce / 737-g) jars tomato pasta sauce
1 tablespoon Italian seasoning
1 teaspoon dried basil
6 cups water
Salt and black pepper, to taste
1 cup baby spinach

1. Set the Instant Pot to Sauté mode, heat the olive oil and brown the beef for 5 minutes.
2. Add the mushrooms, onion, garlic, and sauté for 3 minutes or until soft.
3. Stir in tagliatelle, tomato sauce, Italian seasoning, basil, water, salt, and pepper.
4. Seal the lid, then select the Manual mode and set the time for 5 minutes at High Pressure.
5. Once cooking is complete, do a quick release, then unlock the lid.
6. Select the Sauté mode and add the spinach. Cook for 5 minutes or until wilted. Serve warm.

Beef Carne Guisada

Prep time: 10 minutes | Cook time: 20 minutes | Serves 4

2 tomatoes, chopped
1 red bell pepper, chopped
½ onion, chopped
3 garlic cloves, chopped
1 teaspoon ancho chili powder
1 tablespoon ground cumin
½ teaspoon dried oregano
1 teaspoons salt

1 teaspoon freshly ground black pepper
1 teaspoon smoked paprika
1 pound (454 g) beef chuck, cut into large pieces
¾ cup water, plus 2 tablespoons
¼ teaspoon xanthan gum

1. In a blender, purée the tomatoes, bell pepper, onion, garlic, chili powder, cumin, oregano, salt, pepper, and paprika.
2. Put the beef pieces in the Instant Pot. Pour in the blended mixture.
3. Use ¾ cup of water to wash out the blender and pour the liquid into the pot.
4. Lock the lid. Select Manual mode and set cooking time for 20 minutes on High Pressure.
5. When cooking is complete, quick release the pressure. Unlock the lid.
6. Switch the pot to Sauté mode. Bring the stew to a boil.
7. Put the xanthan gum and 2 tablespoons of water into the boiling stew and stir until it thickens.
8. Serve immediately.

Beef Cheeseburger Pie

Prep time: 15 minutes | Cook time: 30 minutes | Serves 6

1 tablespoon olive oil
1 pound (454 g) ground beef
3 eggs (1 beaten)
½ cup unsweetened tomato purée
2 tablespoons golden flaxseed meal
1 garlic clove, minced
½ teaspoon Italian seasoning blend

½ teaspoon sea salt
½ teaspoon smoked paprika
½ teaspoon onion powder
2 tablespoons heavy cream
½ teaspoon ground mustard
¼ teaspoon ground black pepper
2 cups water
½ cup grated Cheddar cheese

1. Coat a round cake pan with the olive oil.
2. Select Sauté mode. Once the pot is hot, add the ground beef and sauté for 5 minutes or until the beef is browned.
3. Transfer the beef to a large bowl.
4. Add the 1 beaten egg, tomato purée, flaxseed meal, garlic, Italian seasoning, sea salt, smoked paprika, and onion powder to the bowl. Mix until well combined.
5. Transfer the meat mixture to the prepared cake pan and use a knife to spread the mixture into an even layer. Set aside.
6. In a separate medium bowl, combine the 2 remaining eggs, heavy cream, ground mustard, and black pepper. Whisk until combined.
7. Pour the egg mixture over the meat mixture. Tightly cover the pan with a sheet of aluminum foil.
8. Place the trivet in the Instant Pot and add the water to the bottom of the pot. Place the pan on the trivet.
9. Lock the lid. Select Manual mode and set cooking time for 20 minutes on High Pressure.
10. When cooking is complete, allow the pressure to release naturally for 10 minutes and then release the remaining pressure. Allow the pie to rest in the pot for 5 minutes.
11. Preheat the oven broiler to 450°F (235°C).
12. Open the lid, remove the pan from the pot. Remove the foil and sprinkle the Cheddar over top of the pie.
13. Place the pie in the oven and broil for 2 minutes or until the cheese is melted and the top becomes golden brown. Slice into six equal-sized wedges. Serve hot.

Yogurt and Beef Pitas

Prep time: 15 minutes | Cook time: 28 minutes | Serves 4

1 tablespoon olive oil	1 cup beef broth
1 pound (454 g) beef stew meat, cut into strips	1 cucumber, deseeded and chopped
Salt and black pepper, to taste	1 medium tomato, chopped
1 small white onion, chopped	4 whole pita bread, warmed
3 garlic cloves, minced	1 cup Greek yogurt
2 teaspoons hot sauce	1 teaspoon chopped dill

1. Set the Instant Pot to Sauté mode, then heat the olive oil until shimmering.
2. Season the beef with salt, pepper, and brown the beef in the pot for 5 minutes. Remove the beef from the pot and set aside.
3. Add the onion and garlic to oil and sauté for 3 minutes or until softened,. Return the beef to the pot, stir in hot sauce and beef broth.
4. Seal the lid, then select the Manual mode and set the time for 20 minutes at High Pressure.
5. Once cooking is complete, allow a natural release for 5 minutes, then release any remaining pressure. Unlock the lid.
6. Transfer the beef into a bowl. Mix in the cucumber, tomatoes, and spoon the beef mixture into pita bread.
7. In a medium bowl, mix yogurt and dill. Top beef with yogurt mixture and serve immediately.

Beef Rice Noodles

Prep time: 15 minutes | Cook time: 16 minutes | Serves 4

6 cups boiled water	½ cup julienned carrots
8 ounces (227 g) rice noodles	1 yellow onion, sliced
1 tablespoon sesame oil	1 cup shredded green cabbage
1 pound (454 g) ground beef	¼ cup sliced scallions, for garnish
2 cups sliced shitake mushrooms	Sesame seeds, for garnish
Sauce:	
¼ cup tamarind sauce	1 teaspoon grated ginger
1 tablespoon hoisin sauce	1 teaspoon maple syrup

1. In a medium bowl, whisk together the ingredients for the sauce. Set aside.
2. Pour boiling water into a bowl and add rice noodles. Cover the bowl and allow the noodles to soften for 5 minutes. Drain and set aside.
3. Set the Instant Pot to Sauté mode and heat the sesame oil.
4. Cook the beef in the pot for 5 minutes or until browned.
5. Stir in the mushrooms, carrots, onion, and cabbage. Cook for 5 minutes or until softened.
6. Add the noodles. Top with the sauce and mix well. Cook for 1 more minute. Garnish with scallions and sesame seeds and serve immediately.

Veggie and Beef Shawarma Salad Bowls

Prep time: 10 minutes | Cook time: 19 minutes | Serves 4

2 teaspoons olive oil	½ cup Greek yogurt
1½ pounds (680 g) beef flank steak, thinly sliced	2 tablespoons sesame oil
Sea salt and freshly ground black pepper, to taste	1 tablespoon fresh lime juice
1 teaspoon cayenne pepper	2 English cucumbers, chopped
½ teaspoon ground bay leaf	1 cup cherry tomatoes, halved
½ teaspoon ground allspice	1 red onion, thinly sliced
½ teaspoon cumin, divided	½ head romaine lettuce, chopped

1. Press the Sauté button to heat up the Instant Pot. Then, heat the olive oil and cook the beef for about 4 minutes.
2. Add all seasonings, 1½ cups of water, and secure the lid.
3. Choose Manual mode. Set the cook time for 15 minutes on High Pressure.
4. Once cooking is complete, use a natural pressure release. Carefully remove the lid.
5. Allow the beef to cool completely.
6. To make the dressing, whisk Greek yogurt, sesame oil, and lime juice in a mixing bowl.
7. Then, divide cucumbers, tomatoes, red onion, and romaine lettuce among four serving bowls. Dress the salad and top with the reserved beef flank steak. Serve warm.

Sausage and Beef Medley

Prep time: 10 minutes | Cook time: 27 minutes | Serves 8

1 teaspoon butter	broth
2 beef sausages, casing removed and sliced	2 cloves garlic, minced
2 pounds (907 g) beef steak, cubed	1 teaspoon Old Bay seasoning
1 yellow onion, sliced	2 bay leaves
2 fresh ripe tomatoes, puréed	1 sprig thyme
1 jalapeño pepper, chopped	1 sprig rosemary
1 red bell pepper, chopped	½ teaspoon paprika
1½ cups roasted vegetable	Sea salt and ground black pepper, to taste

1. Press the Sauté button to heat up the Instant Pot. Melt the butter and cook the sausage and steak for 4 minutes, stirring periodically. Set aside.
2. Add the onion and sauté for 3 minutes or until softened and translucent. Add the remaining ingredients, including reserved beef and sausage.
3. Secure the lid. Choose Manual mode and set time for 20 minutes on High Pressure.
4. Once cooking is complete, use a quick pressure release. Carefully remove the lid.
5. Serve immediately.

Beef Back Ribs with Barbecue Glaze

Prep time: 10 minutes | Cook time: 35 minutes | Serves 4

½ cup water	¼ teaspoon garlic powder
1 (3-pound / 1.4-kg) rack beef back ribs, prepared with rub of choice	2 teaspoons apple cider vinegar
¼ cup unsweetened tomato purée	¼ teaspoon liquid smoke
¼ teaspoon Worcestershire sauce	¼ teaspoon smoked paprika
	3 tablespoons Swerve
	Dash of cayenne pepper

1. Pour the water in the pot and place the trivet inside.
2. Arrange the ribs on top of the trivet.
3. Close the lid. Select Manual mode and set cooking time for 25 minutes on High Pressure.
4. Meanwhile, prepare the glaze by whisking together the tomato purée, Worcestershire sauce, garlic powder, vinegar, liquid smoke, paprika, Swerve, and cayenne in a medium bowl. Heat the broiler.
5. When timer beeps, quick release the pressure. Open the lid. Remove the ribs and place on a baking sheet.
6. Brush a layer of glaze on the ribs. Put under the broiler for 5 minutes.
7. Remove from the broiler and brush with glaze again. Put back under the broiler for 5 more minutes, or until the tops are sticky.
8. Serve immediately.

Beef Shami Kabob

Prep time: 15 minutes | Cook time: 35 minutes | Serves 4

1 pound (454 g) beef chunks, chopped
1 teaspoon ginger paste
½ teaspoon ground cumin
2 cups water
¼ cup almond flour
1 egg, beaten
1 tablespoon coconut oil

1. Put the beef chunks, ginger paste, ground cumin, and water in the Instant Pot.
2. Select Manual mode and set cooking time for 30 minutes on High Pressure.
3. When timer beeps, make a quick pressure release. Open the lid.
4. Drain the water from the meat. Transfer the beef in the blender. Add the almond flour and beaten egg. Blend until smooth. Shape the mixture into small meatballs.
5. Heat the coconut oil on Sauté mode and put the meatballs inside.
6. Cook for 2 minutes on each side or until golden brown.
7. Serve immediately.

Beef Big Mac Salad

Prep time: 10 minutes | Cook time: 9 minutes | Serves 2

5 ounces (142 g) ground beef
1 teaspoon ground black pepper
1 tablespoon sesame oil
1 cup lettuce, chopped
¼ cup Monterey Jack cheese, shredded
2 ounces (57 g) dill pickles, sliced
1 ounce (28 g) scallions, chopped
1 tablespoon heavy cream

1. In a mixing bowl, combine the ground beef and ground black pepper.shape the mixture into mini burgers.
2. Pour the sesame oil in the Instant Pot and heat for 3 minutes on Sauté mode.
3. Place the mini hamburgers in the hot oil and cook for 3 minutes on each side.
4. Meanwhile, in a salad bowl, mix the chopped lettuce, shredded cheese, dill pickles, scallions, and heavy cream. Toss to mix well.
5. Top the salad with cooked mini burgers. Serve immediately.

Beef Bourguignon

Prep time: 15 minutes | Cook time: 35 minutes | Serves 6

3 ounces (85 g) bacon, chopped
1 pound (454 g) beef tenderloin, chopped
¼ cup apple cider vinegar
¼ teaspoon ground coriander
¼ teaspoon xanthan gum
1 teaspoon dried oregano
1 teaspoon unsweetened tomato purée
1 cup beef broth

1. Put the bacon in the Instant Pot and cook for 5 minutes on Sauté mode. Flip the bacon with a spatula every 1 minute.
2. Add the chopped beef tenderloin, apple cider vinegar, ground coriander, xanthan gum, and dried oregano.
3. Add the tomato purée and beef broth. Stir to mix well and close the lid.
4. Select Manual mode and set cooking time for 30 minutes on High Pressure.
5. When timer beeps, make a quick pressure release. Open the lid.
6. Serve immediately.

Beef Brisket with Cabbage

Prep time: 15 minutes | Cook time: 1 hour 7 minutes | Serves 8

3 pounds (1.4 kg) corned beef brisket
4 cups water
3 garlic cloves, minced
2 teaspoons yellow mustard seed
2 teaspoons black peppercorns
3 celery stalks, chopped
½ large white onion, chopped
1 green cabbage, cut into quarters

1. Add the brisket to the Instant Pot. Pour the water into the pot. Add the garlic, mustard seed, and black peppercorns.
2. Lock the lid. Select Meat/Stew mode and set cooking time for 50 minutes on High Pressure.
3. When cooking is complete, allow the pressure to release naturally for 20 minutes, then release any remaining pressure. Open the lid and transfer only the brisket to a platter.
4. Add the celery, onion, and cabbage to the pot.
5. Lock the lid. Select Soup mode and set cooking time for 12 minutes on High Pressure.
6. When cooking is complete, quick release the pressure. Open the lid, add the brisket back to the pot and let warm in the pot for 5 minutes.
7. Transfer the warmed brisket back to the platter and thinly slice. Transfer the vegetables to the platter. Serve hot.

Creamy Delmonico Steak

Prep time: 10 minutes | Cook time: 20 minutes | Serves 4

1 tablespoon butter
1 pound (454 g) Delmonico steak, cubed
½ cup double cream
½ cup beef broth
1 clove garlic, minced
¼ cup sour cream
1 teaspoon cayenne pepper
Sea salt and ground black pepper, to taste
¼ cup gorgonzola cheese, shredded

1. Press the Sauté button of the Instant Pot. Melt the butter and brown the beef cubes in batches for about 4 minutes per batch.
2. Add the double cream, broth, garlic, and sour cream to the Instant Pot, then season with cayenne pepper, salt, and black pepper.
3. Secure the lid. Choose the Manual mode and set the cooking time for 10 minutes at High pressure.
4. Once cooking is complete, use a quick pressure release. Carefully open the lid.
5. Top with gorgonzola cheese and serve.

Beef with Garlic

Prep time: 12 mins, Cook time: 10 mins, Servings: 4

1½ lbs. beef sirloin
1 tbsp. sea salt
1 tbsp. extra virgin olive oil
5 garlic cloves, chopped
1 cup heavy cream

1. On a clean work surface, rub the beef with salt.
2. Set the Instant Pot to Sauté mode. Add the olive oil and heat until shimmering.
3. Add the beef and sear for 3 minutes until lightly browned.
4. Add garlic and sauté for 30 seconds or until fragrant.
5. Mix in the heavy cream.
6. Lock the lid. Set the pot to Manual setting and set the timer for 10 minutes at High Pressure.
7. When the timer beeps, press Cancel, then use a natural pressure release for 10 minutes, and then release any remaining pressure.
8. Carefully open the lid. Allow to cool for a few minutes. Transfer them on a large plate and serve immediately.

Gingered Beef Tenderloin

Prep time: 12 mins, Cook Time: 1 hour, Servings: 8

2 tbsps. olive oil	¼ cup soy sauce
2 tbsps. minced garlic	Salt and pepper, to taste
2 tbsps. thinly sliced ginger	1 cup water
4 fillet mignon steaks	

1. Press the Sauté button on the Instant Pot and heat the olive oil.
2. Sauté the garlic for 1 minute until fragrant.
3. Add the ginger and fillet mignon and allow to sear for 4 minutes or until lightly browned.
4. Drizzle with the soy sauce. Add salt and pepper to taste. Pour in a cup of water.
5. Lock the lid and select the Meat/Stew mode and set the timer to 1 hour at High Pressure.
6. Once cooking is complete, use a natural pressure release for 10 minutes, then release any remaining pressure.
7. Carefully open the lid. Allow to cool for a few minutes. Transfer them on a large plate and discard the bay leaf, then serve.

Instant Pot Rib Roast

Prep time: 6 mins, Cook Time: 2 hours 30 mins, Servings: 12

5 lbs. beef rib roast	1 tbsp. olive oil
1 tsp. garlic powder	Salt and pepper, to taste
1 bay leaf	1 cup water

1. Put all the ingredients in the Instant Pot. Stir to mix well.
2. Lock the lid. Set the pot to Meat/Stew mode and set the timer to 2 hours 30 minutes at High Pressure.
3. Once cooking is complete, use a natural pressure release for 10 to 20 minutes, then release any remaining pressure.
4. Carefully open the lid. Allow to cool for a few minutes. Transfer them on a large plate and discard the bay leaf, then serve.

Beef Tips with Portobello Mushrooms

Prep time: 20 minutes | Cook time: 16 minutes | Serves 4

2 teaspoons olive oil	portobello mushrooms
1 beef top sirloin steak (1-pound / 454-g), cubed	1 small onion, halved and sliced
½ teaspoon salt	2 cups beef broth
¼ teaspoon ground black pepper	1 tablespoon Worcestershire sauce
⅓ cup dry red wine	3 to 4 tablespoons cornstarch
½ pound (227 g) sliced baby	¼ cup cold water

1. Select the Sauté setting of the Instant Pot. Add the olive oil.
2. Sprinkle the beef with salt and pepper. Brown meat in batches in the pot for 10 minutes. Flip constantly. Transfer meat to a bowl.
3. Add the wine to the pot. Return beef to the pot and add mushrooms, onion, broth, and Worcestershire sauce.
4. Lock the lid. Select the Manual setting and set the cooking time for 15 minutes at High Pressure.
5. When timer beeps, quick release the pressure. Carefully open the lid.
6. Select the Sauté setting and bring to a boil.
7. Meanwhile, in a small bowl, mix cornstarch and water until smooth.
8. Gradually stir the cornstarch into beef mixture. Sauté for 1 more minute or until sauce is thickened. Serve immediately.

Beef Clod Vindaloo

Prep time: 15 minutes | Cook time: 15 minutes | Serves 2

½ Serrano pepper, chopped	¼ teaspoon ground paprika
¼ teaspoon cumin seeds	1 cup water
¼ teaspoon minced ginger	9 ounces (255 g) beef clod, chopped
¼ teaspoon cayenne pepper	
¼ teaspoon salt	

1. Put Serrano pepper, cumin seeds, minced ginger, cayenne pepper, salt, ground paprika, and water in a food processor. Blend the mixture until smooth.
2. Transfer the mixture in a bowl and add the chopped beef clod. Toss to coat well.
3. Transfer the beef clod and the mixture in the Instant Pot and close the lid.
4. Select Manual mode and set cooking time for 15 minutes on High Pressure.
5. When timer beeps, use a natural pressure release for 10 minutes, then release any remaining pressure. Open the lid.
6. Serve immediately.

Beef Meatballs with Roasted Tomatoes

Prep time: 15 minutes | Cook time: 16 minutes | Serves 4

2 tablespoons avocado oil	pepper
1 pound (454 g) ground beef	½ teaspoon kosher salt
½ teaspoon dried basil	½ teaspoon freshly ground black pepper
½ teaspoon crushed red pepper	2 (14-ounce / 397-g) cans fire roasted tomatoes
½ teaspoon ground cayenne	

1. Set the Instant Pot to Sauté mode and heat the avocado oil.
2. In a large bowl, mix the remaining ingredients, except for the tomatoes. Form the mixture into 1½-inch meatballs and place them into the Instant Pot. Spread the tomatoes evenly over the meatballs.
3. Close the lid. Select the Manual mode, set the cooking time for 16 minutes on High Pressure.
4. When timer beeps, perform a natural pressure release for 5 minutes, then release any remaining pressure.
5. Open the lid and serve.

Beef Meatballs with Tomato

Prep time: 12 mins, Cook Time: 10 mins, Servings: 4

1 lb. lean ground beef	1 tbsp. olive oil
2 large eggs	2 cups diced tomatoes
3 tbsps. all-purpose flour	1 cup water
Salt and pepper, to taste	

1. In a large bowl, thoroughly mix the beef, eggs, and flour, then sprinkle with salt and pepper. Mix well and make 6 meatballs of 1½ inch.
2. Grease a baking dish with olive oil and add the meatballs. Add the tomatoes and tightly wrap with a foil.
3. Pour the water in the Instant pot. Arrange the trivet or steamer basket inside, then place the dish on the trivet/basket.
4. Lock the lid. Press Manual. Set the timer to 10 minutes at High Pressure.
5. When the timer goes off, press Cancel, then use a quick pressure release.
6. Carefully open the lid. Allow to cool for a few minutes, then serve warm.

Beef Roast with Cauliflower

Prep time: 10 minutes | Cook time: 15 minutes | Serves 2

2 teaspoons sesame oil
12 ounces (340 g) sliced beef roast
Freshly ground black pepper, to taste
½ small onion, chopped
3 garlic cloves, minced
½ cup beef stock
¼ cup soy sauce
2 tablespoons brown sugar
Pinch red pepper flakes
1 tablespoon cornstarch
8 ounces (227 g) fresh cauliflower, cut into florets

1. Set the Instant Pot pot on Sauté mode. Add the sesame oil, beef, and black pepper. Sear for 2 minutes on all sides. Transfer the beef to a plate and set aside.
2. Add the onion and garlic to the pot and sauté for 2 minutes or until softened.
3. Stir in the stock, soy sauce, brown sugar, and red pepper flakes. Stir until the sugar is dissolved, then return the beef to the pot.
4. Secure the lid and set to the Manual mode. Set the cooking time for 10 minutes on High Pressure.
5. When timer beeps, quick release the pressure and open the lid. Set to the Sauté mode.
6. Transfer 2 tablespoons of liquid from the pot to a small bowl. Whisk it with the cornstarch, then add back to the pot along with the cauliflower.
7. Cover the lid and let simmer for 3 to 4 minutes, or until the sauce is thickened and the cauliflower is softened.
8. Serve the beef and cauliflower.

Corned Beef

Prep time: 6 mins, Cook Time: 1 hour 30 mins, Servings: 4

12 oz. beer
1 cup water
3 garlic cloves, minced
3 lbs. corned beef brisket
Salt and pepper, to taste

1. Pour the beer and water into the Instant Pot. Add the garlic and mix to combine well.
2. Put the steamer basket inside.
3. Add the beef to the basket and season with salt and pepper.
4. Cover the pot. Select the Meat/Stew mode and cook at High Pressure for 90 minutes.
5. Once cooking is complete, do a quick pressure release for 10 minutes, and then release any remaining pressure. Carefully open the lid.
6. Transfer the beef to a baking pan and cover it with foil.
7. Let it rest for 15 minutes before slicing to serve.

Sweet Potato Beef

Prep time: 12 mins, Cook Time: 40 mins, Servings: 4

1 tbsp. olive oil
1 lb. lean beef stew meat
4 cups low-sodium beef stock
1 small sweet potato, diced
1 tomato, roughly chopped
2 bell peppers, sliced
Salt and pepper, to taste

1. Press Sauté on Instant Pot. Grease the pot with the olive oil.
2. Add the beef and sauté for 4 to 5 minutes to evenly brown.
3. Mix in the remaining ingredients.
4. Lock the lid. Press Manual. Set the timer to 35 minutes at High Pressure.
5. When the timer beeps, press Cancel, then use a quick pressure release.
6. Open the lid, transfer them in 4 plates and serve warm.

Garlicky Prime Rib

Prep time: 12 mins, Cook Time: 1 hour, Servings: 10

2 tbsps. olive oil
10 garlic cloves, minced
4 lbs. prime rib roast
2 tsps. dried thyme
Salt and pepper, to taste
1 cup water

1. Press the Sauté button on the Instant Pot and heat the oil.
2. Add and sauté the garlic for 1 to 2 minutes until fragrant.
3. Add the prime rib roast and sear on all sides for 3 minutes until lightly browned.
4. Sprinkle with thyme, salt and pepper.
5. Pour in the water and remove the browning at the bottom.
6. Lock the lid. Set the pot to Meat/Stew mode and set the timer to 1 hour at High Pressure.
7. Once cooking is complete, use a natural pressure release for 10 minutes, then release any remaining pressure.
8. Carefully open the lid. Allow to cool for a few minutes. Transfer them on a large plate and serve immediately.

Mushroom Beef Stroganoff

Prep time: 25 minutes | Cook time: 20 minutes | Serves 8

2 pounds (907 g) ground beef, divided
1½ teaspoons salt, divided
1 teaspoon ground black pepper, divided
½ pound (227 g) sliced fresh mushrooms
1 tablespoon butter
2 medium onions, chopped
2 garlic cloves, minced
1 (10½-ounce / 298-g) can condensed beef consomme, undiluted
⅓ cup all-purpose flour
2 tablespoons tomato paste
1½ cups sour cream
Hot cooked noodles, for serving

1. Select the Sauté setting of the Instant Pot. Add half of ground beef, salt and pepper. Sauté for 8 minutes or until no longer pink. Remove the beef. Repeat with remaining ground beef, salt and pepper.
2. Add mushrooms, butter, and onions to Instant Pot. Sauté for 6 minutes or until mushrooms are tender. Add garlic and sauté for 1 minute more until fragrant. Return the beef to the pot.
3. Lock the lid. Select the Manual setting and set the cooking time for 5 minutes at High Pressure.
4. When timer beeps, quick release pressure. Carefully open the lid. Select the Sauté setting.
5. In a small bowl, whisk together consomme, flour and tomato paste. Pour over the beef and stir to combine.
6. Sauté for 3 more minutes or until thickened. Stir in sour cream; cook for a minute more until heated through. Serve with noodles.

Lemon Beef Meal

Prep time: 12 mins, Cook Time: 10 mins, Servings: 2

1 tbsp. olive oil
2 beef steaks
½ tsp. garlic salt
1 garlic clove, crushed
2 tbsps. lemon juice

1. Press Sauté on the Instant Pot. Heat the olive oil in the pot until shimmering.
2. Add the beef and garlic salt and sauté for 4 to 5 minutes to evenly brown.
3. Add the garlic and sauté for 1 minute until fragrant.
4. Serve with lemon juice on top.

Beef Shoulder Roast

Prep time: 15 minutes | Cook time: 46 minutes | Serves 6

2 tablespoons peanut oil
2 pounds (907 g) shoulder roast
¼ cup coconut aminos
1 teaspoon porcini powder
1 teaspoon garlic powder
1 cup beef broth
2 cloves garlic, minced

2 tablespoons champagne vinegar
½ teaspoon hot sauce
1 teaspoon celery seeds
1 cup purple onions, cut into wedges
1 tablespoon flaxseed meal, plus 2 tablespoons water

1. Press the Sauté button to heat up the Instant Pot. Then, heat the peanut oil and cook the beef shoulder roast for 3 minutes on each side.
2. In a mixing dish, combine coconut aminos, porcini powder, garlic powder, broth, garlic, vinegar, hot sauce, and celery seeds.
3. Pour the broth mixture into the Instant Pot. Add the onions to the top.
4. Secure the lid. Choose Meat/Stew mode and set cooking time for 40 minutes on High Pressure.
5. Once cooking is complete, use a natural pressure release for 15 minutes, then release any remaining pressure. Carefully remove the lid.
6. Make the slurry by mixing flaxseed meal with 2 tablespoons of water. Add the slurry to the Instant Pot.
7. Press the Sauté button and allow it to cook until the cooking liquid is reduced and thickened slightly. Serve warm.

Herbed Sirloin Tip Roast

Prep time: 5 mins, Cook Time: 1 hour 30 mins, Servings: 6

2 tbsps. mixed herbs
1 tsp. garlic powder
3 lbs. sirloin tip roast

1¼ tsps. paprika
1 cup water
Salt and pepper, to taste

1. In the Instant Pot, combine all the ingredients. Stir to mix well.
2. Lock the lid. Set the pot to Meat/Stew mode and set the timer to 1 hour 30 minutes at High Pressure.
3. Once cooking is complete, use a natural pressure release for 10 minutes, then release any remaining pressure.
4. Carefully open the lid. Allow to cool for a few minutes. Transfer them on a large plate and discard the bay leaf, then serve.

Super Beef Chili

Prep time: 12 mins, Cook Time: 8 mins, Servings: 4

1 lb. ground beef
1½ tsps. sea salt
1 medium onion, chopped
2 cups tomato purée

2 cups zucchini, peeled and rinsed, cut into 1-inch bites
1 cup water
1 tsp. chili spice powder

1. Select the Instant Pot to Sauté setting. Coat the pot with olive oil and heat until shimmering.
2. Add the beef, salt and onion, then sauté for 4 minutes or until the beef is lightly browned.
3. Add the tomato purée, zucchini, water and chili spice powder. Stir to mix well.
4. Lock the lid. Set the Instant Pot to Manual setting and set the timer for 8 minutes at High Pressure.
5. Once cooking is complete, use a quick pressure release.
6. Carefully open the lid. Allow to cool for a few minutes. Transfer them on a large plate and serve immediately.

Beef Steaks with Mushrooms

Prep time: 15 minutes | Cook time: 25 minutes | Serves 2

2 beef steaks, boneless
Salt and black pepper, to taste
2 tablespoons olive oil
4 ounces (113 g) mushrooms, sliced

½ onion, chopped
1 garlic clove, minced
1 cup vegetable soup
1½ tablespoons cornstarch
1 tablespoon half-and-half

1. Rub the beef steaks with salt and pepper on a clean work surface.
2. Set the Instant Pot to Sauté mode and warm the olive oil until shimmering.
3. Sear the beef for 2 minutes per side until browned. Transfer to a plate.
4. Add the mushrooms and sauté for 5 minutes or until soft. Add the onion and garlic and sauté for 2 minutes until fragrant.
5. Return the steaks to the pot and pour in the soup. Seal the lid, select the Manual mode, and set the time to 15 minutes on High Pressure.
6. When cooking is complete, do a quick pressure release and unlock the lid and transfer the chops to a plate. Press the Sauté button.
7. In a bowl, combine the cornstarch and half-and-half and mix well. Pour the mixture into the pot and cook until the sauce is thickened. Serve warm.

Sautéed Beef and Green Beans

Prep time: 12 mins, Cook Time: 5 mins, Servings: 4

1 tbsp. olive oil
10 oz. fat removed beef sirloin
2 spring onions, chopped

7 oz. canned green beans
2 tbsps. soy sauce
Salt and pepper, to taste

1. Press Sauté on the Instant Pot. Grease the pot with the olive oil.
2. Add the beef and sauté for 2 to 3 minutes to evenly brown.
3. Add the onions, green beans, and soy sauce, then sauté for another 2 to 3 minutes until the beans are soft. Sprinkle with salt and pepper.
4. Serve warm.

Sloppy Joes

Prep time: 10 minutes | Cook time: 19 minutes | Serves 4

1 pound (454 g) ground beef, divided
½ cup chopped onion
½ cup chopped green bell pepper
¼ cup water
2 teaspoons Worcestershire sauce

1 garlic clove, minced
1 tablespoon Dijon mustard
¾ cup ketchup
2 teaspoons brown sugar
¼ teaspoon sea salt
½ teaspoon hot sauce
4 soft hamburger buns

1. Select the Sauté mode of the Instant Pot. Put about ½ cup of the ground beef in the pot and cook for about 4 minutes or until browned.
2. Stir in the onion, bell pepper, and water. Add the remaining beef and cook for about 3 minutes or until well browned.
3. Mix in the Worcestershire sauce, garlic, mustard, ketchup, brown sugar, and salt.
4. Lock the lid. Select the Manual mode. Set the time for 12 minutes at High Pressure.
5. When timer beeps, quick release the pressure, then unlock the lid.
6. Stir in the hot sauce. Select the Sauté mode and simmer until lightly thickened. Spoon the meat and sauce into the buns. Serve immediately.

Ginger Short Ribs

Prep time: 12 mins, Cook Time: 25 mins, Servings: 6

4 beef short ribs
1 tsp. salt
3 tbsps. extra virgin olive oil, plus 1 tbsp. for coating

1 large onion, diced
2-inch knob of ginger, grated
¾ cup water

1. On a clean work surface, rub the ribs with salt.
2. Lightly coat the Instant Pot with olive oil and set the setting to Sauté.
3. Add the onion and ginger, then sauté for a minute
4. Add the ribs and brown for 4 to 5 minutes. Pour in the water.
5. Lock the lid. Set to Manual mode and set the cooking time for 25 minutes at High Pressure.
6. Once cooking is complete, use a natural pressure release for 10 minutes, then release any remaining pressure.
7. Carefully open the lid. Allow to cool for a few minutes. Transfer them on a large plate and serve immediately.

Greek Beef and Spinach Ravioli

Prep time: 15 minutes | Cook time: 20 minutes | Serves 4

1 cup cheese ravioli
3 cups water
Salt, to taste
1 tablespoon olive oil
1 pound (454 g) ground beef
1 cup canned diced tomatoes

1 tablespoon dried mixed herbs
3 cups chicken broth
1 cup baby spinach
¼ cup Kalamata olives, sliced
¼ cup crumbled feta cheese

1. Put ravioli, water, and salt in Instant Pot. Seal the lid, select the Manual mode and set the time for 3 minutes at High Pressure.
2. Once cooking is complete, do a quick pressure release. Carefully open the lid. Drain the ravioli through a colander and set aside.
3. Set the pot to Sauté mode, then heat the olive oil. Add and brown the beef for 5 minutes.
4. Mix in the tomatoes, mixed herbs, and chicken broth. Seal the lid, select the Manual mode and set cooking time for 10 minutes on High Pressure.
5. When timer beeps, do a quick pressure release. Carefully open the lid.
6. Set the pot to Sauté mode, then mix in ravioli, spinach, olives and cook for 2 minutes or until spinach wilts. Stir in the feta cheese and serve.

Beef Ribs with Leek

Prep time: 40 minutes | Cook time: 1 hour 40 minutes | Serves 4

1 pound (454 g) beef short ribs, bone-in
½ medium leek, sliced
½ teaspoon celery seeds
1 teaspoon onion soup mix
1 clove garlic, sliced

1 sprig thyme
1 sprig rosemary
1 tablespoon olive oil
Sea salt and ground black pepper, to taste
1 cup water

1. Place all ingredients in the Instant Pot.
2. Secure the lid. Choose the Manual mode and set the cooking time for 90 minutes at High pressure.
3. Once cooking is complete, do a natural pressure release for 30 minutes, then release any remaining pressure. Carefully open the lid.
4. Transfer the short ribs in the broiler and broil for 10 minutes or until crispy.
5. Transfer the ribs to a platter and serve.

Slow Cooked Beef Steak

Prep time: 10 minutes | Cook time: 7 hours | Serves 4

½ cup butter, softened
1 pound (454 g) beef steak

1 teaspoon ground nutmeg
½ teaspoon salt

1. Heat the butter in the Instant Pot on Sauté mode.
2. When the butter is melted, add beef steak, ground nutmeg, and salt.
3. Close the lid and select Slow Cook mode and set cooking time for 7 hours on Less.
4. When cooking is complete, allow to cool for half an hour and serve warm.

Sirloin with Snap Peas

Prep time: 15 minutes | Cook time: 8 minutes | Serves 4

½ teaspoon hot sauce
1 teaspoon balsamic vinegar
1 cup chicken stock
¼ cup soy sauce
2 tablespoons sesame oil, divided
2 tablespoons maple syrup

½ cup plus 2 teaspoons cornstarch, divided
1 pound (454 g) beef sirloin, sliced
2 cups snap peas
3 garlic cloves, minced
3 scallions, sliced

1. In a bowl, combine the hot sauce, vinegar, stock, soy sauce, 1 tablespoon of sesame oil, maple syrup, and 2 tablespoons of cornstarch. Set aside.
2. Pour the remaining cornstarch on a plate. Season beef with salt, and pepper; toss lightly in cornstarch.
3. Set the Instant Pot to Sauté mode, heat the remaining sesame oil and fry the beef in batches for 5 minutes or until browned and crispy. Remove the beef from the pot and set aside.
4. Wipe the Instant Pot clean and pour in hot sauce mixture. Return meat to the pot, then add snow peas and garlic.
5. Seal the lid, select the Manual mode and set the time for 3 minutes on High Pressure.
6. When cooking is complete, perform natural pressure release for 10 minutes, then release the remaining pressure. Unlock the lid.
7. Dish out and garnish with scallions.

Indian Spicy Beef with Basmati

Prep time: 15 minutes | Cook time: 15 minutes | Serves 4

1 tablespoon olive oil
1 pound (454 g) beef stew meat, cubed
Salt and black pepper, to taste
½ teaspoon garam masala powder
½ teaspoon grated ginger
2 white onions, sliced
2 garlic cloves, minced
1 tablespoon cilantro leaves

½ teaspoon red chili powder
1 teaspoon cumin powder
¼ teaspoon turmeric powder
1 cup basmati rice
1 cup grated carrots
2 cups beef broth
¼ cup cashew nuts
¼ cup coconut yogurt, for serving

1. Set the Instant Pot to Sauté mode, then heat the olive oil.
2. Season the beef with salt and pepper, and brown both sides for 5 minutes. Transfer to a plate and set aside.
3. Add and sauté the garam masala, ginger, onions, garlic, cilantro, red chili, cumin, turmeric, salt, and pepper for 2 minutes.
4. Stir in beef, rice, carrots, and broth. Seal the lid, select the Manual mode, and set the time to 6 minutes on High Pressure.
5. When cooking is complete, do a natural pressure release for 5 minutes, then release any remaining pressure. Unlock the lid.
6. Fluff the rice and stir in cashews. Serve with coconut yogurt.

Citrus Beef Carnitas

Prep time: 15 minutes | Cook time: 25 minutes | Serves 8

2½ pounds (1.1 kg) bone-in country ribs
Salt, to taste
¼ cup orange juice
1½ cups beef stock
1 onion, cut into wedges
2 garlic cloves, smashed and peeled
1 teaspoon chili powder
1 cup shredded Jack cheese

1. Season the ribs with salt on a clean work surface.
2. In the Instant Pot, combine the orange juice and stock. Fold in the onion and garlic. Put the ribs in the pot. Sprinkle with chili powder.
3. Seal the lid, select the Manual mode and set the cooking time for 25 minutes at High Pressure.
4. Once cooking is complete, do a natural pressure release for 10 minutes, then release any remaining pressure. Carefully open the lid. Transfer beef to a plate to cool.
5. Remove and discard the bones. Shred the ribs with two forks. Top the beef with the sauce remains in the pot. Sprinkled with cheese and serve.

Mexican Beef Shred

Prep time: 20 minutes | Cook time: 30 minutes | Serves 4

1 pound (454 g) tender chuck roast, cut into half
3 tablespoons chipotle sauce
1 (8-ounce / 227-g) can tomato sauce
1 cup beef broth
½ cup chopped cilantro
1 lime, zested and juiced
2 teaspoons cumin powder
1 teaspoon cayenne pepper
Salt and ground black pepper, to taste
½ teaspoon garlic powder
1 tablespoon olive oil

1. In the Instant Pot, add the beef, chipotle sauce, tomato sauce, beef broth, cilantro, lime zest, lime juice, cumin powder, cayenne pepper, salt, pepper, and garlic powder.
2. Seal the lid, then select the Manual mode and set the cooking time for 30 minutes at High Pressure.
3. Once cooking is complete, allow a natural pressure release for 10 minutes, then release any remaining pressure.
4. Unlock the lid and using two forks to shred the beef into strands. Stir in the olive oil. Serve warm.

Ribeye Steak with Cauliflower Rice

Prep time: 15 minutes | Cook time: 20 minutes | Serves 4

1 cup water
1 ribeye steak
½ teaspoon dried parsley
½ teaspoon ground cumin
½ teaspoon ground turmeric
½ teaspoon paprika
½ teaspoon freshly ground black pepper
½ teaspoon kosher salt
1 head cauliflower, riced
2 tablespoons butter, softened

1. Pour the water into the Instant Pot, then insert a trivet.
2. In a small bowl, mix the parsley, cumin, turmeric, paprika, black pepper, and salt. Coat the steak evenly with the mixture.
3. Place the steak into a greased baking pan. Arrange the cauliflower rice beside the steak.
4. Place the pan onto the trivet, and cover with aluminum foil. Close the lid, then select the Manual mode. Set the cooking time for 20 minutes on High Pressure.
5. When timer beeps, naturally release the pressure for about 10 minutes, then release any remaining pressure. Carefully open the lid.
6. Remove the pan. Add the butter to the steak. Serve immediately.

Philly Steak Sub

Prep time: 20 minutes | Cook time: 13 minutes | Serves 4

1½ pounds (680 g) flat iron steak
1 tablespoon olive oil
4 teaspoons garlic seasoning
1 cup beef broth
1 large red bell pepper, cut into
1-inch-wide strips
2 tablespoons soy sauce
4 crusty sub sandwich rolls, split lengthwise
4 slices provolone cheese

1. Select the Sauté mode. Brush the steak with the olive oil and rub with garlic seasoning.
2. Add the steaks in batches to the pot and cook for 8 minutes until well browned. Flip the steaks halfway through.
3. Transfer the steaks to a cutting board and slice into ¼- to ½-inch-thick slices. Return the meat to the pot. Add the broth, bell peppers, and soy sauce.
4. Lock the lid, select the Manual function, and set the cooking time for 5 minutes on High Pressure.
5. When timer beeps, let the pressure release naturally for 10 minutes, then release any remaining pressure. Carefully open the lid.
6. Remove the beef and vegetables from the pot. Mound the beef and peppers on the rolls. Top with slices of cheese and serve.

Classic Pot Roast

Prep time: 15 minutes | Cook time: 1 hour 8 minutes | Serves 6

¼ cup dry red wine
1 tablespoon dried thyme
1½ cups beef broth
½ tablespoon dried rosemary
1 teaspoon paprika
1 teaspoon garlic powder
1½ teaspoons sea salt
½ teaspoon ground black pepper
3 pounds (1.4 kg) boneless
chuck roast
1½ tablespoons avocado oil
2 tablespoons unsalted butter
½ medium yellow onion, chopped
2 garlic cloves, minced
1 cup sliced mushrooms
4 stalks celery, chopped
2 sprigs fresh thyme
1 bay leaf

1. In a medium bowl, combine the wine, dried thyme, beef broth, and dried rosemary. Stir to combine. Set aside.
2. In a small bowl, combine the paprika, garlic powder, sea salt, and black pepper. Mix well. Generously rub the dry spice mixture into the roast. Set aside.
3. Select Sauté mode. Once the pot becomes hot, add the avocado oil and butter and heat until the butter is melted, about 2 minutes.
4. Add the roast to the pot. Sauté for 3 minutes per side or until a crust is formed. Transfer the browned roast to a plate and set aside.
5. Add the onions and garlic to the pot. Sauté for 3 minutes or until the onions soften and the garlic becomes fragrant.
6. Add half the broth and wine mixture to the pot.
7. Place the trivet in the Instant Pot and place the roast on top of the trivet. Add the mushrooms and celery to the pot, and pour the remaining broth and wine mixture over the roast. Place the thyme sprigs and bay leaf on top of the roast.
8. Lock the lid. Select Manual mode and set cooking time for 1 hour on High Pressure.
9. When cooking is complete, allow the pressure to release naturally for 10 minutes and then release the remaining pressure.
10. Open the lid, discard the bay leaf and thyme sprigs. Transfer the roast to a serving platter.
11. Transfer the vegetables to the platter and spoon the remaining broth over the roast and vegetables.
12. Slice the roast and ladle ¼ cup of the broth over each serving. Serve hot.

Winter Beef Roast Pot

Prep time: 15 minutes | Cook time: 40 minutes | Serves 6

2 tablespoons olive oil
1 (3-pound / 1.4-kg) chuck roast
½ cup dry red wine
1 (1-pound / 454-g) butternut squash, chopped
2 carrots, chopped
¾ cup pearl onions
1 teaspoon dried oregano leaves
1 bay leaf
1½ cups beef broth
Salt and black pepper, to taste
1 small red onion, quartered

1. Select the Sauté mode of the Instant Pot and heat the olive oil.
2. Season the beef with salt and sear in the pot for 3 minutes per side or until well browned.
3. Mix in the wine. Bring to a boil and cook for 2 more minutes or until the wine has reduced by half.
4. Mix in the butternut squash, carrots, pearl onions, oregano, bay leaf, broth, black pepper, and red onion. Stir to combine and add the beef.
5. Seal the lid, then select the Manual mode and set the time for 35 minutes on High Pressure.
6. Once cooking is complete, do a quick pressure release. Carefully open the lid.
7. Remove the beef and slice. Spoon over the sauce and vegetables to serve.

Steak, Pepper, and Lettuce Salad

Prep time: 20 minutes | Cook time: 25 minutes | Serves 4

¾ pound (340 g) steak
¼ cup red wine
½ teaspoon red pepper flakes
Sea salt and ground black pepper, to taste
¾ cup water
2 tablespoons olive oil
1 tablespoon wine vinegar
1 sweet pepper, cut into strips
½ red onion, sliced
1 butterhead lettuce, separate into leaves
¼ cup feta cheese, crumbled
¼ cup black olives, pitted and sliced

1. Add the steak, red wine, red pepper, salt, black pepper, and water to the Instant Pot.
2. Secure the lid. Choose the Manual mode and set the cooking time for 25 minutes at High pressure.
3. Once cooking is complete, perform a natural pressure release for 10 minutes. Carefully open the lid.
4. Thinly slice the steak and transfer to a salad bowl. Toss with the olive oil and vinegar.
5. Add the peppers, red onion, and lettuce, then toss to combine well. Top with cheese and olives and serve.

Braised Tri-Tip Steak

Prep time: 20 minutes | Cook time: 54 minutes | Serves 4

2 pounds (907 g) tri-tip steak, patted dry
2 teaspoons coarse sea salt
3 tablespoons avocado oil
½ medium onion, diced
2 cloves garlic, smashed
1 tablespoon unsweetened tomato purée
1½ cups dry red wine
½ tablespoon dried thyme
2 bay leaves
1 Roma (plum) tomato, diced
1 stalk celery, including leaves, chopped
1 small turnip, chopped
½ cup water

1. Season the tri-tip with the coarse salt. Set the Instant Pot to Sauté mode and heat the avocado oil until shimmering.
2. Cook the steak in the pot for 2 minutes per side or until well browned. Remove the steak from the pot and place it in a shallow bowl. Set aside.

3. Add the onion to the pot and sauté for 3 minutes. Add the garlic and sauté for 1 minute. Add the unsweetened tomato purée and cook for 1 minute, stirring constantly.
4. Pour in the red wine. Stir in the thyme and bay leaves.
5. Return the tri-tip steak to the pot. Scatter the tomato, celery, and turnip around the steak. Pour in the water.
6. Secure the lid. Press the Manual button and set cooking time for 35 minutes on High Pressure.
7. When timer beeps, allow the pressure to release naturally for 20 minutes, then release any remaining pressure. Open the lid. Discard the bay leaves.
8. Remove the steak and place in a dish. Press the Sauté button and bring the braising liquid to a boil. Cook for 10 minutes or until the liquid is reduced by about half.
9. Slice the steak thinly and serve with braising liquid over.

Korean Beef Ribs

Prep time: 10 minutes | Cook time: 15 minutes | Serves 6

3 pounds (1.4 kg) beef short ribs
1 cup beef broth
Sauce:
½ teaspoon gochujang
½ cup rice wine
½ cup soy sauce
½ teaspoon garlic powder
2 green onions, sliced
1 tablespoon toasted sesame seeds
½ teaspoon ground ginger
½ cup pure maple syrup
1 teaspoon white pepper
1 tablespoon sesame oil

1. In a large bowl, combine the ingredients for the sauce. Dunk the rib in the bowl and press to coat well. Cover the bowl in plastic and refrigerate for at least an hour.
2. Add the beef broth to the Instant Pot. Insert a trivet. Arrange the ribs standing upright over the trivet. Lock the lid.
3. Press the Manual button and set the cooking time for 25 minutes at High Pressure.
4. When timer beeps, let pressure release naturally for 10 minutes, then release any remaining pressure. Unlock the lid.
5. Transfer ribs to a serving platter and garnish with green onions and sesame seeds. Serve immediately.

Saucy Short Ribs

Prep time: 20 minutes | Cook time: 40 minutes | Serves 4

2 tablespoons olive oil
1½ pounds (680 g) large beef short ribs
Salt and ground black pepper, to taste
3 garlic cloves, minced
1 medium onion, finely
chopped
½ cup apple cider vinegar
1 tablespoon honey
1 cup beef broth
2 tablespoons tomato paste
1 tablespoon cornstarch

1. Select the Sauté mode of the Instant Pot, then heat the olive oil.
2. Season ribs with salt and pepper, and fry in the pot for 8 minutes or until browned. Remove from the pot and set aside.
3. Sauté the garlic, onion, and cook for 4 minutes until fragrant.
4. Stir in apple cider vinegar, honey, broth, tomato paste. Bring to a simmer.
5. Add ribs. Seal the lid, then select the Manual mode and set the time for 25 minutes at High Pressure.
6. Once cooking is complete, allow a natural pressure release for 10 minutes, then release any remaining pressure. Unlock the lid.
7. Transfer the ribs to serving plates. Stir cornstarch into the sauce in the pot and stir for 1 minute or until thickened, on Sauté mode.
8. Spoon sauce over ribs and serve.

Mongolian Arrowroot Glazed Beef

Prep time: 15 minutes | Cook time: 20 minutes | Serves 4

1 tablespoon sesame oil
1 (2-pound / 907-g) skirt steak, sliced into thin strips
½ cup pure maple syrup
¼ cup soy sauce
4 cloves garlic, minced
1-inch knob fresh ginger root, peeled and grated
½ cup plus 2 tablespoons water, divided
2 tablespoons arrowroot powder

1.Press the Sauté button on the Instant Pot. Heat the sesame oil.
2.Add and sear the steak strips for 3 minutes on all sides.
3.In a medium bowl, whisk together maple syrup, soy sauce, garlic, ginger, and ½ cup water. Pour the mixture over beef. Lock the lid.
4.Press the Manual button and set the cooking time for 10 minutes at High Pressure.
5.When timer beeps, quick release the pressure, then unlock the lid.
6.Meanwhile, in a small dish, whisk together the arrowroot and 2 tablespoons water until smooth and chunky.
7.Stir the arrowroot into the beef mixture. Press the Sauté button and simmer for 5 minutes or until the sauce thickens.
8.Ladle the beef and sauce on plates and serve.

New York Strip with Heavy Cream

Prep time: 15 minutes | Cook time: 30 minutes | Serves 4

1 tablespoon sesame oil
1 pound (454 g) New York strip, sliced into thin strips
½ leek, sliced
1 carrot, sliced
⅓ cup dry red wine
½ tablespoon tamari
½ cup cream of mushroom soup
1 clove garlic, sliced
Kosher salt and ground black pepper, to taste
¼ cup heavy cream

1.Press the Sauté button of the Instant Pot. Heat the sesame oil until sizzling.
2.Add and brown the beef strips in batches for 4 minutes. Stir in the remaining ingredients, except for the heavy cream.
3.Secure the lid. Choose the Manual mode and set the cooking time for 20 minutes at High pressure.
4.Once cooking is complete, use a quick pressure release. Carefully open the lid.
5.Transfer the beef on a serving plate. Mash the vegetables in the pot with a potato masher.
6.Press the Sauté button. Bring to a boil, then Stir in the heavy cream.
7.Spoon the mixture over the New York strip and serve immediately.

Italian Beef Chuck

Prep time: 10 minutes | Cook time: 19 minutes | Serves 6

1 tablespoon olive oil
1 pound (454 g) 95% lean ground chuck
1 medium yellow onion, chopped
3 tablespoons tomato paste
3 medium garlic cloves,
chopped
2 teaspoons Italian seasoning
1 (28-ounce / 794-g) can tomatoes, chopped, with juice
½ cup beef broth
Salt and freshly ground black pepper, to taste

1.Put the olive oil in the pot, select the Sauté mode.
2.Add the ground beef and onion and sauté for 8 minutes or until the beef is browned.

3.Push the meat and onion mixture to one side of the pot. Add the tomato paste, garlic, and Italian seasoning to the other side of the pot and sauté for 1 minute or until fragrant.
4.Add the tomatoes and the broth to the pot. Lock on the lid, select the Manual function, and set the cooking time for 10 minutes on High Pressure.
5.When the cooking time is up, quick release the pressure. Season with salt and pepper and serve.

Herbed Beef Chuck Roast

Prep time: 15 minutes | Cook time: 1 hour | Serves 8

2 tablespoons coconut oil
3 pounds (1.4 kg) beef chuck roast
1 cup water
½ teaspoon dried parsley
½ teaspoon dried basil
½ teaspoon chili powder
½ teaspoon fresh paprika
1 cup butter
½ teaspoon kosher salt
½ teaspoon freshly ground black pepper

1.Set the Instant Pot to Sauté mode and melt the coconut oil.
2.Add and sear the roast for 4 minutes or until browned on both sides. Flip the roast halfway through, then remove from the pot.
3.Pour the water into the Instant Pot, then add the parsley, basil, chili powder, paprika, butter, salt, and black pepper. Return the beef to the pot.
4.Close the lid. Select the Manual mode, set the cooking time for 55 minutes on High Pressure.
5.When timer beeps, naturally release the pressure for about 10 minutes, then release any remaining pressure. Open the lid.
6.Serve immediately.

Slow Cooked Beef Pizza Casserole

Prep time: 15 minutes | Cook time: 3 hours 4 minutes | Serves 6

2 tablespoons olive oil, divided
1 pound (454 g) ground beef
2 cups shredded whole Mozzarella cheese, divided
1 tablespoon Italian seasoning blend, divided
1 teaspoon garlic powder, divided
½ cup unsweetened tomato purée
¼ teaspoon dried oregano
¼ teaspoon sea salt
15 slices pepperoni
2 tablespoons sliced black olives

1.Select Sauté mode. Once the pot is hot, add 1 tablespoon olive oil and crumble the ground beef into the pot. Sauté for 4 minutes until the meat is browned.
2.Place a colander over a large bowl. Transfer the meat to the colander to drain and then transfer the drained meat to a large mixing bowl.
3.To the bowl with the meat, add 1 cup Mozzarella, ½ tablespoon Italian seasoning, and ½ teaspoon garlic powder. Mix until well combined. Set aside.
4.In a small bowl, combine the tomato purée, remaining Italian seasoning, remaining garlic powder, oregano, and sea salt. Mix well. Set aside.
5.Coat the bottom of the Instant Pot with the remaining olive oil. Press the meat mixture into the bottom of the pot.
6.Add the tomato purée mixture to the pot and use a spoon to evenly distribute the sauce over the meat. Add the pepperoni over the sauce. Sprinkle the remaining Mozzarella over and then top with the olives.
7.Lock the lid. Select Slow Cook mode and set cooking time for 3 hours on Normal.
8.When cooking is complete, open the lid and transfer the casserole to a serving platter. Slice into six equal-sized wedges. Serve hot.

Steak and Bell Pepper Fajitas

Prep time: 15 minutes | Cook time: 45 minutes | Serves 6

1 (2-pound / 907-g) skirt steak
1 medium red bell pepper, deseeded and diced
1 medium green bell pepper, deseeded and diced
1 small onion, diced
1 cup beef broth
Sauce:
1 tablespoon fish sauce
¼ cup soy sauce
1 teaspoon ground cumin
2 tablespoons tomato paste
1 teaspoon chili powder
½ teaspoon sea salt
⅛ cup avocado oil

1. In a small bowl, combine the ingredients for the sauce. Spread ¾ of the sauce on all sides of the beef on a clean work surface. Reserve the remaining sauce.
2. Press the Sauté button on Instant Pot. Add skirt steak and sear on each side for about 5 minutes. Remove the meat and set aside.
3. Add the bell peppers and onion with reserved sauce. Sauté for 3 to 5 minutes or until the onions are translucent.
4. Pour in the beef broth. Set the beef over the onion and peppers. Lock the lid.
5. Press the Meat / Stew button and set the cooking time for 35 minutes at High Pressure.
6. When timer beeps, let the pressure release naturally for 15 minutes, then release any remaining pressure. Unlock the lid.
7. Using a slotted spoon, remove the meat and vegetables to a serving platter. Thinly slice the skirt steak and serve.

Osso Buco with Gremolata

Prep time: 35 minutes | Cook time: 1 hour 2 minutes | Serves 6

4 bone-in beef shanks
Sea salt, to taste
2 tablespoons avocado oil
1 small turnip, diced
1 medium onion, diced
1 medium stalk celery, diced
4 cloves garlic, smashed
1 tablespoon unsweetened tomato purée
½ cup dry white wine
1 cup chicken broth
1 sprig fresh rosemary
2 sprigs fresh thyme
3 Roma tomatoes, diced
For the Gremolata:
½ cup loosely packed parsley leaves
1 clove garlic, crushed
Grated zest of 2 lemons

1. On a clean work surface, season the shanks all over with salt.
2. Set the Instant Pot to Sauté and add the oil. When the oil shimmers, add 2 shanks and sear for 4 minutes per side. Remove the shanks to a bowl and repeat with the remaining shanks. Set aside.
3. Add the turnip, onion, and celery to the pot and cook for 5 minutes or until softened.
4. Add the garlic and unsweetened tomato purée and cook 1 minute more, stirring frequently.
5. Deglaze the pot with the wine, scraping the bottom with a wooden spoon to loosen any browned bits. Bring to a boil.
6. Add the broth, rosemary, thyme, and shanks, then add the tomatoes on top of the shanks.
7. Secure the lid. Press the Manual button and set cooking time for 40 minutes on High Pressure.
8. Meanwhile, for the gremolata: In a small food processor, combine the parsley, garlic, and lemon zest and pulse until the parsley is finely chopped. Refrigerate until ready to use.
9. When timer beeps, allow the pressure to release naturally for 20 minutes, then release any remaining pressure. Open the lid.
10. To serve, transfer the shanks to large, shallow serving bowl. Ladle the braising sauce over the top and sprinkle with the gremolata.

Beef and Mushroom Meal

Prep time: 12 mins, Cook Time: 40 mins, Servings: 4

1 lb. fat removed beef ribs
Salt, to taste
3 cups low-sodium beef stock
1 bacon slice, chopped
2 cups button mushrooms slices

1. On a clean work surface, rub the beef ribs with salt.
2. Add the ribs and stock to the Instant Pot. Stir to combine well.
3. Lock the lid. Press Manual. Set the timer to 30 minutes at High Pressure.
4. When the timer goes off, press Cancel, then use a natural pressure release for 10 minutes, and then release any remaining pressure.
5. Take out the beef and shred with a knife.
6. Put the shredded beef back to the pot, add the bacon and mushrooms; gently stir to combine.
7. Lock the lid. Press Manual. Set the timer to 7 minutes at High Pressure.
8. Once the timer goes off, press Cancel, then use a quick pressure release.
9. Open the lid, transfer them on 4 plates and serve.

Bacon Stuffed Meatloaf

Prep time: 15 minutes | Cook time: 32 minutes | Serves 4

1 pound (454 g) ground beef
1 large egg, beaten
½ cup unsweetened tomato purée
2 tablespoons golden flaxseed meal
1 teaspoon garlic powder
1 teaspoon sea salt
½ teaspoon paprika
¼ teaspoon ground black pepper
4 slices uncooked bacon
⅓ cup shredded Cheddar cheese
1 cup water
For The Glaze:
⅓ cup unsweetened tomato purée
1 teaspoon apple cider vinegar
¼ teaspoon onion powder
¼ teaspoon garlic powder
2 teaspoons erythritol
⅛ teaspoon sea salt
⅛ teaspoon allspice

1. In a large bowl, combine the ground beef, egg, tomato purée, flaxseed meal, garlic powder, sea salt, paprika, and black pepper. Mix to combine well.
2. Place a sheet of aluminum foil on a flat surface. Place half of the meat mixture in the center of the foil sheet and use the hands to mold the mixture into a flat oval shape that is about 6 inches long.
3. Place the bacon slices on top of the meat and sprinkle the Cheddar over. Place the remaining meat mixture on top and shape the mixture into an oval-shaped loaf.
4. Fold the sides of the foil up and around the sides of the meatloaf to form a loaf pan. Set aside.
5. Make the tomato glaze by combining the tomato purée, vinegar, onion powder, garlic powder, erythritol, sea salt, and allspice in a small bowl. Mix well. Spoon the glaze over the meatloaf.
6. Add the water to the Instant Pot. Place the loaf on the trivet and lower the trivet into the pot.
7. Lock the lid. Select Manual mode and set cooking time for 30 minutes on High Pressure.
8. While the meatloaf is cooking, preheat the oven broiler to 550°F (288°C).
9. When cooking time is complete, quick release the pressure, then open the lid and carefully remove the meatloaf from the pot.
10. Transfer the loaf pan to a large baking sheet. Place the meatloaf under the broiler to brown for 2 minutes or until the glaze is bubbling.
11. Transfer the browned meatloaf to a serving plate, discard the foil, and cut the loaf into 8 equal-sized slices. Serve hot.

Tequila Short Ribs

Prep time: 3 hours 25 minutes | Cook time: 35 minutes | Serves 4

1 pound (454 g) chuck short ribs
1 shot tequila
½ tablespoon stone ground mustard
½ tablespoon Sriracha sauce
½ cup apple cider
1 tablespoon tomato paste
1 tablespoon honey
½ teaspoon marjoram
½ teaspoon garlic powder
½ teaspoon shallot powder
½ teaspoon paprika
Kosher salt and cracked black pepper, to taste
¾ cup beef bone broth

1. Place all ingredients, except for the beef broth, in a large bowl. Cover with a foil and let it marinate for 3 hours in the refrigerator.
2. Pour the beef along with the marinade in the Instant Pot. Pour in the beef bone broth.
3. Secure the lid. Choose the Meat / Stew mode and set the cooking time for 35 minutes at High pressure.
4. Once cooking is complete, do a natural pressure release for 15 minutes, then release any remaining pressure. Carefully open the lid.
5. Serve immediately.

Sumptuous Beef and Tomato Biryani

Prep time: 10 minutes | Cook time: 25 minutes | Serves 6

1 tablespoon ghee
1 small onion, sliced
1 pound (454 g) top round, cut into strips
1 (28-ounce / 794-g) can whole stewed tomatoes, with juice
1 cup plain Greek yogurt
1 tablespoon minced fresh ginger root
2 cloves garlic, minced
½ teaspoon ground cloves
½ teaspoon ground cumin
½ teaspoon ground coriander
½ teaspoon ground cinnamon
½ teaspoon ground cardamom
1 teaspoon salt
½ teaspoon ground black pepper
2 cups cooked basmati rice

1. Press the Sauté button on Instant Pot. Melt the ghee.
2. Add the onion and sauté for 3 to 5 minutes or until translucent.
3. Add the remaining ingredients, except for the rice, to the Instant Pot. Lock the lid.
4. Press the Manual button and set the cooking time for 10 minutes at High Pressure.
5. When timer beeps, quick release the pressure, then unlock the lid.
6. Press the Sauté button and simmer for about 10 minutes or until most of the liquid has evaporated. Serve over cooked basmati rice.

Thai Coconut Beef with Snap Peas

Prep time: 30 minutes | Cook time: 40 minutes | Serves 10

1 (3-pound / 1.4-kg) boneless beef chuck roast, halved
1 teaspoon salt
1 teaspoon ground black pepper
2 tablespoons canola oil
1 (14-ounce / 397-g) can coconut milk
½ cup creamy peanut butter
¼ cup red curry paste
2 tablespoons honey
¾ cup beef stock
2 tablespoons soy sauce
2 teaspoons minced fresh ginger root
1 large sweet red pepper, sliced
½ pound (227 g) fresh sugar snap peas, trimmed
¼ cup minced fresh cilantro

1. Sprinkle the beef with salt and pepper on a clean work surface. Select the Sauté setting of the Instant Pot. Add the canola oil and heat.
2. Add one roast half. Brown on all sides for about 5 minutes. Remove and repeat with remaining beef half.

3. Meanwhile, in a bowl, whisk the coconut milk with peanut butter, curry paste, honey, beef stock, soy sauce, and ginger root.
4. Put all the beef halves into the Instant Pot, then add red pepper and pour the coconut milk mixture over the beef.
5. Lock the lid. Select the Manual setting and set the cooking time for 35 minutes at High Pressure.
6. When timer beeps, quick release the pressure. Carefully open the lid.
7. Add the sugar snap peas and set the cooking time for 5 minutes at High Pressure.
8. When timer beeps, naturally release the pressure for 10 minutes, then release any remaining pressure. Unlock the lid.
9. Remove beef from the pot. Skim fat from cooking juices. Shred beef with forks. Stir in cilantro and serve.

Sweet Apricot Beef

Prep time: 12 mins, Cook Time: 30 mins, Servings: 4

1½ lbs. beef tenderloin
1 tsp. sea salt
1 tbsp. coconut oil
4 apricots, pitted and sliced
thinly
½ cup chopped almonds
1 cup water

1. On a clean work surface, sprinkle the beef with salt and cut into 1-inch thick slices.
2. Set the Instant Pot to Sauté setting, then add coconut oil and heat until melted.
3. Add the beef and sauté for 4 to 5 minutes or until browned.
4. Add the apricot and sauté for a minute. Add the chopped almonds. Pour in the water.
5. Lock the lid. Press the Manual setting and set the timer at 30 minutes at High Pressure.
6. When the timer beeps, press Cancel, then use a quick pressure release.
7. Carefully open the lid and allow to cool for a few minutes. Serve warm.

Lemongrass Rice and Beef Pot

Prep time: 45 minutes | Cook time: 15 minutes | Serves 4

1 pound (454 g) beef stew meat, cut into cubes
2 tablespoons olive oil
1 green bell pepper, chopped
1 red bell pepper, chopped
1 lemongrass stalk, sliced
Marinade:
1 tablespoon rice wine
½ teaspoon Five-spice
½ teaspoon miso paste
1 teaspoon garlic purée
1 teaspoon chili powder
1 teaspoon cumin powder
1 onion, chopped
2 garlic cloves, minced
1 cup jasmine rice
2 cups chicken broth
2 tablespoons chopped parsley, for garnish

1 tablespoon soy sauce
1 teaspoon plus ½ tablespoon ginger paste, divided
½ teaspoon sesame oil
Salt and black pepper, to taste

1. In a bowl, add beef and top with the ingredients for the marinade. Mix and wrap the bowl in plastic. Marinate in the refrigerate for 30 minutes.
2. Set the Instant Pot to Sauté mode, then heat the olive oil.
3. Drain beef from marinade and brown in the pot for 5 minutes. Flip frequently.
4. Stir in bell peppers, lemongrass, onion, and garlic. Sauté for 3 minutes.
5. Stir in rice, cook for 1 minute. Pour in the broth. Seal the lid, select the Manual mode and set the time for 5 minutes on High Pressure.
6. When timer beeps, perform a quick pressure release. Carefully open the lid.
7. Dish out and garnish with parsley. Serve warm.

Chapter 7 Pork

Albóndigas Sinaloenses

Prep time: 15 minutes | Cook time: 10 minutes | Serves 6

1 pound (454 g) ground pork
½ pound (227 g) Italian sausage, crumbled
2 tablespoons yellow onion, finely chopped
½ teaspoon dried oregano
1 sprig fresh mint, finely minced
½ teaspoon ground cumin
2 garlic cloves, finely minced
¼ teaspoon fresh ginger,
grated
Seasoned salt and ground black pepper, to taste
1 tablespoon olive oil
½ cup yellow onions, finely chopped
2 chipotle chilies in adobo
2 tomatoes, puréed
2 tablespoons tomato passata
1 cup chicken broth

1. In a mixing bowl, combine the pork, sausage, 2 tablespoons of yellow onion, oregano, mint, cumin, garlic, ginger, salt, and black pepper.
2. Roll the mixture into meatballs and reserve.
3. Press the Sauté button to heat up the Instant Pot. Heat the olive oil and cook the meatballs for 4 minutes, stirring continuously.
4. Stir in ½ cup of yellow onions, chilies in adobo, tomatoes passata, and broth. Add reserved meatballs.
5. Secure the lid. Choose the Manual mode and set cooking time for 6 minutes at High pressure.
6. Once cooking is complete, use a quick pressure release. Carefully remove the lid.
7. Serve immediately.

Apple and Pumpkin Ham

Prep time: 10 minutes | Cook time: 10 minutes | Serves 6

1 cup apple cider vinegar
1 pound (454 g) ham, cooked
2 tablespoons erythritol
1 tablespoon avocado oil
2 tablespoons butter
½ teaspoon pumpkin pie spices

1. Pour apple cider vinegar in the Instant Pot and insert the trivet.
2. Rub the ham with erythritol avocado oil,, butter, and pumpkin pie spices.
3. Put the ham on the trivet. Close the lid.
4. Select Manual mode and set cooking time for 10 minutes on High Pressure.
5. When timer beeps, use a natural pressure release for 5 minutes, then release any remaining pressure and open the lid.
6. Slice the ham and serve.

Pork Steak Curry

Prep time: 15 minutes | Cook time: 8 minutes | Serves 6

½ teaspoon mustard seeds
1 teaspoon fennel seeds
1 teaspoon cumin seeds
2 chili peppers, deseeded and minced
½ teaspoon ground bay leaf
1 teaspoon mixed peppercorns
1 tablespoon sesame oil
1½ pounds (680 g) pork steak, sliced
2 cloves garlic, finely minced
2 tablespoons scallions,
chopped
1 teaspoon fresh ginger, grated
1 teaspoon curry powder
1 cup chicken broth
2 tablespoons balsamic vinegar
3 tablespoons coconut cream
¼ teaspoon red pepper flakes, crushed
Sea salt, to taste
¼ teaspoon ground black pepper

1. Heat a skillet over medium-high heat. Once hot, roast the mustard seeds, fennel seeds, cumin seeds, chili peppers, ground bay leaf, and peppercorns for 1 or 2 minutes or until aromatic.
2. Press the Sauté button to heat up the Instant Pot. Heat the sesame oil until sizzling. Sear pork steak for 5 minutes or until browned.
3. Add the remaining ingredients, including roasted seasonings. Stir to mix well.
4. Secure the lid. Choose the Manual mode and set cooking time for 8 minutes on High pressure.
5. Once cooking is complete, use a quick pressure release. Carefully remove the lid.
6. Serve immediately.

Pork Medallions and Mushrooms

Prep time: 12 mins, Cook time: 8 mins, Servings: 4

2 tsps. extra virgin olive oil
4 pork medallions, rinsed and trimmed
1 tsp. salt
12 oyster mushrooms, quartered
1 onion, diced
1 cup water

1. Set the Instant Pot to Sauté setting, then add the extra virgin olive oil and heat until the oil is shimmering.
2. Add the pork medallions and brown for 3 to 4 minutes.
3. Add the remaining ingredients.
4. Lock the lid. Select the Manual setting and set the timer to 8 minutes at High Pressure.
5. When the timer beeps, press Cancel, then use a quick pressure release.
6. Carefully open the lid. Allow to cool for a few minutes. Transfer them on a large plate and serve immediately.

Bacon-Wrapped Pork Bites

Prep time: 15 minutes | Cook time: 20 minutes | Serves 4

3 tablespoons butter
10 ounces (283 g) pork tenderloin, cubed

6 ounces (170 g) bacon, sliced
½ teaspoon white pepper
¾ cup chicken stock

1. Melt the butter on Sauté mode in the Instant Pot.
2. Meanwhile, wrap the pork tenderloin cubes in the sliced bacon and sprinkle with white pepper. Secure with toothpicks, if necessary.
3. Put the wrapped pork tenderloin in the melted butter and cook for 3 minutes on each side.
4. Add the chicken stock and close the lid.
5. Select Manual mode and set cooking time for 14 minutes on High Pressure.
6. When timer beeps, use a natural pressure release for 5 minutes, then release any remaining pressure. Open the lid.
7. Discard the toothpicks and serve immediately.

Beery Boston-Style Butt

Prep time: 10 minutes | Cook time: 1 hour 1 minutes | Serves 4

1 tablespoon butter
1 pound (454 g) Boston-style butt
½ cup leeks, chopped
¼ cup beer
½ cup chicken stock

Pinch of grated nutmeg
Sea salt, to taste
¼ teaspoon ground black pepper
¼ cup water

1. Press the Sauté button to heat up the Instant Pot. Once hot, melt the butter.
2. Cook the Boston-style butt for 3 minutes on each side. Remove from the pot and reserve.
3. Sauté the leeks for 5 minutes or until fragrant. Add the remaining ingredients and stir to combine.
4. Secure the lid. Choose the Manual mode and set cooking time for 50 minutes on High pressure.
5. Once cooking is complete, use a natural pressure release for 20 minutes, then release any remaining pressure. Carefully remove the lid.
6. Serve immediately.

Mexican Chili Pork

Prep time: 6 mins, Cook Time: 35 mins, Servings: 6

3 tbsps. olive oil
2 tsps. minced garlic
2 lbs. pork sirloin, sliced
2 tsps. ground cumin

1 tbsp. red chili flakes
1 cup water
Salt and pepper, to taste

1. Press the Sauté button on the Instant pot and heat the olive oil until shimmering.
2. Add and sauté the garlic for 30 seconds or until fragrant.
3. Add the pork sirloin and sauté for 3 minutes or until lightly browned.
4. Add the cumin and chili flakes.
5. Pour in the water and sprinkle salt and pepper for seasoning.
6. Lock the lid. Press the Meat/Stew button and set the cooking time to 30 minutes at High Pressure.
7. Once cooking is complete, perform a natural pressure release for 10 minutes, and then release any remaining pressure. Carefully open the lid.
8. Remove the pork from the pot and serve warm.

Blade Pork with Sauerkraut

Prep time: 15 minutes | Cook time: 37 minutes | Serves 6

2 pounds (907 g) blade pork steaks
Sea salt and ground black pepper, to taste
½ teaspoon cayenne pepper
½ teaspoon dried parsley flakes

1 tablespoon butter
1½ cups water
2 cloves garlic, thinly sliced
2 pork sausages, casing removed and sliced
4 cups sauerkraut

1. Season the blade pork steaks with salt, black pepper, cayenne pepper, and dried parsley.
2. Press the Sauté button to heat up the Instant Pot. Melt the butter and sear blade pork steaks for 5 minutes or until browned on all sides.
3. Clean the Instant Pot. Add water and trivet to the bottom of the Instant Pot.
4. Place the blade pork steaks on the trivet. Make small slits over entire pork with a knife. Insert garlic pieces into each slit.
5. Secure the lid. Choose the Meat/Stew mode and set cooking time for 30 minutes on High pressure.
6. Once cooking is complete, use a natural pressure release for 15 minutes, then release any remaining pressure. Carefully remove the lid.
7. Add the sausage and sauerkraut. Press the Sauté button and cook for 2 minutes more or until heated through.
8. Serve immediately.

Paprika Pork with Brussels Sprouts

Prep time: 10 minutes | Cook time: 30 minutes | Serves 4

2 tablespoons olive oil
2 pounds (907 g) pork shoulder, cubed
2 cups Brussels sprouts,

trimmed and halved
1½ cups beef stock
1 tablespoon sweet paprika
1 tablespoon chopped parsley

1. Press the Sauté button on the Instant Pot and heat the olive oil.
2. Add the pork and brown for 5 minutes. Stir in the remaining ingredients.
3. Secure the lid. Select the Manual mode and set the cooking time for 25 minutes at High Pressure.
4. Once cooking is complete, do a natural pressure release for 10 minutes, then release any remaining pressure. Carefully open the lid.
5. Divide the mix between plates and serve warm.

Pork and Mushroom with Mustard

Prep time: 6 mins, Cook Time: 35 mins, Servings: 6

3 tbsps. butter
2 lbs. pork shoulder
3 tbsps. yellow mustard

1 cup water
1 cup sliced mushrooms
Salt and pepper, to taste

1. Press the Sauté button on the Instant Pot and heat the butter until melted.
2. Add the pork shoulder and mustard. Sauté for 3 minutes or until the pork is lightly browned.
3. Stir in water and mushrooms. Sprinkle salt and pepper for seasoning.
4. Lock the lid. Press the Meat/Stew button and set the cooking time to 30 minutes at High Pressure.
5. Once cooking is complete, perform a natural pressure release for 10 minutes, and then release any remaining pressure. Carefully open the lid.
6. Remove the pork from the pot and serve warm.

Jamaican Pork Roast

Prep time: 10 minutes | Cook time: 55 minutes | Serves 6

¼ cup Jamaican jerk spice blend
¾ tablespoon olive oil

2 pounds (907 g) pork shoulder
¼ cup beef broth

1. Rub the jerk spice blend and olive oil all over the pork shoulder and set aside to marinate for 10 minutes.
2. When ready, press the Sauté button on the Instant Pot and add the pork.
3. Sear for 4 minutes. Flip the pork and cook for 4 minutes.
4. Pour the beef broth into the Instant Pot.
5. Secure the lid. Select the Manual mode and set the cooking time for 45 minutes at High Pressure.
6. Once cooking is complete, do a natural pressure release for 10 minutes, then release any remaining pressure. Carefully open the lid.
7. Serve hot.

Maple-Glazed Spareribs

Prep time: 40 minutes | Cook time: 30 minutes | Serves 6

2 racks (about 3 pounds / 1.4 kg) baby back pork ribs, cut into 2-rib sections
1 teaspoon instant coffee crystals
1 teaspoon sea salt
½ teaspoon ground cumin
½ teaspoon chili powder
½ teaspoon ground mustard
½ teaspoon cayenne pepper
½ teaspoon onion powder

½ teaspoon garlic powder
¼ teaspoon ground coriander
¼ cup soy sauce
¼ cup pure maple syrup
2 tablespoons tomato paste
1 tablespoon apple cider vinegar
1 tablespoon olive oil
1 medium onion, peeled and large diced

1. Mix together the coffee, salt, cumin, chili powder, mustard, cayenne pepper, onion powder, garlic powder, and coriander in a mixing bowl. Rub the mixture into the rib sections with your hands. Refrigerate for at least 30 minutes, covered. Set aside.
2. Stir together the soy sauce, maple syrup, tomato paste, and apple cider vinegar in a small mixing bowl.
3. Set your Instant Pot to Sauté and heat the olive oil. Add the onions and sauté for 3 to 5 minutes until translucent.
4. Stir in the soy sauce mixture. Add a few ribs at a time with tongs and gently stir to coat. Arrange the ribs standing upright, meat-side outward. Secure the lid.
5. Select the Manual function and cook for 25 minutes on High Pressure.
6. Once cooking is complete, use a natural pressure release for 10 minutes and then release any remaining pressure. Carefully open the lid.
7. Transfer the ribs to a serving plate and serve warm.

Pulled Pork

Prep time: 6 mins, Cook Time: 1 hour, Servings: 12

4 lbs. pork shoulder
1 tsp. cinnamon
2 tsps. garlic powder
5 tbsps. coconut oil

1 tsp. cumin powder
1½ cups water
Salt and pepper, to taste

1. In the Instant Pot, add all the ingredients. Stir to combine well.
2. Lock the lid. Press the Meat/Stew button and set the cooking time to 1 hour at High Pressure.
3. Once cooking is complete, do a natural pressure release for 10 minutes, and then release any remaining pressure. Carefully open the lid.
4. Remove the meat and shred with two forks to serve.

Paprika Pork Loin Roast

Prep time: 6 mins, Cook Time: 50 mins, Servings: 9

4 tbsps. olive oil
4 garlic cloves
½ cup chopped paprika

3 lbs. pork loin roast
Salt and pepper, to taste
1 cup water

1. Press the Sauté button on the Instant Pot. Coat the pot with olive oil.
2. Add and sauté the garlic and paprika for 1 minute or until fragrant.
3. Add the pork loin roast and sear on all sides for 3 minutes or until lightly browned.
4. Sprinkle salt and pepper for seasoning. Pour in the water.
5. Lock the lid. Press the Meat/Stew button and set the cooking time to 45 minutes at High Pressure.
6. Once cooking is complete, perform a natural pressure release for 10 minutes, and then release any remaining pressure. Carefully open the lid.
7. Allow to cool for a few minutes. Remove the pork from the pot and baste with the juice remains in the pot before serving.

Pork Butt with Pear

Prep time: 12 mins, Cook time: 50 mins, Servings: 12

4 lbs. pork butt
2 tbsps. sea salt
3 tbsps. extra virgin olive oil
4 pears, peeled, stem

removed, deseeded, and cut into ½-inch chunks
1½ cups chicken broth

1. On a clean work surface, rub the pork butt with salt.
2. Set the Instant Pot to Sauté setting, then add and heat the olive oil.
3. Place pork in pot and brown for 5 minutes per side.
4. Add pears and chicken broth. Stir to mix well.
5. Lock the lid. Set the pot to Manual setting and set the timer for 45 minutes at High Pressure.
6. When the timer beeps, press Cancel, then use a quick pressure release.
7. Carefully open the lid and allow to cool for a few minutes. Serve warm.

Chinese Pork

Prep time: 10 mins, Cook Time: 25 mins, Servings: 4

4 tbsps. coconut oil
4 garlic cloves, minced
1 tbsp. fresh ginger
4 boneless pork chops

2 tbsps. soy sauce
Salt and pepper, to taste
1 cup water

1. Press the Sauté button on the Instant Pot and heat the coconut oil until melted.
2. Add and sauté the garlic and ginger for 1 minutes or until fragrant.
3. Add the pork and sauté for 3 minutes or until lightly browned.
4. Pour in the soy sauce and water, then sprinkle salt and pepper for seasoning.
5. Lock the lid. Press the Meat/Stew button and set the cooking time to 20 minutes at High Pressure.
6. Once cooking is complete, perform a natural pressure release for 10 minutes, and then release any remaining pressure. Carefully open the lid.
7. Press the Sauté button and allow to simmer for 3 to 5 minutes or until the sauce has thickened. Keep stirring.
8. Allow to cool for a few minutes. Remove them from the pot and serve warm.

Pine Nut Pork

Prep time: 20 mins, Cook Time: 25 mins, Servings: 4

1½ lbs. pork tenderloin
1 tsp. sea salt
1 tbsp. extra virgin olive oil

1 medium onion, finely sliced
½ cup pine nuts
1 cup pesto sauce

1. On a clean work surface, cut the pork tenderloin into 1-inch thick slices and rub with salt.
2. Place the olive oil in Instant Pot, then set to Sauté setting.
3. Add and brown the pork for 3 minutes, then add onion and sauté for a minute or until translucent.
4. Add the pine nuts and pesto sauce.
5. Lock the lid. Set the pot to Manual mode and set the timer to 20 minutes at High Pressure.
1. Once cooking is complete, use a natural pressure release for 10 minutes, then release any remaining pressure.
6. Carefully open the lid. Allow to cool for a few minutes. Transfer them on a large plate and serve immediately.

Orange and Cinnamon Pork

Prep time: 10 minutes | Cook time: 35 minutes | Serves 4

4 pork chops
1 tablespoon cinnamon powder
3 garlic cloves, minced
½ cup beef stock
Juice of 1 orange

1 tablespoon grated ginger
1 teaspoon dried rosemary
A pinch of salt and black pepper

1. Stir together all the ingredients in your Instant Pot.
2. Secure the lid. Press the Manual button on the Instant Pot and set the cooking time for 35 minutes on High Pressure.
3. Once cooking is complete, perform a natural pressure release for 10 minutes and then release any remaining pressure. Carefully open the lid.
4. Divide the mix among the plates and serve immediately.

Pork Steak Curry

Prep time: 15 minutes | Cook time: 15 minutes | Serves 6

1 teaspoon cumin seeds
1 teaspoon fennel seeds
½ teaspoon mustard seeds
2 chili peppers, deseeded and minced
1 teaspoon mixed peppercorns
½ teaspoon ground bay leaf
1 tablespoon sesame oil
1½ pounds (680 g) pork steak, sliced
1 cup chicken broth
3 tablespoons coconut cream
2 tablespoons balsamic

vinegar
2 tablespoons chopped scallions
2 cloves garlic, finely minced
1 teaspoon curry powder
1 teaspoon grated fresh ginger
¼ teaspoon crushed red pepper flakes
¼ teaspoon ground black pepper
1 cup vegetable broth
Sea salt, to taste

1. Heat a skillet over medium-high heat and roast the cumin seeds, fennel seeds, mustard seeds, peppers, peppercorns, and ground bay leaf and until aromatic.
2. Set the Instant Pot to Sauté. Add and heat the sesame oil until sizzling. Sear the pork steak until nicely browned.
3. Stir in the roasted seasonings and the remaining ingredients.
4. Lock the lid. Select the Manual mode and set the cooking time for 8 minutes at High Pressure.
5. When the timer beeps, do a quick pressure release. Carefully open the lid.
6. Divide the mix among bowls and serve immediately.

Pork and Sweet Potato

Prep time: 20 mins, Cook Time: 25 mins, Servings: 8

2 tbsps. extra virgin olive oil
2 lbs. pork tenderloin, slice into 1-inch bites
1 tsp. sea salt

2 sweet potatoes, peeled and quartered
4 cups beef broth

1. Lightly coat the Instant Pot with the olive oil and set the Sauté mode.
2. Add the pork along with salt and brown for 3 minutes on all sides.
3. Add sweet potatoes with beef broth to the pot.
4. Set the setting to Manual mode and set the cooking time for 25 minutes at High Pressure.
5. Once cooking is complete, use a quick pressure release.
6. Carefully open the lid. Allow to cool for a few minutes. Transfer them on a large plate and serve immediately.

Pork Chops with Peas

Prep time: 12 mins, Cook time: 10 mins, Servings: 4

1 tbsp. olive oil
4 pork chops
1 medium onion, chopped

1 cup peas
½ tsp. salt
1 tsp. curry powder

1. Coat the Instant Pot with olive oil and set to Sauté setting.
2. Add the pork chops and sear for 3 minutes or until lightly browned.
3. Add the onion and sauté for 1 to 2 minutes or until soft.
4. Add peas, salt and curry powder and sauté for 3 to 5 minutes or until peas are tender.
5. Serve them warm on a large plate.

Pork with Mushroom Sauce

Prep time: 10 minutes | Cook time: 15 minutes | Serves 2

1 tablespoon oil
2 bone-in, medium-cut pork chops
Kosher salt and freshly ground black pepper, to taste
4 ounces (113 g) cremini mushrooms, sliced

2 garlic cloves, minced
½ small onion, sliced
Splash of dry white wine
1 cup chicken stock
1 tablespoon cornstarch
1 tablespoon butter
¾ cup sour cream

1. Set your Instant Pot to Sauté. Add and heat the oil.
2. Sprinkle the pork chops generously with the salt and pepper. Sear the pork chops on both sides and transfer to a plate.
3. Add the mushrooms, garlic, and onion and sauté for 3 minutes until soft. Add the white wine and deglaze the pot by scraping up any browned bits on the bottom with a wooden spoon.
4. Stir in the stock. Add the seared pork chops to the pot.
5. Lock the lid. Select the Manual mode and cook for 8 minutes on High Pressure.
6. Once cooking is complete, do a natural pressure release for about 10 minutes. Carefully open the lid.
7. Select the Sauté mode.
8. Transfer the pork chops to a plate. Remove 1 tablespoon of the cooking liquid from the pot and pour in a small bowl with the cornstarch. Stir well and transfer the mixture back to the pot.
9. Mix in the butter and sour cream and stir until mixed. Let simmer for 4 to 5 minutes until thickened. Sprinkle with the salt and pepper if necessary.
10. Transfer to a serving plate and serve.

Blue Pork

Prep time: 5 minutes | Cook time: 20 minutes | Serves 2

1 teaspoon coconut oil
2 pork chops
2 ounces (57 g) blue cheese,
crumbled
1 teaspoon lemon juice
¼ cup heavy cream

1. Heat the coconut oil in the Instant Pot on Sauté mode.
2. Put the pork chops in the Instant Pot and cook on Sauté mode for 5 minutes on each side.
3. Add the lemon juice and crumbled cheese. Stir to mix well.
4. Add heavy cream and close the lid.
5. Select Manual mode and set cooking time for 10 minutes on High Pressure.
6. When timer beeps, perform a natural pressure release for 5 minutes, then release any remaining pressure. Open the lid.
7. Serve immediately.

Bo Ssäm

Prep time: 10 minutes | Cook time: 8 minutes | Serves 6

1 tablespoon vegetable oil
1 pound (454 g) ground pork
2 tablespoons gochujang
1 tablespoon Doubanjiang
½ teaspoon ground Sichuan peppercorns
1 tablespoon minced fresh ginger
1 tablespoon minced garlic
1 tablespoon coconut aminos
1 teaspoon hot sesame oil
1 teaspoon salt
¼ cup water
1 bunch bok choy, chopped (about 4 to 6 cups)

1. Preheat the Instant Pot on Sauté mode. Add the oil and heat until it is shimmering.
2. Add the ground pork, breaking up all lumps, and cook for 4 minutes or until the pork is no longer pink.
3. Add the gochujang, doubanjiang, peppercorns, ginger, garlic, coconut aminos, sesame oil, and salt. Stir to combine.
4. Add the water and bok choy.
5. Lock the lid. Select Manual mode. Set cooking time for 4 minutes on High Pressure.
6. When cooking is complete, quick-release the pressure. Unlock the lid.
7. Serve immediately.

Carolina-Style Pork Barbecue

Prep time: 10 minutes | Cook time: 40 minutes | Serves 4 to 6

1 (4-pound / 1.8-kg) boneless pork shoulder or pork butt roast
3 tablespoons packed brown sugar
1½ teaspoons smoked paprika
1 tablespoon seasoning salt
1 cup ketchup
½ cup water
½ cup cider vinegar

1. On a clean work surface, trim any excess fat off the outside of the pork shoulder, then cut the pork into four large pieces.
2. Mix together the brown sugar, paprika, and seasoning salt in a small bowl. Rub this mixture all over the pork pieces.
3. Place the ketchup, water, and vinegar into the Instant Pot and stir well. Add the pork pieces to the pot, turning to coat.
4. Secure the lid. Select the Manual mode and set the cooking time for 40 minutes at High Pressure.
5. Once cooking is complete, do a natural pressure release for 5 minutes, then release any remaining pressure. Carefully open the lid.
6. Remove the pork pieces from the pot to a cutting board. Using two forks to shred them and discard any large chunks of fat.
7. Spoon the sauce over the pork and serve immediately.

Pork Taco Casserole

Prep time: 15 minutes | Cook time: 30 minutes | Serves 6

½ cup water
2 eggs
3 ounces (85 g) Cottage cheese, at room temperature
¼ cup heavy cream
1 teaspoon taco seasoning
6 ounces (170 g) Cotija cheese, crumbled
¾ pound (340 g) ground pork
½ cup tomatoes, puréed
1 tablespoon taco seasoning
3 ounces (85 g) chopped green chilies
6 ounces (170 g) Queso Manchego cheese, shredded

1. Add the water in the Instant Pot and place in the trivet.
2. In a mixing bowl, combine the eggs, Cottage cheese, heavy cream, and taco seasoning.
3. Lightly grease a casserole dish. Spread the Cotija cheese over the bottom. Stir in the egg mixture.
4. Lower the casserole dish onto the trivet.
5. Secure the lid. Choose Manual mode and set cooking time for 20 minutes on High Pressure.
6. Once cooking is complete, use a quick pressure release. Carefully remove the lid.
7. In the meantime, heat a skillet over a medium-high heat. Brown the ground pork, crumbling with a fork.
8. Add the tomato purée, taco seasoning, and green chilies. Spread the mixture over the prepared cheese crust.
9. Top with shredded Queso Manchego.
10. Secure the lid. Choose Manual mode and set cooking time for 10 minutes on High Pressure.
11. Once cooking is complete, use a quick pressure release. Carefully remove the lid.
12. Serve immediately.

Chile Verde Pulled Pork with Tomatillos

Prep time: 15 minutes | Cook time: 1 hour 3 minutes | Serves 6

2 pounds (907 g) pork shoulder, cut into 6 equal-sized pieces
1 teaspoon sea salt
½ teaspoon ground black pepper
2 jalapeño peppers, deseeded and stemmed
1 pound (454 g) tomatillos, husks removed and quartered
3 garlic cloves
1 tablespoon lime juice
3 tablespoons fresh cilantro, chopped
1 medium white onion, chopped
1 teaspoon ground cumin
½ teaspoon dried oregano
1⅔ cups chicken broth
1½ tablespoons olive oil

1. Season the pork pieces with the salt and pepper. Gently rub the seasonings into the pork cuts. Set aside.
2. Combine the jalapeños, tomatillos, garlic cloves, lime juice, cilantro, onions, cumin, oregano, and chicken broth in the blender. Pulse until well combined. Set aside.
3. Select Sauté mode and add the olive oil to the pot. Once the oil is hot, add the pork cuts and sear for 4 minutes per side or until browned.
4. Pour the jalapeño sauce over the pork and lightly stir to coat well.
5. Lock the lid. Select Manual mode and set cooking time for 55 minutes on High Pressure.
6. When cooking is complete, allow the pressure to release naturally for 10 minutes and then release the remaining pressure.
7. Open the lid. Transfer the pork pieces to a cutting board and use two forks to shred the pork.
8. Transfer the shredded pork back to the pot and stir to combine the pork with the sauce. Transfer to a serving platter. Serve warm.

Cauliflower and Pork Keema

Prep time: 15 minutes | Cook time: 8 minutes | Serves 6

1 tablespoon sesame oil
½ cup yellow onion, chopped
1 garlic cloves, minced
1 (1-inch) piece fresh ginger, minced
1½ pounds (680 g) ground pork
1 cup cauliflower, chopped into small florets
1 ripe tomatoes, puréed
1 jalapeño pepper, seeded and

minced
4 cloves, whole
1 teaspoon garam masala
½ teaspoon ground cumin
¼ teaspoon turmeric powder
1 teaspoon brown mustard seeds
½ teaspoon hot paprika
Sea salt and ground black pepper, to taste
1 cup water

1. Press the Sauté button to heat up the Instant Pot. Heat the sesame oil. Once hot, sauté yellow onion for 3 minutes or until softened.
2. Stir in garlic and ginger; cook for an additional minute. Add the remaining ingredients.
3. Secure the lid. Choose the Manual mode and set cooking time for 5 minutes on High pressure.
4. Once cooking is complete, use a quick pressure release. Carefully remove the lid.
5. Serve immediately.

Chili and Cocoa Pork

Prep time: 10 minutes | Cook time: 30 minutes | Serves 4

4 pork chops
2 tablespoons hot sauce
2 tablespoons cocoa powder
2 teaspoons chili powder
1 cup beef stock

¼ teaspoon ground cumin
1 tablespoon chopped parsley
A pinch of salt and black pepper

1. Stir together all the ingredients in your Instant Pot.
2. Secure the lid. Press the Manual button on the Instant Pot and set the cooking time for 30 minutes on High Pressure.
3. Once cooking is complete, perform a natural pressure release for 10 minutes and then release any remaining pressure. Carefully open the lid.
4. Divide the mix among the plates and serve with a side salad.

Egg Meatloaf

Prep time: 20 minutes | Cook time: 25 minutes | Serves 6

1 tablespoon avocado oil
1½ cup ground pork
1 teaspoon chives
1 teaspoon salt
½ teaspoon ground black

pepper
2 tablespoons coconut flour
3 eggs, hard-boiled, peeled
1 cup water

1. Brush a loaf pan with avocado oil.
2. In the mixing bowl, mix the ground pork, chives, salt, ground black pepper, and coconut flour.
3. Transfer the mixture in the loaf pan and flatten with a spatula.
4. Fill the meatloaf with hard-boiled eggs.
5. Pour water and insert the trivet in the Instant Pot.
6. Lower the loaf pan over the trivet in the Instant Pot. Close the lid.
7. Select Manual mode and set cooking time for 25 minutes on High Pressure.
8. When timer beeps, use a natural pressure release for 10 minutes, then release any remaining pressure. Open the lid.
9. Serve immediately.

Coconut Pork Muffins

Prep time: 5 minutes | Cook time: 9 minutes | Serves 2

1 egg, beaten
2 tablespoons coconut flour
1 teaspoon parsley
¼ teaspoon salt

1 tablespoon coconut cream
4 ounces (113 g) ground pork, fried
1 cup water

1. Whisk together the egg, coconut flour, parsley, salt, and coconut cream. Add the fried ground pork. Mix the the mixture until homogenous.
2. Pour the mixture into a muffin pan.
3. Pour the water in the Instant Pot and place in the trivet.
4. Lower the muffin pan on the trivet and close the Instant Pot lid.
5. Set the Manual mode and set cooking time for 4 minutes on High Pressure.
6. When timer beeps, perform a natural pressure release for 5 minutes, then release any remaining pressure. Open the lid.
7. Serve warm.

Creamy Pork Liver

Prep time: 5 minutes | Cook time: 7 minutes | Serves 3

14 ounces (397 g) pork liver, chopped
1 teaspoon salt
1 teaspoon butter

½ cup heavy cream
3 tablespoons scallions, chopped

1. Rub the liver with the salt on a clean work surface.
2. Put the butter in the Instant Pot and melt on the Sauté mode.
3. Add the heavy cream, scallions, and liver.
4. Stir and close the lid. Select Manual mode and set cooking time for 12 minutes on High Pressure.
5. When timer beeps, perform a natural pressure release for 5 minutes, then release any remaining pressure. Open the lid.
6. Serve immediately.

Pork Steaks with Pico de Gallo

Prep time: 15 minutes | Cook time: 12 minutes | Serves 6

1 tablespoon butter
2 pounds (907 g) pork steaks
1 bell pepper, deseeded and sliced
½ cup shallots, chopped
2 garlic cloves, minced
Pico de Gallo:
1 tomato, chopped
1 chili pepper, seeded and minced
½ cup red onion, chopped

¼ cup dry red wine
1 cup chicken bone broth
¼ cup water
Salt, to taste
¼ teaspoon freshly ground black pepper, or more to taste

2 garlic cloves, minced
1 tablespoon fresh cilantro, finely chopped
Sea salt, to taste

1. Press the Sauté button to heat up the Instant Pot. Melt the butter and sear the pork steaks about 4 minutes or until browned on both sides.
2. Add bell pepper, shallot, garlic, wine, chicken bone broth, water, salt, and black pepper to the Instant Pot.
3. Secure the lid. Choose the Manual mode and set cooking time for 8 minutes at High pressure.
4. Meanwhile, combine the ingredients for the Pico de Gallo in a small bowl. Refrigerate until ready to serve.
5. Once cooking is complete, use a quick pressure release. Carefully remove the lid.
6. Serve warm pork steaks with the chilled Pico de Gallo on the side.

Braised Pork Belly

Prep time: 15 minutes | Cook time: 37 minutes | Serves 4

1 pound (454 g) pork belly
1 tablespoon olive oil
Salt and ground black pepper
to taste
1 clove garlic, minced
1 cup dry white wine
Rosemary sprig

1. Select the Sauté mode on the Instant Pot and heat the oil.
2. Add the pork belly and sauté for 2 minutes per side, until starting to brown.
3. Season the meat with salt and pepper, add the garlic.
4. Pour in the wine and add the rosemary sprig. Bring to a boil.
5. Select the Manual mode and set the cooking time for 35 minutes at High pressure.
6. Once cooking is complete, use a natural pressure release for 10 minutes, then release any remaining pressure. Open the lid.
7. Slice the meat and serve.

Ginger Pork Meatballs

Prep time: 10 minutes | Cook time: 7 minutes | Serves 3

11 ounces (312 g) ground pork
1 teaspoon ginger paste
1 teaspoon lemon juice
¼ teaspoon chili flakes
1 tablespoon butter
¼ cup water

1. Combine the ground pork and ginger paste in a large bowl.
2. Mix in the lemon juice and chili flakes.
3. Put the butter in the Instant Pot and melt on Sauté mode.
4. Meanwhile, shape the mixture into small meatballs.
5. Place the meatballs in the Instant Pot and cook for 2 minutes on each side.
6. Add water and lock the lid.
7. Set the Manual mode and set cooking time for 3 minutes on High Pressure.
8. When timer beeps, perform a quick pressure release. Open the lid.
9. Serve warm.

Pork Cutlets with Creamy Mustard Sauce

Prep time: 20 minutes | Cook time: 13 minutes | Serves 6

6 pork cutlets
½ teaspoon dried rosemary
½ teaspoon dried marjoram
¼ teaspoon paprika
¼ teaspoon cayenne pepper
Kosher salt and ground black
pepper, to taste
2 tablespoons olive oil
½ cup water
½ cup vegetable broth
1 tablespoon butter
1 cup heavy cream
1 tablespoon yellow mustard
½ cup shredded Cheddar
cheese

1. Sprinkle both sides of the pork cutlets with rosemary, marjoram, paprika, cayenne pepper, salt, and black pepper.
2. Press the Sauté button on the Instant Pot and heat the olive oil until sizzling.
3. Add the pork cutlets and sear both sides for about 3 minutes until lightly browned.
4. Pour in the water and vegetable broth.
5. Secure the lid. Select the Manual mode and set the cooking time for 8 minutes at High Pressure.
6. When the timer beeps, perform a quick pressure release. Carefully open the lid. Transfer the pork cutlets to a plate and set aside.
7. Press the Sauté button again and melt the butter.
8. Stir in the heavy cream, mustard, and cheese and cook for another 2 minutes until heated through.
9. Add the pork cutlets to the sauce, turning to coat.
10. Remove from the Instant Pot and serve.

Garlicky Pork Tenderloin

Prep time: 6 mins, Cook Time: 8 hours, Servings: 10

3 tbsps. extra virgin olive oil
¼ cup butter
1 tsp. thyme
1 garlic clove, minced
3 lbs. pork tenderloin
1 cup water
Salt and pepper, to taste

1. Set the Instant Pot on Sauté. Heat the olive oil and butter until the butter is melted.
2. Add and sauté the garlic and thyme for 1 minute or until fragrant.
3. Add the pork tenderloin and sauté for 3 minutes or until lightly browned.
4. Pour in the water and sprinkle salt and pepper for seasoning.
5. Lock the lid. Press the Slow Cook button and set the cooking time to 8 hours at High Pressure.
6. Once cooking is complete, perform a natural pressure release for 10 minutes, and then release any remaining pressure. Carefully open the lid.
7. Allow to cool for a few minutes. Remove the pork from the pot and serve warm.

Golden Bacon Sticks

Prep time: 5 minutes | Cook time: 6 minutes | Serves 4

6 ounces (170 g) bacon, sliced
2 tablespoons almond flour
1 tablespoon water
¾ teaspoon chili pepper

1. Sprinkle the sliced bacon with the almond flour and drizzle with water. Add the chili pepper.
2. Put the bacon in the Instant Pot.
3. Cook on Sauté mode for 3 minutes per side.
4. Serve immediately.

Vinegary Pork Chops with Figs and Pears

Prep time: 10 minutes | Cook time: 10 minutes | Serves 2

2 (1-inch-thick) bone-in pork
chops
1 teaspoon sea salt
1 teaspoon ground black
pepper
¼ cup chicken broth
¼ cup balsamic vinegar
1 tablespoon dried mint
2 tablespoons avocado oil
5 dried figs, stems removed
and halved
3 pears, peeled, cored, and
diced large
1 medium sweet onion, peeled
and sliced

1. Pat the pork chops dry with a paper towel and sprinkle both sides generously with the salt and pepper. Set aside.
2. Stir together the broth, vinegar, and mint in a small bowl. Set aside.
3. Set the Instant Pot to Sauté. Add and heat the oil. Sear the pork chops for 5 minutes on each side and transfer to a plate.
4. Pour in the broth mixture and deglaze the Instant Pot, scraping any browned bits from the pot.
5. Add the onions to the pot and scatter the figs and pears on top. Return the pork chops to the pot.
6. Secure the lid. Select the Steam function and cook for 3 minutes on High Pressure.
7. Once the timer goes off, do a natural pressure release for 10 minutes and then release any remaining pressure. Carefully open the lid.
8. Transfer to a serving dish with a slotted spoon. Serve immediately.

Barbecue-Honey Baby Back Ribs

Prep time: 10 minutes | Cook time: 25 minutes | Serves 4

2 racks baby back ribs (3 pounds / 1.4 kg; about 4 ribs each), cut into 5- to 6-inch portions
2 tablespoons chili powder
2 tablespoons toasted sesame oil
3 tablespoons grainy mustard
1 tablespoon red wine vinegar
1 cup ketchup
⅓ cup honey
½ cup chicken broth

1. Rub the ribs all over with the chili powder.
2. Mix together the remaining ingredients in your Instant Pot and stir until the honey has dissolved.
3. Dip the ribs in the sauce to coat. Using tongs, arrange the ribs standing upright against the sides of the pot.
4. Secure the lid. Select the Manual function and cook for 25 minutes on High Pressure.
5. Preheat the broiler and adjust an oven rack so that it is 4 inches below the broiler element. Line a baking sheet with aluminum foil.
6. When the timer beeps, use a natural pressure release for 15 minutes and then release any remaining pressure. Carefully open the lid.
7. Transfer the ribs with tongs to the prepared baking sheet, meaty side up.
8. Stir the cooking liquid and pour over the ribs with a spoon. Broil the ribs for 5 minutes until browned in places.
9. Transfer the ribs to a serving plate and serve warm.

Indian Roasted Pork

Prep time: 6 mins, Cook Time: 8 hours, Servings: 3

1 tbsp. olive oil
1 lb. pork loin
1 tsp. cumin
2 garlic cloves, roughly
chopped
1 onion, sliced
Salt and pepper, to taste

1. Coat the Instant Pot with olive oil and add the pork loin. Set aside.
2. In a food processor, place the remaining ingredients.
3. Pulse until smooth then pour the mixture over the pork loin.
4. Lock the lid. Press the Slow Cook button and set the cooking time to 8 hours at High Pressure.
5. Once cooking is complete, perform a natural pressure release for 10 minutes, and then release any remaining pressure. Carefully open the lid.
6. Allow to cool for a few minutes. Remove them from the pot and serve warm.

Instant Pot Rib

Prep time: 6 mins, Cook Time: 8 hours, Servings: 3

1 rack baby back rib
1 tbsp. smoked paprika
2 tbsps. olive oil
1 tbsp. onion powder
1 tbsp. garlic powder
Salt and pepper, to taste
½ cup water

1. Prepare a baking sheet. Lay on the ribs. Rub with paprika, olive oil, onion powder, garlic powder, salt, and pepper.
2. Place the well-coated rib in the Instant Pot. Pour in the water.
3. Lock the lid. Press the Slow Cook button and set the cooking time to 8 hours at High Pressure.
4. Once cooking is complete, perform a natural pressure release for 10 minutes, and then release any remaining pressure. Carefully open the lid.
5. Allow to cool for a few minutes. Remove the rib from the pot and serve warm.

Hawaiian Pulled Pork Roast with Cabbage

Prep time: 10 minutes | Cook time: 1 hour 2 minutes minutes | Serves 6

1½ tablespoons olive oil
3 pounds (1.4 kg) pork shoulder roast, cut into 4 equal-sized pieces
3 cloves garlic, minced
1 tablespoon liquid smoke
2 cups water, divided
1 tablespoon sea salt
2 cups shredded cabbage

1. Select Sauté mode and add the olive oil to the Instant Pot. Once the oil is hot, add the pork cuts and sear for 5 minutes per side or until browned. Once browned, transfer the pork to a platter and set aside.
2. Add the garlic, liquid smoke, and 1½ cups water to the Instant Pot. Stir to combine.
3. Return the pork to the pot and sprinkle the salt over top.
4. Lock the lid. Select Manual mode and set cooking time for 1 hour on High Pressure.
5. When cooking is complete, allow the pressure to release naturally for 20 minutes, then release any remaining pressure.
6. Open the lid and transfer the pork to a large platter. Using two forks, shred the pork. Set aside.
7. Add the shredded cabbage and remaining water to the liquid in the pot. Stir.
8. Lock the lid. Select Manual mode and set cooking time for 2 minutes on High Pressure. When cooking is complete, quick release the pressure.
9. Transfer the cabbage to the serving platter with the pork. Serve warm.

Eggplant Pork Lasagna

Prep time: 20 minutes | Cook time: 30 minutes | Serves 6

2 eggplants, sliced
1 teaspoon salt
10 ounces (283 g) ground pork
1 cup Mozzarella, shredded
1 tablespoon unsweetened tomato purée
1 teaspoon butter, softened
1 cup chicken stock

1. Sprinkle the eggplants with salt and let sit for 10 minutes, then pat dry with paper towels.
2. In a mixing bowl, mix the ground pork, butter, and tomato purée.
3. Make a layer of the sliced eggplants in the bottom of the Instant Pot and top with ground pork mixture.
4. Top the ground pork with Mozzarella and repeat with remaining ingredients.
5. Pour in the chicken stock. Close the lid. Select Manual mode and set cooking time for 30 minutes on High Pressure.
6. When timer beeps, use a natural pressure release for 10 minutes, then release the remaining pressure and open the lid.
7. Cool for 10 minutes and serve.

Italian Pork Cutlets

Prep time: 6 mins, Cook Time: 20 mins, Servings: 6

4 tbsps. olive oil
6 pork cutlets
Salt and pepper, to taste
1 tbsp. Italian herb mix
1½ cups water

1. In the Instant Pot, add all the ingredients. Stir to combine well.
2. Lock the lid. Press the Meat/Stew button and set the cooking time to 20 minutes at High Pressure.
3. Once cooking is complete, do a natural pressure release for 10 minutes, and then release any remaining pressure. Carefully open the lid.
4. Remove the meat and serve immediately.

Pork with Bell Peppers

Prep time: 10 minutes | Cook time: 35 minutes | Serves 4

2 tablespoons olive oil
4 pork chops
1 red onion, chopped
3 garlic cloves, minced
1 red bell pepper, roughly chopped

1 green bell pepper, roughly chopped
2 cups beef stock
A pinch of salt and black pepper
1 tablespoon parsley, chopped

1. Press the Sauté on your Instant Pot. Add and heat the oil. Brown the pork chops for 2 minutes.
2. Fold in the onion and garlic and brown for an additional 3 minutes.
3. Stir in the bell peppers, stock, salt, and pepper.
4. Lock the lid. Select the Manual mode and cook for 30 minutes on High Pressure.
5. Once cooking is complete, use a natural pressure release for 10 minutes and then release any remaining pressure. Carefully open the lid.
6. Divide the mix among the plates and serve topped with the parsley.

Pork with Brussels Sprouts

Prep time: 10 minutes | Cook time: 30 minutes | Serves 4

1½ pound (680 g) pork chops
1 pound (454 g) Brussels sprouts, trimmed and halved
2 tablespoons Cajun seasoning

1 cup beef stock
A pinch of salt and black pepper
1 tablespoon parsley, chopped

1. Stir together all the ingredients in your Instant Pot.
2. Secure the lid. Press the Manual button on the Instant Pot and set the cooking time for 30 minutes on High Pressure.
3. Once cooking is complete, perform a natural pressure release for 10 minutes and then release any remaining pressure. Carefully open the lid.
4. Divide the mix among the plates and serve immediately.

Pork Roast with Sweet Potatoes

Prep time: 10 minutes | Cook time: 40 minutes | Serves 4

1 tablespoon olive oil
2 red onions, chopped
2 pounds (907 g) pork shoulder, sliced
2 sweet potatoes, peeled and cubed
1 cup beef stock

1 teaspoon chili powder
½ teaspoon chopped rosemary
A pinch of salt and black pepper
1 cup coconut cream
1 tablespoon chopped parsley

1. Press the Sauté button on the Instant Pot and heat the olive oil.
2. Add the onions and pork and brown for 5 minutes.
3. Stir in the sweet potatoes, beef stock, chili powder, rosemary, salt, and black pepper.
4. Secure the lid. Select the Manual mode and set the cooking time for 25 minutes at High Pressure.
5. Once cooking is complete, do a natural pressure release for 10 minutes, then release any remaining pressure. Carefully open the lid.
6. Press the Sauté button again and add the coconut cream, toss, and cook for an additional 10 minutes.
7. Serve with the parsley sprinkled on top.

Pork Chops with Onions

Prep time: 6 mins, Cook Time: 25 mins, Servings: 4

3 tbsps. butter
4 boneless pork chops
3 onions, chopped

½ cup beef broth
Salt and pepper, to taste
¼ cup heavy cream

1. Press the Sauté button on the Instant Pot.
2. Heat the butter until melted and add the pork chops and onion.
3. Sauté for 3 minutes or until the pork is seared.
4. Stir in the broth and sprinkle salt and pepper for seasoning.
5. Lock the lid. Press the Meat/Stew button and set the cooking time to 20 minutes at High Pressure.
6. Once cooking is complete, perform a natural pressure release for 10 minutes, and then release any remaining pressure. Carefully open the lid.
7. Add the heavy cream. Press the Sauté button and allow to simmer for 5 minutes.
8. Allow to cool for a few minutes. Remove the pork from the pot and serve warm.

Pork, Green Beans, and Corn

Prep time: 10 minutes | Cook time: 35 minutes | Serves 4

2 pounds (907 g) pork shoulder, boneless and cubed
1 cup green beans, trimmed and halved
1 cup corn

1 cup beef stock
2 garlic cloves, minced
1 teaspoon ground cumin
A pinch of salt and black pepper

1. Combine all the ingredients in the Instant Pot.
2. Secure the lid. Select the Manual mode and set the cooking time for 35 minutes at High Pressure.
3. Once cooking is complete, do a natural pressure release for 10 minutes, then release any remaining pressure. Carefully open the lid.
4. Divide the mix among four plates and serve.

Coconut Pork Curry

Prep time: 6 mins, Cook Time: 35 mins, Servings: 6

3 tbsps. coconut oil
3 garlic cloves, minced
1 tbsp. garam masala
2 lbs. pork shoulders, sliced

1 cup freshly squeezed coconut milk
Salt and pepper, to taste

1. Press the Sauté button on the Instant Pot and heat the coconut oil until melted.
2. Add and sauté the garlic and garam masala until fragrant.
3. Add the pork and allow to sear on all sides for 3 minutes or until lightly browned.
4. Pour in the coconut milk. Sprinkle with salt and pepper.
5. Lock the lid. Press the Meat/Stew button and set the cooking time to 30 minutes at High pressure.
6. Once cooking is complete, perform a natural pressure release for 10 minutes, and then release any remaining pressure. Carefully open the lid.
7. Remove the pork from the pot and serve warm.

Pork Potato Lunch

Prep time: 12 mins, Cook Time: 25 mins, Servings: 4

1 tbsp. olive oil
1 onion, chopped
10 oz. fat removed pork neck
3 cups low-sodium beef stock
1 medium sweet potato, chopped
Salt and pepper, to taste

1. Press the Sauté bottom on the Instant Pot. Grease the pot with the olive oil.
2. Add the onion and sauté for 2 minutes until translucent and softened.
3. Add the beef and sauté for 4 to 5 minutes to evenly brown.
4. Add the stock and potatoes. Sprinkle with salt and pepper. Stir to mix well.
5. Lock the lid. Press Manual. Set the timer to 20 minutes at High Pressure.
6. When the timer beeps, press Cancel, then use a quick pressure release.
7. Open the lid, transfer them in a large plate and serve warm.

Pork Shoulder and Celery

Prep time: 10 minutes | Cook time: 30 minutes | Serves 4

2 tablespoons avocado oil
4 garlic cloves, minced
2 pounds (907 g) pork shoulder, boneless and cubed
1½ cups beef stock
2 celery stalks, chopped
2 tablespoons chili powder
1 tablespoon chopped sage
A pinch of salt and black pepper

1. Press the Sauté button on the Instant Pot and heat the avocado oil.
2. Add the garlic and sauté for 2 minutes until fragrant.
3. Stir in the pork and brown for another 3 minutes.
4. Add the remaining ingredients to the Instant Pot and mix well.
5. Secure the lid. Select the Manual mode and set the cooking time for 25 minutes at High Pressure.
6. Once cooking is complete, do a natural pressure release for 10 minutes, then release any remaining pressure. Carefully open the lid.
7. Serve warm.

Pork Tenderloin with Celery

Prep time: 12 mins, Cook Time: 25 mins, Servings: 4

1½ lbs. pork tenderloin
2 tsps. sea salt
½ tsp. rosemary
1 cup heavy cream
4 celery stalks, rinsed, sliced into ½-inch pieces
1 cup water

1. On a clean work surface, rub the pork with salt and rosemary.
2. Slice the well-coated tenderloin into 1-inch thick slices.
3. Set the Instant Pot to Sauté setting.
4. Add the pork and brown for 3 minutes.
5. Add the celery, heavy cream, and water. Stir to combine well.
6. Lock the lid. Set the Instant Pot to Manual mode and set the timer for 20 minutes at High Pressure.
7. Once cooking is complete, use a natural pressure release for 10 minutes, then release any remaining pressure.
8. Carefully open the lid. Allow to cool for a few minutes. Transfer them on a large plate and serve immediately.

Pork Tenderloin with Cherry and Rosemary

Prep time: 5 minutes | Cook time: 25 minutes | Serves 6

2 tablespoons avocado oil
2 (3-pound / 1.4 kg) pork tenderloins, halved
½ cup balsamic vinegar
¼ cup cherry preserves
¼ cup finely chopped fresh
rosemary
¼ cup olive oil
½ teaspoon sea salt
¼ teaspoon ground black pepper
4 garlic cloves, minced

1. Set your Instant Pot to Sauté. Add and heat the oil. Add the pork and brown for about 2 minutes on each side.
2. Stir together the remaining ingredients in a small bowl and pour over the pork. Secure the lid.
3. Select the Manual function and cook for 20 minutes on High Pressure.
4. Once cooking is complete, use a natural pressure release for 5 minutes and then release any remaining pressure. Carefully open the lid.
5. Remove the tenderloin from the Instant Pot to a cutting board. Let stand for 5 minutes.
6. Cut into medallions before serving.

Pork Vindaloo (Curry Pork)

Prep time: 6 mins, Cook Time: 35 mins, Servings: 6

¼ cup coconut oil
2 lbs. pork shoulder, sliced
1 tbsp. garam masala
3 tbsps. freshly squeezed
lemon juice
1 cup water
Salt and pepper, to taste

1. Press the Sauté button on the Instant Pot and heat the coconut oil until melted.
2. Add and sear the pork loin on all sides for 3 minutes or until lightly browned.
3. Add the garam masala and continue sauté for 2 more minutes.
4. Stir in the lemon juice and water. Sprinkle with salt and pepper.
5. Lock the lid. Press the Meat/Stew button and set the cooking time to 30 minutes at High Pressure.
6. Once cooking is complete, perform a natural pressure release for 10 minutes, and then release any remaining pressure. Carefully open the lid.
7. Remove the pork from the pot and serve warm.

Pork with Cherry Sauce

Prep time: 5 minutes | Cook time: 25 minutes | Serves 4

4 pork chops
A pinch of salt and black pepper
1 cup beef stock
1 cup cherries, pitted
1 tablespoon chopped parsley
1 tablespoon balsamic vinegar
1 tablespoon avocado oil

1. Press the Sauté button on the Instant Pot. Add and heat the oil.
2. Brown the pork chops for 2 minutes per side.
3. Stir in the remaining the ingredients. Secure the lid. Press the Manual button and cook for 20 minutes on High Pressure.
4. When the timer goes off, perform a natural pressure release for 5 minutes and then release any remaining pressure. Carefully open the lid.
5. Divide the mix among the plates and serve immediately.

Pork Tenderloin in Salsa

Prep time: 20 minutes | Cook time: 15 minutes | Serves 8

2 teaspoons grapeseed oil
3 pounds (1.4 kg) pork tenderloin, cut into slices
1 teaspoon granulated garlic
½ teaspoon dried marjoram
½ teaspoon dried thyme
1 teaspoon paprika
Salsa:
1 cup puréed tomatoes
1 teaspoon granulated garlic
2 bell peppers, deveined and chopped
1 cup chopped onion

1 teaspoon ground cumin
Sea salt and ground black pepper, to taste
1 cup water
1 avocado, pitted, peeled, and sliced

2 tablespoons minced fresh cilantro
3 teaspoons lime juice
1 minced jalapeño, chopped
Avocado slices, for serving

1. Press the Sauté button on your Instant Pot. Add and hear the oil. Sear the pork until nicely browned on all sides.
2. Stir in the garlic, seasonings, and water.
3. Lock the lid. Select the Manual mode and set the cooking time for 12 minutes at High Pressure.
4. Once the timer beeps, use a natural pressure release for 10 minutes. Carefully open the lid.
5. Remove the tenderloin. Shred with two forks and reserve.
6. Meanwhile, stir together all the ingredients for the salsa in a mixing bowl.
7. Spoon the salsa over the prepared pork.
8. Divide the pork among bowls and serve garnished with the avocado slices.

Pork with Coconut Meat

Prep time: 12 mins, Cook Time: 6 mins, Servings: 4

1 tbsp. olive oil
½ lb. ground pork
1 tsp. salt
6 garlic cloves

2 cups tomato sauce
1 cup water
2 cups coconut meat

1. Set the Instant Pot to Sauté function. Coat the pot with olive oil and heat until the oil is shimmering.
2. Add pork to Instant Pot along with salt and garlic, then sauté for 3 minutes until lightly browned.
3. Add the tomato sauce and water.
4. Lock the lid. Set the Instant Port to Manual function and set the cooking time for 6 minutes at High Pressure.
5. Once cooking is complete, use a natural pressure release for 10 minutes, then release any remaining pressure.
6. Carefully open the lid. Allow to cool for a few minutes. Transfer them on a large plate and serve with coconut meat on top.

Pork Chops with Sauerkraut

Prep time: 15 minutes | Cook time: 30 minutes | Serves 4

2 tablespoons olive oil
4 (1-inch-thick) bone-in pork loin chops
1 teaspoon sea salt
½ teaspoon ground black pepper
4 slices bacon, diced
3 large carrots, peeled and sliced
1 large onion, peeled and diced
1 stalk celery, finely chopped

1 clove garlic, peeled and minced
1 (12-ounce / 340-g) bottle lager
2 medium red apples, peeled, cored, and quartered
4 medium red potatoes, peeled and quartered
1 (1-pound / 454-g) bag high-quality sauerkraut, rinsed and drained
1 tablespoon caraway seeds

1. Set your Instant Pot to Sauté. Add and heat the olive oil.
2. Sprinkle the pork chops with the salt and pepper. Working in batches, sear the pork chops for 1 to 2 minutes on each side. Set aside.
3. Add the bacon, carrots, onion, and celery to the Instant Pot. Sauté for 3 to 5 minutes, or until the onions are translucent.
4. Fold in the garlic and cook for an additional 1 minute. Pour in the beer and deglaze the bottom of the pot by scraping out any browned bits from the pot. Let simmer uncovered for 5 minutes.
5. Mix in the apples, potatoes, and sauerkraut. Sprinkle the caraway seeds on top. Slightly prop pork chops up against the sides of the pot to avoid crowding the pork.
6. Secure the lid. Select the Manual function and cook for 15 minutes on High Pressure.
7. Once the timer goes off, do a natural pressure release for 5 minutes and release any remaining pressure. Carefully remove the lid.
8. Transfer to a serving plate and serve immediately.

Chapter 8 Lamb

Black Bean Minced Lamb

Prep time: 10 minutes | Cook time: 25 minutes | Serves 4 to 6

1 pound (454 g) ground lamb
2 tablespoons vegetable oil
½ cup chopped onion
½ teaspoon salt
2 cans drained black beans
1 can undrained diced
tomatoes

1 can chopped and undrained
green chillies
1½ cups chicken broth
1½ tablespoons tomato paste
1½ tablespoons chili powder
2 teaspoons cumin
½ teaspoon cayenne

1. Set the Instant Pot to the Sauté mode and heat the oil. Add the lamb, onion and salt to the pot and sauté for 5 minutes, stirring constantly. Add the remaining ingredients to the pot and stir well.
2. Select the Manual setting and set the cooking time for 20 minutes on High Pressure. Once the timer goes off, use a natural pressure release for 10 minutes, then release any remaining pressure. Carefully open the lid.
3. Serve immediately.

Braised Lamb Ragout

Prep time: 10 minutes | Cook time: 1 hour 8 minutes | Serves 4 to 6

1½ pounds (680 g) lamb,
bone-in
1 teaspoon vegetable oil
4 tomatoes, chopped
2 carrots, sliced
½ pound (227 g) mushrooms,
sliced
1 small yellow onion, chopped

6 cloves garlic, minced
2 tablespoons tomato paste
1 teaspoon dried oregano
Water, as needed
Salt and ground black pepper,
to taste
Handful chopped parsley

1. Press the Sauté button on the Instant Pot and heat the olive oil. Add the lamb and sear for 4 minutes per side, or until browned.
2. Stir in the tomatoes, carrots, mushrooms, onion, garlic, tomato paste, oregano and water. Season with salt and pepper.
3. Set the lid in place. Select the Manual mode and set the cooking time for 60 minutes on High Pressure. Once cooking is complete, perform a quick pressure release. Carefully open the lid.
4. Transfer the lamb to a plate. Discard the bones and shred the meat. Return the shredded lamb to the pot, add the parsley and stir.
5. Serve warm.

Herbed Lamb Shank

Prep time: 15 minutes | Cook time: 35 minutes | Serves 2

2 lamb shanks
1 rosemary spring
1 teaspoon coconut flour
¼ teaspoon onion powder

¼ teaspoon chili powder
¾ teaspoon ground ginger
½ cup beef broth
½ teaspoon avocado oil

1. Put all ingredients in the Instant Pot. Stir to mix well.
2. Close the lid. Select Manual mode and set cooking time for 35 minutes on High Pressure.
3. When timer beeps, use a natural pressure release for 15 minutes, then release any remaining pressure. Open the lid.
4. Discard the rosemary sprig and serve warm.

Lamb Curry

Prep time: 10 minutes | Cook time: 30 minutes | Serves 4

1 teaspoon curry paste
2 tablespoons coconut cream
¼ teaspoon chili powder
1 pound (454 g) lamb shoulder,

chopped
1 tablespoon fresh cilantro,
chopped
½ cup heavy cream

1. In a bowl, mix the curry paste and coconut cream.
2. Add the chili powder and chopped lamb shoulder. Toss to coat the lamb in the curry mixture well.
3. Transfer the lamb and all remaining curry paste mixture in the Instant Pot. Add cilantro and heavy cream.
4. Close the lid and select Manual mode. Set cooking time for 30 minutes on High Pressure.
5. When timer beeps, do a quick pressure release. Open the lid.
6. Serve warm.

Lamb Burgers

Prep time: 10 minutes | Cook time: 14 minutes | Serves 2

10 ounces (283 g) ground lamb
½ teaspoon chili powder
1 teaspoon dried cilantro
1 teaspoon garlic powder

½ teaspoon salt
¼ cup water
1 tablespoon coconut oil

1. In a mixing bowl, mix the ground lamb, chili powder, dried cilantro, garlic powder, salt, and water.
2. Shape the mixture into 2 burgers.
3. Melt the coconut oil on Sauté mode.
4. Put the burgers in the hot oil and cook for 7 minutes on each side or until well browned.
5. Serve immediately.

Indian Lamb Curry

Prep time: 15 minutes | Cook time: 1 hour 3 minutes | Serves 4

2 tablespoons olive oil
1 pound (454 g) lamb meat,
cubed
2 tomatoes, chopped
1 onion, chopped
1-inch piece ginger, grated
2 garlic cloves, minced
½ tablespoon ground cumin

½ tablespoon chili flakes
½ tablespoon ground turmeric
½ teaspoon garam masala
1 cup chicken stock
½ cup coconut milk
¼ cup rice, rinsed
1 tablespoon fish sauce
¼ cup chopped cilantro

1. Set the Instant Pot on the Sauté mode. Heat the olive oil and sear the lamb shoulder on both sides for 8 minutes, or until browned. Transfer the lamb to a plate and set aside.
2. Add the tomatoes, onion, ginger and garlic to the pot and sauté for 5 minutes. Stir in the cumin, chili flakes, turmeric and garam masala. Cook for 10 minutes, or until they form a paste. Whisk in the chicken stock, coconut milk, rice and fish sauce. Return the lamb back to the pot.
3. Lock the lid. Select Meat/Stew mode and set the cooking time for 35 minutes on High Pressure. Once cooking is complete, do a natural pressure release for 10 minutes, then release any remaining pressure. Open the lid and select the Sauté mode. Cook the curry for 5 minutes, or until thickened.
4. Top with the chopped cilantro and serve warm in bowls.

Garlicky Lamb Leg

Prep time: 35 minutes | Cook time: 50 minutes | Serves 6

2 pounds (907 g) lamb leg
6 garlic cloves, minced
1 teaspoon sea salt
1½ teaspoons black pepper
2½ tablespoons olive oil
1½ small onions
1½ cups bone broth
¾ cup orange juice
6 sprigs thyme

1. In a bowl, whisk together the garlic, salt and pepper. Add the lamb leg to the bowl and marinate for 30 minutes.
2. Press the Sauté button on the Instant Pot and heat the olive oil. Add the onions and sauté for 4 minutes. Transfer the onions to a separate bowl.
3. Add the marinated lamb to the pot and sear for 3 minutes on each side, or lightly browned. Whisk in the cooked onions, broth, orange juice and thyme.
4. Close and secure the lid. Set the Instant Pot to the Meat/Stew mode and set the cooking time for 40 minutes on High Pressure. When the timer beeps, use a natural pressure release for 10 minutes, then release any remaining pressure. Carefully open the lid.
5. Divide the dish among 6 serving bowls and serve hot.

Greek Lamb Leg

Prep time: 10 minutes | Cook time: 50 minutes | Serves 4

1 pound (454 g) lamb leg
½ teaspoon dried thyme
1 teaspoon paprika powder
¼ teaspoon cumin seeds
1 tablespoon softened butter
2 garlic cloves
¼ cup water

1. Rub the lamb leg with dried thyme, paprika powder, and cumin seeds on a clean work surface.
2. Brush the leg with softened butter and transfer to the Instant Pot. Add garlic cloves and water.
3. Close the lid. Select Manual mode and set cooking time for 50 minutes on High Pressure.
4. When timer beeps, use a quick pressure release. Open the lid.
5. Serve warm.

Lamb Meatballs

Prep time: 10 minutes | Cook time: 38 minutes | Serves 3

¾ pound (340 g) ground lamb meat
1 teaspoon adobo seasoning
½ tablespoon olive oil
2 small tomatoes, chopped roughly
5 mini bell peppers, deseeded and halved
2 garlic cloves, peeled
½ small yellow onion, chopped roughly
½ cup sugar-free tomato sauce
¼ teaspoon crushed red pepper flakes,
Salt and freshly ground black pepper, to taste

1. Mix the lamb meat and adobo seasoning in a bowl until well combined. Shape the meat mixture into small meatballs.
2. Set the Instant Pot on the Sauté mode and heat the olive oil. Add the meatballs to the pot and cook for 3 minutes, or until golden brown. Transfer the meatballs to bowls.
3. Stir together all the remaining ingredients in the pot. Lock the lid. Select the Meat/Stew mode and set the cooking time for 35 minutes on High Pressure. When the timer beeps, use a natural pressure release for 10 minutes, then release any remaining pressure.
4. Carefully open the lid. Transfer the vegetable mixture to a blender and pulse until smooth. Spread the vegetable paste over the meatballs and serve hot.

Indian Lamb Korma

Prep time: 15 minutes | Cook time: 25 minutes | Serves 6

1 (6-inch) Anaheim chile, minced
1 clove garlic, grated
½ medium onion, chopped
2 tablespoons coconut oil
½ teaspoon grated fresh ginger
1 teaspoon garam masala
¼ teaspoon ground cardamom
Pinch of ground cinnamon
2 teaspoons ground cumin
1 teaspoon coriander seeds
1 teaspoon sea salt
½ teaspoon cayenne pepper
½ tablespoon unsweetened tomato purée
1 cup chicken broth
3 pounds (1.4 kg) lamb shoulder, cut into 1-inch cubes
¼ cup full-fat coconut milk
½ cup full-fat Greek yogurt

1. Preheat the Instant Pot on Sauté mode. Add the chile, garlic, onion, coconut oil, and ginger and sauté for 2 minutes.
2. Add the garam masala, cardamom, cinnamon, cumin, coriander seeds, salt, cayenne, and unsweetened tomato purée and sauté for a minute or until fragrant.
3. Pour in the broth. Add the lamb and stir well.
4. Secure the lid. Press the Manual button and set cooking time for 15 minutes on High Pressure.
5. When timer beeps, quick release the pressure. Open the lid.
6. Stir in the coconut milk and yogurt. Switch to Sauté mode and bring the mixture to a simmer for 5 minutes, stirring occasionally until thickened.
7. Serve hot.

Greek Lamb Loaf

Prep time: 5 minutes | Cook time: 15 minutes | Serves 2

1 pound (454 g) ground lamb meat
4 garlic cloves
½ small onion, chopped
1 teaspoon ground marjoram
1 teaspoon rosemary
¾ teaspoon salt
¼ teaspoon black pepper
¾ cup water

1. In a blender, combine the lamb meat, garlic, onions, marjoram, rosemary, salt and pepper. Pulse until well mixed. Shape the lamb mixture into a compact loaf and cover tightly with aluminium foil. Use a fork to make some holes.
2. Pour the water into the Instant Pot and put a trivet in the pot. Place the lamb loaf on the trivet and lock the lid.
3. Select the Manual mode and set the cooking time for 15 minutes on High Pressure. When the timer goes off, use a quick pressure release.
4. Carefully open the lid. Serve warm.

Lamb Kleftiko with Turnip

Prep time: 25 minutes | Cook time: 50 minutes | Serves 6

¼ cup apple cider vinegar
½ cup chicken broth
1 tablespoon lemon juice
½ teaspoon lemon zest
½ teaspoon fresh thyme
1 pound (454 g) lamb shoulder, chopped
½ cup turnip, chopped

1. In the mixing bowl, mix the apple cider vinegar, chicken broth, lemon juice, lemon zest, and thyme.
2. Put the lamb shoulder in the Instant Pot. Add the lemon juice mixture and turnip.
3. Close the lid. Select Manual mode and set cooking time for 50 minutes on High Pressure.
4. When the time is over, use a natural pressure release for 20 minutes, then release any remaining pressure. Open the lid.
5. Serve warm.

Harissa Lamb

Prep time: 30 minutes | Cook time: 40 minutes | Serves 4

1 tablespoon keto-friendly Harissa sauce
1 teaspoon dried thyme
½ teaspoon salt
1 pound (454 g) lamb shoulder
2 tablespoons sesame oil
2 cups water

1. In a bowl, mix the Harissa, dried thyme, and salt.
2. Rub the lamb shoulder with the Harissa mixture and brush with sesame oil.
3. Heat the the Instant Pot on Sauté mode for 2 minutes and put the lamb shoulder inside.
4. Cook the lamb for 3 minutes on each side, then pour in the water.
5. Close the lid. Select Manual mode and set cooking time for 40 minutes on High Pressure.
6. When timer beeps, use a natural pressure release for 25 minutes, then release any remaining pressure. Open the lid.
7. Serve warm.

Icelandic Lamb with Turnip

Prep time: 5 minutes | Cook time: 45 minutes | Serves 4

12 ounces (340 g) lamb fillet, chopped
4 ounces (113 g) turnip, chopped
3 ounces (85 g) celery ribs, chopped
1 teaspoon unsweetened
tomato purée
¼ cup scallions, chopped
½ teaspoon salt
½ teaspoon ground black pepper
4 cups water

1. Put all ingredients in the Instant Pot and stir well.
2. Close the lid. Select Manual mode and set cooking time for 45 minutes on High Pressure.
3. When timer beeps, use a quick pressure release. Open the lid.
4. Serve hot.

Sauce Glazed Lamb Chops

Prep time: 10 minutes | Cook time: 29 minutes | Serves 2

1½ tablespoons butter
1 pound (454 g) lamb loin chops
½ small onion, sliced
1 garlic clove, crushed
1 cup carrots, peeled and sliced
¾ cup diced sugar-free
tomatoes
½ cup bone broth
¾ teaspoon crushed dried rosemary
Salt and black pepper, to taste
1 tablespoon arrowroot starch
½ tablespoon cold water

1. Select the Sauté mode and heat the butter in the Instant Pot. Add the lamb chops to the pot and cook for 3 minutes on each side, or until lightly browned. Transfer the lamb chops to plates.
2. Add the onion and garlic to the pot and cook for 3 minutes. Stir in the carrots, tomatoes, bone broth, rosemary, salt and pepper.
3. Lock the lid. Select the Manual mode and set the cooking time for 15 minutes at High Pressure. When the timer goes off, do a quick pressure release. Carefully open the lid.
4. In a small bowl, whisk together the arrowroot starch and water. Pour the slurry in the pot. Select the Sauté mode and cook for 5 minutes.
5. Spread the sauce over the cooked chops and serve hot.

Lamb and Tomato Bhuna

Prep time: 15 minutes | Cook time: 20 minutes | Serves 2

¼ teaspoon minced ginger
¼ teaspoon garlic paste
1 teaspoon coconut oil
¼ cup crushed tomatoes
10 ounces (283 g) lamb fillet,
chopped
2 ounces (57 g) scallions, chopped
¼ cup water

1. Put the minced ginger, garlic paste, coconut oil, and crushed tomatoes in the Instant Pot. Sauté for 10 minutes on Sauté mode.
2. Add the chopped lamb fillet, scallions, and water.
3. Select Manual mode and set cooking time for 10 minutes on High Pressure.
4. When timer beeps, use a natural pressure release for 15 minutes, then release any remaining pressure. Open the lid.
5. Serve warm.

Lamb Biryani with Raisins

Prep time: 45 minutes | Cook time: 16 to 17 minutes | Serves 4

1 pound (454 g) lamb leg steak, cut into cubes
1 large brown onion, thinly sliced
1 green bell pepper, sliced
Juice of ½ lime
½ cup Greek yogurt
4 tablespoons ghee, divided
1 tablespoon garlic paste
1 tablespoon grated ginger
3 teaspoons garam masala
1 teaspoon paprika
¼ teaspoon cayenne pepper
½ teaspoon cardamom powder
½ teaspoon turmeric
Salt, to taste
2 cups warm water
1 cup basmati rice, rinsed
½ cup chopped cilantro
½ teaspoon saffron, soaked in 3 tablespoons of hot water
2 tablespoons red raisins

1. In a bowl, stir together the lamb, brown onion and bell pepper.
2. In another bowl, whisk together the lime juice, yogurt, 2 tablespoons of the ghee, garlic, ginger, garam masala, paprika, cayenne pepper, cardamom, turmeric and salt.
3. Spread the mixture over the meat and vegetables. Stir and cover in plastic. Let marinate in the refrigerator for 30 minutes.
4. Remove the meat from the refrigerator and drain the marinade.
5. Press the Sauté button on the Instant Pot and melt the remaining 2 tablespoons of the ghee. Add the lamb and sear for 6 to 7 minutes, or lightly browned. Add the warm water, basmati rice, cilantro and saffron liquid to the pot. Do not stir.
6. Close and secure the lid. Select the Manual mode and set the cooking time for 10 minutes on High Pressure. When the timer goes off, use a natural pressure release for 10 minutes, then release any remaining pressure.
7. Carefully open the lid and stir in raisins. Serve immediately.

Lamb Sirloin Masala

Prep time: 10 minutes | Cook time: 25 minutes | Serves 3

12 ounces (340 g) lamb sirloin, sliced
1 tablespoon garam masala
1 tablespoon lemon juice
1 tablespoon olive oil
¼ cup coconut cream

1. Sprinkle the sliced lamb sirloin with garam masala, lemon juice, olive oil, and coconut cream in a large bowl. Toss to mix well.
2. Transfer the mixture in the Instant Pot. Cook on Sauté mode for 25 minutes. Flip the lamb for every 5 minutes.
3. When cooking is complete, allow to cool for 10 minutes, then serve warm.

Lamb Chops in Picante Sauce

Prep time: 5 minutes | Cook time: 40 minutes | Serves 6

6 lamb chops, bone-in
3 tablespoons all-purpose flour
1¼ apples, peeled and sliced
1¼ cups Picante sauce
3 tablespoons brown sugar
3 tablespoons olive oil

1. 1.In a bowl, place the flour and dip the lamb chops in it to coat well.
2. 2.In another bowl, combine the apples, Picante sauce and brown sugar until well mixed.
3. 3.Press the Sauté button on the Instant Pot and heat the olive oil. Add the coated chops to the pot and sear for 5 minutes, or until lightly browned.
4. 4.Lock the lid. Select the Meat/Stew mode and set the cooking time for 35 minutes on High Pressure.
5. 5.When the timer beeps, use a natural pressure release for 10 minutes, then release any remaining pressure.
6. 6.Open the lid and serve warm.

Milky Lamb with Potatoes

Prep time: 10 minutes | Cook time: 1 hour | Serves 4

2 pounds (907 g) boneless lamb shoulder, cubed
1 pound (454 g) potatoes, cubed
3 carrots, cubed
5 garlic cloves
2 rosemary sprigs
4 cups milk
2 cups water
1 tablespoon Vegeta seasoning
Salt and black pepper, to taste

1.Add all the ingredients to the Instant Pot and stir to combine.
2.Lock the lid. Select the Manual mode and set the cooking time for 60 minutes on High Pressure. Once cooking is complete, use a natural pressure release for 10 minutes, then release any remaining pressure.
3.Carefully open the lid. Remove and discard the rosemary springs. Divide the dish among four serving bowls and serve warm.

Lamb Tagine with Carrots

Prep time: 15 minutes | Cook time: 32 to 34 minutes | Serves 4

2 tablespoons ghee
1½ pounds (680 g) lamb stew meat, cubed
4 large carrots, peeled and chopped
1 large red onion, chopped
6 cloves garlic, minced
2 teaspoons coriander powder
2 teaspoons ginger powder
2 teaspoons cumin powder
½ teaspoon turmeric
¼ teaspoon clove powder
¼ teaspoon cinnamon powder
¼ teaspoon red chili flakes
2 bay leaves
1 lemon, zested and juiced
Salt and black pepper, to taste
2 cups vegetable stock
2 cups green olives, pitted
3 tablespoons chopped parsley

1.Select the Sauté setting. Melt the ghee and add the lamb to the pot. Cook for 6 to 7 minutes, or until the lamb is lightly browned. Stir in the carrots, onion and garlic and cook for 5 minutes, or until the vegetables are tender.
2.Add the coriander, ginger, cumin, turmeric, clove, cinnamon, red chili flakes, bay leaves, lemon zest, lemon juice, salt and pepper to the pot. Cook for 1 to 2 minutes, or until fragrant. Pour the vegetable stock into the pot.
3.Lock the lid. Select Manual mode and set the cooking time for 20 minutes on High Pressure. Once cooking is complete, use a natural pressure release for 10 minutes, then release any remaining pressure. Open the lid. Discard the bay leaves and stir in the green olives and parsley.
4.Divide the dish among 4 serving bowls and serve warm.

Lamb Rogan Josh

Prep time: 15 minutes | Cook time: 35 to 37 minutes | Serves 4

2 tablespoons ghee
1 large onion, chopped
2 pounds (907 g) boneless lamb shoulder, cubed
4 teaspoons chili powder
3 teaspoons coriander powder
2 teaspoons minced ginger
1 teaspoon garam masala
1 teaspoon turmeric
½ teaspoon cinnamon powder
½ teaspoon cardamom powder
¼ teaspoon ground cloves
¼ teaspoon cumin powder
10 garlic cloves, minced
1 bay leaf
Salt and black pepper, to taste
1 (15-ounce / 425-g) can tomato sauce
8 tablespoons plain yogurt
1 cup water
3 tablespoons chopped cilantro

1.Select the Sauté mode. Melt the ghee and add the onion and lamb to the pot. Cook for 6 to 7 minutes, or until the lamb is lightly browned.
2.Add the chili powder, coriander, ginger, garam masala, turmeric, cinnamon, cardamom, cloves, cumin, garlic, bay leaf, salt and pepper to the pot. Cook for 3 minutes, or until fragrant.
3.Stir in the tomato sauce and cook for 2 to 3 minutes. Add the yogurt, 1 tablespoon at a time, stirring to combine. Pour the water in the pot.
4.Lock the lid. Select Manual mode and set the cooking time for 20 minutes on High Pressure.
5.When the timer goes off, do a natural pressure release for 10 minutes, then release any remaining pressure. Open the lid and select the Sauté mode. Cook for another 4 minutes to boil off some liquid until the consistency is stew-like.
6.Divide the dish among 4 bowls. Top with the chopped cilantro and serve warm.

Lamb Rack with Pesto Sauce

Prep time: 15 minutes | Cook time: 45 minutes | Serves 4

1 pound (454 g) lamb rack
2 tablespoons pesto sauce
1 teaspoon chili powder
1 tablespoon coconut oil
1 cup water

1.Rub the lamb rack with pesto sauce and chili powder. Let sit for 15 minutes to marinate.
2.Heat the coconut oil in the Instant Pot on Sauté mode for 3 minutes.
3.Put the marinated lamb in the hot oil and cook on Sauté mode for 4 minutes on each side. Pour in the water.
4.Close the lid. Select Manual mode and set cooking time for 45 minutes on High Pressure.
5.When timer beeps, use a quick pressure release. Open the lid.
6.Serve immediately.

Roasted Lamb Leg

Prep time: 10 minutes | Cook time: 25 minutes | Serves 3

14 ounces (397 g) lamb leg, roughly chopped
1 teaspoon dried thyme
1 teaspoon ground black
pepper
1 tablespoon sesame oil
¼ cup beef broth
½ cup water

1.Rub the lamb leg with thyme, ground black pepper, and sesame oil on a clean work surface.
2.Put the leg in the Instant Pot, add beef broth and water.
3.Close the lid. Select Manual mode and set cooking time for 25 minutes on High Pressure.
4.When timer beeps, make a quick pressure release. Open the lid.
5.Serve warm.

Lamb Curry with Tomatoes

Prep time: 15 minutes | Cook time: 59 minutes | Serves 4

¼ cup olive oil, divided
2 pounds (907 g) lamb shoulder, cubed
4 green onions, sliced
2 tomatoes, peeled and chopped
2 tablespoons garlic paste
1 tablespoon ginger paste
1½ cups vegetable stock
2 teaspoons ground coriander
2 teaspoons allspice

1 teaspoon ground cumin
½ teaspoon ground red chili pepper
½ teaspoon curry powder
1 large carrot, sliced
1 potato, cubed
2 bay leaves
Salt, to taste
2 tablespoons mint leaves, chopped

1. Press the Sauté button on the Instant Pot and heat 2 tablespoons of the olive oil. Add the green onions and sauté for 3 minutes, or until softened, stirring constantly. Transfer the green onions to a blender. Mix in the tomatoes, garlic paste and ginger paste. Blend until smooth.
2. Heat the remaining 2 tablespoons of the olive oil in the pot and add the lamb to the pot. Cook for 6 minutes. Stir in the vegetable stock, coriander, allspice, cumin, red chili pepper, curry powder, carrot, potato, bay leaves and salt.
3. Lock the lid. Select the Manual function and set the cooking time for 50 minutes on High Pressure. When the timer beeps, use a natural pressure release for 10 minutes, then release any remaining pressure. Open the lid. Discard the bay leaves.
4. Top with the mint leaves and serve immediately.

Spicy Minced Lamb Meat

Prep time: 10 minutes | Cook time: 20 minutes | Serves 2

½ pound (227 g) ground lamb meat
½ cup onion, chopped
½ tablespoon minced ginger
½ tablespoon garlic

½ teaspoon salt
¼ teaspoon ground coriander
¼ teaspoon cayenne pepper
¼ teaspoon cumin
¼ teaspoon turmeric

1. Press the Sauté button on the Instant Pot. Add the onion, ginger and garlic to the pot and sauté for 5 minutes. Add the remaining ingredients to the pot and lock the lid.
2. Select the Manual mode and set the cooking time for 15 minutes on High Pressure. Once the timer goes off, perform a natural pressure release for 15 minutes.
3. Open the lid and serve immediately.

Lamb Koobideh

Prep time: 15 minutes | Cook time: 30 minutes | Serves 4

1 pound (454 g) ground lamb
1 egg, beaten
1 tablespoon lemon juice
1 teaspoon ground turmeric
½ teaspoon garlic powder

1 teaspoon chives, chopped
½ teaspoon ground black pepper
1 cup water

1. In a mixing bowl, combine all the ingredients except for water.
2. Shape the mixture into meatballs and press into ellipse shape.
3. Pour the water and insert the trivet in the Instant Pot.
4. Put the prepared ellipse meatballs in a baking pan and transfer on the trivet.
5. Close the lid and select Manual mode. Set cooking time for 30 minutes on High Pressure.
6. When timer beeps, make a quick pressure release. Open the lid.
7. Serve immediately.

Lamb Curry with Zucchini

Prep time: 40 minutes | Cook time: 25 minutes | Serves 3

1 pound (454 g) cubed lamb stew meat
2 garlic cloves, minced
½ cup coconut milk
1 tablespoon grated fresh ginger
½ teaspoon lime juice
¼ teaspoon salt

¼ teaspoon black pepper
1 tablespoon olive oil
1½ medium carrots, sliced
½ medium onion, diced
¾ cup diced tomatoes
½ teaspoon turmeric powder
½ medium zucchini, diced

1. In a bowl, stir together the garlic, coconut milk, ginger, lime juice, salt and pepper. Add the lamb to the bowl and marinate for 30 minutes.
2. Combine the remaining ingredients, except for the zucchini, in the Instant Pot. Add the meat and the marinade to the pot.
3. Set the lid in place. Select the Manual mode and set the cooking time for 20 minutes on High Pressure. Once the timer goes off, use a natural pressure release for 15 minutes, then release any remaining pressure.
4. Open the lid. Add the zucchini to the pot. Select the Sauté mode and cook for 5 minutes.
5. Serve hot.

Lamb Casserole

Prep time: 15 minutes | Cook time: 41 minutes | Serves 2 to 4

1 pound (454 g) lamb stew meat, cubed
1 tablespoon olive oil
3 cloves garlic, minced
2 tomatoes, chopped
2 carrots, chopped
1 onion, chopped
1 pound (454 g) baby potatoes
1 celery stalk, chopped

2 cups chicken stock
2 tablespoons red wine
2 tablespoons ketchup
1 teaspoon ground cumin
1 teaspoon sweet paprika
¼ teaspoon dried rosemary
¼ teaspoon dried oregano
Salt and ground black pepper, to taste

1. Press the Sauté button on the Instant Pot and heat the oil. Add the lamb to the pot and sear for 5 minutes, or until lightly browned. Add the garlic and sauté for 1 minute. Add all the remaining ingredients to the pot.
2. Set the lid in place. Select the Manual mode and set the cooking time for 35 minutes on High Pressure. Once cooking is complete, perform a natural pressure release for 10 minutes, then release any remaining pressure. Carefully open the lid.
3. Serve hot.

Lamb Rostelle

Prep time: 20 minutes | Cook time: 30 minutes | Serves 4

1 pound (454 g) lamb loin, slice into strips
½ teaspoon apple cider vinegar
1 teaspoon ground black

pepper
1 teaspoon olive oil
½ teaspoon salt
1 cup water, for cooking

1. Combine the apple cider vinegar, ground black pepper, olive oil, and salt in a bowl. Stir to mix well.
2. Put the lamb strips in the bowl and toss to coat well.
3. Run the lamb strips through four skewers and put in a baking pan.
4. Pour water in the Instant Pot and then insert the trivet.
5. Put the baking pan on the trivet. Close the lid.
6. Select Manual mode and set cooking time for 30 minutes on High Pressure.
7. When timer beeps, use a natural pressure release for 10 minutes, then release any remaining pressure. Open the lid.
8. Serve immediately.

Lamb Kofta Curry

Prep time: 15 minutes | Cook time: 20 minutes | Serves 4

1 pound (454 g) ground lamb	½ teaspoon chili flakes
4 ounces (113 g) scallions, chopped	1 tablespoon dried cilantro
	1 tablespoon coconut oil
1 tablespoon curry powder, divided	1 cup chicken broth
	⅓ cup coconut cream

1. In a mixing bowl, mix the ground lamb, scallions, and ½ tablespoon of curry powder.
2. Add chili flakes and dried cilantro. Stir the mixture until homogenous and shape the mixture into medium size koftas (meatballs).
3. Heat the coconut oil in the Instant Pot on Sauté mode until melted.
4. Put the koftas in the hot oil and cook for 2 minutes on each side.
5. Meanwhile, mix the chicken broth, coconut cream and remaining curry powder in a small bowl.
6. Pour the mixture over the koftas.
7. Select Manual mode and set timer for 12 minutes on High Pressure.
8. When timer beeps, use a natural pressure release for 10 minutes, then release any remaining pressure. Open the lid.
9. Serve warm.

Lamb with Peppers and Tomatoes

Prep time: 10 minutes | Cook time: 30 minutes | Serves 10

2 tablespoons olive oil	rosemary
2 pounds (907 g) boneless lamb, trimmed	6 garlic cloves, minced
	2 large yellow bell peppers, deseeded and sliced
Salt and black pepper, to taste	
4 cups chopped tomatoes	2 large red bell peppers, deseeded and sliced
3 cups sugar-free tomato sauce	
	2 large green bell peppers, deseeded and sliced
2 cups water	
2 teaspoons crushed dried	

1. Press the Sauté button on the Instant Pot and heat the olive oil. Add the lamb meat to the pot and season with salt and pepper. Cook for 5 minutes. Transfer the lamb meat to a plate.
2. Stir together all the remaining ingredients in the pot and add the lamb meat.
3. Lock the lid. Select the Manual function and set the cooking time for 25 minutes at High Pressure.
4. Once cooking is complete, use a quick pressure release. Open the lid. Serve hot.

Lamb with Anchovies

Prep time: 10 minutes | Cook time: 1 hour 5 minutes | Serves 4

2 tablespoons olive oil	1 teaspoon garlic purée
2 pounds (907 g) boneless lamb shoulder, cut into 4 pieces	3 green chilies, minced
	1 sprig rosemary
	1 teaspoon dried oregano
2 cups chicken stock	Salt, to taste
6 tinned anchovies, chopped	2 tablespoons chopped parsley

1. Press the Sauté button on the Instant Pot. Heat the olive oil and sear the lamb shoulder on both sides for 5 minutes, or until browned. Transfer the lamb to a plate and set aside.
2. Pour the chicken stock into the Instant Pot and add the anchovies and garlic. Return the lamb to the pot and sprinkle the green chilies, rosemary, oregano and salt on top.

3. Set the lid in place, select the Manual mode and set the cooking time for 60 minutes on High Pressure.
4. When the timer goes off, use a natural pressure release for 15 minutes, then release any remaining pressure.
5. Open the lid, shred the lamb with two forks and top with the chopped parsley. Serve warm.

Slow Cooked Lamb Shanks

Prep time: 10 minutes | Cook time: 55 minutes | Serves 4

2 tablespoons olive oil	¾ cup red wine
2 pounds (907 g) lamb shanks	2 cups crushed tomatoes
Salt and black pepper, to taste	1 teaspoon dried oregano
6 garlic cloves, minced	¼ cup chopped parsley, for garnish
1 cup chicken broth	

1. Press the Sauté button on the Instant Pot. Heat the olive oil and add the lamb to the pot. Season with salt and pepper. Sear the lamb on both sides for 6 minutes, or until browned. Transfer the lamb to a plate and set aside.
2. Add the garlic to the pot and sauté for 30 seconds, or until fragrant. Stir in the chicken broth and red wine and cook for 2 minutes, stirring constantly. Add the tomatoes and oregano. Stir and cook for 2 minutes. Return the lamb to the pot and baste with the chicken broth mixture.
3. Lock the lid. Select the Manual setting and set the cooking time for 45 minutes on High Pressure.
4. When the timer beeps, do a natural pressure release for 15 minutes, then release any remaining pressure. Open the lid. Top with the chopped parsley and adjust the taste with salt and pepper.
5. Divide among 4 plates and serve warm.

Spicy Lamb Shoulder

Prep time: 10 minutes | Cook time: 50 minutes | Serves 4

2 pounds (907 g) lamb shoulder	pepper
	1 teaspoon oregano
1 cup chopped fresh thyme	1 teaspoon paprika
¼ cup rice wine	1 teaspoon sugar
¼ cup chicken stock	1 tablespoon olive oil
1 tablespoon turmeric	½ cup water
1 tablespoon ground black	4 tablespoons butter

1. In a large bowl, whisk together the thyme, rice wine, chicken stock, turmeric, black pepper, oregano, paprika and sugar. Rub all sides of the lamb shoulder with the spice mix.
2. Press the Sauté button on the Instant Pot and heat the oil. Add the lamb to the pot and sear for 5 minutes on both sides, or until browned. Add the remaining spice mixture, water and butter to the pot. Stir until the butter is melted.
3. Lock the lid. Select the Manual mode and set the cooking time for 45 minutes on High Pressure. Once cooking is complete, do a natural pressure release for 10 minutes, then release any remaining pressure. Carefully open the lid.
4. Serve hot.

Chapter 9 Pasta and Rice

Parmesan Eggplant Pasta

Prep time: 10 minutes | Cook time: 9 to 10 minutes | Serves 6 to 8

1 (14-ounce / 397-g) can diced tomatoes
3 cloves garlic, minced
4 cups peeled, chopped eggplant
1½ cups water
1 cup diced onion
3 tablespoons unsalted butter, divided
1 tablespoon dried Italian seasoning
1 tablespoon tomato paste
1½ teaspoons kosher salt
1 teaspoon red pepper flakes
9 ounces (255 g) penne pasta
½ cup bread crumbs
⅓ cup shredded Parmesan cheese
1½ cups bocconcini

1. In the Instant Pot, stir together the tomatoes, garlic, eggplant, water, onion, 2 tablespoons of the butter, Italian seasoning, tomato paste, salt and red pepper flakes. Stir in the pasta.
2. Lock the lid. Select the Manual mode and set the cooking time for 7 minutes on High Pressure. Once the timer goes off, perform a natural pressure release for 10 minutes, then release any remaining pressure. Carefully open the lid.
3. Meanwhile, in a small skillet, melt the remaining 1 tablespoon of the butter over medium heat. Add the bread crumbs and mix well. Remove from the heat and let cool. Mix with the Parmesan cheese and set aside.
4. Preheat the broiler to 500ºF (260ºC).
5. Add the bocconcini to the pasta and transfer the pasta to a casserole dish. Sprinkle with the bread crumb mixture and broil for 2 to 3 minutes.
6. Serve hot.

Jollof Rice

Prep time: 10 minutes | Cook time: 22 minutes | Serves 4

1 tablespoon corn oil
2 dried bay leaves
1 onion, finely chopped
2 garlic cloves, finely chopped
1 teaspoon finely chopped fresh ginger
1 jalapeño, seeded and finely chopped
2 tomatoes, coarsely chopped
2 tablespoons tomato paste
1½ teaspoons kosher salt
1 teaspoon paprika
½ teaspoon curry powder
1 cup chopped carrots
1 cup cauliflower florets (7 or 8 florets)
1 cup short-grain white rice, rinsed
2 cups water

1. Press the Sauté button on the Instant Pot and heat the oil.
2. Once hot, add the bay leaves, onion, garlic, ginger, and jalapeños, and sauté for 5 minutes, or until the onion is translucent.
3. Stir in the tomatoes, tomato paste, and salt. Loosely place the lid on top, and cook for 3 minutes, or until the tomatoes are softened. Mix in the paprika and curry powder, then stir in the carrots and cauliflower. Add the rice and water and stir well.
4. Secure the lid. Select the Rice mode and set the cooking time for 12 minutes at Low Pressure.
5. Once cooking is complete, do a natural pressure release for 10 minutes, then release any remaining pressure. Carefully open the lid.
6. Let the rice cool for 15 minutes. Remove the bay leaves. Using a fork, gently fluff the rice and serve hot.

Seafood Pasta with Tomatoes

Prep time: 15 minutes | Cook time: 14 minutes | Serves 4 to 6

1 tablespoon olive oil
2 cloves garlic, chopped
1 medium onion, chopped
1 red bell pepper, chopped
2 tomatoes, chopped
½ cup dry white wine
2 cups macaroni
2 cups vegetable stock
1½ cups frozen mixed seafood
1 tablespoon tomato purée
1 teaspoon mixed herbs
½ teaspoon salt
½ teaspoon ground black pepper
½ cup grated Parmesan cheese

1. Press the Sauté button on your Instant Pot. Add and heat the oil.
2. Add the garlic and onion and cook for 2 minutes, stirring occasionally.
3. Fold in the bell pepper and tomatoes and cook for an additional 2 minutes.
4. Add the wine and stir well. Let simmer for 5 minutes.
5. Add the macaroni, stock, seafood, tomato purée, and herbs. Sprinkle with salt and pepper. Stir until well mixed.
6. Select the Manual mode and cook for 5 minutes on High Pressure.
7. Once the timer goes off, perform a quick pressure release. Carefully remove the lid.
8. Serve topped with the cheese.

Spaghetti with Veggie Bolognese

Prep time: 10 minutes | Cook time: 10 minutes | Serves 6

Pasta:
1 teaspoon extra-virgin olive oil
1 teaspoon kosher salt
8 ounces (227 g) spaghetti
pasta
5 cups water
Sauce:
1 tablespoon extra-virgin olive oil
1 onion, minced
5 garlic cloves, minced
5 mushrooms, roughly minced
2 cups canned crushed tomatoes
1 cup vegetable broth
½ cup dried green lentils
¼ cup finely minced basil leaves
1 teaspoon kosher salt
2 teaspoons freshly ground black pepper
½ cup shredded Parmesan cheese

1. Add all the ingredients for the pasta to the Instant Pot and stir to combine.
2. Lock the lid. Select the Manual mode and set the cooking time for 2 minutes on High Pressure. Once the timer goes off, perform a natural pressure release for 5 minutes, then release any remaining pressure. Carefully open the lid.
3. Drain the pasta and transfer to a bowl..
4. Press the Sauté button on the Instant Pot and heat the oil. Add the onion and garlic to the pot and sauté for 3 minutes. Stir in the remaining ingredients, except for the cheese.
5. Lock the lid. Select the Manual mode and set the cooking time for 5 minutes on High Pressure. Once the timer goes off, perform a natural pressure release for 10 minutes, then release any remaining pressure. Carefully open the lid.
6. Using a potato masher, mash the lentils and tomatoes until it reaches a chunky texture.
7. Stir in the spaghetti, sprinkle with the cheese and serve hot.

Black Bean and Brown Rice Casserole

Prep time: 5 minutes | Cook time: 28 minutes | Serves 4 to 6

2 cups uncooked brown rice
1 cup black beans, soaked for
at least 2 hours and drained
6 ounces (170 g) tomato paste
5 cups water

1 teaspoon garlic
2 teaspoons chili powder
2 teaspoons onion powder
1 teaspoon salt, or more to
taste

1. Place all the ingredients into the Instant Pot and stir to mix well.
2. Lock the lid. Select the Manual mode and set the cooking time for 28 minutes at High Pressure.
3. When the timer beeps, perform a quick pressure release. Carefully remove the lid.
4. Taste and add more salt, if needed. Serve immediately.

Broccoli Fettucine Pasta

Prep time: 10 minutes | Cook time: 8 to 9 minutes | Serves 8

1 teaspoon olive oil
3 garlic cloves, minced
2 cups minced broccoli
4¼ cups water, divided
1 pound (454 g) fettucine pasta
1 tablespoon butter

Salt, to taste
1 cup heavy cream
½ cup shredded Parmesan
cheese
Ground black pepper, to taste
2 tablespoons minced parsley

1. Press the Sauté button on the Instant Pot and heat the oil. Add the garlic to the pot and sauté for 1 minute, or until fragrant. Stir in the broccoli and ¼ cup of the water.
2. Set the lid in place. Select the Manual mode and set the cooking time for 3 minutes on High Pressure. When the timer goes off, do a quick pressure release. Carefully open the lid.
3. Drain the broccoli and transfer to a bowl.
4. Add the remaining 4 cups of the water, pasta, butter and salt to the Instant Pot and stir to combine.
5. Set the lid in place. Select the Manual mode and set the cooking time for 3 minutes on High Pressure. When the timer goes off, do a quick pressure release. Carefully open the lid. Drain any excess liquid from the pot.
6. Select the Sauté mode and stir in the cooked broccoli, heavy cream, Parmesan, salt and black pepper. Cook for 1 to 2 minutes.
7. Serve garnished with the parsley.

Beef Congee

Prep time: 5 minutes | Cook time: 10 minutes | Serves 4

1 tablespoon olive oil
5 cloves garlic, minced
1 cup diced onion
1 pound (454 g) ground beef

1½ cups basmati rice, rinsed
1½ cups chicken or vegetable
stock
Salt, to taste

1. Press the Sauté button on the Instant Pot and heat the olive oil.
2. Add the garlic and sauté for 30 seconds until fragrant.
3. Stir in the diced onion and beef and sauté for about 3 minutes, stirring occasionally, or until the beef begins to brown.
4. Add the basmati rice, stock, and salt to the Instant Pot. Stir well.
5. Lock the lid. Select the Manual mode and set the cooking time for 5 minutes at High Pressure.
6. When the timer beeps, perform a natural pressure release for 10 minutes, then release any remaining pressure. Carefully remove the lid.
7. Serve warm.

Italian Parmesan Chicken Pasta

Prep time: 10 minutes | Cook time: 20 minutes | Serves 2 to 4

8 ounces (227 g) linguine
noodles, halved
½ jar spaghetti sauce
1 cup water
2 chicken breasts, skinless and
boneless
8 ounces (227 g) cherry
tomatoes, halved
3 cloves garlic, chopped

¼ cup parsley, chopped
½ teaspoon Italian seasoning
Salt and crushed red pepper,
to taste
1 tablespoon butter
½ cup Italian bread crumbs
1 cup Parmesan cheese,
grated

1. Stir together the noodles, jar of spaghetti sauce, and water in your Instant Pot.
2. Mix in the chicken breasts, tomatoes, garlic, parsley, Italian seasoning, salt and pepper and stir well.
3. Secure the lid. Press the Manual button on your Instant Pot and cook for 20 minutes on High Pressure.
4. Meantime, melt the butter in a pan and toast the bread crumbs.
5. When the timer goes off, do a quick pressure release. Carefully remove the lid.
6. Stir the dish well. Sprinkle with the bread crumbs and cheese and let sit for 5 minutes.
7. Serve.

Tomato Rice

Prep time: 6 mins, Cook Time:5 mins, Servings: 4

1 tbsp. extra virgin olive oil
2 cups white rice, rinsed and
drained

4½ cups water
1 large, ripe tomato
Salt and pepper, to taste

1. Add olive oil, rice, and water to Instant Pot. Gently stir.
2. Place whole tomato, bottom-side up, in the middle.
3. Lock the lid. Select the Rice mode, then set the timer for 5 minutes at Low Pressure.
4. Once the timer goes off, do a natural pressure release for 3 to 5 minutes, then release any remaining pressure. Carefully open the lid.
5. Using a rice paddle, break up tomato while fluffing up rice. Season with salt and pepper.
6. Serve immediately.

Pea and Carrot Rice

Prep time: 10 minutes | Cook time: 23 minutes | Serves 4 to 6

1 tablespoon olive oil
1 clove garlic, minced
¼ cup chopped shallots
2 cups chicken broth
1½ cups basmati rice, rinsed

1 cup frozen peas
½ cup chopped carrots
2 teaspoons curry powder
Salt and ground black pepper,
to taste

1. Set your Instant Pot to Sauté and heat the olive oil.
2. Add the garlic and shallots and sauté for about 3 minutes until fragrant, stirring occasionally.
3. Add the remaining ingredients to the Instant Pot and stir to incorporate.
4. Lock the lid. Select the Rice mode and set the cooking time for 20 minutes at High Pressure.
5. Once cooking is complete, do a natural pressure release for 10 minutes, then release any remaining pressure. Carefully remove the lid.
6. Fluff the rice with the rice spatula or fork. Serve warm.

Sumptuous One-Pot Garden Pasta

Prep time: 10 minutes | Cook time: 11 minutes | Serves 6

1 tablespoon olive oil
1 cup leeks, sliced thin
3 cloves garlic, crushed and minced
2 cups sliced portabella mushrooms
¼ cup dry red wine
2 cups sliced summer squash
1 teaspoon oregano
1 teaspoon rosemary
1 teaspoon sea salt
1 teaspoon coarse ground black pepper
1 pound (454 g) small pasta of choice
2 cups chopped tomatoes
2 cups vegetable broth
1 cup water
1 tablespoon tomato paste
½ cup chopped fresh basil

1.Press the Sauté button on the Instant Pot and heat the oil. Add the leeks and garlic to the pot and sauté for 3 minutes. Add the mushrooms and red wine and continue to sauté for 3 minutes, or until the wine reduces.
2.Add the summer squash and season with the oregano, rosemary, sea salt and black pepper. Stir in the remaining ingredients, except for the fresh basil.
3.Set the lid in place. Select the Manual mode and set the cooking time for 5 minutes on High Pressure. When the timer goes off, do a quick pressure release. Carefully open the lid.
4.Serve garnished with the fresh basil.

Tomato and Black Bean Rotini

Prep time: 5 minutes | Cook time: 9 to 10 minutes | Serves 4

1 red onion, diced
1 to 2 teaspoons olive oil
1 to 2 teaspoons ground chipotle pepper
1 (28-ounce / 794-g) can crushed tomatoes
8 ounces (227 g) rotini
1 cup water
1½ cups fresh corn
1½ cups cooked black beans
Salt and freshly ground black pepper, to taste

1.Press the Sauté button on the Instant Pot and heat the oil. Add the red onion and cook for 5 to 6 minutes, stirring occasionally, or until the onion is lightly browned.
2.Stir in the chipotle pepper, tomatoes, rotini and water.
3.Lock the lid. Select the Manual mode and set the cooking time for 4 minutes on High Pressure. Once the timer goes off, perform a natural pressure release for 4 minutes, then release any remaining pressure. Carefully open the lid.
4.Stir in the corn and black beans. Taste and season with salt and pepper.
5.Serve immediately.

Tomato Basil Campanelle Pasta

Prep time: 5 minutes | Cook time: 2 minutes | Serves 2

2 cups dried campanelle pasta
1¾ cups vegetable stock
½ teaspoon salt
2 tomatoes, cut into large dices
1 or 2 pinches red pepper flakes
½ teaspoon dried oregano
½ teaspoon garlic powder
10 to 12 fresh sweet basil leaves, finely chopped
Freshly ground black pepper, to taste

1.In the Instant Pot, stir together the pasta, stock, and salt. Spread the tomatoes on top.
2.Set the lid in place. Select the Manual mode and set the cooking time for 2 minutes on High Pressure. When the timer goes off, do a quick pressure release. Carefully open the lid.
3.Stir in the red pepper flakes, oregano and garlic powder.
4.Sprinkle the basil and pepper. Serve immediately.

Tomato Pasta with Capers and Tuna

Prep time: 10 minutes | Cook time: 10 to 11 minutes | Serves 4 to 6

2 tablespoons olive oil
2 cloves garlic, sliced
2 cups pasta of your choice
1½ cups tomatoes, diced
⅛ teaspoon oregano
⅛ teaspoon chili pepper
¾ cup red wine
2 cups water
Salt and ground black pepper, to taste
2 tablespoons capers
1 small can tuna in oil
½ cup grated Parmesan cheese

1.Press the Sauté button on your Instant Pot. Add and heat the oil.
2.Add the garlic and sauté for 1 minute until fragrant.
3.Fold in the pasta and tomatoes and stir well. Season with oregano and chilies.
4.Add the red wine and water. Season with the salt and pepper. Stir to combine.
5.Secure the lid. Press the Manual button on your Instant Pot and cook for 6 minutes on High Pressure.
6.Once the timer beeps, do a quick pressure release. Carefully open the lid.
7.Select the Sauté mode. Stir in the capers and tuna. Sauté for 3 to 4 minutes.
8.Serve topped with the cheese.

Tuna Noodle Casserole with Cheese

Prep time: 10 minutes | Cook time: 3 minutes | Serves 6

12 ounces (340 g) egg noodles
1 (8- to 12-ounce / 227- to 340-g) can tuna albacore chunk preferred, drained
1 cup of frozen peas
1 cup of mushrooms, sliced
3 cup of chicken broth
1 teaspoon of salt
1 teaspoon of garlic powder
½ teaspoon of pepper (optional)
1.5 cup of cheese
1 cup half and half
Hot water and cornstarch as needed

1.Stir together all the ingredients except the cheese and half and half in your Instant Pot.
2.Lock the lid. Press the Manual button and cook for 3 minutes at High Pressure.
3.Once cooking is complete, use a quick pressure release. Carefully remove the lid.
4.Add the cheese and half and half and stir until the cheese has melted. Let stand for about 5 minutes until thickened.
5.Combine some hot water and some cornstarch in a medium bowl and add to the pot to thicken quicker.
6.Serve.

Vegan Rice Pudding

Prep time: 6 mins, Cook Time: 18 mins, Servings: 6

⅔ cup Jasmine rice, rinsed and drained
¼ cup granulated sugar
3 cups almond milk
Salt, to taste
1½ tsps. vanilla extract

1.Add all the ingredients, except vanilla extract, to the Instant Pot.
2.Lock the lid. Select the Manual mode, then set the timer for 18 minutes at Low Pressure.
3.Once the timer goes off, do a natural pressure release for 10 minutes, then release any remaining pressure. Carefully open the lid.
4.Stir in the vanilla extract and cool for 10 minutes, then serve.

Basil Tomato Pasta

Prep time: 10 minutes | Cook time: 10 minutes | Serves 4

1 teaspoon olive oil, plus more for drizzling
1 large Vidalia onion, diced
10 ounces (284 g) penne, rotini, or fusilli
2 cups water
¼ cup sun-dried tomatoes, chopped
½ teaspoon salt, plus more as needed
1 cup cherry tomatoes, halved or quartered
2 tablespoons finely chopped fresh basil
½ teaspoon garlic powder (optional)
Freshly ground black pepper, to taste

1. Set your Instant Pot to Sauté and heat 1 teaspoon of olive oil.
2. Add the onion and sauté for 4 to 5 minutes, stirring occasionally, until the onion is tender.
3. Add the pasta, water, tomatoes, and a pinch of salt. Stir well.
4. Secure the lid. Select the Manual mode and set the cooking time for 4 minutes at High Pressure.
5. Once cooking is complete, do a natural pressure release for 5 minutes, then release any remaining pressure. Carefully open the lid.
6. Set your Instant Pot to Sauté again and stir in the cherry tomatoes, basil, garlic powder (if desired), and another drizzle of olive oil.
7. Taste and season with more salt and pepper, as needed. Serve warm.

Black Olives and Tomato Rice

Prep time: 12 mins, Cook Time:5 mins, Servings: 4

¼ tsp. balsamic vinegar
4½ cups water
¼ cup black olives in brine rings
1 cup ripe tomato, deseeded
and minced
2 cups Basmati rice, rinsed and drained
Salt and pepper, to taste

1. Pour all the ingredients into Instant Pot. Gently stir.
2. Lock the lid. Select the Rice mode, then set the timer for 5 minutes at Low Pressure.
3. Once the timer goes off, do a natural pressure release for 3 to 5 minutes, then release any remaining pressure. Carefully open the lid.
4. Using a rice paddle, fluff up rice.
5. Serve warm.

Broccoli and Cheddar Pasta

Prep time: 5 minutes | Cook time: 6 minutes | Serves 4

2 cups water
½ pound (227 g) pasta
½ cup broccoli
½ cup half and half
8 ounces (227 g) grated Cheddar cheese
Salt, to taste

1. Place the water and pasta in the Instant Pot and insert a steamer basket.
2. Add the broccoli to the basket. Secure the lid.
3. Press the Manual button on the Instant Pot and set the cooking time for 4 minutes on High Pressure.
4. Once cooking is complete, do a quick pressure release. Carefully remove the lid.
5. Take out the broccoli and drain the pasta.
6. Press the Sauté button on the Instant Pot. Add the cooked pasta, broccoli, half and half, and cheese. Stir well. Sprinkle with the salt. Cook the dish for 2 minutes, stirring occasionally.
7. Transfer to a serving dish and serve.

Mushroom and Cabbage Pasta

Prep time: 10 minutes | Cook time: 5 minutes | Serves 4

4 cups chopped green cabbage
2 cups dried bowtie pasta
1½ cups water
1 cup diced onion
1 cup sliced button mushrooms
2 tablespoons butter, melted
1 teaspoon ground marjoram
1 teaspoon kosher salt
1 teaspoon black pepper
1 cup frozen peas and carrots

1. Add all the ingredients, except for the frozen peas and carrots, to the Instant Pot and stir to combine.
2. Scatter the peas and carrots on top of the mixture. Do not stir.
3. Lock the lid. Select the Manual mode and set the cooking time for 5 minutes on High Pressure. Once the timer goes off, perform a natural pressure release for 10 minutes, then release any remaining pressure. Carefully open the lid.
4. Spoon into individual bowls and serve.

Instant Pot Basmati Rice

Prep time: 5 minutes | Cook time: 6 minutes | Serves 4

1 cup white basmati rice, rinsed
1¼ cups water
¼ teaspoon salt
Butter to taste (optional)

1. Combine all the ingredients except the butter in the Instant Pot.
2. Lock the lid. Select the Manual mode and set the cooking time for 6 minutes at High Pressure.
3. Once cooking is complete, do a natural pressure release for 10 minutes, then release any remaining pressure. Carefully remove the lid.
4. Fluff the rice with a fork. You can stir in the butter, if desired. Serve warm.

Parmesan Pea Risotto

Prep time: 10 minutes | Cook time: 15 minutes | Serves 4

1 tablespoon extra-virgin olive oil
2 tablespoons butter, divided
1 yellow onion, chopped
1½ cups Arborio rice
2 tablespoons lemon juice
3½ cups chicken stock, divided
1½ cups frozen peas, thawed
2 tablespoons parsley, finely chopped
2 tablespoons parmesan, finely grated
1 teaspoon grated lemon zest
Salt and ground black pepper, to taste

1. Press the Sauté button on your Instant Pot. Add and heat the oil and 1 tablespoon of butter.
2. Add the onion and cook for 5 minutes, stirring occasionally. Mix in the rice and cook for an additional 3 minutes, stirring occasionally.
3. Stir in the lemon juice and 3 cups of stock.
4. Lock the lid. Select the Manual function and set the cooking time for 5 minutes at High Pressure.
5. Once cooking is complete, do a quick pressure release. Carefully open the lid.
6. Select the Sauté function again. Fold in the remaining ½ cup of stock and the peas and sauté for 2 minutes.
7. Add the remaining 1 tablespoon of butter, parsley, parmesan, lemon zest, salt, and pepper and stir well.
8. Serve.

Pineapple and Cauliflower Rice

Prep time: 20 mins, Cook Time: 20 mins, Servings: 4

2 tsps. extra virgin olive oil
2 cups jasmine rice
1 cauliflower, florets separated and chopped
½ pineapple, peeled and

chopped
4 cups water
Salt and ground black pepper, to taste

1. Mix all the ingredients in your Instant Pot and stir to incorporate.
2. Lock the lid. Select the Manual mode and cook for 20 minutes at Low Pressure.
3. Once cooking is complete, do a natural pressure release for 10 minutes, then release any remaining pressure. Carefully open the lid.
4. Using a fork to fluff the rice and serve in bowls.

Beef and Cheddar Pasta

Prep time: 5 minutes | Cook time: 12 to 13 minutes | Serves 4 to 6

1 teaspoon olive oil
1¼ pound (567 g) ground beef
1 packet onion soup mix
3½ cups hot water
3 beef bouillon cubes
1 pound (454 g) elbow

macaroni
8 ounces (227 g) sharp Cheddar cheese, grated
Salt and ground black pepper, to taste

1. Press the Sauté button on your Instant Pot. Pour in the oil and let heat for 1 minute.
2. Add the ground beef and sauté for 4 to 5 minutes until browned.
3. Mix together the onion soup mix, water, and bouillon cubes in a bowl.
4. Add the mixture and macaroni to the pot and stir to combine.
5. Press the Manual button on your Instant Pot and cook for 7 minutes at High Pressure.
6. When the timer goes off, perform a quick pressure release. Carefully open the lid.
7. Stir in the Cheddar cheese and let stand for 5 minutes.
8. Taste and sprinkle with salt and pepper if needed.
9. Serve.

Pizza Pasta

Prep time: 5 minutes | Cook time: 5 to 8 minutes | Serves 6

4 cups of noodles such as ziti or riganoti
8 cups of water
2 cups of spaghetti sauce

1½ cup of shredded mozzarella cheese
10 pepperoni, cut in half

1. Add the noodles and water to the Instant Pot.
2. Lock the lid. Press the Manual button on the Instant Pot and cook for 3 minutes at High Pressure.
3. Once cooking is complete, perform a quick pressure release. Carefully remove the lid. Drain the cooking liquid.
4. Return the pasta to the Instant Pot. Fold in the spaghetti sauce, shredded cheese, and sliced pepperoni. Stir well.
5. Press the Sauté button on the Instant Pot. Cook for 2 to 3 minutes, or until the sauce starts to bubble and the cheese has melted, stirring occasionally.
6. Serve immediately.

Turkey Spaghetti

Prep time: 10 minutes | Cook time: 16 minutes | Serves 4 to 6

1 teaspoon olive oil
1 pound (454 g) ground turkey
1 clove garlic, minced
¼ onion, diced
8 ounces (227 g) whole wheat spaghetti, halved
1 jar (25-ounce / 709-g) Delallo

Pomodoro Tomato-Basil Sauce (or of your choice)
¾ teaspoon kosher salt
2 cups water
shredded Parmesan cheese (optional)

1. Set your Instant Pot to Sauté. Add and heat the oil.
2. Add the ground turkey and sauté for 3 minutes.
3. Fold in the garlic and onion. Sauté for another 4 minutes.
4. Mix in the spaghetti, sauce and salt. Add the water to the pot and stir to combine.
5. Secure the lid. Press the Manual button on the Instant Pot and cook for 9 minutes on High Pressure.
6. Once the cooking is complete, do a quick pressure release. Carefully remove the lid.
7. Serve topped with the shredded cheese.

Broccoli and Chicken Rice

Prep time: 5 minutes | Cook time: 20 minutes | Serves 4 to 6

2 tablespoons butter
2 cloves garlic, minced
1 onion, chopped
1½ pounds (680 g) boneless chicken breasts, sliced
Salt and ground black pepper,

to taste
1⅓ cups chicken broth
1⅓ cups long grain rice
½ cup milk
1 cup broccoli florets
½ cup grated Cheddar cheese

1. Set your Instant Pot to Sauté and melt the butter.
2. Add the garlic, onion, and chicken pieces to the pot. Season with salt and pepper to taste.
3. Sauté for 5 minutes, stirring occasionally, or until the chicken is lightly browned.
4. Stir in the chicken broth, rice, milk, broccoli, and cheese.
5. Lock the lid. Select the Manual mode and set the cooking time for 15 minutes at High Pressure.
6. When the timer beeps, perform a natural pressure release for 10 minutes, then release any remaining pressure. Carefully remove the lid.
7. Divide into bowls and serve.

Chicken Fettuccine Alfredo

Prep time: 5 minutes | Cook time: 3 minutes | Serves 2

8 ounces (227 g) fettuccine, halved
2 cups water
2 teaspoons chicken seasoning
1 cup cooked and diced

chicken
1 jar (15-ounce / 425-g) Alfredo sauce
Salt and ground black pepper, to taste

1. Add the pasta, water, and chicken seasoning to the Instant Pot and stir to combine.
2. Secure the lid. Press the Manual button on the Instant Pot and set the cooking time for 3 minutes at High Pressure.
3. When the timer goes off, perform a quick pressure release. Carefully remove the lid.
4. Drain the pasta and transfer to a serving bowl.
5. Add the cooked chicken and drizzle the sauce over the top. Sprinkle with salt and pepper.
6. Stir until well mixed and serve.

Tomato and Chickpea Rice
Prep time: 12 mins, Cook Time:25 mins, Servings: 4

½ cup canned chickpeas
4½ cups water
1 cup deseeded and minced ripe tomato

Salt and pepper, to taste
2 cups rinsed and drained white rice

1. Pour all the ingredients into Instant Pot. Gently stir.
2. Lock the lid. Select the Rice mode, then set the timer for 5 minutes at Low Pressure.
3. Once the timer goes off, do a quick pressure release. Carefully open the lid.
4. Using a rice paddle, fluff up rice.
5. Serve immediately.

Chipotle Cilantro Rice
Prep time: 20 mins, Cook Time: 20 mins, Servings: 4

2 cups brown rice, rinsed
4 small bay leaves
2¾ cups water
1½ tbsps. olive oil

½ cup chopped cilantro
1 lime, juiced
1 tsp. salt

1. Place the brown rice, bay leaves, and water in the Instant Pot.
2. Lock the lid. Select the Rice mode and cook for 20 minutes at High Pressure.
3. Once cooking is complete, do a natural pressure release for 10 minutes, then release any remaining pressure. Carefully open the lid.
4. Add the olive oil, cilantro, lime juice, and salt to the pot and stir until well combined. Serve warm.

Cinnamon Brown Rice
Prep time: 5 minutes | Cook time: 25 minutes | Serves 4

1 tablespoon olive oil
3 cloves garlic, crushed and minced
½ cup chopped sweet yellow onion
½ teaspoon cumin
½ teaspoon nutmeg

½ teaspoon cinnamon
½ teaspoon sweet paprika
½ teaspoon sea salt
1½ cups brown rice
2½ cups vegetable broth
½ cup chopped fresh parsley

1. Set your Instant Pot to Sauté and heat the olive oil.
2. Add the garlic, onion, cumin, nutmeg, cinnamon, sweet paprika, and sea salt and sauté for 2 to 3 minutes, stirring frequently, or until the onions are softened.
3. Add the rice and vegetable broth to the Instant Pot.
4. Secure the lid. Select the Manual mode and set the cooking time for 20 minutes at High Pressure.
5. Once cooking is complete, do a quick pressure release. Carefully open the lid.
6. Fluff the rice with a fork and stir in the fresh parsley before serving.

Confetti Rice
Prep time: 5 minutes | Cook time: 12 minutes | Serves 4

3 tablespoons butter
1 small onion, chopped
1 cup long-grain white rice
3 cups frozen peas, thawed
1 cup vegetable broth

¼ cup lemon juice
2 cloves garlic, minced
1 tablespoon cumin powder
½ teaspoon salt
½ teaspoon black pepper

1. Set your Instant Pot to Sauté and melt the butter.
2. Add the onion and sauté for 3 minutes until soft. Add the remaining ingredients to the Instant Pot, stirring well.
3. Secure the lid. Select the Manual mode and set the cooking time for 8 minutes at High Pressure.
4. Once cooking is complete, do a quick pressure release. Carefully open the lid.
5. Fluff the rice and serve hot.

Cilantro Lime Rice
Prep time: 3 minutes; Cook Time: 10 mins, Servings: 2

1¼ cups water
1 cup white rice
Salt, to taste

3 tbsps. fresh chopped cilantro
1 tbsp. fresh lime juice
2 tbsps. vegetable oil

1. Mix the rice and water together in the Instant Pot and stir to combine. Season with salt.
2. Lock the lid. Select the Rice mode, then set the timer for 5 minutes at Low Pressure.
3. Once the timer goes off, do a natural pressure release for 3 to 5 minutes. Carefully open the lid.
4. Use a quick release to get rid of the remaining pressure. Use a fork to fluff up the rice.
5. Mix the lime juice, cilantro, and oil in a bowl.
6. Whisk well and mix into the rice. Serve immediately.

Kimchi Pasta
Prep time: 5 minutes | Cook time: 4 to 5 minutes | Serves 4 to 6

8 ounces (227 g) dried small pasta
2⅓ cups vegetable stock
2 garlic cloves, minced
½ red onion, sliced

½ to 1 teaspoon salt
1¼ cups kimchi, with any larger pieces chopped
½ cup coconut cream

1. In the Instant Pot, combine the pasta, stock, garlic, red onion and salt.
2. Set the lid in place. Select the Manual mode and set the cooking time for 1 minute on High Pressure. When the timer goes off, do a quick pressure release. Carefully open the lid.
3. Select Sauté mode. Stir in the kimchi. Simmer for 3 to 4 minutes. Stir in the coconut cream and serve.

Marsala Tofu Pasta
Prep time: 5 minutes | Cook time: 15 minutes | Serves 2

1 tablespoon butter
2 cups sliced mushrooms
1 small onion, diced
½ cup sun-dried tomatoes
½ cup tofu, diced into chunks
½ teaspoon garlic powder

1 cup white Marsala wine
1½ cups vegetable broth
1 cup Pennette pasta
½ cup grated goat cheese
¼ cup cream

1. Press the Sauté button on the Instant Pot and melt the butter. Add the mushrooms and onion to the pot and cook for 4 minutes. Add the tomatoes and tofu and cook for 3 minutes.
2. Add the garlic powder and cook for 1 minute. Pour in the white wine and cook for 1 minute. Stir in the broth. Add the pasta and don't stir.
3. Set the lid in place. Select the Manual mode and set the cooking time for 6 minutes on High Pressure. When the timer goes off, do a quick pressure release. Carefully open the lid.
4. Add the cheese and cream and let sit for 5 minutes. Serve hot.

Mushroom Alfredo Rice

Prep time: 5 minutes | Cook time: 25 minutes | Serves 4

2 tablespoons olive oil
¾ cup finely chopped onion
2 garlic cloves, minced
1 cup rice
2¾ cups vegetable broth
1½ tablespoons fresh lemon

juice
Salt and black pepper, to taste
2 ounces (57 g) creamy
mushroom Alfredo sauce
¼ cup coarsely chopped
walnuts

1. Set your Instant Pot to Sauté. Add the oil, onion, and garlic to the pot and sauté for 3 minutes. Stir in the rice and broth.
2. Secure the lid. Select the Manual mode and set the cooking time for 22 minutes at High Pressure.
3. Once cooking is complete, do a natural pressure release for 10 minutes, then release any remaining pressure. Carefully open the lid.
4. Add lemon juice, salt, pepper, and sauce and stir to combine. Garnish with the chopped walnuts and serve.

Creamy Tomato Pasta with Spinach

Prep time: 5 minutes | Cook time: 9 minutes | Serves 4

1 (28-ounce / 794-g) can
crushed tomatoes
10 ounces (284 g) penne,
rotini, or fusilli (about 3 cups)
1 tablespoon dried basil
½ teaspoon garlic powder
½ teaspoon salt, plus more as
needed

1½ cups water
1 cup unsweetened coconut
milk
2 cups chopped fresh spinach
(optional)
Freshly ground black pepper,
to taste

1. Combine the tomatoes, pasta, basil, garlic powder, salt, and water in the Instant Pot.
2. Secure the lid. Select the Manual mode and set the cooking time for 4 minutes at High Pressure.
3. Once cooking is complete, do a natural pressure release for 5 minutes, then release any remaining pressure. Carefully open the lid.
4. Stir in the milk and spinach (if desired). Taste and season with more salt and pepper, as needed.
5. Set your Instant Pot to Sauté and let cook for 4 to 5 minutes, or until the sauce is thickened and the greens are wilt. Serve warm.

Spinach and Pine Nut Fusilli Pasta

Prep time: 5 minutes | Cook time: 12 minutes | Serves 4

1 tablespoon butter
2 garlic cloves, crushed
1 pound (454 g) spinach
1 pound (454 g) fusilli pasta
Salt and black pepper, to taste

Water, as needed
2 garlic cloves, chopped
¼ cup chopped pine nuts
Grated cheese, for serving

1. Press the Sauté button on the Instant Pot and melt the butter. Add the crushed garlic and spinach to the pot and sauté for 6 minutes. Add the pasta, salt and pepper. Pour in the water to cover the pasta and mix.
2. Set the lid in place. Select the Manual mode and set the cooking time for 6 minutes on Low Pressure. When the timer goes off, do a quick pressure release. Carefully open the lid.
3. Stir in the chopped garlic and nuts. Garnish with the cheese and serve.

Green Tea Risotto

Prep time: 6 mins, Cook Time: 20 mins, Servings: 4

¼ cup lentils, rinsed
Salt, to taste
3 green tea bags

1 cup brown rice, rinsed
7 cups water

1. In the Instant Pot, add all ingredients and stir gently.
2. Lock the lid. Select the Manual mode, then set the timer for 20 minutes at Low Pressure.
3. Once the timer goes off, do a quick pressure release. Carefully open the lid.
4. Serve immediately.

Ground Beef Pasta

Prep time: 5 minutes | Cook time: 11 to 13 minutes | Serves 4

1 teaspoon olive oil
1 pound (454 g) ground beef
8 ounces (227 g) dried pasta
24 ounces (680 g) pasta sauce

1½ cup water
Salt and ground black pepper,
to taste
Italian seasoning, to taste

1. Press the Sauté button on the Instant Pot. Add the oil and let heat for 1 minute.
2. Fold in the ground beef and cook for 3 to 5 minutes until browned, stirring frequently.
3. Mix in the pasta, sauce and water and stir to combine.
4. Secure the lid. Press the Manual button on the Instant Pot and set the cooking time for 7 minutes on High Pressure.
5. Once cooking is complete, do a quick pressure release. Carefully remove the lid.
6. Stir in salt, pepper, and Italian seasoning and stir well.
7. Transfer to a serving dish and serve immediately.

Duo-Cheese Mushroom Pasta

Prep time: 10 minutes | Cook time: 5 minutes | Serves 4

2 tablespoons butter
3 cloves garlic, minced
1 teaspoon dried thyme
½ teaspoon red pepper flakes
8 ounces (227 g) cremini
mushrooms, trimmed and
sliced
1 cup chopped onion
1¾ cups water
1 teaspoon kosher salt

1 teaspoon black pepper
8 ounces (227 g) fettuccine,
broken in half
8 ounces (227 g) Mascarpone
cheese
1 cup shredded Parmesan
cheese
2 teaspoons fresh thyme
leaves, for garnish

1. Press the Sauté button on the Instant Pot and melt the butter. Add the garlic, thyme, and red pepper flakes to the pot and sauté for 30 seconds. Stir in the mushrooms, onion, water, salt and pepper.
2. Add the fettuccine, pushing it down into the liquid. Add the Mascarpone on top of the pasta. Do not stir.
3. Lock the lid. Select the Manual mode and set the cooking time for 5 minutes on High Pressure. Once the timer goes off, perform a natural pressure release for 5 minutes, then release any remaining pressure. Carefully open the lid.
4. Stir in the Parmesan cheese.
5. Divide the pasta among four dishes, garnish with the thyme and serve.

Pasta Carbonara

Prep time: 10 minutes | Cook time: 8 to 9 minutes | Serves 4

1 pound (454 g) pasta dry such as rigatoni, penne or cavatappi)
4 cups water
¼ teaspoon kosher salt
4 large eggs
1 cup grated Parmesan cheese
Ground black pepper, to taste
8 ounces (227 g) bacon pancetta or guanciale
4 tablespoons heavy cream

1. Place the pasta, water, and salt in your Instant Pot.
2. Secure the lid. Press the Manual button and cook for 5 minutes at High Pressure.
3. Meantime, beat together the eggs, cheese and black pepper in a mixing bowl until well mixed.
4. Cook the bacon on medium heat in a frying pan for 3 minutes until crispy.
5. Once cooking is complete, do a quick pressure release. Carefully remove the lid.
6. Select the Sauté mode. Transfer the bacon to the pot and cook for 30 seconds.
7. Stir in the egg mixture and heavy cream.
8. Secure the lid and let stand for 5 minutes.
9. Transfer to a serving dish and serve.

Instant Pot Jasmine Rice

Prep time: 5 minutes | Cook time: 4 minutes | Serves 4 to 6

2 cups jasmine rice, rinsed
2 teaspoons olive oil
½ teaspoon salt
2 cups water

1. Place all the ingredients into the Instant Pot and give a good stir.
2. Lock the lid. Select the Manual mode and set the cooking time for 4 minutes at High Pressure.
3. Once cooking is complete, do a natural pressure release for 10 minutes, then release any remaining pressure. Remove the lid.
4. Fluff the rice with a fork and serve.

Spinach Lemon Pasta

Prep time: 5 minutes | Cook time: 4 minutes | Serves 6

1 pound (454 g) fusilli pasta
4 cups chopped fresh spinach
4 cups vegetable broth
2 cloves garlic, crushed and minced
1 cup plain coconut milk
1 teaspoon lemon zest
1 teaspoon lemon juice
¼ cup chopped fresh parsley
1 tablespoon chopped fresh mint
½ teaspoon sea salt
½ teaspoon coarse ground black pepper

1. Stir together the fusilli pasta, spinach, vegetable broth and garlic in the Instant Pot.
2. Set the lid in place. Select the Manual mode and set the cooking time for 4 minutes on High Pressure.
3. Meanwhile, whisk together the coconut milk, lemon zest and lemon juice in a bowl.
4. When the timer goes off, do a quick pressure release. Carefully open the lid. Drain off any excess liquid that might remain.
5. Add the coconut milk mixture to the pasta, along with the parsley and mint. Season with salt and pepper.
6. Stir gently and let sit for 5 minutes before serving.

Cauliflower and Pineapple Jasmine Rice Bowl

Prep time: 5 minutes | Cook time: 20 minutes | Serves 4 to 6

4 cups water
2 cups jasmine rice
1 cauliflower, florets separated and chopped
½ pineapple, peeled and
chopped
2 teaspoons extra virgin olive oil
Salt and ground black pepper, to taste

1. Stir together all the ingredients in the Instant Pot.
2. Lock the lid. Select the Manual mode and set the cooking time for 20 minutes at Low Pressure.
3. When the timer beeps, perform a natural pressure release for 10 minutes, then release any remaining pressure. Carefully remove the lid.
4. Fluff with the rice spatula or fork, then serve.

Bow Tie Pasta

Prep time: 5 minutes | Cook time: 11 to 12 minutes | Serves 4 to 5

1 Vidalia onion, diced
2 garlic cloves, minced
1 tablespoon olive oil
3½ cups water
10 ounces (284 g) bow tie pasta
Grated zest and juice of 1 lemon
¼ cup black olives, pitted and chopped
Salt and freshly ground black pepper, to taste

1. Press the Sauté button on the Instant Pot and heat the oil. Add the onion and garlic to the pot. Cook for 7 to 8 minutes, stirring occasionally, or until the onion is lightly browned.
2. Add the water and pasta.
3. Set the lid in place. Select the Manual mode and set the cooking time for 4 minutes on High Pressure. When the timer goes off, do a quick pressure release. Carefully open the lid.
4. Stir the pasta and drain any excess water. Stir in the lemon zest and juice and the olives. Season with salt and pepper.
5. Serve immediately.

Vegetable Basmati Rice

Prep time: 10 minutes | Cook time: 9 to 10 minutes | Serves 6 to 8

3 tablespoons olive oil
3 cloves garlic, minced
1 large onion, finely chopped
3 tablespoons chopped cilantro stalks
1 cup garden peas, frozen
1 cup sweet corn, frozen
2 cups basmati rice, rinsed
1 teaspoon turmeric powder
¼ teaspoon salt
3 cups chicken stock
2 tablespoons butter (optional)

1. Press the Sauté button on the Instant Pot and heat the olive oil.
2. Add the garlic, onion, and cilantro and sauté for 5 to 6 minutes, stirring occasionally, or until the garlic is fragrant.
3. Stir in the peas, sweet corn, and rice. Scatter with the turmeric and salt. Pour in the chicken stock and stir to combine.
4. Lock the lid. Select the Manual mode and set the cooking time for 4 minutes at High Pressure.
5. Once cooking is complete, do a quick pressure release. Carefully open the lid.
6. You can add the butter, if desired. Serve warm.

Zucchini Penne Pasta

Prep time: 10 minutes | Cook time: 10 minutes | Serves 5

1 tablespoon butter
1 yellow onion, thinly sliced
1 shallot, finely chopped
Salt and black pepper, to taste
2 garlic cloves, minced
12 mushrooms, thinly sliced
1 zucchini, thinly sliced
Pinch of dried oregano

Pinch of dried basil
2 cups water
1 cup vegetable stock
2 tablespoons soy sauce
Splash of sherry wine
15 ounces (425 g) penne pasta
5 ounces (142 g) tomato paste

1. Press the Sauté button on the Instant Pot and melt the butter. Add the onion, shallot, salt and pepper to the pot and sauté for 3 minutes. Add the garlic and continue to sauté for 1 minute.
2. Stir in the mushrooms, zucchini, oregano and basil. Cook for 1 minute more. Pour in the water, stock, soy sauce and wine. Add the penne, tomato paste, salt and pepper.
3. Set the lid in place. Select the Manual mode and set the cooking time for 5 minutes on High Pressure. When the timer goes off, do a quick pressure release. Carefully open the lid.
4. Serve hot.

Cherry Tomato Farfalle with Pesto

Prep time: 5 minutes | Cook time: 8 to 9 minutes | Serves 2 to 4

1½ cup farfalle
4 cups water
¾ cup vegan pesto sauce

1 cup cherry tomatoes, quartered

1. Place the farfalle and water in your Instant Pot.
2. Secure the lid. Press the Manual button and cook for 7 minutes at High Pressure.
3. Once cooking is complete, do a quick pressure release. Carefully remove the lid.
4. Drain the pasta and transfer it back to the pot.
5. Stir in the sauce.
6. Press the Sauté button on your Instant Pot and cook for 1 to 2 minutes.
7. Fold in the tomatoes and stir to combine.
8. Transfer to a serving dish and serve immediately.

Pumpkin Risotto

Prep time: 10 minutes | Cook time: 11 to 12 minutes | Serves 4 to 6

2 ounces (57 g) extra virgin olive oil
1 small yellow onion, chopped
2 cloves garlic, minced
4 cups chicken stock
2 cups Arborio rice
¾ cup pumpkin purée

1 teaspoon thyme, chopped
½ teaspoon grated ginger
½ teaspoon cinnamon
½ teaspoon nutmeg
½ cup heavy cream
Salt, to taste

1. Press the Sauté button on your Instant Pot Add and heat the oil.
2. Add the onion and garlic and sauté for 1 to 2 minutes.
3. Stir in the chicken stock, rice, pumpkin purée, thyme, ginger, cinnamon, and nutmeg.
4. Lock the lid. Press the Manual button and cook for 10 minutes at High Pressure.
5. Once cooking is complete, do a quick pressure release. Carefully open the lid.
6. Mix in the heavy cream and salt. Stir well.
7. Serve.

Buttery Raisin Rice

Prep time: 3 mins, Cook Time: 12 mins, Servings: 4

3 cups wild rice, soaked in water overnight and drained
3 cups water

½ cup raisins
¼ cup salted butter
1 tsp. salt

1. Add all the ingredients to the Instant Pot.
2. Lock the lid. Select the Rice mode, then set the timer for 12 minutes at Low Pressure.
3. Once the timer goes off, perform a natural release for 8 to 10 minutes.
4. Carefully open the lid and use a fork to fluff the rice.
5. Serve warm.

Raisins and Almond Rice Bowl

Prep time: 5 minutes | Cook time: 20 minutes | Serves 4

1 cup brown rice
1 cup water
1 cup coconut milk
½ cup coconut chips
½ cup maple syrup

¼ cup raisins
¼ cup almonds
A pinch of cinnamon powder
Salt, to taste

1. Place the rice and water into the Instant Pot and give a stir.
2. Secure the lid. Select the Manual mode and set the cooking time for 15 minutes at High Pressure.
3. When the timer beeps, perform a quick pressure release. Carefully remove the lid.
4. Stir in the coconut milk, coconut chips, maple syrup, raisins, almonds, cinnamon powder, and salt.
5. Lock the lid. Select the Manual mode and set the cooking time for 5 minutes at High Pressure.
6. Once cooking is complete, do a quick pressure release. Open the lid.
7. Serve warm.

Vegetarian Thai Pineapple Fried Rice

Prep time: 10 minutes | Cook time: 10 minutes | Serves 4

1 tablespoon corn oil
3 tablespoons cashews
¼ cup finely chopped onion
¼ cup finely chopped scallions, white parts only
2 green Thai chiles, finely chopped
1 cup canned pineapple chunks

2 tablespoons roughly chopped fresh basil leaves
½ teaspoon curry powder
¼ teaspoon ground turmeric
2 teaspoons soy sauce
1 teaspoon kosher salt
1 cup steamed short-grain white rice
1¼ cups water

1. Press the Sauté button on the Instant Pot and heat the oil.
2. Once hot, add the cashews and stir for 1 minute. Add the onion, scallions, and chiles, and sauté for 3 to 4 minutes, until the onion is translucent.
3. Mix in the pineapple, basil, curry powder, turmeric, soy sauce, and salt. Add the rice and water and stir to combine.
4. Secure the lid. Select the Manual mode and set the cooking time for 3 minutes at High Pressure.
5. Once cooking is complete, do a natural pressure release for 3 minutes, then release any remaining pressure. Carefully open the lid.
6. Let the rice rest for 15 minutes. Remove the bay leaves. Using a fork, fluff the rice and serve hot.

Rice Medley

Prep time: 5 minutes | Cook time: 23 minutes | Serves 4

¾ cup (or more) short grain brown rice, rinsed
3 to 4 tablespoons red, wild or
black rice, rinsed
1½ cups water
¼ teaspoon sea salt

1. Combine all the ingredients in the Instant Pot.
2. Lock the lid. Select the Multigrain mode and set the cooking time for 23 minutes at High Pressure.
3. Once cooking is complete, do a natural pressure release for 15 minutes, then release any remaining pressure. Carefully open the lid.
4. Fluff the rice with a fork and serve.

Shawarma Rice

Prep time: 10 minutes | Cook time: 15 minutes | Serves 6 to 8

1½ cups basmati rice, rinsed and drained
4 cups shredded cabbage
1 pound (454 g) ground beef (chicken, fish, pork, optional), cooked
1½ cups water
1 cup chopped onion
5 cloves garlic, minced
3 tablespoons shawarma spice
1 tablespoon olive oil
1 teaspoon salt
¼ cup chopped cilantro

1. Combine all the ingredients except the cilantro in the Instant Pot.
2. Lock the lid. Select the Manual mode and set the cooking time for 15 minutes at High Pressure.
3. When the timer beeps, perform a natural pressure release for 10 minutes, then release any remaining pressure. Carefully remove the lid.
4. Stir in the cilantro and serve immediately.

Feta and Arugula Pasta Salad

Prep time: 10 minutes | Cook time: 8 minutes | Serves 4 to 6

1 pound (454 g) dry rotini pasta
Water as needed, to cover the pasta
2 cups arugula or spinach, chopped
1 cup feta cheese, diced
2 Roma or plum tomatoes, diced
2 garlic cloves, minced
1 red bell pepper, diced
2 tablespoons white wine vinegar
⅓ cup extra-virgin olive oil
Salt and ground black pepper, to taste

1. Place the pasta and water in your Instant Pot.
2. Secure the lid. Press the Manual button on your Instant Pot and set the cooking time for 8 minutes on High Pressure.
3. Once the timer goes off, do a quick pressure release. Carefully open the lid.
4. Drain the pasta and set aside.
5. Mix together the arugula, feta, tomatoes, garlic, bell pepper, vinegar, and olive oil in a large bowl.
6. Fold in the pasta. Sprinkle with salt and pepper. Stir well.
7. Serve immediately.

Simple Tomato Pasta

Prep time: 5 minutes | Cook time: 8 to 10 minutes | Serves 6

1 tablespoon olive oil
¼ cup minced shallots
¼ cup dry red wine
1 pound (454 g) spaghetti pasta, broken in half
4 cups vegetable broth
3 cups chopped tomatoes
½ cup chopped fresh basil
½ teaspoon salt
1 teaspoon black pepper

1. Press the Sauté button on the Instant Pot and heat the oil. Add the scallions to the pot and sauté for 1 to 2 minutes, or until tender. Pour in the red wine and continue to cook for 2 to 3 minutes, or until the wine reduces. Stir in the remaining ingredients.
2. Set the lid in place. Select the Manual mode and set the cooking time for 5 minutes on High Pressure. When the timer goes off, do a quick pressure release. Carefully open the lid.
3. Stir before serving.

Spanish Rice

Prep time: 5 minutes | Cook time: 14 minutes | Serves 4 to 6

2 tablespoons butter
2 cups long grain rice
8 ounces (227 g) tomato sauce
1½ cups chicken stock or water
1 teaspoon chili powder
1 teaspoon cumin
½ teaspoon onion powder
½ teaspoon garlic powder
½ teaspoon salt

1. Set your Instant Pot to Sauté and melt the butter.
2. Add the rice and sauté for about 4 minutes, stirring occasionally.
3. Add the remaining ingredients to the Instant Pot and stir.
4. Secure the lid. Select the Manual mode and set the cooking time for 10 minutes at High Pressure.
5. When the timer beeps, perform a natural pressure release for 10 minutes, then release any remaining pressure. Carefully remove the lid.
6. Fluff the rice with the rice spatula or fork. Serve warm.

Vegetable Pasta

Prep time: 10 minutes | Cook time: 7 minutes | Serves 4 to 6

2 cups dried pasta
1 cup water
½ jar spaghetti sauce
½ can chickpeas, rinsed and drained
½ can black olives, rinsed and drained

½ cup frozen spinach
½ cup frozen lima beans
½ squash, shredded
½ zucchini, sliced
½ tablespoon Italian seasoning
½ teaspoon cumin
½ teaspoon garlic powder

1. Add all the ingredients to the Instant Pot and stir to combine.
2. Press the Manual button on the Instant Pot and set the cooking time for 7 minutes on High Pressure.
3. Once cooking is complete, perform a natural pressure release for 10 minutes and then release any remaining pressure. Carefully open the lid.
4. Transfer to a serving dish and serve immediately.

Vinegary Brown Rice Noodles

Prep time: 5 minutes | Cook time: 3 minutes | Serves 6

8 ounces (227 g) uncooked brown rice noodles
2 cups water
½ cup soy sauce
2 tablespoons brown sugar
Topping:
Green onions
Peanuts

2 tablespoons white vinegar
2 tablespoons butter
1 tablespoon chili garlic paste
2 red bell peppers, thinly sliced

Sesame seeds

1. Add all the ingredients, except for the red bell peppers, to the Instant Pot and stir to combine.
2. Set the lid in place. Select the Manual mode and set the cooking time for 3 minutes on High Pressure. When the timer goes off, do a quick pressure release. Carefully open the lid.
3. Stir in the red bell peppers. Sprinkle with the green onions, peanuts and sesame seeds. Serve immediately.

Mexican Rice

Prep time: 5 minutes | Cook time: 14 to 16 minutes | Serves 4 to 6

1 tablespoon olive oil
¼ cup diced onion
2 cups long grain white rice

1 cup salsa
2⅓ cups chicken stock
1 teaspoon salt

1. Press the Sauté button on the Instant Pot and heat the olive oil.
2. Add the diced onion and sauté for 2 to 3 minutes until translucent.
3. Add the white rice and cook for an additional 2 to 3 minutes. Stir in the remaining ingredients.
4. Lock the lid. Select the Manual mode and set the cooking time for 10 minutes at High Pressure.
5. Once cooking is complete, do a natural pressure release for 10 minutes, then release any remaining pressure. Carefully open the lid.
6. Fluff the rice with the rice spatula or fork. Serve warm.

Simple Wild Brown Rice

Prep time: 2 mins, Cook Time: 20 mins, Servings: 6 to 8

2 tbsps. olive oil
3¾ cups water

3 cups wild brown rice
Salt, to taste

1. Combine the oil, water, and brown rice in the pot.
2. Season with salt.
3. Lock the lid. Select the Multigrain mode, then set the timer for 20 minutes on Low Pressure.
4. Once the timer goes off, do a natural pressure release for 5 minutes. Carefully open the lid.
5. Fluff the rice with a fork.
6. Serve immediately.

Mustard Macaroni and Cheese

Prep time: 10 minutes | Cook time: 6 minutes | Serves 4 to 6

1 pound (454 g) elbow macaroni
4 cups chicken broth or vegetable broth, low sodium
3 tablespoons unsalted butter
½ cup sour cream
3 cups shredded Cheddar

cheese, about 12 ounces (340 g)
½ cup shredded Parmesan cheese, about 2 ounces (57 g)
1½ teaspoons yellow mustard
⅛ teaspoon cayenne pepper

1. Add the macaroni, broth, and butter to your Instant Pot.
2. Secure the lid. Press the Manual button on the Instant Pot and set the cooking time for 6 minutes on High Pressure.
3. Once cooking is complete, perform a quick pressure release. Carefully remove the lid.
4. Stir in the sour cream, cheese, mustard, and cayenne pepper.
5. Let stand for 5 minutes. Stir well.
6. Serve immediately.

Spinach and Mushroom Pasta
Prep time: 5 minutes | Cook time: 10 minutes | Serves 4

1 tablespoon oil
8 ounces (227 g) mushrooms, minced
½ teaspoon kosher salt
½ teaspoon black ground pepper
8 ounces (227 g) uncooked

spaghetti pasta
1¾ cups water
5 ounces (142 g) spinach
½ cup pesto
⅓ cup grated Parmesan cheese

1.Press the Sauté button on the Instant Pot and heat the oil. Add the mushrooms, salt and pepper to the pot and sauté for 5 minutes. Add the pasta and water.
2.Set the lid in place. Select the Manual mode and set the cooking time for 5 minutes on High Pressure. When the timer goes off, do a quick pressure release. Carefully open the lid.
3.Stir in the spinach, pesto, and cheese. Serve immediately.

Caper and Olive Pasta
Prep time: 10 minutes | Cook time: 5 minutes | Serves 4

3 cloves garlic, minced
4 cups of pasta such as penne or fusilli (short pasta)
4 cups of pasta sauce (homemade or store-bought)
3 cups of water, plus more as needed

1 tablespoon of capers
½ cup of Kalamata olives, sliced
¼ teaspoon. of crushed red pepper flakes
Salt and pepper, to taste

1.Press the Sauté button on your Instant Pot and add the garlic.
2.Add a splash of water and cook for about 30 seconds until fragrant.
3.Mix in the pasta, pasta sauce, water, capers, olives, and crushed red pepper flakes and stir to combine.
4.Lock the lid. Press the Manual button on the Instant Pot and set the cooking time for 5 minutes on High Pressure.
5.Once the timer goes off, use a quick pressure release. Carefully remove the lid.
6.Fold in the pasta and sprinkle with salt and pepper. Stir well.
7.Serve immediately.

Stick of Butter Rice
Prep time: 5 minutes | Cook time: 24 minutes | Serves 4 to 6

1 stick (½ cup) butter
2 cups brown rice

1½ cups French onion soup
1 cups vegetable stock

1.Set your Instant Pot to Sauté and melt the butter.
2.Add the rice, onion soup, and vegetable stock to the Instant Pot and stir until combined.
3.Lock the lid. Select the Manual mode and set the cooking time for 22 minutes at High Pressure.
4.When the timer beeps, perform a natural pressure release for 10 minutes, then release any remaining pressure. Carefully remove the lid.
5.Serve warm.

Penne Pasta with Tomato-Vodka Sauce
Prep time: 5 minutes | Cook time: 4 minutes | Serves 2

½ cup uncooked penne pasta
½ cup crushed tomatoes
1 cup water
⅛ cup coconut oil
1 tablespoon vodka

1 teaspoon garlic powder
½ teaspoon salt
¼ teaspoon paprika
½ cup coconut cream
⅛ cup minced cilantro

1.Add all the ingredients, except for the coconut cream and cilantro, to the Instant Pot and stir to combine.
2.Set the lid in place. Select the Manual mode and set the cooking time for 4 minutes on High Pressure. When the timer goes off, do a quick pressure release. Carefully open the lid.
3.Stir in the coconut cream and fresh cilantro and serve hot.

Wild Rice and Basmati Pilaf
Prep time: 5 minutes | Cook time: 35 minutes | Serves 6

2 tablespoon olive oil
2 brown onions, minced
2 cloves garlic, minced
12 ounces (340 g) mushrooms, sliced
½ teaspoon salt

6 sprigs fresh thyme
2 cups broth
2 cups wild rice and basmati rice mixture
½ cup pine nuts
½ cup minced parsley

1.Set your Instant Pot to Sauté. Add the olive oil and onions and cook for 6 minutes.
2.Add minced garlic and cook for 1 minute more. Place the remaining ingredients, except for nuts and parsley, into the Instant Pot and stir well.
3.Lock the lid. Select the Manual mode and set the cooking time for 28 minutes at High Pressure.
4.When the timer beeps, perform a natural pressure release for 15 minutes, then release any remaining pressure. Carefully remove the lid.
5.Sprinkle with the pine nuts and parsley, then serve.

Chapter 10 Grains and Beans

Acorn Squash Quinoa Pilaf
Prep time: 5 minutes | Cook time: 4 minutes | Serves 2

½ pound (227 g) acorn squash, peeled and sliced
1 sweet onion, thinly sliced
½ tablespoon coconut oil, melted
½ teaspoon chopped fresh ginger
2 cups vegetable stock, divided
1 cup quinoa, rinsed
3 prunes, chopped
1 tablespoon roughly chopped fresh mint leaves

1.Add the acorn squash, sweet onion, coconut oil, ginger and 1 cup of the vegetable stock to the Instant Pot and stir to combine.
2.Lock the lid. Select the Manual mode and set the cooking time for 3 minutes on High Pressure. When the timer goes off, do a quick pressure release. Carefully open the lid.
3.Stir in the remaining 1 cup of the vegetable stock, quinoa and prunes.
4.Lock the lid. Select the Manual mode and set the cooking time for 1 minute on High Pressure. When the timer goes off, do a quick pressure release. Carefully open the lid.
5.Serve garnished with fresh mint leaves.

Vegetable and Adzuki Beans Bowl
Prep time: 5 minutes | Cook time: 25 minutes | Serves 4

1 teaspoon sesame oil
2 cloves garlic, minced
1 teaspoon grated ginger
1 cup dried adzuki beans
½ cup brown rice
½ cup sliced shiitake mushrooms
2 cups shredded collard greens
1-inch strip kombu
3 cups water
3 umeboshi plums, mashed
1 tablespoon lemon juice
1 tablespoon tamari

1.In the Instant Pot, heat the oil on Sauté mode.
2.Add the garlic and ginger and sauté for 2 minutes until the garlic is softened
3. Stir in the adzuki beans, brown rice, mushrooms, greens, kombu, and water.
4.Secure the lid. Select Manual mode and set cooking time for 22 minutes on High Pressure.
5.When timer beeps, use a natural pressure release for 15 minutes, then release any remaining pressure.
6.Remove the cover and stir. Return to the pot, and simmer while stirring in the mashed umeboshi plums, lemon juice, and tamari on Sauté mode for 3 minutes.
7.Serve immediately.

Almond Arborio Risotto
Prep time: 10 mins, Cook Time: 5 mins, Servings: 2

½ cup Arborio rice
2 cups vanilla almond milk
1 tsp. vanilla extract
2 tbsps. agave syrup
¼ cup toasted almond flakes, for garnish

1.Add all the ingredients, except for the almond flakes, to the Instant Pot. Stir to mix well.
2.Lock the lid. Set to the Manual mode, then set the timer for 5 minutes at Low Pressure.
3.Once the timer goes off, perform a natural pressure release. Carefully open the lid.
4.Serve the risotto with almond flakes immediately.

Barley and Apple Salad
Prep time: 10 minutes | Cook time: 20 minutes | Serves 2 to 4

2½ cups water
1 cup pearl barley, rinsed
Salt and white pepper, to taste
1 green apple, chopped
¼ cup chopped celery
¾ cup jarred spinach pesto

1.Combine the water, barley, salt, and white pepper in the Instant Pot.
2.Lock the lid. Select the Manual mode and set the cooking time for 20 minutes at High Pressure.
3.When the timer beeps, perform a quick pressure release. Carefully remove the lid.
4.Drain the barley and transfer to a bowl. Add the chopped apple, celery, and spinach pesto, tossing to coat, and serve.

Balsamic Black Beans with Parsnip
Prep time: 5 minutes | Cook time: 11 minutes | Serves 6

1 cup dried black beans, soaked in water overnight, rinsed and drained
1 teaspoon olive oil
2 cloves garlic, minced
1 cup diced parsnip
½ teaspoon ground coriander
½ teaspoon ground cardamom
2 cups water
2 tablespoons balsamic vinegar

1.In the Instant Pot, heat the oil on Sauté mode. Add the garlic and sauté for a minute or until soft, but not brown.
2.Add the parsnip, coriander, and cardamom and sauté for 5 minutes.
3.Add the black beans and water. Stir to combine.
4.Secure the lid. Select Manual mode and set cooking time for 5 minutes on High Pressure.
5.When timer beeps, use a natural pressure release for 5 minutes, then release any remaining pressure.
6.Remove the lid and stir in 2 tablespoons of the balsamic vinegar. Serve immediately.

Nut Buckwheat Pilaf
Prep time: 10 minutes | Cook time: 11 minutes | Serves 4

1 tablespoon olive oil
4 garlic cloves, minced
1 red bell pepper, diced
2¼ cups chicken broth
1 cup roasted buckwheat groats
½ cup yellow lentils
¾ teaspoon dried thyme
Salt and black pepper, to taste
1 cup chopped dried figs
½ cup toasted walnuts
½ cup chopped dried apricots
½ cup chopped cilantro

1.Press the Sauté button on the Instant Pot and heat the oil. Add the garlic and bell pepper to the pot and sauté for 5 minutes. Stir in the chicken broth, buckwheat groats, lentils, thyme, salt and pepper.
2.Close and secure the lid. Select the Manual mode and set the cooking time for 6 minutes on High Pressure. Once the timer goes off, use a natural pressure release for 10 minutes, then release any remaining pressure. Carefully open the lid.
3.Stir in the figs, walnuts, apricots and cilantro. Spoon the pilaf into bowls and enjoy.

Millet Pilaf with Lime

Prep time: 5 minutes | Cook time: 10 minutes | Serves 4

1 cup chopped green onions
1 cup millet
1 teaspoon kosher salt
1 tablespoon olive oil

1 cup water
1 cup chopped fresh cilantro or parsley
Zest and juice of 1 lime

1. In the Instant Pot, combine the green onions, millet, salt, olive oil, and water.
2. Lock the lid. Select the Manual mode and set the cooking time for 10 minutes at High Pressure.
3. When the timer beeps, perform a natural pressure release for 10 minutes, then release any remaining pressure. Carefully remove the lid.
4. Stir in the cilantro and lime zest and juice and serve.

Lentil and Bulgur Pilaf

Prep time: 5 minutes | Cook time: 10 minutes | Serves 6

2 tablespoons vegetable oil
1 large onion, thinly sliced
1½ teaspoons kosher salt
½ teaspoon ground cinnamon
½ teaspoon ground allspice
1¾ cups water, divided

1 cup whole-grain red wheat bulgur
½ cup dried red lentils
¼ cup chopped fresh parsley
Toasted pine nuts (optional)

1. Press the Sauté button on the Instant Pot and heat the oil.
2. Once the oil is hot, add the onion and salt. Cook, stirring occasionally, until the onion is browned, about 5 minutes.
3. Stir in the cinnamon and allspice and cook for 30 seconds.
4. Add ¼ cup of water to deglaze the pot, scraping up the browned bits. Add the bulgur, lentils, and remaining 1½ cups of water.
5. Lock the lid. Select the Manual mode and set the cooking time for 5 minutes at High Pressure.
6. When the timer beeps, perform a natural pressure release for 10 minutes, then release any remaining pressure. Carefully remove the lid.
7. Stir gently to fluff up the bulgur. Stir in the parsley and pine nuts (if desired), then serve.

Chickpeas Curry

Prep time: 15 minutes | Cook time: 35 minutes | Serves 4

1 cup dried chickpeas
1 tablespoon baking soda
4 cups water, divided
1 teaspoon olive oil
1 clove garlic, minced

¼ cup diced onion
½ teaspoon hot curry powder
¼ teaspoon ground cinnamon
1 bay leaf
½ teaspoon sea salt

1. Add the chickpeas, baking soda, and 2 cups of the water to a large bowl and soak for 1 hour. Rinse the chickpeas and drain.
2. In the Instant Pot, heat the oil on Sauté mode. Add the garlic and onion and sauté for 3 minutes.
3. Add the curry, cinnamon, and bay leaf and stir well. Stir in the chickpeas and 2 cups of the water.
4. Cover the lid. Select Manual mode and set cooking time for 32 minutes on High Pressure.
5. When timer beeps, use a natural pressure release for 15 minutes, then release any remaining pressure.
6. Remove the lid and stir in the sea salt. Remove the bay leaf before serving.

Baked Barbecue Northern Bean

Prep time: 20 minutes | Cook time: 54 minutes | Serves 8

2½ cups (about 1 pound / 454 g) dried great Northern beans, soaked in water for at least 8 hours, rinsed and drained
1 cup barbecue sauce
¼ cup yellow mustard
2 tablespoons maple syrup
1¾ cups water

1½ teaspoons freshly ground black pepper
1½ teaspoons smoked paprika
3 tablespoons avocado oil
1 large yellow onion, diced
2 cloves garlic, minced
1 bay leaf

1. In a small bowl, stir together the barbecue sauce, mustard, maple syrup, water, pepper, and smoked paprika.
2. Select the Sauté setting on the Instant Pot, add the oil, and heat for 2 minutes.
3. Add the onion and sauté for about 10 minutes, stirring often, until it begins to caramelize.
4. Add the garlic and sauté for about 2 minutes more until the garlic is no longer raw.
5. Add the barbecue sauce mixture, beans, and bay leaf. Stir to combine, using a wooden spoon to nudge loose any browned bits from the bottom of the pot.
6. Secure the lid. Select Bean/Chili setting and set the cooking time for 40 minutes at High Pressure.
7. When timer beeps, let the pressure release naturally for 20 minutes, then release any remaining pressure. Open the pot, stir the beans, and discard the bay leaf.
8. Ladle the beans into bowls and serve hot.

Bean Tagine with Ras el Hanout

Prep time: 20 minutes | Cook time: 37 minutes | Serves 8

2½ cups (about 1 pound / 454 g) dried Northern beans, soaked in salted water overnight, rinsed and drained
¼ cup olive oil, plus more for serving
4 cloves garlic, minced
1 yellow onion, sliced
3 cups vegetable broth
8 medium carrots (about 1 pound / 454 g in total), peeled and cut into ½-inch rounds

1 tablespoon tomato paste
1 tablespoon fresh lemon juice
Salt, to taste
2 tablespoons chopped fresh mint
Ras el Hanout:
2 teaspoons paprika
½ teaspoon ground cinnamon
½ teaspoon ground coriander
½ teaspoon ground cumin
¼ teaspoon cayenne pepper.

1. Select the Sauté setting on the Instant Pot, add the oil and garlic, and heat for 2 minutes, until the garlic is bubbling but not browned.
2. Add the onion and sauté for 5 minutes until the onion is softened and the garlic is toasty and brown.
3. Stir in the broth and use a wooden spoon to nudge loose any browned bits from the bottom of the pot.
4. Stir in the carrots, ingredients for the ras el hanout, and salt. Stir in the beans, making sure all of the beans are submerged in the cooking liquid.
5. Secure the lid. Select Bean/Chili setting and set the cooking time for 30 minutes at High Pressure.
6. When timer beeps, let the pressure release naturally for 20 minutes, then release any remaining pressure.
7. Open the pot and stir in the tomato paste and lemon juice.
8. Ladle the tagine into bowls. Drizzle with oil and sprinkle with mint. Serve hot.

Beluga Lentils with Lacinato Kale

Prep time: 15 minutes | Cook time: 40 minutes | Serves 6

¼ cup olive oil, plus more for serving
2 shallots, diced
5 cloves garlic, minced
½ teaspoon red pepper flakes
½ teaspoon ground nutmeg
1 teaspoon fine sea salt
2 bunches (about 1 pound /

454 g) lacinato kale, stems discarded and leaves chopped into 1-inch pieces
2 large carrots, peeled and diced
2½ cups water
1 cup beluga lentils, rinsed

1. Select the Sauté setting on the Instant Pot, add the oil, and heat for 1 minute.
2. Add the shallots and garlic and sauté for about 4 minutes until the shallots soften.
3. Add the red pepper flakes, nutmeg, and salt and sauté for 1 minute more.
4. Stir in the kale and carrots and sauté for about 3 minutes, until the kale fully wilts. Stir in the water and lentils.
5. Secure the lid. Select Bean/Chili setting and set the cooking time for 30 minutes at High Pressure.
6. When timer beeps, let the pressure release naturally for 10 minutes, then release any remaining pressure.
7. Open the pot and give the mixture a stir.
8. Ladle the lentils into serving dishes and drizzle with oil. Serve warm.

Pepper and Black Bean Tacos

Prep time: 10 minutes | Cook time: 23 minutes | Serves 2

1 tablespoon sesame oil
½ onion, chopped
1 teaspoon garlic, minced
1 sweet pepper, deseeded and sliced
1 jalapeño pepper, deseeded and minced
1 teaspoon ground cumin

½ teaspoon ground coriander
8 ounces (227 g) black beans, rinsed
2 (8-inch) whole wheat tortillas, warmed
½ cup cherry tomatoes, halved
⅓ cup coconut cream

1. Press the Sauté button and heat the oil. Cook the onion, garlic, and peppers for 3 minutes or until tender and fragrant.
2. Add the ground cumin, coriander, and beans to the Instant Pot.
3. Secure the lid. Choose the Manual mode and cook for 20 minutes at High Pressure.
4. Once cooking is complete, use a natural pressure release for 10 minutes, then release any remaining pressure. Carefully remove the lid.
5. Serve the bean mixture in the tortillas, then garnish with the cherry tomatoes and coconut cream.

Crumbled Tofu with Black Beans

Prep time: 15 minutes | Cook time: 23 minutes | Serves 2

1 cup canned black beans
2 cups vegetable broth
1 tablespoon avocado oil
1 small red onion, finely chopped
3 garlic cloves, minced
3 tomatoes, chopped

1 (14-ounce / 397-g) extra-firm tofu, crumbled
1 teaspoon turmeric powder
1 teaspoon cumin powder
1 teaspoon smoked paprika
Salt and ground black pepper, to taste

1. Pour the beans and broth in Instant Pot. Seal the lid, select Manual mode, and set cooking time for 10 minutes on High Pressure.

2. When timer beeps, do a quick pressure release. Transfer the beans to a medium bowl. Drain excess liquid and wipe Instant Pot clean.
3. Select Sauté mode. Heat the avocado oil and sauté onion, garlic, and tomatoes until softened, 4 minutes.
4. Crumble the tofu into the pan and cook for 5 minutes.
5. Season with turmeric, cumin, paprika, salt, and black pepper. Cook for 1 minute. Add black beans, stir, and allow heating for 3 minutes.
6. Serve immediately.

Black Chickpea Curry

Prep time: 15 minutes | Cook time: 15 minutes | Serves 6

1 tablespoon olive oil
2 cups minced onion
2 teaspoons garam masala
½ teaspoon ground coriander
2 teaspoons cumin seeds
3 teaspoons minced garlic
½ teaspoon ground turmeric
½ teaspoon ground chile
1 cup black chickpeas, soaked

in water for at least 8 hours, drained
1½ cups diced tomatoes
1½ cups water
2 tablespoons grated ginger
2 teaspoons crushed curry leaves
Salt, to taste

1. Select the Sauté setting on the Instant Pot, and heat the oil until shimmering.
2. Add the onion and sauté for 5 minutes or until transparent.
3. Add the garam masala, coriander, cumin seeds, garlic, turmeric and chile and sauté for 2 minutes.
4. Add the chickpeas, tomatoes, water, ginger and curry leaves, and stir to combine.
5. Put the lid on. Select the Manual setting and set the timer for 8 minutes on High Pressure.
6. When timer beeps, allow the pressure to release naturally for 5 minutes, then release any remaining pressure. Open the lid.
7. Sprinkle with salt and serve.

Kale and Black-Eyed Pea Curry

Prep time: 15 minutes | Cook time: 30 minutes | Serves 4

1 tablespoon olive oil
½ teaspoon cumin seeds
1 medium red onion, chopped
4 cloves garlic, finely chopped
1-inch piece ginger, finely chopped
1 green chili, finely chopped
2 large tomatoes, chopped
½ teaspoon turmeric powder

1 teaspoon coriander powder
¼ teaspoon garam masala
1 teaspoon salt
1 cup dried black-eyed peas, soaked in water for 3 hours, drained
2 cups water
3 cups kale, chopped
2 teaspoons lime juice

1. Press the Sauté button on the Instant Pot. Add the oil and the cumin seeds and let them sizzle for a few seconds.
2. Add the onion and sauté for 2 minutes or until soft.
3. Add the garlic, ginger and green chili and sauté for 1 minute or until golden brown.
4. Add the tomatoes and cook for 3 minutes, or until soft.
5. Add the turmeric powder, coriander powder, garam masala and salt. Cook for 1 minute.
6. Fold in the black-eyed peas and water. Lock the lid.
7. Press the Manual button and set the timer for 20 minutes on High Pressure.
8. When timer beeps, let the pressure release naturally for 10 minutes, then release any remaining pressure.
9. Open the pot and press the Sauté button. Add the kale and simmer for 3 minutes.
10. Stir in the lime juice and serve.

Butternut Squash Arborio Risotto

Prep time: 10 mins, Cook Time: 12 mins, Servings: 4

1 tbsp. olive oil
2 garlic cloves, whole
1 sprig sage, leaves removed
½ butternut squash, diced
1 cup Arborio rice

½ tsp. freshly ground nutmeg
2 tbsps. white wine
1 tsp. sea salt
2 cups water

1. Grease the Instant Pot with olive oil.
2. Set the pot to Sauté mode, then add the garlic and sage. Sauté for 2 minutes or until fragrant.
3. Add the butternut squash and sauté for 5 minutes.
4. Add the remaining ingredients. Stir to mix well.
5. Lock the lid. Set to the Manual mode, then set the timer for 5 minutes at Low Pressure.
6. Once the timer goes off, perform a natural pressure release. Carefully open the lid.
7. Serve immediately.

Swiss Chard with Black-Eyed Peas

Prep time: 15 minutes | Cook time: 10 minutes | Serves 6

1 teaspoon olive oil
1 medium large onion, thinly sliced
1 small jalapeño, minced
1 cup diced red bell pepper
3 cloves garlic, minced
1½ cups dried black-eyed peas, soaked overnight, drained

1 teaspoon chili powder
2 teaspoons smoked paprika
4 dates, finely chopped
1½ cups water
1 (15-ounce / 425-g) can fire-roasted tomatoes with green chiles
2 cups chopped Swiss chard
Salt, to taste

1. Select the Sauté setting of the Instant Pot and heat the oil until shimmering.
2. Add the onion and sauté for 5 minutes or until transparent.
3. Add the peppers and garlic. Sauté for a minute more or until fragrant.
4. Add the black-eyed peas, chili powder, and smoked paprika, and stir. Add the dates and water.
5. Put the lid on. Set to Manual mode and set cooking time for 3 minutes at High Pressure.
6. When timer beeps, let the pressure release naturally for 5 minutes, then release any remaining pressure. Open the lid.
7. Add the tomatoes and Swiss chard. Set cooking time for 1 minute on High Pressure.
8. When cooking is complete, quick release the pressure and open the lid.
9. Sprinkle with salt and serve.

Simple Instant Pot Pearl Barley

Prep time: 2 minutes | Cook time: 25 minutes | Serves 4

3 cups water
1½ cups pearl barley, rinsed
Salt, to taste

Peanut butter, to taste (optional)

1. Combine the water, barley, and salt in the Instant Pot.
2. Lock the lid. Select the Manual mode and set the cooking time for 25 minutes at High Pressure.
3. Once cooking is complete, do a natural pressure release for 15 minutes, then release any remaining pressure. Carefully open the lid.
4. Add the peanut butter to taste, if desired. Serve hot.

Pork and Buckwheat Cabbage Rolls

Prep time: 10 minutes | Cook time: 40 minutes | Serves 4

2 tablespoons butter
½ sweet onion, finely chopped
2 garlic cloves, minced
1 pound (454 g) ground pork
Salt and black pepper, to taste
1 cup buckwheat groats

2 cups beef stock
2 tablespoons chopped cilantro
1 head Savoy cabbage, leaves separated (scraps kept)
1 (23-ounce / 652-g) can chopped tomatoes

1. Set the Instant Pot to the Sauté mode and melt the butter. Add the onion and garlic to the pot and sauté for 4 minutes, or until slightly softened. Add the pork and season with salt and pepper. Cook for 5 minutes, or until the pork is no longer pink. Add the buckwheat groats and beef stock to the pot.
2. Set the lid in place. Select the Manual mode and set the cooking time for 6 minutes at High Pressure. Once the timer goes off, use a quick pressure release. Open the lid. Stir in the chopped cilantro.
3. On a clean work surface, lay the cabbage leaves. Scoop 3 to 4 tablespoons of mixture into the center of each leave and roll up tightly. Clean the pot and spread the cabbage scraps in the bottom. Pour in tomatoes with liquid and arrange cabbage rolls on top.
4. Lock the lid. Select the Manual mode and set the cooking time for 25 minutes on Low Pressure. Once the timer goes off, use a natural pressure release for 10 minutes, then release any remaining pressure. Carefully open the lid. Use a slotted spoon to transfer the cabbage rolls onto serving plates.
5. Serve immediately.

Bulgur Wheat Bowl

Prep time: 5 minutes | Cook time: 14 minutes | Serves 2

1 tablespoon butter
2 shallots, chopped
1 teaspoon minced fresh garlic
1 cup vegetable broth

½ cup bulgur wheat
¼ teaspoon sea salt
¼ teaspoon ground black pepper

1. Set the Instant Pot to the Sauté mode and melt the butter. Add the shallots to the pot and sauté for 3 minutes, or until just tender and fragrant. Add the garlic and sauté for 1 minute, or until fragrant. Stir together the remaining ingredients in the pot.
2. Lock the lid. Select the Manual mode and set the cooking time for 10 minutes on High Pressure. When the timer beeps, perform a natural pressure release for 10 minutes, then release any remaining pressure. Carefully open the lid.
3. Fluff the bulgur wheat with a fork and serve immediately.

Paprika Polenta

Prep time: 2 minutes | Cook time: 9 minutes | Serves 6

10 cups water
3 cups polenta
3 teaspoons salt

3 tablespoons red paprika flakes

1. Combine the water, polenta, salt, and red paprika flakes in the Instant Pot.
2. Lock the lid. Select the Manual mode and set the cooking time for 9 minutes at High Pressure.
3. When the timer beeps, perform a natural pressure release for 15 minutes, then release any remaining pressure. Carefully remove the lid.
4. Cool for 5 minutes and serve.

Chicken and Kamut Platter

Prep time: 10 minutes | Cook time: 12 minutes | Serves 2

½ pound (227 g) boneless and skinless chicken, chopped
½ shallot, chopped
1 sweet pepper, chopped
1 serrano pepper, chopped
½ cup kamut
½ cup tomato purée
½ cup vegetable broth
1 tablespoon butter, melted

1 teaspoon pressed fresh garlic
½ teaspoon basil
½ teaspoon thyme
Sea salt and freshly ground black pepper, to taste
2 ounces (57 g) Colby cheese, shredded

1. Add all the ingredients, except for the Colby cheese, to the Instant Pot and stir to combine.
2. Lock the lid. Select the Manual setting and set the cooking time for 12 minutes on High Pressure. Once the timer goes off, do a quick pressure release. Carefully open the lid.
3. Sprinkle the shredded Colby cheese on top and lock the lid again. Let it sit in the residual heat until the cheese melts. Serve hot.

Chicken and Green Pea Quinoa

Prep time: 10 minutes | Cook time: 12 minutes | Serves 4

2 tablespoons butter
2 leeks, sliced
3 garlic cloves, minced
2 chicken breasts, cut into bite-size pieces
3 cups chicken broth
1½ cups quick-cooking quinoa
1 tablespoon chopped rosemary

1 teaspoon dried basil
Salt and black pepper, to taste
1½ cups green peas, thawed
1 cup ricotta cheese
1 cup grated Parmesan cheese
¼ cup chopped fresh parsley
2 tablespoons lemon juice
2 tablespoons lemon zest

1. Set the Instant Pot to the Sauté mode and melt the butter. Add the leeks to the pot and sauté for 3 minutes, or until bright green and tender. Add the garlic and sauté for 2 minutes, or until fragrant. Stir in the chicken breasts, chicken broth, quinoa, rosemary, basil, salt and black pepper.
2. Close and secure the lid. Select the Manual setting and set the cooking time for 1 minute at High Pressure. Once the timer goes off, use a quick pressure release. Carefully open the lid.
3. Whisk in all the remaining ingredients. Select the Sauté mode and cook for 6 minutes, or until the cheese is melted and the chicken is cooked through.
4. Divide the quinoa into bowls and serve immediately.

Amaranth Egg Pilaf

Prep time: 5 minutes | Cook time: 7 minutes | Serves 2

¾ cup amaranth
2 cups water
½ cup milk
Sea salt and freshly ground black pepper, to taste
1 tablespoon olive oil

2 eggs
½ cup shredded Cheddar cheese
2 tablespoons chopped fresh chives

1. Add the amaranth, water and milk to the Instant Pot.
2. Set the lid in place. Select the Manual mode and set the cooking time for 4 minutes on High Pressure. When the timer goes off, do a quick pressure release. Carefully open the lid. Sprinkle the salt and black pepper to season.
3. Heat the olive oil in a skillet over medium-high heat and fry the eggs for about 3 minutes, or until crispy on the edges.
4. Divide the cooked amaranth between 2 serving bowls. Place the fried eggs, cheese and chives on top. Serve immediately.

Mushroom Farro Bowl

Prep time: 10 minutes | Cook time: 18 to 19 minutes | Serves 2

1 tablespoon olive oil
1 onion, chopped
1 cup sliced mushrooms
1 sweet pepper, chopped
1 garlic clove, minced
½ cup white wine
1½ cups vegetable broth

¾ cup farro
Sea salt and ground black pepper, to taste
⅓ cup grated Swiss cheese
1 tablespoon chopped fresh parsley

1. Set the Instant Pot on the Sauté mode and heat the oil. Add the onion to the pot and sauté for 3 to 4 minutes, or until softened. Add the mushrooms and pepper and sauté for 3 minutes. Stir in the garlic and continue to sauté for 1 minute.
2. Pour in the white wine to deglaze the pan. Stir in the vegetable broth, farro, salt and black pepper.
3. Lock the lid, select the Manual mode and set the cooking time for 11 minutes on High Pressure. When the timer goes off, do a natural pressure release for 10 minutes, then release any remaining pressure. Open the lid.
4. Transfer the dish to bowls and serve topped with the cheese and fresh parsley.

Mushroom Risotto

Prep time: 10 minutes | Cook time: 20 minutes | Serves 4

3 tablespoons butter, divided
1 small red onion, finely chopped
2 garlic cloves, thinly sliced
½ pound (227 g) baby Bella mushrooms, sliced
Salt and black pepper, to taste

1 cup pearl barley
½ cup dry white wine
2½ cups beef broth, hot
2 teaspoons fresh thyme leaves
¼ cup grated Parmesan cheese, plus more for garnish

1. Set the Instant Pot on the Sauté mode and melt 2 tablespoons of the butter. Add the red onion and garlic to the pot and sauté for 5 minutes, or until softened.
2. Add the mushrooms and season with salt and pepper. Cook for 4 minutes, or until the mushrooms are tender.
3. Add the remaining 1 tablespoon of the butter, barley and wine. Cook for 4 minutes, or until the wine is absorbed. Pour the broth in the pot.
4. Lock the lid. Select the Manual mode and set the cooking time for 7 minutes at High Pressure. When the timer goes off, use a natural pressure release for 10 minutes, then release any remaining pressure. Carefully open the lid.
5. Mix in Parmesan cheese to melt and spoon the risotto into serving bowls. Garnish with Parmesan cheese and thyme. Serve warm.

Quinoa with Spinach

Prep time: 5 minutes | Cook time: 2 minutes | Serves 4

1½ cups quinoa, rinsed
1½ cups water
4 cups spinach

1 bell pepper, chopped
3 stalks of celery, chopped
¼ teaspoon salt

1. Combine all ingredients in the Instant Pot.
2. Secure the lid. Select the Manual mode and set the cooking time for 2 minutes at High Pressure.
3. Once cooking is complete, do a natural pressure release for 10 minutes, then release any remaining pressure. Carefully open the lid.
4. Fluff the quinoa and serve.

Quinoa and Chickpea Salad

Prep time: 10 minutes | Cook time: 1 minute | Serves 2

½ cup quinoa, rinsed
1 cup water
1 sweet pepper, deseeded and chopped
1 serrano pepper, deseeded and chopped
½ onion, thinly sliced
½ cup boiled chickpeas

3 tablespoons extra-virgin olive oil, plus more for greasing the pot
1 tablespoon fresh lime juice
¼ teaspoon red pepper flakes
Sea salt and ground black pepper, to taste

1. Grease the Instant Pot with the olive oil. Add the rinsed quinoa and water to the pot.
2. Lock the lid. Select the Manual mode and set the cooking time for 1 minute on High Pressure. When the timer goes off, do a natural pressure release for 10 minutes, then release any remaining pressure. Carefully open the lid.
3. Fluff the quinoa with a fork and let rest for 5 minutes. Toss the cooled quinoa with the remaining ingredients until well combined. Serve immediately.

Cranberry and Almond Quinoa Pilaf

Prep time: 2 minutes | Cook time: 10 minutes | Serves 2 to 4

1 cup quinoa, rinsed
2 cups water
1 cup dried cranberries

½ cup slivered almonds
¼ cup salted sunflower seeds

1. Combine the water and quinoa in the Instant Pot.
2. Lock the lid. Select the Manual mode and set the cooking time for 10 minutes at High Pressure.
3. Once cooking is complete, do a quick pressure release. Carefully open the lid.
4. Add the cranberries, almonds, and sunflower seeds and gently mix until well incorporated. Serve warm.

Black Bean and Quinoa Bowl with Beef

Prep time: 10 minutes | Cook time: 14 to 15 minutes | Serves 4

1 tablespoon olive oil
1 pound (454 g) ground beef
Salt and black pepper, to taste
1 cup fresh corn
1 onion, finely diced
1 red bell pepper, chopped
1 jalapeño pepper, minced
2 garlic cloves, minced
1 teaspoon ground cumin
1 tablespoon chili seasoning

1 (14-ounce / 397-g) can diced tomatoes
1 (8-ounce / 227-g) can black beans, rinsed
2½ cups chicken broth
1 cup quick-cooking quinoa
1 cup grated Cheddar cheese
2 tablespoons chopped cilantro
2 limes, cut into wedges for garnish

1. Press the Sauté button on the Instant Pot and heat the olive oil. Add the beef to the pot and sauté for 5 minutes, or until lightly browned. Season with salt and pepper.
2. Stir in the corn, onion, red bell pepper, jalapeño pepper and garlic. Cook for 5 minutes, or until the bell pepper is tender. Season with the cumin and chili seasoning. Stir in the tomatoes, black beans, chicken broth and quinoa.
3. Lock the lid. Select the Manual setting and set the cooking time for 1 minute at High Pressure. Once the timer goes off, use a quick pressure release. Carefully open the lid.
4. Select the Sauté mode. Sprinkle the food with the Cheddar cheese and 1 tablespoon of the cilantro. Cook for 3 to 4 minutes, or until cheese melts.
5. Spoon quinoa into serving bowls and garnish with the remaining 1 tablespoon of the cilantro and lime wedges. Serve warm.

Khichdi Dal

Prep time: 4 minutes; Cook Time: 12 mins, Servings: 4

1 tbsp. butter
2 cups water
¼ tsp. salt

1 tsp. Balti seasoning
1 cup khichdi mix

1. Set the Instant Pot to Sauté. Add the butter and heat to melt.
2. Mix in the Balti seasoning and cook for 1 minute.
3. Add the Khichdi mix, water, and salt to the pot.
4. Lock the lid. Select the Porridge mode, then set the timer for 10 minutes at High Pressure.
5. Once the timer goes off, do a natural pressure release for 3 to 5 minutes. Carefully open the lid.
6. Fluff the khichdi with a fork and serve warm.

Jackfruit with Chickpeas

Prep time: 20 minutes | Cook time: 15 minutes | Serves 2 to 3

2 teaspoons olive oil
½ teaspoon cumin seeds
½-inch piece cinnamon stick
2 bay leaves
4 cloves, crushed
2 black cardamoms, crushed
4 green cardamoms, crushed
8 black peppercorns, crushed
2 dried red chilies
4 cloves garlic, chopped
2 medium tomatoes, chopped

½ cup split chickpeas, soaked in water for 40 minutes, drained
1 (20-ounce / 567-g) can jackfruit, drained, rinsed and diced
1 teaspoon coriander powder
¾ teaspoon salt
¾ cup water
2 teaspoons lemon juice
Cilantro, for garnish

1. Press the Sauté button on the Instant Pot. Add the oil and then add the cumin seeds, cinnamon stick, bay leaves, crushed spices, and dried red chilies. Sauté for a few seconds until fragrant.
2. Add the chopped garlic and cook for 1 minute or until golden brown and then add the tomato.
3. Cook the tomato for 2 minutes and then add the chickpeas, jackfruit, coriander powder, and salt and mix to combine. Cook for 1 minute and then pour in the water.
4. Lock the lid. Press the Manual button and set the timer for 10 minutes on High Pressure.
5. When timer beeps, let the pressure release naturally for 5 minutes, then release any remaining pressure.
6. Open the pot and press the Sauté button. Stir in the lemon juice, garnish with cilantro and serve.

Greek Quinoa Bowl

Prep time: 10 minutes | Cook time: 13 minutes | Serves 4

1 tablespoon olive oil
3 cloves garlic, minced
1 cup chopped red onion
½ cup quinoa
2 cups chopped tomatoes

2 cups spinach, torn
2 cups chopped zucchini
2 cups vegetable broth
½ cup chopped black olives
½ cup pine nuts

1. Set your Instant Pot to Sauté and heat the olive oil.
2. Add the garlic and onion and sauté for approximately 5 minutes, stirring frequently.
3. Add the remaining ingredients, except for the pine nuts, to the Instant Pot and stir to combine.
4. Secure the lid. Select the Manual mode and set the cooking time for 8 minutes at High Pressure.
5. Once cooking is complete, do a natural pressure release for 10 minutes, then release any remaining pressure. Carefully open the lid.
6. Fluff the quinoa and stir in the pine nuts, then serve.

Bacon and Corn Casserole
Prep time: 10 minutes | Cook time: 25 minutes | Serves 4

8 bacon strips, chopped
2 eggs, beaten
1 (15-ounce / 425-g) can corn, drained
1 (10.5-ounce / 298-g) can sweet corn cream
1 (8.5-ounce / 241-g) package corn muffin mix

1 cup shredded Cheddar cheese
¾ cup heavy cream
¼ cup salted butter, melted
3 tablespoons chopped habanero chilies
Cooking spray
1 cup water

1. Set the Instant Pot on the Sauté mode. Add the bacon to the pot and cook for 5 minutes, or until crispy and brown. Transfer the bacon to a large bowl and clean the pot.
2. In the bacon bowl, stir together all the remaining ingredients. Spritz a bundt pan with cooking spray. Pour the bacon mixture into the bundt pan and cover with the aluminum foil.
3. Pour the water in the pot, fit in a trivet and sit bundt pan on top. Lock the lid, select the Manual mode and set the cooking time for 20 minutes on High Pressure. Once cooking is complete, use a natural pressure release for 10 minutes, then release any remaining pressure.
4. Carefully open the lid and remove the bundt pan. Take off the aluminum foil and transfer the casserole to plates. Serve hot.

Couscous with Spinach
Prep time: 12 mins, Cook Time: 6 mins, Servings: 4

1 tbsp. butter
1 cup couscous
1¼ cups vegetable broth

½ cup chopped spinach, blanched
1½ tomatoes, chopped

1. Set the Instant Pot to Sauté mode, then add and melt the butter.
2. Add the couscous and sauté for 1 minute.
3. Pour in the vegetable broth. Stir to mix well.
4. Lock the lid. Set to the Manual mode, then set the timer for 5 minutes at High Pressure.
5. Once the timer goes off, perform a quick pressure release. Carefully open the lid.
6. Mix in the spinach and tomatoes, then serve warm.

Spicy Pickled Raisins with Chickpea Tagine
Prep time: 30 minutes | Cook time: 25 minutes | Serves 4

1 cup dried chickpeas, soaked in salted water for 8 hours, rinsed and drained
2 teaspoons kosher salt
Spicy Pickled Raisins:
⅓ cup golden raisins
Tagine:
2 tablespoons olive oil
1 large yellow onion, diced
2 medium carrots, diced
5 garlic cloves, minced
2 teaspoons ground cinnamon
2 teaspoons ground coriander
1 teaspoon cumin seeds or ground cumin
1 teaspoon sweet paprika
2 bay leaves
1½ teaspoons kosher salt, plus more to taste
1¼ cups vegetable broth or water

⅓ cup apple cider vinegar
2½ tablespoons organic cane sugar
¼ teaspoon crushed red pepper flakes, to taste

3 cups peeled and finely diced peeled butternut squash (from one 1½-pound / 680-g butternut squash)
¼ cup finely diced dried apricots (about 8 apricots)
1 (14.5-ounce / 411-g) can crushed tomatoes
4 ounces (113 g) Tuscan kale, stems and midribs removed, roughly chopped
¼ cup roughly chopped fresh cilantro
Zest and juice of 1 small lemon

1. Place the raisins in a bowl. In a small saucepan, combine the vinegar, sugar, and pepper flakes and bring to a boil over medium-high heat, whisking until the sugar is dissolved.
2. Remove the vinegar mixture from the heat and carefully pour the hot vinegar mixture over the raisins. Leave the bowl uncovered and allow the mixture to come to room temperature. Set aside.
3. Select the Sauté setting on the Instant Pot and let the pot heat for a few minutes before adding the olive oil.
4. Once the oil is hot, add the onion and carrots. Cook until the vegetables have softened, 4 to 5 minutes.
5. Add the garlic and cook for 1 minute, stirring frequently.
6. Add the cinnamon, coriander, cumin seeds, paprika, bay leaves, and salt. Stir the spices into the vegetables for 30 seconds until the mixture is fragrant.
7. Pour in the broth, drained chickpeas, butternut squash, and dried apricots. Stir to combine all the ingredients. Pour the crushed tomatoes on top, but do not stir, allowing the tomatoes to sit on top.
8. Secure the lid. Select the Manual mode and set the cook time for 12 minutes on High Pressure.
9. When timer beeps, use a natural pressure release for 5 minutes, then release any remaining pressure.
10. Open the pot, discard the bay leaves, and stir in the kale. Select the Sauté setting and cook for 2 to 3 minutes to wilt the kale.
11. Add the cilantro and lemon zest and half of the lemon juice.
12. Transfer the tagine to bowls and add a few spoons of the spicy pickled raisins to each bowl. Serve immediately.

Creamy Grits
Prep time: 5 minutes | Cook time: 10 minutes | Serves 2

¾ cup stone ground grits
1½ cups water
½ teaspoon sea salt
½ cup cream cheese, at room temperature

¼ cup milk
½ teaspoon garlic powder
½ teaspoon paprika
¼ teaspoon porcini powder

1. Add the grits, water and salt to the Instant Pot.
2. Lock the lid. Select the Manual mode and set the cooking time for 10 minutes on High Pressure. When the timer beeps, perform a natural pressure release for 10 minutes, then release any remaining pressure. Carefully open the lid.
3. Whisk in the remaining ingredients and serve warm.

Curried Sorghum with Golden Raisins
Prep time: 10 minutes | Cook time: 20 minutes | Serves 4

1 cup sorghum
3 cups water
Salt, to taste
1 cup milk
2 teaspoons sugar
3 tablespoons rice wine vinegar

1 tablespoon curry powder
½ teaspoon chili powder
2 cups carrots
¼ cup finely chopped green onion
½ cup golden raisins

1. Combine the sorghum, water, and salt in the Instant Pot.
2. Secure the lid. Select the Manual mode and set the cooking time for 20 minutes at High Pressure.
3. Once cooking is complete, do a quick pressure release. Carefully open the lid.
4. In a medium bowl, add the milk, sugar, vinegar, salt, curry powder, and chili powder and whisk well.
5. Drain the sorghum and transfer to a large bowl. Add the milk mixture, carrots, green onion, and raisins. Stir to combine and serve.

Rutabaga and Lentils Rice Bowl

Prep time: 15 minutes | Cook time: 30 minutes | Serves 4

1 tablespoon olive oil
½ cup chopped onion
2 cloves garlic, minced
3½ cups water
1 cup brown lentils
1 cup peeled and diced

rutabaga
1½ cups brown rice
2-inch sprig fresh rosemary
1 tablespoon dried marjoram
Salt and ground black pepper,
to taste

1. Select the Sauté setting of the Instant Pot and heat the oil until shimmering.
2. Add the onion and sauté for 5 minutes or until transparent.
3. Add the garlic and sauté a minute more or until fragrant.
4. Add the lentils, rutabaga, brown rice, rosemary, water, and marjoram to the pot and stir to combine.
5. Put the lid on. Set the Manual mode and set cooking time for 23 minutes at High Pressure.
6. When timer beeps, let the pressure release naturally for 10 minutes, then release any remaining pressure. Open the lid.
7. Sprinkle with salt and pepper before serving.

Farro and Cherry Salad

Prep time: 5 minutes | Cook time: 40 minutes | Serves 4 to 6

3 cups water
1 cup whole grain farro, rinsed
1 tablespoon extra-virgin olive
oil
1 tablespoon apple cider
vinegar

2 cups cherries, cut into halves
¼ cup chopped green onions
1 teaspoon lemon juice
Salt, to taste
10 mint leaves, chopped

1. Combine the water and farro in the Instant Pot.
2. Lock the lid. Select the Manual mode and set the cooking time for 40 minutes at High Pressure.
3. When the timer beeps, perform a quick pressure release. Carefully remove the lid.
4. Drain the farro and transfer to a bowl. Stir in the olive oil, vinegar, cherries, green onions, lemon juice, salt, and mint. Serve immediately.

Mushroom and Leek Risotto

Prep time: 7 minutes | Cook time: 13 minutes | Serves 4 to 6

4 tablespoons butter, divided
1 leek, white and lightest green
parts only, halved and sliced,
rinsed well
12 ounces (340 g) baby bella
mushrooms, sliced
2 garlic cloves, minced
1 cup Arborio rice, rinsed and
drained

2¾ cups vegetable stock
½ teaspoon salt, plus more as
needed
1 teaspoon dried thyme
Juice of ½ lemon
Freshly ground black pepper,
to taste
Chopped fresh parsley, for
garnish

1. Set your Instant Pot to Sauté and heat 2 tablespoons of butter until melted.
2. Add the leek and mushrooms and sauté for about 2 minutes, stirring frequently. Add the garlic and cook for about 30 seconds.
3. Add the rice and toast it for 1 minute. Turn off the Instant Pot.
4. Stir in the stock, thyme, and salt.
5. Secure the lid. Select the Manual mode and set the cooking time for 8 minutes at High Pressure.
6. Once cooking is complete, do a quick pressure release. Carefully open the lid.
7. Stir in the remaining 2 tablespoons of butter and lemon juice. Taste and season with more salt and pepper, as needed. Serve garnished with fresh parsley.

Vegetable Biryani

Prep time: 10 minutes | Cook time: 15 minutes | Serves 6

2 tablespoons butter
3 cardamom seeds
3 whole cloves
2 dried bay leaves
1 (2-inch) cinnamon stick
1 onion, finely chopped
2 garlic cloves, finely chopped
2 teaspoons finely chopped
fresh ginger
1½ cups roughly chopped
fresh mint leaves

2 tomatoes, finely chopped
1½ teaspoons kosher salt
2 teaspoons ground coriander
1 teaspoon red chili powder
2 tablespoons plain Greek
yogurt, plus more for serving
2 cups mixed vegetables
4 tablespoons finely chopped
fresh cilantro, divided
1½ cups basmati rice
2¼ cups water

1. Set your Instant Pot to Sauté and melt the butter.
2. Add the cardamom, cloves, bay leaves, and cinnamon stick. Stir-fry for 30 seconds, then add the onion, garlic, ginger, and mint leaves. Sauté for 3 to 4 minutes until the onion is translucent.
3. Stir in the tomatoes and salt. Loosely place the lid on top and cook for 3 minutes, or until the tomatoes are softened.
4. Add the coriander, chili powder, and yogurt. Mix well and cook for 2 minutes more. Add the mixed vegetables and 2 tablespoons of cilantro, and mix well. Stir in the rice and water.
5. Secure the lid. Select the Manual mode and set the cooking time for 4 minutes at High Pressure.
6. Once cooking is complete, do a natural pressure release for 3 minutes, then release any remaining pressure. Carefully open the lid.
7. Let the rice cool for 15 minutes and remove the bay leaves. Using a fork, fluff the rice and stir in the remaining 2 tablespoons of cilantro. Serve hot with additional yogurt.

Super Bean and Grain Burgers

Prep time: 25 minutes | Cook time: 1 hour 15 minutes | Makes 12 patties

1 tablespoon olive oil
½ cup chopped onion
8 cloves garlic, minced
1 cup dried black beans
Patties:
½ cup ground flaxseed
1 tablespoon dried marjoram
2 teaspoons smoked paprika
2 teaspoons salt

½ cup quinoa, rinsed
½ cup brown rice
4 cups water

1 teaspoon ground black
pepper
1 teaspoon dried thyme

1. Select the Sauté setting of the Instant Pot and heat the oil until shimmering.
2. Add the onion and sauté for 5 minutes or until transparent.
3. Add the garlic and sauté a minute more or until fragrant.
4. Add the black beans, quinoa, rice and water to the onion mixture and stir to combine.
5. Put the lid on. Set to Manual mode. Set cooking time for 34 minutes on High Pressure.
6. When timer beeps, release the pressure naturally for 15 minutes, then release any remaining pressure. Open the lid.
7. Preheat the oven to 350°F (180°C) and line 2 baking sheets with parchment paper.
8. Mash the beans in the pot, then mix in the ground flaxseed, marjoram, paprika, salt, pepper and thyme.
9. Divide and shape the mixture into 12 patties and put on the baking sheet.
10. Cook in the preheated oven for 35 minutes or until firmed up. Flip the patties halfway through the cooking time.
11. Serve immediately.

Pepper and Egg Oatmeal Bowl

Prep time: 5 minutes | Cook time: 6 to 7 minutes | Serves 2

1½ cups vegetable broth
½ cup steel-cut oats
1 tomato, puréed
Kosher salt and freshly ground
black pepper, to taste

2 teaspoons olive oil
1 onion, chopped
2 bell peppers, deseeded and
sliced
2 eggs, beaten

1. Add the vegetable broth, oats, tomato, salt and black pepper to the Instant Pot and stir to combine.
2. Set the lid in place. Select the Manual setting and set the cooking time for 3 minutes on High Pressure. When the timer goes off, perform a natural pressure release for 20 minutes, then release any remaining pressure. Open the lid. Transfer the oatmeal to bowls.
3. Heat the olive oil in a skillet over medium-high heat. Add the onion and peppers to the skillet and sauté for 3 to 4 minutes, or until tender. Add the beaten eggs and continue to cook until they are set.
4. Spread the egg mixture over the oatmeal and serve warm.

Beetroot with Green Beans

Prep time: 15 minutes | Cook time: 5 minutes | Serves 2 to 3

1 cup water
1 cup green beans, cut into
½-inch pieces
1 large beetroot, diced small,
around ½-inch pieces
1½ tablespoons olive oil
½ teaspoon mustard seeds
2 teaspoons split and

dehusked black gram lentils
2 teaspoons chickpeas
2 dried red chilies, broken
⅛ teaspoon asafetida
12 curry leaves
⅛ teaspoon turmeric powder
½ teaspoon salt
⅓ cup fresh grated coconut

1. Pour the water in the Instant Pot. Put the chopped green beans and beetroot in a steamer basket and then put the steamer basket in the pot.
2. Close the lid. Press the Steam button and set the time to 2 minutes on High Pressure.
3. When timer beeps, do a quick pressure release. Open the lid. Remove the steamer basket from the pot and transfer the steamed vegetables to a bowl. Set aside.
4. Press the Sauté button, add the oil and mustard seeds. Heat for a few seconds until pop.
5. Add the lentils and chickpeas and cook for 2 minutes, or until golden.
6. Add the dried red chilies and asafetida and sauté for a few seconds.
7. Add the curry leaves, stir, then add the steamed vegetables, turmeric powder and salt.
8. Toss to combine well, then fold in the fresh grated coconut. Transfer to a serving dish and serve.

Asparagus and Green Pea Risotto

Prep time: 10 minutes | Cook time: 10 minutes | Serves 4

1½ cups Arborio rice
4 cups water, divided
1 tablespoon vegetable
bouillon
1 cup fresh sweet green peas
1½ cups chopped asparagus

2 tablespoons nutritional yeast
1 tablespoon lemon juice
Fresh chopped thyme, for
garnish
Salt and ground black pepper,
to taste

1. Add the rice, 3½ cups of water, and vegetable bouillon to the Instant Pot. Put the lid on.
2. Select Manual setting and set a timer for 5 minutes on High Pressure.

3. When timer beeps, perform a natural pressure release for 5 minutes, then release any remaining pressure. Open the lid.
4. Stir in the peas, asparagus, nutritional yeast, remaining water, and lemon juice.
5. Set to Sauté function. Sauté for 5 minutes or until the asparagus and peas are soft.
6. Spread the thyme on top and sprinkle with salt and pepper before serving.

Feta and Red Onion Couscous Pilaf

Prep time: 5 minutes | Cook time: 5 minutes | Serves 4

2 tablespoons vegetable oil
1 teaspoon cumin seeds
1 teaspoon ground turmeric
1 cup frozen peas and carrots
1 cup Israeli couscous
½ cup diced yellow onion

1 teaspoon kosher salt
1 teaspoon garam masala
1 cup water
½ cup chopped red onion
½ cup crumbled feta cheese
Black pepper, to taste

1. Press the Sauté button on the Instant Pot and heat the oil.
2. Once the oil is hot, stir in the cumin seeds and turmeric, allowing them to sizzle for 10 seconds. Turn off the Instant Pot.
3. Add the peas and carrots, couscous, yellow onion, salt, garam masala, and water. Stir to combine.
4. Lock the lid. Select the Manual mode and set the cooking time for 3 minutes at High Pressure.
5. When the timer beeps, perform a natural pressure release for 5 minutes, then release any remaining pressure. Carefully remove the lid.
6. Stir in the red onion and feta cheese. Season to taste with black pepper and serve.

Sausage and Shrimp Grit Bowl

Prep time: 15 minutes | Cook time: 28 minutes | Serves 4

1 tablespoon olive oil
6 ounces (170 g) andouille
sausage, diced
1 yellow onion, diced
2 garlic cloves, minced
1 cup white wine
1 cup corn grits
1 cup chicken broth
1 cup whole milk
1 (8-ounce / 227-g) can diced

tomatoes
1 tablespoon Cajun seasoning
1 teaspoon cayenne pepper
1 tablespoon butter
1 pound (454 g) jumbo shrimp,
peeled and deveined
¼ cup chopped chives
1 tablespoon chopped parsley
¼ cup heavy cream

1. Press the Sauté button on the Instant Pot and heat the olive oil. Add the sausage to the pot and fry for 5 minutes, or until slightly browned on all sides. Add the onion and garlic and sauté for 5 minutes, or until tender and fragrant. Pour in the white wine and cook for 3 minutes, or until it has a thick consistency and reduces about one-third.
2. In a medium heatproof bowl, stir together the grits, chicken broth, milk, tomatoes, Cajun seasoning and cayenne pepper.
3. Place a trivet over the sausage mixture and place the grit bowl on top of the trivet.
4. Lock the lid. Select the Manual mode and set the cooking time for 10 minutes at High Pressure. When the timer goes off, use a natural pressure release for 10 minutes, then release any remaining pressure. Carefully open the lid.
5. Remove the grit bowl from the pot. Mix in the butter and set aside.
6. Remove the trivet. Select the Sauté mode and stir in shrimp, chives and parsley. Cook for 5 minutes and stir in heavy cream. Let rest for 2 minutes.
7. Divide the grits among 4 bowls and spread the shrimp mixture on top. Serve immediately.

Couscous with Veggies

Prep time: 15 minutes | Cook time: 5 minutes | Serves 4 to 6

1 tablespoon olive oil
½ large onion, chopped
2 bay leaves
1 large red bell pepper, chopped
1 cup grated carrot
1¾ cups Israeli couscous

1¾ cups water
½ teaspoon garam masala
2 teaspoons salt, or more to taste
1 tablespoon lemon juice
Chopped cilantro, for garnish

1. Set your Instant Pot to Sauté and heat the olive oil.
2. Add the onion and bay leaves and sauté for 2 minutes.
3. Stir in the bell pepper and carrot and sauté for another 1 minute.
4. Add the couscous, water, garam masala, and salt. Stir to combine well.
5. Lock the lid. Select the Manual mode and set the cooking time for 2 minutes at High Pressure.
6. When the timer beeps, perform a natural pressure release for 10 minutes, then release any remaining pressure. Carefully remove the lid.
7. Fluff the couscous and stir in the lemon juice. Taste and season with more salt, if needed. Garnish with the chopped cilantro and serve hot.

Mushroom Barley Risotto

Prep time: 10 minutes | Cook time: 40 minutes | Serves 6

3 tablespoons butter
1 onion, finely chopped
1 cup coarsely chopped shiitake mushrooms
1 cup coarsely chopped cremini mushrooms
1 cup coarsely chopped brown bella mushrooms
1 teaspoon kosher salt

1 teaspoon freshly ground black pepper
1 teaspoon Italian dried herb seasoning
1 cup pearl barley
1 (32-ounce / 907-g) container vegetable broth
½ cup shredded Parmesan cheese

1. Set your Instant Pot to Sauté and melt the butter.
2. Add the onion and cook for about 3 minutes, or until the onion is translucent. Mix in the mushrooms, salt, pepper, and Italian seasoning. Cook for 5 to 6 minutes or until the mushrooms shrink. Stir in the barley and broth.
3. Secure the lid. Select the Manual mode and set the cooking time for 30 minutes at High Pressure.
4. Once cooking is complete, do a natural pressure release for 10 minutes, then release any remaining pressure. Carefully open the lid.
5. Stir in the Parmesan cheese. Serve hot.

Black-Eyed Peas with Collard

Prep time: 5 minutes | Cook time: 3 to 4 minutes | Serves 4 to 6

1 yellow onion, diced
1 tablespoon olive oil
1 cup dried black-eyed peas
¼ cup chopped sun-dried tomatoes
¼ cup tomato paste

1 teaspoon smoked paprika
2 cups water
4 large collard green leaves
Salt and freshly ground black pepper, to taste

1. In the Instant Pot, select Sauté mode. Add the onion and olive oil and cook for 3 to 4 minutes, stirring occasionally, until the onion is softened.
2. Add the black-eyed peas, tomatoes, tomato paste, paprika, water, and stir to combine.
3. Close the lid, then select Manual mode and set cooking time for 30 minutes on High Pressure.

4. Once the cook time is complete, let the pressure release naturally for about 15 minutes, then release any remaining pressure.
5. Trim off the thick parts of the collard green stems, then slice the leaves lengthwise in half or quarters. Roll them up together, then finely slice into ribbons.
6. Sprinkle the sliced collard greens with salt and massage it into them with hands to soften.
7. Open the lid. Add the collard greens and ½ teaspoon of salt to the pot, stirring to combine and letting the greens wilt in the heat.
8. Serve immediately.

Quinoa Risotto

Prep time: 6 mins, Cook Time: 3 hours, Servings: 4

¾ cup diced onion
1 garlic clove, minced
1 tbsp. butter
Salt and pepper, to taste

2½ cups chicken broth
1 cup rinsed quinoa
¼ cup shredded Parmesan cheese

1. Combine the onion, garlic, and butter in a microwave-safe bowl.
2. Microwave for 5 minutes, stirring every 90 seconds.
3. Put the mixture in the Instant Pot.
4. Add the salt, pepper, broth, and quinoa and stir to combine.
5. Lock the lid. Select the Slow Cook mode, then set the timer for 3 hours at High Pressure.
6. Once the timer goes off, perform a natural release for 10 minutes, then release any remaining pressure. Carefully open the lid.
7. Mix the Parmesan into the mixture. Taste and adjust the seasoning, if needed.

Apple and Pecan Quinoa Salad

Prep time: 7 minutes | Cook time: 8 minutes | Serves 4 to 6

1 cup quinoa, rinsed
1 cup water
¼ teaspoon salt, plus more as needed
2 apples, unpeeled and cut into large dices
2 tablespoons freshly squeezed lemon juice
1 tablespoon white rice vinegar
2 celery stalks, halved lengthwise and chopped
½ bunch scallions, green and

light green parts, sliced
¾ to 1 cup dried cranberries, white raisins, and regular raisins
2 tablespoons avocado oil
½ to 1 teaspoon chili powder, plus more as needed
Pinch freshly ground black pepper
½ to 1 cup chopped pecans
½ cup chopped fresh cilantro

1. Combine the quinoa, water, and salt in the Instant Pot.
2. Secure the lid. Select the Manual mode and set the cooking time for 8 minutes at High Pressure.
3. Once cooking is complete, do a natural pressure release for 10 minutes, then release any remaining pressure. Carefully open the lid.
4. Transfer the quinoa to a large salad bowl. Refrigerate for 5 minutes to cool.
5. Mix the apples, lemon juice, and vinegar in a small resealable container. Cover and shake lightly to coat the apples, then refrigerate.
6. Remove the cooled quinoa and stir in the celery, scallions, cranberry-raisin mix, oil, and chili powder. Taste and season with more salt and pepper, as needed. Add the apples and lemon-vinegar juice into the salad and stir well.
7. Serve topped with the pecans and cilantro.

Ritzy Bean, Pea, and Lentils Mix

Prep time: 20 minutes | Cook time: 11 minutes | Serves 4

1 tablespoon plus 1 teaspoon butter, divided
4 green cardamoms
1 bay leaf
3 cloves
1 teaspoon cumin seeds
2 dried red chilies
¼ teaspoon asafetida
2-inch piece ginger, finely chopped
1 green chili, chopped
1 large tomato, chopped
¼ cup split pigeon peas, rinsed and soaked for 30 minutes, drained
¼ cup split chickpeas, rinsed and soaked for 30 minutes, drained
¼ cup split black beans, rinsed and soaked for 30 minutes, drained
¼ cup split mung beans, rinsed and soaked for 30 minutes, drained
¼ cup split red lentils, rinsed and soaked for 30 minutes, drained
½ teaspoon turmeric powder
1 teaspoon salt
3 cups water
2 tablespoons cilantro, chopped
2 teaspoons lemon juice

1. Press the Sauté button on the Instant Pot. Add 1 tablespoon of butter to the pot and then add the green cardamoms, bay leaf, cloves and cumin seeds. Sauté for a few seconds, until fragrant.
2. Add the dried red chilies and asafetida and sauté for a few seconds.
3. Add the chopped ginger and green chili and cook for a minute.
4. Stir in the tomato and cook for 2 minutes, or until tender.
5. Add the soaked peas, beans, and lentils. Sprinkle with turmeric powder and salt. Mix well.
6. Pour in the water and close the lid. Press the Manual button and set the timer for 7 minutes on High Pressure.
7. When timer beeps, let the pressure release naturally for 10 minutes, then release any remaining pressure.
8. Open the pot, stir and add the remaining 1 teaspoon of butter, cilantro and lemon juice. Serve hot.

Vegetarian Kidney Bean Étouffée

Prep time: 20 minutes | Cook time: 28 minutes | Serves 4

1 tablespoon olive oil
1 cup minced onion
2 cups minced bell pepper
2 teaspoons minced garlic
1 cup dried kidney beans, soaked in water for 8 hours, drained
1½ teaspoons dried thyme
3 bay leaves
2 teaspoons smoked paprika
1 cup water
2 teaspoons dried marjoram
½ teaspoon ground cayenne pepper
1 (14.5-ounce / 411-g) can crushed tomatoes
1 teaspoon dried oregano
Salt and ground black pepper, to taste

1. Select the Sauté setting of the Instant Pot and heat the oil until shimmering.
2. Add the onion and sauté for 5 minutes or until transparent.
3. Add the bell pepper and garlic. Sauté for 5 more minutes or until the bell peppers are tender.
4. Add the beans, thyme, bay leaves, smoked paprika, water, marjoram and cayenne to the pot. Stir to combine.
5. Put the lid on. Select the Manual setting and set the timer for 15 minutes at High Pressure.
6. When timer beeps, use a natural pressure release for 5 minutes, then release any remaining pressure. Open the lid. Remove the bay leaves.
7. Mix in the crushed tomatoes and oregano. Sprinkle with salt and pepper. Set the cooking time for 3 minutes on High Pressure.
8. When timer beeps, release the pressure naturally for 5 minutes, then release any remaining pressure. Open the lid.
9. Serve immediately.

Kidney Beans with Ajwain Sauce

Prep time: 15 minutes | Cook time: 40 minutes | Serves 6

Bean:
2 cups dried kidney beans, soaked for at least 8 hours and drained
6 cups water
1 tablespoon grated ginger
1 teaspoon salt
Sauce:
1 onion, minced
½ teaspoon ajwain seeds
1 teaspoon minced garlic
2 cups finely diced tomatoes
¼ cup yogurt
1 teaspoon ground fenugreek
1 teaspoon garam masala
¾ teaspoon turmeric
2 tablespoons ground coriander
⅛ teaspoon ground red chile pepper

1. Pour the water in the Instant Pot and sprinkle with ginger and salt. Add soak the beans in the water.
2. Set the Manual mode of the pot and set the cooking time for 10 minutes on High Pressure.
3. When timer beeps, allow the pressure to release naturally for 5 minutes, then release any remaining pressure. Open the lid.
4. Carefully pour the beans into a bowl. Let them sit. Clean the Instant Pot.
5. Set the Sauté setting of the pot. Sauté the onion for 4 minutes or until lightly browned.
6. Add the ajwain and garlic and sauté for 1 minute or until fragrant.
7. Mix in the tomatoes and cook until their liquid has evaporated, 5 minutes. Stir in the yogurt, fenugreek, garam masala, turmeric, coriander, and red chile pepper.
8. Drain 2 cups of liquid from the beans and stir 1 cup into the sauce. Add the beans to the sauce and mix well.
9. Simmer on the Sauté setting for 20 minutes or until thickened, stirring occasionally.
10. Transfer to a serving dish and serve.

Mediterranean Couscous Salad

Prep time: 20 minutes | Cook time: 2 minutes | Serves 6

Couscous:
1 cup couscous
Salad:
½ cup salad greens (such as a mix of spinach, arugula, and red and green lettuce leaves)
4 tablespoons finely chopped carrot
4 tablespoons finely chopped black olives
4 tablespoons finely chopped cucumber
½ cup thinly sliced red onion, marinated in 2 tablespoons
2¾ cups water, divided

each of lemon juice and water for 20 minutes, then drained
½ cup shredded red cabbage, marinated in 2 tablespoons each of lemon juice and water for 20 minutes, then drained
1 teaspoon kosher salt
1 teaspoon freshly ground black pepper
2 tablespoons extra-virgin olive oil

1. Combine the couscous and 1¼ of cups water in a heatproof bowl.
2. Pour the remaining 1½ cups of water into the Instant Pot and insert a trivet. Place the bowl on the trivet.
3. Secure the lid. Select the Manual mode and set the cooking time for 2 minutes at High Pressure.
4. Once cooking is complete, do a natural pressure release for 5 minutes, then release any remaining pressure. Carefully open the lid.
5. Let the couscous cool for 15 minutes before fluffing with a fork.
6. Assemble the salad: Add the salad greens, carrot, olives, cucumber, onion, cabbage, salt, pepper, and olive oil to the couscous. Mix gently and serve immediately.

Black Bean Curry

Prep time: 15 minutes | Cook time: 35 minutes | Serves 6

1 tablespoon butter
1 teaspoon cumin seeds
1 onion, minced
1 tablespoon ginger paste
1 tablespoon garlic paste
1 teaspoon chili powder
½ teaspoon garam masala
½ teaspoon ground turmeric

2 teaspoons ground coriander
1 cup black beans, rinsed, soaked in water overnight, drained
2 cups water
1 teaspoon fresh lemon juice
Salt, to taste

1. Add the butter to the Instant Pot and select Sauté mode. Add the cumin seeds and cook for 30 seconds or until pops.
2. Add the onion, ginger paste, garlic paste, chili powder, garam masala, turmeric, and coriander, and cook for 4 minutes.
3. Stir in the chickpeas and water. Secure the lid. Select the Bean/Chili mode and set the timer for 30 minutes on High Pressure.
4. When timer beeps, use a natural pressure release for 15 minutes, then release any remaining pressure.
5. Remove the lid and stir in the lemon juice. Sprinkle with salt and serve.

Lentils with Spinach

Prep time: 15 minutes | Cook time: 15 minutes | Serves 2

1 tablespoon olive oil
½ teaspoon cumin seeds
¼ teaspoon mustard seeds
3 cloves garlic, finely chopped
1 green chili, finely chopped
1 large tomato, chopped
1½ cups spinach, finely chopped

¼ teaspoon turmeric powder
½ teaspoon salt
¼ cup split pigeon peas, rinsed
¼ cup split red lentil, rinsed
1½ cups water
¼ teaspoon garam masala
2 teaspoons lemon juice
Cilantro, for garnish

1. Press the Sauté button on the Instant Pot. Add the oil and then the cumin seeds and mustard seeds.
2. Let the seeds sizzle for a few seconds and then add the garlic and green chili. Sauté for 1 minute or until fragrant.
3. Add the tomato and cook for 1 minute. Add the chopped spinach, turmeric powder and salt, and cook for 2 minutes.
4. Add the rinsed peas and lentils and stir. Pour in the water and put the lid on.
5. Press the Manual button and set the cooking time for 10 minutes on High Pressure.
6. When timer beeps, let the pressure release naturally for 5 minutes, then release any remaining pressure.
7. Open the pot and add the garam masala, lemon juice and cilantro. Serve immediately.

Moong Bean with Cabbage

Prep time: 10 minutes | Cook time: 8 minutes | Serves 2

2 teaspoons olive oil
½ teaspoon mustard seeds
1 small red onion, chopped
2 green chilies, sliced
5 cups cabbage, shredded
½ cup split moong bean, rinsed

½ teaspoon turmeric powder
½ teaspoon salt
⅓ cup water
¼ cup fresh dill, chopped
Garam masala, for topping

1. Press the Sauté button on the Instant Pot. Add the oil and the mustard seeds. Heat for a few seconds until the mustard seeds pop.
2. Add the onion and sliced green chilies. Sauté for 2 minutes or until softened.
3. Add the shredded cabbage and sauté for 1 minute.

4. Add the moong bean, turmeric powder, and salt and mix well.
5. Pour in the water and close the pot. Press the Manual button and set the timer for 5 minutes on High Pressure.
6. When timer beeps, let the pressure release naturally for 5 minutes, then release any remaining pressure.
7. Open the pot, add the chopped dill, and sprinkle with garam masala. Stir to mix well. Serve hot.

Mujadara (Lebanese Lentils and Rice)

Prep time: 5 minutes | Cook time: 15 minutes | Serves 6

⅓ cup dried brown lentils
2 tablespoons vegetable oil
1 large yellow onion, sliced
1 teaspoon kosher salt, or more to taste

1 cup basmati rice, rinsed and drained
½ teaspoon ground cumin
½ teaspoon ground coriander
2 cups water

1. Place the lentils in a small bowl. Cover with hot water and soak for 15 to 20 minutes, then drain.
2. Press the Sauté button on the Instant Pot and heat the oil.
3. Add the onion and season with a little salt and cook, stirring, until the onions begin to crisp around the edges but are not burned, 5 to 10 minutes. Remove half the onions from the pot and reserve as a garnish.
4. Add the soaked lentils, rice, cumin, coriander, salt, and water, stirring well.
5. Lock the lid. Select the Manual mode and set the cooking time for 6 minutes at High Pressure.
6. When the timer beeps, perform a natural pressure release for 10 minutes, then release any remaining pressure. Carefully remove the lid.
7. Transfer to a serving dish. Sprinkle with the reserved cooked onions and serve.

Red Lentils with Butternut Squash

Prep time: 15 minutes | Cook time: 12 minutes | Serves 4

2 teaspoons olive oil
½ teaspoon mustard seeds
½ teaspoon cumin seeds
⅛ teaspoon asafetida
1 green chili, sliced
2 dried red chilies, broken
1½ teaspoons ginger, finely chopped
12 curry leaves

2 medium tomatoes, chopped
2 cups butternut squash, diced into 1-inch pieces
¾ cup split red lentils
2½ cups water, divided
½ teaspoon turmeric powder
1 teaspoon salt
1 tablespoon cilantro, chopped
1½ teaspoons lemon juice

1. Press the Sauté button of the Instant Pot. Add the oil, mustard seeds and cumin seeds. Let the mustard seeds pop for a few seconds.
2. Add the asafetida, green chili and broken dried red chilies. Sauté for a few seconds.
3. Add the ginger and curry leaves and cook for a minute or until the ginger is golden brown.
4. Stir in the tomatoes and squash. Cook for 2 minutes. Add the lentils and mix well. Pour in 1 cup of the water, turmeric powder and salt and mix well.
5. Secure the lid, press the Manual button. Set cooking time for 6 minutes on High Pressure.
6. When timer beeps, naturally release the pressure for 5 minutes, then release any remaining pressure.
7. Open the pot, press the Sauté button and add the remaining 1½ cups of water, cilantro and lemon juice. Simmer for 2 minutes.
8. Serve warm.

Farro Risotto with Mushroom

Prep time: 10 minutes | Cook time: 30 minutes | Serves 3

½ cup farro
2 tablespoons barley
3 cups chopped mushrooms
1 tablespoon red curry paste
1 jalapeño pepper, seeded and chopped
1 tablespoon shallot powder

2 tablespoons onion powder
Salt and pepper, to taste
4 garlic cloves, minced
1½ cups water
2 tomatoes, diced
Chopped cilantro, for serving
Chopped scallions, for serving

1. Combine all the ingredients, except for the tomatoes, cilantro, and scallion, in the Instant Pot.
2. Secure the lid. Select the Manual mode and set the cooking time for 30 minutes at High Pressure.
3. Once cooking is complete, do a quick pressure release. Carefully open the lid.
4. Stir in the tomatoes and let sit for 2 to 3 minutes until warmed through. Sprinkle with the cilantro and scallions and serve.

Black-Eyed Pea Rice Bowl

Prep time: 15 minutes | Cook time: 14 minutes | Serves 4

1 teaspoon extra-virgin olive oil
1 large onion, diced
2 carrots, diced
3 celery stalks, diced
3 cloves garlic, minced
1 cup dried black-eyed peas
½ cup white rice
1 medium tomato, diced
1 teaspoon dried oregano

1 teaspoon dried parsley
¼ teaspoon ground cumin
1 teaspoon crushed red pepper
¼ teaspoon ground black pepper
¼ cup tomato paste
2½ cups vegetable broth
2 tablespoons lemon juice
Salt, to taste

1. Select the Sauté setting of the Instant Pot and heat the oil until shimmering.
2. Add the onion, carrots, celery and garlic and sauté for 6 minutes or until tender.
3. Add the black-eyed peas, rice, tomato, oregano, parsley, cumin red and black peppers, tomato paste and broth to the onion mixture and stir to combine.
4. Put the lid on. Select the Manual setting and set the timer for 8 minutes at High Pressure.
5. When timer beeps, let the pressure release naturally for 5 minutes, then release any remaining pressure. Open the lid.
6. Mix in the lemon juice and salt before serving.

Spicy Manchego Buckwheat

Prep time: 5 minutes | Cook time: 8 to 9 minutes | Serves 2

1 teaspoon olive oil
1 shallot, chopped
1 teaspoon minced garlic
1 bell pepper, chopped
1 Chile de árbol, chopped

1 cup buckwheat
1 cup chicken broth
1 cup water
⅓ cup grated Manchego curado

1. Set the Instant Pot to the Sauté mode and heat the oil. Add the shallot to the pot and sauté for 3 minutes, or until just softened. Add the garlic, bell pepper and Chile de árbol and sauté for 2 to 3 minutes, or until fragrant. Stir in the buckwheat, chicken broth and water to the pot.
2. Set the lid in place. Select the Manual mode and set the cooking time for 3 minutes on High Pressure. When the timer goes off, perform a quick pressure release. Carefully open the lid.
3. Serve garnished with cheese.

Parmesan Risotto

Prep time: 6 mins, Cook Time: 20 mins, Servings: 4

4 cups chicken broth, divided
4 tbsps. butter
1 small onion, diced
2 garlic cloves, minced

1½ cups Arborio rice
Salt and pepper, to taste
¼ cup shredded Parmesan cheese

1. Set the Instant Pot to sauté and melt the butter.
2. Mix the onions in and let them cook for 2 minutes until they have become soft.
3. Add the garlic and rice and stir. Cook for 1 more minute.
4. Add 1 cup of broth and cook about 3 minutes, or until the broth is absorbed.
5. Add 3 cups of broth, salt, and pepper.
6. Sprinkle with Parmesan cheese.
7. Lock the lid. Select the Manual mode, then set the timer for 10 minutes at Low Pressure.
8. Once the timer goes off, perform a natural release for 5 minutes, then release any remaining pressure. Carefully open the lid.
9. Ladle the rice into bowls and serve.

Mint and Pea Risotto

Prep time: 5 minutes | Cook time: 20 minutes | Serves 2

2 tablespoons coconut oil
1 onion, peeled and diced
½ teaspoon garlic powder
½ cup barley
1 cup vegetable broth, divided

Salt and pepper, to taste
½ cup fresh peas
¼ teaspoon lime zest
¼ cup chopped fresh mint leaves

1. Press the Sauté button on the Instant Pot and heat the oil.
2. Add the onion and stir-fry for 5 minutes.
3. Add garlic powder and barley and cook for 1 minute more.
4. Pour in ½ cup of vegetable broth and stir for 3 minutes until it is absorbed by barley.
5. Add the remaining ½ cup of broth, salt, and pepper.
6. Secure the lid. Select the Manual mode and set the cooking time for 10 minutes at High Pressure.
7. Once cooking is complete, do a natural pressure release for 10 minutes, then release any remaining pressure. Carefully open the lid.
8. Stir in peas, lime zest, and mint and let sit for 3 minutes until heated through. Serve immediately.

Pearl Barley with Peppers

Prep time: 5 minutes | Cook time: 25 minutes | Serves 2

1 tablespoon sesame oil
½ yellow onion, chopped
1 garlic clove, minced
1 bell pepper, deseeded and chopped

1 jalapeño pepper, deseeded and chopped
1½ cups vegetable broth
¾ cup pearl barley, rinsed
2 tablespoons chopped chives

1. Set the Instant Pot to the Sauté mode and heat the oil. Add the onion to the pot and sauté for 3 minutes, or until just tender and fragrant. Add the garlic, bell pepper and jalapeño pepper to the pot and sauté for 2 minutes, or until fragrant. Stir in the vegetable broth and pearl barley.
2. Lock the lid. Select the Multigrain mode and set the cooking time for 20 minutes on High Pressure. When the timer goes off, perform a quick pressure release. Carefully open the lid.
3. Fluff the pearl barley mixture with a fork. Serve garnished with the chopped chives.

Mushroom Polenta
Prep time: 5 minutes | Cook time: 23 minutes | Serves 4

1 cup yellow cornmeal
4 cups vegetable broth
1 tablespoon butter
2 portobello mushrooms caps, finely chopped
1 teaspoon onion powder
1 teaspoon kosher salt
1 teaspoon freshly ground black pepper

1. In a large bowl, whisk together the cornmeal and broth until there are no lumps. Set aside.
2. Set your Instant Pot to Sauté and melt the butter.
3. Add the mushrooms, onion powder, salt, and pepper, and sauté for 2 minutes. Add the cornmeal mix to the Instant Pot, stirring well.
4. Lock the lid. Select the Porridge mode and set the cooking time for 20 minutes at High Pressure.
5. When the timer beeps, perform a natural pressure release for 10 minutes, then release any remaining pressure. Carefully remove the lid.
6. Stir the polenta and serve hot.

Shrimp and Broccoli Quinoa Bowl
Prep time: 10 minutes | Cook time: 11 minutes | Serves 4

2 tablespoons butter
1 red bell pepper, chopped
1 medium white onion, finely diced
4 garlic cloves, minced
2 teaspoons smoked paprika
1½ cups quick-cooking quinoa
3 cups chicken broth
Salt and black pepper, to taste
1 pound (454 g) jumbo shrimp, peeled and deveined
2 cups broccoli florets
1 lemon, zested and juiced
3 scallions, chopped

1. Set the Instant Pot to the Sauté mode and melt the butter. Add the bell pepper and onion to the pot and sauté for 4 minutes. Add the garlic and paprika, and sauté for 1 minute. Stir in the quinoa, chicken broth, salt and pepper.
2. Lock the lid. Select the Manual mode and set the cooking time for 1 minute on High Pressure. Once cooking is complete, use a quick pressure release. Carefully open the lid.
3. Add the shrimp, broccoli, lemon zest and juice to the pot. Select the Sauté mode and cook for 5 minutes, or until shrimp are pink.
4. Garnish with the chopped scallions and serve.

Sautéed Beluga Lentil and Zucchinis
Prep time: 15 minutes | Cook time: 10 minutes | Serves 4

2 tablespoons olive oil
2 large zucchinis, chopped
4 garlic cloves, minced
½ tablespoon dried oregano
½ tablespoon curry powder
Salt and ground black pepper, to taste
2 cups canned beluga lentils,
drained
¼ cup chopped parsley, divided
½ cup chopped basil
1 small red onion, diced
2 tablespoons balsamic vinegar
1 teaspoon Dijon mustard

1. Set the Instant Pot to Sauté mode. Heat the oil and sauté the zucchinis until tender.
2. Mix in the garlic and cook until fragrant, 30 seconds. Top with oregano, curry, salt, and pepper. Allow to combine for 1 minute, stirring frequently.
3. Pour in lentils, cook for 3 minutes, and stir in half of parsley, basil, and onion. Sauté until onion softens, about 5 minutes.
4. Meanwhile, in a bowl, combine vinegar with mustard and pour mixture over lentils. Plate and garnish with remaining parsley.

Scarlet Runner Bean and Potato Hash
Prep time: 5 minutes | Cook time: 20 minutes | Serves 4

1 tablespoon avocado oil
3 cups diced potatoes
2 cups diced red and yellow pepper
4 cloves garlic, minced
1 cup diced celery
1 cup Scarlet Runner beans,
soaked in water overnight, rinsed and drained
2 vegetable broth
1 tablespoon dried oregano
1 teaspoon chili powder
Salt, to taste

1. Heat the oil in the Instant Pot on the Sauté function.
2. Add the potatoes, peppers, garlic, and celery, and sauté for 4 minutes.
3. Add the beans. Begin adding broth until cover the beans. Stir in the dried oregano and chili powder.
4. Cover the pot. Select Manual mode and set cooking time for 12 minutes on High Pressure.
5. When timer beeps, use a natural pressure release for 5 minutes, then release any remaining pressure.
6. Remove the cover. Sprinkle with salt and serve.

Spicy Chicken Bulgur
Prep time: 10 minutes | Cook time: 19 to 20 minutes | Serves 2

½ tablespoon sesame oil
½ pound (227 g) chicken breasts, boneless and skinless, cut into bite-sized pieces
½ onion, chopped
1 teaspoon minced fresh garlic
1-inch ginger, peeled and sliced
1 Bird's-eye chili pepper, deseeded and minced
1 cup chicken stock
½ cup coconut milk
½ cup bulgur
1 teaspoon garam masala
½ teaspoon turmeric powder
½ teaspoon ground cumin
Sea salt and ground black pepper, to taste
1 tablespoon chopped fresh coriander

1. Set the Instant Pot to the Sauté mode and heat the sesame oil. Add the chicken breasts to the pot and sear for 3 to 4 minutes, or until lightly browned. Transfer to a plate and set aside.
2. Add the onion to the pot and sauté for 5 minutes, or until just softened and fragrant. Stir in the garlic and continue to sauté for 1 minute.
3. Return the cooked chicken breasts to the pot and stir in the remaining ingredients, except for the coriander.
4. Set the lid in place. Select the Manual setting and set the cooking time for 10 minutes on High Pressure. When the timer goes off, perform a natural pressure release for 10 minutes, then release any remaining pressure. Open the lid.
5. Transfer the chicken mixture to bowls and serve topped with fresh coriander

Spinach and Tomato Couscous
Prep time: 10 minutes | Cook time: 8 minutes | Serves 4

2 tablespoons butter
1 cup couscous
1¼ cups water
½ cup chopped spinach
1½ tomatoes, chopped

1. Set your Instant Pot to Sauté and melt the butter.
2. Add the couscous and cook for 1 minute.
3. Pour in the water and stir well.
4. Lock the lid. Select the Manual mode and set the cooking time for 5 minutes at High Pressure.
5. When the timer beeps, perform a quick pressure release. Carefully remove the lid.
6. Transfer the couscous to a large bowl. Add the spinach and tomatoes, stir, and serve.

Sumptuous Navy Beans

Prep time: 20 minutes | Cook time: 50 minutes | Serves 10

2 tablespoons extra-virgin olive oil
1 green bell pepper, deseeded and chopped
1 onion, minced
1 jalapeño pepper, minced
3 garlic cloves, minced
6 ounces (170 g) tomato paste
¼ cup molasses
1 teaspoon balsamic vinegar
2 cups vegetable broth

1 tablespoon mustard
¼ teaspoon smoked paprika
¼ cup sugar
¼ teaspoon ground black pepper
1 pound (454 g) navy beans, soaked in water for at least 4 hours, drained
2 cups water
Salt, to taste

1. Add the butter to the Instant Pot and select Sauté setting.
2. Add the bell pepper and onion and cook for 4 minutes or until the onion is translucent.
3. Add the jalapeño and garlic and cook for 1 minute or until fragrant.
4. Meanwhile, combine remaining ingredients in a bowl, except the beans and water, and beat until smooth to make the sauce.
5. Stir the beans, water and sauce mixture in the pot. Secure the lid.
6. Set on Manual mode and set cooking time for 45 minutes on High Pressure.
7. When timer beeps, allow a natural pressure release for 15 minutes, then release any remaining pressure.
8. Remove the lid and stir in the salt before serving.

Vegetable Fried Millet

Prep time: 10 minutes | Cook time: 25 minutes | Serves 4

1 teaspoon vegetable oil
½ cup thinly sliced oyster mushrooms
1 cup finely chopped leeks
2 garlic cloves, minced
½ cup green lentils, rinsed
1 cup millet, soaked and drained

½ cup sliced bok choy
1 cup chopped asparagus
1 cup chopped snow peas
2¼ cups vegetable stock
Salt and black pepper, to taste
A drizzle of lemon juice
¼ cup mixed chives and parsley, finely chopped

1. Press the Sauté button on the Instant Pot and heat the oil.
2. Cook the mushrooms, leeks, and garlic for 3 minutes. Add lentils and millet, stir, and cook for 4 minutes.
3. Stir in the bok choy, asparagus, snow peas, and vegetable stock.
4. Secure the lid. Select the Manual mode and set the cooking time for 10 minutes at High Pressure.
5. Once cooking is complete, do a quick pressure release. Carefully open the lid.
6. Season to taste with salt and pepper. Serve sprinkled with the lemon juice, chives, and parsley.

White Beans with Poblano and Tomatillos

Prep time: 15 minutes | Cook time: 39 minutes | Serves 6

1 cup chopped poblano, deseeded and stem removed
2 cups chopped tomatillos
1 cup chopped onion
½ jalapeño, deseeded
1½ teaspoons ground cumin

1½ cups dried white beans, soaked for 8 hours, drained
2 teaspoons dried oregano
1½ cups water
Salt and ground black pepper, to taste

1. Add the poblano, tomatillos, onion and jalapeño to a food processor. Pulse to break them into tiny pieces.
2. Set the Sauté setting of the Instant Pot and pour in the blended mixture.

3. Fold in the cumin. Sauté for 4 minutes or until the onion is translucent.
4. Stir in the beans, oregano, and water. Put the lid on.
5. Select the Manual setting and set cooking time for 35 minutes at High Pressure.
6. When timer beeps, allow the pressure to release naturally for 15 minutes, then release any remaining pressure. Open the lid.
7. Sprinkle with salt and pepper before serving.

Za'atar-Spiced Bulgur Wheat Salad

Prep time: 10 minutes | Cook time: 2 minutes | Serves 6

Bulgur Wheat:
1 cup bulgur wheat
Salad:
¼ cup finely chopped cucumber
¼ cup finely chopped fresh parsley
2 tablespoons finely chopped fresh mint
2 tablespoons extra-virgin olive oil

2¼ cups water, divided

2 tablespoons freshly squeezed lemon juice
5 cherry tomatoes, finely chopped
1 teaspoon kosher salt
½ teaspoon freshly ground black pepper
1 teaspoon za'atar spice blend

1. Combine the bulgur wheat and 1¼ cups of water in a heatproof bowl.
2. Pour the remaining 1 cup of water into the Instant Pot and insert a trivet. Place the bowl on the trivet.
3. Secure the lid. Select the Manual mode and set the cooking time for 2 minutes at High Pressure.
4. Once cooking is complete, do a natural pressure release for 5 minutes, then release any remaining pressure. Carefully open the lid.
5. Let the bulgur wheat cool for 20 minutes before fluffing it with a fork.
6. Assemble the salad: Add the cucumber, parsley, mint, olive oil, lemon juice, tomatoes, salt, pepper, and za'atar seasoning to the bulgur wheat. Mix gently and serve immediately.

Artichoke Corn Risotto

Prep time: 15 minutes | Cook time: 13 minutes | Serves 4

2 tablespoons olive oil
2 large white onions, chopped
1 medium zucchini, chopped
4 garlic cloves, minced
Salt and black pepper, to taste
1 cup Arborio rice
½ cup white wine
2½ cups chicken stock
2 cups corn kernels

1 (6-ounce / 170-g) can artichokes, drained and chopped
1 cup grated Parmesan cheese
3 tablespoons lemon juice
1 tablespoon lemon zest
¼ cup chopped basil, plus more for garnish

1. Set the Instant Pot on the Sauté function and heat the olive oil. Add the onions, zucchini and garlic to the pot and sauté for 5 minutes, or until tender. Season with salt and pepper. Stir in the rice and cook for 2 minutes, or until translucent.
2. Pour in the white wine and keep cooking until it has a thick consistency and reduces about one-third. Stir in the chicken stock, corn, salt and pepper.
3. Lock the lid. Select the Manual mode and set the cooking time for 6 minutes at High Pressure. When the timer goes off, use a natural pressure release for 15 minutes, then release any remaining pressure. Carefully open the lid.
4. Add the artichokes, cheese, lemon juice and zest and whisk until risotto is sticky. Stir in the chopped basil and transfer the risotto into bowls. Serve garnished with the basil.

Chapter 11 Soups, Stews, and Chilis

African Peanut and Yam Stew

Prep time: 20 minutes | Cook time: 60 minutes | Serves 4

3 yams, chopped
1 white onion, roughly chopped
1 teaspoon minced ginger root
1 teaspoon garlic, diced
1 tablespoon almond butter
1 teaspoon cilantro
1 teaspoon oregano
1 teaspoon cayenne pepper
1 teaspoon onion powder

1 teaspoon ground black pepper
1 teaspoon cumin
¼ cup peanuts, chopped
1 bell pepper, chopped
1 cup collard greens, chopped
3 tablespoons peanut butter
½ cup almond milk
2 cups water

1. Select the Instant Pot to Sauté mode. Add the yams, onion, minced ginger root, and diced garlic with almond butter for 5 minutes. Stir constantly.
2. Meanwhile, mix up together the cilantro, oregano, cayenne pepper, onion powder, ground black pepper, and cumin in a small bowl.
3. Add the mixture in the Instant Pot, then add the peanuts, bell pepper, collard, and peanut butter. Add almond milk and water.
4. Close the lid. Set Meat/Stew mode and set cooking time for 50 minutes on High Pressure.
5. When timer beeps, use a quick pressure release. Open the lid.
6. Let the stew sit for at least 15 minutes before serving.

Beef T-Bone Broth

Prep time: 20 minutes | Cook time: 50 minutes | Serves 4

1 pound (454 g) T-bone beef steak, chopped
1 bay leaf

1 teaspoon peppercorns
1 teaspoon salt
3 cups water

1. Put all ingredients in the Instant Pot. Stir to mix well. Close the lid.
2. Set Manual mode and set cooking time for 50 minutes on High Pressure.
3. When timer beeps, use a natural pressure release for 15 minutes, then release the remaining pressure and open the lid.
4. Strain the cooked mixture and shred the meat. Serve the beef broth with the shredded beef.

Cauliflower and Beef Soup

Prep time: 10 minutes | Cook time: 14 minutes | Serves 4

1 cup ground beef
½ cup cauliflower, shredded
1 teaspoon unsweetened tomato purée
¼ cup coconut milk

1 teaspoon minced garlic
1 teaspoon dried oregano
½ teaspoon salt
4 cups water

1. Put all ingredients in the Instant Pot and stir well.
2. Close the lid. Select Manual mode and set cooking time for 14 minutes on High Pressure.
3. When timer beeps, make a quick pressure release and open the lid.
4. Blend with an immersion blender until smooth.
5. Serve warm.

Chickpea and Artichoke Soup

Prep time: 5 minutes | Cook time: 6 minutes | Serves 4

1 large potato, diced
3 cloves garlic, minced
½ package extra-firm tofu, pressed, drained, and diced
1 (14-ounce / 397-g) can artichoke hearts, drained
1 (14-ounce / 397-g) can chickpeas, rinsed and drained

5 cups vegetable broth
1 tomato, diced
2 stalks celery, chopped
1 teaspoon turmeric
1 teaspoon paprika
¼ teaspoon ground black pepper
¼ cup capers, for garnish

1. Combine all the ingredients except the black pepper and capers in the Instant Pot.
2. Secure the lid. Select the Manual mode and set the cooking time for 6 minutes at High Pressure.
3. Once cooking is complete, do a quick pressure release. Carefully open the lid and stir in the black pepper.
4. Garnish with the capers and serve hot.

Pozole

Prep time: 20 minutes | Cook time: 53 minutes | Serves 6

2½ pounds (1.1 kg) boneless pork shoulder, cut into pieces
1 teaspoon salt, divided
1 teaspoon ground black pepper, divided
2 tablespoons vegetable oil
2 medium yellow onions, peeled and chopped
2 medium poblano peppers, deseeded and diced
1 chipotle pepper in adobo, minced
4 cloves garlic, peeled and minced

1 cinnamon stick
1 tablespoon smoked paprika
2 teaspoons chili powder
1 teaspoon dried oregano
1 teaspoon ground cumin
½ teaspoon ground coriander
1 (12-ounce / 340-g) can lager-style beer
4 cups chicken broth
2 (15-ounce / 425-g) cans hominy, drained and rinsed
1 tablespoon lime juice
½ cup chopped cilantro

1. Season the pork pieces with ½ teaspoon of the salt and ½ teaspoon of the pepper.
2. Press the Sauté button on the Instant Pot and heat the oil. Add half the pork to the pot in an even layer, making sure there is space between pieces to prevent steam from forming. Sear the pork for 3 minutes on each side, or until lightly browned. Remove the pork to a plate. Repeat with the remaining pork.
3. Add the onions and poblano peppers to the pot and sauté for 5 minutes, or until just softened. Add the chipotle pepper, garlic, cinnamon, paprika, chili powder, oregano, cumin and coriander to the pot. Sauté for 1 minute, or until fragrant.
4. Return the pork to the pot and turn to coat with the spices. Pour in the beer and chicken broth.
5. Lock the lid. Select the Manual mode and set the cooking time for 35 minutes on High Pressure. When the timer beeps, perform a natural pressure release for 20 minutes, then release any remaining pressure. Carefully open the lid.
6. Season with the remaining ½ teaspoon of the salt and ½ teaspoon of the pepper. Stir in the hominy, lime juice and cilantro. Serve hot.

Serrano Chile and Avocado Soup

Prep time: 10 minutes | Cook time: 7 minutes | Serves 4

2 avocados
1 small fresh tomatillo, quartered
2 cups chicken broth
2 tablespoons avocado oil
1 tablespoon butter
2 tablespoons finely minced onion
1 clove garlic, minced

½ Serrano chile, deseeded and ribs removed, minced, plus thin slices for garnish
¼ teaspoon sea salt
Pinch of ground white pepper
½ cup full-fat coconut milk
Fresh cilantro sprigs, for garnish

1. Scoop the avocado flesh into a food processor. Add the tomatillo and chicken broth and purée until smooth. Set aside.
2. Set the Instant Pot to Sauté mode and add the avocado oil and butter. When the butter melts, add the onion and garlic and sauté for a minute or until softened. Add the Serrano chile and sauté for 1 minute more.
3. Pour the puréed avocado mixture into the pot, add the salt and pepper, and stir to combine.
4. Secure the lid. Press the Manual button and set cooking time for 5 minutes on High Pressure.
5. When timer beeps, use a quick pressure release. Open the lid and stir in the coconut milk.
6. Serve hot topped with thin slices of Serrano chile, and cilantro sprigs.

Tomato and Bean Stew

Prep time: 12 mins, Cook Time: 20 mins, Servings: 4

1 tbsp. olive oil
1 large onion, chopped
2 large tomatoes, roughly chopped
1 lb. green beans

2 cups low-sodium chicken stock
Salt and pepper, to taste
¼ cup Parmesan cheese

1. Press the Sauté bottom on the Instant Pot.
2. Add and heat the olive oil.
3. Add the onions and sauté for 2 minutes until translucent and softened.
4. Add the tomatoes and sauté for 3 to 4 minutes or until soft.
5. Add the beans and stock. Sprinkle with salt and pepper.
6. Lock the lid. Press Manual. Set the timer to 15 minutes at High Pressure.
7. Once the timer goes off, press Cancel. Do a quick pressure release.
8. Open the lid, transfer them in a large bowl and serve with Parmesan cheese on top.

Cabbage and Pork Soup

Prep time: 10 minutes | Cook time: 12 minutes | Serves 3

1 teaspoon butter
½ cup shredded white cabbage
½ teaspoon ground coriander
½ teaspoon salt

½ teaspoon chili flakes
2 cups chicken broth
½ cup ground pork

1. Melt the butter in the Instant Pot on Sauté mode.
2. Add cabbage and sprinkle with ground coriander, salt, and chili flakes.
3. Fold in the chicken broth and ground pork.
4. Close the lid and select Manual mode. Set cooking time for 12 minutes on High Pressure.
5. When timer beeps, use a quick pressure release. Open the lid.
6. Ladle the soup and serve warm.

Blue Cheese Mushroom Soup

Prep time: 15 minutes | Cook time: 20 minutes | Serves 4

2 cups chopped white mushrooms
3 tablespoons cream cheese
4 ounces (113 g) scallions, diced
4 cups chicken broth

1 teaspoon olive oil
½ teaspoon ground cumin
1 teaspoon salt
2 ounces (57 g) blue cheese, crumbled

1. Combine the mushrooms, cream cheese, scallions, chicken broth, olive oil, and ground cumin in the Instant Pot.
2. Seal the lid. Select Manual mode and set cooking time for 20 minutes on High Pressure.
3. When timer beeps, use a quick pressure release and open the lid.
4. Add the salt and blend the soup with an immersion blender.
5. Ladle the soup in the bowls and top with blue cheese. Serve warm.

Bacon Curry Soup

Prep time: 10 minutes | Cook time: 20 minutes | Serves 4

3 ounces (85 g) bacon, chopped
1 tablespoon chopped scallions
1 teaspoon curry powder

1 cup coconut milk
3 cups beef broth
1 cup Cheddar cheese, shredded

1. Heat the the Instant Pot on Sauté mode for 3 minutes and add bacon. Cook for 5 minutes. Flip constantly.
2. Add the scallions and curry powder. Sauté for 5 minutes more.
3. Pour in the coconut milk and beef broth. Add the Cheddar cheese and stir to mix well.
4. Select Manual mode and set cooking time for 10 minutes on High Pressure.
5. When timer beeps, use a quick pressure release. Open the lid.
6. Blend the soup with an immersion blender until smooth. Serve warm.

Carrot and Bean Chili

Prep time: 10 minutes | Cook time: 41 minutes | Serves 4

1 tablespoon olive oil
1 small red onion, peeled and diced
1 medium green bell pepper, deseeded and diced
1 large carrot, peeled and diced
4 cloves garlic, peeled and minced
1 small jalapeño, deseeded and diced
1 (28-ounce / 794-g) can diced tomatoes, undrained

1 (15-ounce / 425-g) can cannellini beans, drained and rinsed
1 (15-ounce / 425-g) can kidney beans, drained and rinsed
1 (15-ounce / 425-g) can black beans, drained and rinsed
2 tablespoons chili powder
1 teaspoon ground cumin
1 teaspoon salt
¼ cup vegetable broth

1. Press the Sauté button on the Instant Pot and heat the oil. Add the onion, bell pepper and carrot to the pot and sauté for 5 minutes, or until the onion is translucent. Add the garlic and sauté for 1 minute.
2. Stir in the remaining ingredients.
3. Set the lid in place. Select the Meat/Stew setting and set the cooking time for 35 minutes on High Pressure. When the timer goes off, perform a natural pressure release for 15 minutes, then release any remaining pressure. Open the lid.
4. Ladle the chili into 4 bowls and serve warm.

Millet and Brown Lentil Chili

Prep time: 10 minutes | Cook time: 20 minutes | Serves 6

2 tablespoons olive oil
1 cup finely diced yellow onion
2 cloves garlic, minced
1 seeded and finely diced fresh jalapeño
½ teaspoon ground cinnamon
1 teaspoon chili powder
1 teaspoon ground cumin
1 cup dried brown lentils, rinsed and drained
1 cup millet, rinsed and drained
½ cup diced summer squash
4 cups diced fresh tomatoes
2 cups bite-size pieces kale
1 bay leaf
2 cups vegetable broth
4 cups water
Juice of 1 lemon
1 tablespoon chopped fresh sweet basil
½ teaspoon sea salt

1. Heat the olive oil in the Instant Pot. Add the onion and cook for 3 to 4 minutes, stirring occasionally, until softened.
2. Add the garlic, stir, then add the jalapeño, cinnamon, chili powder, and cumin and sauté for a few minutes more, until the jalapeño softens.
3. Add the lentils, millet, squash, tomatoes, kale, bay leaf, broth, and water and stir to combine.
4. Cover the lid. Select Manual mode and set cooking time for 8 minutes on High Pressure.
5. When timer beeps, use a natural pressure release for 15 minutes, then release any remaining pressure.
6. Carefully remove the lid. Select Sauté mode and bring to a simmer, then add the lemon juice, basil, and salt.
7. Stir and let simmer for a few minutes more. Serve immediately.

Spinach and Beef Stew

Prep time: 20 minutes | Cook time: 30 minutes | Serves 4

1 pound (454 g) beef sirloin, chopped
2 cups spinach, chopped
3 cups chicken broth
1 cup coconut milk
1 teaspoon allspices
1 teaspoon coconut aminos

1. Put all ingredients in the Instant Pot. Stir to mix well.
2. Close the lid. Set the Manual mode and set cooking time for 30 minutes on High Pressure.
3. When timer beeps, use a natural pressure release for 10 minutes, then release any remaining pressure. Open the lid.
4. Blend with an immersion blender until smooth.
5. Serve warm.

Pork and Beef Chili

Prep time: 10 minutes | Cook time: 40 minutes | Serves 4

1 tablespoon olive oil
½ pound (227 g) ground beef
½ pound (227 g) ground pork
1 medium onion, peeled and diced
1 (28-ounce / 794-g) can puréed tomatoes, undrained
1 large carrot, peeled and diced
1 small green bell pepper, deseeded and diced
1 small jalapeño, deseeded and diced
3 cloves garlic, minced
2 tablespoons chili powder
1 teaspoon sea salt
2 teaspoons ground black pepper

1. Press the Sauté button on the Instant Pot and heat the olive oil. Add the ground beef, ground pork and onion to the pot and sauté for 5 minutes, or until the pork is no longer pink.
2. Stir in the remaining ingredients.
3. Close and secure the lid. Select the Meat/Stew setting and set the cooking time for 35 minutes on High Pressure. Once cooking is complete, use a natural pressure release for 15 minutes, then release any remaining pressure. Open the lid.
4. Serve warm.

Bacon, Leek, and Cauliflower Soup

Prep time: 15 minutes | Cook time: 15 minutes | Serves 6

6 slices bacon
1 leek, remove the dark green end and roots, sliced in half lengthwise, rinsed, cut into ½-inch-thick slices crosswise
½ medium yellow onion, sliced
4 cloves garlic, minced
3 cups chicken broth
1 large head cauliflower,
roughly chopped into florets
1 cup water
1 teaspoon kosher salt
1 teaspoon ground black pepper
⅔ cup shredded sharp Cheddar cheese, divided
½ cup heavy whipping cream

1. Set the Instant Pot to Sauté mode. When heated, place the bacon on the bottom of the pot and cook for 5 minutes or until crispy.
2. Transfer the bacon slices to a plate. Let stand until cool enough to handle, crumble it with forks.
3. Add the leek and onion to the bacon fat remaining in the pot. Sauté for 5 minutes or until fragrant and the onion begins to caramelize. Add the garlic and sauté for 30 seconds more or until fragrant.
4. Stir in the chicken broth, cauliflower florets, water, salt, pepper, and three-quarters of the crumbled bacon.
5. Secure the lid. Press the Manual button and set cooking time for 3 minutes on High Pressure.
6. When timer beeps, perform a quick pressure release. Open the lid.
7. Stir in ½ cup of the Cheddar and the cream. Use an immersion blender to purée the soup until smooth.
8. Ladle into bowls and garnish with the remaining Cheddar and crumbled bacon. Serve immediately.

Beef and Eggplant Tagine

Prep time: 15 minutes | Cook time: 25 minutes | Serves 6

1 pound (454 g) beef fillet, chopped
1 eggplant, chopped
6 ounces (170 g) scallions, chopped
4 cups beef broth
1 teaspoon ground allspices
1 teaspoon erythritol
1 teaspoon coconut oil

1. Put all ingredients in the Instant Pot. Stir to mix well.
2. Close the lid. Select Manual mode and set cooking time for 25 minutes on High Pressure.
3. When timer beeps, use a natural pressure release for 15 minutes, then release any remaining pressure. Open the lid.
4. Serve warm.

Okra and Beef Stew

Prep time: 15 minutes | Cook time: 25 minutes | Serves 3

8 ounces (227 g) beef sirloin, chopped
¼ teaspoon cumin seeds
1 teaspoon dried basil
1 tablespoon avocado oil
¼ cup coconut cream
1 cup water
6 ounces (170 g) okra, chopped

1. Sprinkle the beef sirloin with cumin seeds and dried basil and put in the Instant Pot.
2. Add avocado oil and roast the meat on Sauté mode for 5 minutes. Flip occasionally.
3. Add coconut cream, water, and okra.
4. Close the lid and select Manual mode. Set cooking time for 25 minutes on High Pressure.
5. When timer beeps, use a natural pressure release for 10 minutes, the release any remaining pressure. Open the lid.
6. Serve warm.

Mushroom and Beef Chili

Prep time: 15 minutes | Cook time: 40 minutes | Serves 6

1 tablespoon olive oil	diced tomatoes, undrained
1 pound (454 g) beef stew cubes	2 cups sliced mushrooms
1 medium onion, peeled and diced	2 tablespoons tomato paste
4 cloves garlic, minced	2 tablespoons chili powder
½ cup beef broth	1 tablespoon Italian seasoning
1 (16-ounce / 454-g) can chili beans, undrained	1 teaspoon red pepper flakes
1 (14.5-ounce / 411-g) can	1 teaspoon sea salt
	½ teaspoon ground black pepper

1. Press the Sauté button on the Instant Pot and heat the oil. Add the beef stew cubes and onion to the pot and sauté for 3 minutes, or until the beef is lightly browned and the onion is translucent. Add the garlic to the pot and sauté for 2 minutes.
2. Pour in the beef broth and deglaze by scraping any of the bits from the bottom and sides of the pot. Stir in the remaining ingredients.
3. Set the lid in place. Select the Meat/Stew setting and set the cooking time for 35 minutes on High Pressure. Once cooking is complete, do a natural pressure release for 15 minutes, then release any remaining pressure. Open the lid.
4. Ladle the chili into individual bowls and serve warm.

Black Bean, Pumpkin, and Kale Chili

Prep time: 10 minutes | Cook time: 12 minutes | Serves 4

¾ cup dried black beans, soaked in water overnight, rinsed and drained	2 tablespoons chili powder
	1 teaspoon onion powder
2 cups chopped pumpkin	3 cups water
1 (28-ounce / 794-g) can crushed tomatoes	½ teaspoon garlic powder
	2 cups finely shredded kale
	½ teaspoon salt

1. Combine the black beans, pumpkin, tomatoes, chili powder, onion powder, water, and garlic powder.
2. Close the lid, then select Manual mode and set cooking time for 10 minutes on High Pressure.
3. Once the cook time is complete, let the pressure release naturally for about 20 minutes, then release any remaining pressure. Open the lid.
4. Stir in the kale to wilt on Sauté mode for 2 minutes more. Season with salt. Serve warm.

Calamari Stew

Prep time: 12 mins, Cook Time: 32 mins, Servings: 3

1 tbsp. olive oil	½ bunch parsley, chopped
1 lb. separated calamari	7 oz. tomatoes, chopped
¼ cup white wine	

1. Set the Instant Pot to Sauté and add the oil and calamari. Stir to combine well.
2. Lock the lid. Select the Manual mode, then set the timer for 9 minutes at Low Pressure.
3. Once the timer goes off, do a quick pressure release. Carefully open the lid.
4. Add the wine, tomatoes and half of the parsley, and stir well.
5. Lock the lid. Select the Manual mode, then set the timer for 25 minutes at High Pressure.
6. Once the timer goes off, do a quick pressure release. Carefully open the lid.
7. Sprinkle the remaining parsley on top. Divide the soup into bowls and serve.

Vegetable and Beef Stew

Prep time: 15 minutes | Cook time: 46 minutes | Serves 6

2 tablespoons olive oil	2 medium Russet potatoes, scrubbed and small-diced
2 pounds (907 g) beef stew cubes	1 stalk celery, chopped
1 medium sweet onion, peeled and diced	2 tablespoons chopped fresh rosemary
4 cloves garlic, peeled and minced	1 teaspoon salt
3 cups beef broth	½ teaspoon ground black pepper
½ cup dry red wine	2 tablespoons gluten-free all-purpose flour
1 (14.5-ounce / 411-g) can crushed tomatoes, undrained	4 tablespoons water
2 medium carrots, peeled and diced	¼ cup chopped fresh Italian flat-leaf parsley

1. Press the Sauté button on the Instant Pot and heat the oil. Add the beef and onion to the pot and sauté for 5 minutes, or until the beef is seared and the onion is translucent. Add the garlic and sauté for 1 minute.
2. Pour in the beef broth and wine and deglaze the pot by scraping up any bits from the sides and bottom of the pot.
3. Stir in the tomatoes with juice, carrots, potatoes, celery, rosemary, salt and pepper.
4. Set the lid in place. Select the Meat/Stew setting and set the cooking time for 35 minutes on High Pressure. When the timer goes off, perform a natural pressure release for 10 minutes, then release any remaining pressure. Open the lid.
5. Create a slurry by whisking together the flour and water in a small bowl. Add the slurry to the pot. Select the Sauté mode and let simmer for 5 minutes, stirring constantly.
6. Ladle the stew into 6 bowls and serve topped with the parsley.

Beef and Onion Chili

Prep time: 20 minutes | Cook time: 19 minutes | Serves 8

2 pounds (907 g) 90% lean ground beef	2 tablespoons red wine vinegar
3 large yellow onions, peeled and diced, divided	2 tablespoons chili powder
	1 tablespoon pumpkin pie spice
3 cloves garlic, peeled and minced	1 teaspoon ground cumin
2 (16-ounce / 454-g) cans kidney beans, rinsed and drained	½ teaspoon ground cardamom
	½ teaspoon salt
1 (15-ounce / 425-g) can tomato sauce	½ teaspoon freshly cracked black pepper
1 cup beef broth	¼ teaspoon ground cloves
2 tablespoons semisweet chocolate chips	1 pound (454 g) cooked spaghetti
2 tablespoons honey	4 cups shredded Cheddar cheese

1. Press the Sauté button on the Instant Pot. Add the ground beef and ¾ of the diced onions to the pot and sauté for 8 minutes, or until the beef is browned and the onions are transparent. Drain the beef mixture and discard any excess fat. Add the garlic to the pot and sauté for 30 seconds.
2. Stir in the remaining ingredients, except for the reserved onions, spaghetti and cheese. Cook for 1 minute, or until fragrant.
3. Set the lid in place. Select the Manual mode and set the cooking time for 10 minutes on High Pressure. When the timer goes off, perform a quick pressure release. Carefully open the lid.
4. Serve over the cooked spaghetti and top with the reserved onions and cheese.

Beef Chili with Pinto Beans

Prep time: 20 minutes | Cook time: 40 minutes | Serves 8

1 pound (454 g) 80% lean ground beef
1 medium onion, peeled and chopped
2 cloves garlic, peeled and minced
¼ cup chili powder
2 tablespoons brown sugar
1 teaspoon ground cumin
½ teaspoon ground coriander
½ teaspoon salt
½ teaspoon ground black pepper
1 (14.5-ounce / 411-g) can diced tomatoes
2 cups dried pinto beans, soaked overnight in water and drained
2 cups beef broth
1 tablespoon lime juice

1. Press the Sauté button on the Instant Pot and brown the beef for 10 minutes, or until no pink remains. Add the onion, garlic, chili powder, brown sugar, cumin, coriander, salt and pepper to the pot and sauté for 10 minutes, or until the onion is just softened.
2. Stir in the tomatoes, soaked beans and beef broth.
3. Lock the lid. Select the Manual mode and set the cooking time for 20 minutes on High Pressure. When the timer goes off, do a natural pressure release for 20 minutes, then release any remaining pressure. Carefully open the lid.
4. Add the lime juice and stir well. Serve hot.

Red Feta and Broccoli Soup

Prep time: 10 minutes | Cook time: 25 minutes | Serves 4

1 cup broccoli, chopped
½ cup coconut cream
1 teaspoon unsweetened tomato purée
4 cups beef broth
1 teaspoon chili flakes
6 ounces (170 g) feta, crumbled

1. Put broccoli, coconut cream, tomato purée, and beef broth in the Instant Pot. Sprinkle with chili flakes and stir to mix well.
2. Close the lid and select Manual mode. Set cooking time for 8 minutes on High Pressure.
3. When timer beeps, make a quick pressure release and open the lid.
4. Add the feta cheese and stir the soup on Sauté mode for 5 minutes or until the cheese melt.
5. Serve immediately.

Chicken Soup with Egg Noodles

Prep time: 15 minutes | Cook time: 24 minutes | Serves 8

1 (3½-pound / 1.5-kg) chicken, cut into pieces
4 cups low-sodium chicken broth
3 stalks celery, chopped
2 medium carrots, peeled and chopped
1 medium yellow onion, peeled and chopped
1 clove garlic, and smashed
1 bay leaf
1 teaspoon poultry seasoning
½ teaspoon dried thyme
1 teaspoon salt
¼ teaspoon ground black pepper
4 ounces (113 g) dried egg noodles

1. Add all the ingredients, except for the egg noodles, to the Instant Pot and stir to combine.
2. Set the lid in place. Select the Soup mode and set the cooking time for 20 minutes at High Pressure. Once cooking is complete, use a natural pressure release for 20 to 25 minutes, then release any remaining pressure. Carefully open the lid.
3. Remove and discard the bay leaf. Transfer the chicken to a clean work surface. Shred chicken and discard the skin and bones. Return the shredded chicken to the pot and stir to combine. Stir in the noodles.

4. Lock the lid. Select the Manual mode and set the cooking time for 4 minutes at High Pressure. Once cooking is complete, use a quick pressure release. Carefully open the lid.
5. Serve hot.

Buffalo Chicken Soup

Prep time: 7 minutes | Cook time: 10 minutes | Serves 2

1 ounce (28 g) celery stalk, chopped
4 tablespoons coconut milk
¾ teaspoon salt
¼ teaspoon white pepper
1 cup water
2 ounces (57 g) Mozzarella, shredded
6 ounces (170 g) cooked chicken, shredded
2 tablespoons keto-friendly Buffalo sauce

1. Place the chopped celery stalk, coconut milk, salt, white pepper, water, and Mozzarella in the Instant Pot. Stir to mix well.
2. Set the Manual mode and set timer for 7 minutes on High Pressure.
3. When timer beeps, use a quick pressure release and open the lid.
4. Transfer the soup on the bowls. Stir in the chicken and Buffalo sauce. Serve warm.

Butternut Squash and Cauliflower Soup

Prep time: 5 minutes | Cook time: 25 minutes | Serves 3

2 teaspoons olive oil
1 garlic clove, minced
½ medium onion, diced
1 cup vegetable broth
½ pound (227 g) frozen cauliflower
½ pound (227 g) frozen, cubed, butternut squash
½ teaspoon paprika
¼ teaspoon dried thyme
2 pinches of sea salt
½ cup coconut milk

1. Set your Instant Pot to Sauté and heat the olive oil.
2. Add the garlic and onion and cook for 2 minutes.
3. Add the broth, cauliflower, butternut, and all the spices to the Instant Pot, stirring well.
4. Secure the lid. Select the Manual mode and set the cooking time for 5 minutes at High Pressure.
5. Once cooking is complete, do a quick pressure release. Carefully open the lid.
6. Add the milk to the soup and blend with an immersion blender until creamy.
7. Serve hot.

Chicken Tomato Stew

Prep time: 12 mins, Cook Time: 30 mins, Servings: 8

4 onions, chopped
1 tbsp. olive oil
10 oz. chicken breast
1 cup diced tomatoes
4 cups low-sodium chicken stock
¼ cup water

1. Press the Sauté bottom on the Instant Pot.
2. Add and heat the olive oil.
3. Add the onions and sauté for 1 to 2 minutes until turn translucent and softened.
4. Add the chicken and evenly brown for 4 to 5 minutes.
5. Add the tomatoes and sauté for 2 minutes or until soft.
6. Pour in the stock and water.
7. Lock the lid. Press Manual. Set the timer to 20 minutes at High Pressure.
8. Once the timer goes off, press Cancel. Do a quick pressure release.
9. Open the lid, transfer them in a large bowl and serve.

Beef Meatball Minestrone

Prep time: 5 minutes | Cook time: 35 minutes | Serves 6

1 pound (454 g) ground beef
1 large egg
1½ tablespoons golden flaxseed meal
⅓ cup shredded Mozzarella cheese
¼ cup unsweetened tomato purée
1½ tablespoons Italian seasoning, divided
1½ teaspoons garlic powder, divided
1½ teaspoons sea salt, divided
1 tablespoon olive oil

2 garlic cloves, minced
½ medium yellow onion, minced
¼ cup pancetta, diced
1 cup sliced yellow squash
1 cup sliced zucchini
½ cup sliced turnips
4 cups beef broth
14 ounces (397 g) can diced tomatoes
½ teaspoon ground black pepper
3 tablespoons shredded Parmesan cheese

1. Preheat the oven to 400°F (205°C) and line a large baking sheet with aluminum foil.
2. In a large bowl, combine the ground beef, egg, flaxseed meal, Mozzarella, unsweetened tomato purée, ½ tablespoon of Italian seasoning, ½ teaspoon of garlic powder, and ½ teaspoon of sea salt. Mix the ingredients until well combined.
3. Make the meatballs by shaping 1 heaping tablespoon of the ground beef mixture into a meatball. Repeat with the remaining mixture and then transfer the meatballs to the prepared baking sheet.
4. Place the meatballs in the oven and bake for 15 minutes. When the baking time is complete, remove from the oven and set aside.
5. Select Sauté mode of the Instant Pot. Once the pot is hot, add the olive oil, garlic, onion, and pancetta. Sauté for 2 minutes or until the garlic becomes fragrant and the onions begin to soften.
6. Add the yellow squash, zucchini, and turnips to the pot. Sauté for 3 more minutes.
7. Add the beef broth, diced tomatoes, black pepper, and remaining garlic powder, sea salt, and Italian seasoning to the pot. Stir to combine and then add the meatballs.
8. Lock the lid. Select Manual mode and set cooking time for 15 minutes on High Pressure.
9. When cooking is complete, allow the pressure to release naturally for 10 minutes and then release the remaining pressure.
10. Open the lid and gently stir the soup. Ladle into serving bowls and top with Parmesan. Serve hot.

Veal and Kale Stew

Prep time: 12 mins, Cook Time: 35 mins, Servings: 6

1 tbsp. olive oil
2 large onions, finely chopped
1 small sweet potato, diced
4 cups low-sodium beef stock

10 oz. fat removed and chopped veal shoulder
1 lb. fresh kale, chopped
Salt and pepper, to taste

1. Press the Sauté bottom on the Instant Pot.
2. Add and heat the olive oil.
3. Add the onions and sauté for 3 minutes until turn translucent and softened.
4. Add the sweet potato and ¼ cup of stock. Sauté for 5 minutes or until soft.
5. Add the remaining stock, veal shoulder, and kale to the Instant Pot. Sprinkle with salt and pepper. Combine to mix well.
6. Lock the lid. Press Manual. Set the timer to 25 minutes at High pressure.
7. Once the timer goes off, press Cancel. Do a quick pressure release.
8. Open the lid, transfer them in a large bowl and serve

Beef Tomato Stew

Prep time: 12 mins, Cook Time: 30 mins, Servings: 4

2 tsps. olive oil
1 lb. lean beef stew meat
2 cups diced tomatoes

2 spring onions, chopped
4 cups low-sodium beef broth
Salt and pepper, to taste

1. Press the Sauté bottom on the Instant Pot.
2. Add and heat the olive oil.
3. Add the meat and sauté for 3 to 4 minutes to evenly brown.
4. Add the tomatoes and onions, then sauté for 3 to 4 minutes or until soft.
5. Pour in the broth. Sprinkle with salt and pepper.
6. Lock the lid. Press Meat/Stew bottom. Set the timer to 20 minutes at High Pressure.
7. Once the timer goes off, press Cancel. Do a quick pressure release.
8. Open the lid, transfer them in a large bowl and serve.

Beer Chipotle Chili

Prep time: 15 minutes | Cook time: 55 minutes | Serves 8

2 pounds (907 g) chili meat, made from chuck roast
1 medium onion, peeled and chopped
3 cloves garlic, peeled and minced
3 tablespoons minced chipotle in adobo
2 tablespoons chili powder
2 tablespoons light brown sugar

1 teaspoon ground cumin
½ teaspoon ground coriander
½ teaspoon salt
½ teaspoon ground black pepper
2 cups beef broth
1 (12-ounce / 340-g) bottle lager-style beer
½ cup water
¼ cup corn masa
1 tablespoon lime juice

1. Press the Sauté button on the Instant Pot and brown the chili meat for 10 minutes. Add the onion, garlic, chipotle, chili powder, brown sugar, cumin, coriander, salt and pepper to the pot and cook for 10 minutes, or until the onion is just softened.
2. Pour in the beef broth and beer and stir well.
3. Lock the lid. Select the Bean/Chili mode and set the cooking time for 30 minutes on High Pressure. When the timer goes off, perform a quick pressure release. Carefully open the lid.
4. Select the Sauté mode. Whisk in the water and masa and cook for 5 minutes, stirring constantly, or until it starts to thicken.
5. Stir in the lime juice. Serve hot.

Shrimp and Chicken Thigh Stock

Prep time: 10 minutes | Cook time: 15 minutes | Serves 4

2 chicken thighs, boneless, chopped
4 ounces (113 g) shrimps, peeled
3 ounces (85 g) sausages, chopped

½ bell pepper, chopped
1 cup beef broth
1 teaspoon unsweetened tomato purée
1 celery stalk, chopped
½ teaspoon Cajun seasonings

1. Heat the the Instant Pot on Sauté mode for 3 minutes.
2. Add the chicken thighs, shrimps, sausages, bell pepper, beef broth, unsweetened tomato purée, celery stalk, and Cajun seasonings.
3. Gently mix the the ingredients and close the lid.
4. Select Manual mode and set time to 15 minutes on High Pressure.
5. When cooking is complete, use a quick pressure release and open the lid.
6. Serve immediately.

Black Bean and Quinoa Chili

Prep time: 10 minutes | Cook time: 16 minutes | Serves 6

1 tablespoon vegetable oil
1 medium onion, peeled and chopped
1 medium red bell pepper, deseeded and chopped
2 cloves garlic, peeled and minced
3 tablespoons chili powder
1 teaspoon ground cumin
½ teaspoon salt
½ teaspoon ground black pepper
2 cups vegetable broth
1 cup water
¾ cup quinoa
2 (15-ounce / 425-g) cans black beans, drained and rinsed

1. Press the Sauté button on the Instant Pot and heat the oil. Add the onion and bell pepper to the pot and sauté for 5 minutes, or until tender. Add the garlic, chili powder, cumin, salt and black pepper to the pot and sauté for 1 minute, or until fragrant.
2. Stir in the remaining ingredients.
3. Lock the lid. Select the Manual mode and set the cooking time for 10 minutes on High Pressure. When the timer goes off, do a quick pressure release. Carefully open the lid.
4. Serve hot.

Quinoa and Chicken Stew

Prep time: 30 mins, Cook Time: 23 mins, Servings: 6

1¼ lbs. chicken thigh fillets
4 cups chicken stock
4 cups chopped butternut
squash
1 cup chopped onion
½ cup uncooked quinoa

1. Put the chicken in the Instant Pot. Add the chicken thigh fillets, stock, squash and chopped onion.
2. Lock the lid. Select the Manual mode, then set the timer for 8 minutes at High Pressure.
3. Once the timer goes off, do a quick pressure release. Carefully open the lid.
4. Stir the quinoa into the stew.
5. Set the Instant Pot to Sauté and cook for about 15 minutes, stirring occasionally.
6. Serve the stew in a large serving bowl.

Butternut Squash and Kale Chili

Prep time: 10 minutes | Cook time: 20 minutes | Serves 6

1 teaspoon vegetable oil
2 cloves garlic, minced
½ cup diced onion
¼ cup diced green bell pepper
3 cups diced butternut squash (½-inch cubes)
1 teaspoon chili powder
1½ teaspoons cumin
1 tablespoon Sriracha sauce
1 cup dried brown lentils, rinsed and drained
2 tomatoes, diced
3 cups vegetable broth
4 cups loosely packed kale, cut or torn into bite-size pieces
1 tablespoon lemon juice
Salt and ground black pepper, to taste

1. In the Instant Pot, heat the oil on Sauté mode.
2. Add the garlic, onion, and bell pepper and sauté for 2 minutes, until the onion softens.
3. Add the squash, chili powder, cumin, and Sriracha and sauté for 4 minutes. Stir in the lentils and tomatoes.
4. Add the vegetable broth to cover by 1 inch. Add the kale and stir to combine.
5. Cover the lid. Select Manual mode and set cooking time for 10 minutes on High Pressure.
6. When timer beeps, use a natural pressure release for 15 minutes, then release any remaining pressure.
7. Remove the lid. Stir in the lemon juice. Add salt and ground black pepper and serve.

Zoodle and Chicken Soup

Prep time: 25 minutes | Cook time: 15 minutes | Serves 2

2 cups water
6 ounces (170 g) chicken fillet, chopped
1 teaspoon salt
2 ounces (57 g) zucchini, spiralized
1 tablespoon coconut aminos

1. Pour water in the Instant Pot. Add chopped chicken fillet and salt. Close the lid.
2. Select Manual mode and set cooking time for 15 minutes on High Pressure.
3. When cooking is complete, perform a natural pressure release for 10 minutes, then release any remaining pressure. Open the lid.
4. Fold in the zoodles and coconut aminos.
5. Leave the soup for 10 minutes to rest. Serve warm.

Broccoli and Bacon Cheese Soup

Prep time: 6 minutes | Cook time: 10 minutes | Serves 6

3 tablespoons butter
2 stalks celery, diced
½ yellow onion, diced
3 garlic cloves, minced
3½ cups chicken stock
4 cups chopped fresh broccoli florets
3 ounces (85 g) block-style cream cheese, softened and cubed
½ teaspoon ground nutmeg
½ teaspoon sea salt
1 teaspoon ground black pepper
3 cups shredded Cheddar cheese
½ cup shredded Monterey Jack cheese
2 cups heavy cream
4 slices cooked bacon, crumbled
1 tablespoon finely chopped chives

1. Select Sauté mode. Once the Instant Pot is hot, add the butter and heat until the butter is melted.
2. Add the celery, onions, and garlic. Continue sautéing for 5 minutes or until the vegetables are softened.
3. Add the chicken stock and broccoli florets to the pot. Bring the liquid to a boil.
4. Lock the lid,. Select Manual mode and set cooking time for 5 minutes on High Pressure.
5. When cooking is complete, allow the pressure to release naturally for 10 minutes and then release the remaining pressure.
6. Open the lid and add the cream cheese, nutmeg, sea salt, and black pepper. Stir to combine.
7. Select Sauté mode. Bring the soup to a boil and then slowly stir in the Cheddar and Jack cheeses. Once the cheese has melted, stir in the heavy cream.
8. Ladle the soup into serving bowls and top with bacon and chives. Serve hot.

Cauliflower and Provolone Soup

Prep time: 10 minutes | Cook time: 6 minutes | Serves 4

2 cups chopped cauliflower
2 tablespoons fresh cilantro
1 cup coconut cream
2 cups beef broth
3 ounces (85 g) Provolone cheese, chopped

1. Put cauliflower, cilantro, coconut cream, beef broth, and cheese in the Instant Pot. Stir to mix well.
2. Select Manual mode and set cooking time for 6 minutes on High Pressure.
3. When timer beeps, allow a natural pressure release for 4 minutes, then release any remaining pressure. Open the lid.
4. Blend the soup and ladle in bowls to serve.

Carrot and Cabbage Beef Stew

Prep time: 10 minutes | Cook time: 19 minutes | Serves 4 to 6

3 tablespoons extra-virgin olive oil
2 large carrots, peeled and sliced into ¼-inch disks and then quartered
1 large Spanish onion, diced
2 pounds (907 g) ground beef
3 cloves garlic, minced
1 (46-ounce / 1.3-kg) can tomato juice
2 cups vegetable broth

Juice of 2 lemons
1 head cabbage, cored and roughly chopped
½ cup jasmine rice
¼ cup dark brown sugar
1 tablespoon Worcestershire sauce
2 teaspoons seasoned salt
1 teaspoon black pepper
3 bay leaves

1. Set the Instant Pot to the Sauté mode and heat the oil for 3 minutes. Add the carrots and onion to the pot and sauté for 3 minutes, or until just tender. Add the ground beef and garlic to the pot and sauté for 3 minutes, or until the beef is lightly browned. Stir in the remaining ingredients.
2. Lock the lid. Select the Manual mode and set the cooking time for 10 minutes on High Pressure. When the timer goes off, perform a quick pressure release. Carefully open the lid.
3. Let rest for 5 minutes to thicken and cool before serving.

Chicken Chili Verde Soup

Prep time: 10 minutes | Cook time: 25 minutes | Serves 4

1 pound (454 g) chicken breast, skinless, boneless
5 cups chicken broth
½ cup Cheddar cheese,

shredded
2 ounces (57 g) chili Verde sauce
1 tablespoon dried cilantro

1. Put chicken breast and chicken broth in the Instant Pot.
2. Add the cilantro, Close the lid. Select Manual mode and set cooking time for 15 minutes on High Pressure.
3. When timer beeps, make a quick pressure release and open the lid.
4. Shred the chicken breast with a fork.
5. Add the Cheddar and chili Verde sauce in the soup and cook on Sauté mode for 10 minutes.
6. Mix in the dried cilantro. Serve immediately.

Orzo Veggie Soup

Prep time: 15 minutes | Cook time: 10 minutes | Serves 4

1 medium potato, peeled and small-diced
1 medium zucchini, diced
1 small carrot, peeled and diced
1 small yellow onion, peeled and diced
2 stalks celery, diced
1 (15-ounce / 425-g) can diced tomatoes, undrained
2 cloves garlic, peeled and minced

½ cup gluten-free orzo
5 cups vegetable broth
2 teaspoons dried oregano leaves
2 teaspoons dried thyme leaves
1 teaspoon salt
1 teaspoon ground black pepper
3 cups fresh baby spinach
4 tablespoons grated Parmesan cheese

1. Add all the ingredients, except for the spinach and Parmesan cheese, to the Instant Pot.
2. Lock the lid. Select the Manual setting and set the cooking time for 10 minutes at High Pressure. Once the timer goes off, use a quick pressure release. Carefully open the lid.
3. Stir in the spinach until wilted.
4. Ladle the soup into four bowls and garnish with the Parmesan cheese. Serve warm.

Cauliflower Rice and Chicken Thigh Soup

Prep time: 15 minutes | Cook time: 13 minutes | Serves 5

2 cups cauliflower florets
1 pound (454 g) boneless, skinless chicken thighs
4½ cups chicken broth
½ yellow onion, chopped
2 garlic cloves, minced
1 tablespoon unflavored gelatin powder
2 teaspoons sea salt
½ teaspoon ground black

pepper
½ cup sliced zucchini
⅓ cup sliced turnips
1 teaspoon dried parsley
3 celery stalks, chopped
1 teaspoon ground turmeric
½ teaspoon dried marjoram
1 teaspoon dried thyme
½ teaspoon dried oregano

1. Add the cauliflower florets to a food processor and pulse until a ricelike consistency is achieved. Set aside.
2. Add the chicken thighs, chicken broth, onions, garlic, gelatin powder, sea salt, and black pepper to the pot. Gently stir to combine.
3. Lock the lid. Select Manual mode and set cooking time for 10 minutes on High Pressure.
4. When cooking is complete, quick release the pressure and open the lid.
5. Transfer the chicken thighs to a cutting board. Chop the chicken into bite-sized pieces and then return the chopped chicken to the pot.
6. Add the cauliflower rice, zucchini, turnips, parsley, celery, turmeric, marjoram, thyme, and oregano to the pot. Stir to combine.
7. Lock the lid. Select Manual mode and set cooking time for 3 minutes on High Pressure.
8. When cooking is complete, quick release the pressure.
9. Open the lid. Ladle the soup into serving bowls. Serve hot.

Kidney Bean Stew

Prep time: 15 mins, Cook Time: 15 mins, Servings: 2

1 cup tomato passata
3 tbsps. Italian herbs

1lb. cooked kidney beans
1 cup low-sodium beef broth

1. Mix all the ingredients in the Instant Pot.
2. Lock the lid. Select the Bean/Chili mode, then set the timer for 15 minutes at High Pressure.
3. Once the timer goes off, do a natural pressure release for 10 minutes, then release any remaining pressure. Carefully open the lid.
4. Serve warm.

Chicken Chipotle Stew

Prep time: 15 minutes | Cook time: 10 minutes | Serves 3

9 ounces (255 g) chicken fillet, chopped
2 chipotle chili in adobo sauce, chopped
2 tablespoons sesame seeds

1 ounce (28 g) fresh cilantro, chopped
1 teaspoon ground paprika
¼ teaspoon salt
1 cup chicken broth

1. In a mixing bowl, combine the chicken fillet, chipotle chili, sesame seeds, cilantro, ground paprika, and salt.
2. Transfer the mixture in the Instant Pot and pour in the chicken broth.
3. Select Manual mode and set cooking time for 10 minutes on High Pressure.
4. When timer beeps, use a natural pressure release for 10 minutes, then release any remaining pressure. Open the lid.
5. Serve warm.

Beef and Cheese Soup

Prep time: 10 minutes | Cook time: 16 minutes | Serves 4

1 tablespoon olive oil
1 pound (454 g) ground beef
1 medium yellow onion, peeled and diced
1 small green bell pepper, deseeded and diced
1 medium carrot peeled and shredded
1 (15-ounce / 425-g) can diced tomatoes, undrained

2 teaspoons yellow mustard
1 teaspoon garlic powder
1 teaspoon smoked paprika
½ teaspoon salt
4 cups beef broth
2 cups shredded iceberg lettuce
1 cup shredded Cheddar cheese, divided
½ cup diced dill pickles

1. Set the Instant Pot to the Sauté mode and heat the olive oil for 30 seconds. Add the beef, onion and green bell pepper to the pot and sauté for 5 minutes, or until the beef is lightly browned. Add the carrot and sauté for 1 minute.
2. Stir in the tomatoes with juice, mustard, garlic powder, paprika, salt and beef broth.
3. Close and secure the lid. Select the Manual mode and set the cooking time for 7 minutes on High Pressure. When the timer goes off, use a quick pressure release. Carefully open the lid.
4. Whisk in the lettuce and ½ cup of the cheese. Select the Sauté mode and cook for 3 minutes.
5. Divide the soup among 4 bowls and serve topped with the remaining ½ cup of the cheese and dill pickles.

Salmon Head Soup

Prep time: 6 mins, Cook Time: 12 mins, Servings: 1

1 tsp. coconut oil
1 onion, sliced
3 cups water

1 salmon head
3-inch ginger piece, slivered
Salt and pepper, to taste

1. Press the Sauté button on the Instant Pot and heat the coconut oil.
2. Sauté the onion for 3 minutes or until translucent.
3. Pour in the water, then add the salmon head and ginger.
4. Sprinkle salt and pepper for seasoning.
5. Lock the lid. Set on the Manual mode, then set the timer to 10 minutes at Low Pressure.
6. When the timer goes off, perform a quick release.
7. Carefully open the lid. Allow to cool before serving.

Kale and Chicken Soup

Prep time: 6 mins, Cook Time: 20 mins, Servings: 4

1 tbsp. coconut oil
1 onion, diced
2 celery stalks, chopped
1 lb. boneless chicken breasts

3 cups water
Salt and pepper, to taste
4 cups chopped kale

1. Press the Sauté button on the Instant Pot and heat the coconut oil.
2. Sauté the onions and celery for 2 minutes until soft.
3. Add the chicken breasts and sear for 2 minutes on each side or until lightly browned.
4. Pour in the water and sprinkle salt and pepper for seasoning.
5. Lock the lid. Set to Poultry mode and set the timer to 15 minutes at High Pressure.
6. When the timer goes off, do a natural pressure release for 10 minutes, then release any remaining pressure.
7. Carefully open the lid. Press the Sauté button and add the kale.
8. Allow to simmer for 3 minutes.
9. Serve warm.

Lamb and Chickpea Soup

Prep time: 10 minutes | Cook time: 13 minutes | Serves 4

1 tablespoon olive oil
1 pound (454 g) ground lamb
1 medium red onion, peeled and diced
1 medium carrot, peeled and shredded
3 cloves garlic, peeled and minced
1 (15-ounce / 425-g) can diced tomatoes, undrained

1 (15.5-ounce / 439-g) can chickpeas, rinsed and drained
4 cups chicken broth
½ teaspoon ground ginger
½ teaspoon turmeric
½ teaspoon salt
¼ teaspoon ground cinnamon
½ cup chopped fresh cilantro
4 tablespoons plain full-fat Greek yogurt

1. Set the Instant Pot to the Sauté mode and heat the olive oil. Add the lamb and onion to the pot and sauté for 5 minutes, or until the lamb is lightly browned. Add the carrot and garlic to the pot and sauté for 1 minute.
2. Stir in the remaining ingredients, except for the cilantro and Greek yogurt.
3. Set the lid in place. Select the Manual mode and set the cooking time for 7 minutes on High Pressure. When the timer goes off, perform a quick pressure release. Carefully open the lid.
4. Ladle the soup into 4 bowls and garnish with the cilantro and yogurt. Serve warm.

Thai Tom Saap Pork Ribs Soup

Prep time: 6 mins, Cook Time: 30 mins, Servings: 4

1 lb. pork spare ribs
4 lemongrass stalks
10 galangal slices
10 kaffir lime leaves

6 cups water
Salt and pepper, to taste
1 tbsp. sesame oil
Cilantro, to taste

1. In the Instant Pot, place the spare ribs, lemongrass, galangal, and kaffir lime leaves.
2. Pour in the water and sprinkle salt and pepper for seasoning.
3. Lock the lid. Set on the Manual mode, then set the timer to 30 minutes at High Pressure.
4. When the timer goes off, do a natural pressure release, then release any remaining pressure.
5. Carefully open the lid. Drizzle with sesame oil and garnish with cilantro before serving.

Chuck Roast and Cabbage Stew

Prep time: 6 mins, Cook Time: 36 mins, Servings: 10

2 tbsps. olive oil
2 onions, sliced
1 garlic clove, minced
3 lbs. chuck roast

6 cups water
Salt and pepper, to taste
1 small cabbage head, chopped

1. Press the Sauté button on the Instant Pot and heat the olive oil.
2. Sauté the onions and garlic for 2 minutes until fragrant.
3. Add the chuck roast and sauté for 3 minutes or until lightly browned.
4. Pour in the water and sprinkle salt and pepper for seasoning.
5. Lock the lid. Set on the Manual mode, then set the timer to 30 minutes at High Pressure.
6. When the timer goes off, do a natural pressure release, then release any remaining pressure.
7. Carefully open the lid. Press the Sauté button and add the cabbage.
8. Allow to simmer for 3 minutes.
9. Serve warm.

Chinese Pork Belly Stew

Prep time: 10 minutes | Cook time: 42 minutes | Serves 8

½ cup plus 2 tablespoons soy sauce, divided
¼ cup Chinese cooking wine
½ cup packed light brown sugar
2 pounds (907 g) pork belly, skinned and cubed

12 scallions, cut into pieces
3 cloves garlic, minced
3 tablespoons vegetable oil
1 teaspoon Chinese five-spice powder
2 cups vegetable broth
4 cups cooked white rice

1. In a large bowl, whisk together ½ cup of the soy sauce, wine and brown sugar. Place the pork into the bowl and turn to coat evenly. Cover in plastic and refrigerate for at least 4 hours. Drain the pork and pat dry. Reserve the marinade.
2. Press the Sauté button on the Instant Pot and heat the oil. Add half the pork to the pot in an even layer, making sure there is space between pork cubes to prevent steam from forming. Sear the pork for 3 minutes on each side, or until lightly browned. Transfer the browned pork to a plate. Repeat with the remaining pork.
3. Stir in the remaining ingredients, except for the rice. Return the browned pork to the pot with the reserved marinade.
4. Lock the lid. Select the Manual mode and set the cooking time for 30 minutes on High Pressure. When the timer beeps, perform a natural pressure release for 20 minutes, then release any remaining pressure. Carefully open the lid.
5. Serve hot over cooked rice.

Rutabaga and Seitan Stew

Prep time: 10 minutes | Cook time: 15 minutes | Serves 4 to 6

1 pound (454 g) seitan, patted dry
¼ teaspoon fine sea salt
½ teaspoon freshly ground black pepper
1 tablespoon avocado oil
1 yellow onion, diced
4 cloves garlic, minced
½ cup red wine
1 teaspoon fresh thyme leaves
1 teaspoon chopped fresh sage leaves
1 teaspoon chopped fresh

rosemary
1 cup vegetable broth
2 teaspoons Dijon mustard
1 (1-pound / 454-g) large rutabaga, peeled and cut into 1-inch pieces
4 medium carrots (about 8 ounces / 227 g in total), peeled and sliced into 1-inch rounds
3 waxy potatoes (about 1 pound / 454 g in total), cut into 1-inch pieces
1 tablespoon tomato paste

1. Sprinkle the seitan with the salt and pepper.
2. Select the Sauté setting on the Instant Pot, add the oil, and heat for 2 minutes.
3. Add the seitan and sear for 4 minutes until golden brown. Flip and sear for 3 minutes more. Transfer the seitan to a dish and set aside.
4. Add the onion and garlic to the pot and sauté for 4 minutes until the onion softens.
5. Stir in the wine. Let the wine simmer until it has mostly evaporated, about 4 minutes.
6. Add the thyme, sage, and rosemary, and sauté for 1 minute more. Add the broth and mustard and stir to dissolve.
7. Bring the mixture up to a simmer, then stir in the seitan, rutabaga, carrots, and potatoes. Add the tomato paste on top. Do not stir.
8. Secure the lid. Select the Meat/Stew setting and set the cooking time for 4 minutes at High Pressure.
9. When timer beeps, perform a quick pressure release. Open the pot and gently stir the stew to incorporate the tomato paste and make sure everything is coated with the cooking liquid.
10. Ladle the stew into bowls and serve hot.

Borscht

Prep time: 15 minutes | Cook time: 15 minutes | Serves 7

4 tablespoons olive oil
2 medium white onions, chopped
2 large grated carrots
4 medium beets
4 large white potatoes, peeled and diced
½ medium white cabbage, thinly sliced
8 medium cloves garlic, diced

10 cups water
4 cups vegetable stock
½ cup dried porcini mushrooms
4 tablespoons apple cider vinegar
3 tablespoons tomato paste
2 teaspoons salt
1 teaspoon pepper
Fresh parsley, for garnish

1. Press the Sauté button on the Instant Pot and add the oil and onions. Cook for 3 minutes, stirring frequently.
2. Add the carrots, beets, potatoes, and cabbage, and sauté for 1 minute.
3. Add the remaining ingredients except the parsley to the Instant Pot and stir well.
4. Secure the lid. Select the Manual mode and set the cooking time for 10 minutes at High Pressure.
5. Once cooking is complete, do a natural pressure release for 10 minutes, then release any remaining pressure. Carefully open the lid.
6. Garnish with the parsley and serve.

Thai Coconut Shrimp Soup

Prep time: 6 mins, Cook Time: 6 mins, Servings: 2

6 oz. shrimps, shelled and deveined
2 cups water

Juice of 3 kaffir limes
1½ cups coconut milk
1 cup fresh cilantro

1. In the Instant Pot, add all the ingredients excluding cilantro.
2. Lock the lid. Set on the Manual mode and set the timer to 6 minutes at Low Pressure.
3. When the timer goes off, perform a quick release.
4. Carefully open the lid. Garnish with the fresh cilantro and serve immediately.

Coconut Red Bean Soup

Prep time: 10 minutes | Cook time: 50 minutes | Serves 4

2 teaspoons olive oil
3 slices bacon, diced
2 large carrots, peeled and diced
5 green onions, sliced
1 stalk celery, chopped
1 Scotch bonnet, deseeded, veins removed and minced
1 (15-ounce / 425-g) can diced tomatoes, undrained
½ pound (227 g) dried small

red beans
1 (13.5-ounce / 383-g) can coconut milk
2 cups chicken broth
1 tablespoon Jamaican jerk seasoning
1 teaspoon salt
4 cups cooked basmati rice
1 cup chopped fresh parsley
1 lime, quartered

1. Press the Sauté button on the Instant Pot and heat the oil. Add the bacon, carrots, onions, celery and Scotch bonnet to the pot and sauté for 5 minutes, or until the onions are translucent.
2. Stir in the tomatoes with juice, red beans, coconut milk, chicken broth, Jamaican jerk seasoning and salt.
3. Lock the lid. Select the Manual mode and set the cooking time for 45 minutes on High Pressure. When the timer goes off, do a natural pressure release for 10 minutes, then release any remaining pressure. Carefully open the lid.
4. Ladle the soup into four bowls over cooked rice and garnish with parsley. Squeeze a quarter of lime over each bowl. Serve warm.

Kidney Bean and Corn Chili

Prep time: 5 minutes | Cook time: 10 minutes | Serves 4

1 teaspoon olive oil
½ cup diced carrot
1 cup diced onion
3 cloves garlic, minced
½ cup chopped celery
1 (14.5-ounce / 411-g) can whole kernel corn, drained
1 cup diced green bell pepper
1 cup diced red bell pepper
1 teaspoon chili powder
½ teaspoon ground cumin

1 (28-ounce / 794-g) can diced tomatoes
2 tablespoons tomato paste
2 cups vegetable broth
1 fresh jalapeño, deseeded and finely diced
½ teaspoon cayenne pepper
1 teaspoon red pepper flakes
1 cup water
1½ cups red kidney beans, rinsed and drained

1. In the Instant Pot, heat the oil on Sauté mode.
2. Add the carrot, onion, garlic, and celery and sauté for 3 minutes.
3. Add the corn, bell peppers, chili powder, cumin, diced tomatoes, tomato paste, broth, jalapeño, cayenne, red pepper flakes, water, and beans.
4. Secure the lid. Select Manual mode and set cooking time for 6 minutes at Low Pressure.
5. When timer beeps, use a natural pressure release for 15 minutes, then release any remaining pressure. Open the lid.
6. Serve immediately.

Broccoli Soup with Bacon

Prep time: 15 minutes | Cook time: 30 minutes | Serves 4

2 teaspoons unsalted butter
6 slices bacon, diced
1 large carrot, peeled and diced
1 medium sweet onion, peeled and diced
1 small Russet potato, scrubbed and diced
1 pound (454 g) fresh broccoli,

chopped
¼ cup grated Cheddar cheese
1 tablespoon Dijon mustard
1 teaspoon salt
1 teaspoon ground black pepper
4 cups chicken broth
¼ cup whole milk
4 tablespoons sour cream

1. Set the Instant Pot to the Sauté mode and melt the butter. Add the bacon to the pot and sear for 5 minutes, or until crispy. Transfer the bacon to a plate lined with paper towels and let rest for 5 minutes. Crumble the bacon when cooled.
2. Add the carrot, onion and potato to the pot. Sauté for 5 minutes, or until the onion is translucent. Stir in the remaining ingredients, except for the milk and sour cream.
3. Set the lid in place. Select the Soup mode and set the cooking time for 20 minutes at High Pressure. Once cooking is complete, use a quick pressure release. Carefully open the lid.
4. Pour the milk into the pot. Use an immersion blender to blend the soup in the pot until it achieves the desired smoothness.
5. Ladle the soup into 4 bowls and garnish with the crumbled bacon and sour cream. Serve warm.

Crab Soup

Prep time: 10 minutes | Cook time: 21 minutes | Serves 4

4 tablespoons unsalted butter
2 large carrots, peeled and diced
1 cup chopped leeks
2 stalks celery, chopped
4 cloves garlic, peeled and minced
2 teaspoons Italian seasoning

1 teaspoon salt
5 cups vegetable broth
1 pound (454 g) lump crabmeat, divided
2 tablespoons cooking sherry
¼ cup heavy cream
2 tablespoons fresh thyme leaves

1. Press the Sauté button on the Instant Pot and melt the butter. Add the carrots, leeks and celery to the pot and sauté for 5 minutes, or until the leeks are translucent. Add the garlic and sauté for 1 minute.
2. Stir in the Italian seasoning, salt, vegetable broth and ½ pound (227 g) of the crabmeat.
3. Lock the lid, select the Manual mode and set the cooking time for 15 minutes on High Pressure. Once cooking is complete, use a natural pressure release for 10 minutes, then release any remaining pressure. Carefully open the lid.
4. Use an immersion blender to blend the soup in the pot until smooth. Stir in the remaining ½ pound (227 g) of the crabmeat, sherry and heavy cream.
5. Ladle soup into four bowls and serve garnished with the thyme

Tofu and Vegetable Soup

Prep time: 5 minutes | Cook time: 10 minutes | Serves 8

2 to 3 tablespoons butter
3 cloves garlic, minced
1 (14-ounce / 397-g) package soft tofu
1 cup almond milk
2 tablespoons lemon juice
1 teaspoon dried dill
½ teaspoon salt

4 cups diced potatoes
2 cups sliced mushrooms
2 cups sliced onion, cut into half-moons
1 cup chopped celery
1 cup chopped carrot
4 cups vegetable broth
Ground black pepper, to taste

1. Set your Instant Pot to Sauté and melt the butter.
2. Add the garlic and sauté for 1 minute.
3. Pulse the tofu, almond milk, lemon juice, salt, and dill in a food processor until creamy.
4. Add the potatoes, mushrooms, onion, carrots, and celery to the Instant Pot, stirring well. Pour the tofu mixture into the pot and stir in the vegetable broth.
5. Secure the lid. Select the Manual mode and set the cooking time for 5 minutes at High Pressure.
6. Once cooking is complete, do a quick pressure release. Carefully open the lid.
7. Season to taste with black pepper and serve.

Acorn Squash Chili

Prep time: 15 minutes | Cook time: 16 minutes | Serves 6

1 tablespoon olive oil
½ cup chopped onion
1 cup sliced carrots
1 large celery stalks, chopped
2 cloves garlic, minced
1½ cups cubed acorn squash
10 ounces (283 g) can red kidney beans, drained
10 ounces (283 g) can cannellini beans, drained

2 (10-ounce / 283-g) can crushed tomatoes
¾ cup corn kernels
1 teaspoon Tabasco sauce
1 teaspoon mesquite powder
1 teaspoon chili flakes
1 teaspoon dried oregano
1 teaspoon ground cumin
1 teaspoon smoked paprika

1. Heat the oil in the Instant pot on Sauté mode.
2. Add the onion and carrots. Sauté for 3 minutes or until soft.
3. Add the celery and sauté for 2 minutes. Add the garlic and sauté for 1 minute.
4. Add the remaining ingredients and lock the lid.
5. Select Manual mode and set cooking time for 10 minutes on High Pressure.
6. When timer beeps, use a natural pressure release for 5 minutes, then release any remaining pressure. Open the lid.
7. Serve warm.

Quinoa and Bean Chili

Prep time: 10 minutes | Cook time: 7 minutes | Serves 6

1 tablespoon olive oil
1 large yellow onion, diced
3 cloves garlic, minced
1 green bell pepper, deseeded and diced
1 cup peeled and diced sweet potato cubes (about 1 inch)
1 (15-ounce / 425-g) can black beans, drained and rinsed
1 (15-ounce / 425-g) can kidney beans, drained and rinsed
½ cup uncooked quinoa, rinsed

and drained
1 (4-ounce / 113-g) can diced green chiles
1 (26-ounce / 737-g) box chopped or diced tomatoes
1½ tablespoons chili powder
1 tablespoon ground cumin
½ teaspoon smoked paprika
½ teaspoon sea salt
2 cups vegetable broth
Fresh cilantro leaves, for garnish
1 avocado, sliced, for garnish

1. Select Sauté mode, and heat the oil in the Instant Pot until hot.
2. Add the onion and sauté for 1 minute. Add the garlic, bell pepper, and sweet potatoes, and sauté 1 minute more.
3. Add the black beans, kidney beans, quinoa, chiles, tomatoes, chili powder, cumin, paprika, salt, and broth, and stir.
4. Lock the lid. Select Manual mode and set the cook time for 5 minutes on High Pressure.
5. Once the cook time is complete, quick release the pressure and carefully remove the lid.
6. Serve warm, garnished with cilantro and avocado.

Fish and Carrot Stew

Prep time: 10 minutes | Cook time: 14 minutes | Serves 4

1 tablespoon olive oil
1 large carrot, peeled and diced
1 stalk celery, diced
1 small yellow onion, peeled and diced
4 cloves garlic, peeled and minced
2 cups baby red potatoes, scrubbed and small-diced

1 (28-ounce / 794-g) can diced tomatoes, undrained
1 pound (454 g) skinless cod, cut into cubes
1 (8-ounce / 227-g) bottle clam juice
2 cups water
1 tablespoon Italian seasoning
1 teaspoon salt
1 bay leaf

1. Press the Sauté button on the Instant Pot and heat the oil. Add the carrot, celery and onion to the pot and sauté for 5 minutes, or until the onion is translucent. Add the garlic and sauté for 1 minute. Stir in the remaining ingredients.
2. Set the lid in place. Select the Manual setting and set the cooking time for 8 minutes on High Pressure. Once cooking is complete, perform a natural pressure release for 10 minutes, then release any remaining pressure. Open the lid.
3. Ladle the stew into 4 bowls and serve warm.

Swiss Chard and Leek Soup

Prep time: 12 mins, Cook Time: 6 mins, Servings: 4

8 cups chopped Swiss chard
3 leeks, chopped
Salt, to taste

1½ cups chicken stock
1 cup coconut milk

1. In the Instant Pot, mix the chard with leeks, salt, stock and coconut milk, stir to combine well.
2. Lock the lid. Select the Manual mode, then set the timer for 6 minutes at High Pressure.
3. Once the timer goes off, do a quick pressure release.
4. Carefully open the lid. Allow to cool for a few minutes, then pour the soup in an immersion blender and process until smooth. Ladle the soup into bowls and serve.

Collard and Black-Eyed Pea Chili

Prep time: 10 minutes | Cook time: 20 minutes | Serves 4

1 teaspoon olive oil
½ cup diced red onion
3 cloves garlic, minced
2 cups chopped carrot
2 cups chopped celery
4 large collard green leaves, halved, center ribs removed, cut into ¼-inch wide strips
½ teaspoon ground coriander
1 teaspoon ground cinnamon
1 tablespoon dried oregano
2 tablespoons chili powder
1 teaspoon ground cumin

1 teaspoon deseeded and diced fresh jalapeño
2 cups dried black-eyed peas, rinsed and drained
1 (28-ounce / 794-g) can diced tomatoes
1 (8-ounce / 227-g) can tomato sauce
2 bay leaves
2 cups vegetable broth
1 cup water
¼ teaspoon sea salt

1. In the Instant Pot heat the oil on Sauté mode.
2. Add the onion and garlic and sauté for about 2 minutes until the onion begins to soften.
3. Add the carrots and celery and continue to sauté for another 3 to 5 minutes.
4. Add the collard greens, coriander, cinnamon, oregano, chili powder, cumin, and jalapeño and sauté for a minute.
5. Add the black-eyed peas, diced tomatoes, tomato sauce, bay leaves, broth, and water. Stir to combine.
6. Secure the lid. Select Manual mode and set cooking time for 10 minutes on High Pressure.
7. When timer beeps, use a natural pressure release for 15 minutes, then release any remaining pressure.
8. Remove the cover. Add salt to taste. Remove the bay leaves before serving.

Turkey with Ginger and Turmeric Soup

Prep time: 6 mins, Cook Time: 17 mins, Servings: 4

1 tbsp. coconut oil
2 celery stalks, chopped
1 thumb-size ginger, sliced
1 tsp. turmeric powder

1 lb. turkey meat, chopped
3 cups water
Salt and pepper, to taste

1. Press the Sauté button on the Instant Pot and heat the coconut oil.
2. Add the celery, ginger, and turmeric powder and sauté for 3 minutes or until fragrant and the celery is tender.
3. Add the turkey meat and stir for another 3 minutes until lightly browned.
4. Pour in the water and sprinkle salt and pepper for seasoning.
5. Lock the lid. Set on the Manual mode, then set the timer to 15 minutes at High Pressure.
6. When the timer goes off, do a natural pressure release, then release any remaining pressure.
7. Carefully open the lid. Serve warm.

Turmeric Chicken Soup

Prep time: 6 mins, Cook Time: 15 mins, Servings: 3

3 boneless chicken breasts
1 bay leaf
½ cup coconut milk

2½ tsps. turmeric powder
4 cups water

1. Place all the ingredients in the Instant Pot. Stir to combine well.
2. Lock the lid. Set to Poultry mode and set the timer to 15 minutes at High Pressure.
1. When the timer goes off, perform a natural pressure release for 10 minutes, then release any remaining pressure.
3. Carefully open the lid. Allow to cool for a few minutes, then serve immediately.

Lentil Soup with Garam Masala

Prep time: 5 minutes | Cook time: 15 minutes | Serves 6

1 tablespoon vegetable oil
2 tablespoons finely diced shallot
1 cup diced carrots
1 cup diced celery
½ teaspoon garam masala
½ teaspoon ground cinnamon
½ teaspoon cumin
1 bay leaf
1¾ cups dried brown or green lentils, rinsed and drained
2 cups vegetable broth
3 cups water
¼ to ½ teaspoon sea salt (optional)
Freshly ground black pepper, to taste

1. Set your Instant Pot to Sauté and heat the oil.
2. Add the shallot, carrots, and celery and sauté for 3 to 5 minutes, until the shallot and celery are tender, stirring occasionally.
3. Add the garam masala, cinnamon, cumin, bay leaf, and lentils and stir well. Pour in the vegetable broth and water and stir to mix well.
4. Secure the lid. Select the Manual mode and set the cooking time for 8 minutes at High Pressure.
5. Once cooking is complete, do a natural pressure release for 10 minutes, then release any remaining pressure. Carefully open the lid.
6. Remove the bay leaf and sprinkle with salt (if desired). Season to taste with black pepper and serve.

Tofu and Kale Miso Soup

Prep time: 5 minutes | Cook time: 10 minutes | Serves 6

1 to 2 teaspoons vegetable oil
4 cloves garlic, cut in half
1 small sweet onion, quartered
2 medium carrots, cut into 2- to 3-inch pieces
4 cups low-sodium vegetable broth
1 (12-ounce / 340-g) package silken (light firm) tofu
1 bunch kale (off the stem), plus a few leaves for garnish
¼ cup yellow miso
Ground black pepper, to taste

1. Press the Sauté button on the Instant Pot and heat the oil.
2. Add the garlic, onion, and carrots and sauté for 5 minutes, stirring occasionally.
3. Add the vegetable broth and tofu. Crumble the tofu into pieces with a spoon. Add the kale and stir to incorporate.
4. Secure the lid. Select the Manual mode and set the cooking time for 4 minutes at High Pressure.
5. Once cooking is complete, do a natural pressure release for 10 minutes, then release any remaining pressure. Carefully open the lid.
6. Stir in the miso and blend the soup with an immersion blender until smooth.
7. Season to taste with black pepper and serve garnished with extra kale.

Vegetable Quinoa Stew

Prep time: 10 minutes | Cook time: 15 minutes | Serves 4

2 teaspoons corn oil
1 yellow onion, minced
3 Roma tomatoes, minced
¼ cup frozen corn kernels, thawed to room temperature
1 zucchini, cut into 1-inch chunks
½ cup chopped red bell pepper
1½ cups broccoli florets
¼ cup diced carrot
½ cup quinoa, rinsed
1 teaspoon ground coriander
½ teaspoon paprika
½ teaspoon ground cumin
1 (32-ounce / 907-g) container vegetable broth
2 teaspoons kosher salt
4 tablespoons minced fresh cilantro, divided

1. Press the Sauté button on the Instant Pot and heat the oil. Once hot, add the onion and sauté 5 minutes, stirring occasionally.
2. Add the tomatoes, corn, zucchini, bell pepper, broccoli, and carrot and mix well. Stir in the quinoa, coriander, paprika, cumin, broth, salt, and 2 tablespoons of cilantro.
3. Secure the lid. Select the Manual mode and set the cooking time for 8 minutes at High Pressure.
4. Once cooking is complete, do a natural pressure release for 5 minutes, then release any remaining pressure. Carefully open the lid.
5. Stir in the remaining 2 tablespoons of cilantro and serve hot.

Summer Chili

Prep time: 10 minutes | Cook time: 15 minutes | Serves 6

2 tablespoons olive oil
1 poblano chile or green bell pepper, deseeded and diced
1 jalapeño chile, deseeded and diced
1 celery stalk, diced
2 cloves garlic, minced
1 yellow onion, diced
½ teaspoon fine sea salt, plus more as needed
2 tablespoons chili powder
1 teaspoon dried oregano
½ teaspoon ground cumin
¼ teaspoon cayenne pepper
2 zucchini, diced
1 (15-ounce / 425-g) can peruano beans, rinsed and drained
1 (12-ounce / 340-g) bag frozen corn
1 cup vegetable broth
1 (14.5-ounce / 411-g) can diced fire-roasted tomatoes
¼ cup chopped fresh cilantro
2 green onions, white and tender green parts, thinly sliced

1. Select the Sauté setting on the Instant Pot, add the oil, and heat for 1 minute.
2. Add the poblano and jalapeño chiles, celery, garlic, onion, and salt, and sauté for about 5 minutes, until the vegetables soften.
3. Add the chili powder, oregano, cumin, and cayenne and sauté for about 1 minute more.
4. Add the zucchini, beans, corn, and broth and stir to combine. Pour the tomatoes and their liquid over the top. Do not stir.
5. Secure the lid. Select Manual mode and set the cooking time for 5 minutes at High Pressure.
6. When timer beeps, perform a quick pressure release. Open the pot, give a stir.
7. Ladle the chili into bowls and sprinkle with cilantro and green onions. Serve hot.

Lentil and Vegetable Soup

Prep time: 30 mins, Cook Time: 20 mins, Servings: 5

1 tbsp. olive oil
6 cups chicken stock
1¼ cup green lentils
6 garlic cloves, minced
5 tbsps. mixed spices
Salt, to taste
4 cups mixed vegetables

1. Set the Instant Pot to Sauté and heat the olive oil. Cook the garlic for 2 minutes or until fragrant.
2. Add the vegetables and spices. Season with salt and cook for 5 minutes more.
3. Add the stock and lentils and stir well.
4. Lock the lid. Select the Manual mode, then set the timer for 12 minutes at High Pressure.
5. Once the timer goes off, do a natural pressure release for 10 minutes, then release any remaining pressure. Carefully open the lid.
6. Serve immediately.

Salsa Verde Cannellini Bean Chili

Prep time: 10 minutes | Cook time: 10 minutes | Serves 4 to 6

1 tablespoon olive oil
1 yellow onion, diced
1 green bell pepper, deseeded and diced
1 jalapeño pepper, deseeded and diced
1 clove garlic, grated
2 (15.5-ounce / 439-g) cans cannellini beans, drained and rinsed

1 cup salsa verde
1 teaspoon ground cumin
1 teaspoon ground coriander
¼ teaspoon cayenne pepper
4 cups vegetable stock
Salt and freshly ground black pepper, to taste
4 ounces (113 g) plant-based cheese, softened

1. Press Sauté button on the Instant Pot and allow the pot to heat for 2 minutes.
2. Add the oil, onion, bell pepper and jalapeño to the pot. Sauté for 3 minutes. Stir in the garlic.
3. Add the beans, salsa verde, cumin, coriander, cayenne, stock, and salt and black pepper, to taste. Stir to combine.
4. Secure the lid. Press Manual button and set cooking time for 5 minutes on High Pressure.
5. When timer beeps, quick release the pressure. Remove the lid and mix in the plant-based cheese.
6. Serve immediately.

Salmon Stew

Prep time: 6 mins, Cook Time:13 mins, Servings: 9

2 tbsps. olive oil
3 garlic cloves, minced
3 cups water

3 lbs. salmon fillets
Salt and pepper, to taste
3 cups spinach leaves

1. Press the Sauté button on the Instant Pot and heat the olive oil.
2. Sauté the garlic for a minute until fragrant.
3. Add the water and salmon fillets. Sprinkle salt and pepper for seasoning.
4. Lock the lid. Set on the Manual mode, then set the timer to 10 minutes at Low Pressure.
5. When the timer goes off, perform a quick release.
6. Carefully open the lid. Press the Sauté button and add the spinach.
7. Allow to simmer for 3 minutes.
8. Serve warm.

Tuscan Sausage and Kale Soup

Prep time: 15 minutes | Cook time: 13 minutes | Serves 3

1 bacon slice, chopped
6 ounces (170 g) Italian sausages, chopped
2 ounces (57 g) scallions, diced

½ teaspoon garlic powder
¼ cup cauliflower, chopped
1 cup kale, chopped
3 cups chicken broth
¼ cup heavy cream

1. Heat the the Instant Pot on Sauté mode for 3 minutes.
2. Add chopped bacon and cook for 2 minutes on Sauté mode until curls and buckles.
3. Mix in the Italian sausages, scallions, garlic powder, and cauliflower.
4. Cook for 5 minutes on Sauté mode.
5. Add kale, chicken broth, and heavy cream.
6. Select Manual mode and set cooking time for 6 minutes on High Pressure.
7. When timer beeps, make a quick pressure release. Open the lid.
8. Serve immediately.

White Bean Green Soup

Prep time: 5 minutes | Cook time: 20 minutes | Serves 6

1 tablespoon vegetable oil
4 large cloves garlic, minced
2 cups diced carrots
1 cup diced onion
1 cup diced celery
2 cups sliced cremini, shiitake, maitake, or baby bella mushrooms
2 tablespoons dried herbes de Provence
1 bay leaf
1 teaspoon red pepper flakes
½ teaspoon freshly ground

black pepper, plus additional for serving
5 cups vegetable broth
2 cups water
¼ cup tomato paste
1½ cups dried cannellini beans, soaked for 12 hours or overnight, rinsed
8 cups loosely packed greens
Juice of 1 large lemon (about 3 tablespoons)
1 to 1½ teaspoons salt (optional)

1. Press the Sauté button on the Instant Pot and heat the oil.
2. Add the garlic, carrots, onion, and celery and sauté for 3 minutes.
3. Add the mushrooms and seasonings and sauté for 3 to 5 minutes more. Add the vegetable broth, water, and tomato paste. Stir well.
4. Stir in the beans and greens.
5. Secure the lid. Select the Manual mode and set the cooking time for 8 minutes at High Pressure.
6. Once cooking is complete, do a natural pressure release for 10 minutes, then release any remaining pressure. Carefully open the lid.
7. Stir in the lemon juice and taste before adding salt. Remove the bay leaf and serve with additional black pepper.

Veggie Stew

Prep time: 40 mins, Cook Time: 20 mins, Servings: 4

1 tbsp. olive oil
1 onion, minced
1 package mixed frozen vegetables

4 cups vegetable broth
20 oz. tomato sauce
2 tsps. Italian seasoning
Salt and pepper, to taste

1. Set the Instant Pot to Sauté and heat the olive oil.
2. Cook the onion for 1 minute until translucent. Add the frozen vegetables and cook for 5 minutes, stirring frequently.
3. Add the remaining ingredients and stir to combine.
4. Lock the lid. Select the Manual mode, then set the timer for 15 minutes at High Pressure.
5. Once the timer goes off, do a quick pressure release. Carefully open the lid.
6. Serve immediately.

Kale and White Bean Soup

Prep time: 30 mins, Cook Time: 13 mins, Servings: 10

3 tbsps. olive oil
1 (28 oz) can diced tomatoes
4 cups kale

1 white onion, chopped
30 oz. white cannellini beans
4 cups vegetable stock

1. Set the Instant Pot to Sauté and heat the olive oil.
2. Sauté the white onion for 3 minutes, stirring occasionally.
3. Add the tomatoes, beans, and vegetable stock, and whisk well.
4. Lock the lid. Select the Manual mode, then set the timer for 10 minutes at High Pressure.
5. Once the timer goes off, do a quick pressure release. Carefully open the lid.
6. Stir in the kale.
7. Cover the pot and let rest for a few minutes until the kale is wilted. Serve warm.

Winter Chili

Prep time: 10 minutes | Cook time: 15 minutes | Serves 4 to 6

3 tablespoons olive oil
2 cloves garlic, minced
2 leeks, white and tender green parts, halved lengthwise and thinly sliced
2 jalapeño chiles, deseeded and diced
1 teaspoon fine sea salt
1 canned chipotle chile in adobo sauce, minced
3 tablespoons chili powder

1 cup vegetable broth
2 carrots, peeled and diced
1 (15-ounce / 425-g) can black beans, rinsed and drained
1 (1-pound / 454-g) delicata squash, deseeded and diced
1 (14.5-ounce / 411-g) can diced fire-roasted tomatoes
Chopped fresh cilantro, for serving

1. Select the Sauté setting on the Instant Pot, add the oil and garlic, and heat for 2 minutes, until the garlic is bubbling.
2. Add the leeks, jalapeños, and salt and sauté for 5 minutes, until the leeks are wilted.
3. Add the chipotle chile and chili powder and sauté for 1 minute more. Stir in the broth.
4. Add the carrots, beans and the squash. Pour the tomatoes and their liquid over the top. Do not stir.
5. Secure the lid. Select Manual mode and set the cooking time for 5 minutes at High Pressure.
6. When timer beeps, perform a quick pressure release. Open the pot, give a stir.
7. Ladle the chili into bowls and sprinkle with cilantro. Serve hot.

Swiss Chard and White Bean Stew

Prep time: 6 minutes | Cook time: 10 minutes | Serves 4 to 6

1 tablespoon olive oil
2 carrots, sliced, with thicker end cut into half-moons
1 celery stalk, sliced
½ onion, cut into large dices
2 or 3 garlic cloves, minced
3 tomatoes, chopped
¼ to ½ teaspoon red pepper flakes
½ teaspoon dried oregano
½ teaspoon dried rosemary

½ teaspoon salt, plus more as needed
¼ teaspoon dried basil
Pinch freshly ground black pepper, plus more as needed
2 cups cooked great northern beans
1 small bunch Swiss chard leaves, chopped
Nutritional yeast, for sprinkling (optional)

1. Set your Instant Pot to Sauté and heat the olive oil until it shimmers.
2. Add the carrots, celery, and onion. Sauté for 2 to 3 minutes, stirring occasionally. Add the garlic and cook for 30 seconds more. Turn off the Instant Pot.
3. Stir in the tomatoes, red pepper flakes, oregano, rosemary, salt, basil, black pepper, and beans.
4. Secure the lid. Select the Manual mode and set the cooking time for 4 minutes at High Pressure.
5. Once cooking is complete, do a quick pressure release. Carefully open the lid.
6. Stir in the Swiss chard and let sit for 2 to 3 minutes until wilted. Taste and season with salt and pepper, as needed. Sprinkle the nutritional yeast over individual servings, if desired.

Spring Veggie Chili

Prep time: 3 minutes | Cook time: 9 minutes | Serves 4

1 (8-ounce / 227-g) can cannellini beans, rinsed
2 radishes, trimmed, sliced
1 cup sliced carrots
1 cup fennel bulb, sliced
¼ cup onion, chopped
2 tablespoon shallots, chopped
¼ cup chopped celery
2 cloves garlic, chopped
1 cup tomato paste
1 teaspoon chipotle powder

½ cup vegetable broth
½ teaspoon cumin
1 teaspoon dried oregano
Pinch of rosemary
Pinch of cayenne
Salt and ground black pepper, to taste
1 medium zucchini, cubed
½ cup corn kernels
2 cherry tomatoes, quartered

1. Combine all ingredients, into the Instant pot, except the zucchinis, corn, and cherry tomatoes.
2. Lock the lid and select Manual mode. Set cooking time for 8 minutes on High Pressure.
3. When timer beeps, use a natural pressure release for 5 minutes, then release any remaining pressure. Open the lid.
4. Stir in the zucchinis, corn, and tomatoes. Lock the lid and set cooking time for 1 minute on High Pressure on Manual mode.
5. When timer beeps, perform a quick pressure release and open the lid.
6. Serve warm.

Veal and Buckwheat Groat Stew

Prep time: 12 mins, Cook Time: 50 mins, Servings: 4

¼ cup buckwheat groats
1 tsp. olive oil
1 onion, chopped

7 oz. veal shoulder
3 cups low-sodium beef stock
Salt and pepper, to taste

1. Add the buckwheat and pour in enough water to cover the buckwheat in the Instant Pot. Stir the ingredients to combine well.
2. Lock the lid. Press Manual. Set the timer to 12 minutes at Low Pressure.
3. Once the timer goes off, press Cancel. Do a natural pressure release, then release any remaining pressure.
4. Drain water and set the buckwheat aside.
5. Press the Sauté bottom on the Instant Pot.
6. Add and heat the olive oil.
7. Add the onions and cook for 3 minutes until translucent.
8. Add the veal shoulder and sauté for 4 to 5 minutes to evenly brown.
9. Pour in the beef stock. Sprinkle with salt and pepper.
10. Lock the lid. Press Manual. Set the timer to 30 minutes at High Pressure.
11. Once the timer goes off, press Cancel. Do a natural pressure release for 8 to 10 minutes.
12. Open the lid, mix in the buckwheat and transfer them in a large bowl and serve.

Flageolet Bean and Millet Stew

Prep time: 10 minutes | Cook time: 20 minutes | Serves 6

1 teaspoon olive oil
¼ cup sliced shallot
1 apple, diced
½ cup diced parsnip
1 golden beet, diced
1½ cups dried flageolet beans, soaked in water overnight, rinsed and drained
½ cup millet
1 (14-ounce / 398-g) can diced

tomatoes
1 bay leaf
1 teaspoon whole fennel seed, crumbled
1 teaspoon dried thyme
1 teaspoon dried sweet basil
2½ cups vegetable broth
2½ cups water
1 to 2 tablespoons lemon juice
¼ teaspoon black pepper

1. In the Instant Pot, heat the oil on Sauté mode.
2. Add the shallot and sauté for 1 minute to soften a bit.
3. Add the apple, parsnip, and beet and sauté for 4 minutes.
4. Add the beans, millet, diced tomatoes, bay leaf, fennel, thyme, and basil. Stir to combine.
5. Cover the vegetables and beans with broth and water by 3 inches.
6. Secure the lid. Select Manual mode and set cooking time for 10 minutes on High Pressure.
7. When timer beeps, use a natural pressure release for 15 minutes, then release any remaining pressure.
8. Remove the lid and stir in the lemon juice. Remove the bay leaf before serving. Add ground pepper and serve.

Black Bean and Sweet Potato Stew

Prep time: 5 minutes | Cook time: 30 minutes | Serves 6

2 tablespoons avocado oil
4 cups vegetable broth
½ cup chopped onion
4 cloves garlic, minced
2 carrots, chopped
1 large sweet potato, diced into equal, bite-size pieces
2 small tomatoes, diced

3 stalks celery, chopped
½ teaspoon ground cinnamon
1 teaspoon garam masala
1 cup dried black beans, rinsed and drained
2 bay leaves
½ teaspoon sea salt
¼ teaspoon black pepper

1. In the Instant Pot, heat the oil on Sauté mode.
2. Add the onion and garlic and sauté for 2 minutes until the onion is soft.
3. Add the carrots and sweet potato and sauté for another 3 minutes.
4. Add the tomatoes, celery, cinnamon, and garam masala and stir to coat all the vegetables with the spices.
5. Add the black beans, bay leaves, and vegetable broth. Stir to combine.
6. Secure the lid. Select Manual mode and set cooking time for 24 minutes.
7. When timer beeps, use a natural pressure release for 15 minutes, then release any remaining pressure.
8. Remove the lid, remove the bay leaves, stir in the salt and pepper, and serve.

West African Chickpea Stew

Prep time: 5 minutes | Cook time: 7 minutes | Serves 6

1½ tablespoons refined coconut oil
1 large yellow onion, diced
6 garlic cloves, minced
2-inch piece fresh ginger, grated or minced
1 Scotch bonnet pepper, deseeded and minced
1 teaspoon ground coriander
1 teaspoon ground turmeric
¼ teaspoon ground cinnamon
½ teaspoon dried thyme
1½ teaspoons ground cumin
½ teaspoon freshly cracked black pepper
¼ teaspoon ground cloves
2 cups vegetable broth

1 pound (454 g) sweet potatoes, peeled and cut into ¾-inch cubes
1½ teaspoons kosher salt
½ cup peanut butter
1 (15-ounce / 425-g) can chickpeas, drained and rinsed
1 (28-ounce / 794-g) can crushed tomatoes
3 tablespoons tomato paste
4 cups kale, stems and midribs removed and sliced into strips
½ cup fresh cilantro, roughly chopped
1 tablespoon fresh lime juice
⅓ cup roasted peanuts, roughly chopped

1. Select the Sauté setting on the Instant Pot and let the pot heat for a few minutes before adding the oil.
2. Once the oil is hot, add the onion. Cook until the onion is softened, about 3 to 4 minutes.
3. Add the garlic, ginger, and chile pepper and cook for 1 minute, tossing frequently.
4. Add the coriander, turmeric, cinnamon, thyme, cumin, black pepper, and cloves. Stir the spices into the vegetables and cook until the mixture is fragrant, about 30 seconds.
5. Pour in the vegetable broth to deglaze the pan, using a wooden spoon to scrape up any browned bits on the bottom of the pot.
6. Add the sweet potatoes, salt, peanut butter, and chickpeas. Stir to combine.
7. Pour the crushed tomatoes and tomato paste on top, but do not stir, allowing the tomatoes and paste to sit on top.
8. Secure the lid. Select the Manual mode and set the cook time to 5 minutes on High Pressure.
9. When timer beeps, allow a natural pressure release for 5 minutes, then release any remaining pressure.
10. Open the pot and stir in the kale. Select the Sauté setting and cook until wilted and cooked through, about 2 minutes. Stir in the cilantro and lime juice.
11. Transfer the stew to bowls and garnish with the roasted peanuts. Serve immediately.

Chapter 12 Appetizers and Snacks

Bacon Stuffed Mini Peppers

Prep time: 15 minutes | Cook time: 16 minutes | Serves 4

1 ounce (28 g) bacon, chopped
1 garlic clove, minced
2 tablespoons chopped onion
½ teaspoon Worcestershire sauce
2 ounces (57 g) Mexican cheese blend, crumbled
½ teaspoon Taco seasoning
4 mini sweet bell peppers, deseeded and membranes removed
1 cup water
1 tablespoon fresh cilantro, chopped

1.Press the Sauté button of the Instant Pot. Add and cook the bacon for 8 minutes or until it is crisp. Flip the bacon halfway through and crumble with a spatula. Set aside.
2.Add and cook the garlic and onion for 3 minutes or until tender and fragrant.
3.Add the Worcestershire sauce, cheese, and Taco seasoning. Stir in the reserved bacon.
4.Divide the mixture among the peppers on a clean work surface.
5.Pour the water in the Instant Pot. Arrange a trivet over the water. Place the stuffed peppers onto the trivet.
6.Secure the lid. Choose the Manual mode and set the cooking time for 5 minutes at High pressure.
7.Once cooking is complete, perform a natural pressure release for 5 minutes, then release any remaining pressure. Carefully open the lid.
8.Serve the bacon stuffed pepper on a platter garnished with fresh cilantro.

Wheat Berry and Celery Salad

Prep time: 15 minutes | Cook time: 40 minutes | Serves 12

1½ tablespoons vegetable oil
6¾ cups water
1½ cups wheat berries
1½ teaspoons Dijon mustard
1 teaspoon granulated sugar
1 teaspoon sea salt
½ teaspoon freshly ground black pepper
¼ cup white wine vinegar
½ cup extra-virgin olive oil
½ small red onion, peeled and diced
2 medium stalks celery, finely diced
1 medium zucchini, peeled, grated and drained
1 medium red bell pepper, deseeded and diced
4 green onions, diced
1⅓ cups frozen corn, thawed
¼ cup diced sun-dried tomatoes
¼ cup chopped fresh Italian flat-leaf parsley

1.Add the vegetable oil, water, and wheat berries to the Instant Pot.
2.Set the lid in place. Select the Multigrain mode and set the cooking time for 40 minutes on High Pressure. When the timer goes off, do a quick pressure release. Carefully open the lid.
3.Fluff the wheat berries with a fork. Drain and transfer to a large bowl.
4.Make the dressing by processing the mustard, sugar, salt, pepper, vinegar, olive oil, and red onion in a food processor until smooth.
5.Stir ½ cup of the dressing into the cooled wheat berries. Toss the seasoned wheat berries with the remaining ingredients.
6.Serve immediately. Cover and refrigerate any leftover dressing up to 3 days.

Bacon Wrapped Wieners

Prep time: 15 minutes | Cook time: 3 minutes | Serves 10

1 pound (454 g) cocktail wieners
½ pound (227 g) bacon, cut into slices
2 tablespoons apple cider vinegar
¼ cup ketchup
1 tablespoon ground mustard
1 tablespoon onion powder
½ cup chicken broth
Salt and ground black pepper, to taste
½ cup water

1.Wrap each cocktail wiener with a slice of bacon and secure with a toothpick.
2.Lay the bacon-wrapped cocktail wieners in the bottom of the Instant Pot. Repeat with the remaining cocktail wieners.
3.In a bowl, combine the remaining ingredients. Stir to mix well. Pour the mixture over the bacon-wrapped cocktail wieners.
4.Secure the lid. Choose the Manual mode and set the cooking time for 3 minutes on Low Pressure.
5.Once cooking is complete, perform a natural pressure release for 5 minutes, then release any remaining pressure. Carefully open the lid.
6.Serve immediately.

Beery Shrimp with Thai Sauce

Prep time: 10 minutes | Cook time: 10 minutes | Serves 10

Thai Sauce:
¼ cup Thai sweet chili sauce
1 tablespoon Sriracha sauce
¼ cup sour cream
2 teaspoons lime juice
½ cup mayonnaise
Shrimp:
1 (12-ounce / 340-g) bottle beer
4 pounds (1.8 kg) large shrimp, shelled and deveined

1.Combine ingredients for the Thai sauce in a small bowl. Cover the bowl in plastic and refrigerate until ready to serve.
2.Pour the beer into the Instant Pot and insert the steamer basket. Place shrimp in basket.
3.Lock the lid. Press the Steam button and set the cook time for 10 minutes on Low Pressure.
4.When timer beeps, quick release the pressure and then unlock the lid.
5.Transfer shrimp to a serving dish and serve with the Thai sauce.

Crab Spread

Prep time: 12 mins, Cook Time: 15 mins, Servings: 4

1 tsp. Worcestershire sauce
½ bunch scallions, chopped
½ cup sour cream
¼ cup half-and-half
8 oz. crab meat

1.In the Instant Pot, mix the crabmeat with sour cream, half-and-half, scallions and Worcestershire sauce, and stir to combine well.
2.Lock the lid. Select the Manual mode, then set the timer for 15 minutes at Low Pressure.
3.Once the timer goes off, do a quick pressure release. Carefully open the lid.
4.Allow the spread cool for a few minutes and serve.

Bacon and Broccoli Salad

Prep time: 12 mins, Cook Time: 12 mins, Servings: 4

1½ cups water
½ tbsp. apple cider vinegar
¼ cup chopped cilantro

2 tbsps. olive oil
1 head broccoli, cut into florets
4 bacon slices, chopped

1. Add the water and steamer basket to the Instant Pot. Arrange the broccoli florets in the basket.
2. Lock the lid. Select the Manual mode, then set the timer for 3 minutes at High Pressure.
3. Once the timer goes off, do a quick pressure release. Carefully open the lid.
4. Drain the broccoli and transfer to a bowl.
5. Clean the pot and set it to Sauté. Add the bacon, stir and cook for 4 minutes per side until it's crispy.
6. Roughly chop broccoli and return it to the Instant Pot. Stir and cook for 1 minute more.
7. Add the oil, cilantro and vinegar, and mix well. Remove from the heat to a plate and serve.

Apple and Brussels Sprout Appetizer

Prep time: 12 mins, Cook Time: 6 mins, Servings: 4

1½ cups water
1 lb. halved Brussels sprouts
1 cup dried cranberries
2 tbsps. canola oil

1 green apple, cored and
roughly chopped
2 tbsps. lemon juice

1. Pour the water into the Instant Pot and arrange the steamer basket in the pot, then add Brussels sprouts.
2. Lock the lid. Select the Manual mode, then set the timer for 4 minutes at High Pressure.
3. Once the timer goes off, do a quick pressure release. Carefully open the lid.
4. Drain the Brussels sprouts and transfer to a bowl.
5. Clean the pot and set it to Sauté. Heat the oil and add Brussels sprouts, stir and cook for 1 minute.
6. Stir in apple, cranberries and lemon juice, and cook for 1 minute. Serve warm.

Cauliflower Tots

Prep time: 15 minutes | Cook time: 23 minutes | Serves 6

1 cup water
1 head cauliflower, broken into
florets
2 eggs, beaten
½ cup grated Parmesan
cheese

½ cup grated Swiss cheese
2 tablespoons fresh coriander,
chopped
1 shallot, chopped
Sea salt and ground black
pepper, to taste

1. Add the water to the Instant Pot. Set a steamer basket in the pot.
2. Arrange the cauliflower florets in the steamer basket.
3. Secure the lid. Choose the Manual mode and set the cooking time for 3 minutes at High Pressure.
4. Once cooking is complete, perform a quick pressure release. Carefully open the lid.
5. Mash the cauliflower in a food processor and add the remaining ingredients. Pulse to combine well.
6. Form the mixture into a tater-tot shape with oiled hands.
7. Place cauliflower tots on a lightly greased baking sheet. Bake in the preheated oven at 400°F (205°C) for about 20 minutes. Flip halfway through the cooking time.
8. Serve immediately.

Broccoli and Brussels Sprout Salad

Prep time: 12 mins, Cook Time: 6 mins, Servings: 6

1½ cups water
2 tsps. mustard
1 head broccoli, cut into florets

½ cup walnut oil
1 lb. halved Brussels sprouts
¼ cup balsamic vinegar

1. Put the water in the Instant Pot and arrange the steamer basket in the pot, then add broccoli and Brussels sprouts.
2. Lock the lid. Select the Manual mode, then set the timer for 4 minutes at High Pressure.
3. Once the timer goes off, do a quick pressure release. Carefully open the lid.
4. Drain the vegetables and transfer to a bowl.
5. Clean the pot and set it to Sauté. Heat the oil and add broccoli and Brussels sprouts. Stir and cook for 1 minute.
6. Drizzle with the vinegar and cook for 1 minute more, then transfer to a bowl.
7. Add the mustard and toss well. Serve immediately or refrigerate to chill.

Beet and Carrot Spread

Prep time: 12 mins, Cook Time: 12 mins, Servings: 6

1 bunch basil, chopped
8 carrots, chopped
¼ cup lemon juice

4 beets, peeled and chopped
1 cup vegetable stock

1. In the Instant Pot, combine the beets with stock and carrots.
2. Lock the lid. Select the Manual mode and set the cooking time for 12 minutes at High Pressure.
3. Once cooking is complete, do a quick pressure release. Carefully open the lid.
4. Blend the ingredients with an immersion blender, and add the lemon juice and basil, and whisk well. Serve immediately.

Cashew and Hummus Spread

Prep time: 12 mins, Cook Time: 6 mins, Servings: 8

¼ cup nutritional yeast
¼ tsp. garlic powder
½ cup soaked and drained

cashews
10 oz. hummus
½ cup water

1. In the Instant Pot, combine the cashews and water.
2. Lock the lid. Select the Manual mode, then set the timer for 6 minutes at High Pressure.
3. Once the timer goes off, do a quick pressure release. Carefully open the lid.
4. Transfer the cashews to the blender, and add hummus, yeast and garlic powder, and pulse until well combined. Serve immediately.

Barbecue Chicken Meatballs

Prep time: 6 mins, Cook Time: 15 mins, Servings: 8

24 oz. frozen chicken meatballs
½ tsp. crushed red pepper
12 oz. barbecue sauce

¼ cup water
12 oz. apricot preserves

1. Add all the ingredients to the Instant Pot. Stir to mix well.
2. Lock the lid. Select the Manual mode, then set the timer for 5 minutes at High Pressure.
3. Once the timer goes off, do a quick pressure release. Carefully open the lid.
4. Serve the meatballs on a platter.

Broccoli and Cheddar Salad
Prep time: 12 mins, Cook Time: 4 mins, Servings: 4

1½ cups water
2 tbsps. balsamic vinegar
4 oz. cubed Cheddar cheese

1 cup mayonnaise
1 head broccoli, cut into florets
⅛ cup pumpkin seeds

1. Put the water into the Instant Pot and arrange the steamer basket in the pot, then add the broccoli.
2. Lock the lid. Select the Manual mode, then set the timer for 3 minutes at High Pressure.
3. Once the timer goes off, do a quick pressure release. Carefully open the lid.
4. Drain the broccoli and chop, then transfer to a bowl.
5. Add the cheese, pumpkin seeds, mayo and vinegar, and toss to combine. Serve immediately.

Shrimp and Tomatoes
Prep time: 12 mins, Cook Time: 4 mins, Servings: 6

1 lb. shrimp, shelled and deveined
2 tbsps. butter
1 cup crumbled feta cheese

1½ cups chopped onion
15 oz. chopped canned tomatoes

1. Set the Instant Pot to Sauté and melt the butter.
2. Add the onion, stir, and cook for 2 minutes.
3. Add the shrimp and tomatoes and mix well.
4. Lock the lid. Select the Manual mode, then set the timer for 2 minutes at Low Pressure.
5. Once the timer goes off, do a quick pressure release. Carefully open the lid.
6. Divide shrimp and tomatoes mixture into small bowls. Top with feta cheese and serve.

Chili Endives Platter
Prep time: 12 mins, Cook Time: 7 mins, Servings: 4

¼ tsp. chili powder
1 tbsp. butter
4 trimmed and halved endives

1 tbsp. lemon juice
Salt, to taste

1. Set the Instant Pot to Sauté and melt the butter. Add the endives, salt, chili powder and lemon juice to the pot.
2. Lock the lid. Select the Manual mode, then set the timer for 7 minutes at High Pressure.
3. Once the timer goes off, do a quick pressure release. Carefully open the lid.
4. Divide the endives into bowls. Drizzle some cooking juice over them and serve.

Carrot Salad
Prep time: 12 mins, Cook Time: 3 mins, Servings: 4

1 lb. carrots, grated
¼ cup water
Salt, to taste

1 tbsp. lemon juice
1 tsp. red pepper flakes
1 tbsp. chopped parsley

1. In the Instant Pot, mix the carrots with water and salt.
2. Lock the lid. Select the Manual mode, then set the timer for 3 minutes at High Pressure.
3. Once the timer goes off, do a quick pressure release. Carefully open the lid.
4. Drain the carrots and cool them in a bowl.
5. Add the lemon juice, pepper flakes and parsley to the bowl, and toss well. Serve immediately.

Vegetable Chicken Skewers
Prep time: 15 minutes | Cook time: 5 minutes | Serves 4

1 cup water
1 pound (454 g) chicken breast halves, boneless and skinless
Celery salt and ground black pepper, to taste
½ teaspoon Sriracha sauce

1 zucchini, cut into thick slices
1 cup cherry tomatoes, halved
1 red onion, cut into wedges
¼ cup olives, pitted
1 tablespoon fresh lemon juice
2 tablespoons olive oil

Special Equipment:
4 bamboo skewers

1. Pour the water in the Instant Pot. Arrange a trivet in the pot. Place the chicken on the trivet.
2. Secure the lid. Choose Poultry mode and set the cooking time for 5 minutes at High Pressure.
3. Once cooking is complete, perform a natural pressure release for 5 minutes, then release any remaining pressure. Carefully open the lid.
4. Slice the chicken into cubes. Sprinkle chicken cubes with salt, pepper, and drizzle with Sriracha.
5. Thread the chicken cubes, zucchini, cherry tomatoes, onion, and olives onto bamboo skewers. Drizzle the lemon juice and olive oil over and serve.

Egg-Crusted Zucchini
Prep time: 5 minutes | Cook time: 5 minutes | Serves 2

1 zucchini, cut into ½-inch round slices
½ teaspoon dried dill
½ teaspoon paprika
1 egg

1½ tablespoons coconut flour
1 tablespoon milk
Salt and black pepper, to taste
1 tablespoon coconut oil

1. Whisk egg and milk in a bowl. Mix the salt, black pepper, paprika, dried dill, and flour in another bowl. Dip the zucchini slices in the egg mixture, then in the dry mixture.
2. Press the Sauté button on the Instant Pot and heat the oil. Add the zucchini slices to the pot and sauté for 5 minutes.
3. Serve immediately.

Cheesy Crab and Bacon Dip
Prep time: 30 minutes | Cook time: 14 minutes | Serves 8

8 bacon strips, sliced
½ cup coconut cream
1 cup grated Parmesan cheese, divided
2 poblano pepper, chopped
½ cup mayonnaise
2 tablespoons lemon juice

8 ounces (227 g) cream cheese
4 garlic cloves, minced
4 green onions, minced
Salt and black pepper, to taste
12 ounces (340 g) crab meat

1. Set the Instant Pot on sauté mode. Add the bacon and cook for 8 minutes or until crispy. Transfer onto a plate and pat dry with paper towels. Set aside.
2. In a bowl, mix the coconut cream with half of the Parmesan, poblano peppers, mayo, lemon juice, cream cheese, garlic, green onions, salt, pepper, crab meat and bacon and stir well.
3. Add the mixture to the Instant Pot. Spread the remaining Parmesan on top. Seal the Instant Pot lid and select the Manual mode. Set the cooking time 14 minutes on High Pressure.
4. Once cooking is complete, perform a quick pressure release. Carefully open the lid.
5. Divide into 8 bowls and serve immediately.

Pork and Beef Chili Nachos

Prep time: 25 minutes | Cook time: 45 minutes | Serves 8

1 tablespoon olive oil
1 medium green bell pepper, seeded and diced
1 small red onion, peeled and diced
4 ounces (113 g) ground pork
½ pound (227 g) ground beef
1 (4-ounce / 113-g) can chopped green chiles, with juice
1 (14.5-ounce / 411-g) can diced tomatoes, with juice

1 teaspoon garlic powder
1 tablespoon chili powder
1 teaspoon ground cumin
1 teaspoon salt
4 ounces (113 g) cream cheese
2 Roma tomatoes, deseeded and diced
½ cup shredded Cheddar cheese
4 scallions, sliced
1 bag corn tortilla chips

1. Press the Sauté button on the Instant Pot. Heat the olive oil until shimmering.
2. Add the bell pepper and onion to pot. Sauté for 5 minutes or until onions are translucent. Add the pork and beef and sauté for 5 more minutes.
3. Add the chiles with juice, tomatoes with juice, garlic powder, chili powder, cumin, and salt to pot and stir to combine.
4. Lock the lid. Press the Meat / Stew button and set the time for 35 minutes on High Pressure. When the timer beeps, let pressure release naturally for 10 minutes, then release any remaining pressure.
5. Unlock the lid. Stir in cream cheese until melted and evenly distributed.
6. Transfer chili mixture to a serving dish. Garnish with Roma tomatoes, Cheddar, and scallions. Serve warm with chips.

Guacamole

Prep time: 5 minutes | Cook time: 9 minutes | Serves 4

1 large onion, finely diced
4 tablespoons lemon juice
¼ cup cilantro, chopped
4 avocados, peeled and diced

3 tablespoons olive oil
3 jalapeños, finely diced
Salt and black pepper, to taste

1. Press the Sauté button on the Instant Pot and heat the oil. Add the onions to the pot and sauté for 3 minutes, or until tender. Stir in the remaining ingredients.
2. Set the lid in place. Select the Manual mode and set the cooking time for 6 minutes on High Pressure. When the timer goes off, do a quick pressure release. Carefully open the lid.
3. Serve immediately.

Brussels Sprout Salad

Prep time: 12 mins, Cook Time: 6 mins, Servings: 4

2 tbsps. apple cider vinegar
1 lb. halved Brussels sprouts
1 tbsp. olive oil

½ cup chopped pecans
1 tbsp. brown sugar
1½ cups water

1. Place the water in the Instant Pot and arrange the steamer basket in the pot, then add Brussels sprouts.
2. Lock the lid. Select the Manual mode, then set the timer for 4 minutes at High Pressure.
3. Once the timer goes off, do a quick pressure release. Carefully open the lid.
4. Drain the Brussels sprouts and transfer to a bowl.
5. Clean the pot and set it to Sauté. Heat the olive oil and add Brussels sprouts and vinegar, stir and cook for 1 minute.
6. Add the sugar and pecans, stir, and cook for 30 seconds more. Remove from the pot to a plate and serve.

Olive and Eggplant Spread

Prep time: 20 minutes | Cook time: 8 minutes | Serves 6

¼ cup olive oil
2 pounds (907 g) eggplant, peeled and cut into medium chunks
4 garlic cloves, minced
½ cup water

Salt and black pepper, to taste
1 tablespoon sesame seed paste
¼ cup lemon juice
1 bunch thyme, chopped
3 olives, pitted and sliced

1. Set the Instant Pot on Sauté mode. Add the olive oil and heat until shimmering.
2. Add eggplant pieces and Sauté for 5 minutes. Add the garlic, water, salt and pepper, then stir well.
3. Close the lid, set to the Manual mode and set the cooking time for 3 minutes on High Pressure.
4. Once cooking is complete, perform a quick pressure release. Carefully open the lid.
5. Transfer to a blender, then add sesame seed paste, lemon juice and thyme, pulse to combine well.
6. Transfer to bowls, sprinkle olive slices on top and serve.

Veggie and Egg Mix

Prep time: 5 minutes | Cook time: 8 minutes | Serves 8

16 eggs, beaten
2 sweet potatoes, peeled and shredded
2 red bell peppers, deseeded and chopped
2 onions, chopped

2 garlic cloves, minced
4 teaspoons chopped fresh basil
Salt and black pepper, to taste
2 tablespoons oil

1. Add all the ingredients to the Instant Pot and stir to combine.
2. Set the lid in place. Select the Manual mode and set the cooking time for 8 minutes on High Pressure. When the timer goes off, do a quick pressure release. Carefully open the lid.
3. Serve immediately.

Red Pepper Hummus

Prep time: 10 minutes | Cook time: 30 minutes | Makes 1½ cups

½ cup dried chickpeas
2 cups water
1 cup jarred roasted red peppers with liquid, chopped and divided
1 tablespoon tahini paste
1 tablespoon lemon juice
1 teaspoon lemon zest

¼ teaspoon ground cumin
2 cloves garlic, minced
¼ teaspoon smoked paprika
⅛ teaspoon cayenne pepper
¼ teaspoon salt
1 teaspoon sesame oil
1 tablespoon olive oil

1. Add chickpeas and water to the Instant Pot. Drain liquid from the roasted peppers into the pot. Set aside the drained peppers.
2. Lock the lid. Press the Beans / Chili button and set the time to 30 minutes on High Pressure. When the timer beeps, let pressure release naturally for 5 minutes, then release any remaining pressure. Unlock the lid.
3. Drain pot, reserving the liquid in a small bowl.
4. Make the hummus: Transfer the chickpeas into a food processor. Add ¼ cup of chopped red peppers, tahini paste, lemon juice and zest, cumin, garlic, smoked paprika, cayenne pepper, salt, sesame oil, and olive oil. If consistency is too thick, slowly add reserved liquid, 1 tablespoon at a time until it has a loose paste consistency.
5. Transfer the hummus to a serving dish. Garnish with remaining chopped roasted red peppers and serve.

Avocado Spread

Prep time: 12 mins, Cook Time: 2 mins, Servings: 4

1 cup coconut milk
2 pitted, peeled and halved
avocados
Juice of 2 limes
½ cup chopped cilantro
¼ tsp. stevia
1 cup water

1. In the Instant Pot, add the water and steamer basket. Place the avocados in the basket.
2. Lock the lid. Select the Manual mode and set the cooking time for 2 minutes at High Pressure.
3. Once cooking is complete, do a quick pressure release. Carefully open the lid.
4. Transfer the avocados to your blender, and add the cilantro, stevia, lime juice, and coconut milk, and blend, or until it reaches your desired consistency. Serve immediately or refrigerate to chill until ready to use.

Broccoli Appetizer

Prep time: 12 mins, Cook Time: 3 mins, Servings: 4

1 cup water
2 tbsps. mayonnaise
1 tbsp. honey
½ cup Greek yogurt
1 head broccoli, cut into florets
1 apple, cored and sliced

1. In the Instant Pot, add the water. Arrange the steamer basket in the pot, then add the broccoli inside.
2. Lock the lid. Select the Manual mode, then set the timer for 3 minutes at Low Pressure.
3. Once the timer goes off, do a quick pressure release. Carefully open the lid.
4. Drain the broccoli florets and transfer to a bowl. Add the apple, mayo, yogurt and honey, and toss well. Serve immediately.

Chinese Flavor Chicken Wings

Prep time: 10 minutes | Cook time: 16 minutes | Serves 6

1 teaspoon Sriracha sauce
2 teaspoons Chinese five-spice powder
¼ cup tamari
¼ cup apple cider vinegar
3 cloves garlic, minced
1 tablespoon light brown sugar
2 tablespoons sesame oil
5 scallions, sliced and separated into whites and greens
3 pounds (1.4 kg) chicken wings, separated at the joint
1 cup water
¼ cup toasted sesame seeds

1. In a large bowl, combine the Sriracha, Chinese five-spice powder, tamari, apple cider vinegar, garlic, brown sugar, sesame oil, and whites of scallions. Stir to mix well. Transfer 2 tablespoons of the sauce mixture to a small bowl and reserve until ready to use.
2. Add wings to the remaining sauce and toss to coat well. Wrap the bowl in plastic and refrigerate for at least 1 hour or up to overnight.
3. Add the water to the Instant Pot and insert a steamer basket. Place the chicken wings in the single layer in the steamer basket. Lock the lid.
4. Press the Manual button and set the cook time for 10 minutes on High Pressure. When the timer beeps, let pressure release naturally for 5 minutes, then release any additional pressure and unlock the lid.
5. Using a slotted spoon, transfer the wings to a baking sheet. Brush with 2 tablespoons of reserved sauce. Broil the wings in the oven for 3 minutes on each side to crisp the chicken.
6. Transfer the wings to a serving dish and garnish with sesame seeds and greens of scallions. Serve immediately.

Endive Salad

Prep time: 12 mins, Cook Time: 18 mins, Servings: 3

1 cup vegetable soup
3 big endives, roughly chopped
3 tbsps. heavy cream
2 tbsps. extra virgin olive oil
½ yellow onion, chopped

1. Set the Instant Pot to Sauté and heat the olive oil. Add the onion, stir and cook for 4 minutes until tender.
2. Add the endives, stir and cook for 4 minutes more. Pour in the stock and whisk to combine.
3. Lock the lid. Select the Manual mode, then set the timer for 10 minutes at High Pressure.
4. Once the timer goes off, do a quick pressure release. Carefully open the lid.
5. Stir in the heavy cream and cook for 1 minute. Remove from the pot and serve in bowls.

Chicken in Lettuce

Prep time: 15 minutes | Cook time: 13 to 15 minutes | Serves 4

6 ounces (170 g) chicken breasts
1 cup water
1 teaspoon sesame oil
½ small onion, finely diced
1 garlic clove, minced
½ teaspoon ginger, minced
Kosher salt and ground black pepper, to taste
1 tablespoon hoisin sauce
½ tablespoon soy sauce
1 tablespoon rice vinegar
½ head butter lettuce, leaves separated

1. Add the chicken breasts and water to the Instant Pot.
2. Secure the lid. Choose the Manual mode and set the cooking time for 8 minutes at High pressure.
3. Once cooking is complete, perform a quick pressure release. Carefully open the lid. Shred the chicken with forks.
4. Press the Sauté button and heat the sesame oil.
5. Add and cook the garlic and onion for 3 to 4 minutes or until softened.
6. Add the chicken and cook for 2 to 3 minutes more.
7. Stir in the hoisin sauce, rice vinegar, soy sauce, ginger, salt, and black pepper. Cook for another minute.
8. Spoon the chicken mixture over the lettuce leaves on a large plate, wrap and serve immediately.

Hungarian Squares

Prep time: 15 minutes | Cook time: 55 minutes | Serves 4

1¼ cup water, divided
1 cup yellow cornmeal
1 cup yogurt
1 egg, beaten
½ cups sour cream
1 teaspoon baking soda
2 tablespoons safflower oil
¼ teaspoon salt
4 tablespoons plum jam

1. Pour 1 cup of water in the Instant Pot. Set a trivet in the pot. Spritz a baking pan with cooking spray.
2. Combine the cornmeal, yogurt, egg, sour cream, baking soda, ¼ cup of water, safflower oil, and salt in a large bowl. Stir to mix well.
3. Pour the mixture into the prepared baking pan. Spread the plum jam over. Cover with aluminum foil. Lower the pan onto the trivet.
4. Secure the lid. Choose the Manual mode and set the cooking time for 55 minutes at High pressure. Once cooking is complete, perform a quick pressure release, carefully open the lid.
5. Transfer the corn meal chunk onto a cooling rack and allow to cool for 10 minutes. Slice into squares and serve.

Three Bean Salad with Parsley

Prep time: 10 minutes | Cook time: 30 minutes | Serves 8

⅓ cup apple cider vinegar
¼ cup granulated sugar
2½ teaspoons salt, divided
½ teaspoon freshly ground
black pepper
¼ cup olive oil
½ cup dried chickpeas
½ cup dried kidney beans
1 cup frozen green beans
pieces
4 cups water
1 tablespoon vegetable oil
1 cup chopped fresh Italian
flat-leaf parsley
½ cup peeled and diced
cucumber
½ cup diced red onion

1. For the dressing: In a small bowl, whisk together the vinegar, sugar, 1½ teaspoons of the salt and pepper. While whisking continuously, slowly add the olive oil. Once well combined, cover in plastic and refrigerate.
2. Add the chickpeas, kidney beans, green beans, water, vegetable oil, and the remaining 1 teaspoon of the salt to the Instant Pot. Stir to combine.
3. Lock the lid. Select the Manual mode and set the cooking time for 30 minutes on High Pressure. Once the timer goes off, perform a natural pressure release for 10 minutes, then release any remaining pressure. Carefully open the lid.
4. Transfer the cooked beans to a large mixing bowl. Stir in all the remaining ingredients along with the dressing. Toss to combine thoroughly. Cover and refrigerate for 2 hours before serving.

Wild Rice and Kale Salad

Prep time: 12 mins, Cook Time: 25 mins, Servings: 4

1 tsp. olive oil
1 avocado, peeled, pitted and
chopped
3 oz. goat cheese, crumbled
1 cup cooked wild rice
1 bunch kale, roughly chopped

1. Set the Instant Pot to Sauté and heat the olive oil.
2. Add the rice and toast for 2 to 3 minutes, stirring often.
3. Add kale and stir well.
4. Lock the lid. Select the Manual mode, then set the timer for 20 minutes at Low Pressure.
5. Once the timer goes off, do a natural pressure release for 10 minutes, then release any remaining pressure. Carefully open the lid.
6. Add avocado and toss well. Sprinkle the cheese on top and serve.

Pear and Apple Crisp

Prep time: 5 minutes | Cook time: 5 minutes | Serves 4

3 tablespoons butter, melted
1 teaspoon ground cinnamon
½ cup packed brown sugar
½ cup all-purpose flour
½ cup old-fashioned rolled oats
½ teaspoon freshly grated
nutmeg
2 apples, peeled and sliced
2 pears, peeled and sliced
½ cup water

1. Take a bowl and mix together the brown sugar, butter, oats, flour, cinnamon, and nutmeg.
2. Evenly layer the apples and pears in the inner pot. Then evenly spread the oat mixture on top of the fruit and pour the water on top of the oat mixture.
3. Set the lid in place. Select the Manual mode and set the cooking time for 5 minutes on High Pressure. When the timer goes off, do a quick pressure release. Carefully open the lid.
4. Stir the crisp. Select the Sauté mode and cook until it bubbles.
5. Serve warm.

Mushroom Lettuce Cups

Prep time: 5 minutes | Cook time: 9 minutes | Serves 4

1 tablespoon vegetable oil
¼ cup minced shallots
2 tablespoons cooking sherry
4 cups cremini mushrooms,
quartered
½ cup chopped water
chestnuts
¼ cup low-sodium soy sauce
¼ cup vegetable broth
¼ cup fresh basil
8 butter lettuce leaves

1. Press the Sauté button on the Instant Pot and heat the oil. Add the scallions to the pot and sauté for 3 minutes, or until tender. Add the cooking sherry and continue to cook for 2 minutes. Stir in the remaining ingredients, except for the lettuce leaves.
2. Set the lid in place. Select the Manual mode and set the cooking time for 4 minutes on High Pressure. When the timer goes off, do a quick pressure release. Carefully open the lid.
3. Select the Sauté mode and cook the mushroom mixture, stirring frequently, until the sauce thickens. Let cool for 5 minutes.
4. Spoon equal amounts of the mushroom mixture into lettuce leaves and serve.

Endives and Lemon Juice Appetizer

Prep time: 12 mins, Cook Time: 13 mins, Servings: 4

3 tbsps. olive oil
½ cup chicken stock
Juice of ½ lemon
2 tbsps. chopped parsley
8 endives, trimmed

1. Set the Instant Pot to Sauté and heat the olive oil. Add the endives and cook them for 3 minutes.
2. Add lemon juice and stock, and whisk well.
3. Lock the lid. Select the Manual mode, then set the timer for 10 minutes at High Pressure.
4. Once the timer goes off, do a quick pressure release. Carefully open the lid.
5. Transfer the endives to a large bowl. Drizzle some cooking juices all over and sprinkle with the chopped parsley before serving.

Citrus Buckwheat and Barley Salad

Prep time: 10 minutes | Cook time: 35 minutes | Serves 4

1 cup wheat berries
1 cup pearl barley
3 cups vegetable broth
¼ cup minced shallots
¼ cup olive oil
¼ cup lemon juice
2 cloves garlic, crushed and
minced
¼ cup pine nuts
1 cup finely chopped kale
1 cup chopped tomatoes
½ teaspoon salt
½ teaspoon black pepper

1. In the Instant Pot, combine the wheat berries, pearl barley, vegetable broth and shallots. Mix well.
2. Lock the lid. Select the Manual mode and set the cooking time for 35 minutes on High Pressure. Once the timer goes off, perform a natural pressure release for 20 minutes, then release any remaining pressure. Carefully open the lid.
3. Meanwhile, combine the olive oil, lemon juice and garlic in a bowl. Whisk until well combined.
4. Remove the grains from the cooker and transfer them to a large bowl. Allow them to sit out long enough to cool slightly.
5. Add the dressing, pine nuts, kale and tomatoes to the grains and stir.
6. Season with salt and black pepper, as desired.
7. Serve warm or cover and chill until ready to serve.

Carrot Fish Balls
Prep time: 12 mins, Cook Time: 10 mins, Servings: 16

¼ cup cornstarch
1 carrot, grated
1½ cups fish stock

3 egg whites
1½ lbs. skinless, boneless and ground pike fillets

1. In a bowl, mix the fillets with egg whites, cornstarch and carrot. Form the mixture into equal-sized balls with your hands.
2. Put the stock and fish balls into the Instant pot.
3. Lock the lid. Select the Manual function and cook for 10 minutes at Low Pressure.
4. Once cooking is complete, do a quick pressure release. Carefully open the lid.
5. Drain the fish balls and arrange them on a platter and serve.

Garlic-Ginger Egg Potatoes
Prep time: 5 minutes | Cook time: 10 minutes | Serves 3

2 eggs, whisked
1 teaspoon ground turmeric
1 teaspoon cumin seeds
2 tablespoons olive oil
2 potatoes, peeled and diced

1 onion, finely chopped
2 teaspoons ginger-garlic paste
½ teaspoon red chili powder
Salt and black pepper, to taste

1. Press the Sauté button on the Instant Pot and heat the oil. Add the cumin seed, ginger-garlic paste, and onions to the pot and sauté for 4 minutes. Stir in the remaining ingredients.
2. Set the lid in place. Select the Manual mode and set the cooking time for 6 minutes on High Pressure. When the timer goes off, do a quick pressure release. Carefully open the lid.
3. Serve immediately.

Green Olive Pâté
Prep time: 12 mins, Cook Time: 2 mins, Servings: 4

½ cup olive oil
2 anchovy fillets
1 tbsp. chopped capers

2 cups pitted green olives
2 garlic cloves, minced

1. In a food processor, process the olives with anchovy fillets, garlic, capers and olive oil, then transfer to the Instant Pot.
2. Lock the lid. Select the Manual mode, then set the timer for 2 minutes at Low Pressure.
3. Once the timer goes off, do a quick pressure release. Carefully open the lid.
4. Remove from the pot and serve warm.

Green Bean Salad
Prep time: 12 mins, Cook Time: 2 mins, Servings: 4

1 tbsp. red wine vinegar
1 lb. green beans
½ cup water

2 sliced red onions
1 tbsp. olive oil
1 tbsp. Creole mustard

1. In the Instant Pot, mix green beans with water.
2. Lock the lid. Select the Manual mode, then set the timer for 2 minutes at High Pressure.
3. Once the timer goes off, do a quick pressure release. Carefully open the lid.
4. Drain the green beans and transfer to a bowl. Add the onion slices, mustard, vinegar, and oil, and gently toss to combine. Serve immediately.

Greek Beef Meatballs
Prep time: 12 mins, Cook Time: 12 mins, Servings: 10

1 egg, whisked
¼ cup chopped mint
1 lb. ground beef

3 tbsps. olive oil
¼ cup white vinegar

1. In a bowl, mix the beef with mint and egg, and whisk well. Shape the beef mixture into 10 meatballs with your hands.
2. Set the Instant Pot to Sauté and heat the olive oil.
3. Add the beef meatballs and brown them for about 4 minutes on each side.
4. Add the vinegar and stir to mix well.
5. Lock the lid. Select the Manual mode, then set the timer for 4 minutes at High Pressure.
6. Once the timer goes off, do a quick pressure release. Carefully open the lid.
7. Divide the meatballs among plates and serve them with a yogurt dip on the side.

Jalapeño Peanuts
Prep time: 3 hours 20 minutes | Cook time: 45 minutes | Serves 4

4 ounces (113 g) raw peanuts in the shell
1 jalapeño, sliced
1 tablespoon Creole seasoning

½ tablespoon cayenne pepper
½ tablespoon garlic powder
1 tablespoon salt

1. Add all ingredients to the Instant Pot. Pour in enough water to cover. Stir to mix well. Use a steamer to gently press down the peanuts.
2. Secure the lid. Choose the Manual mode and set the cooking time for 45 minutes at High pressure.
3. Once cooking is complete, perform a natural pressure release for 15 minutes, then release any remaining pressure. Carefully open the lid.
4. Transfer the peanut and the liquid in a bowl, then refrigerate for 3 hours before serving.

Beef Patties with Lentil
Prep time: 25 minutes | Cook time: 25 minutes | Makes 15 patties

1 cup dried yellow lentils
2 cups beef broth
½ pound (227 g) 80/20 ground beef
½ cup chopped old-fashioned oats

2 large eggs, beaten
2 teaspoons Sriracha sauce
2 tablespoons diced yellow onion
½ teaspoon salt

1. Add the lentils and broth to the Instant Pot. Lock the lid.
2. Press the Manual button and set the cook time for 15 minutes on High Pressure. When the timer beeps, let pressure release naturally for 10 minutes, then release any remaining pressure. Unlock the lid.
3. Transfer the lentils to a medium bowl with a slotted spoon. Smash most of the lentils with the back of a spoon until chunky.
4. Add beef, oats, eggs, Sriracha, onion, and salt. Whisk to combine them well. Form the mixture into 15 patties.
5. Cook in a skillet on stovetop over medium-high heat in batches for 10 minutes. Flip the patties halfway through.
6. Transfer patties to serving dish and serve warm.

Carrot and Kale Salad

Prep time: 12 mins, Cook Time: 7 mins, Servings: 4

1 tbsp. olive oil
3 carrots, sliced
1 red onion, chopped
10 oz. kale, roughly chopped
½ cup chicken stock

1. Set the Instant Pot to Sauté and heat the olive oil.
2. Add the onion and carrots, stir, and cook for 1 to 2 minutes.
3. Stir in stock and kale.
4. Lock the lid. Select the Manual mode, then set the timer for 5 minutes at High Pressure.
5. Once the timer goes off, do a quick pressure release. Carefully open the lid.
6. Divide the vegetables among four bowls and serve.

Minty Kale and Pineapple Salad

Prep time: 12 mins, Cook Time: 3 mins, Servings: 4

2 tbsps. lemon juice
2 tbsps. chopped mint
1 bunch kale, roughly chopped
1 tsp. sesame oil
1 cup chopped pineapple

1. Set the Instant Pot to Sauté and heat the oil.
2. Add kale, stir, and cook for 1 minute.
3. Add pineapple, lemon juice and mint, and stir well. Divide the salad among plates and serve.

Mustard Flavored Artichokes

Prep time: 5 minutes | Cook time: 12 minutes | Serves 3

3 artichokes
3 tablespoons mayonnaise
1 cup water, for the pot
2 pinches paprika
2 lemons, sliced in half
2 teaspoons Dijon mustard

1. Mix mayonnaise, paprika, and mustard.
2. Pour the water and insert the trivet in the Instant Pot. Place the artichokes upwards and arrange the lemon slices on it.
3. Set the lid in place. Select the Manual mode and set the cooking time for 12 minutes on High Pressure. When the timer goes off, do a quick pressure release. Carefully open the lid.
4. Put the artichokes in the mayonnaise mixture. Serve.

Mussel Appetizer

Prep time: 20 minutes | Cook time: 10 minutes | Serves 4

¼ cup olive oil
28 ounces (794 g) canned tomatoes, chopped
2 jalapeño peppers, chopped
½ cup chopped white onion
¼ cup balsamic vinegar
¼ cup veggie stock
2 garlic cloves, minced
2 tablespoons crushed red pepper flakes
2 pounds (907 g) mussels, scrubbed
½ cup chopped basil
Salt, to taste

1. Press the Sauté button on the Instant Pot and heat the olive oil.
2. Add the tomatoes, jalapeño, onion, vinegar, veggie stock, garlic, and red pepper flakes and stir well. Cook for 5 minutes. Stir in the mussels.
3. Secure the lid. Select the Manual mode and set the cooking time for 4 minutes at Low Pressure.
4. Once cooking is complete, do a quick pressure release. Carefully open the lid.
5. Sprinkle with the basil and salt and stir well. Divide the mussels among four bowls and serve.

Herbed Button Mushrooms

Prep time: 10 minutes | Cook time: 4 minutes | Serves 4

6 ounces (170 g) button mushrooms, rinsed and drained
1 clove garlic, minced
½ cup vegetable broth
½ teaspoon dried basil
½ teaspoon onion powder
½ teaspoon dried oregano
⅓ teaspoon dried rosemary
½ teaspoon smoked paprika
Coarse sea salt and ground black pepper, to taste
1 tablespoon tomato paste
1 tablespoon butter

1. Put all the ingredients, except for the tomato paste and butter, in the Instant Pot. Stir to mix well.
2. Secure the lid. Choose the Manual mode and set the cooking time for 4 minutes at High pressure.
3. Once cooking is complete, perform a quick pressure release. Carefully open the lid.
4. Stir in the tomato paste and butter. Serve immediately.

Herbed Polenta Squares

Prep time: 1 hour 15 minutes | Cook time: 15 minutes | Serves 4

½ cup cornmeal
½ cup milk
1½ cups water
½ teaspoon kosher salt
½ tablespoon butter
⅓ cup cream cheese
1 tablespoon chives, finely chopped
1 tablespoon cilantro, finely chopped
½ teaspoon basil
½ tablespoon thyme
½ teaspoon rosemary
⅓ cup bread crumbs
1 tablespoon olive oil

1. Make the polenta: Add the cornmeal, milk, water, and salt to the Instant Pot. Stir to mix well.
2. Press the Sauté button and bring the mixture to a simmer.
3. Secure the lid. Choose the Manual mode and set the cooking time for 8 minutes at High pressure.
4. Once cooking is complete, perform a quick pressure release. Carefully open the lid.
5. Grease a baking pan with butter. Add the cream cheese and herbs to the polenta.
6. Scoop the polenta into the prepared baking pan and refrigerate for an hour or until firm. Cut into small squares. Spread the breadcrumbs on a large plate, coat the polenta squares with breadcrumbs.
7. Heat the olive oil in a skillet over medium heat.
8. Cook the polenta squares in the skillet for about 3 minutes per side or until golden brown. Serve immediately.

Honey Raisins and Carrots

Prep time: 5 minutes | Cook time: 5 minutes | Serves 3

1 pound (454 g) carrots, peeled and cut into chunks
2 tablespoons golden raisins
½ cup water
½ tablespoon honey
⅔ teaspoon crushed red pepper flakes
½ tablespoon melted butter
Salt, to taste

1. Add the carrots, raisins, and water to the Instant Pot
2. Secure the lid and select the Manual function. Set the cooking time for 5 minutes on Low Pressure.
3. When the timer beeps, do a quick release, then open the lid.
4. Strain the carrots and transfer them to a large bowl.
5. Put the remaining ingredients into the bowl and toss well.
6. Serve warm.

Honey Carrots

Prep time: 5 minutes | Cook time: 6 minutes | Serves 4

8 medium carrots
1 cup water
1 clove garlic, finely chopped
1 tablespoon honey
2 tablespoons soy sauce

½ tablespoon sesame seeds
Salt, to taste
Chopped green onions, for garnish

1. Add the carrots and water to the Instant Pot.
2. Set the lid in place. Select the Manual mode and set the cooking time for 3 minutes on High Pressure. When the timer goes off, do a quick pressure release. Carefully open the lid.
3. Remove the carrots. Drain the water.
4. Select the Sauté mode and add the remaining ingredients, except for the green onions and sesame seeds. Cook for 3 minutes, or until sticky.
5. Put the carrots back into the pot and coat well. Sprinkle with the green onions and seeds and serve.

Potato Cubes

Prep time: 5 minutes | Cook time: 10 minutes | Serves 2

2½ medium potatoes, scrubbed and cubed
1 tablespoon chopped fresh rosemary
½ tablespoon olive oil

Freshly ground black pepper, to taste
1 tablespoon fresh lemon juice
½ cup vegetable broth

1. Put the potatoes, rosemary, oil, and pepper to the Instant Pot. Stir to mix well.
2. Set to the Sauté mode and sauté for 4 minutes.
3. Fold in the remaining ingredients.
4. Secure the lid and select the Manual function. Set the cooking time for 6 minutes at High Pressure.
5. Once cooking is complete, do a quick release, then open the lid.
6. Serve warm.

Tomato and Parsley Quinoa Salad

Prep time: 5 minutes | Cook time: 21 minutes | Serves 4

2 tablespoons olive oil
2 cloves garlic, minced
1 cup diced tomatoes
¼ cup chopped fresh Italian flat-leaf parsley

1 tablespoon fresh lemon juice
1 cup quinoa
2 cups water
1 teaspoon salt

1. Press the Sauté button on the Instant Pot and heat the olive oil. Add the garlic and sauté for 30 seconds. Add the tomatoes, parsley and lemon juice. Sauté for an additional minute. Transfer the tomato mixture to a small bowl.
2. Add the quinoa and water to the Instant Pot.
3. Lock the lid. Select the Manual mode and set the cooking time for 20 minutes on High Pressure. Once the timer goes off, perform a natural pressure release for 10 minutes, then release any remaining pressure. Carefully open the lid.
4. Fluff the cooked quinoa with a fork. Stir in the tomato mixture and salt.
5. Serve immediately.

Watercress Appetizer Salad

Prep time: 12 mins, Cook Time: 2 mins, Servings: 4

1 bunch watercress, roughly torn
½ cup water
1 tbsp. lemon juice

1 cubed watermelon
1 tbsp. olive oil
2 peaches, pitted and sliced

1. In the Instant Pot, mix watercress with water.
2. Lock the lid. Select the Manual mode, then set the timer for 2 minutes at High Pressure.
3. Once the timer goes off, do a quick pressure release. Carefully open the lid.
4. Drain the watercress and transfer to a bowl. Add peaches, watermelon, oil, and lemon juice, and toss well. Divide the salad into salad bowls and serve.

Little Smokies with Grape Jelly

Prep time: 10 minutes | Cook time: 2 minutes | Serves 4

3 ounces (85 g) little smokies
2 ounces (57 g) grape jelly
¼ teaspoon jalapeño, minced
¼ cup light beer

¼ cup chili sauce
1 tablespoon white vinegar
½ cup roasted vegetable broth
2 tablespoons brown sugar

1. Place all ingredients in the Instant Pot. Stir to mix.
2. Secure the lid. Choose the Manual mode and set the cooking time for 2 minutes at High pressure.
3. Once cooking is complete, perform a quick pressure release. Carefully open the lid.
4. Serve hot.

Pinto Bean Dip

Prep time: 12 mins, Cook Time: 8 mins, Servings: 4

2 tbsps. chopped tomatoes
1 (8 oz) can pinto beans, drained

3 tbsps. lemon juice
1¼ cup chopped parsley
4 rosemary sprigs, chopped

1. In the Instant Pot, mix pinto beans with rosemary and tomatoes.
2. Lock the lid. Select the Manual mode, then set the timer for 8 minutes at High Pressure.
3. Once the timer goes off, do a quick pressure release. Carefully open the lid.
4. Blend the mixture with an immersion blender. Add the parsley and lemon juice, and pulse until well combined.
5. Store in an airtight container in the fridge until ready to serve.

Thyme Carrots

Prep time: 5 minutes | Cook time: 2 minutes | Serves 2

4 carrots, peeled and cut into sticks
1½ teaspoon fresh thyme

2 tablespoons butter
½ cup water
Salt, to taste

1. Press the Sauté button on the Instant Pot and melt the butter. Add the carrots, thyme, salt, and water to the pot.
2. Set the lid in place. Select the Manual mode and set the cooking time for 2 minutes on High Pressure. When the timer goes off, do a quick pressure release. Carefully open the lid.
3. Serve hot.

Red Wine Poached Pears

Prep time: 5 minutes | Cook time: 8 minutes | Serves 3

3 firm pears
½ teaspoon grated ginger
½ bottle red wine

½ grated cinnamon
1 cup granulated sugar
1 bay laurel leaf

1.Add all the ingredients to the Instant Pot and stir to combine.
2.Lock the lid. Select the Manual mode and set the cooking time for 8 minutes on High Pressure. Once the timer goes off, perform a natural pressure release for 10 minutes, then release any remaining pressure.
3.Carefully open the lid and transfer the pears to a bowl.
4.Select the Sauté mode and let the mixture simmer for 10 more minutes to reduce its consistency and drizzle the red wine sauce on pears.
5.Serve immediately.

Rhubarb Strawberry Tarts

Prep time: 5 minutes | Cook time: 5 minutes | Serves 12

1 pound (454 g) rhubarb, cut into small pieces
½ pound (227 g) strawberries
¼ cup minced crystallized ginger

½ cup honey
1 cup water
12 tart shells, short crust
½ cup whipped cream

1.Add all the ingredients, except for the tart shells and whipped cream, to the Instant Pot and stir to combine.
2.Lock the lid. Select the Manual mode and set the cooking time for 5 minutes on High Pressure. Once the timer goes off, perform a natural pressure release for 10 minutes, then release any remaining pressure. Carefully open the lid.
3.Place the mixture in the tart shells. Top with whipped cream and serve.

Vinegary Pearl Onion

Prep time: 5 minutes | Cook time: 5 minutes | Serves 4

1 pound (454 g) pearl onions, peeled
Pinch of salt and black pepper
½ cup water
1 bay leaf

4 tablespoons balsamic vinegar
1 tablespoon coconut flour
1 tablespoon stevia

1.In the pot, mix the pearl onions with salt, pepper, water, and bay leaf.
2.Set the lid in place. Select the Manual mode and set the cooking time for 5 minutes on Low Pressure. When the timer goes off, do a quick pressure release. Carefully open the lid.
3.Meanwhile, in a pan, add the vinegar, stevia, and flour. Mix and bring to a simmer. Remove from the heat. Pour over the pearl onions. Mix and serve.

Scallion and Mayo Spread

Prep time: 12 mins, Cook Time: 3 mins, Servings: 6

3 tbsps. chopped dill
1 cup sour cream
1 tbsp. grated lemon zest

½ cup chopped scallions
¼ cup mayonnaise

1.Set the Instant Pot to Sauté and add the scallions. Stir and cook for 1 minute.
2.Add the sour cream and stir to combine well.
3.Lock the lid. Select the Manual mode, then set the timer for 2 minutes at High Pressure.
4.Once the timer goes off, do a quick pressure release. Carefully open the lid.
5.Leave this mixture to rest until cooled completely. Add the mayo, dill, and lemon zest, and stir well. You can serve this with tortilla chips on the side.

Egg Spread

Prep time: 12 mins, Cook Time: 5 mins, Servings: 4

1 tbsp. olive oil
4 eggs
1 cup water

Salt, to taste
½ cup mayonnaise
2 green onions, chopped

1.Grease a baking dish with olive oil and crack the eggs in it.
2.Add the water and trivet to the Instant Pot. Place the baking dish on the trivet.
3.Lock the lid. Select the Manual mode, then set the timer for 5 minutes at High Pressure.
4.Once the timer goes off, do a natural pressure release for 3 to 5 minutes. Carefully open the lid.
5.Cool eggs down and mash them with a fork. Sprinkle with salt, mayo, and green onions. Stir well and serve immediately.

Ranch Spread

Prep time: 12 mins, Cook Time: 10 mins, Servings: 12

4 green onions, chopped
1 cup sour cream
1 lb. bacon, chopped

1 cup shredded Monterey Jack cheese
1 cup mayonnaise

1.Set the Instant Pot to Sauté and cook the bacon for about 4 minutes on each side until it is crispy.
2.Add the sour cream and green onions, and stir to mix well.
3.Lock the lid. Select the Manual mode, then set the timer for 6 minutes at High Pressure.
4.Once the timer goes off, do a natural pressure release for 5 minutes. Carefully open the lid.
5.Add the cheese and mayo and stir. Allow to cool for a few minutes and serve.

Spinach Mushroom Treat

Prep time: 5 minutes | Cook time: 11 minutes | Serves 3

½ cup spinach
½ pound (227 g) fresh mushrooms, sliced
2 garlic cloves, minced
2 tablespoons chopped fresh thyme
1 onion, chopped
1 tablespoon olive oil
1 tablespoon chopped fresh cilantro, for garnish
Salt and black pepper, to taste

1. Press the Sauté button on the Instant Pot and heat the oil. Add the garlic and onions to the pot and sauté for 4 minutes. Stir in the remaining ingredients.
2. Set the lid in place. Select the Manual mode and set the cooking time for 7 minutes on High Pressure. When the timer goes off, do a quick pressure release. Carefully open the lid.
3. Serve garnished with the cilantro.

Steamed Asparagus with Mustard Dip

Prep time: 7 mins, Cook Time: 8 mins, Servings: 4

1 tsp. Dijon mustard
2 tbsps. mayonnaise
Salt and black pepper, to taste
1 cup water
12 asparagus stems
3 tbsps. lemon juice

1. Mix the Dijon mustard, mayonnaise, salt and black pepper in a bowl. Set aside.
2. Set trivet to the Instant Pot and add the water.
3. Place asparagus stems on the trivet and drizzle with lemon juice.
4. Lock the lid. Select the Manual mode, then set the timer for 8 minutes at High Pressure.
5. Once the timer goes off, do a quick pressure release. Carefully open the lid.
6. Dip the asparagus into mustard mixture.

Stuffed Eggs

Prep time: 5 minutes | Cook time: 6 minutes | Serves 4

4 eggs
1½ tablespoons Greek yogurt
1½ tablespoons mayonnaise
½ teaspoon chopped jalapeño
¼ teaspoon onion powder
¼ teaspoon paprika
¼ teaspoon lemon zests
Salt and black pepper, to taste
1 cup water, for the pot

1. Pour the water and insert the trivet in the Instant Pot. Place the eggs on the trivet.
2. Set the lid in place. Select the Manual mode and set the cooking time for 6 minutes on High Pressure. When the timer goes off, do a quick pressure release. Carefully open the lid.
3. Place the eggs into ice-cold water. Peel the eggs, and cut in half, lengthwise. Scoop out the egg yolks and mix them with the remaining ingredients. Fill the hollow eggs with the mixture and serve.

Sweet Roasted Cashews

Prep time: 5 minutes | Cook time: 20 minutes | Serves 2

¾ cup cashews
¼ teaspoon salt
¼ teaspoon ginger powder
1 teaspoon minced orange
zest
4 tablespoons honey
1 cup water, for the pot

1. Stir together the honey, orange zest, ginger powder, and salt in a bowl. Add the cashews to the mixture and place it in a ramekin.
2. Pour the water and insert the trivet in the Instant Pot. Place the ramekin on the trivet.
3. Set the lid in place. Select the Manual mode and set the cooking time for 20 minutes on High Pressure. When the timer goes off, do a quick pressure release. Carefully open the lid.
4. Serve immediately.

Vanilla Rice Pudding

Prep time: 5 minutes | Cook time: 20 minutes | Serves 4

2 cups whole milk
1¼ cups water
1 teaspoon cinnamon
½ teaspoon grated nutmeg
Pinch of salt
1 cup long-grain rice, rinsed and drained
1 teaspoon vanilla extract
1 can (14-ounce / 397-g) condensed milk

1. Add the whole milk, water, cinnamon, nutmeg and salt into the Instant Pot.
2. Add rice and stir to combine.
3. Lock the lid. Select the Porridge mode and set the cooking time for 20 minutes on High Pressure. Once the timer goes off, perform a natural pressure release for 10 minutes, then release any remaining pressure. Carefully open the lid.
4. Add the vanilla extract and condensed milk. Stir well until creamy and serve.

Zucchini Spread

Prep time: 12 mins, Cook Time: 9 mins, Servings: 6

½ cup water
1 tbsp. olive oil
1 bunch basil, chopped
1½ lbs. zucchinis, chopped
2 garlic cloves, minced

1. Set the Instant Pot to Sauté and heat the olive oil. Cook the garlic cloves for 3 minutes, stirring occasionally.
2. Add zucchinis and water, and mix well.
3. Lock the lid. Select the Manual mode, then set the timer for 3 minutes at High Pressure.
4. Once the timer goes off, do a quick pressure release. Carefully open the lid.
5. Add the basil and blend the mixture with an immersion blender until smooth.
6. Select the Simmer mode and cook for 2 minutes more.
7. Transfer to a bowl and serve warm.

Chapter 13 Side Dishes

Adobo-Style Eggplant with Bell Pepper

Prep time: 10 minutes | Cook time: 6 minutes | Serves 4

1 (1-pound / 454-g) eggplant, cut into 1-inch pieces
1 teaspoon fine sea salt
¼ cup low-sodium soy sauce
2 tablespoons palm vinegar
2 tablespoons avocado oil
4 cloves garlic, minced
1 large shallot, diced
1 red bell pepper, deseeded and cut into 1-inch squares
½ teaspoon freshly ground black pepper
2 tablespoons water
Hot steamed rice, for serving
1 green onion, tender green part only, thinly sliced

1. In a colander, toss the eggplant with the salt. Let sit in the sink or on top of a dish for 30 minutes (some liquid will release from the eggplant as it sits), then rinse the eggplant well under running water. Pat the pieces dry with paper towels.
2. In a small bowl, combine the soy sauce and vinegar. Set aside.
3. Press the Sauté button on the Instant Pot and heat the oil for 1 minute. Add the garlic and shallot and sauté for 3 minutes, or until the shallot softens and the garlic begins to color.
4. Add the eggplant, bell pepper, and black pepper, and stir to coat the vegetables with the oil. Pour in the vinegar mixture and water.
5. Set the lid in place. Select the Manual mode and set the cooking time for 2 minutes on Low Pressure. When the timer goes off, do a quick pressure release. Carefully open the lid.
6. Give the vegetables a gentle stir to coat with the sauce, then let sit for a minute or two.
7. Spoon over bowls of steamed rice and sprinkle green onions on top. Serve hot.

Black-Eyed Peas with Greens

Prep time: 10 minutes | Cook time: 15 minutes | Serves 2

1 tablespoon oil
½ yellow onion, diced
2 garlic cloves, minced
½ pound (227 g) dried black-eyed peas
2 cups chopped Swiss chard or kale
1 cup chicken stock
1½ teaspoons red pepper flakes
½ teaspoon dried thyme or 2 fresh thyme sprigs
½ tablespoon kosher salt
¼ teaspoon freshly ground black pepper
1 tablespoon apple cider vinegar
1 to 2 teaspoons hot sauce (optional)

1. Press the Sauté button on the Instant Pot and heat the oil until shimmering.
2. Add the onion and cook for 2 minutes until tender, stirring frequently.
3. Stir in the garlic and cook for about 1 minute until fragrant.
4. Add the peas, Swiss chard, chicken stock, red pepper flakes, thyme, salt, and pepper. Using a wooden spoon, scrape the bottom of the pot, then mix well.
5. Lock the lid. Select the Manual mode and set the cooking time for 10 minutes at High Pressure.
6. Once cooking is complete, do a natural pressure release for 10 minutes, then release any remaining pressure. Carefully open the lid.
7. Whisk in the vinegar and hot sauce, if desired. Taste and adjust the seasoning, if needed. Serve warm.

Artichokes with Mayonnaise Dip

Prep time: 10 minutes | Cook time: 15 minutes | Serves 4

2 large artichokes, rinsed
1 medium lemon, halved
¾ teaspoon salt, divided
Mayonnaise Dip:
3 tablespoons mayonnaise
⅛ teaspoon black pepper
3 cloves garlic, crushed
1 cup water

¼ teaspoon chili powder

1. Cut off top ½ inch of each artichoke.
2. Slice one half of the lemon into wedges and set the other half aside.
3. Add the lemon wedges, ½ teaspoon of salt, garlic, and water to your Instant Pot.
4. Put the trivet in the bottom of the pot and place the artichokes on top. Lock the lid. You may need to trim the artichoke stems to secure the lid.
5. Press the Manual button on your Instant Pot and set the cooking time for 15 minutes at High Pressure.
6. Once cooking is complete, do a quick pressure release. Carefully open the lid and remove the artichokes.
7. Meanwhile, make the mayonnaise dip by stirring together the juice from the remaining ½ lemon, the remaining ¼ teaspoon of salt, mayonnaise pepper, and chili powder in a small bowl.
8. Cut the artichokes in half and serve alongside the mayonnaise dip.

Garlicky Broccoli

Prep time: 5 minutes | Cook time: 9 minutes | Serves 4

3 tablespoons olive oil
2 medium heads broccoli, cut into florets
½ teaspoon salt
½ teaspoon black pepper
4 cloves garlic, minced

1. Press the Sauté button on your Instant Pot. Add the oil and let heat for 1 minute.
2. Add the broccoli and sprinkle with the salt and pepper. Secure the lid and sauté for 4 minutes.
3. Stir in the garlic and lock the lid. Sauté for another 4 minutes.
4. Transfer to a serving bowl and serve hot.

Caramelized Sweet Potatoes

Prep time: 5 minutes | Cook time: 19 minutes | Serves 2

2 sweet potatoes, scrubbed
1 cup water
2 tablespoons coconut oil
Pinch of salt and black pepper
Pinch of chili powder

1. Pour the water and insert the trivet in the Instant Pot. Put the pan on the trivet.
2. Pour the water to the Instant Pot and place the steamer basket at the bottom. Add the sweet potatoes to the basket.
3. Set the lid in place. Select the Manual mode and set the cooking time for 15 minutes on High Pressure. When the timer goes off, do a quick pressure release. Carefully open the lid.
4. Remove and slice the potatoes. Clean the pot.
5. Press the Sauté button on the Instant Pot and heat the oil. Add the sliced sweet potatoes. Season with salt, pepper and chili powder and brown for 2 minutes on each side.
6. Serve hot.

Brussels Sprouts with Sesame Seeds

Prep time: 5 minutes | Cook time: 4 minutes | Serves 4

25 Brussels sprouts, halved lengthwise
1 cup water
1 tablespoon extra-virgin olive oil
2 garlic cloves, finely chopped

1 tablespoon balsamic vinegar
1 teaspoon kosher salt
½ teaspoon freshly ground black pepper
1 tablespoon roasted sesame seeds

1. Place the Brussels sprouts in the steamer basket. Pour the water and insert the trivet in the Instant Pot. Place the basket on the trivet.
2. Set the lid in place. Select the Manual mode and set the cooking time for 1 minute on High Pressure. When the timer goes off, do a quick pressure release. Carefully open the lid.
3. Using tongs, carefully transfer the Brussels sprouts to a serving plate. Discard the water and wipe the inner pot dry.
4. Press the Sauté button on the Instant Pot and heat the oil. Add the garlic and sauté for 1 minute. Add the Brussels sprouts, vinegar, salt, and pepper, and sauté for 2 minutes. Sprinkle with the roasted sesame seeds and serve hot.

Braised Cabbage

Prep time: 5 minutes | Cook time: 7 to 8 minutes | Serves 4

1 tablespoon olive oil
¼ cup minced shallots
¼ cup white wine

4 cups savoy cabbage
1 cup vegetable broth

1. Press the Sauté button on the Instant Pot and heat the oil. Add in the shallots and sauté for 3 minutes. Add the white wine and cook for 1 to 2 minutes, or until the wine reduces. Add the savoy cabbage and the vegetable broth to the pot.
2. Lock the lid. Select the Manual mode and set the cooking time for 3 minutes on High Pressure. Once the timer goes off, perform a natural pressure release for 5 minutes, then release any remaining pressure. Carefully open the lid.
3. Serve immediately.

Asparagus with Sauce Gribiche

Prep time: 10 minutes | Cook time: 5 minutes | Serves 4

2 large eggs
1½ cups water
1 pound (454 g) asparagus, trimmed and cut into 1-inch pieces
1 tablespoon Dijon mustard
¼ cup vegetable oil
1 tablespoon apple cider

vinegar
2 to 3 tablespoons chopped dill pickle
1 tablespoon chopped fresh parsley
1 teaspoon granulated sugar
½ teaspoon kosher salt
½ teaspoon black pepper

1. Pour the water and insert the trivet in the Instant Pot. Place the eggs on one side of the trivet.
2. Tightly wrap the asparagus in foil and place on the trivet next to the eggs.
3. Set the lid in place. Select the Manual mode and set the cooking time for 5 minutes on High Pressure. When the timer goes off, do a quick pressure release. Carefully open the lid.
4. Meanwhile, fill a medium bowl with ice cubes and water.
5. Remove the eggs and place them in the ice water bath for 5 minutes. Peel and finely dice the eggs.
6. In a small bowl, combine the mustard, oil, vinegar, pickle, parsley, sugar, salt, and pepper. Stir in the chopped eggs.
7. Place the asparagus on a serving platter and spoon the gribiche on top. Serve.

Beet and Corn Salad

Prep time: 10 minutes | Cook time: 8 minutes | Serves 6

2 medium red beets, peeled
1 corn on the cob, husks removed, washed
1½ cups water
¼ cup finely chopped onion
¼ cup finely chopped fresh cilantro
3 tablespoons mayonnaise
1 tablespoon extra-virgin olive

oil
2 teaspoons freshly squeezed lemon juice
1 teaspoon grated lemon zest
1 teaspoon sugar
1 teaspoon kosher salt
1 teaspoon freshly ground black pepper

1. Place the whole beets and corn in the steamer rack. Pour the water and insert the trivet in the Instant Pot. Place the steamer rack on the trivet.
2. Set the lid in place. Select the Manual mode and set the cooking time for 4 minutes on High Pressure. When the timer goes off, do a quick pressure release. Carefully open the lid.
3. Using tongs, transfer the corn to a plate and set aside to cool.
4. Set the lid in place again. Select the Manual mode and set the cooking time for 4 minutes on High Pressure. When the timer goes off, do a quick pressure release. Carefully open the lid.
5. Using tongs, transfer the beets to the plate with the corn and set aside to cool.
6. Using a knife, carefully remove the corn kernels from the cob. Cut the beets into ½-inch cubes.
7. In a large bowl, combine the beets, corn, onion, cilantro, mayonnaise, olive oil, lemon juice and zest, sugar, salt, and pepper. Mix thoroughly and chill in the refrigerator for 1 hour.
8. Serve chilled.

Curred Cauliflower

Prep time: 5 minutes | Cook time: 13 minutes | Serves 4

2 tablespoons olive oil
1 medium head cauliflower, cut into florets

½ teaspoon curry powder
⅛ teaspoon salt
⅛ teaspoon black pepper

1. Press the Sauté button on your Instant Pot. Add the oil and let heat for 1 minute.
2. Add the remaining ingredients and stir well. Lock the lid and sauté for 12 minutes, or until the florets are crisp-tender.
3. Transfer to a plate and serve hot.

Artichoke-Spinach Dip

Prep time: 10 minutes | Cook time: 10 to 11 minutes | Serves 8

2 teaspoons corn oil
¼ cup chopped onion
2 garlic cloves, finely chopped
8 ounces (227 g) fresh spinach, roughly chopped
½ teaspoon kosher salt
1 teaspoon freshly ground black pepper
5 ounces (142 g) cream

cheese
1 (8½-ounce / 241-g) can water-packed artichoke hearts, drained and quartered
⅓ cup heavy cream
⅓ cup water
Chips or sliced veggies, for serving

1. Press the Sauté button on the Instant Pot and heat the oil. Add the onion and garlic and sauté for 1 minute. Add the spinach, salt, and pepper. Continue to sauté for 2 to 3 minutes, or until the spinach is wilted. Add the cream cheese, artichokes, cream, and water and mix thoroughly.
2. Set the lid in place. Select the Manual mode and set the cooking time for 7 minutes on High Pressure. When the timer goes off, do a quick pressure release. Carefully open the lid.
3. Stir the dip, then let cool for 5 minutes. Transfer to a serving bowl and serve with chips or sliced veggies.

Bacon with Red Cabbage

Prep time: 10 minutes | Cook time: 18 minutes | Serves 4

1 tablespoon olive oil
1 small onion, peeled and diced
3 slices bacon, diced
5 cups chopped red cabbage
1 small apple, peeled, cored,

and diced
½ cup apple cider vinegar
1 cup chicken broth
½ teaspoon sea salt
¼ cup crumbled goat cheese

1. Set your Instant Pot to Sauté and heat the oil.
2. Add the onion and sauté until translucent, 3 to 5 minutes. Add the bacon and sauté for 3 minutes more, stirring occasionally, or until the bacon begins to crisp. Stir in the cabbage, apple, chicken broth, and vinegar.
3. Secure the lid. Select the Manual mode and set the cooking time for 10 minutes at High Pressure.
4. Once cooking is complete, do a quick pressure release. Carefully open the lid.
5. Remove from the Instant Pot to a plate and season with salt. Sprinkle the goat cheese on top for garnish before serving.

Balsamic Brussels Sprouts with Cranberries

Prep time: 5 minutes | Cook time: 5 minutes | Serves 4 to 6

2 tablespoons (¼ stick) salted butter
2 shallots, diced
2 to 3 pounds (907 g to 1.4 kg) Brussels sprouts, stems trimmed and halved

¼ cup maple syrup
⅓ cup balsamic vinegar
10 to 20 almonds, crushed
1 cup dried cranberries
Balsamic glaze, for topping (optional)

1. Set your Instant Pot to Sauté and melt the butter.
2. Add the shallots and sauté until slightly softened, about 3 minutes.
3. Add the Brussels sprouts, maple syrup, vinegar, almonds, and cranberries and stir until the Brussels sprouts are fully coated in the sauce.
4. Lock the lid. Select the Manual mode and set the cooking time for 1 minute at High Pressure.
5. Once cooking is complete, do a quick pressure release. Carefully open the lid.
6. Transfer the Brussels sprouts to a platter, along with their sauce. Serve with a drizzle of balsamic glaze, if desired.

BBQ Baked Beans

Prep time: 5 minutes | Cook time: 33 minutes | Serves 8

16 ounces (454 g) dried great northern beans, soaked overnight and drained
2 cups water
1 medium onion, chopped
2 teaspoons garlic powder, divided

2 teaspoons onion powder, divided
1 cup barbecue sauce
¾ cup packed brown sugar
½ teaspoon ground nutmeg
¼ teaspoon ground cloves
2 teaspoons hot pepper sauce

1. In the pot, combine the beans, water, onion, 1 teaspoon of the garlic powder and 1 teaspoon of the onion powder.
2. Set the lid in place. Select the Manual mode and set the cooking time for 30 minutes on High Pressure. When the timer goes off, do a quick pressure release. Carefully open the lid.
3. Stir in the barbecue sauce, sugar, nutmeg, cloves, hot pepper sauce, and the remaining garlic and onion powder.
4. Set the lid in place. Select the Manual mode and set the cooking time for 3 minutes on High Pressure. When the timer goes off, do a quick pressure release. Carefully open the lid.
5. Serve hot.

Sumptuous Beet Salad with Vinaigrette

Prep time: 10 minutes | Cook time: 20 minutes | Serves 4

Salad:

1 pound (454 g) beets, each about 2½ inches in diameter
2 navel oranges, peeled and cut into segments
1 large avocados, pitted, peeled and sliced

1 (5- to 6-ounce / 142- to 170- g) bag baby spinach
4 sprigs fresh mint, leaves removed and torn if large
¾ cup Feta cheese
1 cup water

Vinaigrette:

¼ cup extra-virgin olive oil
2 tablespoons fresh lemon juice
½ teaspoon dried oregano

¼ teaspoon fine sea salt
¼ teaspoon freshly ground black pepper
1 clove garlic, minced

1. Pour the water into the Instant Pot and place the wire metal steam rack in the pot. Arrange the beets in a single layer on the steam rack.
2. Set the lid in place. Select the Manual mode and set the cooking time for 20 minutes on High Pressure.
3. While the beets are cooking, prepare an ice bath.
4. To make the vinaigrette: In a widemouthed 1-pint jar, combine the oil, lemon juice, oregano, salt, pepper, and garlic. Using an immersion blender, blend until an emulsified vinaigrette forms. Set aside.
5. When the timer goes off, do a quick pressure release. Carefully open the lid. Using tongs, transfer the beets to the ice bath and let cool for 10 minutes.
6. Using a paring knife, remove the skins from the beets; they should peel off very easily. Trim and discard the ends of the beets, then slice them into wedges.
7. In a large bowl, toss the spinach with half of the vinaigrette. Arrange the spinach on a large serving plate or on individual salad plates, then top with the beets, oranges, avocado, and mint.
8. Using a pair of spoons, scoop bite-sized pieces of the feta out of its container and dollop it onto the salad. Spoon the rest of the vinaigrette over the salad and serve immediately.

Sweet Potato and Marshmallow Casserole

Prep time: 5 minutes | Cook time: 30 to 35 minutes | Serves 6 to 8

3 pounds (1.4 kg) sweet potatoes, peeled and cut into 1-inch pieces
¼ cup coconut oil
¼ cup dark maple syrup

1 teaspoon fine sea salt
½ teaspoon ground cinnamon
10 marshmallows, cut in half lengthwise
1 cup water

1. Pour the water into the Instant Pot and place a steamer basket in the pot. Add the sweet potatoes to the basket.
2. Set the lid in place. Select the Manual mode and set the cooking time for 5 minutes on High Pressure.
3. While the sweet potatoes are steaming, preheat the oven to 325ºF (163ºC). Grease a baking dish with coconut oil and line a baking sheet with aluminum foil.
4. When the timer goes off, do a quick pressure release. Carefully open the lid. Wearing heat-resistant mitts, lift out the steamer basket. Lift out the inner pot and discard the water.
5. Return the sweet potatoes to the still-warm inner pot. Add the coconut oil, maple syrup, salt, and cinnamon, then use a potato masher to mash the sweet potatoes until smooth.
6. Spoon the mashed potatoes into the baking dish. Top with a single layer of the marshmallows, cut side down. Place the dish on the prepared baking sheet. Bake for 25 to 30 minutes, until the marshmallows are puffed and golden brown on top. Serve warm.

Braised Kale

Prep time: 5 minutes | Cook time: 5 minutes | Serves 4

1 large bunch kale
2 tablespoons extra-virgin olive oil
6 cloves garlic, thinly sliced crosswise
½ cup vegetable broth
¼ teaspoon sea salt
Freshly ground black pepper, to taste

1. Remove and discard the middle stems from the kale and roughly chop the leafy parts. Rinse and drain the kale.
2. Press the Sauté button on the Instant Pot and heat the oil. Add the garlic and sauté for about 2 minutes until tender and golden. Transfer the garlic and oil to a small bowl and set aside.
3. Add the broth to the inner pot. Place the kale on top and sprinkle with salt and pepper.
4. Set the lid in place. Select the Manual mode and set the cooking time for 3 minutes on Low Pressure. When the timer goes off, do a quick pressure release. Carefully open the lid.
5. Return the garlic and oil to the pot, and toss to combine.
6. Serve immediately.

Maple Glazed Brussels Sprouts

Prep time: 10 minutes | Cook time: 3 minutes | Serves 10

2 pounds (907 g) fresh Brussels sprouts, sliced
⅓ cup dried cranberries
2 large apples (Fuji or Braeburn), chopped
8 bacon strips, cooked and crumbled, divided
¼ cup maple syrup
2 tablespoons olive oil
⅓ cup cider vinegar
1 teaspoon salt
½ teaspoon coarsely ground pepper
¾ cup chopped hazelnuts or pecans, toasted

1. In a large bowl, mix together the Brussels sprouts, cranberries, apples, and 4 slices of bacon.
2. In a small bowl, stir together the syrup, oil, vinegar, salt, and pepper. Pour this mixture over the Brussels sprouts mixture and toss until well coated.
3. Transfer to the Instant Pot. Secure the lid.
4. Press the Manual on the Instant Pot and set the cooking time for 3 minutes on High Pressure.
5. Once cooking is complete, use a quick pressure release. Carefully remove the lid.
6. Serve sprinkled with the remaining 4 slices of bacon and hazelnuts.

Creamy Spinach with Mushrooms

Prep time: 10 minutes | Cook time: 10 minutes | Serves 4

1 tablespoon olive oil
1 cup sliced fennel
2 cloves garlic, crushed and minced
¼ cup white wine
10 cups fresh spinach
2 cups sliced portabella mushrooms,
1 cup coconut milk
½ cup vegetable broth
½ teaspoon salt
1 teaspoon coarse ground black pepper
1 teaspoon nutmeg
½ teaspoon thyme

1. Press the Sauté button on the Instant Pot and heat the oil. Add the fennel and garlic. Sauté the mixture for 3 minutes.
2. Add the white wine and sauté an additional 2 minutes, or until the wine reduces. Add the remaining ingredients and stir.
3. Lock the lid. Select the Manual mode and set the cooking time for 5 minutes on High Pressure. Once the timer goes off, perform a natural pressure release for 10 minutes, then release any remaining pressure. Carefully open the lid.
4. Stir before serving.

Mushroom Pilaf

Prep time: 20 minutes | Cook time: 10 minutes | Serves 6

¼ cup butter
1 cup medium grain rice
1 cup water
4 teaspoon beef base
2 garlic cloves, minced
6 green onions, chopped
½ pound (227 g) baby portobello mushrooms, sliced

1. Set your Instant Pot to Sauté and melt the butter.
2. Add the rice and cook for 3 to 5 minutes, stirring frequently, or until lightly browned.
3. Meanwhile, whisk together the water and beef base in a small bowl.
4. Add the garlic, green onions, and mushrooms to the Instant Pot and stir well. Pour the sauce over the top of the rice mixture.
5. Secure the lid. Select the Manual mode and set the cooking time for 4 minutes at High Pressure.
6. Once cooking is complete, do a natural pressure release for 10 minutes, then release any remaining pressure. Carefully open the lid.
7. Allow to cool for 5 minutes before serving.

Gold Potatoes with Buffalo Wing Sauce

Prep time: 15 minutes | Cook time: 5 minutes | Serves 6

1 cup water
2 pounds (907 g) Yukon Gold potatoes, cut into 1-inch cubes
½ small red onion, chopped
1 small sweet yellow pepper,
chopped
¼ cup Buffalo wing sauce
½ cup shredded Cheddar cheese
Optional Toppings:
Sliced green onions
Sour cream
Crumbled cooked bacon

1. Add the water to your Instant Pot and insert a steamer basket.
2. Place the potatoes, onion and yellow pepper in the basket. Secure the lid.
3. Select the Manual mode and set the cooking time for 3 minutes on High Pressure. Once cooking is complete, perform a quick pressure release. Remove the vegetables to a bowl.
4. Drain the cooking liquid and discard.
5. Drizzle the vegetables with the Buffalo wing sauce and stir until coated. Scatter the cheese on top and let stand covered for 1 to 2 minutes, or until the cheese has melted.
6. Top with toppings of your choice and serve immediately.

Black-Eyed Peas With Ham

Prep time: 10 minutes | Cook time: 18 minutes | Serves 10

4 cups water
1 package (16-ounce / 454-g) dried black-eyed peas, rinsed
1 cup cubed fully cooked ham
3 garlic cloves, minced
1 medium onion, finely
chopped
2 teaspoons seasoned salt
1 teaspoon pepper
Thinly sliced green onions, for garnish (optional)

1. Combine all the ingredients except the green onions in the Instant Pot.
2. Lock the lid. Select the Manual mode and set the cooking time for 18 minutes at High Pressure.
3. Once cooking is complete, do a natural pressure release for 10 minutes, then release any remaining pressure. Carefully open the lid.
4. Serve garnished with the sliced green onions, if desired.

Corn and Zucchini Casserole

Prep time: 15 minutes | Cook time: 1 hour 5 minutes | Serves 6

1½ cups water
Cooking spray
2 teaspoons baking powder
¾ cup cornmeal
1½ cups all-purpose flour
1 teaspoon salt
¼ teaspoon black pepper

1 cup whole milk
¼ cup vegetable oil
2 large eggs, beaten
4 cups shredded zucchini
1½ cups Monterey Jack cheese

1. Add the water to your Instant Pot and put the trivet in the bottom of the pot. Spritz a cake pan with cooking spray and set aside.
2. Stir together the baking powder, cornmeal, flour, salt, and pepper in a large bowl.
3. Create a well inside the dry mixture and pour in the milk, oil, and egg. Stir well to combine.
4. Fold in the zucchini and stir until well mixed. Then stir in the cheese.
5. Pour the casserole batter into the prepared cake pan. Place a paper towel on top and wrap top of the pan in aluminum foil. Create a foil sling and carefully lower the cake pan into your Instant Pot.
6. Lock the lid.
7. Press the Manual button on your Instant Pot and set the cooking time for 65 minutes on High Pressure.
8. When the timer goes off, do a quick pressure release. Carefully open the lid.
9. Remove the cake pan from your Instant Pot using the foil sling and serve hot.

Lemony Peas

Prep time: 5 minutes | Cook time: 2 minutes | Serves 4

4 cups fresh peas, not in pods
1 cup vegetable broth
1 tablespoon coconut oil, melted

¼ cup chopped fresh mint
¼ cup chopped fresh parsley
1 teaspoon lemon zest

1. Combine the peas and vegetable broth in the Instant Pot.
2. Set the lid in place. Select the Manual mode and set the cooking time for 2 minutes on High Pressure. When the timer goes off, do a quick pressure release. Carefully open the lid.
3. Drain off the excess liquid from the peas and place them in a bowl.
4. Drizzle the peas with the melted coconut oil and toss to coat.
5. Add the mint, parsley and lemon zest to the bowl and stir.
6. Serve immediately.

Strawberry Applesauce

Prep time: 10 minutes | Cook time: 5 minutes | Serves 6

4 cups frozen strawberries
6 cups roughly chopped Gala apples

½ cup water
½ cup granulated sugar
¼ teaspoon salt

1. Place the strawberries and apples in your Instant Pot.
2. Mix in the water, sugar, and salt and stir well. Lock the lid.
3. Press the Manual button on your Instant Pot and cook for 5 minutes at High Pressure.
4. Once cooking is complete, perform a natural pressure release for 15 minutes and then release any remaining pressure. Carefully open the lid.
5. Blend the mixture with an immersion blender until smooth.
6. Place in the refrigerator for 2 hours.
7. Serve chilled.

Mashed Potatoes

Prep time: 10 minutes | Cook time: 8 minutes | Serves 4

2½ pounds (1.1 kg) russet potatoes, peeled
½ teaspoon salt
1 cup chicken broth

¾ cup whole milk, warm
2 tablespoons butter
5 cloves garlic, minced

1. Add the potatoes, salt, and broth to the Instant Pot. Lock the lid.
2. Press the Manual button on the Instant Pot and cook for 8 minutes on High Pressure.
3. Once cooking is complete, use a quick pressure release and then carefully open the lid.
4. Drain the broth and discard.
5. Mash the potatoes in the pot with a potato masher. Mix in the warm milk and stir well.
6. Stir in the butter until melted. Add garlic and stir again.
7. Transfer to a plate and serve warm.

Spanish Risotto

Prep time: 5 minutes | Cook time: 10 minutes | Serves 6

3 tablespoons olive oil
1 cup chopped yellow onion
2 garlic cloves, minced
2 cups white rice
2½ cups vegetable stock

¾ cup crushed tomatoes
½ teaspoon chili powder
¼ cup chopped cilantro
Salt and black pepper, to taste

1. Press the Sauté button on the Instant Pot and heat the oil. Add the onion and garlic and cook for 4 minutes. Add the rice and cook for 2 minutes. Stir in the stock, tomatoes, and chili powder.
2. Set the lid in place. Select the Manual mode and set the cooking time for 4 minutes on High Pressure. When the timer goes off, do a quick pressure release. Carefully open the lid.
3. Sprinkle with the cilantro and season with salt and pepper. Stir and serve.

Instant Pot Pinto Beans

Prep time: 10 minutes | Cook time: 20 minutes | Serves 4

3 cups water
1 cup dried pinto beans, soaked for 8 hours and drained
2 cloves garlic, minced
½ yellow onion, chopped
1 teaspoon chili powder
1 teaspoon ground cumin
¼ teaspoon freshly ground

black pepper
½ fine sea salt, or more to taste
Pinch of cayenne pepper (optional)
Chopped fresh cilantro, for garnish
Lime wedges, for garnish

1. In the Instant Pot, combine the water, beans, garlic, and onion.
2. Lock the lid. Select the Manual mode and set the cooking time for 20 minutes at High Pressure.
3. Once cooking is complete, do a natural pressure release for 10 minutes, then release any remaining pressure. Carefully open the lid.
4. Drain the beans and reserve the liquid.
5. Return the cooked beans to the pot and stir in ½ cup of the reserved liquid. Add the chili powder, cumin, black pepper, salt, and cayenne pepper (if desired) and stir well. Using a potato masher, mash the beans until smooth, leaving some texture if you like. If you prefer a more smooth texture, you can purée the beans with an immersion blender.
6. Taste and add more salt, if desired. Garnish with the cilantro and lime wedges and serve warm.

Chow-Chow Relish

Prep time: 15 minutes | Cook time: 20 minutes | Serves 8

2 large green bell peppers, deseeded and diced small
1 large red bell pepper, deseeded and diced small
2 cups finely diced cabbage
2 large green tomatoes, diced small
1 large sweet onion, peeled and diced small
1 cup water
1 cup apple cider vinegar
½ cup granulated sugar
½ cup packed dark brown sugar
1 tablespoon ground mustard
1 tablespoon sea salt
2 teaspoons celery seed
2 teaspoons red pepper flakes
2 teaspoons ground ginger
1 teaspoon ground turmeric

1. Combine all the ingredients in the Instant Pot.
2. Secure the lid. Select the Manual mode and set the cooking time for 20 minutes at High Pressure.
3. Once cooking is complete, do a natural pressure release for 10 minutes, then release any remaining pressure. Carefully open the lid.
4. Give the mixture a good stir and transfer to a bowl. Serve warm.

Citrus Brussels Sprouts with Bacon

Prep time: 5 minutes | Cook time: 7 to 9 minutes | Serves 4

1 tablespoon avocado oil
2 slices bacon, diced
½ cup water
½ cup freshly squeezed orange
juice
1 pound (454 g) Brussels sprouts, trimmed and halved
2 teaspoons orange zest

1. Press the Sauté button on your Instant Pot. Add the avocado oil and let heat for 1 minute.
2. Add the bacon. Sauté for 3 to 5 minutes, or until the bacon is almost crisp and the fat is rendered. Pour in the water and orange juice and deglaze the Instant Pot by scraping the bits from the pot.
3. Fold in the Brussels sprouts. Secure the lid.
4. Press the Manual button on your Instant Pot and set the cooking time for 3 minutes at High Pressure.
5. Once the timer goes off, use a quick pressure release and then release any remaining pressure. Carefully open the lid.
6. Remove the Brussels sprouts from the Instant Pot to a serving dish with a slotted spoon.
7. Serve warm garnished with the orange zest.

Green Beans with Shallots

Prep time: 5 minutes | Cook time: 6 minutes | Serves 4

¾ teaspoon salt, divided
1 cup water
1 pound (454 g) green beans, trimmed
2 tablespoons olive oil
1 medium shallot, peeled and minced
½ teaspoon black pepper

1. Add ½ teaspoon of salt and the water to the Instant Pot and insert a steamer basket. Place green beans on top of the basket. Lock the lid.
2. Press the Steam button on the Instant Pot and set the cooking time for 0 minutes on High Pressure.
3. When the timer goes off, do a quick pressure release and then carefully open the lid. Remove the green beans and drain the cooking liquid.
4. Select the Sauté mode and add the oil to the pot.
5. Add the green beans and shallot and sauté for 6 minutes, or until the green beans are crisp-tender.
6. Sprinkle with the remaining ¼ teaspoon of salt and pepper.
7. Transfer to a serving plate and serve.

Brussels Sprouts with Walnuts

Prep time: 10 minutes | Cook time: 10 to 12 minutes | Serves 4

1 tablespoon olive oil
¼ cup minced shallots
4 cups halved Brussels sprouts
1 cup orange juice
¼ cup cranberry juice
2 tablespoons maple syrup
¼ cup chopped dried cranberries
¼ cup chopped walnuts

1. Combine the orange juice, cranberry juice and maple syrup in a small bowl. Whisk together until well blended.
2. Press the Sauté button on the Instant Pot and heat the oil. Add in the shallots and sauté them for 3 minutes. Add the sauce and the Brussels sprouts to the pot.
3. Set the lid in place. Select the Manual mode and set the cooking time for 4 minutes on High Pressure. When the timer goes off, do a quick pressure release. Carefully open the lid.
4. Use a slotted spoon to remove the Brussels sprouts from the pot and transfer them to a serving plate or bowl.
5. Press the Sauté button on the Instant Pot and cook the remaining sauce for 3 to 5 minutes, or until it thickens slightly and reduces.
6. Pour the sauce over the Brussels sprouts and toss to coat.
7. Garnish the Brussels sprouts with the dried cranberries and walnuts before serving.

Succotash

Prep time: 5 minutes | Cook time: 10 minutes | Serves 6 to 8

2 tablespoons extra-virgin olive oil
1 clove garlic, minced
1 yellow onion, diced
1 (16-ounce / 454-g) bag frozen baby lima beans
1 (12-ounce / 340-g) bag frozen corn kernels
1 (14½-ounce / 411-g) can diced tomatoes
½ cup low-sodium vegetable broth
½ teaspoon dried thyme
½ teaspoon fine sea salt
¼ teaspoon freshly ground black pepper

1. Select the Sauté setting on the Instant Pot, add the oil and garlic, and heat for 2 minutes, or until the garlic is bubbling but not browned. Add the onion and sauté for about 5 minutes, or until the onion softens. Add the lima beans, corn, tomatoes and their liquid, broth, thyme, salt, and pepper, and vegetable broth. Stir to combine.
2. Set the lid in place. Select the Manual mode and set the cooking time for 3 minutes on High Pressure. When the timer goes off, do a quick pressure release. Carefully open the lid.
3. Stir the succotash, then transfer to a serving bowl. Serve warm.

Maple-Glazed Carrots

Prep time: 10 minutes | Cook time: 5 minutes | Serves 6

1 pound (454 g) carrots, peeled and diced large
1 tablespoon pure maple syrup
1 tablespoon ghee
1 tablespoon minced fresh dill
1 cup water
½ teaspoon sea salt

1. Place all the ingredients in the Instant Pot. Secure the lid.
2. Select the Manual mode and set the cooking time for 5 minutes on High Pressure.
3. Once cooking is complete, perform a natural pressure release for 10 minutes and then release any remaining pressure. Carefully open the lid.
4. Transfer to a serving dish and serve immediately.

Corn on the Cob

Prep time: 5 minutes | Cook time: 5 minutes | Serves 4

1 cup water
¼ teaspoon salt

4 ears corn

1. Add the water and salt to the Instant Pot. Put the trivet in the bottom of the pot.
2. Lay the ears of corn on the trivet.
3. Lock the lid.
4. Set the Instant Pot to Manual and set the cooking time for 5 minutes on High Pressure.
5. Once cooking is complete, perform a quick pressure release. Carefully open the lid.
6. Transfer the corn to a plate and serve.

Corn with Crab

Prep time: 5 minutes | Cook time: 1 minute | Serves 4 to 6

1 cup water
30 ounces (850 g) frozen corn
½ pound (227 g) lump crabmeat
4 ounces (113 g) cream cheese, cut into chunky cubes
½ cup grated Parmesan

cheese
½ cup heavy cream or half-and-half
1½ teaspoons granulated sugar
1 teaspoon black pepper
3 tablespoons salted butter

1. Add the water to your Instant Pot and insert a steamer basket. Arrange the corn in the basket.
2. Lock the lid. Press the Manual button on your Instant Pot and set the cooking time for 1 minute at High Pressure.
3. When the timer goes off, use a quick pressure release. Carefully open the lid.
4. Drain the corn and dump back into the pot.
5. Add the remaining ingredients and stir until the cream cheese has melted completely.
6. Serve immediately.

Mac & Cheese

Prep time: 5 minutes | Cook time: 7 minutes | Serves 2

6 ounces (170 g) elbow macaroni
¾ cup vegetable stock, plus more as needed
½ teaspoon kosher salt
1 tablespoon unsalted butter
2 ounces (57 g) cream cheese
⅓ cup whole milk
½ tablespoon Dijon mustard
½ tablespoon hot sauce

(optional)
⅓ cup shredded Gruyère cheese
⅓ cup shredded fontina cheese
⅓ cup shredded Cheddar cheese
Salt and freshly ground black pepper, to taste

1. Combine the macaroni, vegetable stock, and kosher salt in the Instant Pot.
2. Lock the lid. Select the Manual mode and set the cooking time for 5 minutes at High Pressure.
3. Once cooking is complete, do a quick pressure release. Carefully open the lid.
4. Set your Instant Pot to Sauté and stir in the butter until melted.
5. Add the cream cheese, milk, mustard, and hot sauce (if desired) and stir well.
6. Add the shredded cheeses, about ⅓ cup at a time, mixing well after each addition.
7. Sprinkle with the salt and pepper and serve.

Mashed Cauliflower

Prep time: 5 minutes | Cook time: 4 minutes | Serves 4 to 6

1 cup chicken or vegetable broth
1 head cauliflower, stalk and green leaves removed, cut into large chunks
2 tablespoons (¼ stick) salted

butter
½ cup milk, heavy cream, or half-and-half
Seasoned salt and black pepper, to taste
Chopped chives, for garnish

1. Place the trivet in the bottom of your Instant Pot, add in the broth, and layer the cauliflower on top.
2. Lock the lid and press the Manual button your Instant Pot and set the cooking time for 4 minutes on High Pressure. When the timer beeps, perform a quick pressure release.
3. Transfer the cauliflower to a food processor. Add in about ⅓ of the broth from the pot and purée until smooth.
4. Fold in the butter, milk, seasoned salt, and pepper. Purée again until totally creamy.
5. Transfer to a plate and serve garnished with chives.

Deviled Potatoes

Prep time: 10 minutes | Cook time: 10 minutes | Serves 6

6 medium Yukon Gold potatoes, halved
1 cup water
5 tablespoons mayonnaise
1 teaspoon Dijon mustard
1 tablespoon sweet pickle relish
1 teaspoon sugar

½ teaspoon freshly squeezed lemon juice
½ teaspoon kosher salt
½ teaspoon freshly ground black pepper
1 tablespoon finely chopped fresh cilantro
1 teaspoon paprika

1. Place the halved potatoes in the steamer rack. Pour the water and insert the trivet in the Instant Pot. Place the steamer rack on the trivet.
2. Set the lid in place. Select the Manual mode and set the cooking time for 10 minutes on High Pressure. When the timer goes off, do a quick pressure release. Carefully open the lid.
3. Using tongs, carefully transfer the potatoes to a platter. Set aside to cool for 15 minutes.
4. In a medium bowl, stir together the mayonnaise, mustard, relish, sugar, lemon juice, salt and pepper.
5. Using a melon scooper or spoon, remove the middle part of the potatoes, creating a well. Spoon 1 to 1½ teaspoons of the mayonnaise mixture into each potato. Garnish each deviled potato with the cilantro and paprika before serving.

Beet and Grapefruit Salad

Prep time: 5 minutes | Cook time: 20 minutes | Serves 8

6 medium fresh beets
1½ cups water
¼ cup extra-virgin olive oil
3 tablespoons lemon juice
2 tablespoons cider vinegar
2 tablespoons honey

¼ teaspoon salt
¼ teaspoon black pepper
2 large grapefruits, peeled and sectioned
2 small red onions, halved and sliced

1. Scrub the beets, trimming the tops to 1 inch.
2. Pour the water and insert the trivet in the Instant Pot. Place the beets on the trivet.
3. Set the lid in place. Select the Manual mode and set the cooking time for 20 minutes on High Pressure. When the timer goes off, do a quick pressure release. Carefully open the lid.
4. Whisk together the remaining ingredients, except for the grapefruits and onion. Pour over beets. Stir in the grapefruits and onion and serve.

Steamed Broccoli

Prep time: 5 minutes | Cook time: 0 minutes | Serves 4

1 cup water
1 medium head broccoli, chopped

2 teaspoons ghee
1 teaspoon lemon juice
½ teaspoon sea salt

1. Add the water to the Instant Pot. Place a steamer basket and layer the broccoli on top. Secure the lid.
2. Select the Steam mode and set the cooking time for 0 minutes on High Pressure.
3. When the timer goes off, do a quick pressure release. Carefully open the lid.
4. Remove the broccoli from the steamer basket to a serving dish. Mix in the ghee, lemon juice, and salt and toss to combine.
5. Serve warm.

Root Vegetable Medley

Prep time: 15 minutes | Cook time: 5 minutes | Serves 4

2 medium parsnips, peeled and diced
2 medium turnips, peeled and diced
3 cloves garlic, peeled and halved
1 large Yukon gold potato, peeled and diced
1 medium shallot, peeled and quartered

½ cup chicken broth, plus more as needed
1 cup water
2 tablespoons ghee
¼ cup unsweetened almond milk
½ teaspoon sea salt
½ teaspoon ground black pepper

1. Place the parsnips, turnips, garlic, potato, shallot, broth, and water in the Instant Pot. Secure the lid.
2. Select the Manual mode and set the cooking time for 5 minutes on High Pressure.
3. Once the timer goes off, use a natural pressure release for 10 minutes and then release any remaining pressure. Carefully open the lid.
4. Remove the vegetables from the pot to a medium bowl.
5. Stir in the ghee, milk, salt, and pepper. Blitz the mixture with an immersion blender until smooth. Add more broth, 1 tablespoon at a time, from the Instant Pot if a thinner consistency is desired.
6. Transfer to a serving plate and serve warm.

Green Bean Stir-Fry

Prep time: 5 minutes | Cook time: 4 minutes | Serves 4

12 ounces (340 g) green beans, trimmed
1 cup water
2 tablespoons corn oil
2 garlic cloves, finely chopped

3 tablespoons crushed peanuts
2 tablespoons soy sauce
¼ teaspoon kosher salt
½ teaspoon cane sugar
2 teaspoons chili flakes

1. Place the beans in the steamer basket. Pour the water and insert the trivet in the Instant Pot. Place the basket on the trivet.
2. Set the lid in place. Select the Manual mode and set the cooking time for 1 minute on High Pressure. When the timer goes off, do a quick pressure release. Carefully open the lid.
3. Drain the beans and wipe the inner pot dry.
4. Press the Sauté button on the Instant Pot and heat the oil. Add the garlic and sauté for 1 minute. Add the peanuts and soy sauce and sauté for 2 more minutes.
5. In a large bowl, combine the green beans, garlic, peanuts, salt, and sugar. Mix until the sugar and salt are dissolved. Sprinkle with the chili flakes and serve hot.

Gingery Mashed Sweet Potatoes

Prep time: 10 minutes | Cook time: 10 minutes | Serves 6

2½ pounds (1.1 kg) sweet potatoes, peeled and diced large
2 cups water
1 tablespoon minced fresh

ginger
1 tablespoon butter
1 tablespoon pure maple syrup
½ teaspoon sea salt
¼ cup milk

1. Add the potatoes and water to your Instant Pot. Secure the lid.
2. Select the Manual mode and set the cooking time for 10 minutes at High Pressure.
3. Once the timer goes off, use a natural pressure release for 10 minutes and then release any remaining pressure. Carefully open the lid.
4. Drain the water and add the remaining ingredients to the potatoes. Blend until desired consistency with an immersion blender.
5. Transfer to a serving plate and serve warm.

Mexican Corn

Prep time: 5 minutes | Cook time: 3 minutes | Serves 4

4 cups fresh corn kernels
1 cup water
½ teaspoon salt
1 tablespoon olive oil

1 teaspoon cumin
1 teaspoon smoked paprika
¼ cup fresh cilantro
1 tablespoon lime juice

1. Place the corn kernels, water and salt in the Instant Pot.
2. Lock the lid. Select the Manual mode and set the cooking time for 3 minutes on High Pressure.
3. While the corn is in the pot, combine the olive oil, cumin and paprika in a small saucepan or microwave-safe bowl. Heat just until warmed through and the oil is infused with the spices.
4. Once the timer goes off, perform a natural pressure release for 5 minutes, then release any remaining pressure. Carefully open the lid. Remove the corn from the pot and drain off any excess liquid.
5. Pour the spice-infused oil over the corn and toss to coat.
6. Add in the cilantro and lime juice and stir.
7. Serve immediately.

Smoky Carrots and Collard Greens

Prep time: 10 minutes | Cook time: 12 minutes | Serves 4 to 6

1 tablespoon extra-virgin olive oil
1 yellow onion, diced
8 ounces (227 g) carrots, peeled and diced
2 bunches collard greens, stems discarded and leaves sliced into 1-inch ribbons

½ teaspoon smoked paprika
½ teaspoon fine sea salt, plus more as needed
¼ teaspoon freshly ground black pepper
½ cup water
1 tablespoon tomato paste

1. Select the Sauté setting on the Instant Pot, add the oil, and heat for 1 minute. Add the onion and carrots and sauté for about 4 minutes, or until the onion begins to soften. Stir in the collards and sauté for about 2 minutes, or until wilted. Stir in the smoked paprika, salt, pepper, and water. Dollop the tomato paste on top, but do not stir it in.
2. Set the lid in place. Select the Manual mode and set the cooking time for 5 minutes on High Pressure. When the timer goes off, do a quick pressure release. Carefully open the lid.
3. Stir to incorporate the tomato paste. Taste and adjust the seasoning with salt, if needed.
4. Spoon the collards into a serving bowl or onto serving plates. Serve warm.

Smokey Garbanzo Mash

Prep time: 5 minutes | Cook time: 20 minutes | Serves 6

2 cups dried garbanzo beans
1 tablespoon liquid smoke
½ teaspoon salt
1 teaspoon black pepper
1 teaspoon smoked paprika
½ teaspoon cayenne powder
¼ cup fresh parsley
¼ cup coconut milk

1. Place the garbanzo beans in the Instant Pot and add enough water just to cover. Sprinkle in the liquid smoke and stir.
2. Lock the lid. Select the Bean/Chili mode and set the cooking time for 20 minutes on High Pressure. Once the timer goes off, perform a natural pressure release for 10 minutes, then release any remaining pressure. Carefully open the lid. Drain off any excess liquid.
3. Add the salt, black pepper, smoked paprika, cayenne powder, fresh parsley and coconut milk to the garbanzo beans.
4. Use an immersion blender or a potato masher to mash the garbanzo beans to a desired consistency.
5. Serve immediately.

Spicy Green Beans

Prep time: 5 minutes | Cook time: 3 minutes | Serves 4 to 6

1½ pounds (680 g) green beans, ends trimmed
¼ cup low-sodium soy sauce
¼ cup vegetable or garlic broth
3 cloves garlic, minced
2 tablespoons sriracha
2 tablespoons sesame oil
1 tablespoon paprika
1 tablespoon rice vinegar
2 teaspoons garlic powder
1 teaspoon onion powder
2 tablespoons chopped almonds (optional)
¼ teaspoon crushed red pepper flakes (optional)
¼ teaspoon cayenne pepper (optional)

1. Stir together all the ingredients in the Instant Pot.
2. Lock the lid. Select the Manual mode and set the cooking time for 3 minutes at High Pressure.
3. Once cooking is complete, do a quick pressure release. Carefully open the lid.
4. Serve warm.

Zucchini-Parmesan Cheese Fritters

Prep time: 15 minutes | Cook time: 24 minutes | Serves 4

4 cups shredded zucchini
1 teaspoon salt
⅓ cup shredded Parmesan cheese
⅓ cup all-purpose flour
1 large egg, beaten
2 cloves garlic, minced
½ teaspoon black pepper
6 tablespoons olive oil, plus more as needed

1. In a colander, add the zucchini and lightly sprinkle with the salt. Let stand for 10 minutes.
2. Remove from the colander and pat the zucchini dry using a paper towel to gently press as much moisture out as you can.
3. In a large bowl, mix together the zucchini, Parmesan, flour, egg, garlic, and pepper and stir well.
4. Press the Sauté button on the Instant Pot. Add 2 tablespoons of the oil into the pot.
5. Working in batches, scoop out tablespoonfuls of the zucchini mixture and add to the Instant Pot, pressing down gently with the back of a spoon to create 2½ rounds.
6. Cook for 4 minutes per side until lightly browned on both sides.
7. Remove the zucchini fritters with a slotted spatula. Repeat with the remaining zucchini mixture, adding more oil, if needed, with each batch.
8. Allow to cool for 5 minutes before serving.

Sweet-and-Sour Kale and Beets

Prep time: 10 minutes | Cook time: 10 minutes | Serves 6

4 cups quartered beets
3 cups roughly chopped kale
1 cup sliced onion
1½ cups water
¼ cup walnut oil
¼ cup apple cider vinegar
1 tablespoon brown sugar
½ teaspoon salt
1 teaspoon black pepper

1. Combine the beets and the water in the Instant Pot.
2. Set the lid in place. Select the Manual mode and set the cooking time for 5 minutes on High Pressure. When the timer goes off, do a quick pressure release. Carefully open the lid.
3. Add in the kale and the onion.
4. Lock the lid again. Select the Manual mode and set the cooking time for 5 minutes on High Pressure. Once the timer goes off, perform a natural pressure release for 5 minutes, then release any remaining pressure.
5. While the steam is releasing, combine the walnut oil, apple cider vinegar, brown sugar, salt and black pepper. Whisk together until well blended.
6. Carefully open the lid. Remove the vegetables from the pot and thoroughly drain them.
7. Transfer the vegetables to a bowl and add in the dressing. Toss to coat.
8. Serve warm, or cover and refrigerate for several hours for a chilled side dish.

Sriracha Collard Greens

Prep time: 10 minutes | Cook time: 10 minutes | Serves 6

2 pounds (907 g) collard greens, washed, spines removed, and chopped
1 cup chicken broth
1 small onion, peeled and diced
¼ cup apple cider vinegar
1 slice bacon
1 teaspoon sriracha
½ teaspoon sea salt
¼ teaspoon ground black pepper

1. Combine all the ingredients in Instant Pot.
2. Secure the lid. Select the Manual mode and set the cooking time for 10 minutes at High Pressure.
3. Once cooking is complete, do a natural pressure release for 10 minutes, then release any remaining pressure. Carefully open the lid.
4. Discard the bacon and transfer the collard greens to a bowl. Serve immediately.

Sweet Potato Mash with Sage

Prep time: 5 minutes | Cook time: 5 minutes | Serves 4

4 cups peeled sweet potato chunks
1 cup water
3 tablespoon butter
4 sage leaves, thinly sliced
Sea salt, to taste
Freshly ground black pepper, to taste

1. Fit the inner pot with a steamer basket and add 1 cup water. Place the sweet potato chunks into the basket.
2. Set the lid in place. Select the Manual mode and set the cooking time for 3 minutes on High Pressure. When the timer goes off, do a quick pressure release. Carefully open the lid.
3. Use tongs to carefully remove the steamer basket and potatoes. Discard the water and return the inner pot to the Instant Pot.
4. Press the Sauté button on the Instant Pot and melt the butter. Sauté the sage leaves until fragrant, about 2 minutes. Add the sweet potatoes to the pot and mash with a potato masher to the desired consistency. Season to taste with salt and pepper.
5. Serve immediately.

Steamed Leeks with Tomato Sauce

Prep time: 10 minutes | Cook time: 2 minutes | Serves 6

1 large tomato, chopped
1 small navel orange, chopped
2 tablespoons minced fresh parsley
2 tablespoons sliced olives
1 teaspoon capers, drained
1 teaspoon red wine vinegar
1 teaspoon olive oil

½ teaspoon grated orange zest
½ teaspoon pepper
6 medium leeks, white portion only, halved lengthwise and cleaned
Crumbled Feta cheese, for serving
1 cup water, for the pot

1. In a bowl, stir together all the ingredients, except for the leeks, cheese and water. Set aside.
2. Pour the water and insert the trivet in the Instant Pot. Place the leeks on the trivet.
3. Set the lid in place. Select the Manual mode and set the cooking time for 2 minutes on High Pressure. When the timer goes off, do a quick pressure release. Carefully open the lid.
4. Transfer the leeks to a platter. Spoon the tomato mixture on top. Sprinkle with the cheese and serve.

Szechuan Honey-Glazed Asparagus

Prep time: 5 minutes | Cook time: 1 minute | Serves 4

2 bunches asparagus, woody ends removed
1 tablespoon extra-virgin olive oil
½ teaspoon kosher salt

½ teaspoon freshly ground black pepper
1 cup water
2 tablespoons honey
1 tablespoon Szechuan sauce

1. Place the asparagus in a large bowl. Drizzle with the olive oil, salt, and pepper, and toss to combine.
2. Place the asparagus in the steaming rack. Pour the water and insert the trivet in the Instant Pot. Place the steamer rack on the trivet. Lock the lid into place.
3. Set the lid in place. Select the Manual mode and set the cooking time for 1 minute on High Pressure. When the timer goes off, do a quick pressure release. Carefully open the lid.
4. Using tongs, transfer the asparagus to a serving bowl.
5. In a small bowl, combine the honey and Szechuan sauce. Drizzle over the asparagus and serve hot.

Summer Squash and Tomatoes

Prep time: 20 minutes | Cook time: 1 minute | Serves 8

1 pound (454 g) medium yellow summer squash, cut into ¼-inch-thick slices
2 medium tomatoes, chopped
¼ cup thinly sliced green onions
1 cup vegetable broth
¼ teaspoon pepper

½ teaspoon salt
1½ cups coarsely crushed Caesar salad croutons, for serving
4 bacon strips, cooked and crumbled, for serving
½ cup shredded Cheddar cheese, for serving

1. Combine all the ingredients except the croutons, bacon, and cheese in the Instant Pot.
2. Secure the lid. Select the Manual mode and set the cooking time for 1 minute at High Pressure.
3. Once cooking is complete, do a quick pressure release. Carefully open the lid.
4. Remove the squash from the Instant Pot to a plate. Serve topped with the croutons, bacon, and cheese.

Ratatouille

Prep time: 15 minutes | Cook time: 8 minutes | Serves 6

1 (1-pound / 454-g) globe eggplant, cut into 1-inch pieces
3 zucchinis, cut into 1-inch pieces
1 teaspoon fine sea salt
2 tablespoons extra-virgin olive oil, plus more for serving
1 large yellow onion, cut into 1-inch pieces
2 cloves garlic, minced
1 teaspoon dried basil
½ teaspoon freshly ground

black pepper
½ teaspoon dried thyme
½ teaspoon red pepper flakes
1 bay leaf
3 red bell peppers, stemmed, deseeded and cut into 1-inch pieces
1 (14½-ounce / 411-g) can diced tomatoes
¼ cup dry white wine
Fresh basil leaves, for serving
Crusty bread, for serving

1. In a large bowl, toss together the eggplant and zucchini with the salt. Let stand for 15 minutes.
2. Select the Sauté setting on the Instant Pot, add the oil, and heat for 1 minute. Add the onion and garlic and sauté for about 4 minutes, or until the onion softens. Add the basil, black pepper, thyme, red pepper flakes, and bay leaf and sauté for about 1 minute. Add the eggplant-zucchini mixture and any liquid that has pooled in the bottom of the bowl, along with the bell peppers, tomatoes and their liquid, and wine. Stir to combine.
3. Set the lid in place. Select the Manual mode and set the cooking time for 2 minutes on Low Pressure. When the timer goes off, do a quick pressure release. Carefully open the lid.
4. Discard the bay leaf. Spoon the ratatouille into a serving bowl.
5. Drizzle the ratatouille with oil and sprinkle with fresh basil. Serve warm, with crusty bread.

Steamed Artichoke with Aioli Sauce

Prep time: 10 minutes | Cook time: 15 minutes | Serves 2

1 large artichoke
1 cup water
The Aioli Dipping Sauce:
½ cup raw cashews, soaked overnight or 2 hours in hot water
1½ tablespoons Dijon mustard
1 tablespoon apple cider vinegar

Juice of ½ lemon

Juice of ½ lemon
2 cloves garlic
Pinch of ground turmeric
½ teaspoon sea salt
⅓ cup water

1. Fit the inner pot with the trivet and add 1 cup water. Trim the artichoke stem so that it is 1 to 2 inches long, and trim about 1 inch off the top. Squeeze the lemon juice over the top of the artichoke and add the lemon rind to the water. Place the artichoke, top-side down, on the trivet.
2. Set the lid in place. Select the Steam mode and set the cooking time for 15 minutes on High Pressure. When the timer goes off, do a quick pressure release. Carefully open the lid.
3. Check for doneness. Leaves should be easy to remove and the "meat" at the base of each leaf should be tender.
4. Meanwhile, make the aioli dipping sauce. Drain the cashews and place them in a blender. Add the Dijon, vinegar, lemon juice, garlic, turmeric, and sea salt. Add half the water and blend. Continue adding water as you blend until the sauce is smooth and creamy. Transfer the sauce to a small bowl or jar. Refrigerate until ready to use.
5. Use tongs to remove the hot artichoke and place on a serving dish. Serve the artichoke warm with the aioli.

Spaghetti Squash with Olives

Prep time: 15 minutes | Cook time: 10 minutes | Serves 10

1 cup water
1 medium spaghetti squash, halved lengthwise and seeds removed
¼ cup sliced green olives with pimientos
1 can (14-ounce / 397-g) diced tomatoes, drained

1 teaspoon dried oregano
½ teaspoon salt
½ teaspoon pepper
½ cup shredded Cheddar cheese, for serving
¼ cup minced fresh basil, for serving

1. Pour the water into the Instant Pot and insert a trivet. Place the spaghetti squash on top of the trivet.
2. Secure the lid. Select the Manual mode and set the cooking time for 7 minutes at High Pressure.
3. Once cooking is complete, do a quick pressure release. Carefully open the lid.
4. Remove the spaghetti squash and trivet from the Instant Pot. Drain the cooking liquid from the pot.
5. Separate the squash into strands resembling spaghetti with a fork and discard the skin.
6. Return the squash to the Instant Pot. Add the olives, tomatoes, oregano, salt, and pepper and stir to combine.
7. Press the Sauté button on the Instant Pot and cook for about 3 minutes until heated through.
8. Serve topped with the cheese and basil.

Pesto Spaghetti Squash

Prep time: 5 minutes | Cook time: 12 minutes | Serves 6

1½ cups plus 3 tablespoons water, divided
1 (3-pound / 1.4-kg) spaghetti

squash, pierced with a knife about 10 times
¼ cup pesto

1. Pour 1½ cups of the water and insert the trivet in the Instant Pot. Put the pan on the trivet. Place the squash on the trivet.
2. Lock the lid. Select the Manual mode and set the cooking time for 12 minutes on High Pressure. Once the timer goes off, perform a natural pressure release for 10 minutes, then release any remaining pressure. Carefully open the lid.
3. Using tongs, carefully transfer the squash to a cutting board to cool for about 10 minutes.
4. Halve the spaghetti squash lengthwise. Using a spoon, scoop out and discard the seeds. Using a fork, scrape the flesh of the squash and shred into long "noodles". Place the noodles in a medium serving bowl.
5. In a small bowl, mix the pesto with the remaining 3 tablespoons of the water. Drizzle over the squash, toss to combine, and serve warm.

Sweet Turnip Greens

Prep time: 5 minutes | Cook time: 5 minutes | Serves 10

2 pounds (907 g) turnips, peeled and chopped
12 ounces (340 g) fresh turnip greens

1 medium onion, chopped
2 tablespoons sugar
Salt and pepper, to taste
5 cups vegetable broth

1. Add all the ingredients to the Instant Pot and stir to combine.
2. Set the lid in place. Select the Manual mode and set the cooking time for 5 minutes on High Pressure. When the timer goes off, do a quick pressure release. Carefully open the lid.
3. Serve hot.

Spiced Orange Carrots

Prep time: 5 minutes | Cook time: 4 to 5 minutes | Serves 6

2 pounds (907 g) medium carrots or baby carrots, cut into ¾-inch pieces
½ cup orange juice
½ cup packed brown sugar
2 tablespoons butter

¾ teaspoon ground cinnamon
¼ teaspoon ground nutmeg
½ teaspoon salt
¼ cup cold water
1 tablespoon cornstarch

1. Mix together all the ingredients except the water and cornstarch in your Instant Pot.
2. Secure the lid. Press the Manual button on your Instant Pot and cook for 3 minutes on Low Pressure.
3. When the timer goes off, use a quick pressure release. Carefully remove the lid.
4. Press the sauté button on your Instant Pot and bring the liquid to a boil. Fold in the water and cornstarch and stir until smooth.
5. Continue to cook for 1 to 2 minutes and stir until the sauce is thickened.
6. Transfer to a serving dish and serve immediately.

Steamed Leeks with Orange

Prep time: 10 minutes | Cook time: 2 minutes | Serves 6

1 large tomato, chopped
1 small navel orange, peeled, sectioned, and chopped
2 tablespoons sliced Greek olives
2 tablespoons minced fresh parsley
1 teaspoon red wine vinegar
1 teaspoon capers, drained

1 teaspoon olive oil
½ teaspoon pepper
½ teaspoon grated orange zest
1 cup water
6 medium leeks (white part only), halved lengthwise, cleaned
Crumbled feta cheese, for serving

1. Stir together the tomato, orange, olives, parsley, vinegar, capers, olive oil, pepper, and orange zest in a large bowl and set aside.
2. Pour the water into the Instant Pot and insert a trivet. Place the leeks on top of the trivet.
3. Secure the lid. Select the Steam mode and set the cooking time for 2 minutes at High Pressure.
4. Once cooking is complete, do a quick pressure release. Carefully open the lid.
5. Transfer the leeks to a serving plate and spoon the tomato mixture over top. Scatter with the feta cheese and serve immediately.

Sweet and Sour Beet Salad

Prep time: 15 minutes | Cook time: 20 minutes | Serves 8

1½ cups water
6 medium fresh beets (about 2 pounds / 907 g), scrubbed and tops trimmed
Sauce:
¼ cup extra virgin olive oil
3 tablespoons lemon juice
2 tablespoons honey

2 small red onions, halved and thinly sliced
2 large ruby red grapefruit, peeled and sectioned

2 tablespoons cider vinegar
¼ teaspoon pepper
¼ teaspoon salt

1.Pour the water into the Instant Pot and insert a trivet. Place the beets on top of the trivet.
2.Secure the lid. Select the Manual mode and set the cooking time for 20 minutes at High Pressure.
3.Once cooking is complete, do a natural pressure release for 10 minutes, then release any remaining pressure. Carefully open the lid.
4.Remove the beets from the Instant Pot and let cool to room temperature before peeling, halving and thinly slicing them. Transfer the beets to a salad bowl.
5.Whisk together all the ingredients for the sauce in a small bowl until smooth. Pour the sauce over the beets and add the red onions and grapefruit. Toss gently to coat and serve immediately.

Sweet Potato Gratin

Prep time: 20 minutes | Cook time: 30 minutes | Serves 8

2 medium sweet potatoes, peeled and thinly sliced
2 tablespoons extra-virgin olive oil
1 teaspoon kosher salt
1 teaspoon freshly ground black pepper
1 tablespoon dried basil

1 tablespoon dried thyme
1 tablespoon butter, melted
½ cup heavy cream
1 cup Mexican-blend shredded cheese
2 tablespoons panko bread crumbs
1 cup water

1.In a large bowl, drizzle the olive oil over the sweet potato slices. Season with the salt, pepper, basil, and thyme. Mix thoroughly to coat the sweet potatoes. Set aside.
2.In a small bowl, mix the butter and cream.
3.In a springform pan, arrange a single layer of sweet potatoes. Spread about 2 tablespoons of the cream-butter mixture on top and sprinkle with 4 to 5 tablespoons of the cheese. Repeat these steps until all the sweet potato slices have been used, about three layers. After the last layer, sprinkle the bread crumbs on top. Cover the pan with aluminum foil.
4.Pour the water and insert the trivet in the Instant Pot. Place the springform pan on the trivet.
5.Lock the lid. Select the Manual mode and set the cooking time for 30 minutes on High Pressure. Once the timer goes off, perform a natural pressure release for 15 minutes, then release any remaining pressure. Carefully open the lid.
6.Carefully remove the pan. Let the sweet potatoes cool for at least 1 hour before serving so the cheese sets.

Zucchini and Chickpea Tagine

Prep time: 30 minutes | Cook time: 5 minutes | Serves 12

2 tablespoons olive oil
2 garlic cloves, minced
2 teaspoons paprika
1 teaspoon ground cumin
1 teaspoon ground ginger
½ teaspoon salt
¼ teaspoon ground cinnamon
¼ teaspoon pepper
2 medium zucchini, cut into ½-inch pieces
1 small butternut squash, peeled and cut into ½-inch cubes
1 can (15-ounce / 425-g) chickpeas or garbanzo beans,

rinsed and drained
12 dried apricots, halved
½ cup water
1 medium sweet red pepper, coarsely chopped
1 medium onion, coarsely chopped
2 teaspoons honey
2 to 3 teaspoon harissa chili paste
1 can (14.5-ounce / 411-g) crushed tomatoes, undrained
¼ cup chopped fresh mint leaves

1.Press the Sauté button on the Instant Pot and heat the olive oil until it shimmers.
2.Add the garlic, paprika, cumin, ginger, salt, cinnamon, and pepper and cook for about 1 minute until fragrant. Add the remaining ingredients except the tomatoes and mint to the Instant Pot and stir to combine.
3.Secure the lid. Select the Manual mode and set the cooking time for 3 minutes at High Pressure.
4.Once cooking is complete, do a quick pressure release. Carefully open the lid.
5.Stir in the tomatoes and mint until heated though. Serve warm.

Ginger-Garlic Spicy Kale

Prep time: 5 minutes | Cook time: 6 minutes | Serves 4

1 tablespoon olive oil
5 cloves garlic
1 tablespoon fresh grated ginger
1 tablespoon crushed red

pepper flakes
8 cups kale, stems removed and chopped
1½ cups vegetable broth
1 tablespoon garlic chili paste

1.Press the Sauté button on the Instant Pot and heat the oil. Add in the garlic, ginger and crushed red pepper flakes. Sauté the mixture for 2 minutes or until highly fragrant.
2.Add in the vegetable broth and garlic chili paste. Whisk until well blended. Add in the kale and stir.
3.Lock the lid. Select the Manual mode and set the cooking time for 4 minutes on High Pressure. Once the timer goes off, perform a natural pressure release for 5 minutes, then release any remaining pressure. Carefully open the lid.
4.Stir before serving.

Chapter 14 Sauce and Broth

Andouille Sausage

Prep time: 10 minutes | Cook time: 35 minutes | Makes 8 large links

1½ cups vital wheat gluten flour
¼ cup nutritional yeast
1 teaspoon garlic powder
1 teaspoon cayenne powder
1 teaspoon dried marjoram
1 teaspoon onion powder

1 teaspoon dried thyme
1 teaspoon salt
½ teaspoon ground black pepper
¼ teaspoon ground allspice
1½ cups plus 1 cup water, divided

1.Add all the ingredients, except for 1 cup water to a mixer and mix on low speed for about 5 minutes. Knead in a bread maker or by hand until the dough begins to smooth out.
2.Cut into 8 equal pieces and roll into logs. Wrap in parchment paper and add to a large foil packet.
3.Add the trivet to the Instant Pot and pour in 1 cup of the water. Place the packets on top.
4.Lock the lid. Select the Manual mode and set the cooking time for 35 minutes on High Pressure. Once the timer goes off, perform a natural pressure release for 20 minutes, then release any remaining pressure. Carefully open the lid.
5.Serve.

Baked Potato

Prep time: 1 minute | Cook time: 15 minutes | Serves 4 to 6

1 cup water
4 to 6 medium Russet or Idaho potatoes, rinsed, scrubbed,

with skins pierced all over with a fork

1.Put a trivet in the Instant Pot and pour in the water, then place the pierced potatoes on the trivet.
2.Lock the lid. Press the Manual button on the Instant Pot and set the cooking time for 15 minutes at High Pressure.
3.When the timer beeps, perform a natural pressure release for 10 minutes, then release any remaining pressure. Carefully remove the lid.
4.Using tongs, remove the potatoes from the pot to a plate. Cool for 5 minutes before serving.

BBQ Sauce

Prep time: 5 minutes | Cook time: 5 minutes | Serves 6

8 ounces (227 g) Heinz ketchup
4 ounces (113 g) water
2 ounces (57 g) apple cider vinegar
½ ounce (14 g) lemon juice
½ ounce (14 g) light corn syrup
½ ounce (14 g) Worcestershire sauce

2½ tablespoons white sugar
2½ tablespoons brown sugar
½ tablespoon jerk rub
¼ tablespoon onion powder
¼ tablespoon dry mustard powder
¼ tablespoon freshly ground black pepper

1.Combine all the ingredients in the Instant Pot.
2.Lock the lid. Press the Manual button on the Instant Pot and set the cooking time for 5 minutes at High Pressure.
3.Once cooking is complete, do a natural pressure release for 10 minutes, then release any remaining pressure. Carefully open the lid.
4.Serve chilled or at room temperature.

Caesar Salad Dressing

Prep time: 6 mins, Cook Time: 3 hours, Servings: 6

½ cup olive oil
1 tbsp. Dijon mustard
½ cup grated Parmesan cheese
⅔ oz. chopped anchovies

½ freshly squeezed lemon juice
¼ cup water
Salt and pepper, to taste

1.Place all the ingredients in the Instant Pot and stir to incorporate.
2.Lock the lid. Select the Slow Cook mode, then set the timer for 3 hours at High Pressure.
3.Once the timer goes off, do a quick pressure release. Carefully open the lid.
4.You can use the Caesar dressing to marinate the meat or dress the salad, or you can use it as a dipping sauce for crudités.

Spinach and Artichoke Dip

Prep time: 5 minutes | Cook time: 4 minutes | Makes 2½ cups

1 cup raw cashews
1 cup unsweetened coconut milk
1 tablespoon nutritional yeast
1½ tablespoons apple cider vinegar
1 teaspoon onion powder

½ teaspoon garlic powder
½ to 1 teaspoon salt
1 (14-ounce / 397-g) can artichoke hearts in water
2 cups fresh spinach
1 cup water

1.In a blender, combine the cashews, milk, nutritional yeast, vinegar, onion powder, garlic powder, and salt. Purée until smooth and creamy, about 1 minute. Add the artichoke hearts and spinach and pulse a few times to chop up a bit. Pour the mixture into a baking pan.
2.Pour the water and insert the trivet in the Instant Pot. Put the pan on the trivet.
3.Lock the lid. Select the Manual mode and set the cooking time for 4 minutes on High Pressure. Once the timer goes off, perform a natural pressure release for 10 minutes, then release any remaining pressure. Carefully open the lid.
4.Let the baking pan cool for a few minutes before carefully lifting it out of the pot with oven mitts.
5.Transfer the dip to a bowl and serve.

Béarnaise Sauce

Prep time: 6 mins, Cook Time: 3 mins, Servings: 4

2 tsps. freshly squeezed lemon juice
2 tbsps. fresh tarragon

4 beaten egg yolks
¼ tsp. onion powder
⅔ lb. butter

1.Press the Sauté button on the Instant Pot and melt the butter.
2.Transfer the melted butter to a mixing bowl.
3.Slowly add the egg yolks to the bowl while whisking.
4.Continue stirring so that no lumps form.
5.Add the lemon juice, onion powder, and fresh tarragon, and whisk well.
6.Béarnaise sauce is suitable for many dishes, you can serve it with roasted beef chops, grilled pork chops, or chicken tenderloin.

Baby Bella Mushroom Gravy

Prep time: 5 minutes | Cook time: 24 to 26 minutes | Serves 4 to 6

1 tablespoon olive oil
8 ounces (227 g) baby bella mushrooms, diced
½ small sweet onion, diced
2 garlic cloves, minced
2 tablespoons Worcestershire sauce

1 teaspoon Dijon mustard
1 teaspoon rubbed sage
1¼ cups vegetable stock, divided
¼ cup red wine
1 tablespoon cornstarch

1.Press the Sauté button on the Instant Pot and heat the oil. Add the mushrooms and onion. Sauté for 2 to 3 minutes, stirring frequently. Add the garlic. Cook, stirring so it doesn't burn, for 30 seconds more.
2.Add the Worcestershire sauce, mustard, sage, ¾ cup of the stock and the red wine.
3.Lock the lid. Select the Manual mode and set the cooking time for 20 minutes on High Pressure. Once the timer goes off, perform a natural pressure release for 10 minutes, then release any remaining pressure.
4.In a small bowl, whisk the remaining ½ cup of the stock and cornstarch. Carefully remove the lid and stir this slurry into the gravy.
5.Select Sauté mode again and simmer the gravy for 2 to 3 minutes, or until thickened.

Caramel Sauce

Prep time: 5 minutes | Cook time: 15 minutes | Serves 4

1 cup sugar
⅓ cup water
3 tablespoons coconut oil

⅓ cup condensed coconut milk
1 teaspoon vanilla extract

1.Press the Sauté button on the Instant Pot and add the sugar and water. Stir well.
2.Sauté the mixture for 12 minutes, stirring occasionally.
3.Add the coconut oil, coconut milk, and vanilla and keep whisking until smooth.
4.Let the sauce stand for 10 minutes. Serve warm or refrigerate until chilled.

Balsamic Tomato Sauce

Prep time: 5 minutes | Cook time: 20 minutes | Makes 4 cups

2 tablespoons olive oil
2 cloves garlic, minced
2½ pounds (1.1 kg) vine-ripened tomatoes, peeled, diced and juice retained
1 tablespoon balsamic vinegar

1 teaspoon dried basil
1 teaspoon dried parsley
½ teaspoon granulated sugar
Pinch of salt
Pinch of freshly ground black pepper

1.Press the Sauté button on the Instant Pot and heat the oil. Add the garlic to the pot and sauté for 30 seconds, or until fragrant.
2.Add the tomatoes to the pot along with their juice. Add the remaining ingredients to the pot.
3.Lock the lid. Select the Manual mode and set the cooking time for 10 minutes on High Pressure. Once the timer goes off, perform a natural pressure release for 15 minutes, then release any remaining pressure. Carefully open the lid.
4.Stir the sauce. If you prefer a thicker sauce, press the Sauté button and simmer uncovered for 10 minutes, or until it reaches the desired thickness.
5.Serve immediately or refrigerate until ready to use.

Beef Stock

Prep time: 10 minutes | Cook time: 1 hour 30 minutes | Makes 4 cups

1 tablespoon oil
2 pounds (907 g) meaty beef bones

¼ teaspoon kosher salt (optional)
8 cups water

1.Press the Sauté button on the Instant Pot and heat the oil until shimmering.
2.Working in batches, arrange the beef bones in a single layer and sear each side for 6 to 8 minutes. Season with salt (if desired).
3.Add the water to the Instant Pot, making sure the bones are fully submerged.
4.Lock the lid. Select the Manual mode and set the cooking time for 75 minutes at High Pressure.
5.Once cooking is complete, do a natural pressure release for 15 minutes, then release any remaining pressure. Remove the lid.
6.Carefully pour the stock through a fine-mesh strainer into a large bowl.
7.Serve immediately or store in an airtight container in the refrigerator for up to 4 days or in the freezer for 6 to 12 months.

Citrus Berry Sauce

Prep time: 5 minutes | Cook time: 5 minutes | Serves 6

1 pound (454 g) cranberries (fresh or frozen)
10 strawberries, chopped
1 apple, cored and chopped
Juice from 1 lemon
Juice from 1 orange

1 teaspoon grated lemon zest
1 teaspoon grated orange zest
1 cup sugar
¼ cup water
1 cinnamon stick

1.Combine all the ingredients in the Instant Pot.
2.Secure the lid. Select the Manual mode and set the cooking time for 5 minutes at High Pressure.
3.Once cooking is complete, do a natural pressure release for 10 minutes, then release any remaining pressure. Carefully open the lid.
4.Serve immediately or refrigerate until ready to use.

Beef Bone Broth

Prep time: 5 minutes | Cook time: 2 hours | Serves 8

8 cups water
4 pounds (1.8 kg) beef bones
5 cloves garlic, smashed
2 carrots, peeled and sliced in half
2 ribs celery, sliced in half
1 medium yellow onion, with skin-on, quartered

10 whole black peppercorns
1 tablespoon apple cider vinegar
1 teaspoon poultry seasoning
1 teaspoon kosher salt
2 sprigs rosemary
2 sprigs thyme
2 bay leaves

1.Add all the ingredients to the Instant Pot and stir to combine.
2.Lock the lid. Press the Manual button on the Instant Pot and set the cooking time for 2 hours at High Pressure.
3.When the timer beeps, perform a natural pressure release for 30 minutes, then release any remaining pressure. Carefully remove the lid.
4.Let the broth cool for 15 minutes. Strain the broth through a fine-mesh strainer and discard all the solids.
5.Serve immediately or store in a sealed container in the refrigerator for 1 week or in the freezer for up to 3 months.

White Bean and Carrot Dip

Prep time: 10 minutes | Cook time: 3 minutes | Makes 3 cups

2 cups cooked white beans	Grated zest and juice of 1 lime
4 or 5 carrots, scrubbed or peeled and chopped	1 teaspoon smoked paprika
1 cup water	1 to 2 tablespoons olive oil
1 or 2 jalapeño peppers, deseeded and chopped	½ to ¾ teaspoon salt
2 tablespoons tahini	Freshly ground black pepper, to taste

1. In the Instant Pot, combine the white beans, carrots, and water.
2. Set the lid in place. Select the Manual mode and set the cooking time for 3 minutes on High Pressure. When the timer goes off, do a quick pressure release. Carefully open the lid.
3. Drain any excess water and transfer the beans and carrots to a food processor.
4. Add the jalapeños, tahini, lime zest and juice, and paprika. Purée, adding the olive oil, 1 tablespoon at a time, to achieve the desired texture. Taste and season with the salt and pepper.
5. Serve immediately or refrigerate until ready to use.

Cashew and Cauliflower Sour Cream

Prep time: 5 minutes | Cook time: 3 minutes | Makes 1 cup

2 cups cauliflower florets	1 teaspoon lemon juice
2 cups water	½ teaspoon apple cider vinegar
3 tablespoon cashews	Salt, to taste
1 teaspoon nutritional yeast	

1. Add the cauliflower, water and cashews to the Instant Pot.
2. Set the lid in place. Select the Manual mode and set the cooking time for 3 minutes on High Pressure. When the timer goes off, do a quick pressure release. Carefully open the lid.
3. Drain, reserving the liquid for blending.
4. In a blender, combine the cauliflower and cashews along with the nutritional yeast, lemon juice, apple cider vinegar and 1 teaspoon of the cooking liquid. Blend, scrape down the sides and add more cooking liquid if needed. Blend until smooth. Season with salt.
5. Serve immediately or refrigerate until ready to use.

Carrot and Celery Broth

Prep time: 5 minutes | Cook time: 30 minutes | Makes 4 cups

3 large stalks celery, cut in half	10 whole peppercorns
2 large yellow onions, peeled and halved	1 head garlic, cloves separated and peeled
2 medium carrots, peeled and cut into large pieces	1 bay leaf
	6 cups water

1. Add all the ingredients to the Instant Pot and stir to combine.
2. Lock the lid. Select the Manual mode and set the cooking time for 30 minutes on High Pressure. Once the timer goes off, perform a natural pressure release for 20 minutes, then release any remaining pressure. Carefully open the lid.
3. Strain the stock through a fine-mesh strainer or through cheesecloth placed in a colander.
4. Store in an airtight container in the refrigerator for 2 to 3 days, or in the freezer for up to 3 months.

Celery and Pepper Red Beans

Prep time: 10 minutes | Cook time: 43 to 45 minutes | Serves 8

3 tablespoons butter	1 teaspoon liquid smoke
1 cup diced white onion	½ teaspoon Worcestershire sauce
1 cup diced green bell pepper	1 teaspoon hot sauce
1 cup diced celery	½ teaspoon dried thyme
2 cloves garlic, minced	1 teaspoon cayenne pepper
2¼ cups dried red kidney beans	2 bay leaves
5 cups vegetable broth	2 teaspoons salt

1. Press the Sauté button on the Instant Pot and melt the butter. Add the onions, bell pepper, celery, and garlic. Stir-fry for 3 to 5 minutes, or until onions are translucent.
2. Stir in the remaining ingredients.
3. Lock the lid. Select the Bean/Chili mode and set the cooking time for 30 minutes on High Pressure. Once the timer goes off, perform a natural pressure release for 10 minutes, then release any remaining pressure. Carefully open the lid.
4. If a thicker consistency is desired, press the Sauté button and simmer the bean mixture for 10 minutes to thicken.
5. Remove the bay leaves before serving. Serve immediately.

Mushroom Chicken Stock

Prep time: 5 minutes | Cook time: 1 hour | Serves 8

2½ pounds (1.1 kg) chicken, bones only	1 teaspoon dried bay leaf
1 cup diced cremini mushrooms	1 teaspoon kosher salt
	½ teaspoon white pepper
1 small onion, unpeeled and halved	½ teaspoon whole black peppercorns
1 leek, finely chopped	8 cups water

1. Place all the ingredients into the Instant Pot and stir well.
2. Lock the lid. Select the Manual mode and set the cooking time for 1 hour at High Pressure.
3. Once cooking is complete, do a natural pressure release for 10 minutes, then release any remaining pressure. Carefully open the lid.
4. Strain the stock through a fine-mesh strainer and discard all the solids. Remove the layer of fat that forms on the top, if desired.
5. Serve immediately or store in an airtight container in the refrigerator for 3 to 4 days or in the freezer for up to 6 months.

Chicken Bone Broth

Prep time: 12 mins, Cook time: 2 to 3 hours, Servings: 4

1 lb. bones of one whole chicken	2 cloves garlic, minced
	8 cups water
2 tbsps. apple cider vinegar	1 tsp. sea salt

1. Add all the ingredients to the Instant Pot.
2. Lock the lid. Select the Soup mode, then set the timer for 2 to 3 hours at High Pressure.
3. Once the timer goes off, do a natural pressure release for 10 to 20 minutes, then release any remaining pressure. Carefully open the lid.
4. Strain the liquid and transfer the broth to an airtight container to store in the refrigerator for up to 5 days. Bone soup is healthy and recommended for those with a leaky gut.

Chicken Stock

Prep time: 5 minutes | Cook time: 1 hour | Makes 4 cups

2 pounds (907 g) chicken
bones and parts
1 large garlic clove, smashed
(optional)

¼ teaspoon kosher salt
(optional)
8 cups water

1.Place the chicken bones and parts and the garlic (if desired)
into the Instant Pot. Sprinkle with the salt, if desired.
2.Add the water to the Instant Pot, making sure the chicken is
fully submerged.
3.Lock the lid. Select the Manual mode and cook for 1 hour at
High Pressure.
4.Once cooking is complete, do a natural pressure release for
15 minutes, then release any remaining pressure. Remove the
lid.
5.Carefully pour the stock through a fine-mesh strainer into a
large bowl.
6.Serve immediately or refrigerate in an airtight container for up
to 4 days.

Chili Aioli

Prep time: 6 mins, Cook Time: 2 mins, Servings: 6

½ tsp. chili flakes
1 tbsp. lemon juice
1 egg yolk

2 garlic cloves, minced
¾ cup avocado oil

1.Put all ingredients in the Instant Pot and whisk vigorously.
2.Press the Sauté button and allow to heat for 2 minutes while
stirring. Do not bring to a boil.
3.You can serve the chili aioli on top of the seafood or salad.

Creamy Alfredo

Prep time: 5 minutes | Cook time: 6 minutes | Serves 4

½ pound (227 g) dry linguine
noodles, break in half
1½ cups vegetable broth
1½ cups heavy cream

¾ cup shredded Parmesan
cheese
1 teaspoon minced garlic
Salt and pepper, to taste

1.Combine all the ingredients in the Instant Pot.
2.Secure the lid. Select the Manual mode and set the cooking
time for 6 minutes at High Pressure.
3.Once cooking is complete, do a quick pressure release.
Carefully open the lid.
4.Cool for 5 minutes before serving.

Cauliflower Sauce

Prep time: 5 minutes | Cook time: 3 minutes | Serves 4

12 ounces (340 g) cauliflower
florets
½ cup water

¼ teaspoon pepper
¼ teaspoon garlic salt
2 tablespoons almond milk

1.Except for the almond milk, combine all the ingredients in the
Instant Pot.
2.Secure the lid. Select the Manual mode and set the cooking
time for 3 minutes at High Pressure.
3.Once cooking is complete, do a quick pressure release.
Remove the lid.
4.Purée the mixture with an immersion blender until smooth.
5.Pour in the almond milk and whisk to combine.
6.Serve chilled or at room temperature.

Chili Sauce

Prep time: 5 minutes | Cook time: 8 minutes | Serves 4

4 medium-sized Ancho chili
peppers, stems and seeds
removed
2 teaspoons kosher salt
1½ teaspoons sugar
½ teaspoon ground dried
oregano

½ teaspoon ground cumin
1½ cups water
2 cloves garlic, crushed
2 tablespoons heavy cream
2 tablespoons apple cider
vinegar

1.On your cutting board, chop the peppers into small pieces.
2.Place the pepper pieces into the Instant Pot along with the
salt, sugar, oregano, and cumin. Pour in the water and stir to
combine.
3.Lock the lid. Press the Manual button on the Instant Pot and
set the cooking time for 8 minutes at High Pressure.
4.Once cooking is complete, do a natural pressure release for
10 minutes, then release any remaining pressure. Carefully
open the lid.
5.Transfer the mixture to a food processor. Add the garlic, heavy
cream, and apple cider vinegar. Process until smooth and
creamy.
6.Serve chilled or at room temperature.

Chimichurri Sauce

Prep time: 6 mins, Cook Time: 3 hours, Servings: 6

2 garlic cloves, minced
1 green chili pepper, chopped
1 lemon, juice and zest

2 tbsps. olive oil
½ yellow bell pepper, chopped
1 tbsp. white wine vinegar

1.Place all ingredients in the Instant Pot and stir to combine.
2.Lock the lid. Select the Slow Cook mode, then set the timer
for 3 hours at High Pressure.
3.Once the timer goes off, do a quick pressure release. Carefully
open the lid.
4.Allow to cool for 30 minutes and serve with grilled meats,
steaks, or sausages.

Marinara Sauce

Prep time: 5 minutes | Cook time: 13 minutes | Makes 4 cups

2 tablespoons oil
1 medium onion, grated
3 garlic cloves, roughly
chopped
1 (28-ounce / 794-g) can
or carton whole or crushed
tomatoes
1 teaspoon kosher salt, plus

more as needed
Freshly ground black pepper,
to taste
½ teaspoon dried oregano or 2
oregano sprigs
Pinch granulated or raw sugar
(optional)

1.Press the Sauté button on the Instant Pot and heat the oil until
it shimmers.
2.Add the grated onion and sauté for 2 minutes until tender. Add
the garlic and sauté for 1 minute.
3.Fold in the tomatoes, salt, oregano, and pepper and stir well.
4.Secure the lid. Select the Manual mode and set the cooking
time for 10 minutes at High Pressure.
5.Once cooking is complete, do a quick pressure release.
Carefully open the lid.
6.Taste and adjust the seasoning, if needed. Add the sugar to
balance the acidity of the tomatoes, if desired.
7.Store in an airtight container in the refrigerator for up to 4 days
or freeze for up to 6 months.

Coconut Milk Custard

Prep time:5 minutes | Cook time: 30 minutes | Serves 4

3 eggs
1 cup coconut milk
⅓ cup Swerve

1 teaspoon vanilla extract
Cooking spray
2 cups water

1. Spritz a baking dish with cooking spray. Set aside.
2. Beat together the eggs, coconut milk, Swerve, and vanilla and in a large mixing bowl until well incorporated.
3. Transfer the egg mixture to the prepared baking dish and cover with foil.
4. Add the water and trivet to the Instant Pot, then place the baking dish on top of the trivet.
5. Secure the lid. Select the Manual mode and set the cooking time for 30 minutes at High Pressure.
6. Once cooking is complete, do a natural pressure release for 10 minutes, then release any remaining pressure. Carefully open the lid.
7. Allow to cool for 5 to 10 minutes before removing and serving.

Cheese Sauce

Prep time: 6 mins, Cook Time: 4 hours, Servings: 4

¼ cup cream cheese
¼ cup heavy whipping cream
2 tbsps. melted butter

Salt and pepper, to taste
½ cup grated Cheddar cheese

1. Put all the ingredients in the Instant Pot and stir to combine.
2. Lock the lid. Select the Slow Cook mode, then set the timer for 4 hours at High Pressure.
3. Once the timer goes off, do a quick pressure release. Carefully open the lid.
4. You can serve this cheese sauce with French fries, Nachos, chicken nuggets, or pretzels.

Hollandaise Sauce

Prep time: 6 mins, Cook Time: 5 mins, Servings: 4

⅔ lb. butter
4 egg yolks, beaten

2 tbsps. lemon juice
Salt and pepper, to taste

1. Press the Sauté button on the Instant Pot.
2. Add the butter and heat to melt.
3. Whisk vigorously while adding the yolks. Cook for 1 minute.
4. Continue stirring and add the lemon juice, salt, and pepper.
5. You can serve the hollandaise sauce with poached or grilled fish or chicken.

Keto Gravy

Prep time: 6 mins, Cook Time: 10 mins, Servings: 6

2 tbsps. butter
1 white onion, chopped
2 cups chicken bone broth

1 tbsp. balsamic vinegar
¼ cup coconut milk

1. Press the Sauté button on the Instant Pot.
2. Melt the butter and sauté the onions for 2 minutes.
3. Add the remaining ingredients. Stir constantly for 5 minutes or until slightly thickened.
4. You can serve the gravy on top of any roasted steaks, meats, or seafoods. You can even use it as a dressing for your salad.

Fish Stock

Prep time: 5 minutes | Cook time: 50 minutes | Serves 10

1 tablespoon olive oil
2 salmon heads, cut into quarters, rinsed, and patted dry
2 cloves garlic, sliced
1 cup roughly chopped celery

1 cup roughly chopped carrots
2 lemongrass stalks, roughly chopped
8 cups water
Handful fresh thyme, including stems

1. Press the Sauté button on the Instant Pot and heat the oil.
2. Add the salmon to the Instant Pot and lightly sear the fish on both sides, about 4 minutes.
3. Add the remaining ingredients to the Instant Pot and stir to combine.
4. Secure the lid. Select the Soup mode and set the cooking time for 45 minutes at High Pressure.
5. Once cooking is complete, do a natural pressure release for 15 minutes, then release any remaining pressure. Remove the lid.
6. Over a large bowl, carefully strain the stock through a fine-mesh strainer.
7. Serve immediately or refrigerate until ready to use.

Garden Tomato Salsa

Prep time: 5 minutes | Cook time: 5 minutes | Makes 6 to 8 cups

8 large tomatoes, roughly chopped
6 garlic cloves, finely diced
2 jalapeño peppers, deseeded and diced
1 red bell pepper, diced
1 small red onion, diced
1 small yellow onion, diced
1 tablespoon ground cumin

3 to 4 teaspoons salt
½ teaspoon freshly ground black pepper
½ teaspoon baking soda
¼ cup tomato paste
2 tablespoons freshly squeezed lime juice
1 teaspoon chopped fresh cilantro leaves

1. In the Instant Pot, stir together the tomatoes, garlic, jalapeños, bell pepper, red onion, yellow onion, cumin, salt, pepper, and baking soda.
2. Lock the lid. Select the Manual mode and set the cooking time for 5 minutes on High Pressure. Once the timer goes off, perform a natural pressure release for 10 minutes, then release any remaining pressure. Carefully open the lid.
3. Stir in the tomato paste, lime juice and cilantro.
4. Serve chilled or at room temperature.

White or Brown Rice

Prep time: 2 minutes | Cook time: 3 or 25 minutes | Serves 4

1 cup white or brown rice (do not use instant or ready rice)

1 cup water or broth of your choice

1. Put the rice in a fine-mesh strainer and rinse it under cold running water for 1 minute, shaking it around until the water coming through goes from cloudy to clear.
2. Place the rice and pour water into the Instant Pot and stir well.
3. Secure the lid. Select the Manual mode and set the cooking time for 3 minutes at High Pressure for white rice, 25 minutes for brown rice.
4. Once cooking is complete, do a natural pressure release for 10 minutes, then release any remaining pressure. Carefully remove the lid.
5. Fluff the rice with a fork and serve warm.

Hard-Boiled Eggs

Prep time: 1 minute | Cook time: 5 minutes | Serves 6

8 to 10 large eggs | 1 cup water

1. Add the water and trivet to the Instant Pot, then place the eggs on top of the trivet.
2. Lock the lid. Select the Manual mode and set the cooking time for 5 minutes at High Pressure.
3. When the timer beeps, perform a natural pressure release for 5 minutes, then release any remaining pressure. Carefully remove the lid.
4. Transfer the eggs to a bowl of ice water to cool for at least 1 minute. Once cooled, peel and serve immediately.

Vegetable Bouillon

Prep time: 5 minutes | Cook time: 10 minutes | Makes 4 cups

2 large onions, quartered
½ cup water
6 medium carrots, cut into lengths to fit the Instant Pot
4 celery stalks, cut into lengths
to fit the Instant Pot
8 sprigs fresh thyme
1 sprig fresh rosemary
1 cup nutritional yeast
Salt, to taste (optional)

1. Add the onions, water, carrots, celery, thyme and rosemary to the Instant Pot.
2. Lock the lid. Select the Manual mode and set the cooking time for 10 minutes on High Pressure. Once the timer goes off, perform a natural pressure release for 10 minutes, then release any remaining pressure. Carefully open the lid.
3. Scoop the cooked veggies and broth into a blender and add the nutritional yeast. Blend until smooth. Add salt and blend again.
4. Store in the refrigerator up to a week or put in ice-cube trays and freeze.

Satay Sauce

Prep time: 6 mins, Cook Time: 3 hours, Servings: 6

⅓ cup peanut butter
1 red chili pepper, finely chopped
4 tbsps. soy sauce
1 cup coconut milk
1 garlic clove, minced

1. Place all ingredients in the Instant Pot and stir until everything is well combined.
2. Lock the lid. Select the Slow Cook mode, then set the timer for 3 hours at High Pressure.
3. Once the timer goes off, do a quick pressure release. Carefully open the lid.
4. Serve the satay sauce with beef kebabs or chicken skewers, or you can serve it as dipping sauce.

Soy Yogurt

Prep time: 5 minutes | Cook time: 8 hours | Makes 4 cups

1 (32-ounce / 907-g) container plain unsweetened soy milk
1 packet yogurt starter
1 tablespoon tapioca starch

1. Whisk together the soy milk, starter and starch in a mixing bowl. Pour the mixture into small glass jars. Sit them right on the pot bottom.
2. Set the lid in place. Select the Yogurt mode and set the cooking time for 8 hours. When the timer goes off, do a quick pressure release. Carefully open the lid.
3. Serve chilled. Store in the fridge for up to 10 days.

Carrot and Mushroom Broth

Prep time: 10 minutes | Cook time: 20 minutes | Makes 8 cups

4 medium carrots, peeled and cut into large pieces
2 large leeks, trimmed and cut into large pieces
2 large yellow onions, peeled and quartered
1 large stalk celery, chopped
2 cups sliced button mushrooms
5 whole cloves garlic
Pinch of dried red pepper flakes
8½ cups water

1. Add all the ingredients to the Instant Pot and stir to combine.
2. Lock the lid. Select the Manual mode and set the cooking time for 20 minutes on High Pressure. Once the timer goes off, perform a natural pressure release for 15 minutes, then release any remaining pressure. Carefully open the lid.
3. Strain the broth through a fine-mesh strainer or through cheesecloth placed in a colander.
4. Store in a covered container in the refrigerator or freezer.

Corn and Mushroom Stock

Prep time: 10 minutes | Cook time: 15 minutes | Serves 8

4 large mushrooms, diced
2 cobs of corns
1 small onion, unpeeled and halved
1 celery stalk, chopped into thirds
1 teaspoon dried bay leaf
1 teaspoon grated ginger
1 sprig fresh parsley
1 teaspoon kosher salt
½ teaspoon ground turmeric
½ teaspoon whole black peppercorns
8 cups water

1. Place all the ingredients into the Instant Pot and stir well.
2. Lock the lid. Press the Manual button on the Instant Pot and set the cooking time for 15 minutes at High Pressure.
3. Once cooking is complete, do a natural pressure release for 10 minutes, then release any remaining pressure. Carefully open the lid.
4. Strain the stock through a fine-mesh strainer and discard all the solids.
5. Serve immediately or refrigerate in an airtight container for 3 to 4 days.

Mushroom Broth

Prep time: 5 minutes | Cook time: 15 minutes | Serves 8

4 ounces (113 g) dried mushrooms, soaked and rinsed
½ cup celery, chopped
½ cup carrots, chopped
4 cloves garlic, crushed
4 bay leaves
1 onion, quartered
8 cups water
Salt and ground black pepper, to taste.

1. Add all the ingredients except the salt and pepper to the Instant Pot and stir well.
2. Lock the lid. Press the Manual button on the Instant Pot and set the cooking time for 15 minutes at High Pressure.
3. Once cooking is complete, do a quick pressure release. Open the lid.
4. Add the salt and pepper to taste.
5. Over a large bowl, carefully strain the stock through a fine-mesh strainer. Discard all the solids.
6. Serve immediately or store in a sealed container in the refrigerator for 4 to 5 days or in the freezer for up to 6 months.

Pork and Carrot Broth

Prep time: 5 minutes | Cook time: 1 hour | Serves 8

3 pounds (1.4 kg) pork bones
3 large carrots, cut into large chunks
3 large stalks celery, cut into large chunks
2 cloves garlic, sliced
1 bay leaf
1 tablespoon apple cider vinegar
8 cups water
1 teaspoon whole peppercorns
Salt, to taste

1. Place all the ingredients into the Instant Pot and stir to incorporate.
2. Secure the lid. Select the Manual mode and set the cooking time for 1 hour at High Pressure.
3. When the timer beeps, perform a natural pressure release for 10 minutes, then release any remaining pressure. Carefully remove the lid.
4. Allow the broth to cool for 10 to 15 minutes. Strain the broth through a fine-mesh strainer and discard all the solids.
5. Serve immediately or store in a sealed container in the refrigerator for 4 to 5 days or in the freezer for up to 6 months.

Ranch Dip

Prep time: 6 mins, Cook Time: 2 mins, Servings: 8

1 cup olive oil
Salt and pepper, to taste
1 cup beaten egg whites
1 tsp. mustard paste
Juice of 1 lemon

1. In the Instant Pot, add all the ingredients and mix well.
2. Press the Sauté button and heat for 2 minutes while stirring. Do not bring to a simmer.
3. You can serve the ranch dip with chicken nuggets, French fries, or green salad.

Seafood Stock

Prep time: 5 minutes | Cook time: 30 minutes | Serves 8

8 cups water
Shells and heads from ½ pound (227 g) prawns
3 cloves garlic, sliced
4 carrots, cut into chunks
4 onions, quartered
2 bay leaves
1 teaspoon whole black peppercorns

1. Place all the ingredients into the Instant Pot.
2. Secure the lid. Select the Manual mode and set the cooking time for 30 minutes at High Pressure.
3. Once cooking is complete, do a natural pressure release for 15 minutes, then release any remaining pressure. Remove the lid.
4. Over a large bowl, carefully strain the stock through a fine-mesh strainer.
5. Serve immediately or store in an airtight container in the refrigerator for 3 days or in the freezer for up to 3 months.

Almond Milk

Prep time: 5 minutes | Cook time: 10 minutes | Makes 4 cups

1 cup almonds
6 cups water, divided

1. Add the almonds and 2 cups of the water to the Instant Pot.
2. Lock the lid. Select the Manual mode and set the cooking time for 10 minutes on High Pressure.
3. Once the timer goes off, perform a natural pressure release for 10 minutes, then release any remaining pressure. Carefully open the lid. Drain the almonds.
4. In a blender, combine the almonds and 4 cups of the water and blend well. Strain through a nut milk bag and store in the refrigerator.

Thousand Island Dressing

Prep time: 10 mins, Cook Time: 2 hours, Servings: 4

1 tsp. tabasco
1 shallot, finely chopped
1 cup mayonnaise
4 tbsps. chopped dill pickles
1 tbsp. freshly squeezed lemon juice
¼ cup water
Salt and pepper, to taste

1. Place all the ingredients in the Instant Pot and whisk to combine.
2. Lock the lid. Select the Slow Cook mode, then set the timer for 2 hours at High Pressure.
3. Once the timer goes off, do a quick pressure release. Carefully open the lid.
4. You can use this dressing to serve the burgers, sandwiches, or salads.

Tomato Salsa

Prep time: 10 minutes | Cook time: 30 minutes | Serves 6

6 cups fresh tomatoes, diced, peeled, and deseeded
1½ (6-ounce / 170-g) cans tomato paste
1½ green bell peppers, diced
1 cup jalapeño peppers, deseeded and chopped
¼ cup vinegar
2 yellow onions, diced
½ tablespoon kosher salt
1½ tablespoons sugar
1 tablespoon cayenne pepper
1 tablespoon garlic powder

1. Place all the ingredients into the Instant Pot and stir to incorporate.
2. Secure the lid. Select the Manual mode and set the cooking time for 30 minutes at High Pressure.
3. Once cooking is complete, do a natural pressure release for 10 minutes, then release any remaining pressure. Carefully open the lid.
4. Serve immediately or refrigerate in an airtight container for up to 5 days.

Caramel Sauce

Prep time: 5 minutes | Cook time: 45 minutes | Serves 4 to 6

1 (11-ounce / 312-g) can sweetened condensed coconut milk

1 cup water
1 teaspoon coarse sea salt (optional)

1. Peel the label off the can and place the can on a trivet and into your Instant Pot. Pour in the water.
2. Lock the lid. Select the Manual mode and set the cooking time for 45 minutes on High Pressure. Once the timer goes off, perform a natural pressure release for 20 minutes, then release any remaining pressure. Carefully open the lid.
3. Remove the can and trivet. Set aside until cool enough to handle.
4. Once cooled, open the can and pour the caramel sauce into a glass jar for storage. For a salted caramel, stir in the sea salt.

Tabasco Sauce

Prep time: 5 minutes | Cook time: 1 hour | Makes 2 cups

18 ounces (510 g) fresh hot peppers or any kind, stems removed and chopped

1¾ cups apple cider
3 teaspoons smoked or plain salt

1. Combine all the ingredients in the Instant Pot.
2. Lock the lid. Press the Manual button on the Instant Pot and set the cooking time for 1 hour at High Pressure.
3. Once cooking is complete, do a natural pressure release for 15 minutes, then release any remaining pressure. Carefully open the lid.
4. Purée the mixture with an immersion blender until smooth.
5. Serve immediately or refrigerate until ready to use.

Basil Tomato Sauce

Prep time: 5 minutes | Cook time: 16 minutes | Serves 4

1 tablespoon olive oil
3 cloves garlic, minced
2½ pounds (1.1 kg) Roma tomatoes, diced

½ cup chopped basil
¼ cup vegetable broth
Salt, to taste

1. Set your Instant Pot to Sauté and heat the olive oil.
2. Add the minced garlic and sauté for 1 minute until fragrant. Stir in the tomatoes, basil, and vegetable broth.
3. Lock the lid. Press the Manual button on the Instant Pot and cook for 10 minutes at High Pressure.
4. Once cooking is complete, do a quick pressure release. Carefully open the lid.
5. Set your Instant Pot to Sauté again and cook for another 5 minutes.
6. Blend the mixture with an immersion blender until smooth.
7. Season with salt to taste. Serve chilled or at room temperature.

Cinnamon-Vanilla Applesauce

Prep time: 10 minutes | Cook time: 5 minutes | Serves 6 to 8

3 pounds (1.4 kg) apples, cored and quartered
⅓ cup water
1 teaspoon ground cinnamon

1 teaspoon freshly squeezed lemon juice
1 teaspoon vanilla extract
½ teaspoon salt

1. Add all the ingredients to the Instant Pot and stir to combine.
2. Lock the lid. Select the Manual mode and set the cooking time for 5 minutes on High Pressure. Once the timer goes off, perform a natural pressure release for 10 minutes, then release any remaining pressure. Carefully open the lid.
3. Using an immersion blender, blend the applesauce until smooth.
4. Serve immediately or refrigerate until ready to use.

Vegetable Stock

Prep time: 5 minutes | Cook time: 30 minutes | Serves 8

8 cups water
4 celery stalks, cut into chunks
4 carrots, cut into chunks
4 thyme sprigs
6 parsley sprigs

2 teaspoons chopped garlic
2 bay leaves
2 green onions, sliced
10 whole black peppercorns
1½ teaspoons salt

1. Except for the salt, add all the ingredients to the Instant Pot.
2. Secure the lid. Select the Soup mode and set the cooking time for 30 minutes at High Pressure.
3. Once cooking is complete, do a natural pressure release for 15 minutes, then release any remaining pressure. Remove the lid.
4. Sprinkle with the salt and whisk well.
5. Over a large bowl, carefully strain the stock through a fine-mesh strainer.
6. Serve immediately or store in an airtight container in the refrigerator for 4 to 5 days or in the freezer for up to 3 months.

Chapter 15 Desserts

Chocolate Almond Fudge

Prep time: 5 minutes | Cook time: 5 minutes | Serves 30

2½ cups Swerve
1¾ cups unsweetened almond milk
1½ cups almond butter
8 ounces (227 g) unsweetened

baking chocolate, finely chopped
1 teaspoon almond or vanilla extract
¼ teaspoon fine sea salt

1. Line a baking dish with greased parchment paper.
2. Place the sweetener, almond milk, almond butter, and chocolate in the Instant Pot. Stir well. Select the Sauté mode and cook for 2 minutes.
3. Set the Instant Pot to Keep Warm for 3 minutes, or until the fudge mixture is completely melted and well mixed. Fold in the extract and salt and stir well.
4. Pour the fudge mixture into the prepared baking dish, cover, and refrigerate until firm, about 4 hours.
5. Cut the fudge into 30 equal-sized pieces and serve.

Apple and Oatmeal Crisps

Prep time: 15 minutes | Cook time: 5 minutes | Serves 4

5 apples, cored and chopped
1 tablespoon honey
2 teaspoons cinnamon powder
½ teaspoon nutmeg powder
1 cup water
¾ cup old fashioned rolled oats
¼ cup all-purpose flour

4 tablespoons unsalted butter, melted
½ teaspoon salt
¼ cup brown sugar
1 cup vanilla ice cream, for topping

1. In the Instant Pot, mix the apples, honey, cinnamon, nutmeg, and water.
2. In a medium bowl, combine the rolled oats, flour, butter, salt, and brown sugar. Drizzle the mixture over the apples.
3. Seal the lid, set to the Manual mode and set the cooking time for 5 minutes on High Pressure.
4. When cooking is complete, allow a natural pressure release for 10 minutes, then release any remaining pressure. Carefully open the lid.
5. Spoon the apple into serving bowls, top with vanilla ice cream and serve immediately.

Simple Chocolate Cake

Prep time: 12 mins, Cook Time: 6 mins, Servings: 3

4 tbsps. self-raising flour
1 egg
4 tbsps. sugar
4 tbsps. milk

1 tbsp. cocoa powder
1 tbsp. melted coconut oil
1 cup water

1. In a bowl, combine the flour, egg, sugar, milk and cocoa powder, stir well and set the mixture to a cake pan greased with coconut oil.
2. Add the water to the Instant Pot, add steamer basket, add cake inside.
3. Lock the lid. Set the Instant Pot to Manual mode, then set the timer for 6 minutes at High Pressure.
4. When the timer goes off, perform a natural release for 5 minutes, then release any remaining pressure. Carefully open the lid.
5. Serve the cake warm.

Apricots Dulce de Leche

Prep time: 15 minutes | Cook time: 25 minutes | Serves 6

5 cups water
2 cups sweetened condensed milk

4 apricots, halved, cored, and sliced

1. Pour the water in the Instant Pot and fit in a trivet. Divide condensed milk into 6 medium jars and close with lids. Place jars on trivet.
2. Seal the lid, set to the Manual mode and set the timer for 25 minutes at High Pressure.
3. When cooking is complete, use a natural pressure release for 10 minutes, then release any remaining pressure. Unlock the lid.
4. Use a fork to whisk until creamy. Serve with sliced apricots.

Bulletproof Hot Choco

Prep time: 6 mins, Cook Time: 5 mins, Servings: 1

2 tbsps. coconut oil, divided
½ cup coconut milk
½ cup water
2 tbsps. unsweetened cocoa

powder
Dash of cinnamon
1 tsp. erythritol

1. Place 1 tablespoon of coconut oil and milk in the Instant Pot and pour in the water.
2. Lock the lid. Set the Instant Pot to Manual mode, then set the timer for 5 minutes at High Pressure.
3. When the timer goes off, perform a quick release.
4. Open the lid and press the Sauté button.
5. Add 1 tablespoon of coconut oil, cocoa powder, cinnamon and erythritol. Stir to combine well and the mixture has a thick consistency.
6. Transfer the mixture on a baking sheet, then put the sheet in the refrigerator for several hours. Serve chilled.

Caramel Apple Cobbler

Prep time: 30 minutes | Cook time: 2 minutes | Serves 4

5 apples, cored, peeled, and cut into 1-inch cubes, at room temperature
2 tablespoons caramel syrup
½ teaspoon ground nutmeg
2 teaspoons ground cinnamon
2 tablespoons maple syrup
½ cup water

¾ cup old-fashioned oats
¼ cup all-purpose flour
⅓ cup brown sugar
4 tablespoons salted butter, softened
½ teaspoon sea salt
Vanilla ice cream, for serving

1. Place the apples in the Instant Pot and top with the caramel syrup, nutmeg, cinnamon, maple syrup, and water. Stir to coat well.
2. Combine the oats, flour, brown sugar, butter and salt in a large bowl. Mix well and pour over the apple mixture in the pot.
3. Secure the lid, then select the Manual mode and set the cooking time for 2 minutes on High Pressure.
4. When cooking is complete, perform a natural pressure release for 20minutes, then release any remaining pressure. Carefully open the lid.
5. Transfer the cobbler to a plate, then topped with vanilla ice cream and serve.

Apple Bread

Prep time: 12 mins, Cook Time: 1 hour, Servings: 4

1 tbsp. baking powder
3 eggs
1½ cups sweetened condensed milk
2½ cups white flour
3 apples, peeled, cored and chopped
1 tbsp. melted coconut oil
1 cup water

1. In a bowl, mix the baking powder with eggs and whisk well.
2. Add the milk, flour and apple pieces, whisk well and pour into a loaf pan greased with coconut oil.
3. In the Instant Pot, add the water. Arrange a trivet in the pot, then place the loaf pan on the trivet.
4. Lock the lid. Set the Instant Pot to Slow Cook mode, then set the timer for 1 hour at High Pressure.
5. When the timer goes off, perform a natural release for 10 minutes, then release any remaining pressure. Carefully open the lid.
6. Leave apple bread to cool down, slice and serve.

Apple Wontons

Prep time: 10 minutes | Cook time: 12 minutes | Serves 8

1 (8-ounce / 227-g) can refrigerated crescent rolls
1 large apple, peeled, cored, and cut into 8 wedges
4 tablespoons unsalted butter
2 teaspoons ground cinnamon
¼ teaspoon ground nutmeg
½ cup brown sugar
1 teaspoon vanilla extract
¾ cup orange juice

1. Make the dumplings: Unfold the crescent rolls on a clean work surface, then separate into the 8 triangles. Place 1 apple wedge on each crescent roll triangle and fold the dough around the apple to enclose it. Set aside.
2. Select the Sauté mode of the Instant Pot. Add the butter and heat for 2 minutes until melted.
3. Add the cinnamon, nutmeg, sugar, and vanilla, heating and stirring until melted.
4. Place the dumplings in the Instant Pot and mix in the orange juice.
5. Lock the lid. Select the Manual mode. Set the time for 10 minutes at High Pressure.
6. When cooking is complete, let the pressure release naturally for 5 minutes, then release any remaining pressure. Unlock the lid.
7. Serve immediately.

Chocolate Mug Cake

Prep time: 12 mins, Cook Time: 10 mins, Servings: 1

1 cup water
6 drops liquid stevia
1½ tbsps. cocoa powder
1 egg, beaten
¼ tsp. baking powder
¼ cup almond powder
Salt, to taste

1. Place a steam rack in the Instant Pot and pour in the water.
2. In a bowl, add all the remaining ingredients.
3. Mix until well combined.
4. Pour into a heat-proof mug.
5. Place the mug on the steam rack.
6. Lock the lid. Set the Instant Pot to Steam mode, then set the timer for 10 minutes at High Pressure.
7. When the timer goes off, perform a quick release. Carefully open the lid.
8. Serve the cake immediately.

Beer Poached Pears

Prep time: 5 minutes | Cook time: 10 minutes | Serves 2

3 peeled (stem on) firm pears
1½ cups (1 bottle) stout beer
½ cup packed brown sugar
1 vanilla bean, split lengthwise and seeds scraped

1. Slice a thin layer from the bottom of each pear so they can stand upright. Use a melon baller to scoop out the seeds and core from the bottom.
2. Stir together the beer, brown sugar, and vanilla bean and seeds in the Instant Pot until combined. Place the pears upright in the pot.
3. Lock the lid. Select the Manual mode and set the cooking time for 9 minutes at High Pressure.
4. When the timer beeps, perform a quick pressure release. Carefully remove the lid.
5. Using tongs, carefully remove the pears by their stems and transfer to a plate and set aside.
6. Set the Instant Pot to Sauté and simmer until the liquid in the Instant Pot is reduced by half.
7. Strain the liquid into a bowl through a fine-mesh sieve, then pour over the pears.
8. Serve at room temperature or chilled.

Coconut Boosters

Prep time: 2 hours, Cook Time: 5 mins, Servings: 5

1 cup coconut oil
½ cup chia seeds
1 tsp. vanilla extract
1 tsp. erythritol
¼ cup unsweetened dried coconut flakes

1. Press the Sauté button on the Instant Pot.
2. Heat the coconut oil and add the chia seeds, vanilla extract, erythritol, and coconut flakes and sauté for 5 minutes.
3. Allow to cool and remove the mixture from the pot. Form the mixture into balls and set on a baking sheet.
4. Allow to set in the refrigerator for 2 hours before serving.

Oat and Black Bean Brownies

Prep time: 5 minutes | Cook time: 25 minutes | Serves 4

1½ cups canned black beans, drained
½ cup steel-cut oats
½ teaspoon salt
3 tablespoons unsweetened cocoa powder
½ cup maple syrup
¼ cup coconut oil
¾ teaspoon baking powder
½ cup chocolate chips
Cooking spray
1½ cups water

1. Pulse the black beans, oats, salt, cocoa powder, maple syrup, coconut oil, and baking powder in a food processor until very smooth.
2. Pour the batter into a medium bowl and fold in the chocolate chips.
3. Spray a 7-inch springform pan with cooking spray and pour in the batter. Cover the pan with aluminum foil.
4. Pour the water into the Instant Pot and insert a trivet. Place the pan on the trivet.
5. Lock the lid. Select the Manual mode and set the cooking time for 25 minutes at High Pressure.
6. When the timer beeps, perform a natural pressure release for 10 minutes, then release any remaining pressure. Carefully remove the lid.
7. Let cool for 5 minutes, then transfer to the fridge to chill for 1 to 2 hours.
8. Cut the brownies into squares and serve.

Bourbon and Date Pudding Cake

Prep time: 15 minutes | Cook time: 25 minutes | Serves 4

¾ cup all-purpose flour
¼ teaspoon allspice
½ teaspoon baking soda
¼ teaspoon cloves powder
½ teaspoon cinnamon powder
¼ teaspoon salt
1 teaspoon baking powder
2 tablespoons bourbon

3 tablespoons unsalted butter, melted
6 tablespoons hot water
2 tablespoons whole milk
1 egg, beaten
½ cup chopped dates
1 cup water
½ cup caramel sauce

1. In a bowl, combine the flour, allspice, baking soda, cloves, cinnamon, salt, and baking powder.
2. In another bowl, mix the bourbon, butter, hot water, and milk. Pour the bourbon mixture into the flour mixture and mix until well mixed. Whisk in egg and fold in dates.
3. Spritz 4 medium ramekins with cooking spray. Divide the mixture among them, and cover with foil.
4. Pour the water in the Instant Pot, then fit in a trivet and place ramekins on top.
5. Seal the lid, select the Manual mode and set the cooking time for 25 minutes at High Pressure.
6. When cooking is complete, perform a natural pressure release for 10 minutes, then release any remaining pressure.
7. Unlock the lid and carefully remove ramekins, invert onto plates, and drizzle caramel sauce on top. Serve warm.

Coconut Brown Rice Pudding

Prep time: 15 minutes | Cook time: 22 minutes | Serves 6

1 cup long-grain brown rice, rinsed
2 cups water
1 (15-ounce / 425-g) can full-fat coconut milk

½ teaspoon pure vanilla extract
½ teaspoon ground cinnamon
⅓ cup maple syrup
Pinch fine sea salt

1. Combine the rice and water in the Instant Pot and secure the lid. Select the Manual mode and set the cooking time for 22 minutes on Low Pressure.
2. When timer beeps, allow the pressure to naturally release for 10 minutes, then release any remaining pressure. Carefully open the lid.
3. Add the coconut milk, vanilla, cinnamon, maple syrup, and salt. Stir well to combine.
4. Use an immersion blender to pulse the pudding until creamy. Serve warm or you can refrigerate the pudding for an hour before serving.

Caramel Popcorns

Prep time: 5 minutes | Cook time: 7 minutes | Serves 4

4 tablespoons butter
1 cup sweet corn kernels

3 tablespoons brown sugar
¼ cup whole milk

1. Set the Instant Pot to Sauté mode, melt butter and mix in the corn kernels, heat for 1 minute or until the corn is popping.
2. Cover the lid, and keep cooking for 3 more minutes or until the corn stops popping. Open the lid and transfer the popcorns to a bowl.
3. Combine brown sugar and milk in the pot and cook for 3 minutes or until sugar dissolves. Stir constantly.
4. Drizzle caramel sauce over corns and toss to coat thoroughly. Serve warm.

Cardamom and Pistachio Rice Pudding

Prep time: 15 minutes | Cook time: 10 minutes | Makes 4 cups

½ cup long-grain basmati rice
1½ cups water
1 (13.5-ounce / 383-g) can coconut milk
1 small (5¼-ounce / 149-g) can coconut cream

½ cup brown rice syrup or agave nectar
½ teaspoon ground cardamom
¼ teaspoon fine sea salt
¼ cup currants
¼ cup chopped pistachios

1. Combine the rice and water in the Instant Pot. Secure the lid. Select Manual mode and set the cooking time for 5 minutes at High Pressure.
2. Meanwhile, in a blender, combine the coconut milk, coconut cream, brown rice syrup, cardamom, and salt. Blend at medium speed for about 30 seconds, until smooth. Set aside.
3. When timer beeps, let the pressure release naturally for 10 minutes, then release any remaining pressure. Open the pot and use a whisk to break up the cooked rice. Whisking constantly, pour the coconut milk mixture in a thin stream into the rice.
4. Select the Sauté setting. Cook the pudding for about 5 minutes, whisking constantly, until it is thickened and bubbling.
5. Sit the pudding until set. Remove the pudding from the pot. Stir in the currants.
6. Pour the pudding into a glass or ceramic dish or into individual serving bowls. Cover and refrigerate the pudding for at least 4 hours.
7. Sprinkle the pudding with chopped pistachios. Serve chilled.

Cinnamon Glaze Apple Cake

Prep time: 20 minutes | Cook time: 30 minutes | Serves 4

Apple Cake:

2 tablespoons flaxseed meal plus 6 tablespoons water
1½ cups all-purpose flour
½ tablespoon baking powder
½ teaspoon salt
3 cups apples
½ tablespoon cinnamon

powder
¾ cup beet sugar
½ cup butter, melted
2 tablespoons orange juice
1 teaspoon vanilla extract
Cooking spray
1 cup water

Cinnamon Glaze:

1 cup beet powdered sugar
½ teaspoon cinnamon powder

1 tablespoon coconut milk

1. In a bowl, mix the flaxseed meal with the water and set aside. Allow to sit for 15 minutes to thicken.
2. In a separate bowl, combine the flour, baking powder, and salt.
3. In a third bowl, mix the apples, cinnamon, and beet sugar.
4. When the flax egg is ready, whisk in the butter, orange juice, and vanilla. Stir together all three ingredients until well mixed.
5. Lightly spray a springform pan with cooking spray and pour the batter into the pan.
6. Add the water to the Instant Pot and insert a trivet. Place the springform pan on the trivet.
7. Lock the lid. Select the Manual mode and set the cooking time for 30 minutes at High Pressure.
8. When the timer beeps, perform a natural pressure release for 15 minutes, then release any remaining pressure. Carefully remove the lid.
9. Remove the cake pan, the trivet and discard the water. Leave the cake cool for 5 to 10 minutes in the pan.
10. Meanwhile, in a bowl, make the cinnamon glaze by whisking the sugar, cinnamon powder, and coconut milk until mixed.
11. Remove the cake from the pan and cut into slices. Serve drizzled with the cinnamon glaze.

Chocolate Chip Brownies

Prep time: 10 minutes | Cook time: 33 minutes | Serves 8

1½ cups almond flour
⅓ cup unsweetened cocoa powder
¾ cup granulated erythritol
1 teaspoon baking powder
2 eggs

1 tablespoon vanilla extract
5 tablespoons butter, melted
¼ cup sugar-free chocolate chips
½ cup water

1. In a large bowl, add the almond flour, cocoa powder, erythritol, and baking powder. Use a hand mixer on low speed to combine and smooth out any lumps.
2. Add the eggs and vanilla and mix until well combined.
3. Add the butter and mix on low speed until well combined. Scrape the bottom and sides of the bowl and mix again if needed. Fold in the chocolate chips.
4. Grease a baking dish with cooking spray. Pour the batter into the dish and smooth with a spatula. Cover tightly with aluminum foil.
5. Pour the water into the pot. Place the trivet in the pot and carefully lower the baking dish onto the trivet.
6. Close the lid. Select Manual mode and set cooking time for 33 minutes on High Pressure.
7. When timer beeps, use a quick pressure release and open the lid.
8. Use the handles to carefully remove the trivet from the pot. Remove the foil from the dish.
9. Let the brownies cool for 10 minutes before turning out onto a plate.

Chia Chocolate Pudding

Prep time: 6 mins, Cook Time: 3 hours, Servings: 4

2 tbsps. cacao powder
¼ tsp. salt
¼ cup chia seeds

½ tsp. liquid stevia
1 cup freshly squeezed coconut milk

1. Pour all the ingredients in the Instant Pot and stir to mix well.
2. Lock the lid. Set the Instant Pot to Slow Cook mode, then set the timer for 3 hours at High Pressure.
3. When the timer goes off, perform a natural release for 10 minutes, then release any remaining pressure. Carefully open the lid.
4. Serve immediately or refrigerate for several hours and serve chilled.

Chocolate Pudding

Prep time: 15 minutes | Cook time: 5 minutes | Serves 4

4 tablespoons cocoa powder
3 medium eggs, cracked
3¼ cups whole milk
¼ cup collagen
1¼ teaspoons gelatin

1½ tablespoons vanilla extract
¼ cup maple syrup
1 tablespoon coconut oil
1 cup water

1. In a blender, combine all the ingredients, except for the water. Process until smooth.
2. Pour the mixture into 4 ramekins and cover with aluminum foil. Pour the water in Instant Pot, fit in a trivet, and place the ramekins on top.
3. Seal the lid, select the Manual mode and set cooking time to 5 minutes on High Pressure.
4. When cooking is complete, allow a natural pressure release for 10 minutes, then release any remaining pressure. Unlock the lid.
5. Refrigerate overnight and serve.

Chocolate Fondue

Prep time: 5 minutes | Cook time: 2 minutes | Serves 4

2 ounces (57 g) unsweetened baking chocolate, finely chopped, divided
1 cup heavy cream, divided

⅓ cup Swerve, divided
Fine sea salt
1 cup cold water

Special Equipment:
Set of fondue forks or wooden skewers

1. Divide the chocolate, cream, and sweetener evenly among four ramekins. Add a pinch of salt to each one and stir well. Cover the ramekins with aluminum foil.
2. Place a trivet in the bottom of your Instant Pot and pour in the water. Place the ramekins on the trivet.
3. Lock the lid. Select the Manual mode and set the cooking time for 2 minutes at High Pressure.
4. When the timer beeps, perform a natural pressure release for 10 minutes. Carefully remove the lid.
5. Use tongs to remove the ramekins from the pot. Use a fork to stir the fondue until smooth.
6. Use immediately.

Cinnamon Butter Bites

Prep time: 6 mins, Cook Time: 5 hours, Servings: 12

5 eggs, beaten
1 cup all-purpose flour
1 grass-fed unsalted butter stick

1 tbsp. cinnamon
¼ cup liquid stevia
¼ cup olive oil
Salt, to taste

1. Mix all ingredients in a mixing bowl, except for the olive oil.
2. Grease the Instant Pot with olive oil.
3. Pour in the batter.
4. Lock the lid. Set the Instant Pot to Slow Cook mode, then set the timer for 5 hours at High Pressure.
5. When the timer goes off, perform a natural release for 10 minutes, then release any remaining pressure. Carefully open the lid.
6. Serve immediately.

Chocolate Lava Cake

Prep time: 5 minutes | Cook time: 5 minutes | Serves 2

1 large egg
4 tablespoons unsweetened raw cocoa powder
2 tablespoons blanched almond flour
2 tablespoons Swerve
2 tablespoons full-fat heavy cream

1 teaspoon vanilla extract
½ teaspoon baking powder
Pinch of sea salt
2 ounces (57 g) dark chocolate (at least 80% cacao), cut into chunks
½ cup water

1. In a small mixing bowl, beat the egg and add the cocoa powder, almond flour, Swerve, heavy cream, vanilla extract, baking powder and sea salt.
2. Transfer half of the batter into a small oven-proof bowl, add the dark chocolate pieces and then the rest of the batter. Loosely cover with aluminum foil.
3. Put the water in the Instant Pot and place the trivet inside. Place the bowl on the trivet.
4. Close the lid. Select on Manual mode and set the timer for 5 minutes on High pressure.
5. When timer beeps, use a natural pressure release for 5 minutes, then release any remaining pressure and open the lid.
6. Remove the bowl, uncover, and serve immediately.

Cardamom Yogurt Pudding

Prep time: 20 minutes | Cook time: 15 minutes | Serves 4

1½ cups Greek yogurt
1 teaspoon cocoa powder
2 cups sweetened condensed milk

1 teaspoon cardamom powder
1 cup water
¼ cup mixed nuts, chopped

1. Spritz 4 medium ramekins with cooking spray. Set aside.
2. In a bowl, combine the Greek yogurt, cocoa powder, condensed milk, and cardamom powder. Pour mixture into ramekins and cover with foil.
3. Pour the water into the Instant Pot, then fit in a trivet, and place ramekins on top.
4. Seal the lid, select the Manual mode and set the cooking time for 15 minutes at High Pressure.
5. When cooking is complete, perform a natural pressure release for 15 minutes, then release any remaining pressure. Unlock the lid.
6. Remove the ramekins from the pot, then take off the foil. Top with mixed nuts and serve immediately.

Coconut Pudding

Prep time: 6 mins, Cook Time: 3 hours, Servings: 2

1 tsp. erythritol
½ cup coconut milk
A dash of vanilla extract
½ tsp. cinnamon powder

¼ cup dried coconut flakes
Salt, to taste
½ cup water

1. Put all ingredients in the Instant Pot.
2. Mix until well combined.
3. Lock the lid. Set the Instant Pot to Slow Cook mode, then set the timer for 3 hours at High Pressure.
4. When the timer goes off, perform a natural release for 10 minutes, then release any remaining pressure. Carefully open the lid.
5. Serve immediately or refrigerate for several hours and serve chilled.

Cinnamon Balls

Prep time: 15 minutes | Cook time: 20 minutes | Serves 8

¼ cup whole-wheat flour
½ cup all-purpose flour
½ teaspoon baking powder
3 tablespoons sugar, divided
¼ teaspoon plus ½ tablespoon cinnamon

¼ teaspoon sea salt
2 tablespoons cold butter, cubed
⅓ cup almond milk
1 cup water

1. Mix the whole-wheat flour, all-purpose flour, baking powder, 1 tablespoon of sugar, ¼ teaspoon of cinnamon, and salt in a medium bowl.
2. Add the butter and use a pastry cutter to cut into butter, breaking it into little pieces until resembling cornmeal. Pour in the milk and mix until the dough forms into a ball.
3. Knead the dough on a flat surface. Divide the dough into 8 pieces and roll each piece into a ball. Put the balls in a greased baking pan with space in between each ball and oil the balls.
4. Pour the water into the Instant Pot. Put in a trivet and place the pan on top.
5. Seal the lid, select Manual mode and set the time for 20 minutes on High Pressure.
6. When timer beeps, perform a natural pressure release for 5 minutes, then release any remaining pressure.
7. In a mixing bowl, combine the remaining sugar and cinnamon. Toss the dough balls in the cinnamon and sugar mixture to serve.

New York Cheesecake

Prep time: 3 hours 45 minutes | Cook time: 40 minutes | Serves 4

12 graham crackers, crushed
2 tablespoons melted salted butter
1½ tablespoons brown sugar
16 ounces (454 g) cream cheese, softened
1 cup granulated sugar

2 eggs
½ cup sour cream
2 tablespoons cornstarch
1 teaspoon vanilla extract
¼ teaspoon salt
1 cup water

1. Mix the crushed graham crackers with butter and brown sugar. Pour mixture into a springform pan and use a spoon to press to fit. Freeze for 15 minutes until firm.
2. In a bowl, beat cream cheese and sugar until smooth. Whisk in the eggs, sour cream, cornstarch, vanilla, and salt.
3. Remove the pan from refrigerator and pour cream cheese mixture on top. Spread evenly using a spatula and cover the pan with foil.
4. Pour the water in Instant Pot, then fit in a trivet, and place cake pan on top.
5. Seal the lid, select the Manual mode and set the cooking time for 40 minutes on High Pressure.
6. When cooking is complete, do a natural pressure release for 10 minutes, then release any remaining pressure.
7. Unlock the lid and carefully remove cake pan. Allow cooling for 10 minutes and chill in refrigerator for 3 hours. Remove from refrigerator, then slice and serve.

Mini Maple Bacon Upside-Down Cheesecakes

Prep time: 15 minutes | Cook time: 10 minutes | Serves 8

3 (8-ounce/ 227-g) packages cream cheese, softened
⅔ cup Swerve
½ cup unsweetened almond milk (or hemp milk for nut-free)
2 teaspoons maple extract
¼ teaspoon fine sea salt

1 large egg
4 slices bacon, chopped, for topping
Sweetened Whipped Cream:
½ cup heavy cream
2 tablespoons Swerve, or more to taste

1. In the bowl of a stand mixer, add the cream cheese, sweetener, milk, maple extract, and salt and blitz until well blended. Add the egg and mix on low speed until very smooth.
2. Pour the batter into 8 ramekins. Gently tap the ramekins against the counter to bring the air bubbles to the surface.
3. Place a trivet in the bottom of the Instant Pot and pour in 1 cup of cold water. Stack the ramekins in two layers on top of the trivet. Cover the top layer of ramekins with 3 large pieces of paper towel to ensure that condensation doesn't leak onto the cheesecakes.
4. Lock the lid. Select the Manual mode and set the cooking time for 6 minutes at High Pressure.
5. When the timer beeps, use a natural pressure release for 10 minutes. Carefully remove the lid.
6. Remove the ramekins with tongs.
7. Place the cheesecakes in the fridge to chill completely, about 4 hours.
8. Meanwhile, make the topping: Cook the bacon in a skillet over medium-high heat for 4 minutes until crisp and cooked through. Place the cooked bacon on a paper towel–lined plate to drain.
9. Add the cream to a medium bowl and use a hand mixer on high speed to mix until soft peaks form. Fold in the sweetener and mix until well combined. Taste and adjust the sweetness to your liking.
10. Drizzle with the sweetened whipped cream and place the bacon on top.
11. Serve.

Chocolate Cake with Ganache

Prep time: 10 minutes | Cook time: 30 minutes | Serves 10

1 cup water	milk
1 cup whole wheat pastry flour	1 teaspoon pure vanilla extract
½ cup unsweetened cocoa powder	1 tablespoon apple cider vinegar
½ cup raw turbinado sugar	¼ cup melted coconut oil
1 teaspoon baking soda	¼ cup chopped, toasted hazelnuts, for garnish
½ teaspoon baking powder	1 cup fresh raspberries, for garnish
½ teaspoon instant coffee	
¼ teaspoon salt	Fresh mint leaves, for garnish
¾ cup unsweetened almond	
For the Ganache:	
¾ cup chopped dairy-free dark chocolate	¼ canned coconut milk

1. Fit the Instant Pot with a trivet and add the water. Coat a springform pan with cooking spray.
2. In a medium bowl, whisk together the flour, cocoa powder, sugar, baking soda, baking powder, instant coffee, and salt.
3. In another medium bowl, whisk together the almond milk, vanilla, vinegar, and oil. Stir the wet mixture into the dry mixture to form a batter.
4. Transfer the batter into the prepared pan and smooth into an even layer with the back of a spoon.
5. Cover the pan with foil and place on the trivet. Lock the lid. Select Manual mode and set the cook time for 30 minutes on High Pressure.
6. Once the cook time is complete, allow the pressure to release naturally for 10 minutes, then quick release any remaining pressure.
7. Carefully remove the lid and the cake pan. Remove the foil and let the cake cool on a cooling rack.
8. Meanwhile, make the ganache: Place the chocolate in a small glass bowl. Heat the coconut milk in a small saucepan, until it just begins to simmer.
9. Carefully pour the coconut milk over the chocolate and stir until all the chocolate has melted and the mixture is smooth.
10. Pour the ganache over the top of the cooled cake, letting it drip down the sides. Serve with the hazelnuts, berries, and mint on top.

Banana Pudding

Prep time: 5 minutes | Cook time: 5 minutes | Serves 4

1 cup whole milk	2 tablespoons cold butter, cut into 4 pieces
2 cups half-and-half	
¾ cup plus 1 tablespoon granulated sugar, divided	1 teaspoon vanilla extract
	2 medium banana, peeled and sliced
4 egg yolks	
3 tablespoon cornstarch	1 cup heavy cream

1. Set the Instant Pot to Sauté mode. Mix the milk, half-and-half, and ½ cup of sugar in the pot.
2. Heat for 3 minutes or until sugar dissolves. Stir constantly.
3. Meanwhile, beat the egg yolks with ¼ cup of sugar in a medium bowl. Add cornstarch and mix well.
4. Scoop ½ cup of milk mixture into egg mixture and whisk until smooth. Pour mixture into Instant Pot.
5. Seal the lid, select the Manual mode and set the cooking time for 2 minutes on High Pressure.
6. When cooking is complete, do a quick pressure release and unlock the lid.
7. Stir in butter and vanilla. Lay banana pieces into 4 bowls and top with pudding.
8. In a bowl, whisk heavy cream with remaining sugar; spoon mixture on top of pudding. Refrigerate for 1 hour before serving.

Cocoa Custard

Prep time: 5 minutes | Cook time: 7 minutes | Serves 4

2 cups heavy cream (or full-fat coconut milk for dairy-free)	unsweetened cocoa powder, or more to taste
4 large egg yolks	½ teaspoon almond extract
¼ cup Swerve, or more to taste	Pinch of fine sea salt
1 tablespoon plus 1 teaspoon	1 cup cold water

1. Heat the cream in a pan over medium-high heat until hot, about 2 minutes.
2. Place the remaining ingredients except the water in a blender and blend until smooth.
3. While the blender is running, slowly pour in the hot cream. Taste and adjust the sweetness to your liking. Add more cocoa powder, if desired.
4. Scoop the custard mixture into four ramekins with a spatula. Cover the ramekins with aluminum foil.
5. Place a trivet in the Instant Pot and pour in the water. Place the ramekins on the trivet.
6. Lock the lid. Select the Manual mode and set the cooking time for 5 minutes at High Pressure.
7. When the timer beeps, use a quick pressure release. Carefully remove the lid.
8. Remove the foil and set the foil aside. Let the custard cool for 15 minutes. Cover the ramekins with the foil again and place in the refrigerator to chill completely, about 2 hours.
9. Serve.

Almond Bread

Prep time: 12 mins, Cook Time: 5 hours, Servings: 10

1½ tsps. baking powder	2½ cups all-purpose flour
1½ cups erythritol	¼ cup olive oil
3 eggs, beaten	Salt, to taste

1. Mix all ingredients in a mixing bowl.
2. Once properly mixed, pour the batter in the greased Instant Pot.
3. Lock the lid. Set the Instant Pot to Slow Cook mode, then set the timer for 5 hours at High Pressure.
4. When the timer goes off, perform a natural release for 10 minutes, then release any remaining pressure. Carefully open the lid.
5. Serve immediately.

Keto Brownies

Prep time: 12 mins, Cook Time: 5 hours, Servings: 9

2 tsps. erythritol	5 beaten eggs
¼ cup all-purpose flour	Salt, to taste
½ cup coconut oil	2 tbsps. olive oil
⅓ cup dark chocolate chips	

1. Place all the ingredients in a mixing bowl, except for the olive oil.
2. Make sure they are well combined.
3. Grese the Instant Pot with olive oil. Pour the mixture into the greased Instant Pot.
4. Lock the lid. Set the Instant Pot to Slow Cook mode, then set the timer for 5 hours at High Pressure.
5. When the timer goes off, perform a natural release for 10 minutes, then release any remaining pressure. Carefully open the lid.
6. Transfer the brownies on a platter and slice to serve.

Super Chocolate Cookies

Prep time: 5 minutes | Cook time: 6 minutes | Serves 8

2 cups blanched almond flour	2 tablespoons pure maple
3 tablespoons arrowroot starch	syrup
1 teaspoon baking soda	1 teaspoon pure vanilla extract
¼ teaspoon sea salt	⅓ cup chopped dairy-free dark
4 tablespoons melted coconut	chocolate
oil	1 cup water

1. In a medium bowl, whisk together the almond flour, arrowroot, baking soda, and salt.
2. Make a well in the middle of the dry ingredients. Pour the coconut oil, maple syrup, and vanilla into the well, and whisk to combine.
3. Stir in the dark chocolate. The mixture may be a little crumbly but should hold together when pressed.
4. Cut out a piece of parchment paper to fit the bottom of a springform pan. Press the dough firmly on top of the parchment. Cover the pan with foil.
5. Fit the Instant Pot with a trivet and add the water. Place the foil-covered springform pan onto the trivet.
6. Lock the lid. Select Manual mode and set the cook time for 6 minutes on High Pressure.
7. Once the cook time is complete, allow the pressure to release naturally for 6 minutes, then quick release any remaining pressure.
8. Preheat the oven broiler.
9. Carefully remove the lid and take the pan out of the Instant Pot. Remove the sides of the springform pan.
10. Transfer the cookie under the broiler for 1 minute, or just until golden on top. Let the cookie cool for 10 minutes, then cut into 8 wedges and serve.

Espresso Cheesecake with Raspberries

Prep time: 5 minutes | Cook time: 35 minutes | Serves 8

1 cup blanched almond flour	16 ounces (454 g) cream
½ cup plus 2 tablespoons	cheese
Swerve	1 cup water
3 tablespoons espresso	6 ounces (170 g) dark
powder, divided	chocolate (at least 80% cacao)
2 tablespoons butter	8 ounces (227 g) full-fat heavy
1 egg	whipping cream
½ cup full-fat heavy cream	2 cups raspberries

1. In a small mixing bowl, combine the almond flour, 2 tablespoons of Swerve, 1 tablespoon of espresso powder and the butter.
2. Line the bottom of a springform pan with parchment paper. Press the almond flour dough flat on the bottom and about 1 inch on the sides. Set aside.
3. In a food processor, mix the egg, heavy cream, cream cheese, remaining Swerve and remaining espresso powder until smooth.
4. Pour the cream cheese mixture into the springform pan. Loosely cover with aluminum foil.
5. Put the water in the Instant Pot and place the trivet inside.
6. Close the lid. Select Manual button and set the timer for 35 minutes on High pressure.
7. When timer beeps, use a natural pressure release for 15 minutes, then release any remaining pressure. Open the lid.
8. Remove the springform pan and place it on a cooling rack for 2 to 3 hours or until it reaches room temperature. Refrigerate overnight.
9. Melt the chocolate and heavy whipping cream in the double boiler. Cool for 15 minutes and drizzle on top of the cheesecake, allowing the chocolate to drip down the sides.
10. Add the raspberries on top of the cheesecake before serving.

Pumpkin Pie

Prep time: 4 hours 20 minutes | Cook time: 35 minutes | Serves 6

½ cup crushed graham	1½ cups canned pumpkin
crackers (about 7 graham	purée
crackers)	1½ teaspoons pumpkin pie
2 tablespoons unsalted butter,	spice
melted	½ teaspoon sea salt
½ cup brown sugar	½ cup evaporated milk
1 large egg	1 cup water

1. Make the crust: In a small bowl, combine the graham cracker crumbs and butter and mix until well combined. Press the mixture into the bottom and 1 inch up the sides of a springform pan. Set aside.
2. In a large mixing bowl, whisk together the egg, pumpkin purée, pumpkin pie spice, sugar, salt, and milk. Pour the filling into the prepared crust. Cover the pan with aluminum foil.
3. Place a trivet in the Instant Pot and pour in the water. Lower the pan onto the trivet.
4. Lock the lid. Select the Manual mode. Set the time for 35 minutes on High Pressure.
5. When timer beeps, let the pressure release naturally for 10 minutes, then release the remaining pressure.
6. Unlock the lid. Remove the pan from the pot and then remove the foil. Allow the pie to cool. Cover with plastic wrap and refrigerate for at least 4 hours before serving.

Milk and Cocoa Pudding

Prep time: 50 mins, Cook Time: 3 mins, Servings: 4

2 cups hot coconut milk	4 tbsps. cocoa powder
4 tbsps. sugar	2 tbsps. gelatin
½ tsp. cinnamon powder	1 cup plus 2 tbsps. water

1. In a bowl, mix the milk with sugar, cinnamon and cocoa powder and stir well.
2. In a bowl, mix gelatin with 2 tablespoons of water, stir well, add to cocoa mix, stir and divide into ramekins.
3. Add 1 cup of water to the Instant Pot, add the steamer basket and ramekins inside.
4. Lock the lid. Set the Instant Pot to Manual mode, then set the timer for 4 minutes at High Pressure.
5. When the timer goes off, perform a natural release. Carefully open the lid.
6. Serve puddings cold.

Avocado and Coconut Pudding

Prep time: 2 hours, Cook Time: 2 mins, Servings: 3

14 oz. canned coconut milk	chopped
1 tbsp. cocoa powder	4 tbsps. sugar
1 avocado, pitted, peeled and	½ cup avocado oil

1. In a bowl, mix oil with cocoa powder and half of the sugar, stir well, transfer to a lined container, keep in the fridge for 1 hour and chop into small pieces.
2. In the Instant Pot, mix coconut milk with avocado and the rest of the sugar, blend using an immersion blender.
3. Lock the lid. Set the Instant Pot to Manual mode, then set the timer for 2 minutes at High Pressure.
4. When the timer goes off, perform a natural release. Carefully open the lid.
5. Add chocolate chips, stir, divide pudding into bowls and keep in the fridge until you serve it.

Lemon Squares

Prep time: 20 minutes | Cook time: 30 minutes | Serves 6

Lemon Squares:
2 tablespoons flaxseed meal plus 6 tablespoons water
1¼ cup almond flour
3 tablespoons coconut flour
1 cup beet sugar
1 large lemon, zested and

juiced
¼ cup butter, melted
2 cups almond milk
Cooking spray
1 cup water

Topping:
5 tablespoons beet sugar

1 lemon, zested and juiced

1. In a bowl, mix the flaxseed meal with water and allow to sit for 15 minutes to thicken.
2. In a separate bowl, combine the almond flour, coconut flour, beet sugar, and lemon zest until mixed. Whisk in lemon juice, butter, milk, and the flax egg.
3. Grease a springform pan lightly with cooking spray and pour the batter into the pan.
4. Pour the water into the Instant Pot and insert a trivet. Place the pan on the trivet.
5. Lock the lid. Select the Manual mode and set the cooking time for 20 minutes at High Pressure.
6. When the timer beeps, perform a natural pressure release for 10 minutes, then release any remaining pressure. Carefully remove the lid.
7. Remove the pan and pierce the top of the cake with a skewer.
8. Make the topping by whisking together the beet sugar, lemon juice, and zest. Sprinkle the mixture on top of the cake and cut into squares to serve.

Deconstructed Tiramisu

Prep time: 5 minutes | Cook time: 9 minutes | Serves 4

1 cup heavy cream (or full-fat coconut milk for dairy-free)
2 large egg yolks
2 tablespoons brewed decaf espresso or strong brewed coffee
2 tablespoons Swerve, or more to taste

1 teaspoon rum extract
1 teaspoon unsweetened cocoa powder, or more to taste
Pinch of fine sea salt
1 cup cold water
4 teaspoons Swerve, for topping

1. Heat the cream in a pan over medium-high heat until hot, about 2 minutes.
2. Place the egg yolks, coffee, sweetener, rum extract, cocoa powder, and salt in a blender and blend until smooth.
3. While the blender is running, slowly pour in the hot cream. Taste and adjust the sweetness to your liking. Add more cocoa powder, if desired.
4. Scoop the mixture into four ramekins with a spatula. Cover the ramekins with aluminum foil.
5. Place a trivet in the bottom of the Instant Pot and pour in the water. Place the ramekins on the trivet.
6. Lock the lid. Select the Manual mode and set the cooking time for 7 minutes at High Pressure.
7. When the timer beeps, use a quick pressure release. Carefully remove the lid.
8. Keep the ramekins covered with the foil and place in the refrigerator for about 2 hours until completely chilled.
9. Sprinkle 1 teaspoon of Swerve on top of each tiramisu. Use the oven broiler to melt the sweetener.
10. Put in the fridge to chill the topping, about 20 minutes.
11. Serve.

Cheesecake

Prep time: 3 hours 40 minutes | Cook time: 40 minutes | Serves 4

2 cups graham crackers, crushed
3 tablespoons brown sugar
¼ cup butter, melted
2 (8 ounce / 227-g) cream cheese, softened

½ cup granulated sugar
2 tablespoons all-purpose flour
1 teaspoon vanilla extract
3 eggs
1 cup water
1 cup caramel sauce

1. Make the crust: Mix the crushed crackers with brown sugar and butter. Spread the mixture at the bottom of a springform pan and use a spoon to press to fit. Freeze in refrigerator for 10 minutes.
2. In a bowl, whisk the cream cheese and sugar until smooth. Mix in the flour and vanilla. Whisk in the eggs. Remove the pan from refrigerator and pour mixture over crust. Cover the pan with foil.
3. Pour the water in Instant Pot, then fit in a trivet and place the pan on top.
4. Seal the lid, select the Manual mode and set the timer for 40 minutes on High Pressure.
5. When cooking is complete, allow a natural pressure release for 10 minutes, then release any remaining pressure. Open the lid.
6. Carefully remove the cake pan and take off the foil. Let cool for 10 minutes. Pour the caramel sauce over and refrigerate for 3 hours.
7. Remove the pan from the refrigerator and invert the cheesecake on a plate. Slice and serve.

Oreo Chocolate Cake

Prep time: 8 hours 35 minutes | Cook time: 35 minutes | Serves 6

12 Oreo cookies, smoothly crushed
2 tablespoons salted butter, melted
16 ounces (454 g) cream cheese, softened
½ cup granulated sugar
2 large eggs
1 tablespoon all-purpose flour

¼ cup heavy cream
2 teaspoons vanilla extract
16 whole Oreo cookies, coarsely crushed
1½ cups water
1 cup whipped cream
2 tablespoons chocolate sauce, for topping

1. Line a springform pan with foil, then spritz with cooking spray.
2. Make the crust: In a bowl, combine smoothly crushed Oreo cookies with butter, then press into bottom of pan. Freeze for 15 minutes.
3. In another bowl, add cream cheese, and beat until smooth. Add sugar to whisk until satiny. Beat in the eggs one by one until mixed. Whisk in flour, heavy cream, and vanilla.
4. Fold in 8 coarsely crushed cookies and pour the mixture onto the crust in the springform pan. Cover pan tightly with foil.
5. Pour the water in the Instant Pot and fit in a trivet. Place the pan on trivet.
6. Seal the lid, set to the Manual mode and set the cooking time for 35 minutes at High Pressure.
7. When cooking is complete, allow a natural pressure release for 10 minutes, then release any remaining pressure. Carefully open the lid.
8. Remove the trivet with cake pan from the pot. Remove foil and transfer to a cooling rack to chill. Refrigerate for 8 hours. Top with whipped cream, remaining cookies, and chocolate sauce. Slice and serve.

Carrot Raisin Halwa

Prep time: 10 minutes | Cook time: 14 minutes | Serves 6

2 tablespoons coconut oil
2 tablespoons raw cashews
2 tablespoons raisins
2 cups shredded carrots
1 cup almond milk

¼ cup sugar
2 tablespoons ground cashews
¼ teaspoon ground cardamom
Chopped pistachios, for garnish

1. Set the Instant Pot to Sauté and melt the coconut oil until it shimmers.
2. Add the cashews and raisins and cook them until the cashews are golden brown, about 4 minutes.
3. Add the carrots, milk, sugar, and ground cashews, and stir to incorporate.
4. Lock the lid. Select the Manual mode and set the cooking time for 10 minutes at High Pressure.
5. When the timer beeps, perform a natural pressure release for 10 minutes, then release any remaining pressure. Carefully remove the lid.
6. Stir well, mashing the carrots together a bit. Set the Instant Pot to Sauté again and cook, stirring, for about 2 to 3 minutes, until thickened.
7. Turn off the Instant Pot. Stir in the cardamom and let the mixture sit for 10 minutes to thicken up.
8. Garnish with the pistachios and serve.

Coconut Cream Pudding

Prep time: 12 mins, Cook Time: 10 mins, Servings: 6

Zest of 1 grated lemon
2 cups coconut cream
5 tbsps. sugar

6 tbsps. flour
1 tsp. cinnamon powder
1 cup water

1. Set the Instant Pot on Sauté mode and add coconut cream, cinnamon and orange zest, then stir.
2. Simmer for 3 minutes then transfer to a bowl and leave aside.
3. Add flour and sugar, stir well and divide this into ramekins.
4. Add the water to the Instant Pot, add steamer basket, add ramekins.
5. Lock the lid. Set the Instant Pot to Manual mode, then set the timer for 10 minutes at Low Pressure.
6. When the timer goes off, perform a natural release for 5 minutes, then release any remaining pressure. Carefully open the lid.
7. Serve cold.

Cream Cheese Pudding

Prep time: 12 mins, Cook Time: 20 mins, Servings: 2 minutes

¼ tsp. vanilla extract
1½ tsps. caramel extract
2 eggs

2 oz. cream cheese
1½ tbsps. sugar
1 cup water

1. Mix cream cheese with eggs, caramel extract, vanilla extract and sugar in a blender and pulse well to divide into greased ramekins.
2. In the Instant Pot, set in the water, add steamer basket and ramekins inside.
3. Lock the lid. Set the Instant Pot to Manual mode, then set the timer for 20 minutes at High Pressure.
4. When the timer goes off, perform a natural release for 10 minutes, then release any remaining pressure. Carefully open the lid.
5. Serve the puddings cold.

Potato Coconut Pudding

Prep time: 5 minutes | Cook time: 10 minutes | Serves 4

1 cup water
1 large sweet potato (about 1 pound / 454 g), peeled and cut into 1-inch pieces
½ cup canned coconut milk

6 tablespoons pure maple syrup
1 teaspoon grated fresh ginger (about ½-inch knob)

1. Pour the water into the Instant Pot and fit in a steamer basket.
2. Place the sweet potato pieces in the steamer basket and secure the lid. Select the Manual mode and set the cooking time for 10 minutes at High Pressure.
3. When timer beeps, use a quick pressure release. Unlock the lid.
4. Transfer the cooked potatoes to a large bowl. Add the coconut milk, maple syrup, and ginger. Use an immersion blender to purée the potatoes into a smooth pudding.
5. Serve the pudding immediately or chill in the refrigerator for an hour before serving.

Cinnamon Cream Puddings

Prep time: 20 mins, Cook Time: 15 mins, Servings: 6

2 cups fresh cream
1 tsp. cinnamon powder
Zest of 1 orange

5 tbsps. sugar
6 egg yolks
2 cups water

1. Set the pot on Sauté mode and heat it up.
2. Add cream, cinnamon and orange zest and sauté for a few minutes and leave aside for 20 minutes.
3. Using a bowl, combine the sugar and egg yolks. Pour the egg yolk mixture in the cream mixture, whisk well, strain the mixture, divide it into ramekins and cover them with tin foil.
4. Clean the pot, add the water, add steamer basket, add ramekins.
5. Lock the lid. Set the Instant Pot to Manual mode, then set the timer for 10 minutes at High Pressure.
6. When the timer goes off, perform a natural release for 5 minutes, then release any remaining pressure. Carefully open the lid.
7. Refrigerate the puddings for several hours, then serve chilled.

Cranberry and Pear Crisps

Prep time: 10 minutes | Cook time: 5 minutes | Serves 6

3 large pears, peeled, cored and diced
1 cup fresh cranberries
1 tablespoon granulated sugar
2 teaspoons ground cinnamon
½ teaspoon ground nutmeg
½ cup water

1 tablespoon pure maple syrup
6 tablespoons almond butter
1 cup old-fashioned rolled oats
⅓ cup dark brown sugar
¼ cup all-purpose flour
½ teaspoon sea salt
½ cup pecans, toasted

1. In the Instant Pot, combine the pears and cranberries and sprinkle with the granulated sugar. Let sit for a few minutes, then sprinkle with the cinnamon and nutmeg. Pour the water and maple syrup on top.
2. In a medium bowl, stir together the almond butter, oats, brown sugar, flour and salt.
3. Spoon the mixture on the fruit in the Instant Pot.
4. Secure the lid. Select Manual mode, and set cooking time for 5 minutes on High Pressure.
5. When timer beeps, use a quick pressure release. Open the lid.
6. Spoon into bowls. Top with pecans and serve.

Pumpkin Pie Spice Pots De Crème

Prep time: 5 minutes | Cook time: 7 minutes | Serves 4

2 cups heavy cream (or full-fat coconut milk for dairy-free)
4 large egg yolks
¼ cup Swerve, or more to taste
2 teaspoons pumpkin pie spice

1 teaspoon vanilla or maple extract
Pinch of fine sea salt
1 cup cold water

1. Heat the cream in a pan over medium-high heat until hot, about 2 minutes.
2. Place the remaining ingredients except the water in a medium bowl and stir until smooth.
3. Slowly pour in the hot cream while stirring. Taste and adjust the sweetness to your liking. Scoop the mixture into four ramekins with a spatula. Cover the ramekins with aluminum foil.
4. Place a trivet in the Instant Pot and pour in the water. Place the ramekins on the trivet.
5. Lock the lid. Select the Manual mode and set the cooking time for 5 minutes at High Pressure.
6. When the timer beeps, use a quick pressure release. Carefully remove the lid.
7. Remove the foil and set the foil aside. Let the pots de crème cool for 15 minutes. Cover the ramekins with the foil again and place in the refrigerator to chill completely, about 2 hours.
8. Serve.

Raspberry and Oat Crumble

Prep time: 10 minutes | Cook time: 20 minutes | Serves 4

2 tablespoons arrowroot starch
½ cup plus 1 tablespoon water, divided
1 teaspoon lemon juice
5 tablespoons sugar, divided
2 cups raspberries

½ cup flour
¼ cup brown sugar
½ cup rolled oats
1 teaspoon cinnamon powder
¼ cup cold butter, cut into pieces

1. In a small bowl, combine the arrowroot starch, lemon juice, 1 tablespoon of water, and 3 tablespoons of sugar. Mix in the raspberries, and toss well. Pour the mixture in a baking pan.
2. In a separate bowl, mix the flour, brown sugar, oats, cinnamon, butter, and remaining sugar, and form crumble. Spread the crumble evenly on the raspberries.
3. Put a trivet in the pot. Cover the pan with foil and pour half cup of water into the pot. Put the pan on the trivet.
4. Seal the lid, select Manual mode, and set cooking time for 20 minutes on High Pressure.
5. When timer beeps, do a quick pressure release. Open the lid.
6. Remove foil and serve.

Rhubarb and Strawberry Compote

Prep time: 10 minutes | Cook time: 5 minutes | Makes 4 cups

1 pound (454 g) rhubarb (about 4 large stalks), trimmed and cut into 1-inch pieces
1 pound (454 g) strawberries,

hulled and quartered lengthwise
½ cup turbinado sugar
½ teaspoon ground cardamom

1. Combine the rhubarb, strawberries, sugar, and cardamom in the Instant Pot and stir well, making sure to coat the rhubarb and strawberries evenly with the sugar. Let the mixture sit for 15 minutes. Stir.
2. Secure the lid. Select Manual mode and set the cooking time for 5 minutes at Low Pressure.
3. When timer beeps, let the pressure release naturally for about 15 minutes, then release any remaining pressure. Open the pot and stir the compote to break down the rhubarb.
4. Serve the compote warm.

Chocolate Pudding with Raspberry Sauce

Prep time: 20 minutes | Cook time: 15 minutes | Serves 4

Chocolate Pudding:
5 tablespoons flaxseed meal plus 1 cup water
6 tablespoons unsweetened cocoa powder
⅓ cup cornstarch

Salt, to taste
4½ cups almond milk
4 ounces (113 g) butter
2 teaspoons vanilla extract

Raspberry Sauce:
1 pound (454 g) fresh raspberries
2 tablespoons freshly

squeezed lemon juice
¼ cup beet sugar
1 tablespoon water

1. In a bowl, mix the flaxseed meal with the water until evenly combined and allow to sit for 15 minutes to thicken.
2. In a separate bowl, combine the cocoa powder, cornstarch, and salt.
3. Press the Sauté button on the Instant Pot and pour in the almond milk. Let simmer for a few seconds, but not to boil.
4. Fetch a tablespoon of the milk into the cocoa powder mixture and stir. Pour the mix into the milk and stir in the flaxseed mixture (flax egg), butter, and vanilla extract. Allow to simmer for 6 minutes, stirring frequently, and spoon into dessert bowls. Turn the pot off and wash the Instant Pot clean.
5. Select the Sauté mode and add the raspberries, lemon juice, sugar, and water. Allow to simmer for 6 minutes.
6. Drain the sauce through a strainer into a bowl. Allow to cool for 5 minutes and spoon the raspberry sauce over the chocolate pudding. Serve immediately.

Pineapple Pudding

Prep time: 12 mins, Cook Time: 5 mins, Servings: 8

1 cup rice
1 tbsp. avocado oil
14 oz. milk

Sugar, to taste
8 oz. chopped canned pineapple

1. In the Instant Pot, mix oil, milk and rice, stir.
2. Lock the lid. Set the Instant Pot to Manual mode, then set the timer for 3 minutes at Low Pressure.
3. When the timer goes off, perform a natural release. Carefully open the lid.
4. Add sugar and pineapple, stir.
5. Lock the lid, then set the timer for 2 minutes at Low Pressure.
6. When the timer goes off, perform a natural release. Carefully open the lid.
7. Divide into dessert bowls and serve.

Banana Cake

Prep time: 12 mins, Cook Time: 1 hour, Servings: 4

1 tsp. nutmeg powder
2 cups flour
1 tsp. cinnamon powder
¼ cup sugar

4 bananas, peeled and mashed
1 cup water

1. In a bowl, mix sugar with flour, bananas, cinnamon and nutmeg, stir, pour into a greased cake pan and cover with tin foil.
2. In the Instant Pot, set in the water, add steamer basket, add cake pan.
3. Lock the lid. Set the Instant Pot to Manual mode, then set the timer for 1 hour at High Pressure.
4. When the timer goes off, perform a natural release for 10 minutes, then release any remaining pressure. Carefully open the lid.
5. Slice and divide between plates to serve cold.

Citrus Apple Crisps with Oat Topping
Prep time: 10 minutes | Cook time: 9 minutes | Serves 4

1 cup water
For the Filling:
3½ cups peeled and diced apples (1-inch chunks)
1 tablespoon fresh lemon juice
1 tablespoon fresh orange juice
½ teaspoon ground cinnamon
2 teaspoons coconut sugar
For the Topping:
½ cup old-fashioned rolled oats
½ cup almond flour
3 tablespoons almond butter
1 tablespoon pure maple syrup
¼ cup coconut sugar
¼ teaspoon sea salt

1. To make the filling: In a medium bowl, toss together all the ingredients. Portion the filling into 4 ramekins, filling all the way to the top. Cover the ramekins with foil.
2. Fit the Instant Pot with a trivet and add the water. Place the ramekins on the trivet.
3. Lock the lid. Select Manual mode and set the cook time for 9 minutes on High Pressure.
4. Once the cook time is complete, quick release the pressure.
5. Meanwhile, make the topping: Place all the ingredients for the topping in the food processor, and pulse to combine. Preheat the oven to 500°F (260°C).
6. Carefully remove the lid and the ramekins. Remove the foil.
7. Spoon the topping evenly over the apple mixture. Transfer the ramekins to the oven, and bake until the topping is golden brown, about 4 minutes.
8. Serve warm.

Flourless Chocolate Brownies
Prep time: 15 minutes | Cook time: 15 minutes | Makes 16 brownies

1 egg
¾ cup almond butter
⅓ cup raw cacao powder
¾ cup coconut sugar
½ teaspoon baking soda
¼ teaspoon fine sea salt
½ teaspoon pure vanilla extract
½ cup dark chocolate chips
1 cup water

1. Line a springform pan with parchment paper. In a large bowl, whisk together the egg, almond butter, cacao powder, coconut sugar, baking soda, salt, and vanilla and stir well until it has a thick consistency.
2. Transfer the batter to the prepared pan and level the batter with a spatula. Sprinkle with the chocolate chips.
3. Pour 1 cup water into the Instant Pot and fit in a trivet. Place the pan on top of the trivet and cover it with an upside-down plate.
4. Secure the lid. Select the Manual mode and set the cooking time for 15 minutes at High Pressure.
5. When timer beeps, let the pressure naturally release for 10 minutes, then release any remaining pressure. Unlock the lid.
6. Slice into 16 brownies and serve.

Flourless Chocolate Tortes
Prep time: 7 minutes | Cook time: 10 minutes | Serves 8

7 ounces (198 g) unsweetened baking chocolate, finely chopped
¾ cup plus 2 tablespoons unsalted butter (or butter-flavored coconut oil for dairy-free)
1¼ cups Swerve, or more to taste
5 large eggs
1 tablespoon coconut flour
2 teaspoons ground cinnamon
Seeds scraped from 1 vanilla bean (about 8 inches long), or 2 teaspoons vanilla extract
Pinch of fine sea salt

1. Grease 8 ramekins. Place the chocolate and butter in a pan over medium heat and stir until the chocolate is completely melted, about 3 minutes.
2. Remove the pan from the heat, then add the remaining ingredients and stir until smooth. Taste and adjust the sweetness to your liking. Pour the batter into the greased ramekins.
3. Place a trivet in the bottom of the Instant Pot and pour in 1 cup of cold water. Place four of the ramekins on the trivet.
4. Lock the lid. Select the Manual mode and set the cooking time for 7 minutes at High Pressure.
5. When the timer beeps, use a quick pressure release. Carefully remove the lid.
6. Use tongs to remove the ramekins. Repeat with the remaining ramekins.
7. Serve the tortes warm or chilled.

Orange Cake
Prep time: 5 minutes | Cook time: 30 minutes | Serves 6

1½ cups orange soda
1 (15.25-ounce / 432-g) box orange cake mix
1 cup water
1 tablespoon caster sugar, for garnish

1. Spritz a bundt pan with cooking spray.
2. In a bowl, mix orange soda and orange cake mix until well combined. Pour into bundt pan, cover with a foil.
3. Pour the water in the Instant Pot, then fit in a trivet, and place the pan on top.
4. Seal the lid, select the Manual mode and set the cooking time for 30 minutes at High Pressure.
5. When cooking is complete, do a quick pressure release. Open the lid.
6. Remove the pan from the pot and allow cooling. Turn over onto a platter, sprinkle with caster sugar. Slice and serve.

Pumpkin Bundt Cake
Prep time: 7 minutes | Cook time: 35 minutes | Serves 12

Cake:
3 cups blanched almond flour
1 teaspoon baking soda
½ teaspoon fine sea salt
2 teaspoons ground cinnamon
1 teaspoon ground nutmeg
1 teaspoon ginger powder
¼ teaspoon ground cloves
6 large eggs
2 cups pumpkin purée
1 cup Swerve
¼ cup (½ stick) unsalted butter (or coconut oil for dairy-free), softened
Glaze:
1 cup (2 sticks) unsalted butter (or coconut oil for dairy-free), melted
½ cup Swerve

1. In a large bowl, stir together the almond flour, baking soda, salt, and spices. In another large bowl, add the eggs, pumpkin, sweetener, and butter and stir until smooth. Pour the wet ingredients into the dry ingredients and stir well.
2. Grease a 6-cup Bundt pan. Pour the batter into the prepared pan and cover with a paper towel and then with aluminum foil.
3. Place a trivet in the bottom of the Instant Pot and pour in 2 cups of cold water. Place the Bundt pan on the trivet.
4. Lock the lid. Select the Manual mode and set the cooking time for 35 minutes at High Pressure.
5. When the timer beeps, use a natural pressure release for 10 minutes. Carefully remove the lid.
6. Let the cake cool in the pot for 10 minutes before removing.
7. While the cake is cooling, make the glaze: In a small bowl, mix the butter and sweetener together. Spoon the glaze over the warm cake.
8. Allow to cool for 5 minutes before slicing and serving.

Pecan Monkey Bread

Prep time: 15 minutes | Cook time: 25 minutes | Serves 6

1½ cinnamon powder
¼ cup brown sugar
¼ cup toasted pecans, chopped
1 pound (454 g) dinner rolls,

cut in half lengthwise
½ cup butter, melted
1 cup water
2 teaspoons whole milk
½ cup powdered sugar

1. Spritz a bundt pan with cooking spray.
2. In a shallow plate, mix the cinnamon, brown sugar, and pecans. Coat the dinner rolls in the mixture, then in butter, and then place in bundt pan, making sure to build layers. Cover pan with foil and allow rising overnight.
3. Pour the water into Instant Pot, then fit in a trivet and place bundt pan on top.
4. Seal the lid, select the Manual mode and set the cooking time for 25 minutes at High Pressure.
5. When cooking is complete, allow a natural release for 10 minutes, then release any remaining pressure.
6. Unlock the lid, remove the pan from the pot, take off the foil, and allow to cool completely.
7. In a bowl, whisk milk with sugar until smooth.
8. Invert the bread on a serving platter and drizzle with sweetened milk.
9. Slice and serve.

Pine Nut Mousse

Prep time: 5 minutes | Cook time: 35 minutes | Serves 8

1 tablespoon butter
1¼ cups pine nuts
1¼ cups full-fat heavy cream
2 large eggs
1 teaspoon vanilla extract

1 cup Swerve, reserve 1 tablespoon
1 c water
1 cup full-fat heavy whipping cream

1. Butter the bottom and the side of a pie pan and set aside.
2. In a food processor, blend the pine nuts and heavy cream. Add the eggs, vanilla extract and Swerve and pulse a few times to incorporate.
3. Pour the batter into the pan and loosely cover with aluminum foil. Pour the water in the Instant Pot and place the trivet inside. Place the pan on top of the trivet.
4. Close the lid. Select Manual mode and set the timer for 35 minutes on High pressure.
5. In a small mixing bowl, whisk the heavy whipping cream and 1 tablespoon of Swerve until a soft peak forms.
6. When timer beeps, use a natural pressure release for 15 minutes, then release any remaining pressure and open the lid.
7. Serve immediately with whipped cream on top.

Lemon Custard Pie

Prep time: 10 minutes | Cook time: 15 minutes | Serves 6

½ cup coconut oil, melted, plus more for greasing the pan
¾ cup coconut flour
½ cup plus 2 tablespoons unrefined sugar, divided
1 (13.5-ounce / 383-g) can full-

fat coconut milk
½ cup freshly squeezed lemon juice (from 4 lemons)
¼ cup cornstarch or arrowroot powder
2 cups water

1. Grease a 6-inch springform pan or pie dish with melted coconut oil.
2. Stir together ½ cup of coconut oil, coconut flour, and 2 tablespoons of sugar in a small bowl. Press the crust into the greased pan.

3. In a medium bowl, whisk together the coconut milk, lemon juice, cornstarch, and remaining ½ cup of sugar until the starch is dissolved. Pour this mixture over the crust. Cover the pan with aluminum foil.
4. Pour the water into the Instant Pot and insert a trivet. Using a foil sling or silicone helper handles, lower the pan onto the trivet.
5. Lock the lid. Select the Manual mode and set the cooking time for 15 minutes at High Pressure.
6. When the timer beeps, perform a quick pressure release. Carefully remove the lid.
7. Serve at room temperature or chilled.

Cinnamon Roll Cheesecake

Prep time: 15 minutes | Cook time: 35 minutes | Serves 12

Crust:
3½ tablespoons unsalted butter or coconut oil
1½ ounces (43 g) unsweetened baking chocolate, chopped
1 large egg, beaten
Filling:
4 (8-ounce / 227-g) packages cream cheese, softened
¾ cup Swerve
½ cup unsweetened almond milk (or hemp milk for nut-free)
Cinnamon Swirl:
6 tablespoons (¾ stick) unsalted butter (or butter flavored coconut oil for dairy-free)
½ cup Swerve
Seeds scraped from ½ vanilla

⅓ cup Swerve
2 teaspoons ground cinnamon
1 teaspoon vanilla extract
¼ teaspoon fine sea salt

1 teaspoon vanilla extract
¼ teaspoon almond extract (omit for nut-free)
¼ teaspoon fine sea salt
3 large eggs

bean (about 8 inches long), or
1 teaspoon vanilla extract
1 tablespoon ground cinnamon
¼ teaspoon fine sea salt
1 cup cold water

1. Line a baking pan with two layers of aluminum foil.
2. Make the crust: Melt the butter in a pan over medium-low heat. Slowly add the chocolate and stir until melted. Stir in the egg, sweetener, cinnamon, vanilla extract, and salt.
3. Transfer the crust mixture to the prepared baking pan, spreading it with your hands to cover the bottom completely.
4. Make the filling: In the bowl of a stand mixer, add the cream cheese, sweetener, milk, extracts, and salt and mix until well blended. Add the eggs, one at a time, mixing on low speed after each addition just until blended. Then blend until the filling is smooth. Pour half of the filling over the crust.
5. Make the cinnamon swirl: Heat the butter over high heat in a pan until the butter froths and brown flecks appear, stirring occasionally. Stir in the sweetener, vanilla seeds, cinnamon, and salt. Remove from the heat and allow to cool slightly.
6. Spoon half of the cinnamon swirl on top of the cheesecake filling in the baking pan. Use a knife to cut the cinnamon swirl through the filling several times for a marbled effect. Top with the rest of the cheesecake filling and cinnamon swirl. Cut the cinnamon swirl through the cheesecake filling again several times.
7. Place a trivet in the bottom of the Instant Pot and pour in the water. Use a foil sling to lower the baking pan onto the trivet. Cover the cheesecake with 3 large sheets of paper towel to ensure that condensation doesn't leak onto it. Tuck in the sides of the sling.
8. Lock the lid. Select the Manual mode and set the cooking time for 26 minutes at High Pressure.
9. When the timer beeps, use a natural pressure release for 10 minutes. Carefully remove the lid.
10. Use the foil sling to lift the pan out of the Instant Pot.
11. Let the cheesecake cool, then place in the refrigerator for 4 hours to chill and set completely before slicing and serving.

Raspberry Cheesecake

Prep time: 3 hours 30 minutes | Cook time: 40 minutes | Serves 4

12 graham crackers, crushed
2 tablespoons melted butter
1 pound (454 g) cream cheese, softened
1 cup granulated sugar
12 large raspberries, plus more for garnish

2 eggs
1 teaspoon vanilla extract
3 tablespoons maple syrup
2 teaspoons cinnamon powder
½ cup heavy cream
1 cup water

1. Make the crust: Mix the crushed graham crackers with butter. Pour the mixture into a springform pan and press to fit with a spoon. Refrigerate for 15 minutes or until firm.
2. In a bowl, whisk the cream cheese and sugar until smooth. Add the raspberries, eggs, vanilla, maple syrup, cinnamon, and heavy cream, and mix until well combined.
3. Remove the cake pan from refrigerator and pour cream cheese mixture on top. Spread evenly and cover pan with foil.
4. Pour the water in Instant Pot, then fit in a trivet, and place cake pan on top.
5. Seal the lid, select the Manual mode and set to 40 minutes on High Pressure.
6. When cooking is complete, allow a natural pressure release for 10 minutes, then release any remaining pressure.
7. Unlock the lid and carefully remove the pan. Allow cooling for 10 minutes and chill in the fridge for 3 hours. Invert the cake on a plate and garnish with more raspberries. Slice and serve.

Cinnamon Mini Monkey Breads

Prep time: 10 minutes | Cook time: 20 minutes | Serves 4

1 (1-pound / 454-g) can buttermilk biscuits, cut into 6 pieces
⅓ cup granulated sugar
Salt, to taste
½ cup crushed cinnamon

crunch cereal, divided, plus more for sprinkling
¼ cup melted unsalted butter
1 cup water
1 cup maple syrup
2 tablespoons almond milk

1. In a bowl, combine the sugar, salt and half of the crushed cereal. Add the cut biscuit pieces to the bowl. Toss to evenly coat.
2. Place 2 tablespoons of the coated biscuits, along with a spoonful of the cereal mixture, in each well of a silicone egg bite mold. Top each pile of coated dough with melted butter.
3. Pour the water into the Instant Pot and insert a trivet. Place the filled mold on top of the trivet.
4. Secure the lid. Press the Manual button and set cooking time for 20 minutes on High Pressure.
5. When timer beeps, quick release the pressure. Remove the lid and take out the silicone mold. Let the monkey breads cool in the mold.
6. Meanwhile, in a medium bowl, mix the milk and maple syrup until smooth.
7. Remove the monkey breads from the mold. Drizzle each monkey bread with milk mixture. Top with a sprinkle of crushed cereal.

Ricotta and Date Cake

Prep time: 30 mins, Cook Time: 20 mins, Servings: 6

1 lb. softened ricotta cheese
4 eggs
4 oz. honey
6 oz. dates, soaked and

drained
Juice of 2 oranges
1 cup water

1. In a bowl, mix soft ricotta with eggs and whisk well.
2. Add honey, dates, and orange juice, whisk, pour into a cake pan and cover with tin foil.
3. Add the water to the Instant Pot, add steamer basket, add cake pan.
4. Lock the lid. Set the Instant Pot to Manual mode, then set the timer for 20 minutes at High Pressure.
5. When the timer goes off, perform a natural release for 10 minutes, then release any remaining pressure. Carefully open the lid.
6. Allow cake to cool down, slice and serve.

Bread Pudding

Prep time: 15 minutes | Cook time: 25 minutes | Serves 8

2 cups milk
5 large eggs
⅓ cup granulated sugar
1 teaspoon vanilla extract

5 cups (about ½ loaf) bread, slice into 2-inch cubes
2 tablespoons unsalted butter, cut into small pieces

1. In a medium bowl, whisk together the eggs, milk, sugar, and vanilla. Add the bread cubes and stir to coat well. Refrigerate for 1 hour.
2. Spritz the Instant Pot with cooking spray. Pour in the bread mixture. Scatter with the butter pieces.
3. Lock the lid. Select the Manual mode. Set the timer for 25 minutes on High Pressure.
4. When timer beeps, let the pressure release naturally for 10 minutes, then release the remaining pressure. Unlock the lid.
5. Serve the pudding immediately or chill in the refrigerator for an hour before serving.

Vanilla Crème Brûlée

Prep time: 7 minutes | Cook time: 9 minutes | Serves 4

1 cup heavy cream (or full-fat coconut milk for dairy-free)
2 large egg yolks
2 tablespoons Swerve, or more to taste
Seeds scraped from ½ vanilla

bean (about 8 inches long), or 1 teaspoon vanilla extract
1 cup cold water
4 teaspoons Swerve, for topping

1. Heat the cream in a pan over medium-high heat until hot, about 2 minutes.
2. Place the egg yolks, Swerve, and vanilla seeds in a blender and blend until smooth.
3. While the blender is running, slowly pour in the hot cream. Taste and adjust the sweetness to your liking.
4. Scoop the mixture into four ramekins with a spatula. Cover the ramekins with aluminum foil.
5. Add the water to the Instant Pot and insert a trivet. Place the ramekins on the trivet.
6. Lock the lid. Select the Manual mode and set the cooking time for 7 minutes at High Pressure.
7. When the timer beeps, perform a quick pressure release. Carefully remove the lid.
8. Keep the ramekins covered with the foil and place in the refrigerator for about 2 hours until completely chilled.
9. Sprinkle 1 teaspoon of Swerve on top of each crème brûlée. Use the oven broiler to melt the sweetener.
10. Allow the topping to cool in the fridge for 5 minutes before serving.

Lemon Mousse

Prep time: 5 minutes | Cook time: 10 minutes | Serves 4

2 tablespoons butter, room temperature
⅓ cup beet sugar
½ cup plus ¼ cup plus ¼ cup plus ¼ cup coconut cream,

whipped
2 lemons, zested and juiced
Pinch of salt
1 cup water
Extra lemon zest, for garnish

1. Whisk the butter with the beet sugar with a hand mixer in a bowl. Beat in ½ cup of coconut cream, lemon zest and juice, and salt. Cover the bowl with aluminum foil.
2. Pour the water into the Instant Pot and insert a trivet. Put the bowl on the trivet.
3. Secure the lid. Select the Manual mode and set the cooking time for 10 minutes at High Pressure.
4. Once cooking is complete, do a natural pressure release for 10 minutes, then release any remaining pressure. Carefully open the lid.
5. Take out the bowl and remove the foil. The mixture will be curdy and clumpy, so whisk until smooth, and strain through a fine mesh into a bowl.
6. Cover the mixture itself with plastic wrap, making sure to press onto the curd. Place in the refrigerator for 2 hours.
7. When ready, remove the wrap and whisk the cream until stiff peak forms. Gently fold in the second portion (¼ cup) of coconut cream, then the third portion, and the last portion. Spoon the mousse into serving bowls.
8. Garnish with the extra lemon zest and serve.

Chocolate Brownies

Prep time: 10 minutes | Cook time: 5 minutes | Makes 3 brownies

2 cups water
3 ounces (85 g) dairy-free dark chocolate
1 tablespoon coconut oil
½ cup applesauce

2 tablespoons unrefined sugar
⅓ cup all-purpose flour
½ teaspoon baking powder
Salt, to taste

1. Pour the water into the Instant Pot and insert a trivet. Set the Instant Pot to Sauté.
2. Stir together the chocolate and coconut oil in a large bowl. Place the bowl on the trivet. Stir occasionally until the chocolate is melted, then turn off the Instant Pot.
3. Stir the applesauce and sugar into the chocolate mixture. Add the flour, baking powder, and salt and stir just until combined. Pour the batter into 3 ramekins. Cover each ramekin with aluminum foil. Using a foil sling or silicone helper handles, lower the ramekins onto the trivet.
4. Lock the lid. Select the Manual mode and set the cooking time for 5 minutes at High Pressure.
5. When the timer beeps, perform a quick pressure release. Carefully remove the lid.
6. Cool for 5 to 10 minutes before serving.

Apricot Cobbler

Prep time: 15 minutes | Cook time: 25 minutes | Serves 4

4 cups sliced apricots
½ cup plus ¼ cup brown sugar, divided
2 tablespoons plus ¾ cup plain flour, divided
½ teaspoon cinnamon powder
¼ teaspoon nutmeg powder

1½ teaspoons salt, divided
1 teaspoon vanilla extract
¼ cup water
½ teaspoon baking powder
½ teaspoon baking soda
3 tablespoons butter, melted
1 cup water

1. In a heatproof bowl, mix the apricots, ½ cup of brown sugar, 2 tablespoons of flour, cinnamon, nutmeg, ½ teaspoon of salt, vanilla, and water; set aside.
2. In another bowl, mix the remaining flour, salt and brown sugar, baking powder and soda, and butter. Spoon mixture over apricot mixture and spread to cover.
3. Pour the water in the pot, fit in a trivet and place heatproof bowl on top.
4. Seal the lid, select Manual mode, and set cooking time for 25 minutes on High Pressure.
5. When timer beeps, allow a natural release for 10 minutes, then release any remaining pressure. Open the lid.
6. Remove bowl and serve.

Crème Brûlée

Prep time: 5 minutes | Cook time: 30 minutes | Serves 4

5 egg yolks
5 tablespoons powdered erythritol

1½ cups heavy cream
2 teaspoons vanilla extract
2 cups water

1. In a small bowl, use a fork to break up the egg yolks. Stir in the erythritol.
2. Pour the cream into a small saucepan over medium-low heat and let it warm up for 3 to 4 minutes. Remove the saucepan from the heat.
3. Temper the egg yolks by slowly adding a small spoonful of the warm cream, keep whisking. Do these three times to make sure the egg yolks are fully tempered.
4. Slowly add the tempered eggs to the cream, whisking the whole time. Add the vanilla and whisk again.
5. Pour the cream mixture into the ramekins. Each ramekin should have ½ cup liquid. Cover each with aluminum foil.
6. Place the trivet inside the Instant Pot. Add the water. Carefully place the ramekins on top of the trivet.
7. Close the lid. Select Manual mode and set cooking time for 11 minutes on High Pressure.
8. When timer beeps, use a natural release for 15 minutes, then release any remaining pressure. Open the lid.
9. Carefully remove a ramekin from the pot. Remove the foil and check for doneness. The custard should be mostly set with a slightly jiggly center.
10. Place all the ramekins in the fridge for 2 hours to chill and set. Serve chilled.

Lush Chocolate Cake

Prep time: 10 minutes | Cook time: 35 minutes | Serves 8

For Cake:

2 cups almond flour	1 teaspoon vanilla extract
⅓ cup unsweetened cocoa powder	½ cup butter, melted and cooled
1½ teaspoons baking powder	6 tablespoons strong coffee, cooled
1 cup granulated erythritol	½ cup water
Pinch of salt	
4 eggs	

For Frosting:

4 ounces (113 g) cream cheese, softened	2½ tablespoons powdered erythritol
½ cup butter, softened	2 tablespoons unsweetened cocoa powder
¼ teaspoon vanilla extract	

1. To make the cake: In a large bowl, whisk together the almond flour, cocoa powder, baking powder, granulated erythritol, and salt. Whisk well to remove any lumps.
2. Add the eggs and vanilla and mix with a hand mixer until combined.
3. With the mixer still on low speed, slowly add the melted butter and mix until well combined.
4. Add the coffee and mix on low speed until the batter is thoroughly combined. Scrape the sides and bottom of the bowl to make sure everything is well mixed.
5. Spray the cake pan with cooking spray. Pour the batter into the pan. Cover tightly with aluminum foil.
6. Add the water to the pot. Place the cake pan on the trivet and carefully lower then pan into the pot.
7. Close the lid. Select Manual mode and set cooking time for 35 minutes on High Pressure.
8. When timer beeps, use a quick pressure release and open the lid.
9. Carefully remove the cake pan from the pot and place on a wire rack to cool. Flip the cake onto a plate once it is cool enough to touch. Cool completely before frosting.
10. To make the frosting: In a medium bowl, use the mixer to whip the cream cheese, butter, and vanilla until light and fluffy, 1 to 2 minutes. With the mixer running, slowly add the powdered erythritol and cocoa powder. Mix until everything is well combined.
11. Once the cake is completely cooled, spread the frosting on the top and down the sides.

Kentucky Butter Cake

Prep time: 5 minutes | Cook time: 35 minutes | Serves 4

2 cups almond flour	1 tablespoon vanilla extract
¾ cup granulated erythritol	½ cup butter, melted
1½ teaspoons baking powder	Cooking spray
4 eggs	½ cup water

1. In a medium bowl, whisk together the almond flour, erythritol, and baking powder. Whisk well to remove any lumps.
2. Add the eggs and vanilla and whisk until combined.
3. Add the butter and whisk until the batter is mostly smooth and well combined.
4. Grease the pan with cooking spray and pour in the batter. Cover tightly with aluminum foil.
5. Add the water to the pot. Place the Bundt pan on the trivet and carefully lower it into the pot using.
6. Set the lid in place. Select the Manual mode and set the cooking time for 35 minutes on High Pressure. When the timer goes off, do a quick pressure release. Carefully open the lid.
7. Remove the pan from the pot. Let the cake cool in the pan before flipping out onto a plate.

Maple-Glazed Zucchini Bundt Cake

Prep time: 7 minutes | Cook time: 40 minutes | Serves 8

Cake:

6 large eggs	2 teaspoons ground cinnamon
1 cup full-fat coconut milk	1 cup coconut flour
¾ cup (1½ sticks) unsalted butter (or butter-flavored coconut oil for dairy-free), melted	1 teaspoon fine sea salt
	1 teaspoon baking powder
	1 cup shredded zucchini
½ cup Swerve	3 teaspoons vanilla extract

Maple Glaze:

½ cup (1 stick) unsalted butter (or butter-flavored coconut oil for dairy-free)	(¼ cup) (or Kite Hill brand cream cheese style spread for dairy-free)
¼ cup Swerve	Chopped raw walnuts, for garnish (omit for nut-free)
2 ounces (57 g) cream cheese	

1. Whisk the eggs with a hand mixer until light and foamy in large bowl. Stir in the coconut milk, melted butter, sweetener, and cinnamon.
2. In another large bowl, stir together the coconut flour, salt, and baking powder. Add the dry ingredients to the wet ingredients and stir well, then fold in the shredded zucchini and extract and stir again.
3. Grease a 6-cup Bundt pan. Pour the batter into the prepared pan and cover the pan with a paper towel and then with aluminum foil.
4. Place a trivet in the bottom of the Instant Pot and pour in 2 cups of cold water. Place the Bundt pan on the trivet.
5. Lock the lid. Select the Manual mode and set the cooking time for 35 minutes at High Pressure.
6. When the timer beeps, use a natural pressure release for 10 minutes. Carefully remove the lid.
7. Let the cake cool in the pot for 10 minutes before removing.
8. Chill the cake in the fridge or freezer before removing from the Bundt pan, about 1 hour.
9. While the cake is cooling, make the glaze: Place the butter in a large pan over high heat and cook for about 5 minutes until brown, stirring occasionally.
10. Remove from the heat. While stirring the browned butter, vigorously, add the sweetener.
11. Carefully add the cream cheese and maple extract to the butter mixture. Allow the glaze to cool for a few minutes, or until it starts to thicken.
12. Transfer the chilled cake to a serving plate and drizzle the glaze over the top. Sprinkle with the walnuts while the glaze is still wet.
13. Place the cake in the fridge to chill completely for an additional 30 minutes before serving.

Tapioca Pudding

Prep time: 12 mins, Cook Time: 15 mins, Servings: 4

1 cup water	tapioca pearls
1¼ cups almond milk	½ cup sugar
¼ cup rinsed and drained seed	½ tsp. lemon zest

1. Pour the water into the Instant Pot.
2. Add the steamer basket inside the pot.
3. In a heat-proof bowl, mix all the ingredients until the sugar has dissolved.
4. Cover with foil and put the bowl on top of the basket.
5. Lock the lid. Set the Instant Pot to Manual mode, then set the timer for 10 minutes at High Pressure.
6. When the timer goes off, perform a natural release for 5 minutes, then release any remaining pressure. Carefully open the lid.
7. Serve immediately or refrigerate for several hours and serve chilled.

Lemon Blueberry Cheesecake

Prep time: 10 minutes | Cook time: 6 minutes | Serves 6

1 tablespoon coconut oil, melted, for greasing the pan	1 cup fresh blueberries
1¼ cups soft pitted Medjool dates, divided	3 tablespoons freshly squeezed lemon juice or lime juice
1 cup gluten-free rolled oats	1¾ cups water
2 cups cashews	Salt, to taste

1. Grease a 6-inch springform pan or pie dish with melted coconut oil.
2. In a food processor, combine 1 cup of dates and the oats. Processor until they form a sticky mixture. Press this mixture into the prepared pan.
3. In a blender, combine the remaining ¼ cup of dates, cashews, blueberries, lemon juice, ¾ cup of water, and a pinch of salt. Blend on high speed for about 1 minute, until smooth and creamy, stopping a couple of times to scrape down the sides. Pour this mixture over the crust. Cover the pan with aluminum foil.
4. Pour the remaining 1 cup of water into the Instant Pot and insert a trivet. Using a foil sling or silicone helper handles, lower the pan onto the trivet.
5. Lock the lid. Select the Manual mode and set the cooking time for 6 minutes at High Pressure.
6. When the timer beeps, perform a natural pressure release for 10 minutes, then release any remaining pressure. Carefully remove the lid.
7. Cool for 5 to 10 minutes before slicing and serving.

Maple Syrup Lemon Pudding

Prep time: 12 mins, Cook Time: 5 mins, Servings: 7

½ cup maple syrup	2 tbsps. gelatin
3 cups milk	Juice of 2 lemons
Lemon zest from 2 grated lemons	1 cup water

1. In the blender, mix milk with lemon juice, lemon zest, maple syrup and gelatin, pulse really well and divide into ramekins.
2. In the Instant Pot, set in the water, add steamer basket, add ramekins inside.
3. Lock the lid. Set the Instant Pot to Manual mode, then set the timer for 5 minutes on High Pressure.
4. When the timer goes off, perform a natural release. Carefully open the lid.
5. Refrigerate and serve the puddings chilled.

Lemon and Ricotta Torte

Prep time: 15 minutes | Cook time: 35 minutes | Serves 12

Cooking spray
Torte:

1⅓ cups Swerve	2½ cups blanched almond flour
½ cup (1 stick) unsalted butter, softened	1¼ (10-ounce / 284-g) cups whole-milk ricotta cheese
2 teaspoons lemon or vanilla extract	¼ cup lemon juice
5 large eggs, separated	1 cup cold water

Lemon Glaze:

½ cup (1 stick) unsalted butter	(¼ cup)
¼ cup Swerve	Grated lemon zest and lemon slices, for garnish
2 tablespoons lemon juice	
2 ounces (57 g) cream cheese	

1. Line a baking pan with parchment paper and spray with cooking spray. Set aside.
2. Make the torte: In the bowl of a stand mixer, place the Swerve, butter, and extract and blend for 8 to 10 minutes until well combined. Scrape down the sides of the bowl as needed.
3. Add the egg yolks and continue to blend until fully combined. Add the almond flour and mix until smooth, then stir in the ricotta and lemon juice.
4. Whisk the egg whites in a separate medium bowl until stiff peaks form. Add the whites to the batter and stir well. Pour the batter into the prepared pan and smooth the top.
5. Place a trivet in the bottom of your Instant Pot and pour in the water. Use a foil sling to lower the baking pan onto the trivet. Tuck in the sides of the sling.
6. Seal the lid, press Pressure Cook or Manual, and set the timer for 30 minutes. Once finished, let the pressure release naturally.
7. Lock the lid. Select the Manual mode and set the cooking time for 30 minutes at High Pressure.
8. When the timer beeps, perform a natural pressure release for 10 minutes. Carefully remove the lid.
9. Use the foil sling to lift the pan out of the Instant Pot. Place the torte in the fridge for 40 minutes to chill before glazing.
10. Meanwhile, make the glaze: Place the butter in a large pan over high heat and cook for about 5 minutes until brown, stirring occasionally. Remove from the heat. While stirring the browned butter, add the Swerve.
11. Carefully add the lemon juice and cream cheese to the butter mixture. Allow the glaze to cool for a few minutes, or until it starts to thicken.
12. Transfer the chilled torte to a serving plate. Pour the glaze over the torte and return it to the fridge to chill for an additional 30 minutes.
13. Scatter the lemon zest on top of the torte and arrange the lemon slices on the plate around the torte.
14. Serve.

Appendix 1 30-Day Meal Plan

	Breakfast	Lunch	Dinner	Snack/ Dessert
1	Pork Quill Egg Cups	Pork Steaks with Pico de Gallo	Beef Bourguignon	Chocolate Brownies
2	Quinoa and Banana Breakfast Bowl	Chipotle Cilantro Rice	Cherry Tomato Farfalle with Pesto	Barbecue Chicken Meatballs
3	Tropical Fruit Chutney	Simple Cauliflower Gnocchi	Bean Tagine with Ras el Hanout	Apple Wontons
4	Carrot and Pineapple Oatmeal	Spinach and Pine Nut Fusilli Pasta	Veggie Stew	Herbed Button Mushrooms
5	Banana and Amaranth Bread with Walnuts	Black Bean and Quinoa Bowl with Beef	Beef Congee	Bacon Wrapped Wieners
6	Asparagus and Gruyère Cheese Frittata	Ratatouille	Millet Pilaf with Lime	Veggie and Egg Mix
7	Vanilla Pancake	Bow Tie Pasta	Tofu and Greens with Fenugreek Sauce	Cauliflower Mash
8	Egg Benedict	Caper and Olive Pasta	Marsala Tofu Pasta	Vegetable Chicken Skewers
9	Strawberry and Pumpkin Spice Quinoa Bowl	Salmon with Dijon Mustard	Curried Sorghum with Golden Raisins	Banana Pudding
10	Rice Pudding	Broccoli and Cheddar Pasta	Fish Fillets with Asparagus	Greek Beef Meatballs
11	Tex Mex Tofu Scramble	Creamy Pork Liver	Mini Tofu and Vegetable Frittatas	Almond Bread
12	Egg Cups with Broccoli	Crumbled Tofu with Black Beans	Lemon and Garlic Cod	Banana Cake
13	Banana and Amaranth Bread with Walnuts	Spaghetti Squash Noodles with Tomatoes	Black Bean and Brown Rice Casserole	Apple and Brussels Sprout Appetizer
14	Spinach and Ham Frittata	Greek Quinoa Bowl	Bacon Stuffed Meatloaf	Citrus Apple Crisps with Oat Topping

15	Coconut Muesli Stuffed Apples	Duo-Cheese Mushroom Pasta	Italian Carrot and Potato Medley	Milk and Cocoa Pudding
16	Quinoa and Banana Breakfast Bowl	Baby Eggplants with Coconut	Pasta Carbonara	Broccoli Appetizer
17	Egg Stuffed Bell Peppers	Herbed Sirloin Tip Roast	Swiss Chard with Black-Eyed Peas	Carrot Raisin Halwa
18	Vanilla Applesauce	Bulgur Wheat Bowl	Salmon with Honey Sauce	Green Olive Pâté
19	Stone Fruit Compote	Pea and Carrot Rice	Couscous with Veggies	Egg-Crusted Zucchini
20	Bacon and Egg Risotto	Fish and Tomato Soup	Vegetable Biryani	Maple-Glazed Zucchini Bundt Cake
21	French Eggs	Bacon and Corn Casserole	Confetti Rice	Pork and Beef Chili Nachos
22	Apple Butter	Seafood Pasta with Tomatoes	Buffalo Wings	Pecan Monkey Bread
23	Sweet Potato and Kale Egg Bites	Chicken Curry	Pizza Pasta	Chicken in Lettuce
24	Eggs En Cocotte	Cauliflower and Pineapple Jasmine Rice Bowl	Soya Granules and Green Pea Tacos	Zucchini Sticks
25	Chicken and Cheddar Casserole	Halibut En Papillote	Ritzy Green Pea and Cauliflower Curry	Beet and Carrot Spread
26	Rhubarb Compote	Chicken Tacos with Cheese Shells	Mushroom Risotto	Chocolate Mug Cake
27	Hawaiian Sweet Potato Hash	Chicken Fettuccine Alfredo	Broccoli with Mushrooms	Espresso Cheesecake with Raspberries
28	Eggs In Purgatory	Jackfruit with Chickpeas	Cod with Orange Sauce	Chinese Flavor Chicken Wings
29	Leek and Asparagus Frittata	Mushrooms with Green Beans	Mustard Macaroni and Cheese	Carrot Fish Balls
30	Buckwheat and Strawberry Pudding	Broccoli Fettucine Pasta	Slow Cooked Beef Steak	Cauliflower Tots

Appendix 2 Measurement Conversion Chart

VOLUME EQUIVALENTS(DRY)

US STANDARD	METRIC (APPROXIMATE)
1/8 teaspoon	0.5 mL
1/4 teaspoon	1 mL
1/2 teaspoon	2 mL
3/4 teaspoon	4 mL
1 teaspoon	5 mL
1 tablespoon	15 mL
1/4 cup	59 mL
1/2 cup	118 mL
3/4 cup	177 mL
1 cup	235 mL
2 cups	475 mL
3 cups	700 mL
4 cups	1 L

WEIGHT EQUIVALENTS

US STANDARD	METRIC (APPROXIMATE)
1 ounce	28 g
2 ounces	57 g
5 ounces	142 g
10 ounces	284 g
15 ounces	425 g
16 ounces (1 pound)	455 g
1.5 pounds	680 g
2 pounds	907 g

VOLUME EQUIVALENTS(LIQUID)

US STANDARD	US STANDARD (OUNCES)	METRIC (APPROXIMATE)
2 tablespoons	1 fl.oz.	30 mL
1/4 cup	2 fl.oz.	60 mL
1/2 cup	4 fl.oz.	120 mL
1 cup	8 fl.oz.	240 mL
1 1/2 cup	12 fl.oz.	355 mL
2 cups or 1 pint	16 fl.oz.	475 mL
4 cups or 1 quart	32 fl.oz.	1 L
1 gallon	128 fl.oz.	4 L

TEMPERATURES EQUIVALENTS

FAHRENHEIT(F)	CELSIUS(C) (APPROXIMATE)
225 °F	107 °C
250 °F	120 °C
275 °F	135 °C
300 °F	150 °C
325 °F	160 °C
350 °F	180 °C
375 °F	190 °C
400 °F	205 °C
425 °F	220 °C
450 °F	235 °C
475 °F	245 °C
500 °F	260 °C

Appendix 3 Recipes Index

CPSIA information can be obtained
at www.ICGtesting.com
Printed in the USA
LVHW111522190122
708732LV00004BA/162